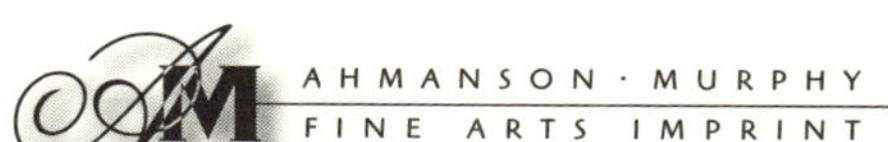

THE AHMANSON FOUNDATION
has endowed this imprint
to honor the memory of
FRANKLIN D. MURPHY
who for half a century
served arts and letters,
beauty and learning, in
equal measure by shaping
with a brilliant devotion
those institutions upon
which they rely.

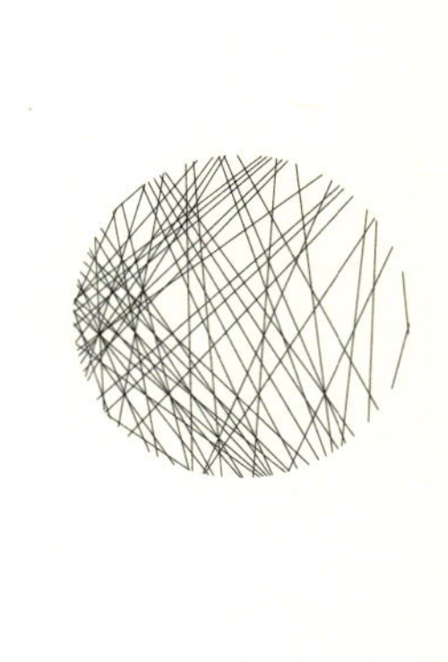

TO LIFE!

ECO ART IN PURSUIT OF A SUSTAINABLE PLANET

Linda Weintraub

UNIVERSITY OF CALIFORNIA PRESS *Berkeley Los Angeles London*

The publisher gratefully acknowledges the generous support of the Art Endowment Fund of the University of California Press Foundation, which was established by a major gift from the Ahmanson Foundation.

The publisher also gratefully acknowledges the generous support of the Richard and Harriett Gold Endowment Fund in Arts and Humanities of the University of California Press Foundation.

University of California Press, one of the most distinguished university presses in the United States, enriches lives around the world by advancing scholarship in the humanities, social sciences, and natural sciences. Its activities are supported by the UC Press Foundation and by philanthropic contributions from individuals and institutions. For more information, visit www.ucpress.edu.

University of California Press
Berkeley and Los Angeles, California

University of California Press, Ltd.
London, England

ISBN 978-0-520-27361-0 (cloth)
ISBN 978-0-520-27362-7 (paper)

Library of Congress Control Number: 2012941645

Manufactured in the United States
19 18 17 16
10 9 8 7 6 5 4 3

Only vegetable-based inks (which are much better for the environment than soy-based inks) were used in the production of this book. The printer burns the plates using lasers instead of the older chemical process. Thomson-Shore also recycles all materials, and the leftover ink is sent back to the ink manufacturer. Thomson-Shore complies with Forest Stewardship Council standards and is the first book manufacturer to sign on with the Green Press Initiative, a watchdog group on environmentally friendly papers.

The paper used in this publication meets the minimum requirements of ANSI/NISO Z39.48-1992 (R 2002) (*Permanence of Paper*).♾

This book is conceived in concern,
invested with hope, and dedicated to the
children of the children of today's children.

Contents

TWENTY-FIRST-CENTURY ECO ART EXPLORERS

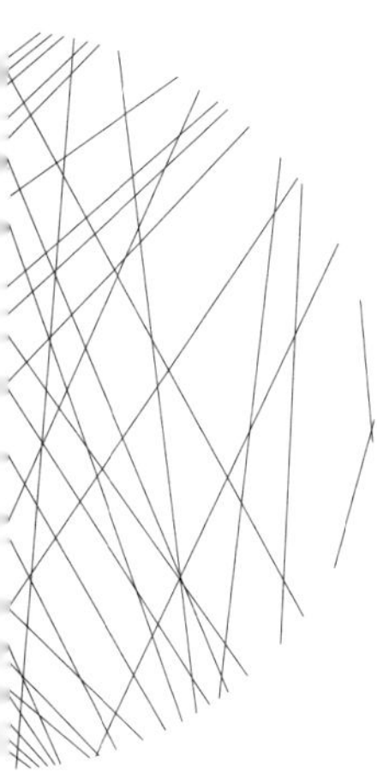

Online Auxiliaries for Instructors and Students

TEACHING GUIDES: UC Press website (www.ucpress.edu)

Studio Art – Level 1 – **ECO ART GENRES**
Art projects introduce bio art, digital art, installation, public art, social practice. Sample syllabus.

Studio Art – Level 2 – **ART STRATEGIES**
Art projects explore eco art visualization, intervention, activation, satirization. Sample syllabus.

Contemporary Art History
Assignments contextualize contemporary eco art within the history of art. Sample syllabus.

Environmental Studies – Level 1 – **ECO ART ISSUES**
Projects address energy, waste, climate change, habitat, sustainability. Sample syllabus.

Environmental Studies – Level 2 – **ECO APPROACHES**
Projects explore conservation, preservation, urban ecology, restoration ecology, deep ecology. Sample syllabus.

STUDENT RESOURCES: Author's website (www.lindaweintraub.com)

a. **Color images** of works discussed in the book.

b. **Links** to videos and artist interviews

c. **Blog** updating artists' careers and the themes they address.

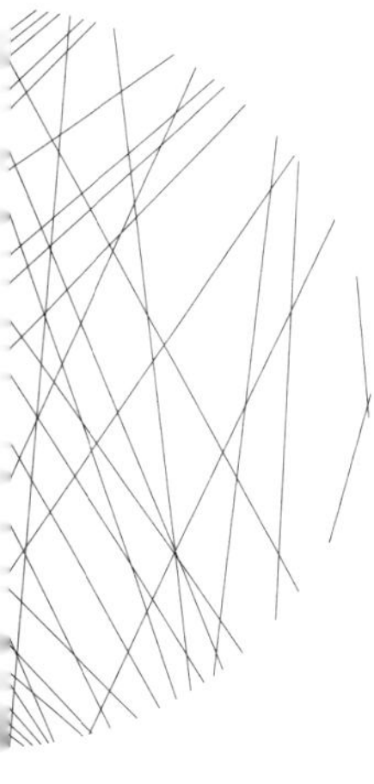

Acknowledgments

TRADITION TAMPERING, replete in this book, is not confined to the remarkable achievements of contemporary eco artists. It has even infiltrated the Acknowledgments, a standard component of every published text. The word *acknowledgment* is objectionable because it is too formal. It seems appropriate for legal documents and official issues of rights and claims, but it does not convey my heartfelt appreciation to the following supporters and participants. I am eager to convey the gratitude, as well as the affection, they have earned.

The artists, first and foremost, are the reason why I describe the arduous task of compiling this volume as a privilege. Besides honoring the brilliance of their creative endeavors, it is my hope that this book will assist them in fulfilling their missions—to awaken eco consciousness, conscience, and consideration.

Rose Robitaille was hired to deal with photo rights and reproduction. She far exceeded her job description by supporting the long and convoluted process of preparing the manuscript. While I am particularly thankful to her for providing the first edit of the text, it is her gracious enthusiasm and persistence that deserve special recognition.

Kari Dahlgren replaced Deborah Kirshman as the book's editor at the University of California Press. Both guided the text's formulation and public presentation. Since this process transpired over multiple years, there was ample opportunity to benefit from their astute supervision and enjoy their generous support.

Dan Franck graced this project with the experience he accumulated over the course of twenty years in educational publishing, science curriculum development, and science content writing. His editing contributions are apparent throughout the text. I am pleased that his generosity has been returned to his alma mater. Dan earned his doctorate in botany at the University of California, Berkeley, the publisher of this volume.

Andrew Weintraub served as a daily sounding board, consultant, counselor, and proponent of this author's efforts. He added much-appreciated affection to his performance in all these roles.

Skip Schuckmann's multiyear tutoring embraced cosmological theories, the minute operations of microclimates, and the wondrous adventures of life on Earth that exist between these extremes.

David Peattie, owner of BookMatters, and copyeditor Lou Doucette joined UC Press marketing manager Lindsie Bear, associate editor Eric Schmidt, and designer Nicole Hayward to benefit this project with their best work. Heidi Neff, Susan Steinman, Laurie Seeman, Dean Drake, and Alex Tuller all contributed to the refinement of the text and its expansion into computer space. I am grateful to them all.

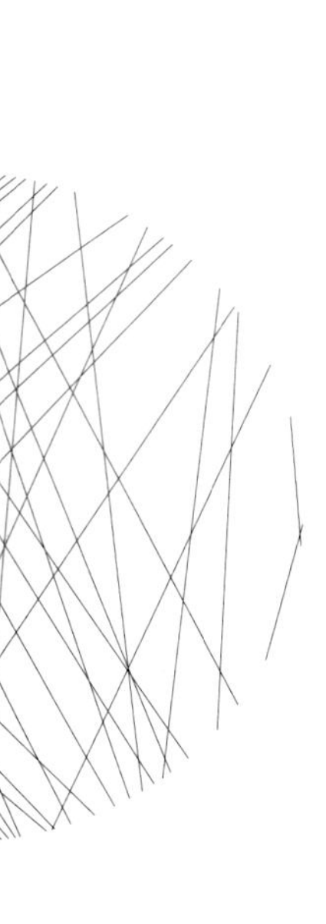

Preface

"IS THAT ALL?" were the words that led to the writing of this text. They were uttered by Skip Schuckmann, a near-stranger at the time, when I told him I had just acquired raw land in the Hudson Valley, New York, and planned to live there the rest of my life. I described the rolling hills, wildflower meadow, forest stream, and a view of the Catskill Mountains to the west. My description culminated in an exuberant, "It's so beautiful!" His question triggered a journey of discovery that ultimately led me to refashion my personal lifestyle and redirect my professional pursuits. Both morphed as I discovered that beauty was not all the site afforded. Its visual qualities were gradually enhanced by previously unrecognized assets. Its botanical and zoological populations, for example, performed wondrous feats of resilience and set exemplary standards of resourcefulness. Over time, the resources that sustain these species have sustained me and my family. At first, we harvested the stone, moss, berries, acorns, deer that were available for harvesting. Then, optimizing the productivity of this habitat became my life mission. I am diligently transforming our eleven acres according to permaculture principles. Water management, soil creation, food production, animal husbandry, forest gardens, composting, fencing, terracing, and winter gardening are hands-on primers in ecology and joy. Over time, I directed this newly acquired appreciation of the hypersensitivity of ecosystems to my profession by founding Artnow Publications. The eco art "textlets" it publishes are produced according to stringent environmental principles.

The thesis and format of the book you are reading are also products of the question, Is that all? When I applied that inquiry to the question, Why write an eco art textbook?, compelling reasons proliferated. They, too, exceeded honoring the beauty that graces our fair planet. Five persuasive answers supplemented the Earth's immense storehouse of visual pleasures. Why write an eco art textbook?

- Because responding to current environmental crises is the singular challenge of the current era.
- Because artists possess astute communication skills that can disseminate existing environmental strategies of reform and preservation.
- Because art's inspirational capacity can activate the behavioral changes and policy reforms of custodial care for our planetary home.
- Because the creative ingenuity that is the special province of art can be directed to life-sustaining problem solving.
- Because art has long served as conscience of a culture.

THESIS

Eco art stands out from the din of environmental warnings, policies, and campaigns because its content is enriched by artistic imagination and its strategies are emboldened by artistic license. All forty-seven artists represented in this book augment humanity's prospects for attaining a sustainable future. By bolstering eco art's status as the current era's definitive artistic movement, they are establishing an entirely new set of standards for measuring an artistic masterwork.

While the previous sentence accurately describes this book's thesis, skeptics are plentiful. They note, with good reason, the many ways the creative individuals the book features jeopardize their status as artists. Driven by the desire to strengthen the planet's weakened defenses and preserve remnants of our planet's vitality, these artists venture beyond conventional art boundaries into uncharted territories. They typically address issues that non-art professionals claim, create works that function like objects with no pretentions as art, conduct processes that do not resemble studio art practices, and share creative responsibility with non-artist collaborators. Another entry on this challenging list is provided by medium. Eco artists replace art store supplies with living plants and microbes, mud and feathers, electronic transmissions and digital imagery, temperature and wind, debris and contaminants. The finale is that eco art is defined as a mission, not a style. For all these reasons, eco artists can be viewed as either defectors from art or as pioneers inaugurating a new art movement.

In all these ways the artists in this book pose the question, Does eco art merit inclusion within the ever-evolving chronicle of art history? The answer may depend upon whether the need to address the pressures currently besetting the planet carries the cultural weight of postwar anxiety in the 1940s that gave rise to a new art movement—abstract expressionism. It will be determined by whether environmental concerns loom with the significance of commodity abundance in the 1960s that spurred another new art movement—pop art. There is no consensus yet on whether chapters exploring contemporary eco art will follow the chapters on abstract expressionism and pop art in future art history texts.

Even before eco art's status within the history of art is resolved, this book advocates for its inclusion within academic curricula. Students benefit by receiving an education that addresses predicaments and crises that are critical to their well-being and to their children's prospects. In a complementary manner, pedagogical attention to eco art benefits the planet by funneling the creative ingenuity of art students into ventures designed to alleviate the innumerable problems that currently beleaguer the Earth and its populations. These benefits can be channeled through courses that focus on critical theory, studio art, art history, social practice, environmental studies, and cultural studies.

Although eco art has been hovering in the wings of the art scene for more than half a century, two phenomena are converging that might ultimately cast it in a leading role in the current era's cultural chronicle. First, its mission is becoming ever more crucial, as the Earth's ability to sustain current and future generations of humans becomes more precarious. Like leaders in education, politics, industry, ethics, legislation, health, commerce, and security, today's eco artists are expanding and intensifying the missions introduced by their predecessors—environmentalists and eco artists of the 1960s and 1970s. Second, the number of international artists rejuvenating the planet has reached a critical mass. My files brim with artists from across the globe who are applying environmental remedies and defenses. Over 300 made the first cut. Forty-seven were ultimately selected for presentation in this text. Thirteen are twentieth-century eco art pioneers. The rest are twenty-first-century eco art explorers. The selection process considered which work of art epitomized an ecological issue or exemplified an ecological art method. Since so many were worthy, decisions ultimately involved differentiating *good* from *better* in order to arrive at *best*. This critical assessment was leveled at works of art, not artists, whose careers are far too varied and extensive to consider in a single volume. Ultimately, the works chosen serve as case studies that encompass the accomplishments of innumerable art colleagues, set standards of environmental integrity, and introduce areas ripe for further exploration.

FORMAT

In order to accommodate contemporary habits of accessing information, this book deviates from publishing conventions. For example, its Table of Contents does not impose a predetermined sequence for accessing the text. Each chapter is a discrete unit of text, able to serve as a building block that can be used to construct individualized reading experiences. In this manner this book is attuned to the electronic communication strategies that have accustomed today's readers to engage with texts that are participatory, expandable, and versatile. These qualities were transferred to book form by utilizing three organizing schemes—banners, schematics, and indexes. Each consolidates and conveys a specific range of environmental concerns or art approaches. These schemes facilitate compare-and-contrast analysis and expedite the reader's selection of text according to individual interest or an instructor's academic discipline.

Banners introduce the artists' chapters. They serve twin purposes. They provide a synopsis of the specific text by identifying the core themes and methods that are particular to the artworks in that chapter. In addition, they establish the context for those artworks by presenting an overview of all the eco art options considered in the book. To respect the interdisciplinary nature of eco art, two banners relay environmental considerations and two are devoted to art considerations:

- Eco issues addressed by eco artists
- Eco approaches adopted by eco artists
- Art genres employed by eco artists
- Art strategies activated by eco artists

Schematics consolidate the information conveyed in the banners into four diagrams: eco issues, eco approaches, art genres, and art strategies. Each banner provides information about the individual chapter. Each diagram provides the broad perspective. The four schematics illustrate the relationships among the artists and identify the distribution of their concerns and methodologies. Schematics construct a visual equivalent of eco art's dynamic interconnections.

Indexes ensure that the information contained in the schematics is easily accessible. They assemble all the artists and group them according to precise eco issues, eco approaches, art genres, and artistic strategies.

In sum, these three schemes serve as signposts for explorations deep into eco art territories.

It is hoped they and the content they support will foster the appreciation and production of eco art so that it can augment humanity's prospects for attaining a sustainable future.

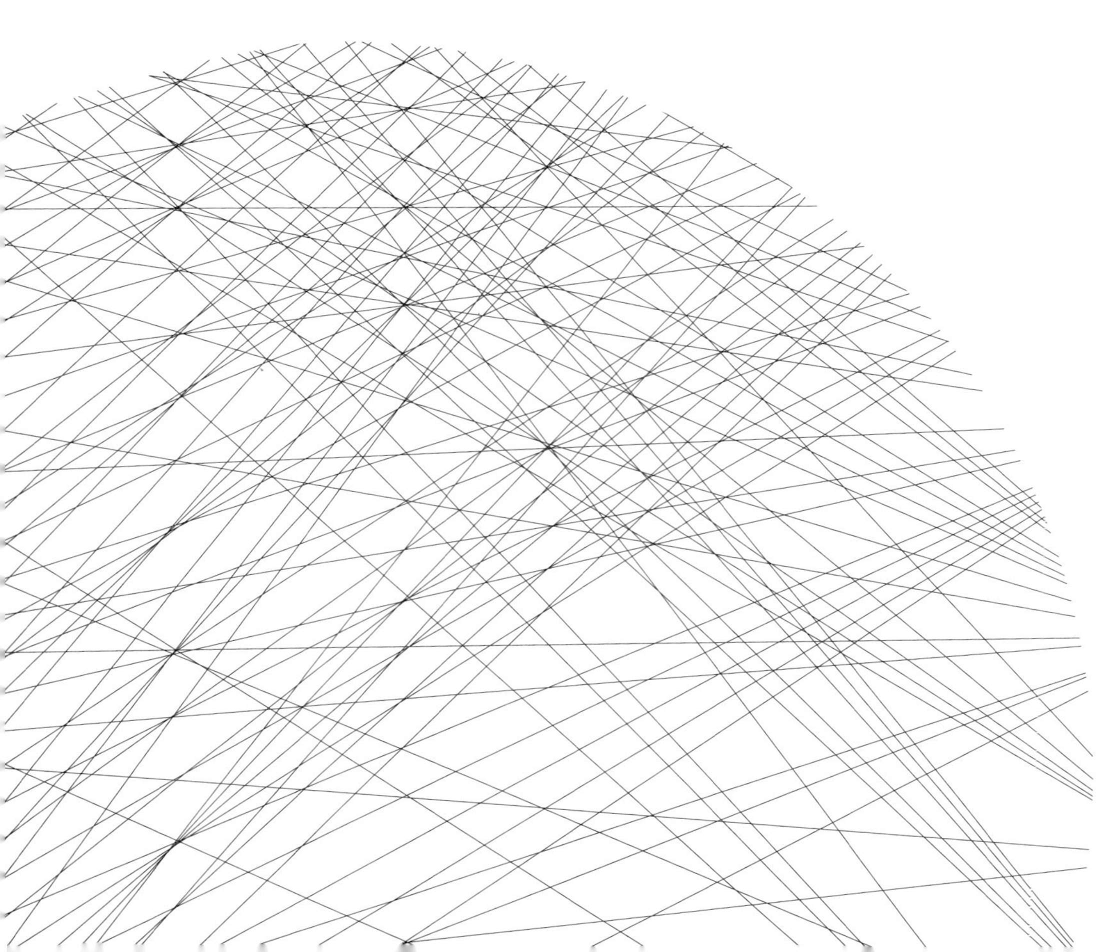

Schematics | Indexes | Glossaries

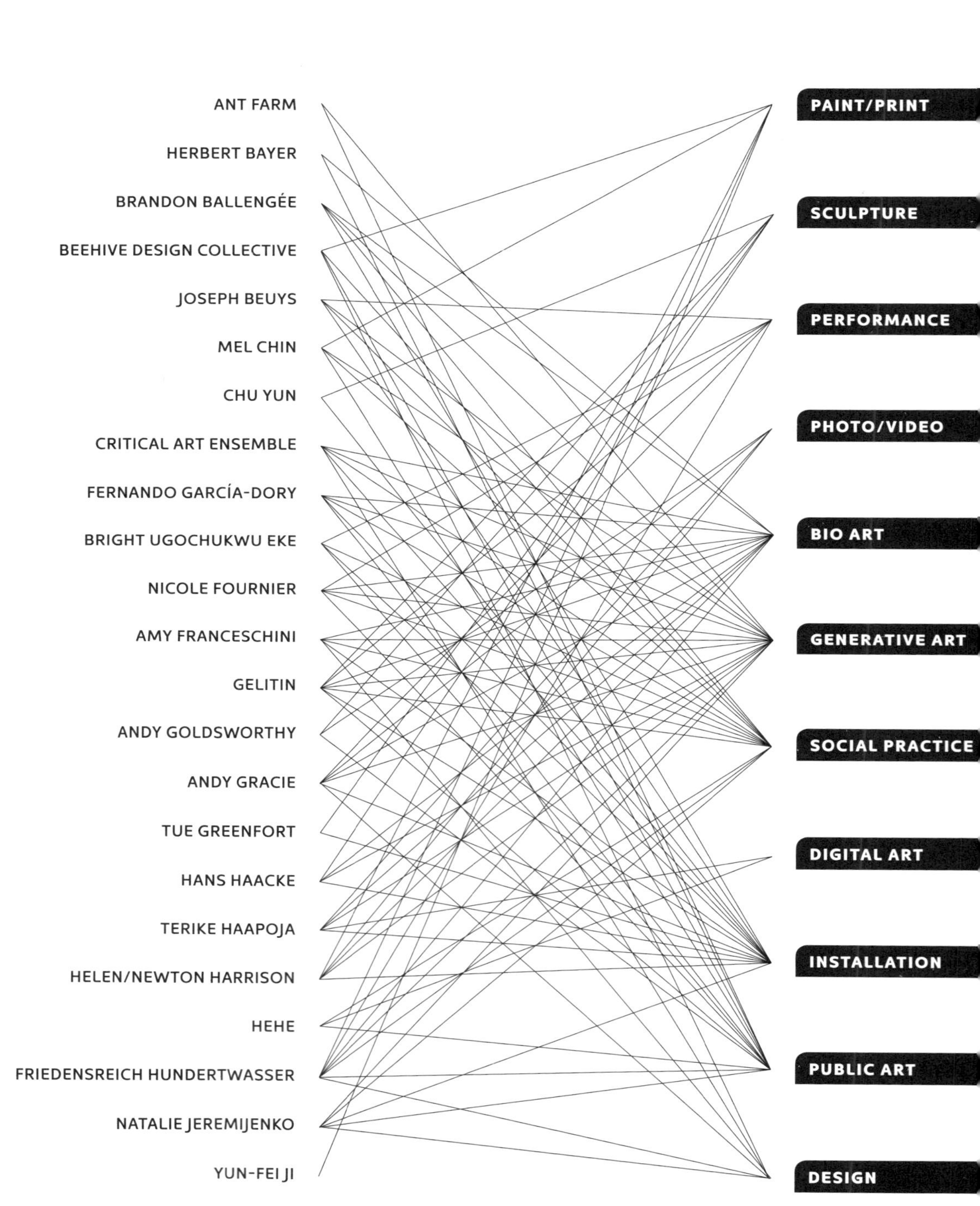
ANT FARM
HERBERT BAYER
BRANDON BALLENGÉE
BEEHIVE DESIGN COLLECTIVE
JOSEPH BEUYS
MEL CHIN
CHU YUN
CRITICAL ART ENSEMBLE
FERNANDO GARCÍA-DORY
BRIGHT UGOCHUKWU EKE
NICOLE FOURNIER
AMY FRANCESCHINI
GELITIN
ANDY GOLDSWORTHY
ANDY GRACIE
TUE GREENFORT
HANS HAACKE
TERIKE HAAPOJA
HELEN/NEWTON HARRISON
HEHE
FRIEDENSREICH HUNDERTWASSER
NATALIE JEREMIJENKO
YUN-FEI JI
PAINT/PRINT
SCULPTURE
PERFORMANCE
PHOTO/VIDEO
BIO ART
GENERATIVE ART
SOCIAL PRACTICE
DIGITAL ART
INSTALLATION
PUBLIC ART
DESIGN

Schematic of ART GENRES

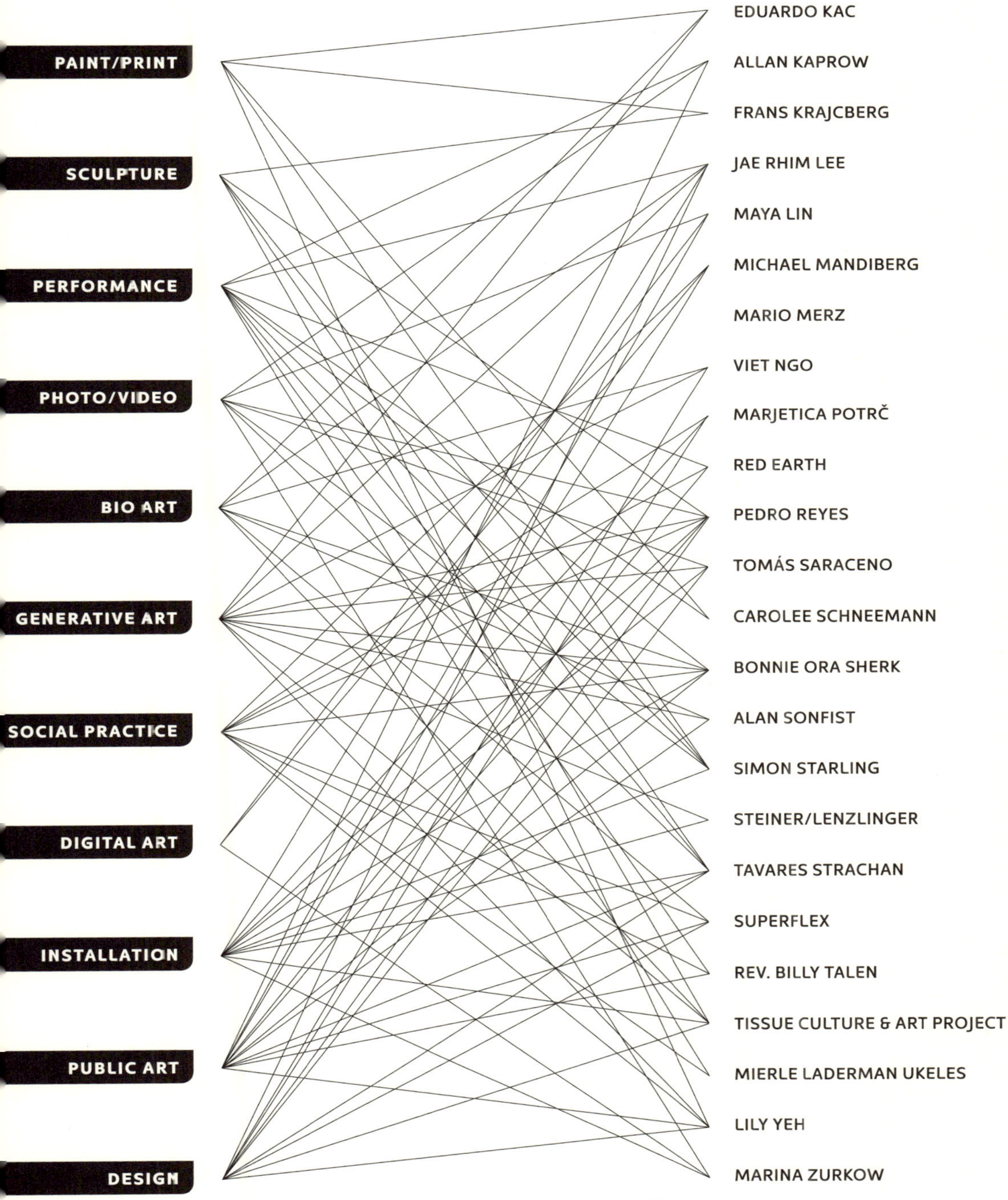

PAINT/PRINT
SCULPTURE
PERFORMANCE
PHOTO/VIDEO
BIO ART
GENERATIVE ART
SOCIAL PRACTICE
DIGITAL ART
INSTALLATION
PUBLIC ART
DESIGN

EDUARDO KAC
ALLAN KAPROW
FRANS KRAJCBERG
JAE RHIM LEE
MAYA LIN
MICHAEL MANDIBERG
MARIO MERZ
VIET NGO
MARJETICA POTRČ
RED EARTH
PEDRO REYES
TOMÁS SARACENO
CAROLEE SCHNEEMANN
BONNIE ORA SHERK
ALAN SONFIST
SIMON STARLING
STEINER/LENZLINGER
TAVARES STRACHAN
SUPERFLEX
REV. BILLY TALEN
TISSUE CULTURE & ART PROJECT
MIERLE LADERMAN UKELES
LILY YEH
MARINA ZURKOW

Index and Glossary of Art Genres

INDEX

PAINT/PRINT BEEHIVE DESIGN COLLECTIVE • MEL CHIN • HELEN AND NEWTON HARRISON • FRIEDENSREICH HUNDERTWASSER • FRANS KRAJCBERG • YUN-FEI JI • EDUARDO KAC • CAROLEE SCHNEEMANN • SIMON STARLING • LILY YEH

SCULPTURE CHU YUN • HANS HAACKE • FRANS KRAJCBERG • GELITIN • ANDY GOLDSWORTHY • TUE GREENFORT • PEDRO REYES • SIMON STARLING • TAVARES STRACHAN • TISSUE CULTURE & ART PROJECT

PERFORMANCE/EVENT JOSEPH BEUYS • BRIGHT UGOCHUKWU EKE • NICOLE FOURNIER • GELITIN • ANDY GRACIE • FRIEDENSREICH HUNDERTWASSER • ALLAN KAPROW • JAE RHIM LEE • RED EARTH • CAROLEE SCHNEEMANN • BONNIE ORA SHERK • SIMON STARLING • TAVARES STRACHAN • REVEREND BILLY TALEN • MIERLE LADERMAN UKELES

PHOTO/VIDEO ANDY GOLDSWORTHY • ANDY GRACIE • TERIKE HAAPOJA • HELEN AND NEWTON HARRISON • ALLAN KAPROW • MAYA LIN • PEDRO REYES • TOMÁS SARACENO • SIMON STARLING • TAVARES STRACHAN • MARINA ZURKOW

BIO ART BRANDON BALLENGÉE • HERBERT BAYER • CRITICAL ART ENSEMBLE • FERNANDO GARCÍA-DORY • NICOLE FOURNIER • AMY FRANCESCHINI • GELITIN • ANDY GRACIE • HANS HAACKE • TERIKE HAAPOJA • HELEN AND NEWTON HARRISON • FRIEDENSREICH HUNDERTWASSER • EDUARDO KAC • JAE RHIM LEE • VIET NGO • BONNIE ORA SHERK • ALAN SONFIST • SUPERFLEX • TISSUE CULTURE & ART PROJECT

GENERATIVE ART ANT FARM • BRANDON BALLENGÉE • JOSEPH BEUYS • MEL CHIN • CRITICAL ART ENSEMBLE • FERNANDO GARCÍA-DORY • NICOLE FOURNIER • AMY FRANCESCHINI • GELITIN • ANDY GRACIE • HANS HAACKE • TERIKE HAAPOJA • HELEN AND NEWTON HARRISON • FRIEDENSREICH HUNDERTWASSER • NATALIE JEREMIJENKO • EDUARDO KAC • JAE RHIM LEE • MARIO MERZ • VIET NGO • PEDRO REYES • TOMÁS SARACENO • BONNIE ORA SHERK • ALAN SONFIST • GERDA STEINER AND JÖRG LENZLINGER • TISSUE CULTURE & ART PROJECT • LILY YEH

SOCIAL PRACTICE JOSEPH BEUYS • BRANDON BALLENGÉE • BEEHIVE DESIGN COLLECTIVE • MEL CHIN • CRITICAL ART ENSEMBLE • FERNANDO GARCÍA-DORY • BRIGHT UGOCHUKWU EKE • NICOLE FOURNIER • AMY FRANCESCHINI • GELITIN • HEHE • FRIEDENSREICH HUNDERTWASSER • NATALIE JEREMIJENKO • MARJETICA POTRČ • MICHAEL MANDIBERG • RED EARTH • PEDRO REYES • SUPERFLEX • REVEREND BILLY TALEN • BONNIE ORA SHERK • MIERLE LADERMAN UKELES • LILY YEH

DIGITAL ART TERIKE HAAPOJA • HEHE • MAYA LIN • MICHAEL MANDIBERG • MARINA ZURKOW

INSTALLATION BRANDON BALLENGÉE • JOSEPH BEUYS • CHU YUN • CRITICAL ART ENSEMBLE • FERNANDO GARCÍA-DORY • BRIGHT UGOCHUKWU EKE • AMY FRANCESCHINI • GELITIN • ANDY GRACIE • TUE GREENFORT • TERIKE HAAPOJA • HANS HAACKE • HELEN AND NEWTON HARRISON • NATALIE JEREMIJENKO • JAE RHIM LEE • MARIO MERZ • MARJETICA POTRČ • PEDRO REYES • TOMÁS SARACENO • SIMON STARLING • GERDA STEINER AND JÖRG LENZLINGER • BONNIE ORA SHERK • TAVARES STRACHAN • TISSUE CULTURE & ART PROJECT • MARINA ZURKOW

PUBLIC ART ANT FARM • HERBERT BAYER • JOSEPH BEUYS • BEEHIVE DESIGN COLLECTIVE • MEL CHIN • FERNANDO GARCÍA-DORY • BRIGHT UGOCHUKWU EKE • NICOLE FOURNIER • GELITIN • ANDY GOLDSWORTHY • HEHE • FRIEDENSREICH HUNDERTWASSER • NATALIE JEREMIJENKO • ALLAN KAPROW • MAYA LIN • MICHAEL MANDIBERG • RED EARTH • PEDRO REYES • BONNIE ORA SHERK • ALAN SONFIST • TAVARES STRACHAN • SUPERFLEX • REVEREND BILLY TALEN • LILY YEH

DESIGN HERBERT BAYER • BEEHIVE DESIGN COLLECTIVE • CRITICAL ART ENSEMBLE • AMY FRANCESCHINI • ANDY GRACIE • FRIEDENSREICH HUNDERTWASSER • NATALIE JEREMIJENKO • JAE RHIM LEE • VIET NGO • MARJETICA POTRČ • PEDRO REYES • TOMÁS SARACENO • TAVARES STRACHAN • SUPERFLEX • TISSUE CULTURE & ART PROJECT • LILY YEH

GLOSSARY

Performance art utilizes the artist's own body as the medium to convey the thematic, stylistic, and compositional components of an artwork. Performance art can be scripted or unscripted. It can occur in an art venue or not. It can engage audience participation or not.

Bio art is distinguished by its medium, which is living matter in the form of tissues, bacteria, fungi, or entire living organisms and their life processes. Gardening, raising animals, and biotechnologies such as genetic engineering, tissue culturing, and cloning are all bio art processes.

Generative art is a process-oriented art practice that evolves in real time through a dynamic, self-contained, semiautonomous operative system. It exhibits a degree of complexity that makes behavioral prediction difficult.

Social practice artists maintain that sustainable environmental practices can succeed only if relationships among people and between people and their surroundings are included. Thus, their artworks are as likely to address human rights and economic opportunities as to address water treatment and forest management. Social practice art is not mediated through an image or a sculpture. Communication proceeds directly from artist to community members, who are often invited to become participants in the artwork.

Digital art is distinguished by the utilization of digital technologies to create imagery and produce art objects. Digital art is also referred to as computer art, multimedia art, and new media art. Eco artists who produce eco visualizations frequently rely upon digital technologies.

Installation art refers to three-dimensional artworks designed to fill interior architectural spaces, as opposed to art that is confined in a frame or set on a pedestal. Installation art can be temporary or permanent and can be presented in art venues or non-art spaces. It typically incorporates a broad range of materials not commonly associated with the production of art.

Public art is distinguished by its location within the public domain, where it is accessible to an entire community. It usually appears in built environments. As opposed to public sculpture's detachment from site, public art emerges from the site's local history, physical conditions, and/or resident populations. Public artists are less concerned with creating objects than in instigating experiences.

Design is characterized by a systematic effort to fulfill a predetermined purpose, which is often functional. Deliberation and forethought replace improvisation and spontaneity.

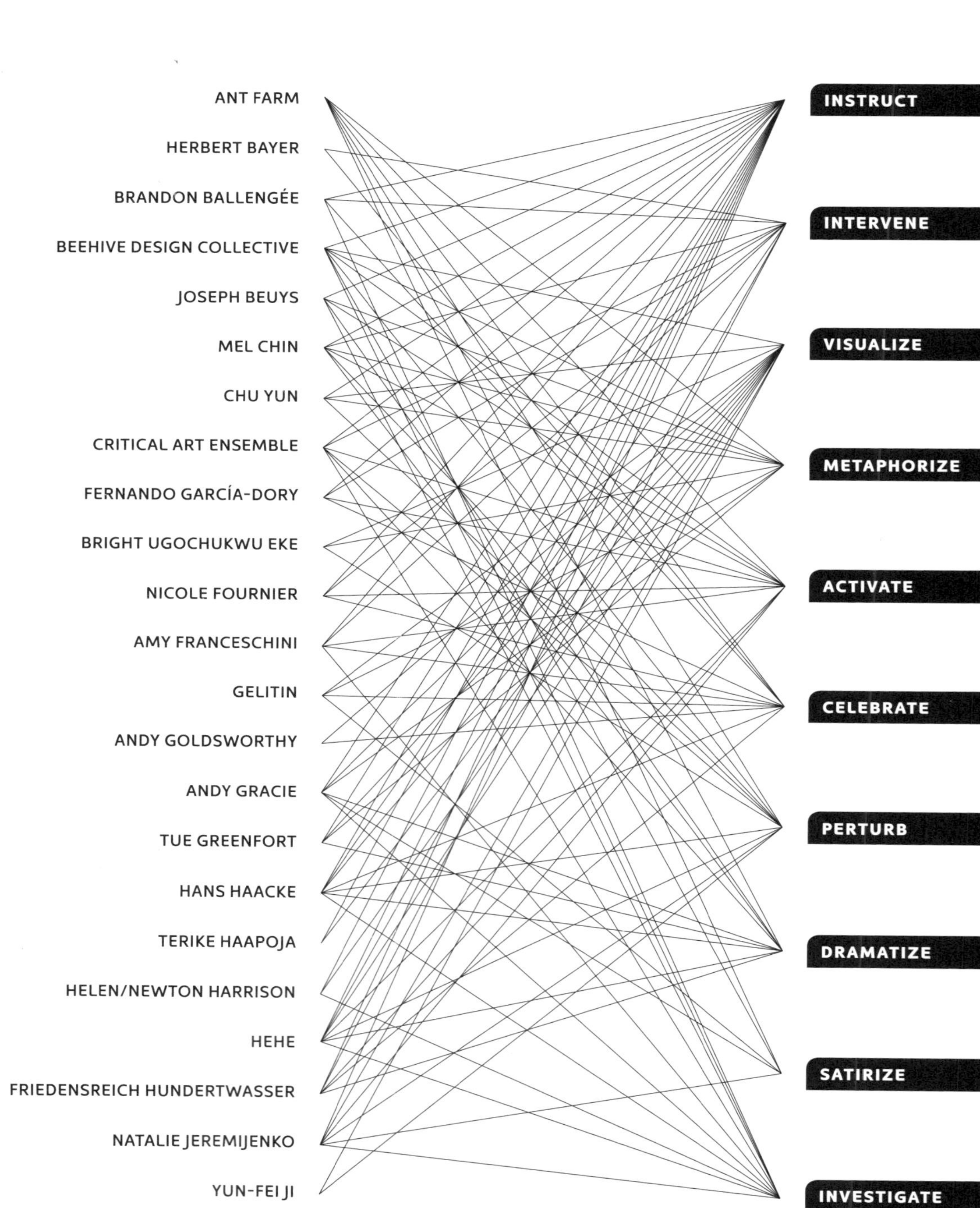

ANT FARM
HERBERT BAYER
BRANDON BALLENGÉE
BEEHIVE DESIGN COLLECTIVE
JOSEPH BEUYS
MEL CHIN
CHU YUN
CRITICAL ART ENSEMBLE
FERNANDO GARCÍA-DORY
BRIGHT UGOCHUKWU EKE
NICOLE FOURNIER
AMY FRANCESCHINI
GELITIN
ANDY GOLDSWORTHY
ANDY GRACIE
TUE GREENFORT
HANS HAACKE
TERIKE HAAPOJA
HELEN/NEWTON HARRISON
HEHE
FRIEDENSREICH HUNDERTWASSER
NATALIE JEREMIJENKO
YUN-FEI JI
INSTRUCT
INTERVENE
VISUALIZE
METAPHORIZE
ACTIVATE
CELEBRATE
PERTURB
DRAMATIZE
SATIRIZE
INVESTIGATE

Schematic of ART STRATEGIES

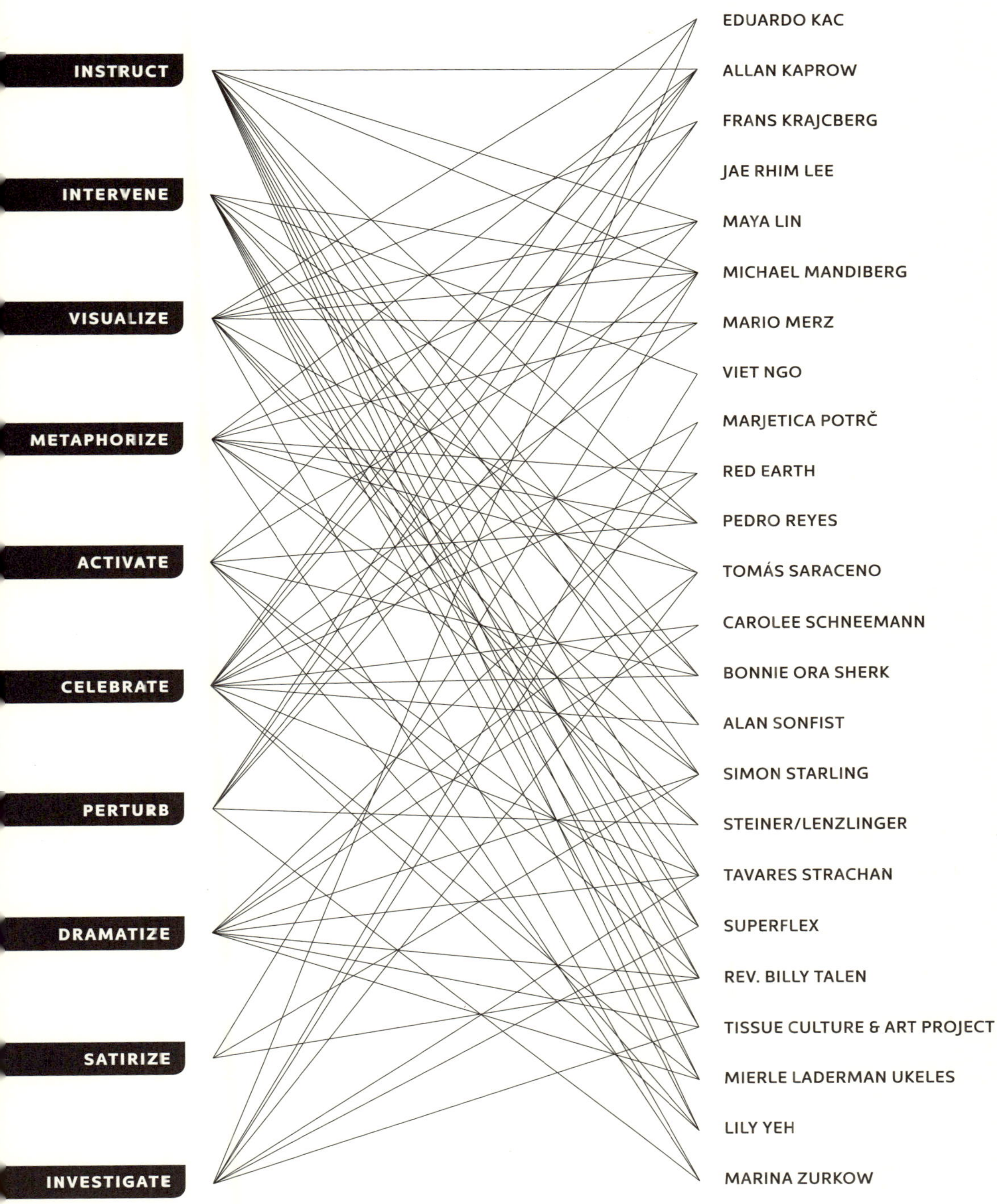

INSTRUCT
INTERVENE
VISUALIZE
METAPHORIZE
ACTIVATE
CELEBRATE
PERTURB
DRAMATIZE
SATIRIZE
INVESTIGATE

EDUARDO KAC
ALLAN KAPROW
FRANS KRAJCBERG
JAE RHIM LEE
MAYA LIN
MICHAEL MANDIBERG
MARIO MERZ
VIET NGO
MARJETICA POTRČ
RED EARTH
PEDRO REYES
TOMÁS SARACENO
CAROLEE SCHNEEMANN
BONNIE ORA SHERK
ALAN SONFIST
SIMON STARLING
STEINER/LENZLINGER
TAVARES STRACHAN
SUPERFLEX
REV. BILLY TALEN
TISSUE CULTURE & ART PROJECT
MIERLE LADERMAN UKELES
LILY YEH
MARINA ZURKOW

Index and Glossary of Art Strategies

INDEX

INSTRUCT JOSEPH BEUYS • BRANDON BALLENGÉE • BEEHIVE DESIGN COLLECTIVE • MEL CHIN • CHU YUN • CRITICAL ART ENSEMBLE • FERNANDO GARCÍA-DORY • NICOLE FOURNIER • AMY FRANCESCHINI • ANDY GRACIE • TUE GREENFORT • HANS HAACKE • TERIKE HAAPOJA • HELEN AND NEWTON HARRISON • HEHE • FRIEDENSREICH HUNDERTWASSER • NATALIE JEREMIJENKO • ALLAN KAPROW • JAE RHIM LEE • MAYA LIN • MICHAEL MANDIBERG • PEDRO REYES • BONNIE ORA SHERK • ALAN SONFIST • SIMON STARLING • TAVARES STRACHAN • SUPERFLEX • REVEREND BILLY TALEN • TISSUE CULTURE & ART PROJECT • MIERLE LADERMAN UKELES • LILY YEH

INTERVENE HERBERT BAYER • BRANDON BALLENGÉE • MEL CHIN • CRITICAL ART ENSEMBLE • FERNANDO GARCÍA-DORY • NICOLE FOURNIER • AMY FRANCESCHINI • HANS HAACKE • FRIEDENSREICH HUNDERTWASSER • HEHE • JAE RHIM LEE • MICHAEL MANDIBERG • VIET NGO • PEDRO REYES • BONNIE ORA SHERK • ALAN SONFIST • SUPERFLEX • REVEREND BILLY TALEN • TISSUE CULTURE & ART PROJECT • MIERLE LADERMAN UKELES • LILY YEH

VISUALIZE BEEHIVE DESIGN COLLECTIVE • CHU YUN • BRIGHT UGOCHUKWU EKE • GELITIN • ANDY GOLDSWORTHY • ANDY GRACIE • TUE GREENFORT • HANS HAACKE • TERIKE HAAPOJA • HELEN AND NEWTON HARRISON • HEHE • NATALIE JEREMIJENKO • YUN-FEI JI • EDUARDO KAC • FRANS KRAJCBERG • JAE RHIM LEE • MAYA LIN • MICHAEL MANDIBERG • MARIO MERZ • TOMÁS SARACENO • SIMON STARLING • GERDA STEINER AND JÖRG LENZLINGER • TAVARES STRACHAN • MARINA ZURKOW

METAPHORIZE ANT FARM • BEEHIVE DESIGN COLLECTIVE • JOSEPH BEUYS • MEL CHIN • CHU YUN • BRIGHT UGOCHUKWU EKE • GELITIN • ANDY GRACIE • TUE GREENFORT • ALLAN KAPROW • MARIO MERZ • MAYA LIN • RED EARTH • PEDRO REYES • TOMÁS SARACENO • SIMON STARLING • GERDA STEINER AND JÖRG LENZLINGER • MARINA ZURKOW

ACTIVATE ANT FARM • BEEHIVE DESIGN COLLECTIVE • JOSEPH BEUYS • MEL CHIN • FERNANDO GARCÍA-DORY • NICOLE FOURNIER • AMY FRANCESCHINI • HEHE • FRIEDENSREICH HUNDERTWASSER • NATALIE JEREMIJENKO • ALLAN KAPROW • BONNIE ORA SHERK • MICHAEL MANDIBERG • PEDRO REYES • SUPERFLEX • LILY YEH

CELEBRATE ANT FARM • HERBERT BAYER • BRANDON BALLENGÉE • FERNANDO GARCÍA-DORY • NICOLE FOURNIER • AMY FRANCESCHINI • GELITIN • ANDY GOLDSWORTHY • HANS HAACKE • TERIKE HAAPOJA • FRIEDENSREICH HUNDERTWASSER • EDUARDO KAC • ALLAN KAPROW • FRANS KRAJCBERG • JAE RHIM LEE • MARIO MERZ • MARJETICA POTRČ • RED EARTH • CAROLEE SCHNEEMANN • BONNIE ORA SHERK • ALAN SONFIST • TAVARES STRACHAN • MIERLE LADERMAN UKELES • LILY YEH

PERTURB ANT FARM • BEEHIVE DESIGN COLLECTIVE • MEL CHIN • CHU YUN • CRITICAL ART ENSEMBLE • BRIGHT UGOCHUKWU EKE • HANS HAACKE • HEHE • NATALIE JEREMIJENKO • YUN-FEI JI • ALLAN KAPROW • FRANS KRAJCBERG • MAYA LIN • MICHAEL MANDIBERG • GERDA STEINER AND JÖRG LENZLINGER • MARINA ZURKOW

DRAMATIZE ANT FARM • JOSEPH BEUYS • MEL CHIN • CRITICAL ART ENSEMBLE • ANDY GRACIE • TUE GREENFORT • HANS HAACKE • FRIEDENSREICH HUNDERTWASSER • HEHE • MARJECTICA POTRČ • RED EARTH • TOMÁS SARACENO • CAROLEE SCHNEEMANN • SIMON STARLING • TAVARES STRACHAN • REVEREND BILLY TALEN • TISSUE CULTURE & ART PROJECT • MIERLE LADERMAN UKELES

SATIRIZE ANT FARM • BEEHIVE DESIGN COLLECTIVE • GELITIN • ANDY GRACIE • NATALIE JEREMIJENKO • MICHAEL MANDIBERG • SIMON STARLING • REVEREND BILLY TALEN

INVESTIGATE BRANDON BALLENGÉE • BEEHIVE DESIGN COLLECTIVE • JOSEPH BEUYS • CRITICAL ART ENSEMBLE • AMY FRANCESCHINI • ANDY GRACIE • HANS HAACKE • HELEN AND NEWTON HARRISON • HEHE • NATALIE JEREMIJENKO • EDUARDO KAC • JAE RHIM LEE • VIET NGO • MARJETICA POTRČ • TOMÁS SARACENO • TAVARES STRACHAN • SUPERFLEX • TISSUE CULTURE & ART PROJECT

GLOSSARY

Visualize refers to an artistic strategy designed to manifest abstract data and invisible forces with the goal of increasing public awareness and motivating modifications in behavior. Typical visualization techniques include photographs, animation, and web applications.

Metaphorize refers to the use of comparison to denote a kind of object, action, or condition.

Activate refers to artworks created for the purpose of energizing the audience to take an action or motivating people to reform behaviors.

Dramatize refers to art that highlights a condition or issue by expressing it so vividly it has an emotional impact on the audience.

Investigate refers to artworks that are the product of extensive research, methodical experimentation, or public inquiry.

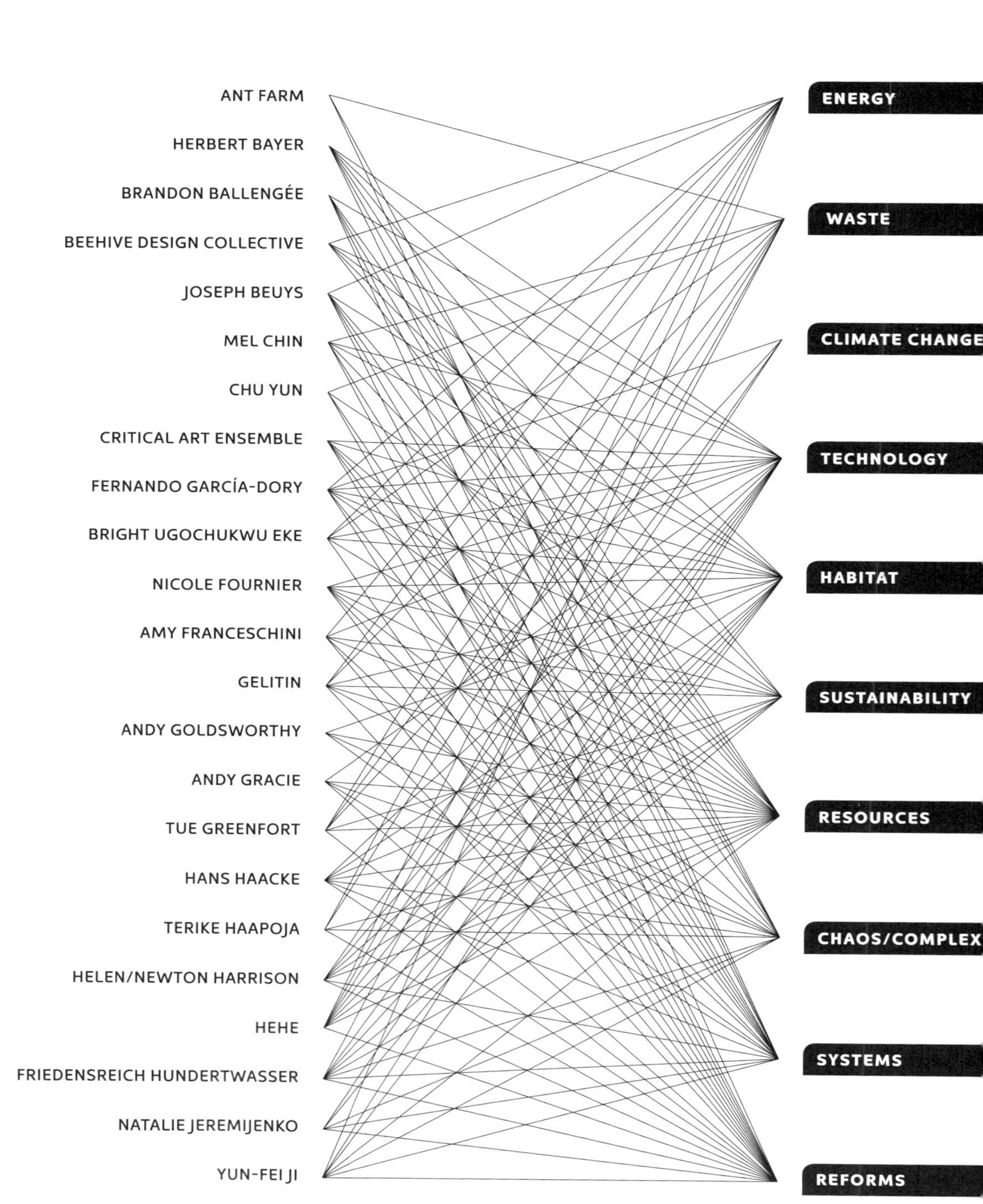
ANT FARM
HERBERT BAYER
BRANDON BALLENGÉE
BEEHIVE DESIGN COLLECTIVE
JOSEPH BEUYS
MEL CHIN
CHU YUN
CRITICAL ART ENSEMBLE
FERNANDO GARCÍA-DORY
BRIGHT UGOCHUKWU EKE
NICOLE FOURNIER
AMY FRANCESCHINI
GELITIN
ANDY GOLDSWORTHY
ANDY GRACIE
TUE GREENFORT
HANS HAACKE
TERIKE HAAPOJA
HELEN/NEWTON HARRISON
HEHE
FRIEDENSREICH HUNDERTWASSER
NATALIE JEREMIJENKO
YUN-FEI JI
ENERGY
WASTE
CLIMATE CHANGE
TECHNOLOGY
HABITAT
SUSTAINABILITY
RESOURCES
CHAOS/COMPLEX
SYSTEMS
REFORMS

Schematic of ECO ISSUES

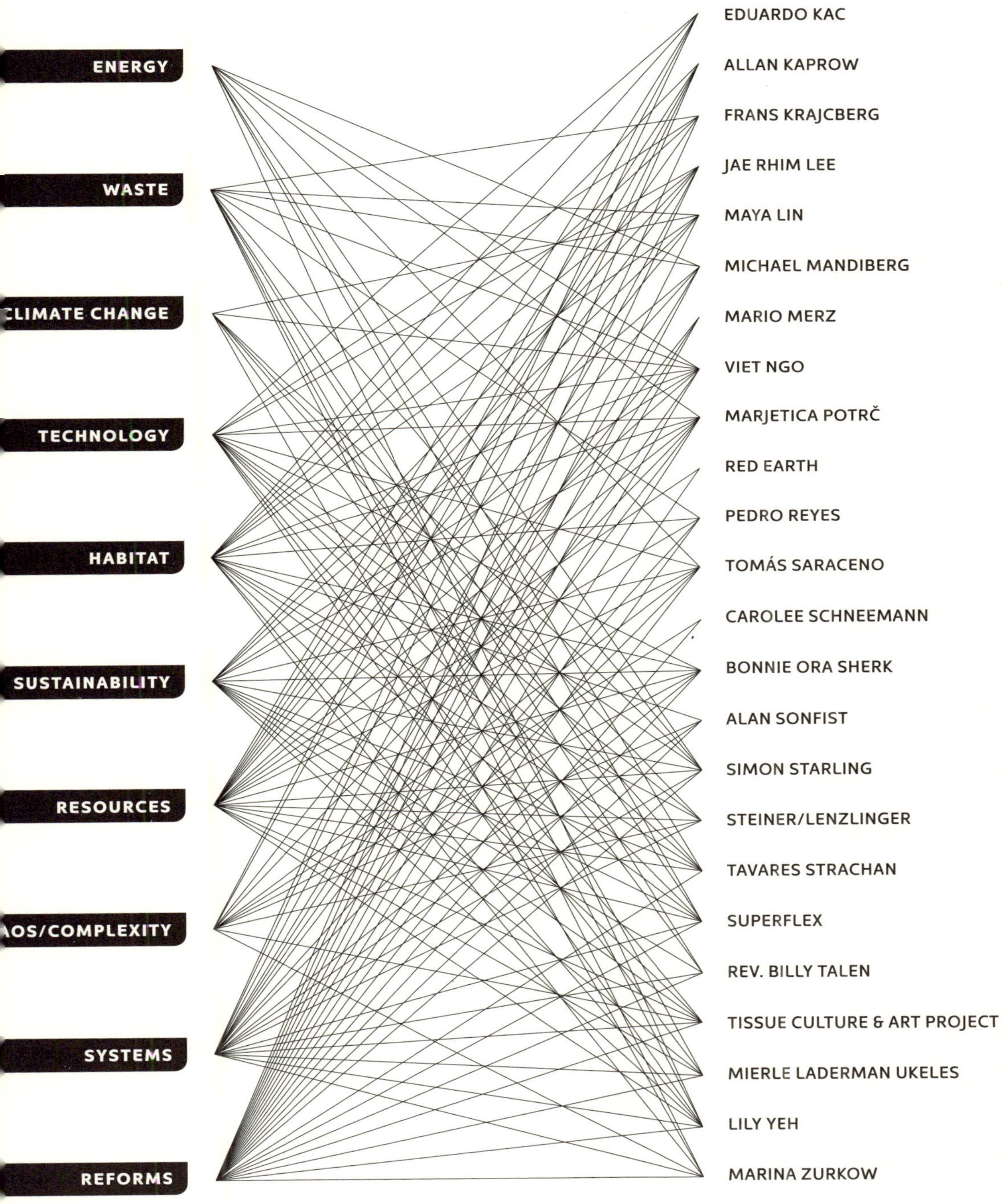

ENERGY

WASTE

CLIMATE CHANGE

TECHNOLOGY

HABITAT

SUSTAINABILITY

RESOURCES

AOS/COMPLEXITY

SYSTEMS

REFORMS

EDUARDO KAC

ALLAN KAPROW

FRANS KRAJCBERG

JAE RHIM LEE

MAYA LIN

MICHAEL MANDIBERG

MARIO MERZ

VIET NGO

MARJETICA POTRČ

RED EARTH

PEDRO REYES

TOMÁS SARACENO

CAROLEE SCHNEEMANN

BONNIE ORA SHERK

ALAN SONFIST

SIMON STARLING

STEINER/LENZLINGER

TAVARES STRACHAN

SUPERFLEX

REV. BILLY TALEN

TISSUE CULTURE & ART PROJECT

MIERLE LADERMAN UKELES

LILY YEH

MARINA ZURKOW

Index of Eco Issues

ENERGY

CONSERVATION TUE GREENFORT • HEHE • MICHAEL MANDIBERG • VIET NGO • SIMON STARLING

DISPERSAL JOSEPH BEUYS • GELITIN • TERIKE HAAPOJA

EXTRACTION BEEHIVE DESIGN COLLECTIVE • BRIGHT UGOCHUKWU EKE

GENERATION JOSEPH BEUYS • AMY FRANCESCHINI • YUN-FEI JI • MARJETICA POTRČ • SIMON STARLING • TAVARES STRACHAN • TOMÁS SARACENO • SUPERFLEX • LILY YEH

WASTE

CONSPICUOUS CONSUMPTION ANT FARM • HEHE • MICHAEL MANDIBERG • REVEREND BILLY TALEN

POSTCONSUMER DISCARDS CHU YUN • BRIGHT UGOCHUKWU EKE • TUE GREENFORT • MAYA LIN • MIERLE LADERMAN UKELES • MARINA ZURKOW

WASTE REGIMENS GELITIN • HANS HAACKE • TERIKE HAAPOJA • HEHE • FRIEDENSREICH HUNDERTWASSER • JAE RHIM LEE • MAYA LIN • VIET NGO • MARJETICA POTRČ • SIMON STARLING • SUPEFLEX • MIERLE LADERMAN UKELES • LILY YEH

DEFORESTATION FRANS KRAJCBERG • MAYA LIN • PEDRO REYES • SUPERFLEX

PEOPLE INCAPACITATED BY ENVIRONMENTAL ILLNESS MEL CHIN • BRIGHT UGOCHUKWU EKE • LILY YEH

CLIMATE CHANGE

ADAPTATION FERNANDO GARCÍA-DORY • HELEN AND NEWTON HARRISON • SIMON STARLING • TAVARES STRACHAN

DEMONSTRATION MAYA LIN • GERDA STEINER AND JÖRG LENZLINGER • MARINA ZURKOW

MITIGATION TUE GREENFORT • HEHE • VIET NGO • REVEREND BILLY TALEN

TECHNOLOGY

BIOLOGICAL REPRODUCTION BRANDON BALLENGÉE • AMY FRANCESCHINI • NATALIE JEREMIJENKO • EDUARDO KAC • JAE RHIM LEE • VIET NGO • TISSUE CULTURE & ART PROJECT

ENERGY PRODUCTION AMY FRANCESCHINI • VIET NGO • MARJETICA POTRČ • TOMÁS SARACENO • SIMON STARLING • TAVARES STRACHAN

FOOD PRODUCTION CRITICAL ART ENSEMBLE • FERNANDO GARCÍA-DORY • NICOLE FOURNIER • HELEN AND NEWTON HARRISON • JAE RHIM LEE • BONNIE ORA SHERK • SUPERFLEX • TISSUE CULTURE & ART PROJECT

GENETIC ENGINEERING/TISSUE CULTURING CRITICAL ART ENSEMBLE • NATALIE JEREMIJENKO • JAE RHIM LEE • TISSUE CULTURE & ART PROJECT

BIOELECTRONICS/BIOMECHANICS/BIOREACTOR AMY FRANCESCHINI • ANDY GRACIE • EDUARDO KAC • TOMÁS SARACENO • SUPERFLEX • TISSUE CULTURE & ART PROJECT

ROBOTICS ANDY GRACIE • NATALIE JEREMIJENKO

HABITAT

SUSTAINABILITY

RESOURCES

CHAOS/COMPLEXITY

SYSTEMS

AGRICULTURAL SYSTEM CRITICAL ART ENSEMBLE • FERNANDO GARCÍA-DORY • NICOLE FOURNIER • HELEN AND NEWTON HARRISON • JAE RHIM LEE

BIOLOGICAL SYSTEM BRANDON BALLENGÉE • CRITICAL ART ENSEMBLE • FERNANDO GARCÍA-DORY • NICOLE FOURNIER • AMY FRANCESCHINI • NATALIE JEREMIJENKO • TERIKE HAAPOJA • EDUARDO KAC • HELEN AND NEWTON HARRISON • JAE RHIM LEE • MARIO MERZ • BONNIE ORA SHERK • ALAN SONFIST • TISSUE CULTURE & ART PROJECT

COMMUNICATION SYSTEM ANDY GRACIE • MICHAEL MANDIBERG • TOMÁS SARACENO • LILY YEH • MARINA ZURKOW

EDUCATION SYSTEM JOSEPH BEUYS • BONNIE ORA SHERK • LILY YEH • BONNIE ORA SHERK • SUPERFLEX • TISSUE CULTURE & ART PROJECT

MARKET SYSTEM ANT FARM • CHU YUN • PEDRO REYES • REVEREND BILLY TALEN

POLITICAL/SOCIAL SYSTEM JOSEPH BEUYS • MEL CHIN • HANS HAACKE • SUPERFLEX • MIERLE LADERMAN UKELES

REMEDIATION SYSTEM MEL CHIN • HANS HAACKE • JAE RHIM LEE • PEDRO REYES • SUPERFLEX • VIET NGO

SANITATION SYSTEM HANS HAACKE • FRIEDENSREICH HUNDERTWASSER • MARJETICA POTRČ • MIERLE LADERMAN UKELES • LILY YEH

WATERSHED SYSTEM HERBERT BAYER • ANDY GOLDSWORTHY • YUN-FEI JI • ALLAN KAPROW • HELEN AND NEWTON HARRISON • GERDA STEINER AND JÖRG LENZLINGER

WEATHER SYSTEM HERBERT BAYER • ANDY GOLDSWORTHY • HANS HAACKE • TOMÁS SARACENO

REFORMS

HERITAGE PRESERVATION FERNANDO GARCÍA-DORY • YUN-FEI JI • RED EARTH • SUPERFLEX • ALAN SONFIST • LILY YEH

SPECIES PRESERVATION BRANDON BALLENGÉE • MAYA LIN

PRUDENCE CHU YUN • BRIGHT UGOCHUKWU EKE • NICOLE FOURNIER • TUE GREENFORT • HEHE • MICHAEL MANDIBERG • SIMON STARLING • REVEREND BILLY TALEN

INTIMACY/REVERENCE JOSEPH BEUYS • NICOLE FOURNIER • ALLAN KAPROW • FRANS KRAJCBERG • MAYA LIN • RED EARTH • CAROLEE SCHNEEMANN

HUMAN/NONHUMAN AFFINITY ANDY GRACIE • TERIKE HAAPOJA • JAE RHIM LEE • RED EARTH • BONNIE ORA SHERK

HUMAN CREATIVITY JOSEPH BEUYS • FRIEDENSREICH HUNDERTWASSER • MARJETICA POTRČ

BIOMIMICRY FRIEDENSREICH HUNDERTWASSER • JAE RHIM LEE • MARIO MERZ • VIET NGO • TOMÁS SARACENO

CITIZEN SCIENCE BRANDON BALLENGÉE • CRITICAL ART ENSEMBLE • NATALIE JEREMIJENKO

COMMUNITY EMPOWERMENT MEL CHIN • FERNANDO GARCÍA-DORY • NICOLE FOURNIER • AMY FRANCESCHINI • MARJETICA POTRČ • BONNIE ORA SHERK • TAVARES STRACHAN • SUPERFLEX • TISSUE CULTURE & ART PROJECT • LILY YEH

GOVERNMENT RESPONSIBILITY MEL CHIN • HANS HAACKE • MARJETICA POTRČ

POWER SHARING CRITICAL ART ENSEMBLE • AMY FRANCESCHINI • NATALIE JEREMIJENKO • HANS HAACKE • MARJETICA POTRČ • PEDRO REYES • SUPERFLEX • BONNIE ORA SHERK • MIERLE LADERMAN UKELES • LILY YEH

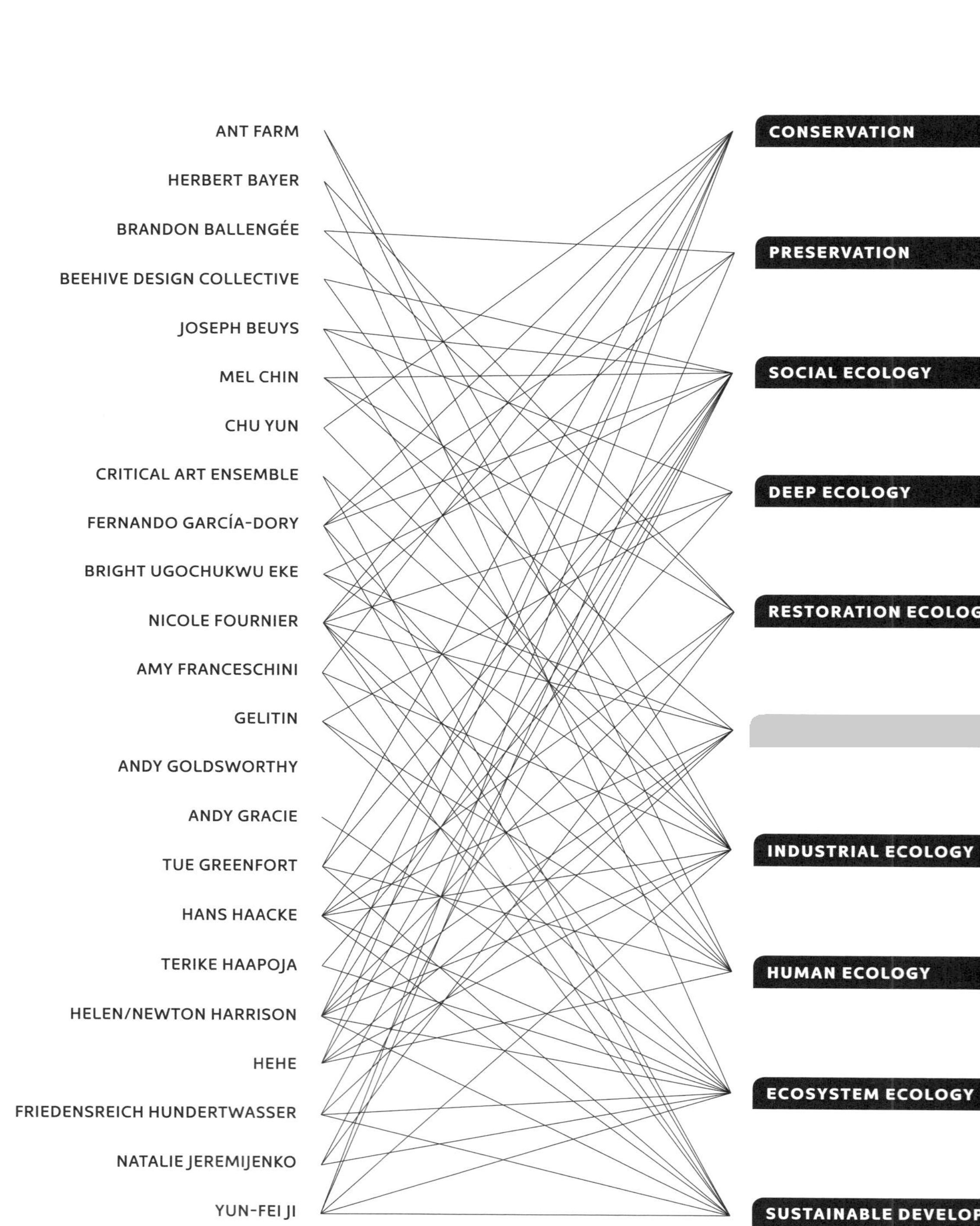
ANT FARM
HERBERT BAYER
BRANDON BALLENGÉE
BEEHIVE DESIGN COLLECTIVE
JOSEPH BEUYS
MEL CHIN
CHU YUN
CRITICAL ART ENSEMBLE
FERNANDO GARCÍA-DORY
BRIGHT UGOCHUKWU EKE
NICOLE FOURNIER
AMY FRANCESCHINI
GELITIN
ANDY GOLDSWORTHY
ANDY GRACIE
TUE GREENFORT
HANS HAACKE
TERIKE HAAPOJA
HELEN/NEWTON HARRISON
HEHE
FRIEDENSREICH HUNDERTWASSER
NATALIE JEREMIJENKO
YUN-FEI JI
CONSERVATION
PRESERVATION
SOCIAL ECOLOGY
DEEP ECOLOGY
RESTORATION ECOLOG
INDUSTRIAL ECOLOGY
HUMAN ECOLOGY
ECOSYSTEM ECOLOGY
SUSTAINABLE DEVELOP

Schematic of ECO APPROACHES

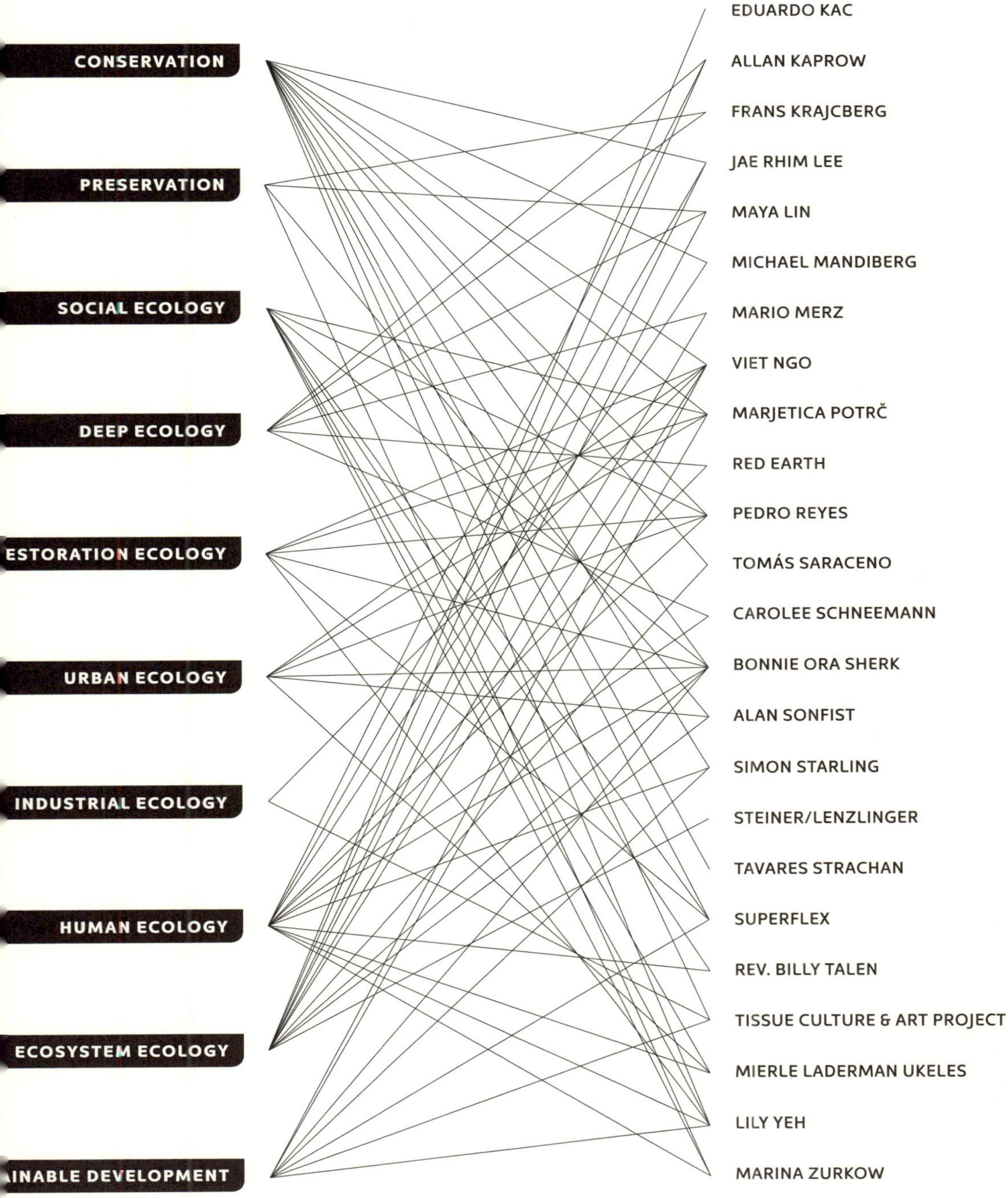

CONSERVATION
PRESERVATION
SOCIAL ECOLOGY
DEEP ECOLOGY
ESTORATION ECOLOGY
URBAN ECOLOGY
INDUSTRIAL ECOLOGY
HUMAN ECOLOGY
ECOSYSTEM ECOLOGY
INABLE DEVELOPMENT

EDUARDO KAC
ALLAN KAPROW
FRANS KRAJCBERG
JAE RHIM LEE
MAYA LIN
MICHAEL MANDIBERG
MARIO MERZ
VIET NGO
MARJETICA POTRČ
RED EARTH
PEDRO REYES
TOMÁS SARACENO
CAROLEE SCHNEEMANN
BONNIE ORA SHERK
ALAN SONFIST
SIMON STARLING
STEINER/LENZLINGER
TAVARES STRACHAN
SUPERFLEX
REV. BILLY TALEN
TISSUE CULTURE & ART PROJECT
MIERLE LADERMAN UKELES
LILY YEH
MARINA ZURKOW

Index and Glosssary of Eco Approaches

INDEX

CONSERVATION CHU YUN • FERNANDO GARCÍA-DORY • NICOLE FOURNIER • AMY FRANCESCHINI • TUE GREENFORT • HELEN AND NEWTON HARRISON • YUN-FEI JI • HEHE • JAE RHIM LEE • MICHAEL MANDIBERG • VIET NGO • MARJETICA POTRČ • PEDRO REYES • TOMÁS SARACENO • BONNIE ORA SHERK • SIMON STARLING • TAVARES STRACHAN • TISSUE CULTURE & ART PROJECT • LILY YEH

PRESERVATION BRANDON BALLENGÉE • FERNANDO GARCÍA-DORY • NICOLE FOURNIER • YUN-FEI JI • MAYA LIN • FRANS KRAJCBERG • ALAN SONFIST • MARINA ZURKOW

SOCIAL ECOLOGY BEEHIVE DESIGN COLLECTIVE • JOSEPH BEUYS • MEL CHIN • FERNANDO GARCÍA-DORY • BRIGHT UGOCHUKWU EKE • TUE GREENFORT • HANS HAACKE • HEHE • HELEN AND NEWTON HARRISON • FRIEDENSCRICH HUNDERTWASSSER • NATALIE JEREMIJENKO • MARJETICA POTRČ • PEDRO REYES • BONNIE ORA SHERK • SUPERFLEX • REVEREND BILLY TALEN • MIERLE LADERMAN UKELES • LILY YEH • MARINA ZURKOW

DEEP ECOLOGY JOSEPH BEUYS • NICOLE FOURNIER • GELITIN • TERIKE HAAPOJA • ALLAN KAPROW • FRANS KRAJCBERG • MAYA LIN • MARIO MERZ • RED EARTH • CAROLEE SCHNEEMANN

RESTORATION ECOLOGY BRANDON BALLENGÉE • HERBERT BAYER • MEL CHIN • HANS HAACKE • HELEN AND NEWTON HARRISON • NATALIE JEREMIJENKO • VIET NGO • MARJETICA POTRČ • BONNIE ORA SHERK • SUPERFLEX • LILY YEH

URBAN ECOLOGY MEL CHIN • BRIGHT UGOCHUKWU EKE • NICOLE FOURNIER • HANS HAACKE • HELEN AND NEWTON HARRISON • HEHE • FRIEDENSREICH HUNDERTWASSER • VIET NGO • MARJETICA POTRČ • PEDRO REYES • BONNIE ORA SHERK • ALAN SONFIST • MIERLE LADERMAN UKELES

INDUSTRIAL ECOLOGY ANT FARM • BEEHIVE DESIGN COLLECTIVE • CHU YUN • CRITICAL ART ENSEMBLE • BRIGHT UGOCHUKWU EKE • AMY FRANCESCHINI • HANS HAACKE • HELEN AND NEWTON HARRISON • HEHE • YUN-FEI JI • VIET NGO • TISSUE CULTURE & ART PROJECT

HUMAN ECOLOGY ANT FARM • JOSEPH BEUYS • FERNANDO GARCÍA-DORY • NICOLE FOURNIER • GELITIN • TUE GREENFORT • HEHE • ALLAN KAPROW • JAE RHIM LEE • MICHAEL MANDIBERG • PEDRO REYES • CAROLEE SCHNEEMANN • BONNIE ORA SHERK • RED EARTH • SIMON STARLING • REVEREND BILLY TALEN • MIERLE LADERMAN UKELES • LILY YEH • MARINA ZURKOW

ECOSYSTEM ECOLOGY HERBERT BAYER • NICOLE FOURNIER • GELITIN • ANDY GRACIE • TERIKE HAAPOJA • HANS HAACKE • HELEN AND NEWTON HARRISON • FRIEDENSREICH HUNDERTWASSER • NATALIE JEREMIJENKO • YUN-FEI JI • EDUARDO KAC • ALLAN KAPROW • JAE RHIM LEE • MAYA LIN • MARIO MERZ • VIET NGO • BONNIE ORA SHERK • ALAN SONFIST • TOMÁS SARACENO • GERDA STEINER AND JÖRG LENZLINGER

SUSTAINABLE DEVELOPMENT CRITICAL ART ENSEMBLE • FERNANDO GARCÍA-DORY • NICOLE FOURNIER • AMY FRANCESCHINI • TUE GREENFORT • HANS HAACKE • HELEN AND NEWTON HARRISON • FRIEDENSREICH HUNDERTWASSER • YUN-FEI JI • VIET NGO • MARJETICA POTRČ • BONNIE ORA SHERK • SIMON STARLING • SUPERFLEX • TISSUE CULTURE & ART PROJECT • LILY YEH

GLOSSARY

Conservation refers to management schemes designed to utilize the planet's resources to derive the most benefit for the most people while minimizing environmental damage and resource depletion.

Preservation is a policy that respects the inherent ability of ecosystems to determine their own optimal compositions and evolution. Preservation strategies often safeguard threatened territories by isolating them from human interference.

Social ecology studies the relationships between human populations and their environments, noting the environmental impacts of social structures such as hierarchical political systems, competitive economic systems, and consumerism, as well as ethnic and gender inequalities, international law, and urban planning. Social ecologists attempt to reformulate such social structures to reverse humanity's negative impact on the environment.

Deep ecology is a philosophy that envisions the universe as unified and interconnected and recognizes the inherent worth of all forms of life without regard for human utility and pleasure. As such, deep ecologists pursue metaphysical unification of humans and their surroundings, as opposed to relying on reason, to guide environmental reform.

Restoration ecology recreates a function or a condition that existed in an ecosystem prior to the onset of a disturbance.

Urban ecology examines the cycling of matter and the flow of energy among plant life, wildlife, and humans in urban habitats. Urban ecologists attend a broad range of city problems, including storm water runoff, smog, heat sinks, and local wildlife.

Industrial ecology is the study of material and energy flows through industrial systems. Industrial ecologists monitor the impacts that industrial activities have on the environment, including the extraction of resources; the transformation of resources into commodities, transport and packaging; and disposing of wastes.

Human ecology investigates the effect of humans on plants, animals, other people, and nonhuman populations, and vice versa. Human ecologists strive to shape living and working spaces, food and clothing, leisure activities and forms of transportation for the betterment of the planet.

Ecosystem ecology studies energy and matter as it courses through locally defined ecosystems. Ecosystem ecologists consider the integrated actions of biotic and abiotic components of ecosystems and their interactions with adjacent ecosystems.

Sustainable development is "development that meets the needs of the present without compromising the ability of future generations to meet their own needs" (www.un-documents.net/ocf-02.htm). In ecosystems, sustainability involves biological systems that remain diverse and productive over time. For humans, sustainability involves long-term maintenance of social and economic systems.

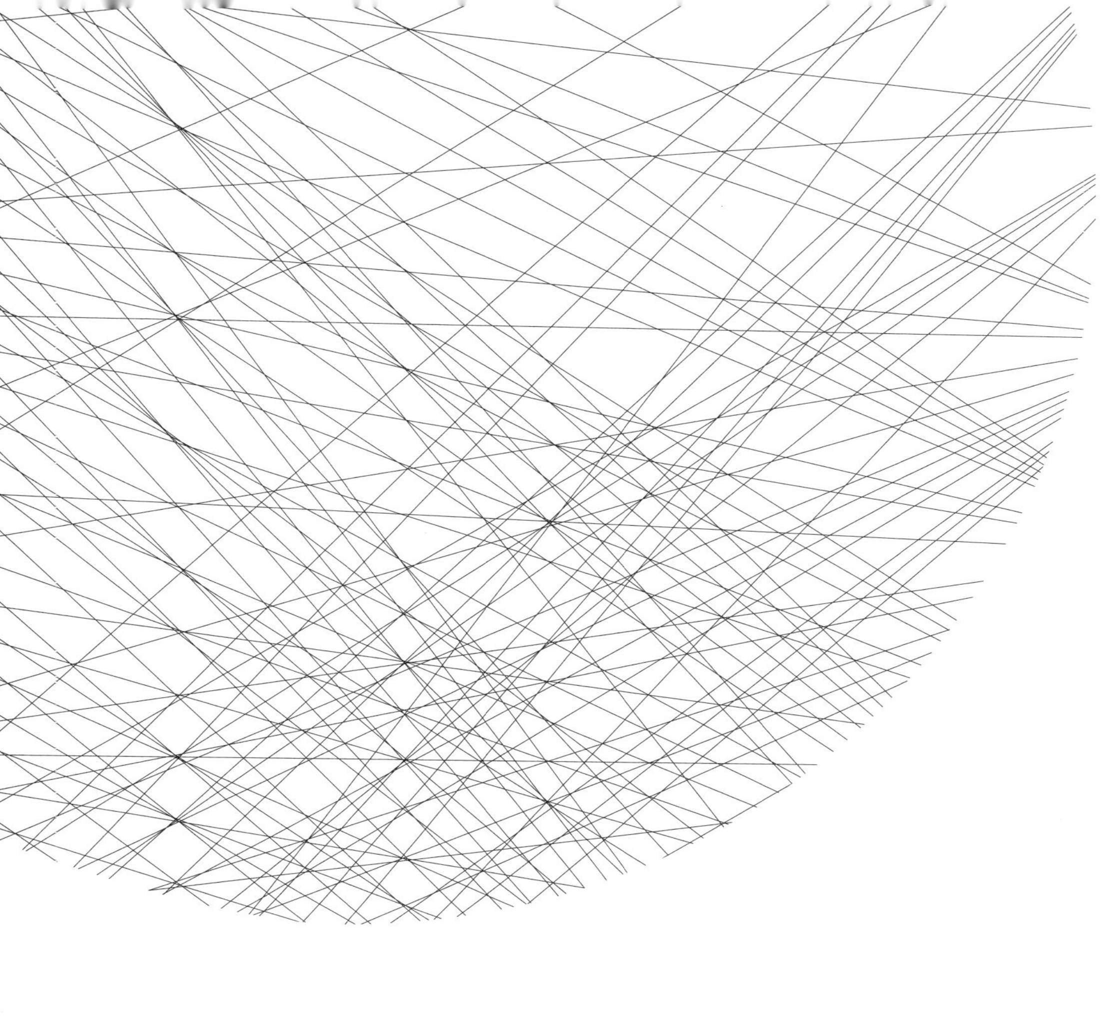

ART: Artistic Infrastructure

Introduction

Eco Art Is / Eco Art Is Not

THE URGE TO GIVE VISUAL FORM to personal sentiments, communal purport, economic conditions, spiritual beliefs, aesthetic values, and institutionalized agendas originated approximately forty thousand years ago. Humans have been creating art ever since, inventing countless devices to manifest their cultures' identity. These impulses are being expressed with a mixture of exuberance and vengeance by today's eco artists. The following chapters chart an advancing course of art today, identifying the contributions of new recruits eager for environmental reform. They also provide examples of the progenitors of today's eco art movement. This exploration begins with the 1960s because those were watershed years when the elements that distinguish eco art in the twenty-first century become palpable. In the 1960s, European and American cultures split into two contrasting camps: "counterculture" and "culture."

"Counterculture" was unified by its opposition to the stultifying conformity and spiritual vacuity of mainstream culture. Otherwise it was a mélange of specialized oppositions to diverse concentrations of authority. White society was attacked by the civil rights movement, commercialism by a new spirituality, universities by student protestors, rationality by psychedelic drugs, patriarchal power by the women's movement, and sexual restraint by the availability of birth control pills.

"Culture" was represented by escalation of the industrial sector, resulting in the rapid expansion of affluence. The word *revolution,* which is often affixed to these changes, was primarily engendered by technology, investment, and engineering. The term is misleading because it conjures images of abrupt and violent overthrows of a system that quickly crumbles, being replaced by an alternative that is so unprecedented it shatters expectations and demands radical adjustments. Twentieth-century technological "revolutions" altered the gadgets, making them bigger, faster, lighter, tougher, and more powerful, but the game remained the same. None challenged the assumption that it was good to amass power over the environment and exercise it to expand the population, longevity, and ease of humans.

The Green Revolution that emerged in this era and that is currently emerging in human societies across the globe may actually warrant the term *revolution* because it reverses this relentless drive. Zero population growth, voluntary simplicity, back-to-the-land movements, organic farming, vegans, birders, solar energy users, recyclers, alternative architectural practices, sustainable land development, community-supported agriculture are all indicators of a wholly new paradigm. These trends acknowledge ecological laws as the basic operants of the planet. They are instigating a profound shift in consciousness that really does seem revolutionary because they reverse the age-old course of human chauvinism. It is replaced with recognition that humans are merely a type of mammal sharing space on the planet with all other species.

Once the meaning of *human* shifts in this manner, all human interactions become eligible for redesign. This entails the observations and data and methods of the ecologist. But it relies equally upon the inventive creativity of the artist. Eco artists are attuned to lead the revolution toward a sustainable future. This book is a rallying cry to readers to join their crusade.

Eco Art Is

"ECO ART IS . . ." IS AN INCOMPLETE SENTENCE that all the pages in this book attempt to resolve. While new concepts are introduced by each chapter, eco art's extraordinary diversity coexists with a thread of commonality. These works share such descriptive nouns as *experiment, exploration*, and *inquiry*, suggesting that eco artists may be testing the limits of art's tolerance for change. Thus, examining eco art raises such quandaries as these:

> Is innovation an essential aspect of a masterwork of art?
>
> Is an understanding of past art a prerequisite for appreciating vanguard art?

These pesky and persistent questions have been swarming around Western art since the collapse of the guilds in Europe after the Middle Ages. That is when cultural attention shifted from the otherworldly domain of infinity and eternity to this-worldly interest in materiality and progress. The transformation established the dynamic course of civilization that has been accelerating and intensifying to this day. Along that course, the pathways of work, family, recreation, governance, and spirituality have resembled lanes, byways, arterials, detours, and occasion dead ends. Comparable routes chart the dynamic course of art.

IS INNOVATION AN ESSENTIAL ASPECT OF A MASTERWORK OF ART?

Most of the artists who have earned enduring esteem have dislodged existing standards of art. Nonetheless, innovation does not ensure renown. History demonstrates that two additional criteria are essential to earning masterwork status—the characteristics of artistic innovation must correlate with the nature of changes occurring in society at that time, and the degree of novelty must be synchronized with the extent and intensity of these changes.

How is this accomplished? Expanding art's mediums is one way artists throughout the ages have fulfilled these criteria; for example, clay and bronze factored into past avant-gardes because they were once novelties. Employing newly invented technologies is another means to introduce meaningful change in art; tube paint, welding guns, and lasers mark a succession of technological adoptions by avant-garde artists. Acknowledging a changed locus of influence is another strategy; for example, art made for domestic interiors instead of cathedrals and castles was innovative in the seventeenth century. Eco art perpetuates this pedigree because the scales, mediums, processes, and themes it is introducing are correlated with compounding environmental woes and humanity's determined efforts to rectify them. Its innovations address the uncertain fate of life currently existing on planet Earth.

Although some eco artworks promote sensory and emotive engagements, the overt functionality of much eco art introduces a particularly disputed form of innovation. Because it frequently seems indistinguishable from engineering, gardening, farming, researching, educating, and so forth, eco art can tamper with the popular assumption that art engages the human spirit. Two responses defend including pragmatic practices within the realm of "art."

First, art that focuses on the practical requirements of survival already appears on the historic trajectory of art innovations. Consider, for example, the many cultures where art functions as offerings to gods who reciprocate the favor by producing rain, multiplying flocks, healing the sick, curdling milk, and raising the sun. Second, artists typically serve the needs of their contemporaries. In the past, art has awakened devotion in times of spiritual unrest and it has aroused protest in times of suppression. Now art innovation is including utilitarian strategies regarding pollution, resource depletion, climate change, escalating populations, and so on, because the strategies that sustain us are threatened.

IS AN UNDERSTANDING OF PAST ART A PREREQUISITE FOR APPRECIATING VANGUARD ART?

Every art interaction is individualized. It is a product of a person's knowledge, intuition, interest, and mood. Familiarity with past art offers one of many ports of entry. Since the far-reaching innovations that eco artists are initiating comprise the content of this book, it is simply a fact that some people will relate this work to poets William Blake and William Wordsworth, or environmentalists Aldo Leopold and John Muir, or painters John Constable and Claude Monet, or philosophers Aristotle and Murray Bookchin. However, readers with none of these reference points need not despair. It also suffices if their context consists of a landscape painted with skill, observed sensitively, and rendered faithfully, or trips to Disney World and the Magic Kingdom, or Discovery Channel specials. All these possibilities provide portals for assessing eco art's explorations with temperature, moisture, sunlight, wind, water, topography, compaction, chemical change, plants, animals, microbes, and human cultural patterns.

In addition to defending its status as art, eco art must also justify its adoption of the prefix *eco-*. On one level, this is satisfied by noting the shared goal between ecologists and artists participating in today's environmental movement—they all actively strive to ensure the vitality of Earth's ecosystems. Four attributes refine the identification of eco art with ecology: topics, interconnection, dynamism, and ecocentrism. These attributes serve as routes for navigating the inspiring profusion of eco artworks. New discoveries are continually being made at their intersections, feeding the ever-evolving expanse of eco art.

Topics that apply to eco art comprise a vast spreadsheet of opportunities that are derived from the rigorous methods of ecologists and the subjective considerations of environmentalists. On the one hand, artists influenced by ecologists glean topics of consideration from three sources: nonhuman organisms, the nonliving environment, and human actions. Every temporal, spatial, behavioral, physical, and chemical possibility on Earth is accounted for within these three categories. On the other hand, artists who behave like environmentalists enrich this topical abundance by adding intuition, opinion, and interpretation. Their shared environmental agenda, however, rarely produces consensus regarding causes of observed phenomena or strategies to protect or rectify them. As a result, eco art encounters are replete with surprises. Some artists, for example, place faith in nature's own healing powers, while others trust human ingenuity. Some focus on local remedies while others adopt global perspectives.

Interconnection is the inescapable law of links and relationships that govern all materials, all processes, and all events on Earth. Eco art that manifests this principle accepts the influences of fluctuating humidity, temperature, sunlight, fungus, bacteria, mice, and humans. Glossaries of ecological terms affirm the centrality of interconnections to this discipline. They reference, for example, *system*, *network*, *synergy*, *coevolution*, *community*, *commensalism*, *mutualism*, *symbiosis*, *competition*, *mimicry*, *feedback*, and *succession*. The ecological axiom that no object is separate and no force is isolated has engendered a host of new disciplines that replace their former separatist identities. They are known as behavioral ecology, urban ecology, social ecology, acoustic ecology, political ecology, industrial ecology, Christian ecology, and media ecology, to name a few. Oddly, the term used to refer to art that embraces the abiding truth of connectivity is *eco art*, not *art ecology*.

Dynamism acknowledges that anything occupying space also transforms through time. Eco works of art that incorporate this attribute submit to the perpetual permutations that account for life on Earth by melting, evaporating, growing, mutating, dying, and so forth. While flux is inevitable, its tempo is variable, determined by the inherent responsiveness of a medium and the intensity of surrounding influences. Some artists choreograph this dynamic duet so that it proceeds according to plan. Others allow their works to yield to conditions they do not predict or wish to control.

Ecocentrism refers to the principle that humans are not more important than other entities on Earth. It is the opposite of anthropocentrism, which interprets reality in terms of human values and experiences. Societies founded on anthropocentrism cultivate "the humanities" and focus on human constructs, not natural systems. Furthermore, they honor "humanitarian" efforts to privilege the welfare of humans, not other living entities. The ecocentric alternative urges humans into alignment with broader environmental directives. It interprets reality as Gaia, the Earth goddess of the ancient Greeks. In 1979 James Lovelock, the renowned independent scientist and author, evoked the Gaia hypothesis that focuses on interdependence and mutuality, as applicable to humans as any other form of life. Ecocentric artists may choose to manifest this theory by inviting living entities and inert forces to create the physical, structural, and functional attributes of their works of art.

In sum, eco art's defining features can be constructed out of these four attributes:

- Topic identifies the dominant idea and determines the work's material and expressive components.
- Interconnections apply to the relationships between the physical constructs of a work of art and between the work of art and the context in which it exists.
- Dynamism emphasizes actions over objects, and changes over ingredients.
- Ecocentrism guides thematic interpretations as well as decisions regarding the resources consumed and the wastes generated at each juncture of the art process.

Since no single work epitomizes all four attributes, and no attribute alone conveys the range of eco art's thematic and material components, this book presents a panorama of examples. The burgeoning arena of contemporary eco art is disclosed, therefore, from two vantage points. Individual works of art delineate the components of this cultural landscape. The overview becomes visible only at their intersections, through relationships, and in combination.

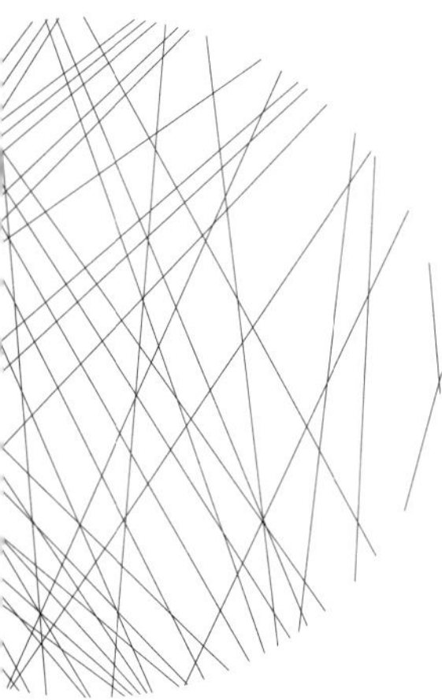

Eco Art Is Not

WHEN "TO LIFE!" RESOUNDS at gatherings of well-wishers and grievers, it is reserved for one particular species—humans. Its exclusivity characterizes anthropocentrism, the perception and interpretation of earthly phenomena in terms of human experience and values.

If, however, ecologists and environmentalists were to exclaim "To life!," the object of their toast would include microbes, plants, animals, and their habitats. Individuals who share ecology's commitment to the perpetually shifting, infinitely layered montage of living entities manifest ecocentrism. The ecocentric worldview honors life's sanctity, augments its diversity, protests its neglect, and optimizes its vitality.

The word *ecocentrism* entered the English language in the 1970s after a zealous minority arose to proclaim that rights belong to all species, not just humans. Ecocentrism envisions humans as components of interconnected systems. These systems are more essential to the planet than any of the individuals or objects found here.

The Twentieth-Century artists who joined this cause established the strategic and perceptual underpinnings of current eco art. These eco art pioneers challenged the assumptions that nonhuman forms of life are important only to the extent that they are useful to humans. The imprint of this anthropocentric supposition defined the cultural norm. It was evident in the era's prevailing notions of utility, beauty, ethics, recreation, spirituality, politics, and so forth. This essay provides a sampling of such anthropocentric notions by exploring three of its manifestations: productivity, longevity, and perspective. Each is revealed through a Twentieth-Century vanguard art movement: pop art, land art, and conceptual art. The individual examples of each were created by artists renowned for being among the originators of these movements: Andy Warhol, Walter De Maria, and On Kawara.

All three vanguard movements revolutionized fine art protocols. Ironically, they accomplished this transformation by affirming the cultural values that mainstream culture absorbed throughout this turbulent era. It is remarkable, therefore, that none of these examples of pop, land, or conceptual art was fueled by cultural dissent. It was left to eco artists to dispute the ethics and prudence of these transformations and implement reforms. Citing these movements, therefore, provides a means to convey the renegade character of eco art. Besides establishing its oppositional stance, such antithesis clarifies the principles that propel eco artists' bold explorations. Thus, the question, What is eco art? is answered in this essay by explaining what eco art is *not*. The text prepares readers to acknowledge eco art's contribution to art of the 1960s and 1970s as a deviation from a cultural norm that, remarkably, included vanguard art. This deviation exists even when Warhol depicts flowers, De Maria engages weather, and Kawara interprets landscape. While these subjects appear related to the considerations that fuel eco art, none of these artists addresses these issues from the vantage of a sustainable planet. Instead, they remain loyal to anthropocentric perspectives.

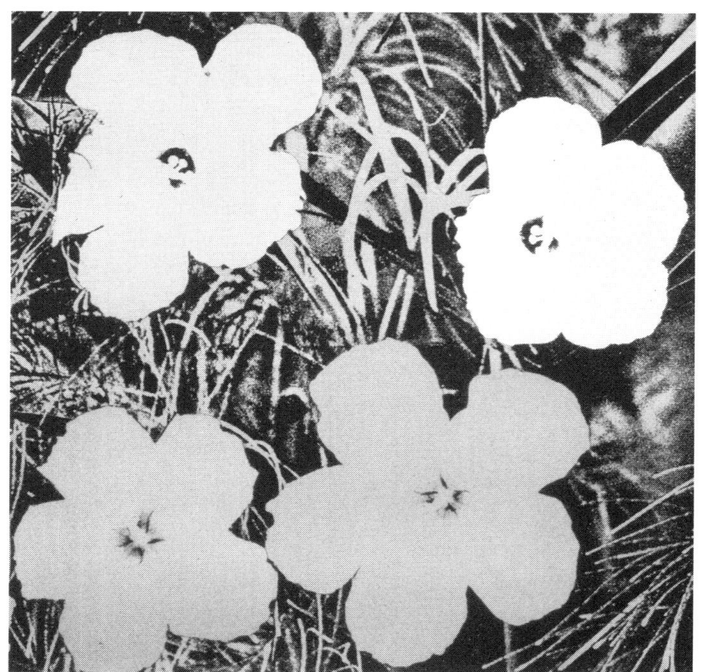

Andy Warhol | Flowers | 1964 Offset lithograph on paper | 23″ × 23″

CREDIT: © 2011 THE ANDY WARHOL FOUNDATION FOR THE VISUAL ARTS INC. / ARTISTS RIGHTS SOCIETY (ARS), NEW YORK / COURTESY ANDY WARHOL MUSEUM, PITTSBURGH; FOUNDING COLLECTION, AND THE RONALD FELDMAN GALLERY, NEW YORK

PRODUCTIVITY: POP ART (ANDY WARHOL)

Andy Warhol demonstrates that paintings of flowers in full bloom in a field don't necessarily evoke the beauty of nature or the concerns of environmentalists. His pop art paintings have more in common with General Electric, Ford, General Motors, Chrysler, IBM, Bell Telephone, US Steel, Pepsi-Cola, DuPont, RCA, and Westinghouse. The unprecedented productive capacity of these industrial giants was being celebrated by lavish displays at the 1964 World's Fair in New York City, the same year Warhol initiated his *Flower* series.

Although Warhol also showcased the abundance that infused American society in the mid-twentieth century, he did not depict a shoppers' paradise. Instead, his attention went behind the scenes to the processes responsible for both the production of cheap goods and the generation of popular imagery. He then reconfigured the production of his art to match the machine's takeover of culture and landscape, replacing the sensibilities, aesthetics, and skills associated with fine art with the mechanized production, assembly-line routines, and commercial strategies of non-art material production. These art practices occurred in a studio he renamed the Factory to indicate his radical artistic goal—to minimize inputs and maximize output. Warhol summed up his artistic intentions when he declared, "The reason I'm painting this way is that I want to be a machine, and I feel that whatever I do and do machine-like is what I want to do."[1]

Between June and July of 1964, Warhol created seven large paintings showing four Mandrinette flowers at peak bloom. The image of this prized hibiscus was mass-produced by a legion of Factory assistants who completed as many as eighty small *Flower* paintings per day. Warhol exclaims, "Friends come over to the Factory and do the work with me. Sometimes there'll be as many as fifteen people in the afternoon, filling in the colors and stretching the canvases."[2] Printmaking, even more than painting, enabled Warhol to exploit factory production strategies. By adopting a simple reproductive technique known as silk screen, the factory accelerated and increased its output of images. Perhaps the most radical confirmation of the industrial ethic was the strategy he devised to demonstrate that in an age of mass production, the multiple takes the place of the original. Warhol signed all the works that emerged from the Factory whether or not he was personally involved in their production.

Warhol's adoption of the cultural norm is apparent in the contemporary context in which he acquired the flowers he painted. Instead of growing in a field or garden, these flowers appeared in the June 1964 issue of *Popular Photography* magazine. The flowers had little connection with living botanicals. Instead, they were captured mechanically with a camera and processed industrially when they were developed and printed.[3] Warhol's process is a tribute to the machine and its takeover of natural occurrences. His style of representation further accentuated these cultural insignia. The images were altered by subtracting the flowers' textures and shading, pressing their spatial complexity into a flat decorative pattern, and then adding the hypersaturated hues common on '60s miniskirts, go-go boots, and psychedelic record album covers. Through these devices Warhol reformulated flowers into the glaringly artificial depictions of nature on tissue boxes and gift wrapping, earning them esteem as emblems of contemporary reliance on industrial manufacture.

Anthropocentric Productivity

The flowers Warhol represented were neither grown like botanicals nor created like art. They were assembled like cars. Their production encapsulates the anthropocentric reliance upon commerce and industry. Warhol's Mandrinette blossoms are as laborsaving as TV dinners, as synthesized as plastic, as processed as breakfast cereals, and as contrived as network news.

Ecocentric Productivity

Ecocentric productivity, on the other hand, is defined by ecologists as the creation of new organic matter by the process of photosynthesis. It bears little relation to anthropocentric focus on mechanical and industrial productivity. Ecocentric productivity is a measure of how much new growth occurs when light energy fuels the metabolic machinery of plants, which enables them to synthesize the new compounds and structures that make cells divide. It is measured by the amount of biomass generated by organisms occupying an ecosystem. In essence, ecocentric productivity is a measure of life. Bonnie Ora Sherk's *The Farm* and Helen and Newton Harrison's *Survival Piece* offer compelling counterpoints to Warhol's Factory. These eco art pioneers engage ecocentric productivity by creating living systems.

LONGEVITY: LAND ART (WALTER DE MARIA)

Unlike some land artists who allow their works to erode over time, Walter De Maria has ensured that his masterwork, *The Lightning Field* (1977), will endure forever. Furthermore, he has made certain that it will not only endure; it will maintain its pristine condition in perpetuity.[4] These guarantees are included in his contract with the work's funders. The stipulations

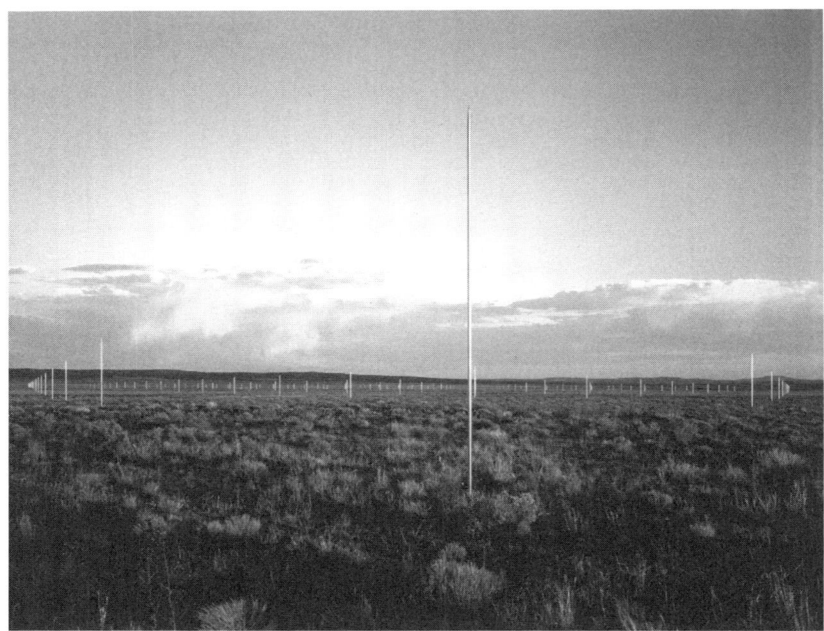

Walter De Maria | Lightning Field (day view) | 1977 A permanent earth sculpture, 400 stainless steel poles arranged in a grid array measuring 1 mile by 1 kilometer, average pole height 20 feet 7 inches | Quemado, New Mexico

PHOTO: JOHN CLIETT / CREDIT: © DIA ART FOUNDATION, NEW YORK / COURTESY DIA ART FOUNDATION, NEW YORK

are common in circumstances where a work of art can be protected while displayed in a climate-controlled exhibition venue and protected in a climate-controlled storage facility. That is not an option regarding *The Lightning Field*, which fulfills the definition of *land art* by existing in, and being inextricably linked to, the landscape. *The Lightning Field* is situated outdoors on a remote desert plateau near Quemado, New Mexico. It is, therefore, subjected to perpetual disturbance by sunshine, wind, rain, heat, frost, solar flares, microbes, plants, animals, humans, and most particularly, lightning.

The flip side of choosing an outdoor context was rejecting art's association with status, entertainment, and investment, the trio of characteristics promoted by commercial art galleries. Furthermore, galleries were too confining to accommodate the grandiose gestures envisioned by land artists who were committed to leaving humanity's mark upon the earth.

The geometrical elegance of *The Lightning Field* is a product of 400 polished stainless steel poles that De Maria had manufactured and delivered to the site. Each pole is 2 inches in diameter and averages 20½ feet tall. The poles are installed at regular 220-foot intervals to form a precise grid that stretches as far as the eye can see. Rectilinear geometry also characterizes their composite shape because the tops of the poles are aligned to produce a precise horizontal plane. The elementary nature of the form belies the complexity of its construction. Because the earth undulates, the height of each pole had to be individually calculated to produce a perfectly level plane. High-resolution stereo photographs, optical machines, laser transits, and electronic distance-measuring equipment enabled De Maria to fulfill the inviolable rules of right-angled geometry, contradicting the site's irregular topography.

Most monuments of human construction that endure through the ages survive as

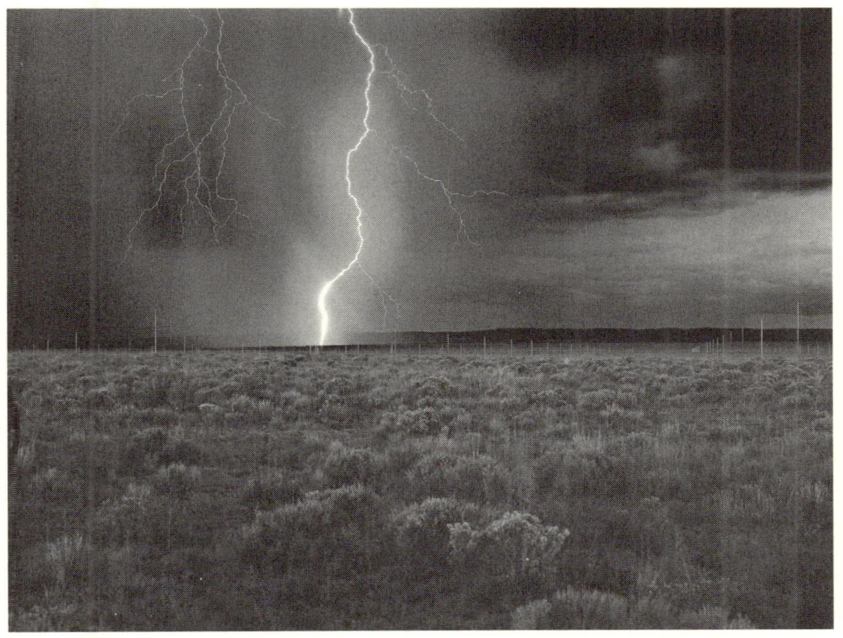

Walter De Maria | Lightning Field (night view) | 1977 A permanent earth sculpture, 400 stainless steel poles arranged in a grid array measuring 1 mile by 1 kilometer, average pole height 20 feet 7 inches | Quemado, New Mexico

PHOTO: JOHN CLIETT / CREDIT: © DIA ART FOUNDATION, NEW YORK / COURTESY DIA ART FOUNDATION, NEW YORK

gradually weathering constructions or as ruins. This was not De Maria's vision of longevity. He devised three strategies to protect *The Lightning Field* from succumbing to wear and tear: durability, resistance, and restoration.

Durability was maximized by implementing the no-compromise engineering specifications devised by Robert Fosdick during the work's planning phase. Fosdick, who directed the construction, comments, "We've taken 120-mile-per-hour winds into consideration, as well as the soil of this area, the storms, everything we can think of. The only change we can expect to happen would be caused if the earth itself moved."[5]

Resistance dictated the choice of medium. Stainless steel is immune to the vulnerabilities that afflict most other materials. It does not chip, fade, or crack; it withstands heat, light, and moisture; it resists fungus, bacteria, and predators.

Restoration is still necessary, despite these precautions, because De Maria intentionally subjects his rods to their one vulnerability. Stainless steel melts at very high temperatures. As the title suggests, De Maria exposes his artwork to lightning, a meteorological force that has stirred terror in the hearts of humans since the beginning of time. Lightning produces temperatures hotter than the surface of the sun. Nonetheless, De Maria beckons lightning to strike his work of art. The payback that justifies this risk takes the form of emblematic and awe-inspiring images of the occasional lightning strikes. These photographs account for the landmark status of this land art project. They depict jagged bolts of electricity hurtling through the skies, illuminating the vast array of steel rods. The linearity and brilliance of lightning is thereby matched by the linearity and brilliance of the stainless steel poles. In this way, lightning's capricious fury appears balanced against the strict logic of human geometry.

In order to fulfill this vision time and again, restoration is included in the site's conservation protocols. Damaged poles are quickly replaced after each strike, returning the work to geometric and material perfection. This guarantee is a profound cultural signifier.

Anthropocentric Longevity

Anthropocentric longevity is expressed as human strategies designed to preserve desirable conditions despite perpetual incursions and assaults by ecosystem forces. De Maria provides a compelling example of human willfulness by pitting the grid (the symbol of humanity's logic) against lightning (the symbol of the almighty force of nature) and then ensuring his work's survival. *The Lightning Field's* defenses against decay and damage confirm the anthropocentric values that extend throughout contemporary culture. Such defiance of ecosystem dynamics also motivates the manufacturers of wood preservatives, food stabilizers, rust retardants, Botox, cryogenics, fluoride treatments, and climate-controlled environments for the storage of art.

Ecocentric Longevity

Ecocentric longevity promotes continuity with the dynamic flux of interacting systems, in contrast to the static principle of endurance espoused by anthropocentric longevity. Ecocentric longevity is known as sustainability. Systems that persist even as individual components die or disappear are sustainable. They remain vital and productive over time by adapting to unanticipated changes. Walter De Maria's contemporary, Alan Sonfist, achieved status as an eco art pioneer by manifesting longevity in the forest he planted as an art project. His dynamic artwork will persist even as nonliving entities naturally accrete, erode, disperse, and dissolve and as living entities grow, die, decompose, evolve, and mutate.

PERSPECTIVE: CONCEPTUAL ART (ON KAWARA)

Perspective is the relationship that persons or cultures form with components of their surroundings. Landscape painters typically evoke their perspectives through aesthetic interpretations of the scenes they observe. Their perspectives can be distanced or immersive, skewed or frontal, oppositional or sympathetic, utilitarian or reverential. Such perspectives are irrelevant to On Kawara's conceptual art practice. His depiction of landscape includes only what he knows, not what he feels or perceives. For this reason he banishes inspiration from his creative process because it is momentary, observation because it is unreliable, sensuality because it is personal, and emotion because it is volatile. Kawara trades all of these appealing components of landscape painting to visualize a site's irrefutable location as prescribed by longitude and latitude, a rational scheme that imposes a grid of equal units upon the irregular complexities of the planet's land masses and water bodies. Latitude lines are equally spaced and parallel to the equator. Longitude lines are equally spaced and measure distances east and west. *Location* (1965) is such a painted landscape. It does not depict topographic or geological formations, nor weather and season, nor flora and fauna. Instead, Kawara reconfigures the landscape-painting tradition to epitomize conceptual objectivity. *Location* fulfills its title because the painted image depicts the numbers and letters that pinpoint an exact position. LAT.31°25′N and LONG.8°41′E denotes a remote region of the Sahara devoid of sentiment and history.

Objectivity also determines Kawara's style and composition. He avoids the whims of

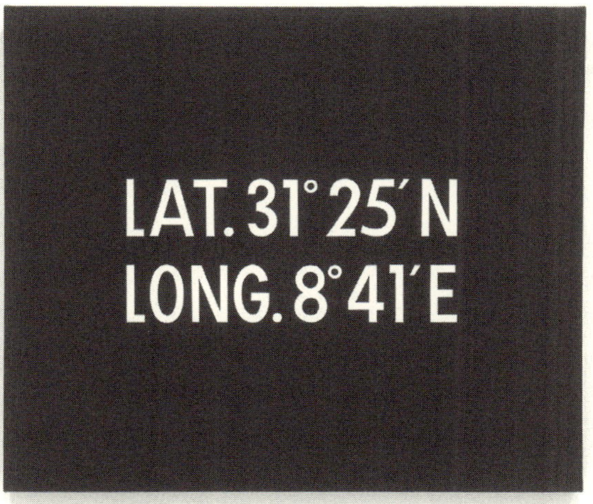

On Kawara | Location | 1965 Lat. 31°25′N, Long. 8°41′E | Acrylic on canvas | 32.9″ × 37.9″

PHOTO: PETER COX, EINDHOVEN, THE NETHERLANDS / COURTESY COLLECTION VAN ABBEMUSEUM, EINDHOVEN, THE NETHERLANDS

mood and taste by painting the numbers and letters in pure white upon a uniform dark green ground, presenting the text in standard Futura typeface, simplifying the composition to two horizontal lines centered between the top and the bottom of the canvas, and employing a methodical painting process undertaken with a predetermined result.

As a reflection of contemporary "perspectives" on the environment, longitude and latitude are culturally significant since they are situated in relation to the equinox and solstice. As such, they apply the remote perspective of the sun to places on the Earth. Thus, when humans use that latitude/longitude grid to answer the question, Where am I?, the answer is found by turning their backs to the earth and looking toward the sun for spatial markers. Recent Global Positioning System technologies and geographic information systems are referred to as "remote" because they, too, promote such emotional distancing.

Nonetheless as a manifestation of human perspective on the environment, Kawara's revision is more an extension of the landscape-painting tradition than a radical innovation. Like other landscape painters, he simplifies nature's inherent complexity, halts the actions of dynamic Earth systems, and ignores their role in humanity's survival. While his landscapes eliminate aesthetic stimulation and vicarious emotional release, they still present the environment as painted representations designed for contemplation.

Anthropocentric Perspective

Kawara's representation of a landscape is anthropocentric because it relies upon an abstract notational system invented by humans to benefit humans in navigating and communicating across the globe, and it disregards the inherent qualities of the location—its textures, shapes, colors, sounds, smells, temperature, humidity, and more. *Location* envisions the dissociated perspective of the many contemporary systems that use numbers to indicate places—zip codes, area codes, transportation routes, and so on. Kawara's version of a landscape encapsulates these aspects of contemporary perspectives.

Ecocentric Perspective

The word *landscape* is absent from ecocentric considerations because painted representations disregard the components of ecosystems that enable them to function: drainage patterns, ranges, biotic regions. They also ignore the interactions occurring within and among rivers, shorelines, mountain ranges, and meadows. These elements of the planet's locations are included in ecological terms like *watershed*, *habitat*, and *biome*. Such terminology considers locations according to their ability to provide resources, manage wastes, and perform dozens of additional services that determine the destinies of their populations. Joseph Beuys, Allan Kaprow, and Frans Krajcberg are among the eco art pioneers whose works embody the holistic character of ecocentric perspectives not indicated by the anthropocentric term *landscape*.

CONCLUSION

Nature is defined as the material world surrounding humankind and existing independently of human activities. This dictionary-like definition suggests that humans don't belong to nature. When humans think of themselves anthropocentrically, as outsiders, they grant themselves the leeway to approach nature as a medium of exchange, a source of wealth, a repository of resources, and a depository for waste. Separateness from nature is viewed as a sign of progress and a mark of civilization.

From an ecocentric perspective, however, the exclusion of humans from nature can justify behaviors that disrupt nature's balance and resilience. Many eco artists apply their communication and visualization skills to expand the definition of *nature* by incorporating human populations, all human technologies, and all the products of their imaginations.

While anthropocentrism and ecocentrism represent divergent worldviews, they are not irreconcilable. Approaches that privilege human-to-human communications and those that integrate nonhuman entities are both included in the toolbox of Twenty-First-Century humans. They may be appropriated separately or integrated, as when ecocentric strategies incorporate human perspectives and when anthropocentric behaviors attend to nonhuman and nonliving components of the environment. Eco artists are experimenting with varied proportions, introducing new recipes to accomplish the ongoing tasks of survival within conditions that are morphing rapidly, intensively, concurrently, and ubiquitously.

NOTES

1 Interview with G.R. Swenson, *Art News*, November 1963: 117.
2 http://www.gallerywarhol.com/andy-warhol-flowers-1970-FS-II.66.htm.
3 The image was taken by nature photographer Patricia Caulfield.
4 Support for maintaining and operating *The Lightning Field* is provided in part by an endowment established by Ray A. Graham III and Lannan Foundation. Support toward the permanent preservation of the undeveloped grasslands surrounding *The Lightning Field* was provided by Dia's board of trustees, Governor Bill Richardson and the State of New Mexico, Helen Winkler Fosdick, and Gucci.
5 http://www.sfaol.com/mccord/lightning.html.

ECO: Ecological Operatives

Introduction

What Is Ecology? What Is Environmentalism?

ART HAS PERFORMED an impressive array of services over the course of human history. It has elevated the stature of leaders, instilled courage to march into battle, inspired piety before gods, celebrated the bounty of the harvest, warned against evil, evoked rapture, and on and on. Today, this impressive list of functions is being extended to attend to the current and future conditions of the planet's waters, soils, atmosphere, and living populations. Some of the creators of these works of art follow the scrupulous scientific methods of ecology; others who behave as advocates, critics, and protestors are proponents of environmentalism. Both explore the fundamental relationships that form the basis of eco art.

Ecologists study the distribution and abundance of living organisms and their interactions with each other and with the nonliving environment. This classical definition of ecology was devised in 1873 by Ernst Haeckel, an eminent biologist, philosopher, physician, and artist. Haeckel's bare-bones definition requires supplementing to convey the uniquely expansive scope of this scientific discipline. For instance, *distribution* includes the oceans, hydrothermal vents, glaciers, vernal pools, intestinal tracts, and every other location on the globe where life survives. *Abundance of living organisms* encompasses over 1.7 million species that have been named and countless more that have yet to be identified. Each species is composed of entire populations, whether of algae, fungi, amphibians, insects, plants, birds, or mammals. Likewise, *interaction* accounts for a broad range of behaviors that include reproducing, migrating, defending, creating shelter, capturing energy, processing waste, and even decomposing. The *nonliving environment* is no less extensive, because it includes energy as well as all forms of inert matter. Even the word *study* must be clarified to distinguish this discipline from scientific pursuits that remove objects being researched from the variability and complexity of normal conditions and relocate them within controlled settings. Ecological study avoids fragmenting systems, isolating phenomena, reducing multiplicity, and suspending time.

Environmentalists, in contrast, contribute attitudes, opinions, and priorities to the verifiable information provided by ecologists. They are at liberty to relate to the Earth's systems by celebrating its splendor, healing its wounds, bolstering its resilience, managing its resources, mimicking its efficiencies, lamenting its infirmities, and the many alternatives evoked by the human imagination. Environmentalism was catalyzed by a convergence of events in the 1960s, beginning with the publication of *Silent Spring* by Rachel Carson. This landmark book unnerved an entire generation by presenting evidence that human activities were causing soils to become infertile, rain to acidify, water to become contaminated, and species to become extinct. Her alarming message was reinforced by a succession of events: people died from extreme air pollution,[1] a chemical-laced river caught fire,[2] and massive oil spills endangered wildlife and habitats.[3] The environmental movement in the United States was officially launched in April 1970 when Congress declared the first Earth Day and then established the Environmental Protection Agency in December of that year. A decade later, however, the movement became stalled by the Reagan administration's opposition to environmental causes, and then by the Clinton administration whose pro-environmental stance had the ironic effect of discouraging citizen activists. It was not until there was evidence of melting ice caps, and back-to-back horrific hurricane seasons in 2004–2005,[4] that planetary conditions rekindled the environmental movement.

NOTES

1 It was reported that 750 people died of smog in London in 1962, and 80 died in 1965 in New York City when a weather inversion created a four-day air pollution incident there.

2 On June 22, 1969, the Cuyahoga River burst into flames reportedly five stories high due to oil and chemical pollution.

3 The *Torrey Canyon* oil tanker crashed off the coast of England in 1967, spilling over 29 million gallons of oil on the coastlines of England and France. An oil well blowout spilled 235,000 gallons of oil that covered 30 miles of beach near Santa Barbara, California, with tar in 1969.

4 2004 was beset with a series of massive hurricanes, all topped in 2005 by Hurricane Katrina, one of the most devastating hurricanes on record in the United States.

Eco Art Themes

THE MENU OF ECO ART THEMES includes fossil fuel dependence, energy conservation, land use, rainwater harvesting, alternative energy, deforestation, extinctions, manufacturing protocols, mining, erosion, loss of topsoil, waste management, herbicides, pesticides, genetically modified crops, oil spills, overharvesting of fish and game, draining of wetlands, acid rain, overpopulation, genetic manipulation, consumerism, monoculture farming, toxic waste, irrigation, introduced species, carbon dioxide emissions, heavy metal accumulations, water contamination, ozone depletion, climate change, smog, species loss, local production, biomimicry, loss of habitat, privatization of natural resources, rights of indigenous peoples, soil contamination, traffic congestion, edible weeds, global warming, bioengineering, desertification, sustainability, radioactive waste, recycling, free trade, mutations, ecofeminism, remediation, restoration, revitalization, preservation, composting, up-scaling, environmental legislation, green architecture, environmental education, organic gardening, hydroponic gardening, urban gardening, and community-sponsored agriculture, to name a few. All these subjects are rooted in real-world conditions that yield consequential outcomes. All can be presented in terms of recorded histories, observable presents, and projected futures. All depend upon research. All are applicable to political policies, manufacturing protocols, lifestyle patterns, ethical quandaries, and cultural expressions.

These themes multiply when contrasting opinions about them are added to the list. Innovations may be honored for accomplishing their intended roles, for example, or derided for their dubious outcomes. Here are some examples:

- Agricultural methods that boost crop yields but exhaust soils and contaminate water
- Technologies that enhance mobility, productivity, communication, comfort, and pleasure but release toxic emissions
- Material abundance that provides luxuries but clogs landfills
- Advanced medicinal regimens that manage diseases but increase resistant bacteria
- Extraction methods that increase output but threaten the resilience of Earth systems

The copious thematic possibilities that introduce this essay were all gleaned from the last four percent of the time that has lapsed since *Homo sapiens* first stood upright and began striding across the Earth. This brief period is crammed with an astounding succession of innovations: agriculture, irrigation, writing, architecture, mathematics, religion, urban planning, metallurgy, trade, money, printing, firearms, combustion engines, nuclear power, eBay, space probes, instant messaging, reggae music, life insurance, and yoga spas.

The three- or four-billion-year history of prehuman forms of life on Earth serves as a lengthy prelude to the evolution of humans. It offers valuable lessons for societies that are inclined toward gulping, grabbing, and guzzling. This is because the temporal enormity of prehuman history demonstrates that plant life did not emerge to feed hungry humans, nor did oxygen originate to support human life, nor did fossils accumulate to power human machines. Ultimately, it proves that humans are dispensable to the biosphere, while the biosphere is indispensable for human survival.

Artists are among the many environmentalists who are scrutinizing humanity's epic expedition on the Earth, weighing each breakthrough against the inadvertent breakdown that may result. The baseline for becoming an eco artist, therefore, entails selecting a theme from within this gaping span of time. Like the process of creating a map, this selection process isolates a component of the Earth's living and nonliving environment. An all-inclusive artwork would be as incomprehensible as a map that simultaneously described roads in Albuquerque, the topography of the African continent, constellations of stars, and tourist destinations in the Champagne Valley.

In order to narrow the field, however, it is first necessary to grasp the vast terrain that ecological and environmental concerns occupy. Options abound. The process of deciding which theme to address may be methodical or intuitive, but in the end it answers two essential questions:

1. Which of these thematic possibilities captivates my attention and inspires my creativity?
2. Which eco theme utilizes my current knowledge and capabilities, or my ability to gather information and develop skills needed to convey this theme?

A bank of super computers would be required to examine the innumerable thematic choices that appear on this list. Instead of attempting this unwieldy undertaking, the following text provides a synopsis of ecological concepts that are so foundational they can accommodate numerous thematic issues. The section for each concept is introduced by an outline of the basic ecological principles relevant to it. The section concludes by enumerating some thematic possibilities the concept suggests.

ECOLOGY: HOME ON EARTH

The *home* referred to in ecology is not composed of huts, cottages, apartments, mansions, nests, dens, or any other lodging. It consists of the entire planet that serves as the home for all living organisms of Earth. This concept can be traced to the origin of the word *ecology*, which is the Greek word *oikos*, meaning *dwelling place*. Over time, *Ökologie* was coined in Germany and became *ecology* in English. While ecologists investigate the functioning of this eco home, environmentalists apply home-care regimes to ecosystems and their human and nonhuman residents. This expanded definition of *home* radically transposes the concept of a stable, self-supporting structure enclosing its residents. To ecologists, home is a vast zone of dynamic, interdependent interactions.

The prefix *dom-*[1] reveals the profound transformation of cultural values that ecology entails. *Domicile* means *house*. But *dom-* also provides the root for the word *dominate*, as when people *dom*esticate a species and *dom*ineer its systems to gain *dom*inion over their environments and claim them as their *dom*ains. The alternative to the propensity to command the systems of the Earth is contained in the prefix *eco-*. *Eco*centric persons are home centered, home involved, and home serving. Their satisfaction is supplied by relationships that extend beyond human-to-human exchanges; they encompass trees, mosses, minerals, sunlight, insects, microbes, soil, and oceans.

Environmentalists often protest examples of human behaviors described by using words beginning with *dom-*. They hope to replace these actions and attitudes with those that comply with eco considerations. Together, they provide a rich territory for art theme explorations.

Ecology offers three variants of *home*: *habitat* refers to place, *range* refers to distance, and *niche* refers to behavior.

HABITAT

Every form of life is married to a context. Divorce is not an option. Habitats sustain life by providing resources to nourish and maintain the body's functions, to build shelter, and to manage wastes. These resources may consist of nonliving substances such as water, sunlight, minerals, oxygen, and carbon dioxide; they are referred to as abiotic. Other resources derive from living and dead microorganisms, plants, animals, and their remains; these are known as biotic.

Habitats are not always reliable storehouses of provisions. They are only hospitable if they offer appropriate resources in appropriate quantities for the populations that are in residence. Acorns, for example, are poisonous for horses but nutritious for pigs, deer, and bears. Likewise, an abundance of water allows frogs to thrive but rabbits to perish. Similarly, for any organism to survive, the quantity and nature of harmful conditions must exist at levels that it can overcome by fighting or learning new behaviors or evolving new traits, can avoid by fleeing or hiding or camouflaging, or can tolerate with antibodies or diet change or protective coverings. Immediate threats are posed by predators, competitors, parasites, and poisons. Eventual threats derive from plate tectonics, climate change, and sunspot activity.

Populations are not merely passive recipients of their habitat's bounties and dangers. Living entities contribute to fluctuations in the habitat's supplies of resources—either diminishing its vitality or enhancing it—by depositing wastes, consuming plants, casting shadows, compressing soil, constructing shelters, reproducing, and so forth. Thus, shaping habitat and being shaped by it are continuous and simultaneous for all organisms on Earth.

Humans and Habitat

Of all the dangers confronting habitats, the greatest threat may be posed by the human species. History provides disturbing evidence of humanity's debilitating effects upon its eco home. In the past, such behaviors were mostly confined to unsustainable agricultural practices and excessive logging/fishing/hunting. The current list of destructive actions has expanded, escalated, compounded, and proliferated. It includes, for example, radioactive waste, the release of bioengineered organisms, and mountaintop removal. Small-scale activities like mowing lawns and drinking bottled water contribute to habitat debasement as well as large-scale installations like coal-fired power plants. However, humanity's toll on habitats is not confined to such practices. Even if everyone pledged to stop driving cars, unplug their gadgets, and compost their waste, humans would still stress the Earth's habitats as never before. This is because keeping seven billion of us alive imposes unprecedented demands upon habitats' capacities to produce resources and manage wastes.

Humanity's impact on habitats provides manifold thematic opportunities for artists. Besides addressing the spectrum of behaviors that impoverish habitats, artists can promote strategies that enhance habitat vitality through conservation measures, recycling strategies, technologies that improve productivity and efficiency, or invention of sustainable approaches.

RANGE

Range is the physical area where a species actually lives. The ranges of most plants and animals are determined by the availability of resources that meet their life requirements within a geographic area. It is small if required resources are plentiful. However, if an endangering shift occurs, organisms are confronted with an ultimatum—they expand their range or migrate to a more congenial location, or they die. Disturbances that compel these alternatives can originate from pests, disease, fire, flooding, wind, contamination, precipitation, introduced species, erosion, and so forth. Climate change seems to be presenting species across the globe with range-related life-and-death dilemmas. Plants, animals, microbes, farmers, vacationers, and scientists are among the organisms that may be scrambling to establish new ranges if and when glaciers melt and waters rise.

Because animals creep, crawl, fly, swim, run, leap, walk, gallop, and saunter, they are able to expand their ranges. However, their mobility is increasingly obstructed by cities and highways that threaten their survivability. Plants, on the other hand, perpetuate their species over a broad range only if their seeds scatter or their roots send up new shoots. Individual plants, however, do not have this option. They are literally rooted in place. This means that their ranges are bounded by how high and wide their leaves pursue the sun, and how deep and wide their roots penetrate the soil. If habitat conditions change, the survival of the species depends on whether seeds are dispersed to more suitable habitats.

Humans and Range

We humans are not inclined to forgo necessities or pleasures simply because they exist outside of the immediate zip codes. Due to our capacity to import goods and export wastes, humanity's range is global. Average citizens enjoy the output of factories in China, forests in Oregon, ranches in Australia, cornfields in Iowa, copper mines in Brazil, lagoons of Thailand, and oil wells in Alaska. An advertisement for MCI serves as a fitting motto for the global dimensions of human ranges: "The world is our home."[2]

Where people live does not determine what they consume, nor does where they live depend upon a location's rainfall, temperature, and soil conditions. Technologies that produce life-sustaining conditions enable us to frolic in Las Vegas, sip beer in the Antarctic, and take naps in outer space.

Eco art themes can be garnered from existing conditions determining range, as well as those that are anticipated. Current predictions of the necessity to expand humanity's range of occupation are based upon escalating human populations and climate change. It may not be long before rockets powered for escape velocity will be launched on adventuresome range-seeking missions, exploring places for humans to live beyond the envelope of Earth's atmosphere.

NICHE

Niche refers to the activities performed by an organism or population within its habitat. Niche studies seek answers to two essential questions: How do organisms glean available resources for their survival? How do organisms defend themselves against competitors, predators, parasites, and pathogens?

Niche strategies that apply to animals include building nests, climbing trees, hiding, setting traps, fighting, and growling at humans. Those that apply to plants include poisons, aromas, camouflage, producing thistles, attracting the enemy of your enemy, and absorbing light energy. For humans, answers might include surfing the Internet for data, mining valuable minerals, and producing medicine, guns, vitamins, and toilets.

Yet these strategies account for only half of the niche equation. Besides gleaning resources and developing defensive strategies, species must maintain the vitality of their habitats. Niche occupation vitalizes a habitat when, for example, pioneer species improve soil, red algae works with coral to build reefs, and fungi recycle plant detritus. However, species that reproduce successfully can also fail the niche test if they compromise the health of their habitat. Invasive plants or animals, for instance, can reproduce so prolifically that they usurp indigenous species and deplete the territory's biodiversity.

Humans and Niche

Soaring human populations provide evidence that the human animal's numerous niche schemes have been remarkably successful. Early humans established the ongoing trend of inventing niche technologies when they learned to forage on the African savanna and then domesticated fire and chiseled flint into blades. These technologies have been continually bolstered by learned and socially transmitted behavior modifiers. Our inventory of tools includes ever more powerful hardware to mine resources and software to mine data. Meanwhile, demands for energy, consumption of resources, and production of damaging by-products escalate. The question now being posed by environmentalists is whether humanity's current niche construction strategies alter the environment to such an extent that they might ultimately decrease our chances of survival.

Concerned citizens are comparing humanity's current niche occupation to a hostile takeover, not a triumph. They are seeking niche roles in which humans, as rational creatures, devise and adapt complementary relationships among members of their own and other species. Eco artists may join this endeavor by devising niche roles for humans that sustain themselves and their fellow Earthlings.

SYSTEMS

There is no straightforward way to describe a system, which indicates its primary characteristic. Systems are complex. Although *system* can be defined as an assemblage of elements that form a composite unit, a system simultaneously has embedded subsystems and is embraced by supersystems that continuously effect and are affected by each other.

Living systems are self-governing and interdependent. Their existence depends upon being equipped with some mechanisms that specialize in resisting change and other mechanisms that are designed to accommodate change. This is because maintaining constancy and permitting modification are equal imperatives for survival. An example of constancy involves maintaining internal temperature when external temperatures vary. An example of modification entails expanding diet when food opportunities shrink. Furthermore, systems must exist in appropriate proportions so that their interconnections are harmonious. If all these conditions are met, a line of kinship extends between subsystems like our own digestive tracts and supersystems like the biosphere. Violating this proportion and harmony unravels the mutuality that supports individuals and entire populations. The disruption of any part threatens the whole.

The word *closed* describes systems in which matter neither enters nor leaves the system; only energy is exchanged, for example as heat or work. Systems are *open* if both matter and energy enter and exit. Consider a house as a closed system. It would have no pipes connecting to a water supply and no need for a driveway. Air would not seep through the cracks, trash would not be deposited on the curb, groceries would not enter, and a contribution to the church bake sale would not exit. A house would only be a closed system if nothing entered except energy, whether as electricity fed through a grid or sunlight streaming through the windows. This analogy applies to our planetary home, which is considered *closed* by scientists who focus exclusively on heat escaping from our atmosphere and solar energy streaming in, but it is referred to as *open* by scientists who emphasize the tons of matter from comets that bombard the surface of the Earth each day.

Many cultures have conceived of their earthly home as a system composed of two pairs of primary elements: stone and air, water and fire. This hallowed concept did not acknowledge energy entering the system from the sun. As a result, the many processes that can be attributed to infusions of solar energy were unexplainable. Such mysteries as the existence of life, evaporation, germination, and rain were credited to supernatural entities whose favor was considered essential to life and prosperity.

Humans and Systems

Humans are a collection of systems. They are composed of reproductive, digestive, muscular, circulatory, and many additional systems. Humans also create systems. The systems they create can be mechanical, electronic, financial, political, religious, military, aesthetic, and so forth. Each of these created systems verifies the human brain's remarkable capacity to organize a world that might otherwise appear to be a chaotic conglomeration of phenomena and formations. Computer technologies are recent additions to humanity's list of created systems. They not only perform an unprecedented range of tasks, they augment humanity's ability to process information, think abstractly, discern patterns, and anticipate outcomes—the prerequisites for inventing ever more intricate systems.

Environmentalists are pooling their cognitive capacities to design systems that emulate ecosystem design efficiencies. Known as biomimicry, this endeavor comprises a great repository of thematic options for eco artists. Artists addressing energy efficiency, for example, might streamline air and fluid movement by aligning with the shape of least resistance in the systems of the universe. Unlike the straight line—the shape that prevails throughout current technological systems—it is a logarithmic spiral.

ENERGY

The sun's energy is trapped by plants, used, and then dispersed as heat. Because it is never cycled, organisms stay alive only if the Earth's energy supply is continually replenished. Ecologists identify two energy processes essential to life:

- Endothermic energy is being absorbed. During this additive process, atoms join into molecules and molecules become more complex, as in photosynthesis.
- Exothermic energy is being released. During this subtractive process, molecules dissociate, as in burning.

Humans and Energy

Energy production and consumption are common measures of standards of living. The analytic route that traces civilization from its inception until today discloses a consistent effort by people to exploit energy's potential to perform work. It also reveals the lengthening of humanity's energy supply line. Before the Industrial Revolution, people satisfied their energy quotients with local resources. They relied upon muscle power and fuels like peat, wood, vegetable starch, and animal fats. Once the Industrial Revolution became established, appetites for energy soared to power industrial machinery. Energy sources increased and supply lines lengthened. Coal was added to the energy menu. Then petroleum was included, and then nuclear sources. Now, nonrenewable fossil fuels are regularly piped across continents and shipped across oceans. They are being mined from deposits that lie miles beneath the Earth's crust and ocean's surface. Nuclear power is extracted from deep within the atomic structure of matter. Meanwhile, the range of fuels is still expanding to ensure supplies in the future. But availability does not equal usability. Energy sources must also be transferred, constrained, processed, and channeled, and their wastes must also be managed.

Environmentalists who acknowledge the effectiveness of these reaping technologies are rarely comforted by them. Establishing efficient, nonpolluting, reliable, inexpensive, renewable, and sustainable energy generation remains an unfulfilled goal. Attempts to satisfy these requirements may involve applying new technologies to such enduring energy sources as the sun, wind, geothermal heat sinks, and waves. Others enlist species like green algae that convert the sun's energy into a form that is usable by us, or split water molecules to release embedded energy. The goal of revising our energy budget and relocating our energy dependencies yields innumerable eco art themes.

LIFE/DEATH/EXTINCTION

For billions of years and throughout the planet's diverse ecosystems, life has been engaged in the continuous process of constructing itself from inputs of energy. In order to execute the fundamental functions of life building, molecules must be organized. But all life carries a death sentence. Even organisms that enjoy optimal living conditions cannot escape this inevitability. Thus, just as continuously, other life-forms are being dismantled. This process begins the instant that active manipulation of energy inputs is halted. Once the organism dies, energy dissipates. Its molecules are broken down and dispersed to be reassembled into new living entities. From an ecocentric perspective, the death of an organism is not an absolute finality, because the molecules of the dead organism don't vanish. They are re-sorted so that they are available for reuse within the vast arena of living forms. For this reason, the hypothetical manual that details ecosystem dynamics allots equal space to the accumulation of energy that increases organization and to the dissipation of energy that decreases organization.

Whereas death is not a terminus within an ecosystem, extinction does constitute an evolutionary and functional end point. Extinction occurs when an entire species ceases to contribute to the pulse of life on the planet. Billions of species have become extinct since the advent of life on the Earth three billion or more years ago. According to fossil records, only two to four percent of the species that have existed on Earth exist today.[3] The majority of these extinctions occurred prior to the evolution of humans. They were driven by cyclic climate change, catastrophic geologic events, and competition from better-adapted species.

Extinction/Biodiversity

Extinctions are proof of species' failure to adapt to environmental change. It follows that every entity that has ever lived is proof of a successful adaption to its particular environment. While the formulas of current evolutionary successes are contained in the gene pools of surviving species, the formulas of past evolutionary successes are contained in the gene pools of extinct species, even if they ultimately succumbed to inhospitable conditions. Thus, each time a species becomes extinct, an adaptation strategy is sacrificed.

When extinction occurs, an ecosystem does not merely lose a species; it also loses the services that the species performed. It may have benefited a system by capturing and storing energy, producing or decomposing organic material, controlling erosion, balancing populations, and conducting countless other useful functions. For this reason, extinctions compromise an ecosystem's ability to accommodate to temporary and enduring environmental changes. Diversified systems are significantly stronger, more productive, more stable, and more resistant to perturbations than simplified systems.

Humans and Extinction/Biodiversity

Recent extinction escalations are being traced to short-sighted activities of humans that cause long-term disruptions of habitats. This state is the unfortunate outcome of polluting the air, waters, and soils; introducing alien species; exploiting species; exhausting resources; and so forth. This trend can be traced back ten thousand years to the advent of agriculture. Cultivating crops means treating most native plants as weeds. Likewise, raising animals involves treating undomesticated animals as pests. Both practices reduce the inherent diversity of ecosystems. Currently, this trend is being accelerated to such an extent that it is known as the "sixth mass extinction" in the planet's history, the only one believed to be caused by the accumulated actions of a single species—humankind—and not a catastrophic geological or meteorological event. If mass murder of humans is called *genocide*, perhaps the mass murder of species by humans should be called *gene-ocide*.

Eco art themes can be derived by evoking extinct species, protecting endangered species, preserving species' habitats, or honoring diversity. Human impediments to biodiversity include the following:

- Introducing nonnative species that outcompete native species
- Overhunting, overfishing, overlogging, overmining
- Monoculture farming
- Paving
- Disrupting migration patterns
- Using pesticides and herbicides

- Dumping toxic waste
- Diverting water

Human strategies to enhance biodiversity include these:

- Planting green roofs and gardens
- Constructing parks, botanical gardens, zoos, and domestic gardens
- Promoting conservation initiatives and wildlife management projects
- Allowing plots of land in rural and urban areas to grow wild
- Remediating contaminated soil and reducing air pollution

Humans and Cultural Diversity

The term *cultural diversity* typically refers to the mixture of human cultural traditions represented in a specific region. As in biological diversity, each culture embodies a successful adaptation to some planetary condition. Because the Earth presents a multiplicity of short- and long-term conditions, cultures develop wide-ranging techniques for procreation, waste management, transportation, communication, governance, architecture, morality, art, and so forth. In this way, cultural diversity optimizes the range of adaptation strategies available to human populations. This asset is especially crucial when ecosystems are transforming, as under conditions of global warming.

Eco artists might find thematic inspiration among the ways humans hinder and improve cultural diversity, especially since the flexibility to achieve sustainability may best be derived from a mosaic of cultural traditions.

Human strategies that reduce cultural diversity include the following:

- Globalization
- Multinational corporations
- World trade organizations
- International monetary funds
- International distribution of films, technologies, music, clothing, and other consumer products

Human strategies that enhance cultural diversity include these:

- Legal mandates to protect and preserve indigenous traditions
- Economic incentives to protect and preserve discrete cultures
- Manufactured products and services that target niche markets
- Localization of crafts, religion, cuisine, architecture, holidays, etc.
- Neighborhood associations
- Regional strategies for growing vegetables, producing energy, making clothing, etc.
- Place-based education
- Decentralized news generation and distribution

SUSTAINABILITY AND CARRYING CAPACITY

Sustainability is a measure of long-term viability that is achieved when the disturbances that afflict a system are balanced by its compensating responses. Disturbances may be as subtle as a speck of dust on an eyelid or as dramatic as an earthquake. They may be as recurrent as lunar tides or as unanticipated as typhoons and meteor strikes.

Carrying capacity measures the limits of an ecosystem's ability to react to a disturbance. A system can be sustainable if three conditions are met: a response must have the opposite effect of the original disturbance; the intensity of a response must match the intensity of the original disturbance; the response must occur within a time frame that enables the system to adjust.

If tolerance levels are exceeded, an individual organism dies, a species becomes extinct, an ecosystem collapses. In the past, fatal disturbances took the form of spewing lava, crashing meteors, and other natural catastrophes. Civilization has updated this executioner's list by adding industrial pollution, genetically modified crops, and atomic fallout, for example.

Humans and Sustainability

Humans commit unsustainable practices when resources and goods are too inefficient to recycle, too contaminating to manage safely, too easily trashed. Such "cradle-to-grave" behaviors occur in domestic kitchens and artists' studios as well as industrial factories, wherever cycles of material use are ignored. "Cradle-to-cradle" practices, on the other hand, balance the use and replenishment of resources, as well as the generation and reuse of waste. Such sustainable solutions are often accomplished by mimicking the strategies that maintain vital ecosystems. Artists can pursue sustainability by avoiding, halting, reversing, and replacing those activities that can be fatal to species and ecosystems, or by bolstering a system's carrying capacity.

EVOLUTION AND MUTATION

Sustainability ensures permanence, but it does not imply stasis. On Earth, flux is omnipresent. Biologically, transformation is driven by evolution. With few exceptions, evolution modifies existing forms of life by progressing in the direction of greater complexity. The tailless, forward-facing, grasping, and imagining organisms known as *Homo sapiens* are presumed to have evolved from infinitesimal clusters of cells enclosed in membranes that comprised the first forms of life on Earth. Evolution, the change in a population's gene frequency over time, is often the product of mutation.

The words *mutate* and *mutant* manifest the duality of outcomes made possible by mutations. Changes that enhance chances of survival because they are suited to available conditions are acknowledged by synonyms for *mutate*: *accommodate*, *innovate*, and *regenerate*. Those that are detrimental and therefore reduce survivability are revealed by synonyms for *mutant*: *aberrant, deviant, grotesque*.

Humans and Evolution

Ingenuity and technological prowess have bolstered humanity's evolutionary advantages beyond spontaneous genetic transformations. The machines we engineer now perform superhuman feats of strength, dexterity, sensitivity, accuracy, endurance, and speed. The electronic devices we construct outperform the human brain's ability to sense, calculate, analyze, and store information. Robots combine these feats. In addition, physical infirmities are accommodated by pacemakers, joint replacements, robotic sensors, contact lenses, performance-enhancing drugs, hearing aids, organ transplants, and so forth. The futuristic character shared by this cache of innovations has progressed so far from evolutionary advances it is sometimes referred to as "post-human." These accomplishments might inspire eco artists to construct body- and mind-altering schemes that result in sustainable outcomes.

HUMANS AND HIERARCHY

Environmentalists of all persuasions are assessing the dividends reaped from the empowering strategies that enable humans to bolster their position on the hierarchy of living creatures, exceeding the peak niche granted by evolution. This ad hoc chorus of concern is seeking answers to the following questions: Have the record-breaking heights of human status made us lose sight of the numerous lower organisms that ensure our existence? Are we undermining chances for our own survival by abusing our base of support? Is there enough room at the top for escalating human populations?

These questions are instigating an interrogation of the current anthropocentric perception of human progress—the ability to control and harvest Earth resources to yield material comfort and convenience. An ecocentric alternative conceives of progress in terms of sustainability and responsibility. Artists might contribute to this reassessment by demonstrating that the "progressive" artist highlights the responsibilities associated with peak hierarchical status by choosing mediums and producing works of art that model sustainable material manipulations.

CONCLUSION

The ecological issues enumerated in this chapter infuse the themes that have received the attention of artists. No theme is exhausted, obsolete, or irrelevant. A representative sampling appears in this book. Many other themes await an artist's presentation and interpretation. Since none come equipped with a ready-made strategy for artistic expression, artists may direct their attention to accusers, defenders, culprits, or troubleshooters. They may behave like shepherds of the planet's life-forms, or technical designers of the planet's systems of production, managers of the planet's habitats, healers of the planet's infirmities, emissaries of the planet's wonders, avengers of the planet's spoilers, and curators of the planet's resources. These many topics and approaches share the goal of achieving the long-term health of the Earth's living systems, and they profit from artists' ingenuity, imagination, and vision.

NOTES

1 The prefix *dom-* is derived from the Latin word *domus*, meaning "house."

2 *New York Times*, November 10, 2003, C7.

3 http://www.encyclopedia.com/article-1G2-2830100848/endangered-species.html.

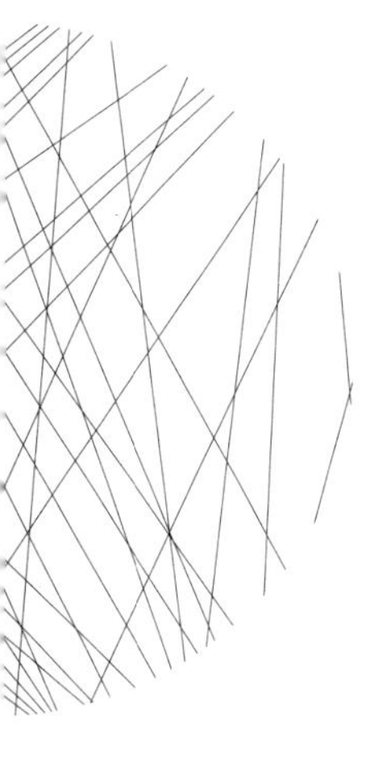

Eco Art Aesthetics

A **GREAT TURNING POINT** in the history of Western art occurred in the Twentieth Century when art's association with beauty first received pummelings from the cubists, futurists, and Dadaists and then was practically exterminated by pop, conceptual, minimal, fluxus, art povera, happenings, and land artists. During these years, those who remained loyal to the goal of achieving beauty were often banished to the outposts of provincialism.

Aesthetics is commonly defined as the study of the mind and the emotions in relation to beauty. Yet aesthetics is a malleable term that has also relinquished its association with beauty to refer generally to the science of sensuous perception. In this regard it perpetuates the tradition by which discoveries in science influence both styles in art and the theories that support them. Renaissance perspective, for example, reflects Galileo's mathematics of motion; impressionist paint dabs coincide with scientific discoveries regarding color and light; cubism's fracturing of form parallels investigations into the atomic structure of matter. Currently, aesthetics is undergoing another revision to keep up with art's continuous reinvention of itself. Eco artists are devising a system of aesthetics to visualize how shapes, colors, and patterns distribute themselves within ecosystems.

The following essay demonstrates that eco-aesthetic investigation is conducted by delving beneath surfaces to discern nature's design efficiencies. Just as past artists dissected bodies to gain an understanding of anatomical structure and skeletal mechanics, artists are now scrutinizing ecosystems to discover how their forms create patterns, how these patterns congeal into constructions, how these constructions comprise networks, and how these networks function as systems.

MULTIPLICITY

The number 2 is the minimum state of multiplicity, yet it introduces manifold conditions that determine the dynamism of events on Earth. It is the numerical baseline that unleashes the drama inherent in relationships of all kinds. Without two of something there would be no separation or contrast, no pressure and friction, nor attraction and repulsion, creativity and conflict, newness and diversity, or likeness and difference. Physically, without at least two, there would be no light, no heat, and no energy. Conceptually, choice and opportunity are introduced by twos. However, the only time *two* actually describes the Earth is when it identifies two kinds of multiplicity: many of the same thing or many different kinds of things.

In the ecological world, *multiplicity* can be used to describe classifications, ecosystems, species, relationships, morphologies, scales, microorganisms, habitats, niches, ranges, fractals, adaptations, life spans, organisms, populations, communities, behaviors, extinctions, traits, environmental pressures, biomes, producers, consumers, decomposers, food webs, networks, vegetation, climate, metabolisms, and so forth.

The two forms of multiplicity characterize the contrasting aesthetic experiences that exist in industrialized societies. Repetition, for example, prevails at the end of industrial assembly lines that produce uniform products and fulfill predetermined intentions. Artists can comment on the huge output of identical units that flood the marketplace by inducing the aesthetic response to repetition—monotony. Great variability, on the other hand, is an inherent component of commerce and popular media where a plethora of quick-paced stimuli compete to capture viewers' attentions. Psychologically, extreme variability generates confusion. Both boredom and confusion are uncomfortable states of being. They lie at far extremes from harmony, the pleasing arrangement of parts. While harmony is lacking in many environments designed by humans, it is easily discovered in outdoor locations like fields and deserts. Such settings avoid monotony because the shape of each object evolves out of adaptations to its exclusive microenvironment, which explains the uniqueness of waves, snowflakes, sunsets, mountains, clouds, frogs, fingerprints, blades of grass, and DNA. At the same time, confusion is reduced outdoors because the elements of an observed scene respond in unison to a given set of forces. The same winds, for example, cause tree limbs to twist, rocks to tumble, earth to erode, clouds to form, and waters to surge. Furthermore, shadows lengthen and shorten together because they are all synchronized with the Earth's rotations. Likewise, the hue and intensity of the light is consistent because it is determined by the weather and time of day.

Applying eco aesthetics to the creation of a work of art can reinforce an artist's theme. In this instance it may be accomplished by determining the intensity and type of multiplicity included in a composition.

LINES

We humans are so attuned to lines that our brains invent them even when they don't exist. Ancient peoples, for example, conceived of constellations by connecting the dots made of stars to resemble bears and dippers and bows. In contrast, the lines that are relevant to eco aesthetics are physical realities, not imaginary. From an ecological perspective, lines that emerge from a pen held by an artist are products of gravity (allows ink to run), viscosity (of the drawing medium), slope (of the application), flow (through the channel), and porosity (of the paper). Such material considerations demonstrate that drawn and painted lines in art are not merely representations. They manifest the same forces that govern rivers coursing through meadows.

OUTLINES: BORDERS

The ability to distinguish one object from another is a vital aid to survival. Navigating a world without such visual separations would be extremely challenging, which is why unified perceptions are typically reserved for extraordinary states like visions, dreams, and hallucinations. However, when eyes observe a scene, they receive a barrage of stimuli that resembles such undifferentiated states. This visual information consists of highlights, shadows, movement, textures, hues, and so on. It requires the active participation of the brain to discern the individual entities within this visual muddle. This is a remarkable feat because the eye is not aided by outlines. Indeed, there are no actual lines circumscribing objects in the real world. Outlines are inventions. They exist in art to define and separate shape. In the physical world, however, shape is produced by borders, not outlines.

Borders prevent the physical universe from blending into uniform consistency. Like outlines, they separate objects from their context. But unlike outlines, borders perform multiple additional functions. For living entities, for example, borders take the form of enclosing membranes. They not only separate one organism from its context, they prevent the internal organs from oozing out. Furthermore, borders protect the organism from being trampled, consumed, or attacked. Borders might also waterproof, insulate, and camouflage their owners. In addition, border functions might be augmented by shell, bark, scale, skin, feather, or fur. In eco aesthetics, borders replace outlines as producers of form.

Eco aesthetics also attends to the characteristics of borders. For example, organisms are neither secure nor safe if their borders resemble impenetrable fortresses. Borders surrounding organisms must be permeable to maintain life. For this reason they resemble busy multilane thoroughfares that provide access routes for such vital resources as air, nutrients, and fluids, and exit lanes for harmful substances like urine, sweat, carbon dioxide, and excess heat. Borders also transmit dispatches about ever-changing environmental conditions to the body's neural pathways. Permeable peripheries are just as essential for skyscrapers and cities, since they too depend upon energy and resources entering and wastes exiting the system.

Within eco aesthetics, the separating function of borders is also applied to states and conditions. The borders separating wet from dry, liquid from gas, tepid from boiling bear little relation to outlines since they are imprecise and gradual. Likewise, calendars may declare the instant that a new season begins, but in ecosystems winter gradually evolves into spring, and summer unfolds into autumn. Clocks may dictate the second a new day starts, but in actuality, night fades into dawn. Even the border transition between being alive and being dead is imprecise, since cells can remain viable long after the body they inhabit is declared dead.

Eco artists may still exploit the capacity of outlines to instruct and describe and clarify. But their other option is to emulate the shape-producing and condition-transitioning strategies discovered in functioning ecosystems.

LINES: TUBES

A line connects two points. When such lines exist in an ecosystem, as opposed to the surface of a drawing or painting, they typically take the form of elongated cylinders that function as tubes. In living entities these tubes include blood vessels, tree trunks, and bones. Those that are engineered include electrical lines, pipelines, and tunnels. Tubes on both lists function as conduits and connectors. Conduits channel oxygen, information, wastes, and so forth. Connectors join the nostrils to the lungs, the sensor to the brain, the toilet to the septic system, and so on. Because tubes maximize extension and minimize volume, they perform these essential functions with utmost efficiency, a core consideration within eco aesthetics.

SHAPES: SPHERES AND BOXES

Copernicus, the celebrated Sixteenth-Century astronomer, expressed why he believed the universe is shaped like spheres. "The reason is either that, of all forms, the sphere is the most perfect, needing no joint and being a complete whole, or that it is the most capacious of figures, best suited to enclose and retain all things, or even that all the separate parts of the universe, I mean the sun, moon, planets, and stars, are seen to be this shape, or that wholes strive to be circumscribed by this boundary, as is apparent in drops of water and other fluid bodies when they seek to be self-contained."[1] Spheres have proliferated since Copernicus proclaimed their attributes. Ecologists situate every living entity in the biosphere that is imbedded in the hydrosphere (the Earth's liquid realm), the atmosphere (gaseous realm), and the lithosphere (outer crust). Astronomers have added the troposphere, stratosphere, mesosphere, thermosphere, and ionosphere.

Nonetheless, humans tend to construct environments that are replete with boxes. Four perpendicular walls contain most settings where we learn, work, sleep, eat, play, and relax. Four right angles form the containers for most of our possessions. When we die, we are placed inside a box, and another box marks our grave. Xbox, mailbox, cable box, batter's box, Unix box—boxes are ubiquitous in the contemporary environment. Three qualities they offer are missing from spheres: efficient means for packing, stability, and strength through rigidity.

Nonetheless, common phrases reveal that when we are trapped, we feel *cornered,* not curved. If we get stymied, we are *boxed in,* not sphered. Attempts to escape our predicaments are referred to as *thinking outside the box,* not in it. Self-improvement strategies entail striving to be *well rounded,* not well angled. When we are doing well, we say we are *on a roll,* not on a plane. And no one likes to be called *square.* These phrases reveal that we still share Copernicus's emotional connection to the sphere despite our culture's alliance with the cube. This alliance reveals the importance of industry and manufacturing as much as an alliance with the sphere connects us with life. Consider, for example, that conception transpires in seeds, eggs, and wombs, all of which are spherical. The social implications of curves and angles are core ingredients of eco-aesthetic analysis.

SPIRALS

The sun at the center of the solar system and our hearts at the center of our bodies are both hubs of spiral vortexes. Kernels, bracts, and needles reveal spiral patterns of growth for corn, pinecone, and cacti. Seashells, electrons, seaweed, hurricanes, blood, lava, fire, whirlpools, and galaxies all revolve in micro and macro cauldrons of spiral movement. As blueprints for beauty and functionality, spirals manifest the cosmos's great canon of design.

All spirals curl around a fixed point with distances that progress at regular intervals, but there are two manners by which they comply with this configuration. One manner is common among objects manufactured by humans, such as coils of rope, clock springs, and paper towel rolls; these expand in fixed increments. The other distinguishes myriad forms marked by growth and transformation, such as seashells, rams' horns, and ear cochleae; they expand exponentially from their source. These expanding spirals are seminal to biological organization. They are also prevalent among artistic representations of physical and spiritual transformation. Artists the world over tend to depict paths to heaven and descents to hell as spiral-shaped passages.

Because spirals constitute the path of least resistance, they are the natural shape of flowing matter. Modern technologies, however, tend to move things in straight lines. Overcoming resistance to this unnatural pattern requires energy inputs and machines to push things along. Fans, propellers, and engines accomplish straight-line movement. Bathtubs manifest these dual forms of movement. Water is pumped through straight pipes to arrive in the faucet, but it spirals when it flows freely down the drain. Eco aesthetics offers artists the opportunity to emulate the Earth's inherent pattern of efficient design—the spiral.

PROGRESSIONS

Divine harmonic proportion, sacred geometry, golden ratios—all these terms honor a particular progression of numbers in which each number is the sum of the two preceding numbers: 1, 1, 2, 3, 5, 8, 13, 21, 34, and so on. Because the sequence accelerates the degree of increase and proceeds infinitely, it forms an expanding spiral when the numbers are plotted. The esteem of this numerical phenomenon is well earned. Physically, the numbers constitute a universal law of progression. Metaphysically, they provide evidence of the interconnectedness of matter at all scales of being. The sequence is known as the Fibonacci numbers after Leonardo Fibonacci, who discovered it in the Thirteenth Century. However, the earliest known proprietors of this knowledge were the Egyptians, who embedded its secrets in the ground plans of their temples, believing it embodied the essence of beauty, harmony, and creation on Earth.

Fibonacci numbers can be retrieved from the shape of our DNA and the measurement of distant galaxies, the rate of radioactive decay and the growth of rabbit populations. Sunflowers manifest the sequence in the number of clockwise and counterclockwise spirals, which are always consecutive Fibonacci numbers such as 21 and 34, or 34 and 55. Furthermore, Fibonacci proportions prevail in such common human constructions as 2" x 3" light switches, 3" x 5" note cards, 8" x 13" legal pads, and such landmark buildings as the Greek Parthenon in Athens and the United Nations headquarters in New York City. But it is not necessary to go any further than your own hand to observe Fibonacci proportions. Each of your five fingers has three parts separated by two knuckles. This eco-aesthetic principle is particularly useful to artists who wish to contrast the dynamic progressions of living forms with the fixed progressions of most engineered products.

COMPLEXITY AND CHAOS

Ecosystem complexity challenges the version of reality described by Euclid, the renowned Greek mathematician who devised the model of the physical world in the Third Century BC that prevailed for centuries. Euclid asserted that the rational mind of humans harmonized with the rational state of the universe, which was, therefore, as logical as pure geometry. Paul Cézanne (1839–1906) confirmed this belief when he described the principle that inspired his paintings, "Everything in nature can be viewed in terms of cones, cylinders, and spheres." In contrast, it is multifaceted complexity that characterizes healthy ecosystems where continuous interactions occur within numerous, sporadic, evolving networks of causations. Eco aesthetics envisions the Earth as home to billions of organisms interacting with each other and responding to fluctuating conditions that emerge every microsecond on every micrometer of the globe.

Chaos is the sister of complexity. The difficulty of envisioning chaotic conditions does not indicate that a condition is tumultuous and haphazard. In ecology, situations are identified as chaotic when the human capacity to understand them is incomplete, thereby subverting predictability. Chaos occurs when causes are too small for humans to detect, too vast to track, and/or too multiple to calculate. Naturally occurring examples of chaos include heart rhythms, fluid dynamics, electrical circuits, weather patterns, and the spread of disease. Human-made chaotic systems account for traffic patterns, public opinion, stock market activity, and even the onset of war.

Whereas geometric representations in art uphold faith in ordered simplicity, artists intent on representing an ecological version of reality acknowledge its complexity and chaos. They practice art in the manner of an ecologist by engaging the fluid intricacies of real-world conditions. Their efforts are as distinguishable from art conventions as ecologists' methods are distinguishable from the formalized research methodologies of other scientific disciplines. These methods involve simplifying the subjects of study by limiting data, dismantling systems, and isolating subjects of observation. Some eco artists also submit their work to real-world dynamic engagements. They express chaos by subjecting their artworks to the vagaries of ongoing physical events instead of attempting to beat the odds against uncertainty by controlling the outcome.

Alternatively, eco artists and ecologists may create simulations of ecosystem complexity through advanced computer technologies. Such ecological studies generate hypotheses and statistical projections, not absolute facts and predictions. In art, they tend to visualize invisible forces and processes.

FRACTALS

Meandering coastlines and clouds forming over the horizon cannot be described using the precise geometries envisioned by Euclid. However, scientists recently discovered that the unfathomable complexity of these and numerous other irregularly shaped entities is neither random nor unfathomable. They exhibit the orderly characteristics of a pattern because the shapes of their parts resemble the shapes of the whole. Patterns that repeat at different scales are called fractals.

Fractal shapes emerge from the bewildering complexity of Earthly shapes that are chaotic. One example is provided by the winding shapes of water coursing through a landscape. They are chaotic because they result from the simultaneous actions of water, heat, moon phases, erosion, evaporation, accretion, animal activity, and so forth. Nonetheless, trickles of water only a few centimeters wide resemble mighty rivers spanning continents. Fractal organization that exhibits such self-similarity can also be observed in broccoli, trees, galaxies, and brains. The repetitive patterning of these complex shapes at different scales accounts for fractals' dazzling appearance.

In addition to introducing a new form of patterning into the visual vocabulary of eco aesthetics, fractals introduce a new standard of measurement. This computing scheme is based upon complexity, not size. Thus, different answers can apply to the measurement of the same fractal form. For example, the circumference of a tree with rough bark is smaller if it is measured with a logger's tape than if it is measured by a two-inch caterpillar. Likewise, the caterpillar's measurement is smaller than the circumference measured by the tiny beetle. This is because the logger's tape skips from high point to high point along the rough surface of the bark, whereas insects travel farther as they move up and down these irregularities to circumnavigate the tree. Fractals demonstrate that no single measurement represents the "true" size of a complex object. The greater the complexity of the shape being measured, the more discrepancy exists using different scales of measurement.

Fractals are not merely curiosities that enrich eco aesthetics by introducing a new category of visual delight. Fractal patterning is being exploited by many new technologies: fractal antennae allow for broadband reception in a compact space; fractal fiber optics reduces distortion; fractal Internet traffic analysis facilitates Internet design; fractal mixers allow fluids to mix at low turbulence. For engineers, biologists, and artists alike, fractal concepts are extremely useful tools for extrapolating information between divergent levels of organization. For instance, through fractal analysis the dynamics of planetary systems might be deduced from the dynamics of molecules.

SCALE

Scales are slippery constructions. They indicate comparisons, not precise quantities. Because they measures degree, magnitude, and ratio, scales always exist in relation to context. Scales can be applied to physical characteristics like size, weight, distance, density, and duration. They pertain to conditions such as temperature, fragility, malleability, and conductivity. Scales can also be assigned to qualities like efficiency, impact, risk, beauty, and equilibrium. As a measure of relationship, scale is an important component of ecological investigations and eco-aesthetic decisions.

Humans' imaginations tend to delight in extremes of scale. The advances in science and technology making headlines tend to report such topics as intergalactic rocket probes and nanoexplorations of subatomic particles. Such explorations of the limits of the universe bypass the mundane scales of everyday life. In fact, the association of the average scales of our world with the commonplace, unimaginative, and dull is apparent in the connection between the word *mundane* and the Latin word *mundus*, meaning "world."

Ecology draws attention back from the extremes of scale and refocuses it on phenomena in our midst. Artists can reinforce ecology's appreciation of phenomena that exist at the scales of unaided human perceptions and unmediated physical interactions.

DYNAMISM

Stasis is an abstract concept that is absent on Earth. Flux rules. Weather is ephemeral. Season is recurrent. Climate evolves. Geological cycles are prolonged. Storms are erratic. Species evolve. Populations flush. Water encapsulates dynamism because it never rests. It travels in an endless cycle from the ocean, to the atmosphere, over the land surface, and back to the sea. Continual motion also applies to the Earth's crust, mantle, and core. Even the term *rock solid* is misleading. Earthquakes and volcanic eruptions provide dramatic evidence that tectonic plates of rock converge, collide, and diverge. Mountain building and ocean trenching are unobservable ever-changing occurrences.

The earliest occupants of the seas provide an epic example of Earth dynamism. They were primitive bacteria that thrived within a primeval soup of sulfurous waters. For ninety-five percent of the four billion years that life has existed, they were the only form of living entity on Earth. Still, stasis was not on Earth's agenda. These bacteria gradually exhausted supplies of carbon dioxide that was essential to their survival and replaced it with oxygen that was poisonous to them. The prolonged accumulation of their minute actions readied the planet to support oxygen-breathing organisms like you and me. The extinction of trillions of bacteria over the course of billions of years engineered the planet for life as we know it. It is just as certain that what we know today will not be known to our distant descendants.

Artists practicing eco aesthetics can expand art's engagement with dynamism beyond painted or sculpted representation by incorporating actual changes within their artworks. Such changes may be inherent to the nature of their mediums, the result of environmental conditions, powered by machines, or instigated by the public. The evolution of these artworks does not necessarily end once the artist's direct engagement ceases.

STABILITY/FLEXIBILITY

That stability optimizes security is a widely held assumption that provides the template for many contemporary systems of governance, education, business, and religion. Structurally, this interpretation of stability tends to resemble a hierarchical pyramid in which authority is concentrated at the peak, communications proceed from the few to the many, decisions are generalized, conformity provides the measure of good conduct, and uniformity comprises the goal of production.

However, this template ensures security only if conditions are predictable, as when a precise task is being performed in an environment that is constant over long periods of time. Such conditions are common in factory production but conspicuously absent from climate, population densities, contagious diseases, and other phenomena characterized by fluctuations arising at random intervals.

Healthy ecosystems, however, are most productive when they function as if they have loose hinges, supple joints, and expandable struts. This flexibility enables them to take advantage of unforeseen opportunities, protect themselves from sudden threats, and adapt to unanticipated occurrences. It even grants them latitude to rewrite their own operating manuals. As such, ecosystems exhibit strategies for coping that have been refined over the course of millennia. These models indicate that stability is gained through flexibility, not rigidity.

The heart provides compelling evidence of this principle. Regular, periodic heart rhythms are optimal only in steady-state conditions. But in the ever-changing environments in which most animals live, vigor and longevity depend upon the heart's ability to beat irregularly.[2] The mechanisms controlling heart rates are intrinsically chaotic.

Online technologies used for banking, lending, shopping, reading news, swapping music, publishing, and communicating incorporate such flexibilities. Eco aesthetics enables artists to emulate them by creating systems that decentralize authority, permit multidirectional communications, and allow spontaneous transformations to occur.

SYSTEMS

Systems are functional groups of elements that are composed of multiple interacting parts. Existing on Earth does not offer the option of disassociating from systems. Humans live nested within biological, social, economic, climatic, geographic, religious, ethical, and many other types of systems. Formally, systems depend upon relationships. Temporally, systems involve change over time. Structurally, systems are complex. Quantitatively and qualitatively, systems depend upon multiplicity. Artistically, systems have infiltrated eco art aesthetics, sources of inspiration, ethical standards, material choices, and creative processes. They conclude this essay because visualizing systems' complexities explains both the originating motive and the culminating goal of eco aesthetics.

NOTES

1 Nicolaus Copernicus, *On the Revolutions of the Heavenly Spheres* (Chapter One, Book I of VI, 1543).
2 "Irregular Heartbeat May Be Normal," *Nutrition Health Review*, Fall 1989. Accessed through Resource Library, FindArticles.com. http://findarticles.com/p/articles/mi_m0876/is_n52/ai_8542487/.

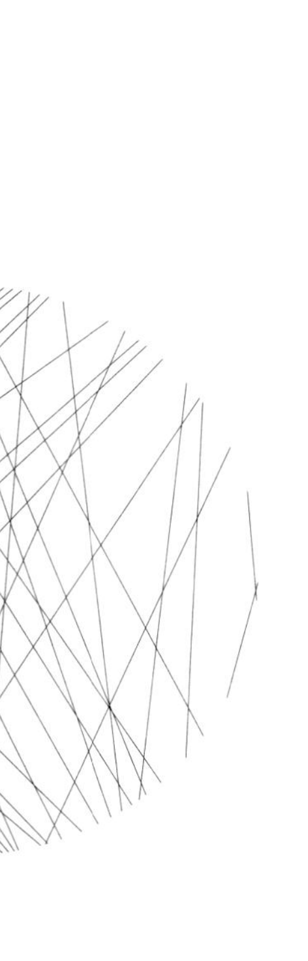

Eco Art Materials

ARTISTS TYPICALLY REFER to the physical component of their artworks as *medium*, capitalizing on the word's double meaning: medium is a physical substance through which an effect is produced, and it is also a person who conveys spiritual messages. Artists' mediums are, therefore, tangible forms of matter that serve as vehicles to express emotions, symbols, and concepts.

This essay asserts the timeliness of highlighting the physical material out of which art is produced. Consciously assessing the physical basis of art allows artists to express concern over the state of the Earth's ecosystems. Thus, in addition to communicating the expressiveness of medium, eco artists address the fact that art is constructed out of matter, its energies are stored in matter, and its processes are manifested in matter. This approach signals a distinct separation from "new media" that manipulate immaterial data through push-button technologies, keyboard operations, and computer-modeled visualizations.

The context for this reevaluation of the physical components of art originates in the markings of early humans that appear on bone, antler, and stone. Material manifestations reign as a distinguishing feature of subsequent art traditions: clay in Mexico, textiles in Vietnam, soapstone in Alaska, fresco in Italy, wood in Africa, porcelain in China, paint on canvas in Europe. In the first half of the Twentieth Century, European and American artists added found objects from the real world to the inventory of art interactions. In all of these versions, matter contributed aesthetic qualities (color, texture, transparency, shininess, etc.), structural possibilities (flexibility, viscosity, brittleness, stickiness, durability, etc.), and thematic content (elegance, rarity, banality, disgust, crudeness, etc.).

Currently, three new material options are being introduced by eco artists. One utilizes sap, pollen, feathers, bark, bone, branches, stones, and innumerable other ingredients that account for the wondrous storehouse of materiality on Earth. Another draws from a profusion of discarded and degraded manufactured materials. The third explores the array of living plants, microbes, and animals. Unlike the remote landscapes that appear on the screens of laptops, iPads, and televisions, eco artists are reclaiming the skills associated with engaging in direct interactions with the Earth's mineral, manufactured, and organic matter. They align art's expressive, narrative, and ethical significance with the physical components of experience.

All three categories of material exploration are motivated by concerns regarding the environmental impact associated with material use of all kinds. Eco artists are assigning as much significance to the material considerations of art as to its aesthetics and theme. Art's visibility and influence provides a privileged opportunity to address the impact of humanity's physical interactions upon the vitality of Earth.

Making material decisions from an ecocentric perspective means acknowledging that a finite stockpile of resources on the Earth comprises humanity's shared inheritance with all other forms of life. What we are and all we own are fabricated out of this common pool.

Even the molecules that comprise our bodies are merely on loan from the ecosystem. Living organisms depend upon the cycling of a shared inventory of raw materials to perpetuate life.

Yet history chronicles examples of humans disrupting these essential processes. Such interruptions generally fall into three categories:

- We increase a substance, such as carbon dioxide, exceeding the system's capacity to recapture it and maintain a balanced state.
- We decrease a resource, such as fish, by overexploitation, and water, by pollution.
- We create new materials such as Teflon, GORE-TEX, and polyester that exist outside the range of the recycling pathways that have evolved over millennia to manage wastes in ecosystems.

The material form of eco artworks represents the culmination of a process of interrogating eco art's environmental impact. Creating eco art, therefore, entails assessing each material option by asking these questions:

- Is it recycled, reused, restored, renewed, polluting, depleting, or keystone?
- Is the energy used to produce it renewable, polluting, local, or depleting?
- Are the wastes and leftovers reusable, beneficial, neutral, or toxic?
- What is its impact on the people who manufacture it and the ecosystems that generated it?

FOOTPRINTS

Footprints measured by environmentalists extend far beyond the toe and the heel of a foot. Ecological footprints measure material resources consumed, energy resources spent, and wastes generated. Footprint calculations compare human use of a resource and disposition of wastes to an ecosystem's ability to regenerate its resources and manage its wastes. This condition is known as its *carrying capacity.* If the use of a resource is supported by the enviroment within its carrying capacity, that practice is sustainable. If use results in permanent depletions of a resource or function, the practice is unsustainable. Footprints apply to nations, species, industries, populations, individuals, and art.

The footprints of works of art measure the environmental impacts of material acquisition, production, storage, crating, transportation, exhibition, promotion, maintenance, and final disposition. Applying such calculations to art raises doubts about spacious studios lavishly outfitted with energy-guzzling technologies, the assumption that monumental proportions are a measure of artistic significance, that it is ethical to lavish fragile artworks with resource-consuming and energy-expending conservation procedures.

All these art protocols perpetuate the expectation of affluence that arose during the first flush of industrial productivity. Eco artists respond to the current era's concern with the Earth's inability to support soaring human populations by demonstrating material accountability for all activities, including the production of art. While footprint considerations may limit artistic license, environmental responsibility does not constitute an impoverishment of creative opportunities. Every artist in this book demonstrates that there exists a vast depot of material ingredients that account for a wondrous uniqueness of the planet we call home. They all await adoption by eco artists.

ECOLOGICAL MATERIALISM

Minimizing art's footprint tampers with the popular notion that artists' primary job is to express the *self*. Footprint-conscious artists downgrade the ego in order to upgrade the eco component of their creative practices. Jane Bennett, a professor of political theory at Johns Hopkins University, proposes a radical strategy to accomplish this cultural conversion. Bennett asserts that people need to be more materialistic, not less!

Bennett named this startling proposition "environmental materialism." She distinguishes it from materialism associated with the kind of consumerism that promotes relationships with material possessions, and may be described as "promiscuous" because they are casual, numerous, and superficial. Consumerism celebrates affordable abundance. It tolerates accelerated obsolescence, upgrades, quick turnovers, and accumulation.

Environmental materialism, on the other hand, involves mindful and purposeful relationships with the material environment. It is based upon "thing-power," the belief that even the common artifacts of daily use have significance.[1] According to Bennett, every thing has power because every material object belongs to the dense web that connects all living and nonliving components of the environment. Respect for things ensures that matter and energy are not exhausted or corrupted as they course through human cultures. Even a plastic bottle is the remarkable summation of resource refinement, engineering proficiency, and design expertise. Even a pinecone is an evolutionary marvel.

Bennett asserts that thing-power yields two positive results. One is enchantment, which she describes poetically as "a sense of having had one's nerves or circulation or concentration powers tuned up and recharged—a shot in the arm, a fleeting return to childlike excitement about life."[2] The other is prudence, which means good judgment in practical matters.[3] Her radical propositions can be applied to artists.

Enchantment

Standardized and anonymous materials manifest industrial and corporate efficiencies, but they offer meager installments of enchantment. Even water loses its allure if it flows predictably from a tap. Likewise, fuel from a pump, heat from a furnace, eggs from a carton, and paint colors squeezed from commercial tubes can all be re-enchanted through cognitive awareness of sources and sensual engagements with systems.

By evoking enchantment, eco artists affirm that the Earth does not merely consist of mute matter available to humans for plundering and exploitation. They stir enchantment by fostering delight regarding the material environment that is unrelated to consumption and possession. A prime example is art that honors the intricate web of responses that produce the statistical miracle known as "life."

Until recently, visual perception has provided art's version of enchantment by delighting the eye's ability to discern colors, shapes, and textures. Currently, many eco artists are extending the art audience's relationship with the physical environment by including material engagements derived from a profusion of attributes not detectable by vision: soft/hard, heavy/light, hot/cold, elastic/rigid, spongy/firm, strong/weak, pliable/stiff, and so on. Such multisensual interactions are powerful generators of material enchantment.

Prudence

The prudent aspect of ecological materialism involves assessing materials according to their current and long-term effects on humans, other species, water, air, soil, and weather. This means that artists' material choices are made with concern for immediate environmental impacts as well as for people they will never meet, places they will never visit, and outcomes they will never experience. Thus, prudence introduces new criteria to assess an artwork's merit. Beyond availability, compliance, and stability, it adds efficiency, renewability, and conservation.

ECO MATERIAL ATTRIBUTES

The materials available for adoption within the eco art avant-garde present such a vast inventory, providing a material assessment of each lies well beyond the realm of possibility within this text. Instead, pairs of characteristics that accompany five considerations of material choices are explored: manufacture, life, reactivity, degradability, and renewability. Together they comprise a periodic chart to guide material interactions in art that ensure enchantment and prudence.

Manufactured Materials Current manufactured materials are predominantly products of industrialized technologies that capitalize on automated production, mechanized processes, and increasingly, electronic controls. Such mechanization streamlines the transformation of raw resources into manufactured commodities, escalates the scale and efficiency of output, and churns out the material abundance many people currently enjoy.

However, contemporary manufacturing processes can also be blamed for many of the environmental predicaments that currently beset the planet. Jeremy Rifkin, an American economist, provides a compelling explanation of this predicament. In his book titled *Entropy*, Rifkin compares the energies and materials consumed by modern technology to its outputs. He discovered many examples of inefficient inputs and undesirable outputs that are credited for consumer abundance. Wasteful outputs, for example, include heat from fuel combustion, solid waste by-products from fabrication or extraction, and effluent discharge from factories. These wastes are rarely recycled or reused in modern production processes. Instead, industry depends on continual supplies of nonrenewable energy and resources. Furthermore, management of wastes is costly and often ineffective. Rifkin concludes that the modern industrial system is hurtling toward a non-sustainable destiny commonly known as "doom."

Manufacturers can implement the following protocols to minimize the footprints of their production methods:

- Fabricating new manufactured products using ingredients recycled from previous human use
- Fabricating new manufactured products with virgin resources that are generated sustainably
- Inventing more efficient technologies to manufacture materials
- Reducing the distances between where resources are gleaned, materials are produced, and products are used

Eco artists can adopt the following protocols in acquiring their materials to support manufacturing reforms:

- Repurposing used manufactured objects
- Dismantling discarded manufactured objects to harvest useful components
- Using overruns of manufacture that would normally be discarded
- Finding uses for stored manufactured items
- Finding uses for obsolete or discarded manufactured items

Nonmanufactured Materials Whereas goods that are the result of industrial production are predictable outcomes of being molded, poured, and stamped along conveyor belts, nonmanufactured materials are not predictable. Instead, they are characterized by infinite variability. There are several categories of nonmanufactured materials that are available for adoption by artists:

- Plants
- Plant parts: stem, leaf, root, shoot, pod, flower, seed, bark, needles, twigs, boughs, juice, sap, charcoal, gum, berries, cones, husks
- Animals
- Animal parts: feathers, bones, hooves, horns, fur, scales, shells
- Mineral elements: stone, metal, glass, water, sand, clay, air

Adopting nonmanufactured substances like plant and animal parts does not automatically guarantee eco materialism. The environmentally conscious act of selection entails discovering whether it produces harmful by-products, consumes non-sustainable ingredients, diminishes ecosystem resilience, utilizes exploitative labor practices, or depletes resources.

Life Art is generally created out of inert materials that are prized for their control, stability, and durability. Eco art introduces a dynamic alternative by adding the option of culturing life or partnering with life. The process of incorporating living entities into art is a complex and unpredictable affair that can be imagined as using paint that is capable of overflowing its container of its own accord, or canvases that can crawl along the studio floor, or brushes that get indigestion.

Lifeless Materials Some lifeless entities were always inert. Others were once alive. Some are manufactured by humans. Others exist without human intervention. Until recently, lifeless materials could not self-initiate actions; they responded to external influences only by accreting, melting, eroding, erupting, falling, drifting, dissolving, and so on. The qualifying phrase "until recently" acknowledges that smart materials are currently being engineered that are rendering past limitations obsolete. For example, engineers are designing "smart" textiles, an entirely new generation of Earthly matter that can cool their wearer when temperatures become uncomfortably hot or repair themselves when they become torn.

Living Materials When artists invite living entities into the repertoire of their interactions, the catalog of art production brims with new possibilities. Living materials can be plant or animal, old or young, endangered or abundant, dangerous or benign. They can be large or microscopic, complex or simple, wild or domesticated, native or introduced, competitive or cooperative, sick or healthy, useful to humans or nuisances. Artists can participate in the creation and perpetuation of life by pruning, selecting, feeding, culling, breeding, grafting, cloning, and so forth. Living entities self-initiate actions by moving, reproducing, eating, drinking, excreting, breathing, and growing.

While nonliving entities are subject to conditions in the surrounding environment, living entities actively respond to their environment with the general goal of maintaining life. Two pairs of responses summarize these massively complex interactions:

- Responses to external stimuli are either products of learned behaviors or inherent and involuntary.
- Responses to external stimuli are either positive or negative. Positive stimuli attract organisms to life-sustaining resources and desirable conditions; for example, flowers seek light and flies seek rotting meat. Negative stimuli repel organisms away from conditions that are harmful to them; for example, deer flee forest fires and salmon avoid warm waters.

Biodegradable Materials Life resembles a multiservice industry. Its tasks include producing oxygen, recycling carbon dioxide, filtering waste, enriching soil, capturing and converting solar energy, and so forth. An often overlooked function of life is decomposing. All forms of life—and all the products that originate in living forms—are biodegradable. The *bio* that performs the job of *degrading* includes bacteria, fungi, worms, and insects. This sanitation crew breaks down complex material from discarded plant matter and animal corpses. It generates the simple compounds that green plants and other producers use to create new organic molecules. In this manner it supplies the nutrients that are distributed among the manifold biotic species that grace planet Earth.

Biological decomposition occurs without human intervention in forests, grasslands, jungles, and gardens, wherever dead organic matter collects. Composting is a human-induced scheme that intensifies the biodegrading process. It is undertaken to reduce pressure on landfills and produce fertile mediums for planting.

Nonbiodegradable Materials Yesterday's royalty could never have imagined the common materials that today's humans discard each day. These materials, concocted to augment power, comfort, and convenience, are created by engineers manipulating minute bits of matter by taking molecules apart and putting them back together. The new materials they devise exceed previous capacities to withstand heat, light, moisture, compaction, compression, percussion, microbes, breakage, and oxidation. Now many substances we throw away are practically impervious to change. They are expanding the age-old list of nonmanufactured products that are minimally degradable, such as stone, crystal, petrified wood, fossilized bone, sand, clay, and water.

Industrially manufactured nonbiodegradable materials are not necessarily blights on the environment. Their longevity becomes an asset when they are assigned a new function. Alternatively, they can be subjected to industrial recycling processes, as when plastic bottles are reused in textiles. This entails dismantling and re-mantling the chemistry that we humans so diligently engineered into existence.

Industrial cycling involves assembling, sorting, transporting, compacting, shipping, and manufacturing before the substances can be returned to the economic stream of production and consumption. For this reason, not all nonbiodegradable manufactured materials are good candidates for industrial recycling. Some degrade in quality when they are recycled; some consume excessive resources during recycling; some are so heavy they are costly to transport; some produce harmful by-products during recycling.

Reactive/Nonreactive Materials

Reactivity is the tendency of materials to undergo chemical change. All materials are subject to external influences. Reactivity measures the tempo of change from fast to slow, not its presence and absence. Materials like ice, paper, and alcohol are highly reactive. But even iron rusts, steel expands and contracts, and stone dissolves.

Humans have devised many strategies to manage reactivity. Some strategies intensify reactivity, as when the military develops materials that ignite, split, and explode as warheads. Other strategies suppress reactivity, such as adding preservatives to bread.

Some eco artists demonstrate consonance with ecosystem dynamics by forgoing protective conservation protocols and allowing their artworks to register natural reactivity to changing environmental conditions.

Renewable/Nonrenewable Materials

Pots of gold that remain full no matter how many coins are removed exist only in fairy tales. Gold is not considered a renewable resource, because it takes so long for the temperature of the volcanic magma to cool and form its minuscule particles. Thus, every ounce of gold that is mined today becomes unavailable for extraction by future generations. Resources like petroleum, coal, and iron ore are nonrenewable because they too take millions of years to form and replenish supplies that have been mined.

Topping the list of renewable resources are solar energy, wind energy, and geothermal power from the earth and the ocean, because they exist in infinite supplies. Other resources such as wood, oxygen, leather, and fish can be regenerated through natural processes. However, these naturally regenerating resources are only renewable if two conditions are satisfied: One, their use over time must equal the rate at which they can be replenished; that is, the rate at which trees are harvested must equal the number of trees that mature over the same time. Two, regenerating these resources must be cost-effective; that is, the monetary and environmental expense of raising and slaughtering cattle must be calculated into the production of meat and leather.

Affordability to current populations explains why the primary sources of energy that power contemporary lifestyles are nonrenewable. Sustainability for future populations explains objections to their use. Three terms have recently entered the discourse to mitigate both economic and environmental concerns:

1. *Carbon credits* manage the emissions of greenhouse gases associated with excessive burning of fossil fuels by trading among countries and organizations.[4] These credits were instituted to postpone peak oil.
2. *Peak oil* refers to the time when the world's crude oil production will reach its maximum output and then steadily decline until the wells run dry.

3. *Natural capital* shifts the concept of capital (a resource that is productive but is not consumed) away from machines, roads, and buildings. It assigns value to minerals, plants, and animals. The term highlights the essential services performed by resources that are not directly consumed by humans.

ACQUISITION

Material selection and use account for a significant component of art's total environmental impact, but not all. The means used to acquire these materials are also implicated in eco-materialistic strategies. Acquisition provides artists with another opportunity to manifest environmental responsibility. Strategies of acquiring materials that reduce dependence on processing, transportation, and packaging include the following:

- Purchasing raw materials and processing them into a useful medium
- Scavenging waste materials, most efficiently undertaken on site
- Collecting renewable resources on site
- Cultivating raw materials
- Processing or crafting your own medium

CONCLUSION

Even after materials that don't survive the scrutiny outlined in this chapter are discarded, the depot of eligible eco art materials still brims with opportunities to perform the marriage between enchantment and prudence. Each marriage of this sort propagates possibilities for *Homo sapiens* to live happily ever after on planet Earth.

NOTES

1 Bennett, Jane, "Thing-Power: Toward an Ecological Materialism," paper presented at the annual meeting of the American Political Science Association, Boston Marriott Copley Place, Sheraton Boston & Hynes Convention Center, Boston, Massachusetts, Aug 28, 2002. http://www.allacademic.com/meta/p65032_index.html.

2 Jane Bennett, *The Enchantment of Modern Life: Attachments, Crossings, and Ethics* (Princeton: Princeton University Press, 2001). http://culturemachine.tees.ac.uk/Reviews/rev27.htm.

3 Jane Bennett, "The Force of Things: Steps toward an Ecology of Matter," *Political Theory* vol. 32, no. 3 (June 2004), 347–372.

4 Quotas were established by the Kyoto Protocol, an international environmental treaty adopted in 1997.

Twentieth-Century Eco Art Pioneers

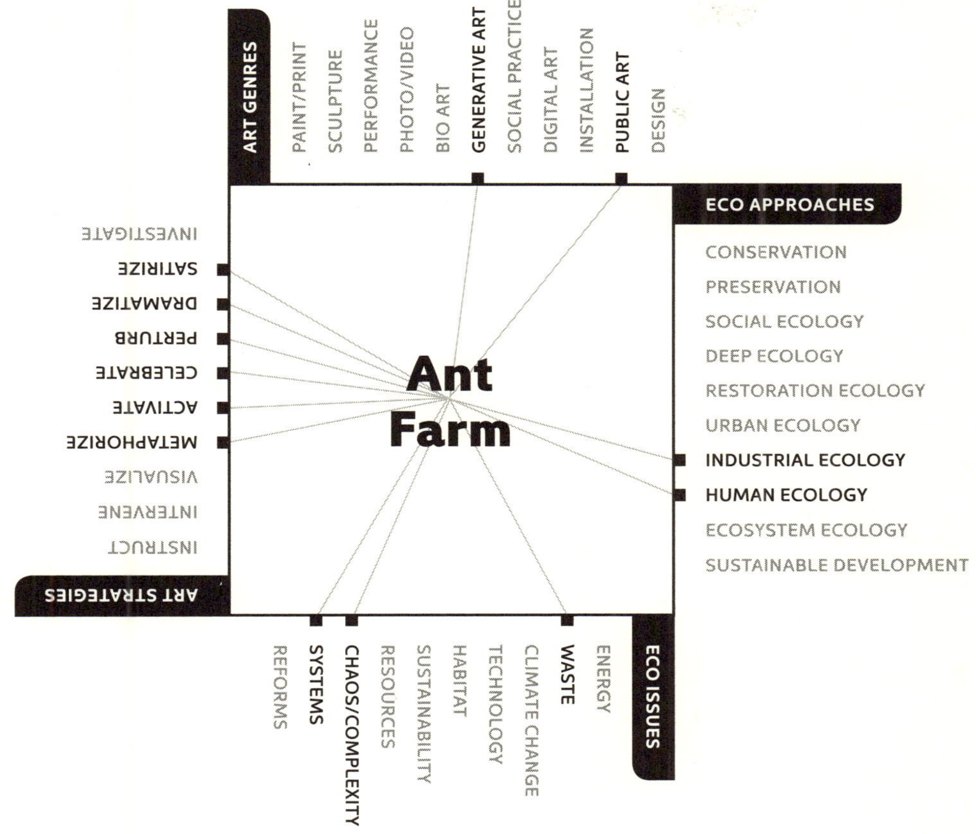

Conspicuous Consumption

Ant Farm founded 1968, California
Doug Michels born 1943, Washington, USA
Died 2003, Eden Bay, Australia
Chip Lord born 1944, Ohio, USA
Hudson Marquez born 1947, Louisiana, USA

WHEN TWO COLLEGE architecture majors (Doug Michels and Chip Lord) and two art majors (Curtis Schreier and Hudson Marquez) were asked if they situated their category-defying practice of the 1970s in the world of art or architecture, they chose a third alternative—the ant world. When asked why, they explained, "We were on our own little planet."[1] They named their collaborative group Ant Farm and began operating in the underground, like ants, in 1968. The group disbanded ten years later after a fire destroyed much of their work. From this self-imposed position off the cultural map, they critiqued the norms of consumer cultures and introduced outlandish inventions that anticipated the future course of eco art and green technologies. Ant Farm designed inflatable structures to serve mobile lifestyles, outfitted a van with solar energy, designed a Clean Air Pod to convey the dangers of air pollution, and created a sea station where humans and dolphins could communicate. In essence, the group functioned as an "art agency that promotes ideas that have no commercial potential, but which we think are important vehicles of cultural introspection."[2]

Ant Farm's radicalism in art reflected the revolutionary zeal of the era's Free Speech Movement, antiwar demonstrations, communal living, sexual liberation, mind-altering drugs, and a do-it-yourself ethos. It was the lighthearted spirit pervading their subversive art practice that captivated art professionals and the general public alike. While their fans rallied behind their satirical escapades, those who were indulging in the practices that they criticized probably emphasized the nuisance aspects of their namesake.

Ant Farm members questioned the value of the era's prosperity that was being heralded as the triumph of capitalism—and perhaps the value of civilization itself. What they discovered was a complicated narrative that originated in the euphoria that spread across the United States at the end of World War II. The country celebrated its victory by churning out the ingredients of the American dream for returning servicemen and their families. This dream surpassed the prewar expectations. Former luxuries like personal cars, televisions, and private homes were reclassified as needs. Factories that had recently produced weapons, tanks, planes, parachutes, and military uniforms began turning out trendy frills and conveniences. Backyard swimming pools replaced wartime Victory Gardens. Economists invented the term *consumer society* to describe this new economy that was driven by the consumption of nonessential goods and services.

By the 1950s, the US economy was booming. An environmental movement arose to absorb the aftershocks from this flood of commodities. Ant Farm joined this endeavor by creating *Cadillac Ranch* (1974), a seminal work that embodies civilization's historic march from scarcity to plenty, and from plenty to excess.

Instead of documenting or correcting the litany of environmental abuses associated with consumerism, Ant Farm identified a single artifact that embodies this critical narrative—the Cadillac tail fin. The ostentatious car appendage evokes an extensive catalog of environmentally significant cultural transformations that were occurring at the time. They include the bulldozing of the countryside for new housing (suburbia), the expanding network of federally funded highways to link suburban residents to places of work (commuting), highway commerce (the mall), automobiles for transport (car culture), and advertisements that enticed people to make frequent purchases (consumerism).

Cadillac Ranch displays a "herd" of ten classic Cadillac automobiles that have been put "out to pasture." Ant Farm installed them diagonally under the blazing Panhandle sun with their hoods buried in the desert sand and their trunks raised high to flaunt their extravagant tail fins. They offered a remarkable sight to unsuspecting motorists whizzing along Route 66 in Amarillo, Texas, a tedious stretch of road interrupted only by grazing cattle and rusting Quonset huts. The work became an immediate roadside attraction. The image of *Cadillac Ranch* has been used—with or without permission—by dozens of companies advertising everything from insurance to restaurants and computers. Although the truth of this assertion is not tested, the artists proudly proclaim, "It's the world's best-selling art postcard."[3]

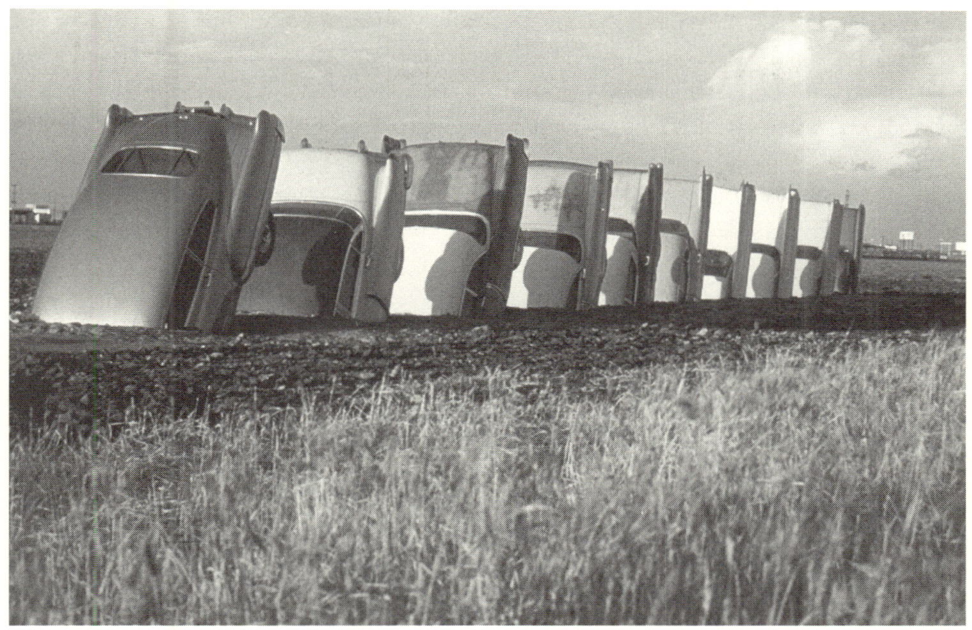

Ant Farm | Chip Lord, Hudson Marquez, and Doug Michels | Cadillac Ranch | 1974 Ten Cadillac cars

PHOTO: CHIP LORD / COURTESY CHIP LORD

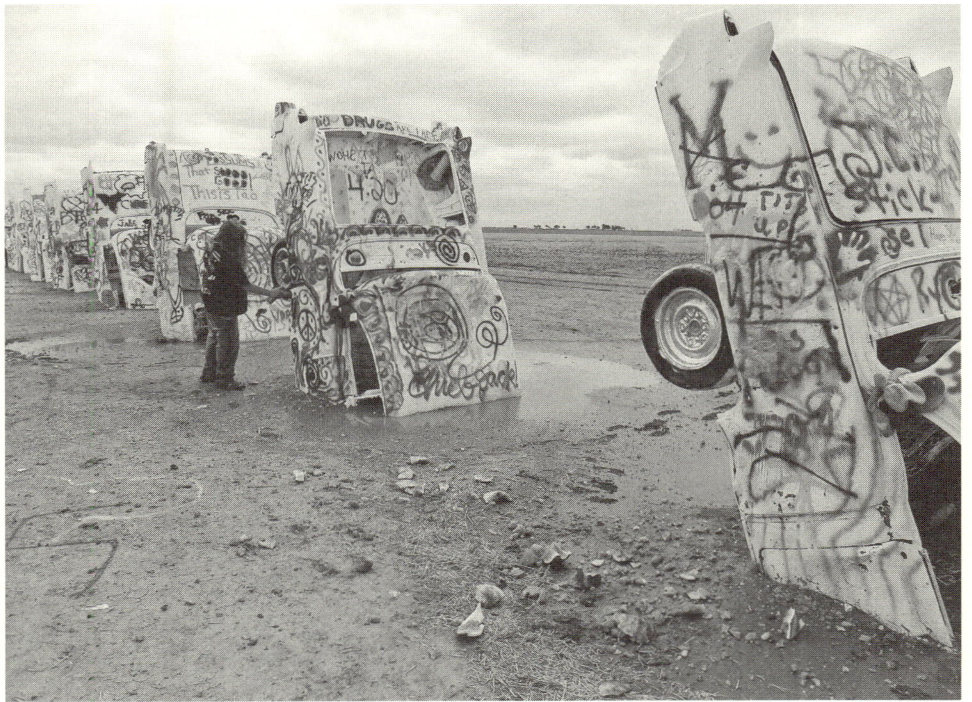

Ant Farm | Chip Lord, Hudson Marquez, and Doug Michels | Cadillac Ranch | 1974–present Ten Cadillac cars

PHOTO: CHIP LORD, TAKEN JUNE 22, 2004 / COURTESY CHIP LORD

The specific cars included in *Cadillac Ranch* represent the signature design shifts that were introduced by Cadillac between 1949, when tail fins were first introduced, and 1964, when they were eliminated. Inspired by new jet-powered aircraft and space-venturing rockets, styling morphed from low, thick, and bulbous to high, slender, and tapered. The artists arranged the bevy of Cadillacs in chronological order so that the expanding proportions of the fins are blatantly displayed. In this manner *Cadillac Ranch* charts the rise of consumerism and the acceleration of obsolescence. Chip Lord observed, "The Detroit design idea was that if you can change the model every year, why change it every three years?"[4] The 1959 version sprouted a set of tail fins that rose forty-two inches off the ground! These appendages served no aerodynamic function, but they served Cadillac owners by flaunting their expendable incomes. Tail fins embodied status in cultures that glorify material consumption.

Cadillac Ranch is a monument to consumerism that could be interpreted as either an endearing homage to the euphoria and optimism of postwar United States or a searing indictment of the waste and extravagance. Lord agrees, "There's an ambiguity as to whether it's a critical piece or a tribute. And it's both. It's a tribute to the tailfin and tailfin culture in a kind and loving way. But there's also a critique of it, because the cars are buried."[5]

This monument to consumerism could not have been accomplished unless the artists themselves indulged in the practice they were critiquing. They purchased the ten luxury cars with obvious relish.

> In May 1974 we went to Amarillo and began buying Cadillacs. It was a white-trash dream come true, buying and driving old Cadillacs on the windswept plains of the Texas Panhandle. In our search we visited every used-car lot in Amarillo and most of the junkyards. We bought a '59 Coupe de Ville at a junkyard for $100 because "it had no papers," as the guy said. "Don't make a shit to us," we said, "if you'll deliver it." He did. We bought a creampuff '62 Sedan de Ville from Guy Mullins Motors. It was a pastel yellow four-door hardtop and it ran so well that it was painful to bury. We found a silver '49 fastback but the guy was asking $700 for it, a price we considered exorbitant (the cars averaged $200 a piece). Stanley suggested we buy it and then smash up the front end with sledgehammers in front of the proud previous owner. So we did in fact smash it, with the cameras rolling as the bewildered owner winced in agony. Our search for Cadillacs took us into people's backyards and private junkyards. At the end of two weeks we had the necessary ten cars and a spare.[6]

Cadillac Ranch did not attain the status of a cultural icon merely as a drive-by experience. From the beginning, visitors were encouraged to park their cars, march through a set of unlocked gates, and enter the private land where the artwork was installed. Ant Farm invites visitors to bring along cans of spray paint to mark the majestic car bodies. To those who worship these consumerist icons, the resulting graffiti constitutes a sacrilege. To counterculture rebels like the members of Ant Farm, it is an irresistible opportunity to obliterate fantasies conjured by the mass media acting in the service of corporate interests. *Cadillac Ranch* signals the triumph of folk culture over mass culture.

Thus, although the original cars were carefully selected for color, their surfaces were quickly obliterated by a free-for-all graffiti spree. The cars have been repainted periodically, most often as a single color, white, pink, sometimes black, in order to provide a clean palette for future renegade markings—political slogans, graffiti tags, blots, and blotches.

In 1997, Ant Farm members and their patron, Stanley Marsh, agreed that the horizon behind *Cadillac Ranch* had become so cluttered with parking lots and malls that the visual impact of the Cadillac silhouettes was being compromised. The artwork needed to be seen against an open horizon. Thus, they "rounded up" the deteriorating car bodies along with the litter that had accumulated around them and moved the monumental mess beyond the city limits. Now the travelers who gawk at and scribble on Ant Farm's classic artwork are driving on Interstate 40.

Even Bruce Springsteen, the celebrated rock musician, was inspired to write an anthem to the work after passing by on tour in 1979. It became a hit single on *The River* album:

> Well, there she sits buddy justa gleaming in the sun
> There to greet a working man when his day is done
> I'm gonna pack my pa and I'm gonna pack my aunt
> I'm gonna take them down to the Cadillac Ranch.[7]

The era that welcomed tail-finned gas guzzlers may seem remote. Carbon emissions and sustainability make tail fins seem like a preposterous reminder of a bygone era. However, Lord explains that the circumstances surrounding the artwork's creation in the 1970s are not that different from today, "There was the first energy crisis in the U.S. and the Arab oil embargo. . . . I mean, that was a big moment and we were in the middle of it and we produced work that responded to it. So now we're in another moment, particular with global warming, when what might have been in a smaller fringe movement in the 70's—well now everybody has to think of this issue of sustainability and climate change and I think it makes sense to look at what was happening in the 70s."[8]

Pioneering Contribution to Eco Art **Instead of chastising consumers or condemning manufacturers, Ant Farm used reverse psychology to temper the euphoria surrounding material abundance. They accomplished this by inviting the public to deface an extravagant example of luxury they might otherwise have coveted. As much as drawing attention to consumerism, this work demonstrates how artists can invent innovative strategies to convey the ethical and ecological consequences of human behaviors.**

NOTES

1 Doug Michels quoted in *Ant Farm 1968–1978* by Constance M. Lewallen and Steve Seid (Berkeley: University of California Press, 2004), 72.
2 Chip Lord interview with Rebecca Cleman, Media Art Resource. http://resourceguide.eai.org/exhibition/ singlechannel/interview_lord.html.
3 Curtis Schreier quoted in *Ant Farm 1968–1978* by Constance M. Lewallen and Steve Seid (Berkeley: University of California Press, 2004), 70.
4 Chip Lord quoted in *Ant Farm 1968–1978* by Constance M. Lewallen and Steve Seid (Berkeley: University of California Press, 2004), 67.
5 Ibid, 43.
6 Chip Lord and Ant Farm, *Automerica: A Trip Down US Highways from World War II to the Future* (New York: Dutton, 1976).
7 Bruce Springsteen, "Cadillac Ranch," *The River* album, 1980.
8 Bruce Tomb, Ant Farm, interview with Jimmy Stamp, "Ant Farm Media Van," *Floater Magazine*. http://www.floatermagazine.com/issue02/Media_Van/.

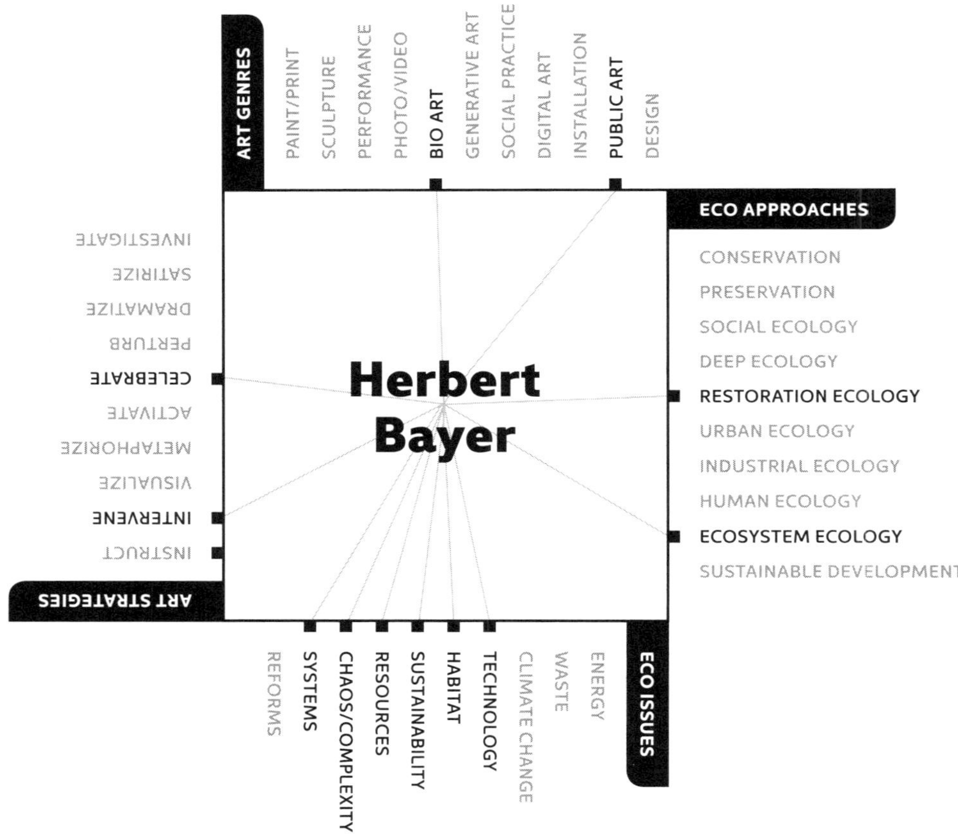

Watershed Management and Beautification

Born 1900, Salzburg, Austria
Died 1984, California, USA

TWO HISTORIC CONFERENCES bracketed the destiny of Herbert Bayer's *Mill Creek Canyon Earthworks* (1982). The first conference entered the annals of Twentieth-Century art because, by facilitating the approval and construction of this adventuresome artwork, it expanded the scope of public art far beyond monumental personal expressions. The later conference determined the artwork's fate twenty-five years after it was made. It, too, may come to be regarded as historic because it exposed the complexities and disputes that public art often provokes. The narrative of these combined events reveals the promise and the pitfalls of restoration ecology.

Ecological restoration is the process of assisting the recovery of an ecosystem that has been degraded, damaged, or destroyed. These interventions are necessary when the abuses are so extreme they exceed the system's inherent compensating mechanisms. Intentional activities that initiate or accelerate the recovery of an ecosystem are developed through the science of restoration ecology, first established in the 1980s. Instead of being passively fatalistic about the negative impact of humans upon the world around them, restorationists are active and optimistic.

The agenda of the 1979 conference, Earthworks: Land Reclamation as Sculpture, consisted of presentations by eight renowned artists. They were invited to propose earthworks in gravel pits, floodplains, surface mines, landfills, and other technologically abused sites. Many of these artists had already produced large-scale earthworks that were aesthetic accessories to the landscape. However, few had considered remediating an unsightly and malfunctioning ecosystem. Strategies to conduct such a technically sophisticated task through public art were explored in public forums, panel discussions, and an exhibition at the Seattle Art Museum. One of two proposals that were realized was Bayer's elegant solution for water erosion and retention on a twenty-acre site in the city of Kent in the state of Washington. It has come to be regarded as a modernist masterpiece.

Bayer was uniquely qualified for this assignment. In 1921, at the age of twenty-one, he moved from Austria to Weimar, Germany, to enroll at the Bauhaus, a radically innovative educational institution that was just two years old at the time. Within a few years, he was promoted to master teacher. Fleeing the repression of Nazi Germany, he arrived in the United States in 1938. Bayer was instrumental in establishing two transformative principles associated with the Bauhaus. One involved establishing the blueprint of supersimplified forms that distinguish "modern" design. The other integrated fine art principles of form into everyday operations of society. Bayer's *Mill Creek Earthwork* was immediately lauded as a grand convergence of these Bauhaus principles—merging the functionality of craft with the elegance of fine art.

At the time of Bayer's tenure at the Bauhaus, there was no such term as *environmental design* and no such art form as an "earthwork." Nonetheless, Bayer explains how the school provided him with the necessary prerequisites to create an artwork that engaged both: "The Bauhaus already saw the function of the artist not only in the shaping of particular objects and issues, but in the totality of all design for an all inclusive environment."[1] The result, Bayer believed, far exceeds artful design. He comments, "Artistic work will expand from the picture frame to the large outdoor spaces where it will eventually assume terrestrial, even cosmic dimension."[2] The commission from the King County Arts Commission and the Department of Public Works allowed Bayer to experiment with this expansive vision of public art.

The town of Kent, Washington is sited precariously in a floodplain between the White and Green Rivers. These watercourses flow downward through a tight canyon that feeds directly into downtown Kent. As the town expanded from an agricultural community to an industrial and commercial city, more and more permeable surfaces were paved, preventing rainwater from being absorbed into the ground. As a result Mill Creek flooded, salmon died, and downtown Kent was waterlogged in the winter. Kent's mayor, Isabel K. Hogan, was dissatisfied with the engineering solution submitted by the URS Corporation because the plan fenced areas off from public access. In a bold move, Hogan solicited a new vision from three unconventional providers of infrastructure design: the county arts commission, the art museum, and an artist.

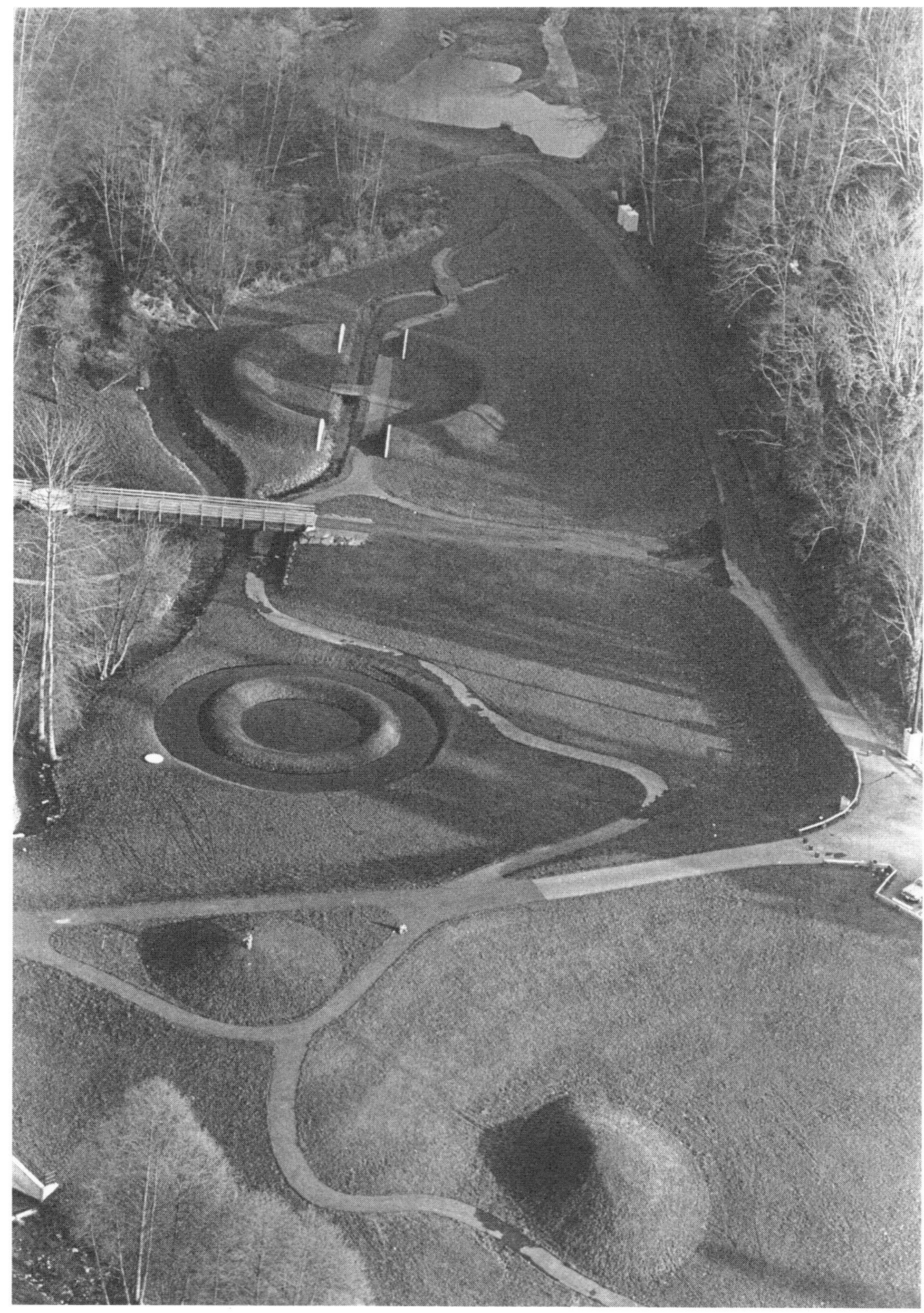

Herbert Bayer | Mill Creek Canyon Earthworks | 1982–present Park and storm water detention dam | Grass, plantings, concrete, wood | 2½ acres, Kent, Washington

PHOTO: CITY OF KENT PUBLIC ART COLLECTION, KENT PUBLIC WORKS / CREDIT: © HERBERT BAYER, MILL CREEK CANYON EARTHWORKS, 1982 / COURTESY CITY OF KENT PUBLIC ART COLLECTION

Bayer's design shaped the land into cones, ridges, and circular berms that were formed out of grass, earth, and concrete to become pools, dams, a bridge, stairs, and pathways. The meticulous contouring of the slopes afforded visitors a refined aesthetic experience and also attended to the hydrologic conditions that needed remedying. The entire work was minimally landscaped with native vegetation and simple rows of poplar trees. The elegance of its geometry gives the earthwork a serene quality even as it improves storm water detention, prevents soil erosion, and rebuilds salmon habitats.

Most often the artwork is dry, but it gets charged by rainstorms. During flooding, the basin becomes a plane of water, the berms protrude like islands, and the surrounding land frames the water. Since 1982 the earthwork has been successfully protecting the town of Kent from the destructive floods that have inundated nearby municipalities. The only flood in Kent has been the flood of goodwill that greeted Bayer's triple plan. Bayer transformed an engineering problem into a tranquil art occurrence, an artwork into a functional solution, and solitary viewing of art into a communal experience. Visitors enjoy evolving views of the work's formal eloquence while climbing the landforms and walking along the paths. Bayer states, "A dam in the ordinary sense constitutes a radical interference with the natural configuration of the land. My intent was, therefore, to give the dams a natural appearance conforming to the landscape (surroundings) and to become integral parts of the landscape being created."[3] Nonetheless, the artwork transcended visual pleasure by reminding visitors of water's fearsome force and its effect upon the canyon, creek, forest, topography, seasons, and weather.

The second conference was held twenty-five years after the work's opening. It was a contentious event designed to resist the revised storm regulations that had just been issued by the Washington State Department of Ecology. The newly established department was launched about the time of Hurricane Katrina, the costliest and most destructive natural disaster in the history of the United States. Bureaucrats reacted to this catastrophe by increasing the safety stipulations for Bayer's water management system a thousand times—from a 100-year-storm requirement to a 10,000-year-storm requirement! Conforming required that the height of the dam, an essential feature of Bayer's meticulous design, had to be raised. Tampering with an earthwork by an acknowledged master of modernism seemed comparable to repainting the nose on the *Mona Lisa*. Richard Haag, an influential American landscape architect, was indignant: "Bureaucrats! It's beyond human resources to set a 10,000 year regulation. There are too many variables at play. Even if they're right, the whole damn system would be overcharged. They can't be serious about this—people have only been building for 5,000 years—the pyramids aren't even 5,000 years old."[4]

The town of Kent responded to the threat by partnering with King County's Office of Historic Preservation, Kent Public Works, students at the University of Washington, and the Kent Arts Commission. Their search for a strategy that would respect Bayer's original concept and design took the form of a symposium with respected artists, landscape architects, and historians in an exhibition they humorously titled "Channeling Herbert" to conjure how Bayer, who died in 1984, might have responded to this dilemma.

Although popular consensus held that the aesthetic loss from raising the height of the dam was far greater than the functional gain, the city capitulated to the new requirements. In the spring of 2008, just weeks after the Kent Arts Commission's nomination of *Mill Creek Canyon Earthworks* for city landmark designation was granted, the city of Kent began construction to raise the height of its earthen berm by two feet.

While Bayer is honored for designing and implementing a large-scale water management project as a work of art, he is also remembered for initiating numerous dilemmas that continue to haunt artists who engage in large-scale restoration. For example, there are numerous reasons why restoration sites may become outdated. Regarding Mill Creek, regulations became stricter. Restoration artworks may also become obsolete because environmental conditions change in an unanticipated manner, or because technical components are refined and improved after the artwork is constructed. These dilemmas introduce three compromises but no solutions: the artwork remains although its function is less than optimal, the artwork's formal integrity is compromised by updating it, the artwork is destroyed and replaced.

Tensions also arise from the dual personality of an artwork that functions as a restoration project. *Mill Creek*'s formalist components conflicted with functional components even before the new regulations were imposed. For instance, sediment and debris that are transported by floodwaters can become trapped in basins, and weeds growing along the banks may benefit fish but look unsightly.

Cultivation versus wildness identifies another restoration quandary that applies to *Mill Creek Canyon Earthworks.* The plantings selected by Bayer create formal beauty, but they limit natural diversity. Therefore they are likely to decrease the ecosystem's resilience against storms and other perturbations. It is possible that the site might function more efficiently if it were not cultivated and maintained as an artwork but allowed to become wild.

Finally, despite his recognition as a pioneering restoration artist, Bayer articulated the unsettling possibility that successful restoration could actually encourage people to degrade ecosystems:

> The most significant implication of art as land reclamation is that art can and should be used to wipe away technological guilt. Do those sites scarred by mining or poisoned by chemicals now seem less like the entropic liabilities of ravenous and shortsighted industry and more like long-awaited aesthetic possibilities? Will it be a little easier in the future to rip up the landscape for one last shovelful of non-renewable energy source if an artist can be found (cheap, mind you) to transform the devastation into an inspiring and modern work of art? Or anyway, into a fun place to be? Well, at the very least, into a tidy, mugger-free park. It would seem that artists participating in art as land reclamation will be forced to make moral as well as aesthetic choices. There may be more choices available than either a cooperative or critical stance for those who participate. But it would perhaps be a misguided assumption to suppose that artists hired to work in industrially blasted landscapes would necessarily and invariably choose to convert such sites into idyllic and reassuring places, thereby socially redeeming those who wasted the landscape in the first place.[5]

Pioneering Contribution to Eco Art **Herbert Bayer's integral approach to watershed restoration dissolved the division between engineering and art, between development schemes and habitat resilience, between environmental solutions and community engagement. Integral thinking is a core ingredient of eco art because partitioned thinking can lead to the nearsighted and shortsighted behaviors that interfere with ecosystem functions. However, Bayer also pioneered the conflicts and quandaries inherent to remedial art.**

NOTES

1 Herbert Bayer (1972) quoted by Gwen F. Chanzit in "Mill Creek Canyon Park and Herbert Bayer's Pioneering Design Strategies," on the Official Website for the City of Kent. http://www.KentWA.gov/content.aspx?id=7328.

2 Ibid.

3 Herbert Bayer quoted in an untitled essay by Brice Maryman on the Official Website for the City of Kent. http://www.KentWA.gov/content.aspx?id=7588.

4 Richard Haag, untitled essay on the Official Website for the City of Kent. http://www.KentWA.gov/content.aspx?id=7488.

5 Herbert Bayer quoted by Robert Morris in "Earthworks: Land Reclamation as Sculpture" (catalog that accompanied the King County Arts Commission symposium, Kent, Washington, 1979).

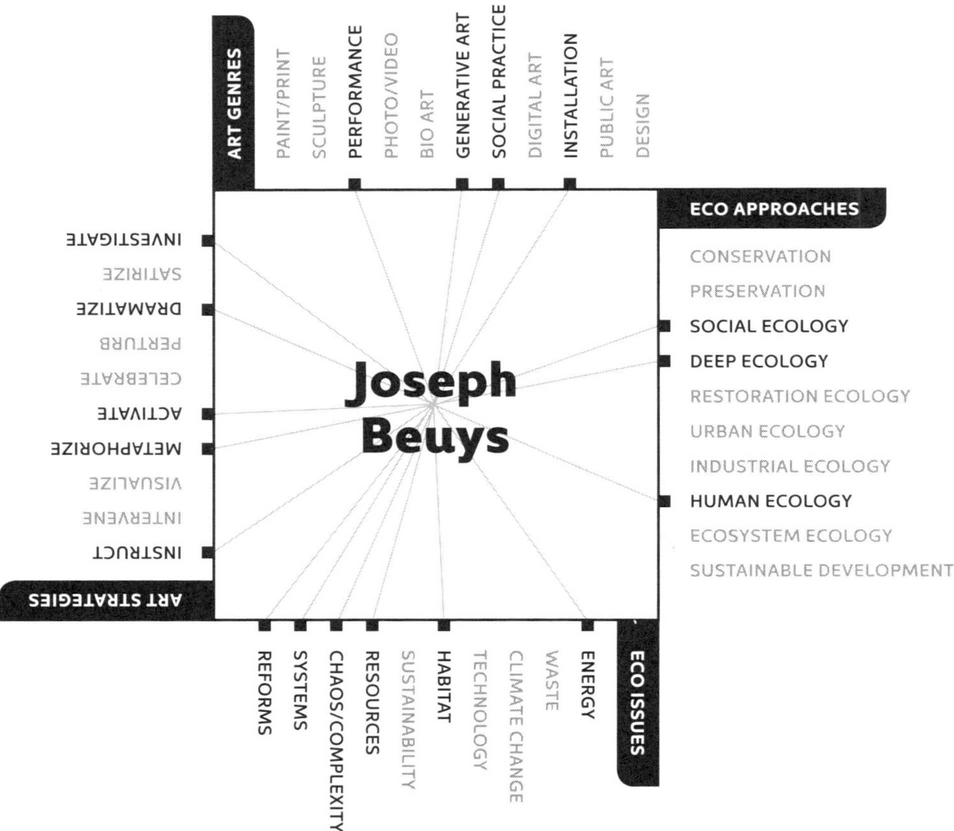

Energy Generation as Social Sculpture

Born 1921, Krefeld, Germany
Died 1986, Düsseldorf, Germany

THE WORD *ENERGY* was emblazoned in capitals beside an image of flaming oil rigs on the cover of the April 1974 issue of *Science Magazine*. The title of the lead article, "Paradise Lost?," reflected the alarm that mounted throughout the '70s regarding the end of the era of energy abundance. The shift was triggered by an Arab oil embargo to the United States, western Europe, and Japan in retaliation for their support of Israel during the Yom Kippur War. People were troubled by shrinking coal and gas reserves, periodic brownouts, occasional blackouts, the escalation of electric utility rates, elevated petroleum product prices, and long lines at the gas pump. The threatened paradises referred to in the headlines included all the economies that depended upon imports to satisfy their energy demands—the United States, Great Britain, Canada, Japan, the Netherlands, Germany, Switzerland, Norway, and others.

The insecurity associated with "oil price shock" triggered extreme reactions on both sides of the political divide. On the one hand, people scrambled to discover ways to limit dependency on oil imports; this spurred research for solar energy, wind power, tidal power, geothermal energy, and ocean thermal conversions. On the other hand, it asserted pressure to relax environmental standards set on emissions from coal and petroleum combustion because they compromised efficiency.

Joseph Beuys, one of the era's seminal artists, performed a simple action that encapsulates this urgent predicament. He thrust a spade into the earth in front of a nuclear power station and titled the artwork *What Is to Be Done?* The question in the title asks which tool ensures the security of humans, the well-being of the environment, and the fragile peace among nations. Is it a simple handheld gardening tool or a mammoth industrial complex involving enriched uranium, fuel rods, chain reactions, nuclear cores, turbines, steam, and electricity?

The alternative energy schemes Beuys ultimately offered differed from those that were occupying most industry experts. Instead of capturing the sun's rays, water, wind, or hydrothermal vents, Beuys liberated the energy of the human spirit. His scheme had no need for cap-and-trade systems, price controls, rationing, and embargoes, because humanity's suppressed creative energies represent an infinite power supply. Unlike most energy schemes that aspire to maintain the status quo, the unlimited energy of human creativity promised unlimited advancements and improvements.

"Warmth = energy = warmth = life"[1] is an equation Beuys constructed to expand the psychological and social meaning of his work. Heat is required to power all forms of life on Earth. Heat is generated from either nutrients that are ingested as food or stored fats that are metabolized as fuel. In the absence of heat, organisms would not grow, or repair themselves, or reproduce. There would be no life on Earth, and life is the ultimate form of creativity.

As a sculptor, Beuys was intrigued by the power of heat to change matter from solid to liquid and from liquid to gas. Within his work, solid matter represents a rigid mind-set, while flowing liquids and swirling gases represent creativity. The necessary catalyst to creativity, therefore, is the addition of heat, which explains Beuys's eccentric choices of medium. He worked with grease, fat, and honey because they readily melt when they are heated. They therefore provide ideal metaphors for the transformation from the hard, orderly mentality devoid of creativity to the flowing and chaotic states of creative thinking.

Within Beuys's theory of sculpture, physical transformations of energy are metaphors that signify the generation of mental and spiritual creativity. Just as photosynthesis converts sun energy into chemical energy, and batteries transform chemical energy into electrical energy, Beuys relied upon thermal energy to indicate a transformation of "thought-power, will-power, powers of sensibility."[2]

Whether it is fact or legend, a dramatic narrative is included in Beuys's biography that explains his use of energy-rich mediums like grease and honey. He is reported to have survived a devastating airplane crash when he served in the German air force during World War II. He parachuted onto the frigid tundra in the Crimea, where he lay unconscious and would have frozen if a tribe of nomadic Tatars hadn't rescued him. The nomads warmed Beuys

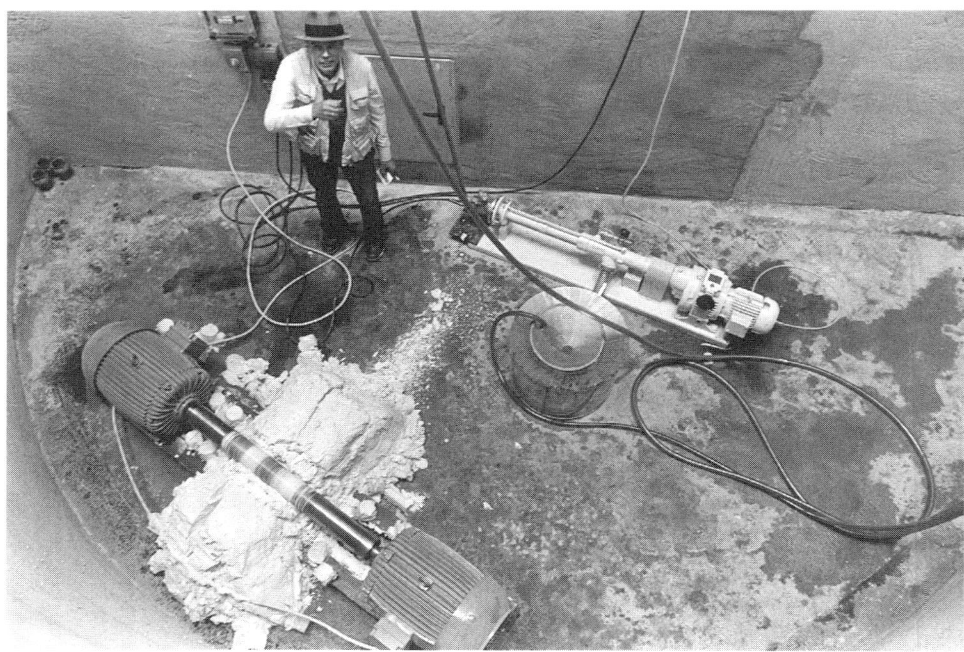

Joseph Beuys | Honeypump at the Working Place | 1977 100 days of Documenta 6, Kassel, West Germany | Two tons of honey, 220 pounds of margarine, two ship's engines, steel container, plastic tubing, three bronze pots | Dimensions: variable

CREDIT: © 2011 ARTISTS RIGHTS SOCIETY (ARS), NEW YORK / VG BILD-KUNST, BONN / COURTESY RONALD FELDMAN GALLERY, NEW YORK

internally by feeding him honey. Then they warmed him externally by covering his body with grease and rolling him in insulating felt blankets. Thermal energy brought him back to life. They also provided Beuys with three precepts that sustained his long and influential art career. The first was ecological: "The question of survival goes beyond the problem of human health and concerns the health of the whole of planet Earth."[3] The second was social: that human opinions, behaviors, and beliefs, as well as physical matter, are activated by warmth/energy. The third was artistic: "Only art is capable of dismantling the repressive effects of a senile social system that continues to totter along the death line: to dismantle in order to build A SOCIAL ORGANISM AS A WORK OF ART."[4]

Beuys demonstrated all three precepts by creating a vast energy stream in an installation entitled *Honeypump at the Working Place* (1977). A real industrial pumping device provided the metaphor for the surge of creative inspiration. It was composed of ship engines, driveshafts, fittings, fuses, switches, and low-pressure pumps. A powerful electric motor rotated a crankshaft that was covered with two hundred pounds of margarine; this thick layer of fat lubricated the machine. A second engine ran a pump that propelled two tons of honey up a pipe that was over fifty feet high. It was connected to a distribution network of plastic tubes that ran throughout the Kunsthalle Fridericianum in Düsseldorf, Germany, a grandiose Eighteenth-Century neoclassical museum. The tubes of honey extended all the way from the basement, up its grand staircase, to the top floor of the museum. The work manifests the equation warmth = energy = life. The pump is the heart. The tubes are arteries and veins. The honey is blood. The honey is warm, liquid, flowing. Conditions are ripe for liberating the energy of inspiration.

Beuys invented the term *social sculpture* to indicate that this grandiose assemblage of pumps and motors and tubes was intended to manufacture a new society. *Honeypump* is, therefore, a social transformation mechanism. Beuys explains that it depends on the creative contributions of all citizens, rebels and conformists alike: "This most modern art discipline—Social Sculpture/Social Architecture—will only reach fruition when every living person becomes a creator, a sculptor or architect of the social organism. . . . Only a conception of art revolutionized to this degree can turn it into a politically productive force, coursing through each person and shaping history."[5]

Beuys hoped this revolutionary vision would be fulfilled in the room where the honey-filled tubes terminated. That is where, throughout the hundred days of the exhibition, Beuys conducted seminars demonstrating radical models for art, education, politics, environmental sciences, law, economics, and research. Such seminars became known as *Energy Plan for Western Man*. The contents of these discourses survive on the large blackboards he covered with diagrams in chalk as he dialogued with the museum visitors. By absorbing the heat of his creative thinking, Beuys hoped, the public's latent energy supplies would be released and a new social structure would emerge in the form of a society that was full-bodied and a populace that was open-minded.

Beuys traced the critical need to reenergize modern society to industrialization, the scientific method, and rationality. Together, these social forces had alienated people from the invisible energies that sustain life. As a result, the human spirit had rigidified and society had become bent on domination. "The metaphor of the earth as nurturing mother would disappear gradually to the same degree as the scientific revolution succeeded in mechanizing and rationalizing the world image. The other metaphor—nature as disturbance and lawlessness—brought forward an important modern thought: the power over nature. Two new ideas, that of mechanism and that of the power over nature, and its conquest, became the central concepts of the modern world. The organic mentality, in which feminine principles were to the fore, was discredited and replaced by a mechanically oriented mentality, that either negated feminine principles or misused them exploitatively."[6] Beuys made this declaration in 1979 when he was the German candidate of the Green Party for the European Parliament. His platform was built upon the conviction that environmental reform depends upon social reform and that social reform depends upon the flexible thinking (warmth) of individuals.

Beuys elevated the importance of recovering a ritual relationship with Earth energies when he performed *Bog Action* (1971). The work survives as two photographs in which he expands the intimate immersion he had experienced among the Tatars in the Crimea. In one, Beuys leaps across a bog, arms wide, in a gesture of joyful abandonment. In the other, he is fully immersed, swimming through the bog's brown waters.

These images are startling because he is shown reveling in a location that is not a popular destination for vacations or a setting for spiritual transport. Bogs tend to repulse people because they are so laden with accumulations of dead plant material that they are brown and spongy. Swimming in chemically laced pools and drinking packaged water—its opposite—suits popular tastes. Indeed, the word *bog* is British slang for *bathroom*. Beuys's action dismissed human perceptions of bogs as disagreeable to highlight their ecological value. Accordingly Beuys states, "Bogs are the liveliest elements in the European landscape, not just from the point of view of flora, fauna, birds, and animals, but as storing places of life, mystery, and chemical change, preservers of ancient history. They are essential to the whole eco-system for water regulation, humidity, ground water, and climate in general."[7] All of these impressive assets were ignored by the developers who scheduled this particular bog for draining and served as the impetus for this art action. The work demonstrates that promoting intimate experiences with the stuff of the earth carries radical political and social consequences.

Pioneering Contribution to Eco Art **As Beuys was expanding the domain of art to include the sculpting of social, political, and economic organizations, he simultaneously expanded the ecological paradigm by implicating human behaviors in the endangerment of forests and bogs. He further augmented ecological considerations by cultivating the primal energies of human consciousness as a form of therapy for humans and the environment. By uniting physical and spiritual, political and artistic, Beuys helped spawn an impressive diversity of today's environmental improvement schemes.**

NOTES

1 Joseph Beuys quoted by Caroline Tisdall, *Joseph Beuys* (London: Thames and Hudson, 1979).
2 Joseph Beuys interviewed Bernard Lamarche-Vadel, August 1979, quoted in *The Essential Joseph Beuys* by Alain Borer (Cambridge, MA: MIT Press, 1977), 15.
3 Joseph Beuys interview with Elizabeth Rona, October 1981, quoted in *The Essential Joseph Beuys* by Alain Borer (Cambridge, MA: MIT Press, 1977), 26.
4 Joseph Beuys quoted by Caroline Tisdall, *Joseph Beuys* (London: Thames and Hudson, 1979), 268.
5 Ibid.
6 Joseph Beuys, *Der Tod der Natur, Ökologie, Frauen und neuzeitliche Naturwissenschaft (The Death of Nature. Woman, Ecology and the Scientific Revolution, 1980)*, translated by Carolyn Merchant (Munich: 1987), 18.
7 Joseph Beuys quoted by Caroline Tisdall, *Joseph Beuys* (London: Thames and Hudson, 1979), 39.

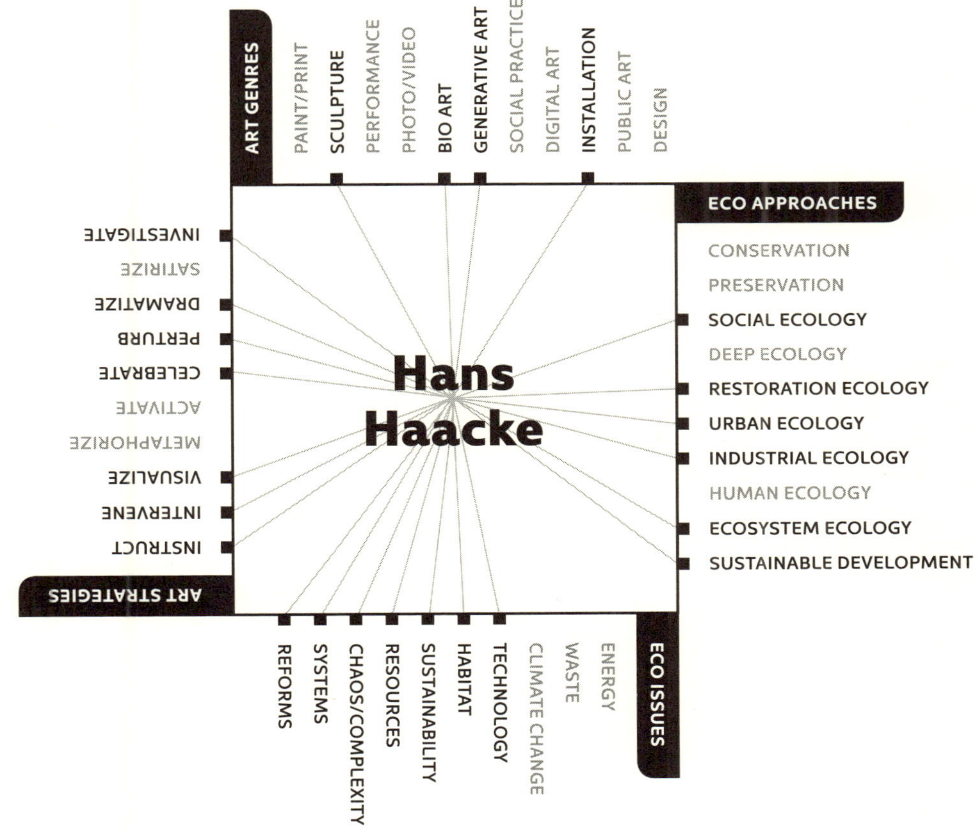

Ecological/Political/ Cultural Systems

Born 1936, Cologne, Germany

PROOF THAT THE EARTH is spherical, not flat, may have allayed peoples' fears about falling into the void if they traveled in one direction across the Earth, but it ruptured basic fifteenth-century assumptions about space, perception, distance, opportunity, and so forth. Currently, the young science of ecology is introducing assertions about our planet that may prove to be equally destabilizing. One challenging ecological concept is that individual entities provide little useful information if they are separated from their contexts. Another warns that events are meaningless if they are divorced from ongoing temporal occurrences. As a result, expectations must be recalibrated to jibe with a planet that consists of myriad composite systems simultaneously evolving and devolving, not objects fixed in space and time. Ecological awareness drives individuals to seek footing upon a perpetually morphing planet.

Hans Haacke joined this planetary reevaluation in the 1960s by dispensing with the static art object. In its place he created real-time systems in which energy flows and materials respond to each other within actual life contexts. Haacke committed himself to this new course by relinquishing conventional art mediums, art tools, self-expression, artistic will, and even the concept of the masterwork. He enumerates his objections in the following statement: "Painters and sculptors of static works are anxious to prevent their works from being influenced by time and environmental conditions. Patina is not looked for as a record of the bronzes' response to atmospheric exposure nor is the darkening and crackle of paintings desirable in order to demonstrate their reaction to environmental conditions. Although physical changes take place, the intention of these artists is to make something that alters as little as possible. Equally, the viewer hopes to see the work as it appeared immediately after its execution."[1] Haacke provides a moderate explanation for the heretical alternatives he introduced: "From the beginning the concept of change has been the ideological basis of my work. All the way down there's absolutely nothing static—nothing that does not change, or instigate real change."[2] In essence, Haacke traded in his affiliation to art history for an alliance with the dynamic systems of the planet.

Condensation Cube (1963–1965) anticipated many Twenty-First-Century eco art practices by responding to fluctuations in the environment. This landmark artwork consists of an elementary form—a clear acrylic box modestly sized at approximately 12" x 12" x 12"—and a simple procedure: Haacke inserted a small quantity of water into the cube and then hermetically sealed it. Although there is no direct interaction between the interior and the exterior of the cube, the water perpetually responds to the temperature, light, moisture, and airflow in the surrounding space. Even visitors' bodies influence the artwork as they emit heat, block light, increase moisture, and interrupt airflow. Droplets trickle, pool, and vapor in concert with fluctuations in the ambient conditions, manifesting the intricate complexities of water in real time and space. Haacke highlighted the environment's role in creating this work when he identified the work's medium as "clear acrylic, water, light, air currents, temperature, climate in exhibition situation."

The self-regulating system that activates the work functions whether or not the artist is present, or viewers are in attendance, or the museum is even open. Indeed, it displaces the artist as sole creator of the physical state of the artwork and the visual experience it provides. Like any viewer, Haacke delights in discovering the marvels that occur as water inside the cube condenses: "A delicate veil of drops begins to develop on the inside walls. At first, they are so small that one can distinguish single drops from only a very close distance. The drops grow—hour by hour—small ones combining with larger ones. The speed of growth depends on the intensity and the angle of the intruding light. After a day, a dense cover of clearly defined drops has developed and they all reflect light. With continuing condensation, some drops reach such a size that their weight overcomes the forces of adhesion and they run down along the walls, leaving a trace. This trace starts to grow together again. Weeks after, manifold traces, running side by side, have developed. According to their respective age, they have drops of varying sizes."[3] The condensation is ongoing and unpredictable. Haacke compares it to a living organism.[4]

While *Condensation Cube* may seem as simple as a grade-school science experiment, it reveals Haacke's propensity to provoke controversy. In this instance, each droplet expos-

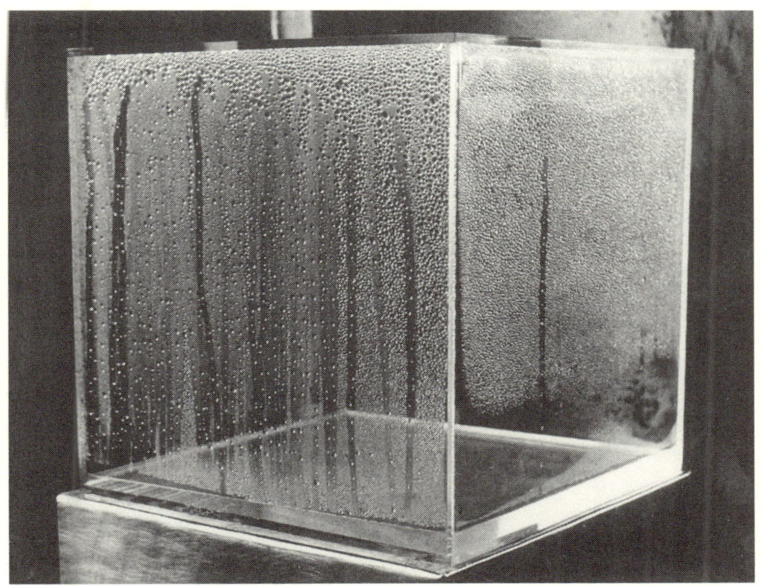

Hans Haacke | Condensation Cube | 1963–65 Clear Plexiglas and distilled water | 12″ × 12″ × 12″

CREDIT: ©HANS HAACKE / ARTISTS RIGHTS SOCIETY (ARS), NEW YORK / COURTESY PAULA COOPER GALLERY, NEW YORK

es the failure of museums to establish the stable environment needed to protect delicate works of art. The work broadcasts the fact that dynamic conditions of ecosystems triumphed over humidifiers, dehumidifiers, heaters, air conditioners, and other sophisticated climate-controlling technologies. Haacke explains, "I was very excited about the subtle communication with a seemingly sealed-off environment and the complexity of interrelated conditions determining the meteorological process. This was an open system, a system responsive to changes in its environment."[5]

In "Untitled Statement" (1965), Haacke delineated the principles devised to create *Condensation Cube*. They provide a concise definition of systems art that continues to distinguish not only his career but the careers of many eco artists:

> Make something which experiences, reacts to its environment, changes, is non stable.
> . . . make something indeterminate, which always looks different, the shape of which cannot be predicted precisely.
> . . . make something which cannot "perform" without the assistance of its environment.
> . . . make something which reacts to light and temperature changes, is subject to air currents and depends, in its functioning, on the forces of gravity.
> . . . make something which the "spectator" handles, with which he plays, and thus animates it.
> . . . make something which lives in time and makes the "spectator" experience time.
> . . . articulate something Natural.[6]

Haacke applied these tenets to a wide range of mediums and topics, explaining, "Such an approach is concerned with the operational structure of organization in which the transfer of

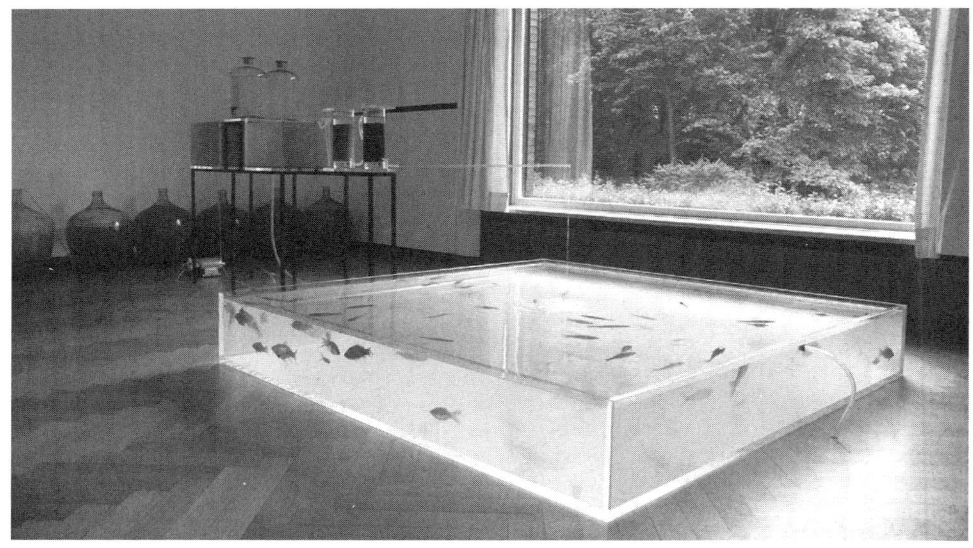

Hans Haacke | Rhinewater Purification Plant | 1972 Installed at Museum Haus Lange, Krefeld, Germany | Glass bottles, water samples, pump, basin, goldfish | Dimensions: variable

CREDIT: ©HANS HAACKE / ARTISTS RIGHTS SOCIETY (ARS), NEW YORK / COURTESY PAULA COOPER GALLERY, NEW YORK

information, energy, and/or material occurs. Systems can be physical, biological, or social; they can be man-made, naturally existing, or a combination of any of the above."[7]

Condensation Cube is an example of a natural system in which inert materials like water display the responsive attributes of living entities. In 1966, Haacke included actual living entities such as grass as his medium. At about the same time, he acknowledged growth as a sculpture process. By the early 1970s, living ants, seagulls, chicks, tortoises, a mynah bird, and a goat were contributing to a series of "Franciscan" works honoring Saint Francis, the patron saint of animals. Ultimately, Haacke migrated to human-designed systems, using the opportunity to expose hypocrisies and indiscretions in the banking system (Deutsche Bank), the business system (Philip Morris, Mobil Oil, Mercedes-Benz), the real estate system (Shapolsky), the art system (Solomon R. Guggenheim Museum), etc.

All these categories of systems converged in *Rhinewater Purification Plant (1972)*, a pioneering remediation art project at the Museum Haus Lange in Krefeld, Germany. The primary physical component of the artwork was Rhine River water that was contaminated by the careless operations of the Krefeld sewage plant located near the museum. Haacke devised a system to purify the water. He used a custom pump to direct the polluted discharged water directly from the river, through a filtering system, into the museum. He displayed the sludge of untreated household and industrial sewage that precipitated out of the river water in large glass bottles, while the cleansed water was diverted to an indoor goldfish tank and the gray water to an outdoor garden.[8] These biological systems played an essential role because they announced the success of the water purification process he was testing. Healthy goldfish were swimming in a tank installed in the museum that was filled with the filtered effluent from the river water. Thriving plants were growing in a garden irrigated with the remaining gray water. The garden was situated outside a large window in the museum so museumgoers could observe evidence of pre- and post-remediation conditions. They observed the problem and its remedy.

The social systems that were integrated into this work included the sewage treatment plant employers and employees who were responsible for turning the river into a sewer, the museum staff who sponsored the artist, and the local municipal authority that provided funding to both the museum and the sewage plant. A scandal erupted when Haacke exposed both the severity of pollution in the local water supply and the culprit that committed the offense. Since the same municipal department funded the host museum, the museum staff found itself in a prickly position. If they supported the protest against the polluter, they would embarrass the municipality and jeopardize their funding. To ignore the pollution, however, was irresponsible. They opted for the latter.

Rhinewater Purification Plant is not merely a tattletale work of art designed to accuse and expose. By demonstrating that the Krefeld sewage plant's murky discharge could be treated and returned safely to the Rhine River, Haacke's real-time decontaminating installation serves as a model remediation project. The work engendered embarrassment among the culprits, hope among the victims, and environmental stewardship everywhere.

Pioneering Contribution to Eco Art **Haacke made a practice of stripping away the protective shields of government authorities and corporate powers. However, his strategy was not merely an impish prank. Acknowledging the connections between economic systems, political systems, cultural systems, and ecological systems tracks the course of disagreeable conditions back to their points of origin, but highlighting these connections also provides keys for networked solutions. His art career is, therefore, distinguished in two manners. On the one hand, it is marked by the censoring of his works,[9] the cancellation of his shows,[10] and the firing of museum staff.[11] On the other, it is honored for introducing the ubiquitous role of systems into art. Haacke's artworks transcend themselves each time they reinforce the notion that interrelationships within systems constitute the workings of the world—inert, living, and social.**

NOTES

1 Hans Haacke, "Previously unpublished 1967," quoted in *Hans Haacke* by Walter Grasskamp (London: Phaidon Press, 2004), 103.

2 Hans Haacke interview with Jeanne Siegel, *Arts Magazine*, vol. 45, no. 7 (May 1971), 18–21. Reprinted in *Hans Haacke for Real: Works 1959–2006*, edited by Matthias Flügge and Robert Fleck (Düsseldorf: Richter, 2006), 253.

3 Hans Haacke, "Notes on *Les Couloirs de Marienbad*" (1965), reproduced in *Hans Haacke for Real: Works 1959–2006*, edited by Matthias Flügge and Robert Fleck (Düsseldorf: Richter, 2006), 85.

4 Ibid.

5 Hans Haacke, "Provisional Remarks," first published in *Hans Haacke: Werkmonographie* by Edward F. Frey (Cologne: DuMont Kunst-Praxis, 1972). Reprinted in *Hans Haacke for Real: Works 1959–2006*, edited by Matthias Flügge and Robert Fleck (Düsseldorf: Richter, 2006), 257.

6 Hans Haacke, "Untitled Statement," quoted in exhibition announcement, Galerie Schmela, Düsseldorf, 1965. Reprinted in *Hans Haacke* by Walter Grasskamp, Molly Nesbit, and Jon Bird (London: Phaidon Press, 2004), 100.

7 Hans Haacke, 1969 announcement at Howard Wise Gallery, New York. Reprinted in *Hans Haacke for Real: Works 1959–2006*, edited by Matthias Flügge and Robert Fleck (Düsseldorf: Richter, 2006), 250.

8 Gray-water reclamation is a technique used by urban planners to reduce strain on drinking water supplies by recycling water from domestic showers and sinks to water plants outdoors.

9 Der Bevolkerung (To the Population), conceived in 1999 as an installation for the Reichstag building in Berlin.

10 Solo show at the Solomon R. Guggenheim Museum scheduled for 1971.

11 The curator, Edward Fry, was fired for supporting Hans Haacke's exhibition at the Solomon R. Guggenheim Museum in 1971.

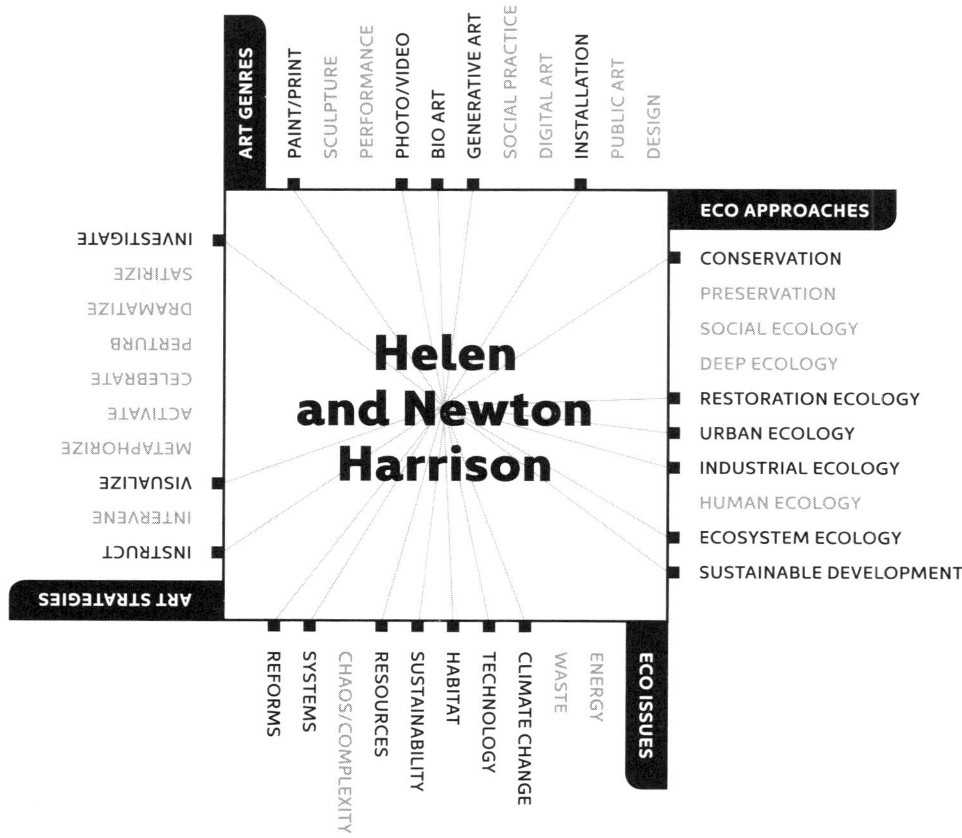

Strategies to Sustain Life

Newton Harrison born 1929, USA
Helen Mayer Harrison born 1932, USA

PARADOXICALLY, Helen Mayer Harrison and Newton Harrison ultimately rejected the innovative installations that earned them esteem as eco art pioneers in the 1970s. The work they abandoned is known collectively as *Survival Piece*, so named because each installation in the series functioned as a productive ecosystem. *Survival Pieces* were exhibited in reputable galleries, commissioned by major museums, praised by influential critics, and studied by distinguished commentators. They were also eligible for inclusion in future histories of art because they heralded art's venture into bio art. Living entities were claimed as art mediums, and biofunctions like waste, procreating, growing, evolving, dying, and decaying were adopted as art processes.

The prefix *bio-* appears in *biology* (the study of life) and *biography* (an account of a life). *Survival Piece* fulfills this double meaning by addressing living entities' imperative to eat. Specifically, it applies this compulsory participation in the food web to humans. The Harrisons explain, "[*Survival Piece* was] done to teach ourselves as urban people how to grow things, principally our own food."[1] Current populations can survive without ever observing the annual rituals of planting/birthing and harvesting/slaughtering. The ingredients for meals are typically grown and harvested at industrial farms far from where they are consumed. Then they are processed and packaged through a global market economy. Because food is fundamental to survival, the Harrisons created museum installations that produced real food.

Most urbanites' and suburbanites' interactions with living entities are limited to caring for houseplants and pets, and exterminating weeds or pests. This artwork awakened awareness of their functional dependence on living entities. The artists bypassed hobby gardening to highlight the growing hindrances to conventional food production. They focused on the far-reaching measures that might be necessary to feed populations in the future.

Newton Harrison describes how this series evolved: "Try to imagine . . . Earth is being wrecked globally, we are in 1968 or 1969. What's Earth? It's where everything grows. But I wanted to see for myself. So I got all kinds of shit, leaves, mulch, sewage, and some other stuff and started to shovel them. They smelled awful. But after a few months of shoveling and watering, the 'earth' smelled so good that you could smell it and taste it as the farmers do! That's when we started to think like farmers and grow plants."[2]

From the start, the Harrisons directed a rigorous process of self-critique to bio art production. Because "the process involved in doing so quickly revealed ethical issues and ecological contradictions,"[3] they ultimately decided to omit biology as their artistic means of expression. However, survival remains the focus of their investigations to this day. Each of the following *Survival Pieces*, therefore, presents one narrative that chronicles the manner in which the artists successfully employed living entities to acquaint their audience with the processes of food production. Then it presents a second narrative that reveals flaws that ultimately led the artists to terminate this series. Referring to themselves, they explain the reason for their career shift: "The Harrisons believe that the core shortcoming in the *Survival Pieces* was that they simply could not carry the complexity of the information necessary to communicate the global ecological trauma they saw on the horizon."[4]

HOG PASTURE, *SURVIVAL PIECE #1*, 1970–71

Description The bleak midwinter timing of the exhibition at the Boston Museum of Fine Arts dramatized the lush, green, sweet-smelling crop of pasture grass growing indoors. The earth had been made by the artists earlier during an earth-making ritual. The grass provided the visual art experience and evidence of the fertility of its medium by growing a half inch each day.

Success This bio artwork offers visitors two treats. One is the visual pleasure of observing the verdant pasture grass the artists planted. The other is appreciation for the fertile soil the artists manufactured by mixing sand, clay, sewage sludge, leaves, and animal manure. These products offered heartening proof that humans could reverse the rampant destruction of topsoil due to farming, industry, mining, and development. Instead of causing deserts, we are capable of creating pastures.

Critique The artists were dissatisfied because museum-scaled situations oversimplify the manner of scientific experiments. They lack the scale and complexity of real life chains. Newton Harrison explains, "In the process we understood that most experimental science that attempted to separate the part from the whole was probably systematically wrong and likely to lead to unfortunate, unexpected consequences while appearing to be valid!"[5]

SHRIMP FARM, *SURVIVAL PIECE #2,* 1971

Description A series of eco art color-field paintings were created by filling four 10′ x 20′ x 8″ containers with water of different salinities. The least salty represented normal seawater, while the most salty was ten times saltier. Each container received populations of several species of algae that differed in their carotene and other pigments as well as their responses to the salinity of water. The ponds' colors changed to blue-green, green-yellow, dark red, and white. Then brine shrimp were introduced. This artwork was designed like a controlled experiment to identify an efficient food source for farm-raised shrimp.

Success This particularly colorful installation took advantage of the fact that algae, simple chlorophyll-containing organisms, are classified according to their dominant photosynthetic pigments: green, brown, and red, with countless variations existing in each category. Botanists have been exploring the causes and functions of these remarkable organisms since the 1800s. Their studies tend to focus on the influence of light or diet. The Harrisons directed this study to salinity. The water turned different colors because different species of algae are adapted to different levels of salinity. More importantly, the experiment was a success because the brine shrimp that were introduced actually ate the algae. Thus, *Shrimp Farm* demonstrated the potential of simple aquaculture systems to increase protein production efficiently and safely. The artists estimate that if this system were employed commercially, it could generate eighteen thousand pounds wet weight per acre.

Critique *Shrimp Farm* excluded humans from this functioning ecosystem. As a result, the work failed to activate a relationship between the consumer of food and the food being consumed. The artists explain that their goal is to create installations "which stand for the place and as meeting ground for discourse, which are models for how to perceive and enact our work."[6]

PORTABLE FISH FARM, *SURVIVAL PIECE #3,* 1971

Description Six large tanks containing a variety of edible fish were exhibited at the Hayward Gallery in London. The bucolic sight of fish swimming about in the tanks was followed by the unsettling inclusion of an electrocution chamber and a skinning and filleting table complete with knives and cleavers. These components enabled the piece to account for the entire food cycle, which included people assuming the role of predators who killed prey in order to survive. Newton Harrison acquainted himself with this particular method of slaughtering fish by training at the fish farms at Brawley, California, where electrocution was adopted as a humane method of killing. He explains, "So I became a worker in their field. They could skin a catfish in 44 seconds. I became accepted when I could skin one in 1 minute and 10 seconds. Then I was tolerated. They showed me how to do all that stuff; so I simply behaved as they behaved for the exhibition, that's the whole story."[7]

Success Protests erupted when the media reported that *Portable Fish Farm* included harvesting and slaughtering. The protests quickly spread to the Royal Society for the Prevention of Cruelty to Animals. Nobel-laureate scientists, celebrities, and even the British Parliament debated the ethics of the Harrisons' action. The dispute persisted until one defender of the project announced that many of the protestors had recently feasted on catfish and hush puppies at a public function. The controversy bolstered the success of the project by highlighting contemporary urbanites' estrangement from the standard farming activities that supply their food.

Critique Despite its name, the work was too expensive and wasteful to be portable. The installation depended heavily upon energy-consuming technologies to power the pumps and to transport approximately two hundred fish from California to London. Furthermore, the journey was so stressful to the fish, many died en route.

PORTABLE ORCHARD, *SURVIVAL PIECE #5*, 1972–73

Description Assorted dwarf citrus trees were planted in twelve 4′ x 3′ hexagonal redwood boxes and arranged under hanging hexagonal light boxes. The artwork tested which trees could survive within artificial conditions.

Success Some trees thrived, but the meaning of the work was most effectively conveyed by the trees that withered. They confronted museumgoers with evidence that, unlike engineered manufacturing, engineered farming does not guarantee predictable outcomes. Furthermore, viewers were led to ask why such a drastic measure as growing fruit indoors was undertaken. The practice signaled two environmental problems that are endemic to contemporary lifestyles—trees may be brought indoors because croplands are being usurped by suburban and industrial development, or they might be relocated to escape the smog, acid rain, and polluted soils outdoors.

Critique The Harrisons were concerned that *Portable Orchard* gave the mistaken impression that a simple strategy could solve a compound environmental problem. In actuality, rectifying these problems involves science, politics, sociology, architecture, city planning, ecology, and more. As a result, the artists sought a way to use the full expressive potential of their profession to invent the radical schemes that might be needed to address such pragmatic issues. "The signals became clear. We decided to choose a direction other than simple sculptural installations with farming systems. We began improvising ways to present whole systems by adding text, photographic and drawn or painted images and narrative to the work in a new format."[8]

A whole-systems approach was required to solve the whole-systems problems they now tackled. The Harrisons initiated their career change by gathering voluminous amounts of information to accommodate the enlargement of their temporal and spatial considerations.

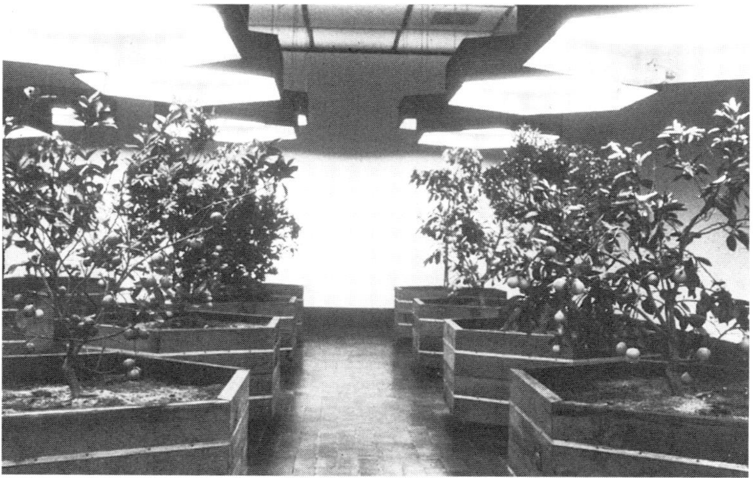

Helen Mayer Harrison and Newton Harrison | Portable Orchard: Survival Piece #5 | 1972–73 Twelve 4′ × 3′ hexagonal redwood boxes, assorted citrus trees, hexagonal redwood light boxes | Dimensions: 3′ deep

COURTESY RONALD FELDMAN FINE ARTS, NEW YORK

Then they devised multiple schemes to disseminate this information. For gallery settings the information was judiciously distributed among painted images, maps, satellite images, statistics, text, and listening pads. To reach audiences beyond the gallery setting, they exploited the communicating power of the media. Posters, billboards, public television, radio, and graffiti were supplemented by personal columns in local newspapers, where they posted incisive advice to government officials.

The Harrisons initiated this new program in 1977 when they developed *Meditations on the Sacramento River, the Delta and Bays at San Francisco*. As the title indicates, their concerns encompassed the vast watersheds of California's two largest rivers: the Sacramento and the San Joaquin. The *water* part of watersheds included river water, subsurface water, and surface runoff. The *shed* components were riverbanks and valleys in the surrounding landscape that drain water, sediment, and dissolved materials. Forests, lakes, estuaries, and marine systems; their soils, minerals, and populations of plants and animals; and government, corporations, and the military were all implicated in the Harrisons' project because they were all dependent on the same source of freshwater. The Harrisons amassed data on all these components and then set about conveying how current water practices create water crises. "The idea was to present a vision that would explode in the mind of the interested person."[9]

At the time, agricultural lands of California's Central Valley were beset with ill-conceived dams, ill-advised irrigation systems, and ill-managed agricultural practices. The Harrisons condensed this disturbing narrative into nine hand-worked maps that they presented as an installation. Each map conveyed a unique perspective on the watersheds: the distanced perspective of a satellite camera, the cultural perspective of Native Americans, the engineering perspective of dams and pumping stations, and so forth. Hopeful solutions accompanied alarming messages. "Meditations" then invited audiences to meditate upon constructive alternatives: creating nature reserves, planting forests, installing vegetative flood controls, and so on.

The monumental implications of this artwork are not confined to the Sacramento River

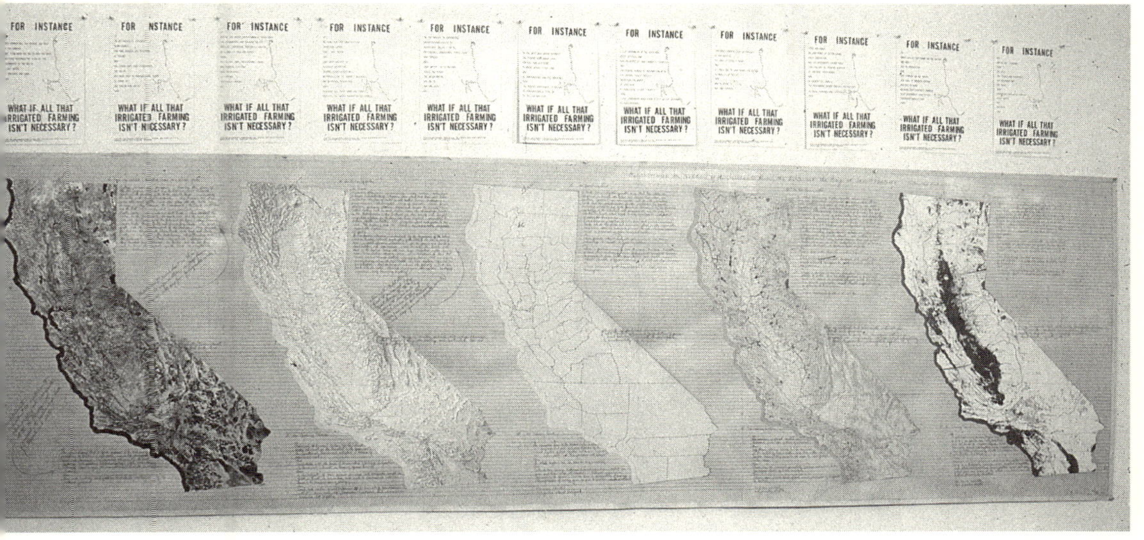

Helen Mayer Harrison and Newton Harrison | Meditations on the Sacramento River, the Delta and Bays at San Francisco | 1976 Photography, graphite, collage, and ink | 4′2″ × 13′2″

COURTESY RONALD FELDMAN FINE ARTS, NEW YORK

watershed. The artists explain, "The work became a guiding metaphor, a lens through which many existing cultural landscapes in the process of being transformed into industrial landscapes could be dealt with by ourselves as artists, with the idea that new and different possible histories could become available and open for exploration and criticism."[10]

Over forty years have passed, and the Harrisons remain committed to their exploratory and critical mission. However, the focus of their recent work has shifted from industrial development to climate change, a problem they describe as "so compelling in the near term, so potentially catastrophic in the long term, and so obviously destabilizing to the environment."[11] *Greenhouse Britain: Losing Ground, Gaining Wisdom*[12] (2007–2009) is a multimedia installation that charts the future impact of global warming upon the United Kingdom. A bleak scenario of rising waters, storm surges, and shrinking coastlines is balanced by ingenious proposals to cope with these disruptions and avert an apocalyptic collapse. Unconventional information-disseminating schemes are utilized to convey this scrupulously researched data, such as video projections simulating rising waters along the shorelines that are projected onto a huge map of the region. Recorded voices repeat phrases like "the news is not good, and it's getting worse." This ominous forecast is balanced by multiple solution-oriented strategies: relocating low-lying villages to the mountains, creating dams to control storm surges, sequestering carbon, diverting rivers, and generally overhauling current living practices to adapt to the troublesome conditions humans may have helped cause.

Contribution to Eco Art **The Harrisons' creative imaginations come in two scales—bio, which deals with individual organisms and their immediate environs, and watersheds, which encompass multitudes of organisms and their extended environs. With these scales, they helped initiate spatial parameters of eco art explorations. If bio and watershed are envisioned as the horizontal axis for**

eco art explorations, a vertical axis was also established by the Harrisons. It marks the contrasting focuses of eco art—problems and solutions. If this graph were conceived of in the third dimension, the Harrisons' contributions would also appear, as the temporal unit—current and eventual. Despite the impressive range of their conceptualizations, the artists describe themselves modestly: "We're just two people putting one foot in front of the other, asking for reasonably ethical behavior. . . . The most important thing is to begin anywhere, and get cracking."[13]

NOTES

1 Helen Mayer Harrison and Newton Harrison, "From There to Here" (published by Helen Mayer Harrison and Newton Harrison, 2001).

2 Newton Harrison quoted in "Helen and Newton Harrison in Conversation with Brandon Ballengee," *Transdiscourse 1: Mediated Environments*, by Andrea Gleiniger, Angelika Hilbeck, and Jill Scott (Springer Vienna Architecture, December 1, 2010), 47.

3 Helen Mayer Harrison and Newton Harrison, "From There to Here" (published by Helen Mayer Harrison and Newton Harrison, 2001).

4 Helen Mayer and Newton Harrison correspondence with the author, October 27, 2010.

5 Newton Harrison quoted in "Helen and Newton Harrison in Conversation with Brandon Ballengee," *Transdiscourse 1: Mediated Environments*, by Andrea Gleiniger, Angelika Hilbeck, and Jill Scott (Springer Vienna Architecture, December 1, 2010), 56.

6 Helen Mayer Harrison and Newton Harrison quoted by Arlene Raven, "Two Lines of Sight and An Unexpected Connection: The Art of Helen Mayer Harrison and Newton Harrison." http://www.communityarts.net/readingroom/archivefiles/2002/09/two_lines_of_si.php.

7 Newton Harrison quoted in "Helen and Newton Harrison in Conversation with Brandon Ballengee," *Transdiscourse 1: Mediated Environments*, by Andrea Gleiniger, Angelika Hilbeck, and Jill Scott (Springer Vienna Architecture, December 1, 2010), 58.

8 Helen Mayer Harrison and Newton Harrison, "From There to Here" (published by Helen Mayer Harrison and Newton Harrison, 2001).

9 Ibid.

10 Ibid.

11 Greenhouse Britain (2007), "New Publication from the Harrison Studio–Greenhouse Britain: Losing Ground and Gaining Wisdom." http://greenhousebritain.greenmuseum.org/2007/08/04/new-publication-from-harrison-studio-greenhouse-britain-losing-ground-gaining-wisdom/.

12 Collaborators include David Haley, Christopher Fremantle, and Gabriel Harrison.

13 Helen Mayer and Newton Harrison quoted in *Two Lines of Sight and an Unexpected Connection: The Art of Helen Mayer Harrison and Newton Harrison* by Arlene Raven (2002). http://www.communityarts.net/readingroom/archivefiles/2002/09/two_lines_of_si.php.

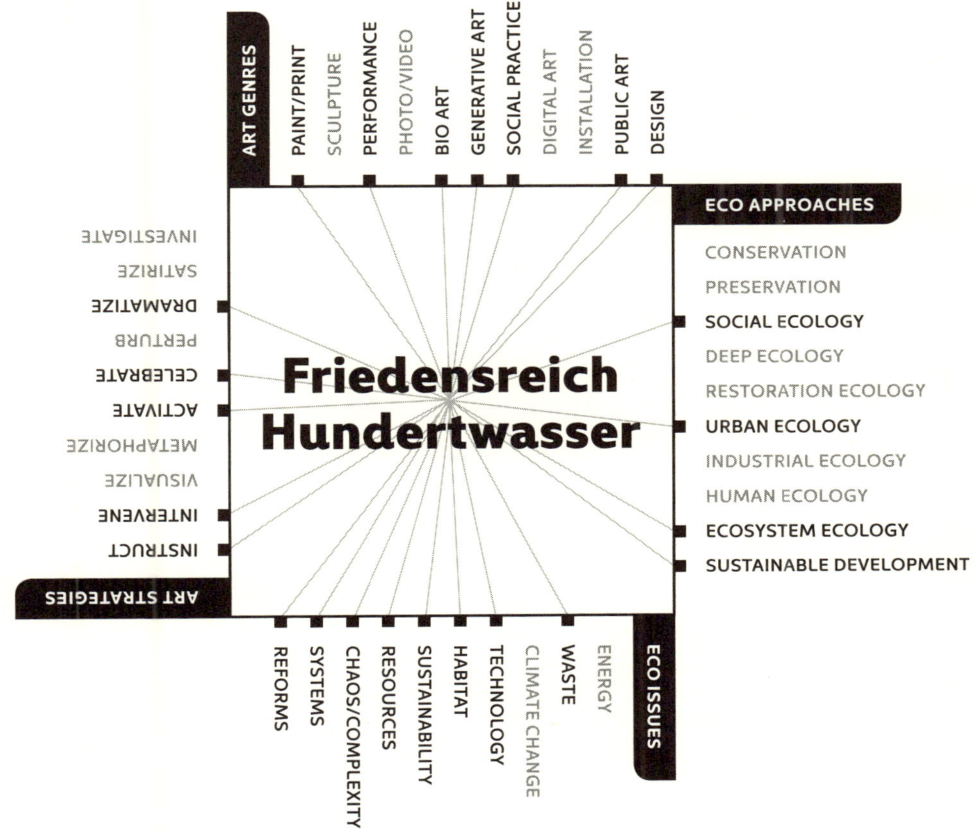

Built Environments as Living Systems

Born 1928, Vienna, Austria
Died 2000, aboard the ship *Queen Elizabeth 2*; buried in the Garden of the Happy Dead in New Zealand

FRIEDENSREICH REGENTAG DUNKELBUNT HUNDERTWASSER is the unusual name Friedrich Stowasser chose for himself to manifest his spirited defiance of cultural and social conventions. *Friedensreich* means "peaceland." *Regentag* means "rainy day." *Dunkelbunt* means "darkly multicolored." *Hundertwasser* means "hundred-water." Combine them and they embody the audacity he displayed throughout his career. He was not even averse to denouncing his fellow architects who had earned international acclaim in the 1950s and 1960s. He condemned them for alienating architecture from bi-

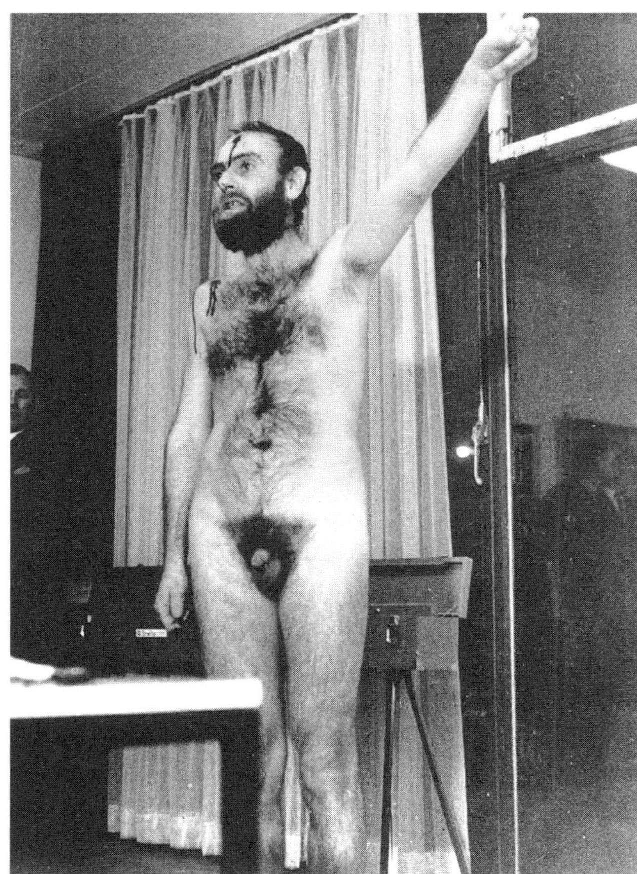

Friedensreich Hundertwasser | Nude Demonstration Against Rationalism in Architecture at the Internationales Studentenheim, Vienna | 1968 Photograph

CREDIT: © HUNDERTWASSER ARCHIVE, VIENNA / COURTESY HUNDERTWASSER ARCHIVE, VIENNA

ology by aligning their designs to industry. While they were being praised for their spare design, unadorned facades, and rectilinear forms, Hundertwasser was declaring, "The tangible and material uninhabitability of slums is preferable to the moral uninhabitability of utilitarian, functional architecture. In the so-called slums only the human body can be oppressed, but in our modern functional architecture, man's soul is perishing, oppressed."[1] Essentially Hundertwasser's career can be characterized as an attack upon modernism's veneration of technology, engineering, and industry. The provocative question he posed was this: are people happier living in environments that resemble machines or meadows?

Hundertwasser's rejection of progressive and modernist architecture did not lead him into a nostalgic replay of historic styles. His version of progress was infused with a renegade's imagination and the fervor of a crusader. He not only wrote ecstatic manifestos proclaiming the benefits of integrating biological systems into urban settings, he delivered this rhetoric to audiences stark naked. "Speech in the Nude for the Right to a Third Skin" (1967) was not just an attention-getting prank. It illustrated Hundertwasser's conviction that biology, not industry, embodies design excellence. His nudity provided an opportunity for the audience to observe its functional and aesthetic components. Hundertwasser explains, "The human being has three layers between himself and the world. The first layer is the skin. The second layer is the clothing. The third layer is the architecture. Over the centuries we have . . .

perverted and distorted the second and the third layers to such a degree they no longer suit our needs."[2] Subsequently, Hundertwasser expanded his renegade tactics by adding two more layers to the "world" humans occupy. In addition to skin, clothes, and architecture, he added the social environment as the fourth skin, and the global environment as the fifth. Together they comprise a holistic approach known as *ecological*.

Hundertwasser's outlandish architectural schemes made their public debut in 1972 when he showed models on Eurovision TV's *Make a Wish*, a popular television show. Then, in 1985, one model materialized as an extravagantly colored, patterned, and shaped edifice known as *Hundertwasser House*, one of thirty-four innovative architectural projects he designed in his lifetime. This low-income apartment complex in Vienna houses about 200 people. It is owned by the city and rented to individuals just like any other public-housing project. However, nothing but the rental scheme is ordinary about the complex. It was so ahead of its time that tourists continue to flock there to revel in its exuberant deviations from architectural norms. These deviations can also be appreciated as confirmations of the aesthetic and functional components of the "first skin," the naked human body:

- Straight lines and flat planes were banished because there are no straight lines and flat planes in the human body. This principle determined the vertical facade of *Hundertwasser House*, which undulates in perpetually surprising volumes. The formation of the first skin even determined the building's horizontal surfaces. The floors undulate too! Hundertwasser explains, "The flat floor is an invention of architects. . . . It fits engines—not human beings. . . . If people are forced to walk on flat asphalt and concrete floors, estranged from the age-old relationship and contact with earth, a crucial part of humanity withers and dies."[3]
- Tenants are encouraged to alter the exterior of the building by loading a brush with paint and leaning out their windows, depositing paint as far as they can reach in any manner they desire. This policy helps account for the brilliant colors, copious embellishment, and bold irregularities that enliven the facades of the building. These "window rights" are part of the rental contracts of *Hundertwasser House* residents. The uniqueness of each window decoration mirrors the uniqueness of each component of the human body. Modernist architecture may be constituted of perfect symmetries and modular forms, but bodies are not.
- The roof at *Hundertwasser House* supports 900 tons of earthen terraces planted with vegetation to absorb rainwater, provide insulation, create a habitat for wildlife, and reduce air temperatures and air pollution in the urban setting. To Hundertwasser, green roofs are architectural versions of hair growing on peoples' heads that protects the scalp against the sun and helps hold body heat. The materials used in these sustainable architectural elements fostered growth. They were blatant rejections of the modernist preference for glass and steel, two materials engineered as obstacles to biological processes. In all, the building boasts approximately 250 trees and plants within its structure.[4]
- Hundertwasser stipulated that humans are not eligible to rent all of the units in his apartment complex. Some are reserved for "tree tenants." The trees' roots are planted in pots inside the building, but their limbs and branches ex-

tend through open windows where they freely seek the sun and are touched by the rain. As a result, fresh air enters the building and stale air exits. Even moisture and temperature are exchanged between inside and outside. In contrast, modernist architecture is a sealed container that barricades against the intrusion of outside forces. Tree tenants and open windows emulate the skin that encloses the human body. Portals such as pores, nostrils, and mouths allow air, nutrients, and fluids to enter the system, and sweat, carbon dioxide, and heat to exit.

- Sewage technologies also mimic biology. Hundertwasser introduced no-flush humus toilets that collect and compost human solid waste on site. Microbes do the job of breaking these substances down into a stable, odorless, soil-like material that is used as fertilizer for the plants growing on the roof. The artist proclaimed the magnificence of this substance when he wrote the manifesto *Shit Culture—Holy Shit* (1980). In it he declares, "Ever since man could think, he has sought immortality. Man wants to have a soul. Shit is our soul. Shit will enable us to survive. Shit will enable us to be immortal. . . . The person who uses a humus toilet has no fear of death, for our shit makes future life and rebirth possible."[5]
- Household waste waters like urine and wash water are incorporated into a biological water-purification system on site. It replaces conventional methods that entail long trips to chemical-infused treatment facilities. The liquid waste enters the system at the top of the building. It flows down to tiers planted with special botanicals capable of removing impurities. By the time it reaches the bottom, it is cleansed.

Hundertwasser also reveled in one aspect of human skin that nudity does not reveal—the vast populations of microscopic organisms that normally reside there. He recognized that all living organisms coexist with millions of invisible fellow creatures. Because they are essential to our survival, Hundertwasser welcomed them, too, into his audacious defiance of cultural norms. He expressed this intention in 1958 when he delivered "Mould Manifesto against Rationalism in Architecture." In it he explains, "When rust sets in on a razor blade, when a wall starts to get 'mouldy,' when moss grows in a corner of a room, rounding its geometric angles, we should be glad because, together with the microbes and fungi, life is moving into the house and through this process we can more consciously become witnesses of architectural changes from which we have much to learn."[6] Hundertwasser actually proposed rescuing modernist architecture by pouring a decomposing solution over its smooth and anonymous surfaces that commit "mass murder by premeditated sterilization."[7]

The daring proposal to reserve entire floors in high-rise apartment complexes so they could become meadows and forests where animals grazed and raised their young was never realized. But this and other precedent-defying innovations remain within the visionary vocabulary of sustainable architecture to this day. "If we want to survive, we must bring nature into things i.e., let other energies do their work besides just us. . . . Our cities are so ugly because we don't let nature paint, because we want to kill off nature the minute it manifests itself somewhere because of an error or for whatever reason. . . . We must conclude a peace treaty with nature. We must give territories back to nature which we misappropriated

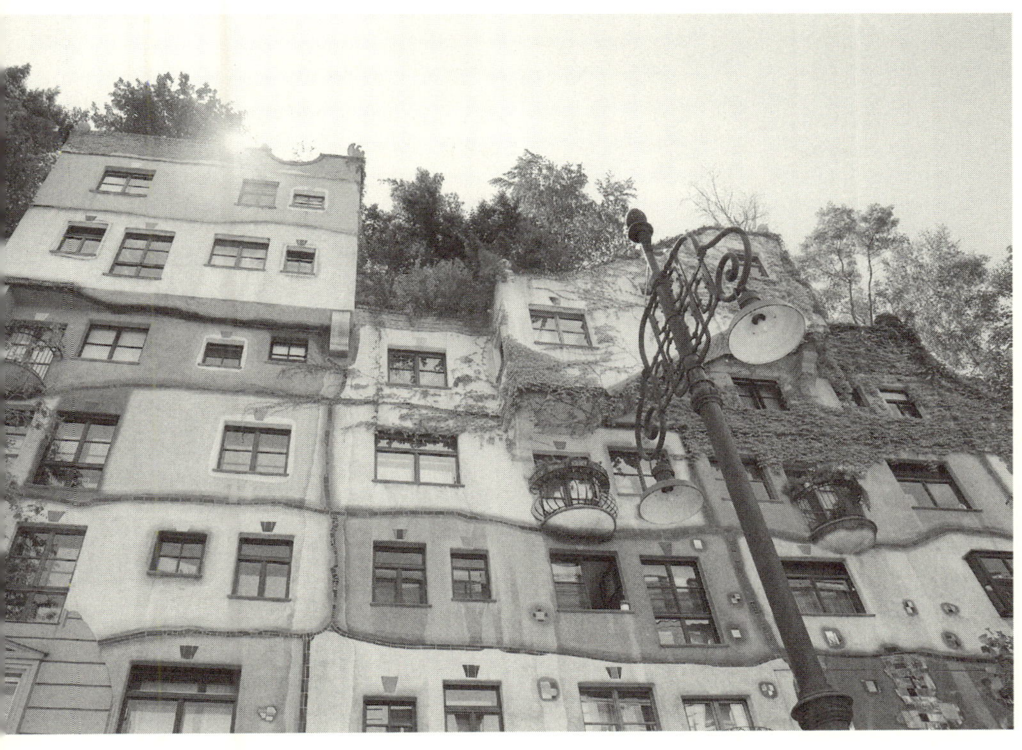

Friedensreich Hundertwasser, idea and concept | Architect and original coauthor: em.o. Univ.-Professor DI J.Krawina | Architect and planning: DI Peter Pelikan, architect | Hundertwasser House, Vienna | 1985

PHOTO: GERHARD DEUTSCH / CREDIT: © HUNDERTWASSER ARCHIVE, VIENNA / COURTESY HUNDERTWASSER ARCHIVE, VIENNA

long ago. Spontaneous vegetation, spontaneous weathering must be reinstated in their old rights."[8]

Hundertwasser was as defiant of the lifeless inhumanity of industrial prefabrication regarding the "second skin"—clothing—as he was regarding the "third skin," architecture. He is famous for his wardrobe that featured outrageous floppy headgear extending around a bushy beard, peppermint-striped slacks hugging his spindly legs, one bright green sock and one bright orange one, and a threadbare cut-velvet jacket. Once again, his outrageous behavior expressed the principle that the human spirit needs to be unsterilized by reconnecting with the messy and vibrant qualities of life. This is not accomplished by dressing like a bureaucrat. He preferred to be known as "the magician of vegetation."[9]

Pioneering Contribution to Eco Art **For millennia, architects have acquired principles of elegant proportion by observing living entities. Likewise, painters have discovered the formal attributes of beauty in biological and geological formations. When Hundertwasser added function to the influence of nature in art, he became an early practitioner of biomimicry, a practice that attempts to solve human problems by studying the designs and processes of animals, plants, and microbes, the Earth's consummate engineers.**

NOTES

1 Friedensreich Hundertwasser, "Mould Manifesto against Rationalism in Architecture" (read by Hundertwasser at Seckau Abbey, Styria, July 4, 1958; read in Galerie Van de Loo, Munich, July 11, 1958, and Galerie Parnass, Wuppertal, July 26, 1958; published in a signed and numbered brochure, 1958). http://www.hundertwasser.at/english/texts/philo_verschimmelungsmanifest.php.

2 Friedensreich Hundertwasser, "Nude Demonstration," *The Oeuvre*. http://www.hundertwasser.at/english/oeuvre/arch/architektur.php.

3 Friedensreich Hundertwasser, "Art and Connections: Hundertwasser's District Heating Plant" (Boulder: Ideas LLC, 1998–2011). http://www.ideapete.com/Hundertwasser.html.

4 Michael Felton-O'Brien, "Amazing Architecture: Vienna's Hundertwasserhaus," EscapeArtists.com (1996–April 13, 2011). http://www.escapeartist.com/OREQ16/Vienna.html.

5 Friedensreich Hundertwasser, "Shit Culture—Holy Shit," *Humus Toilet* (1980). http://www.thepoopproject.org/wp-content/uploads/2010/06/hundertwasser.pdf.

6 Friedensreich Hundertwasser, "Mould Manifesto against Rationalism in Architecture" (read by Hundertwasser at Seckau Abbey, Styria, July 4, 1958; read in Galerie Van de Loo, Munich, July 11, 1958, and Galerie Parnass, Wuppertal, July 26, 1958; published in a signed and numbered brochure, 1958). http://www.hundertwasser.at/english/texts/philo_verschimmelungsmanifest.php.

7 Ibid.

8 Friedensreich Hundertwasser, "Hundertwasser Architecture: For a More Human Architecture in Harmony with Nature," *Colour in Architecture* (Cologne: Taschen, 1997), 66.

9 Friedensreich Hundertwasser, "Art Encyclopedia: Friedensreich Hundertwasser." http://www.artgalleryartist.com/friedensreich-hundertwasser/.

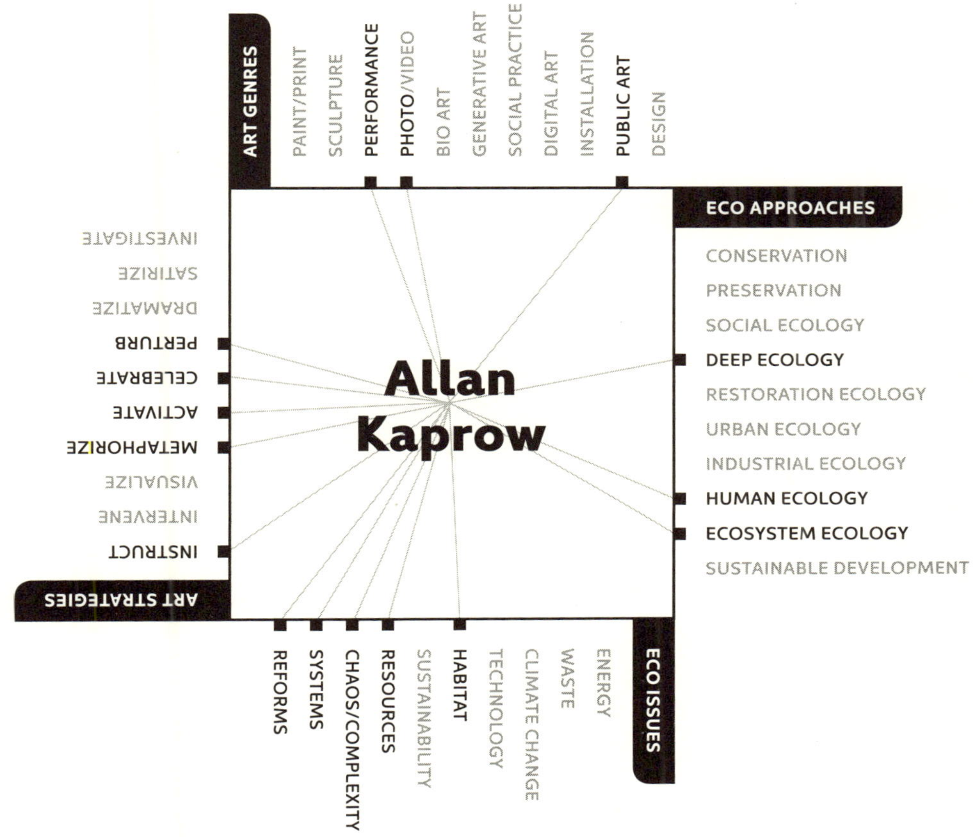

Performing a River

Born 1927, New Jersey, USA
Died 2006, California, USA

ALLAN KAPROW SUMMARIZES his noteworthy contribution to Twentieth-Century art by declaring, "I separated the action of action painting from the painting part of it, and in a sense jumped into life."[1] Eliminating painting from art involved repudiating his training with two renowned advocates of modernist art: Hans Hofmann, a distinguished member of the abstract expressionist school of painters, and Meyer Schapiro, an eminent art historian. Kaprow's defection was initiated when he discarded paint and replaced it with straw, newspaper, and twine in a technique he termed "action collage." Kaprow explains:

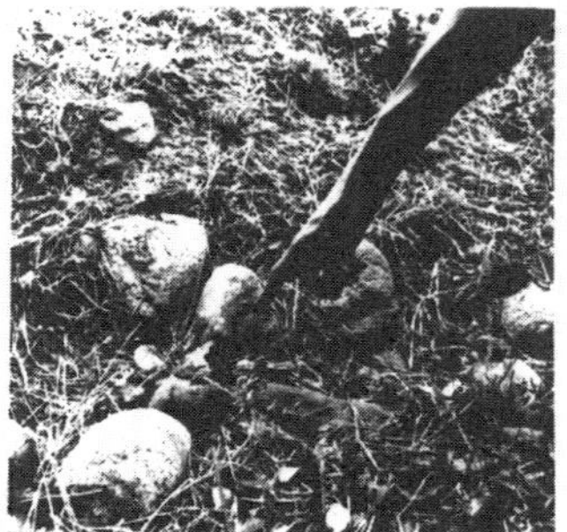

choosing another stone there

Allan Kaprow | EASY (Choosing Another Stone There) | 1972 Activity booklet
PHOTO: ALVIN COMITER / COURTESY ALLAN KAPROW ESTATE AND HAUSER & WIRTH GALLERY, ZURICH AND LONDON

The action collages then became bigger, and I introduced flashing lights and thicker hunks of matter. These parts projected further and further from the wall into the room, and included more and more audible elements: sounds of ringing buzzers, bells, toys, etc., until I had accumulated nearly all the sensory elements I was to work with during the following years. . . . I immediately saw that every visitor to the environment was part of it. And so I gave him opportunities like moving something, turning switches on—just a few things. Increasingly during 1957 and 1958, this suggested a more "scored" responsibility for the visitor. I offered him more and more to do until there developed

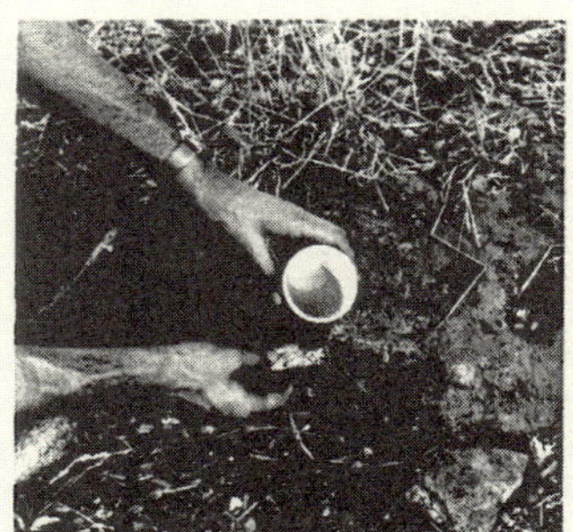

wetting a stone

Allan Kaprow | EASY (Wetting a Stone) | 1972 Activity booklet

PHOTO: ALVIN COMITER / COURTESY ALLAN KAPROW ESTATE AND HAUSER & WIRTH GALLERY, ZURICH AND LONDON

the Happening. . . . The integration of all elements—environment, constructed sections, time, space, and people—has been my main technical problem ever since.[2]

Happenings are events that transpire on streets, fields, alleyways—anywhere but on a stage. While they are performed, there are no scripts, no costumes, no sets, no lighting, no roles, nor any other form of artificiality used in conventional theater. The substance and the context of Happenings are continuous with everyday reality. This continuity applies to the performers. Happenings are enacted by people who would otherwise be viewers and observers. They retain their own personalities as they proceed according to a loose set of instructions from an artist. Allan Kaprow is acknowledged as an originator of this art form.

Everyday components converged in the 1968 Happening, *EASY*, when Kaprow gave the following instructions to students at CalArts who gathered at a dry streambed not far from campus to participate in his Happening:

> *(dry stream bed)*
> *wetting a stone*
> *carrying it downstream until dry*
> *dropping it*
> *choosing another stone there*
> *wetting it*
> *carrying it upstream until dry*
> *dropping it.*

Kaprow provides a compelling description of *EASY* in the following text:

> Each person walked along the stream bed until he or she selected a stone. Finding that stone was a personal matter. No one found his or her stone in the same place or at the same time as the others. The stone was moistened with a paper cup of water brought along and was carried in the hand slowly downstream. It was a clear, hot day. Periodically the stone was examined to see how much it had dried. One began to see that one had a certain amount of control over this process, depending on whether one peeked through a crack in the fingers or boldly opened the hand, exposing the stone to the sun directly. So for some, the drying happened in a few hundred yards, if they held the stone lightly or if the stone was small or nonabsorbent. For others it took a long time, their walking perhaps a mile and a half, since at least a few of the group discovered that the day's heat caused their palms to sweat and add moisture to that already on the stone. Exactly when the condition of dryness was reached was of course up to the individual to decide.
>
> At that point the stone was dropped. It was at a place where no one else dropped his or hers. Now a second stone was required for the walk upstream. As reported in discussion afterwards, this choice was a little more difficult because the first stone had become a sort of token of the self or at least a "possession" on some dim level. The general feeling was that, as one wandered around looking, the second choice was going to be the second best. Anyway, it too, was wetted with the remaining water and the upstream meander began.
>
> Since everybody was a lot hotter by then, the time elapsed and distance traveled until the stones were dry were as different from those of the trip downstream as they were from individual to individual. There was no correlation, no pattern. Yet the second stones had become, if not as private as the first, fond adoptions like the second car, and when they were dropped onto the dry sand of the steam bed, the satisfaction of completing the event easily was mingled with small regrets.[3]

EASY could have earned its name because it used elemental ingredients like stone and water, or because it involved the simple act of walking, or because it excluded sophisticated technologies. But stripping the Happening to such elemental phenomena cleared the way for the students to experience multifarious sensations they might otherwise ignore. For example, the work's simplicity enabled them to monitor subtle shifts in temperature, wind, and humidity. These complex and invisible environmental factors are typically engulfed by the clamor and speed of urban/industrial lifestyles. Likewise, *EASY*'s elemental conditions sensitized the participants to the subtle ways their behavior retarded or accelerated the rate of evaporation.

Neither was there anything easy about the conceptual implications of this Happening. The task of moistening a stone in an arid streambed led the students to interrogate their lack of familiarity with water beyond spigots and faucets; the construction and land development in the vicinity that diverted the water from the stream; the possibility that the drying of the stream was a normal seasonal phenomenon; the correlation between the rocks/water/riverbed with the stone/sweat/palm; that lack of flowing liquid indicated the absence of a habitat for many living entities. Kaprow explains, "Needless to say, on the natural side of things, the group was imitating in condensed time some typical geological changes of the earth's surface: the land rises, and water erodes it, carrying up what was down and down what was up."[4]

There was also nothing simplistic about the pooling of creative inputs to generate *EASY*. The students were fully implicated in the Happening's unfolding narrative. Kaprow established the work's parameters, but it was the participants whose movements constituted its composition, whose tempos determined its duration, and whose experiences constructed its meaning. Furthermore, Kaprow allowed the processes and interactions that drive ecosystems to play formative roles in his work. The porosity of stone, the angle of the sun, and the strength of the wind determined his work's duration. In this manner participants who were accustomed to think of intervals in social terms—three-act play, eight-hour workday, two-week vacation, one-year membership, and twenty-year mortgage—became tuned to temporal units inherent to ecosystems.

The final disposition of *EASY* is ultimately disruptive to art conventions. Kaprow insisted that Happenings only endure as "unplanned gossip" told by the participants.[5] The photographs and text that present *EASY* are not documentation of the event with the students. They were shot later as a score enabling people to construct the Happening at some future date, as musicians write scores of music. Furthermore, Kaprow presented these visuals as instruction manuals, not art. In this manner the Happening never becomes congealed into an iconic instance. Instead, it remains embedded in the flow of real-life occurrences.

Happenings diverged in so many ways from convention that Kaprow frequently referred to this new art form as "unart." He explains, "It means casting our values (our habits) over the edge of great heights, smiling as we hear them clatter to pieces down below like so much crockery—because now we must get up and invent something again."[6] The radical parameters of "un-arting" welcomed the messy unpredictability of ordinary life that had long been banished from art. At the same time, they discarded art's look-but-don't-touch protocols. By activating the body's full capacity for sensual interaction with the material world, Happenings incorporated visual, aural, olfactory, tactile, taste, temperature, and kinesthetic experiences as they occurred in real time.

In sum, the apparent absurdity of Happenings barely camouflages the sophisticated examination of the prevailing cultural attitudes they convey. Kaprow comments, "I have taken my cue from those rare screwballs that emerge every once in a while in unexpected places, who are crazy to transform themselves into the Essential Absolute of each moment that passes through them and who are perhaps in that manner the purest living forms of art. . . .

They leave no monuments (and I am tired of monuments, those tokens to eternity), no testimonials, but they know more about renewal than the rest of us. . . . I am convinced that the only human 'virtue' is the continuous rebirth of the Self. And this is what a new art is."[7]

Pioneering Contribution to Eco Art By welcoming life into his creative practice, Kaprow eliminated art-ifice and art-ificiality from art. As he was digging this fissure into the edifice of Western art conventions, he was constructing the footing upon which much environmental art now stands. From the scientific perspective, Happenings are amalgamations of multiple art forms just as ecology is a composite of individual scientific disciplines. Both embrace the ever-changing, multifaceted complexity of real time and space events. From a philosophic perspective, *EASY* reestablishes intimate human/nonhuman connections that deep ecology also promotes. In both instances these intimacies are cultivated as a means to suppress the human tendency to disrupt viable ecosystems through, for example, irresponsible damming, irrigation, farming, and manufacturing that can cause rivers to run dry. This theme has grown in significance and urgency since Kaprow helped introduce it into eco art.

NOTES

1 Allan Kaprow interview at the Dallas Public Library Cable Access Studio (1988). http://www.mailartist.com/johnheldjr/InterviewWithAlanKaprow.html.
2 Allan Kaprow (1965). http://www.lichtensteinfoundation.org/allankaprow.htm.
3 Allan Kaprow, "Easy," *Art in America*, July/August,1974, 73.
4 Ibid.
5 Allan Kaprow interview with Robert C. Morgan, *Journal of Contemporary Art*. http://www.jca-online.com/kaprow.html.
6 Allan Kaprow, *Untitled Essay and Other Works Allan Kaprow* (1958), originally published as a Great Bear Pamphlet (New Brunswick: Something Else Press, 1967), 5.
7 Ibid.

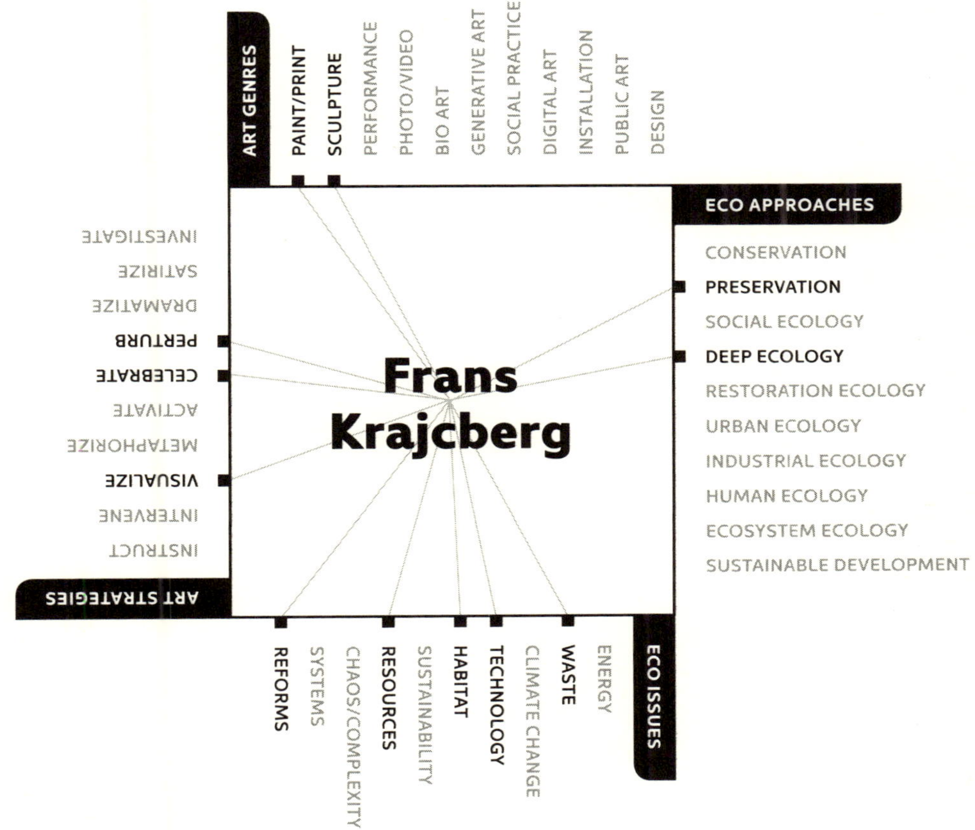

Integral Naturalism

Born 1921, Kozienice, Poland

IF YOU FLIP THROUGH ANY SURVEY of art history book, you will encounter landscapes depicted in realistic, expressionistic, romantic, abstract, pointillist, surreal, pop, neoclassical, and many more styles of artistic expression. Physically, however, they are not varied. All of these stylistic interpretations of landscape appear as two-dimensional paintings. Why not sculpture?

The answer might be traced to the fact that painting a landscape resembles perceiving a landscape. When a scene is perceived, information about it is received by the eye and then transmitted to the brain, where it is deciphered as a flat picture. In similar manner, painters render multidimensional mountains, sunsets, streams, and other elements of landscape as two-dimensional depictions. Vision and painting are formal and emotional experiences. They do not engage the material components of the setting: weight, texture, moisture, pliability, and temperature. However, these are precisely the qualities that account for ecosystems' ability to function, which is why physical conditions, not images, are of principal importance to ecologists, environmentalists, and many eco artists.

Frans Krajcberg is credited with a succession of innovative techniques that expand the artist's interaction with landscape beyond a visual presentation of colors and forms. He explains, "I do not seek the landscape but the matter of which it is made."[1] And again, "For the first time I felt the need to feel the matter, not the painting."[2] Since existing traditions of art lacked precedents for capturing the materiality of earth, forests, and beaches, Krajcberg invented them.

One of his signature techniques involved printing directly from slabs of wood and trunks of trees found in the forest. Unlike traditional woodblock printing in which the artist gouges out patterns and pictures, Krajcberg inked the wood and then transferred the impressions of its textures and patterns directly to paper. The resulting prints reveal the tree's biography as it has been configured by growth, weather, climate, wounds, illnesses, and the animals that took up residence in its bark. In this way the tree's experiences take precedence over the artist's interpretation and observation.

Krajcberg also exceeded visual perception by placing a rectangular frame directly on the beach at ebb tide. He then poured liquid plaster into the frame to capture a direct impression of the rhythmic, arching patterns that the tides made in the sand. Krajcberg used the cast as a mold by laying moistened paper on it and allowing the paper to dry into a relief he referred to as "gravures." Their subject coincided with their form—the actual topography of the beach and its actual textures. In a similar manner, he made molds of the intricate and cadenced patterns of material conditions formed by rain and wind. Krajcberg explains his deviation from the tradition of landscape art: "I made impressions of earth and of stones. . . . There was no pictorial gesture. They were impressions, reliefs, pieces of nature."[3]

Krajcberg added a chromatic dimension to his textural and topographical explorations after he moved to Brazil in 1948 and ultimately set up a studio among the iron-mining fields at the foot of Itabirito Hill in 1964. It served as his base for venturing into the rain forests of the Amazon, where he became dazzled by the perpetually unfolding kaleidoscope of colors he encountered—ochers, grays, browns, greens, and reds. Instead of representing the luxuriant vegetation and minerals in commercial paint, Krajcberg enlisted the actual plants, soils, and stones to generate the tints, hues, and tones. The resulting works of art were not *about* the rain forest's colorful profusion, they *produced* this profusion.

Yet even this strategy did not fulfill Krajcberg's unequivocal pursuit of a new form of landscape art that utilized the raw ingredients of habitat. The new tactic consisted of gluing soil directly to a canvas, not as a medium to represent some other phenomenon, but as a source of visual delight and functional significance worthy of attention. He called the results "earth pictures." The uniting of subject, form, and medium make it necessary to dispense with the prefix *re-* in describing these works of art. The earth pictures did not re-present, replicate, or re-produce. They consisted of an actual component of the location.

Medium as subject expanded into the third dimension in the 1960s when Krajcberg began gathering dead tree trunks from the rain forest for his sculptures. The unprocessed wood was deeply imprinted with the effects of the ever-changing conditions in lush, primordial rain forests.

Creating art that was equivalent to the actualities of habitat was so unprecedented at the time that it inspired the renowned French art critic Pierre Restany to draft "The Rio Negro Manifesto of Integral Naturalism" to announce this historic contribution to artistic production. It was cosigned by Krajcberg and the artist Sepp Baendereck in 1978. The significance of Krajcberg's methods became apparent to Restany when he journeyed with the artist through the upper Negro River in the heart of the Amazonian rain forests. The manifesto describes the distinctive kind of art engendered by intense environmental awareness, and it declares its culture-shifting implications. Integral naturalism, he maintained, replaces humanity's long-standing lust for power with respect for the sovereign role of planet Earth. It declares that all forms of life and all forms of matter are subject to this rule, including humans and the products of civilization. The manifesto declared that the new art is not realistic, it is not metaphoric, and not expressionistic. Instead, it "represents a discipline of perception, a full availability toward the direct and spontaneous message from the immediate data of consciousness. . . . To practice this availability to that which is 'naturally granted' is to admit the modesty of human perception, and its very own limitations in relation to a whole that is an end in itself."[4]

The exultant language that Krajcberg summons to express direct contact with virgin forest and windswept beaches conveys how humanity is both enlarged and humbled by such integration. By purifying the senses and the thoughts, such experiences prepare people to receive the Earth's vital energies. "I walked through the forest and discovered life. Pure life: to be, change, continue, receive light, heat, humidity. When with nature I think the truth, I speak the truth, I demand of myself to be true. When I look at it, I feel in rhythm with birth, death, life's continuity."[5]

Such sensitivity to habitat does not guarantee uplifting and vitalizing experiences. Intense emotional identification also intensifies concern for a site's well-being. For Krajcberg, celebration of the creative forces of the planet succumbed to anguish when he discovered that the great rain forest was being logged, burned, and cleared for development. That is when integral naturalism ceased inspiring joy and spurred outrage regarding humanity's destructive rampage. He explains, "The sun was always red and the sky never blue. There was smoke day and night. One day I was invited to the North of Parana. The trees were like men calcined by war. I could not bear it."[6]

The image of the Amazon as the quintessence of vitality was crushed by evidence of the slaughter of forests to open land for coffee plantations. It no longer provided the antidote for memories that drove Krajcberg from Europe in the 1950s. He was seeking refuge from the brutality of civilization that he experienced as a Polish Jew whose parents and all four siblings were murdered in the Nazi extermination camps during the Holocaust. Krajcberg grieved the loss of each tree as the murder of another innocent victim. To him, the destruction of a forest was equivalent to genocide. The scorched trees and understory from this incineration were as horrific as ashes from a crematorium.

In his youth Krajcberg protested persecution by joining the Red Army and then leading the insurrection of the Warsaw Ghetto in Vilnius in 1939. The plight of the Amazon inflamed this spirit of revolt once again. This time, Krajcberg protested by creating art decrying environmental abuse. His subsequent life's work is a heart-wrenching plea to rescue the forest from human assault. Krajcberg explains, "The forest is dying in the Amazon before my frightened eyes, under the fierceness of the fire and the power saw. The prodigious strength of its green succumbs to a cruel treatment. It is a long agony but the most precious source of life in the planet is diminishing, tree after tree. Birds become insane and the singing ceases. Orchids, butterflies, the uirapuru, the moss, they are all becoming cinder. It is horrible to see that the murderers of the forest are men—men who lack humanity, like those responsible for the malignant gases that are killing our Earth, our mother, the home of all people (including the assassins)."[7]

Krajcberg's grief and outrage were funneled into a series of massive burnt wood constructions. "I do not try to sculpt; I seek shapes for my cry. This burnt husk is me. I feel myself in wood and in stone. Animistic? Yes! Visionary? No! I am a participant in the moment. My only wish is to express all I feel. It is a struggle without truce."[8]

Krajcberg's ninetieth birthday was celebrated in 2011 with the award of medals, exhibitions, speaking engagements and a full-scale retrospective at the Salvador de Bahia Rodin Museum in Brazil. The title of the catalog that accompanied this exhibition reveals that his anguish regarding the destruction of forests has not abated. It is called *A Cry*.

Pioneering Contribution to Eco Art **Krajcberg's immersion into the mutable matter of Brazil's forests greatly expanded the domain of art's materials, forms, and creative processes. But his contribution to eco art exceeds engagement with the formal, textural, and chromatic opulence discovered in jungle habitats. By avoiding the distanced perspective that characterizes landscape art, Krajcberg was instrumental in promoting sensual, emotional, and ethical connections with air, water, soil, animals, plants that reflect ecocentric sensibilities in general, and deep ecology in particular. The result for Krajcberg was anguish about the destruction of the sources of these wonders. Thus, joy and horror, celebration and disgust, healing and pain are twin pillars of "integral naturalism." The environmental movement and many eco artists are also driven by these disparities.**

NOTES

1 Frans Krajcberg quoted in *Frans Krajcberg: Imagens Do Fogo*, Museue de Arte Moderna Do Rio de Janeiro, Museu de Arte Moderna de Bahia (1992), 74.

2 Ibid, 58.

3 Ibid.

4 Pierre Restany, "The Rio Negro Manifesto." http://www.frans-krajcberg.com/fkmanifesteenglish.html.

5 Frans Krajcberg quoted in "Frans Krajcberg: Brazil's Eco Sculptor" by Leon Kaplan, reproduced from *Artfocus/67* (©Artfocus Magazine, Fall 1999). http://www.artfocus.com/Krajcberg.html.

6 Frans Krajcberg quoted in *Frans Krajcberg: Imagens Do Fogo*, Museue de Arte Moderna Do Rio de Janeiro, Museu de Arte Moderna de Bahia (1992), 58.

7 Frans Krajcberg quoted in *Manifesto do Rio Negro Do Naturalistmo Integral* (Editora Index: Rio de Janeiro, 1992).

8 Frans Krajcberg quoted in "Frans Krajcberg: Brazil's Eco Sculptor" by Leon Kaplan, reproduced from *Artfocus 67* (©Artfocus Magazine, Fall 1999). http://www.artfocus.com/Krajcberg.html.

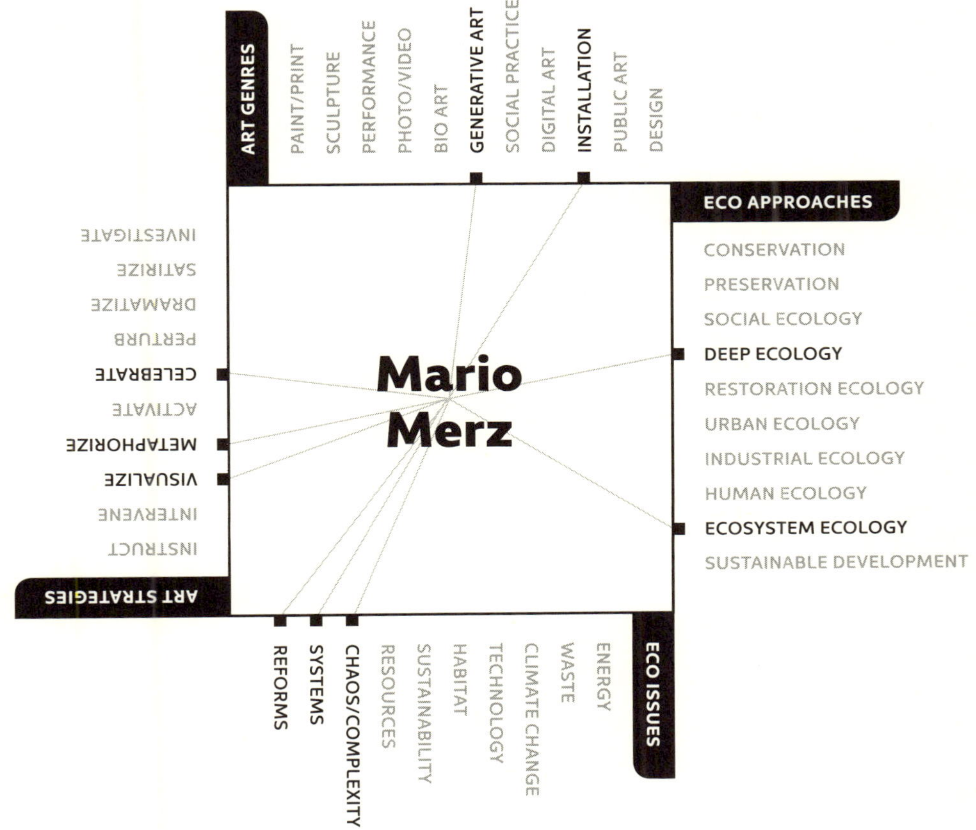

Template of Life and Dynamism

Born 1925, Milan, Italy
Died 2003, Milan, Italy

A JOKE IN THE COMIC STRIP *FoxTrot*[1] depicts Jason Fox, an annoyingly nerdy ten-year-old, and his best friend Marcus Jones. They are eating nachos. First they take one nacho from a bowl, then one more, then two more, then three, then five, then eight. The punch line is, "They call it Fibonacho!" Did you laugh? If you didn't get the joke, here is a clue. The *FoxTrot* comic is connected to the chorus of the song "Astronomy (8th Light)" by the rap group Black Star. The lyrics are, "Now everybody hop on the one, the sounds of the two. It's the third eye vision, five side dimension The 8th Light, is gonna shine bright tonight."[2]

Both pop culture sources refer to the Fibonacci series, a numerical sequence in which each new entry is the sum of the two previous numbers: 1, 1, 2, 3, 5, 8, 13, 21, 34, 55, without end. Because it accelerates to infinity, this simple sequence has asserted profound philosophical, cultural, and ecological significance since the Pisan monk, Leonardo Fibonacci, discovered it in the Thirteenth Century. When these numbers are plotted geometrically, they form an expanding spiral. The thrust of the spiral can assume any radius, size, direction, and rate of progression while maintaining a common pattern.

In the late 1960s, the artist Mario Merz became obsessed with the Fibonacci numbers. For him, the infinite proliferation of the sequence was not merely a mathematical or geometrical curiosity. It was remarkable because the spiral that it generated was the essence of biological growth and cosmic structure. It governs movements of planets, cycles of nature, regenerative forces of life inherent to the growth patterns of most living things, and flows of energy throughout the universe.

Merz believed that deriving his compositions from the Fibonacci sequence imbued his works with the aura of mystical significance. Because the sequence manifests the underlying structure of the universe and the universal principles of creation, Merz adopted it to access the transcendent state of universality. He explains, "The spiral is the form of the void, the spiral is the form of the solid, the spiral is the pause of the void, the spiral is the tension of the solid, the spiral is by opposites the tension and the pause in an organic that is also musical also pictorial; to begin again the most imaginary form of the void is still the spiral."[3]

Merz attempted to reestablish harmony with the patterns of the universe, and thereby reinvigorate the human spirit, by avoiding the rigid geometry of the right angle that constitutes a prevailing principle of human design. He explains his oppositional stance, "The emptiness of today's man of technology must be opposed to a non-emptiness reaching far back."[4] He evokes this thought in verse:

". . . 1,1,2,3,5,8,13,21,34,55 . . .
writing and making these numbers
is to frustrate the progression
of the numbers in their logic of temporal
and spatial succession
frustrating the straight line . . ."[5]

The harmony Merz discovered in this eminent principle of mathematics assumes many guises. The eccentric elements that recur in his installations, for example, all reflect sources of human subsistence on Earth that are as elemental as the Fibonacci spiral. Dried twigs are a primeval form of fuel; fresh fruits and vegetables represent a basic form of nourishment; tables are elemental facilitators of communication; igloos are an elemental form of architecture. These choices encompass the four basic functions upon which all humans, and perhaps all life, depends: keeping warm, eating, communicating, and being sheltered. In all these ways Merz diverts viewers away from the alienating alternatives contrived by humans and leads them toward primeval experiences that are as tuned by the planet and the cosmos as the Fibonacci numbers.

The installation entitled *Travolo a spirale in tubolare di ferro per festino di giornali datati il giorno del fesino*[6] (1976) incorporates Merz's signature themes, forms, and mediums. A flow of energy courses between the diverse components as through all Earthly phenomena.

A glass-topped, spiral-shaped table dominates this room-size installation. It manifests

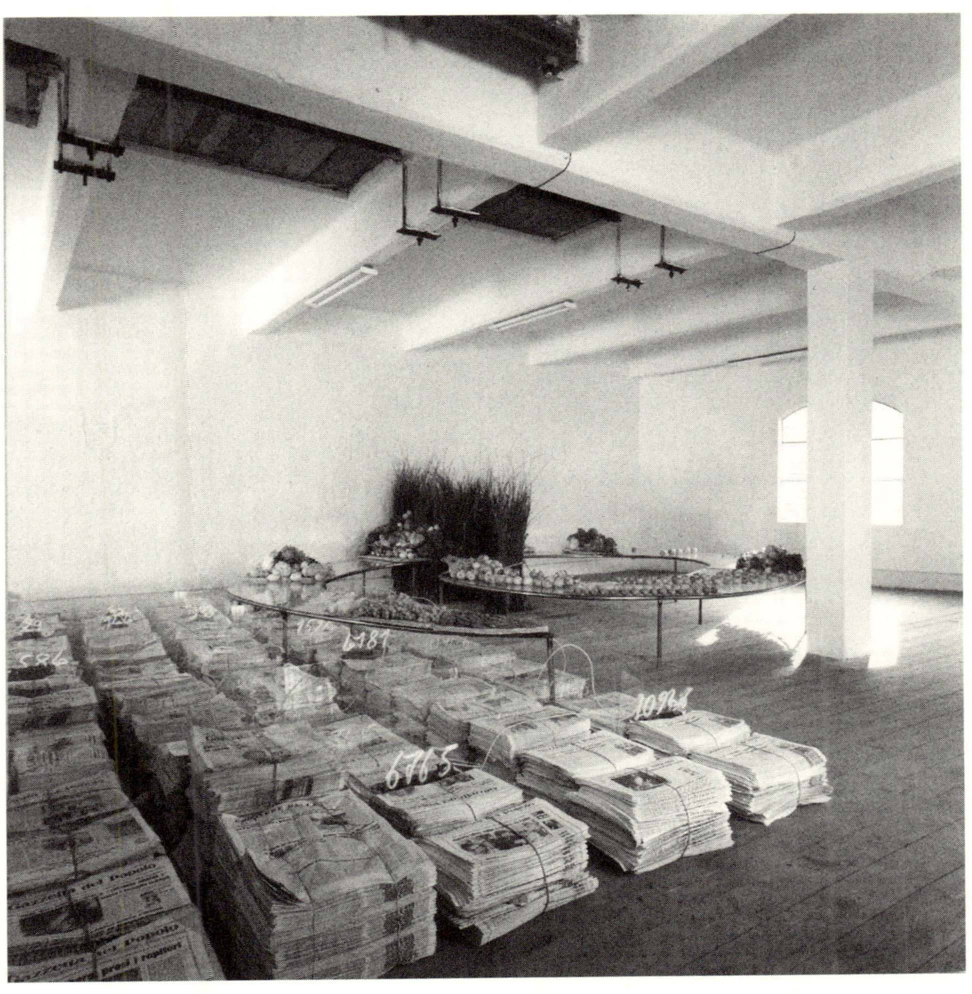

Mario Merz | Travolo a spirale in tubolare di ferro per festino di giornali datati il giorno del festino | 1976 Installation at Kunstmuseum Wolfsburg, Wolfsburg, Germany | Aluminum, glass, fruit, vegetables, branches, beeswax, newspapers, neon numbers | Dimensions: variable

a Fibonacci spiral. Its horizontal sweep is balanced by the vertical thrust of a large bundle of dried faggots positioned at its fulcrum. The table is laden with meticulously arranged lemons, apples, cabbages, peppers, cauliflower, and red cabbages. The fruits and vegetables materialize the abstract principle of nature's reproductive capacity inherent to the Fibonacci series.

The Fibonacci sequence appears as illuminated neon numerals. They are arranged on a grid of bundled newspapers. This pairing invites viewers to compare and contrast possible forms of perception and interaction. At one end of the spectrum of possibility exists the newspapers stacked in a rectangular pile. Thematically they embody an industrial form of proliferation used to disseminate human observations. Formally they comprise a rigid, right-angled solid. The formal and thematic opposite is provided by the expanding numbers in the Fibonacci series that start with the number 1 and expand to the number 10,946. The numbers are formed out of electrified neon lights and appear as dramatic bolts of blue light.

They embody the dynamically unfolding spiral that is fundamental to biological metamorphosis. As such, the infinite, enduring, universal principles of the Fibonacci sequences are pitted against the transitory facts, individual opinions, and disparate ideologies represented by newspapers.

Merz summed up his distinguished art practice by writing a five-line ode to the Fibonacci sequence. It starts with a singular plant and escalates with breathless speed to encapsulate the universe:

> THE PLANT PROLIFERATIONS . . .
> ITS SPACE OF GROWTH POURS INTO INFINITE SPACE . . .
> ITS TIME OF GROWTH POURS INTO INFINITE TIME . . .
> NUMBERS THAT PROLIFERATE RISING IN THE VOID . . .
> FROM ONE TO INFINITY.[7]

Merz grew up in Italy during the most horrendous years of Mussolini's dictatorship. His faith in the healing power of art was engendered by the needs of war-weary citizens. Over the years this belief escalated to embrace all people who are divorced from the sources of vitality on Earth. The visual language he developed is as unifying as wars are divisive, and as elemental as industrialization is contrived. His flowing hair, jagged profile, resolute jaw, and piercing eyes typecast him for this missionary role.

Pioneering Contribution to Eco Art **While many eco artists delve directly into the messy complexity of ecosystem functions and choose the words *complex, unpredictable,* and *chaotic* to describe the functioning of Earth systems, Merz paves an alternative route that can be described as elemental, unified, and knowable. The precise numerical and structural constancy that he highlights seems as prevalent throughout the cosmos as the functions described by chaos theory. In a similar manner, life on Earth depends on stabilizing homeostasis and dynamic evolution. Thus Merz establishes an important conceptual base of operations from which eco artists can launch projects designed to avoid the collapse of Earth habitats and their endangered populations.**

NOTES

1 February 8, 2009, *FoxTrot* cartoon by Bill Amend
2 Black Star, *Mos Def & Talib Kweli Are Black Star* album (New York: Rawkus Records, 1998).
3 Mario Merz, *Mario Merz*, Centro per l'Arte Contemporanea Luigi Pecci, Museo d'Art Contemporanea Prato (Firenze: Hopefulmonster, 1990), 79.
4 Mario Merz, *Mario Merz*, Galleria Civica di Arte Contemporanea (Trento: Hopefulmonster, 1995).
5 Ibid.
6 Approximate translation: Iron tubular spiral table with newspapers dated the Day of the Feast.
7 Mario Merz, *Mario Merz*, Castello di Rivoli Galleria Civica d'Art Moderna e Contemporanea, Museo d'Art Contemporanea, Fondazione Merz (2006), 105.

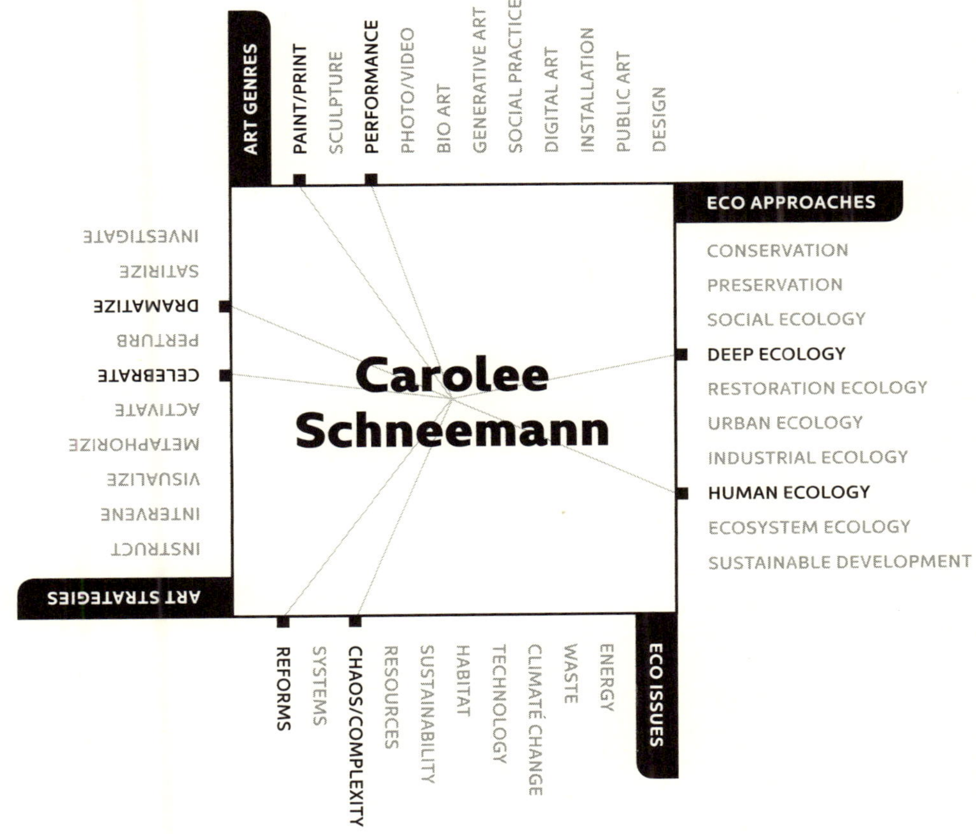

Primal Immersions

Born 1939, Pennsylvania, USA

D*IRTY JOBS*, the Mike Rowe television program that airs on the Discovery Channel, was being advertised on bus shelters all over New York City in 2008. A large poster promising "the worst is yet to come" displayed Rowe's greatly enlarged face crusted with blobs of yucky gunk. His taut lips were formed into an apprehensive smile. Each glop was accompanied by an arrow directing the eye to a label identifying the dirty job that involved the offensive substance. The overwhelming majority involved interactions with biological matter: dead geese, live kelp, bugs, leeches, maggots, fish, and body parts like tripe. Evidently, Rowe considers them more dirty than repairing

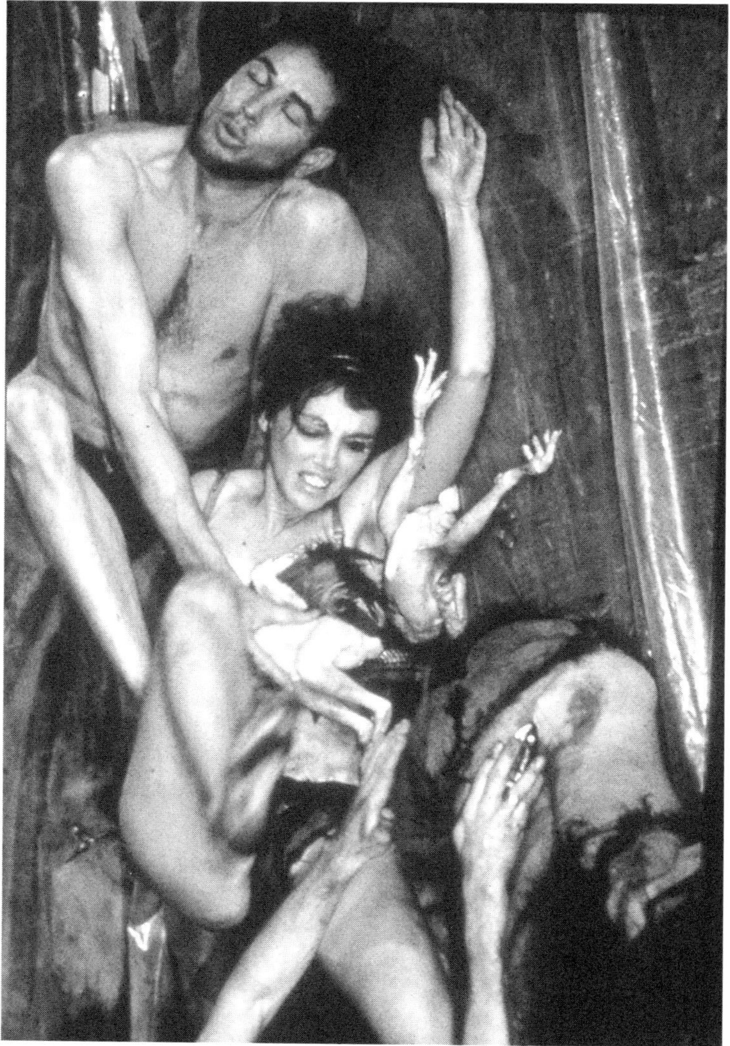

Carolee Schneemann | Meat Joy | 1964 Performance | Raw fish, chickens, sausages, wet paint, plastic, rope, paper scrap

PHOTO: AL GIESE / COURTESY CAROLEE SCHNEEMANN AND ARTISTS RIGHTS SOCIETY (ARS), NEW YORK

greasy engines. The poster indicates that holding a "dirty job" is mostly reserved for those who engage with the solid and fluid components of life.

The artist Carolee Schneemann ventured into this zone by creating paintings, drawings, films, and performances that pay tribute to material immersions with the flesh of human, nonhuman, and nonliving bodies. She did not symbolize the emancipating power of such material contacts; she actualized them by engaging in full-body encounters that exceeded existing art conventions and defied norms of behavior. They anticipated environmentalism's revolutionary implications.

The final ten minutes of a single performance work would be sufficient to explain why Schneemann has earned legendary status in the annals of Twentieth-Century art. *Meat Joy* is an elaborate performance work created in 1964.[1] Conservatives condemned it as perversity, while progressives celebrated the work as courageous liberation. However, there was no disagreement regarding the actions contained within this work. Both adversaries and advocates concurred that they went beyond acceptable displays of sensual material interactions; *Meat Joy* was blatantly erotic. The work celebrated the exultant pleasures induced when human flesh comes into contact with the materials that currently constitute "dirty jobs."

Widely circulated photographs of *Meat Joy* depict nine seminude performers reveling in their interactions with such unlikely props as chunks of raw meat and dead mackerel fish. These close-up images and the artist's descriptive text depict being situated in the midst of the work's boisterous festivities. Audience members were seated on the floor, gaining "ringside" proximity to the exultant actions of the orgiastic performers in the midst of the clamor of taped sounds of a ticking clock, popular songs, traffic noise, and vendors selling fish, chickens, vegetables, and flowers. One witness described the action he observed by stating, "I remember two highly emotional moments very close to each other. Carolee sucking fish—and a man handling a fish and following with it the contours of Rita's body, undulating, first tenderly and then wildly."[2]

The renowned poet Jerome Rothenberg attended the New York performance of *Meat Joy*. He admitted that he was "unprepared for the sensual/kinetic intensity of (the) work" that he described this way:

> Living bodies upon which materials were sent to work, beautiful or shocking/painful. Bodies among rolls of paper, packaged, papers pressed against their legs, their hips; or bodies under plastic sheets, a play of flashlights over them; or bodies painting bodies, dripping sponges of wet paint; or bodies moving, tying bodies; or bodies living, holding the remains of other bodies: chicken, fish, and sausage, the raw meat that we become. But it was beautiful for all of that, almost austere and not an imposition, an exploitation of dead flesh, like a "mere cruelty"—but tender . . . in its proposition "that we become what we see what we touch" and what she (Schneemann) elsewhere wrote: "a certain tenderness or empathy is pervasive even to the most violent action." And the perception that a body under plastic is a body under plastic, in a theater or in the white counter of the supermarket butcher—for "we are a part of nature and of all visible and invisible forms."[3]

Direct interaction between the performers and forbidden materials is emphasized in Schneemann's own description of the work: "*Meat Joy* has the character of an erotic rite: excessive, indulgent, a celebration of flesh as material: raw fish, chickens, sausages, wet paint, transparent plastic, rope, brushes, paper scrap. Its propulsion is toward the ecstatic—shifting and turning between tenderness, wildness, precision, abandon: qualities which could at any moment be sensual, comic, joyous, repellent."[4]

Schneemann prepared audience members for the raucous conclusion of *Meat Joy* by disclosing the elaborate preparatory process during the weeks preceding the performance. The goal of this training was to ensure that the actions of the performers were the products of authentic hormone-driven surges, not acted pretense. Some exercises heightened the performers' responsiveness. Others sharpened their awareness of the body's muscular, chemical, and kinetic processes. Still others delved into their dreams, personal narratives, and paranormal experiences. Schneemann enacted an additional strategy that guaranteed that the work elicited genuine and spontaneous sensuality. She withheld the actual props (paint, dead fish and chickens, and hot dogs) until the day of the performance, stating, "The real dance is with the material."[5]

Schneemann notes that people tend to acquire the characteristics of the materials with which they interact. She suggests that today's populace is just as lifeless as polyethylene, propylene, and urethane. "Wild things/wild life confuses them, makes them uneasy: bugs, birds, snakes. Mud, dirt and dust discourage their control over the world."[6] Schneemann identifies visceral immediacy as "nature." "From childhood—without any break—I felt myself a part of nature; saw the world as animate, expressive, alive and sometimes responsive to my own desires; but always the natural world was intoxicating, giving my senses information which feed emotions for personal relationships which might one day have the rich wheeling of unpredictable qualities. My sense of my own physical life and of making things within the life were always united."[7]

In *Meat Joy,* materials are not representations. Emotions are not enacted. Wetness, weight, and texture are not illusions. The work returns humans to a state of integration and wholeness by embracing the full range of Earth substances in their raw state—human and nonhuman, living and dead. Schneemann sums up her disdain for abstractions and representation when she notes with irony, "As if paint, plaster, celluloid, stone, paper, exist to convince us of a life force as vital as our own flesh and blood . . . and subject to social moralities! This is as child-like as spanking our dolls for making imaginary pee-pee."[8]

Pioneering Contribution to Eco Art **Efforts to reacquaint citizens of an industrialized culture with biotic processes and materials are included in the reform strategies currently being instituted by many environmentalists and eco artists. *Meat Joy* introduced this ecological paradigm into art by locating the source of inspiration and production in corporeal interactions. In this manner Schneemann offers an antidote to the rampant alienation from the world of physicality by engaging the soft, supple, moist, and gooey—the qualities shared by life itself. The transformation from an environmentally neglectful to an environmentally responsible culture may ultimately be marked by acceptance of eco materialism that Schneemann helped introduce into art.**

NOTES

1 Meat Joy was performed on May 29 at the Festival de la Libre Expression, Paris; June 8 at Dennison Hall, London; November 16, 17, 18 at Judson Church, New York City.

2 Perre Restany, Paris (1977) quoted in *More than Meat Joy: Performance Works and Selected Writings* (Kingston, NY: McPherson & Company, 1979, 1999), 279.

3 Jerome Rothenberg (1977) quoted in *More than Meat Joy: Performance Works and Selected Writings* (Kingston, NY: McPherson & Company, 1979, 1999), 281.

4 Carolee Schneemann, *More than Meat Joy: Performance Works and Selected Writings* (Kingston, NY: McPherson & Company, 1979, 1999), 63.

5 Carolee Schneemann interviewed with Carl Heyward in *Interventions and Provocations: Conversations on Art, Culture, and Resistance* (State University of New York Press, 1998), 198.

6 Carolee Schneemann, *More than Meat Joy: Performance Works and Selected Writings* (Kingston, NY: McPherson & Company, 1979, 1999), 59.

7 Ibid, 12.

8 Ibid.

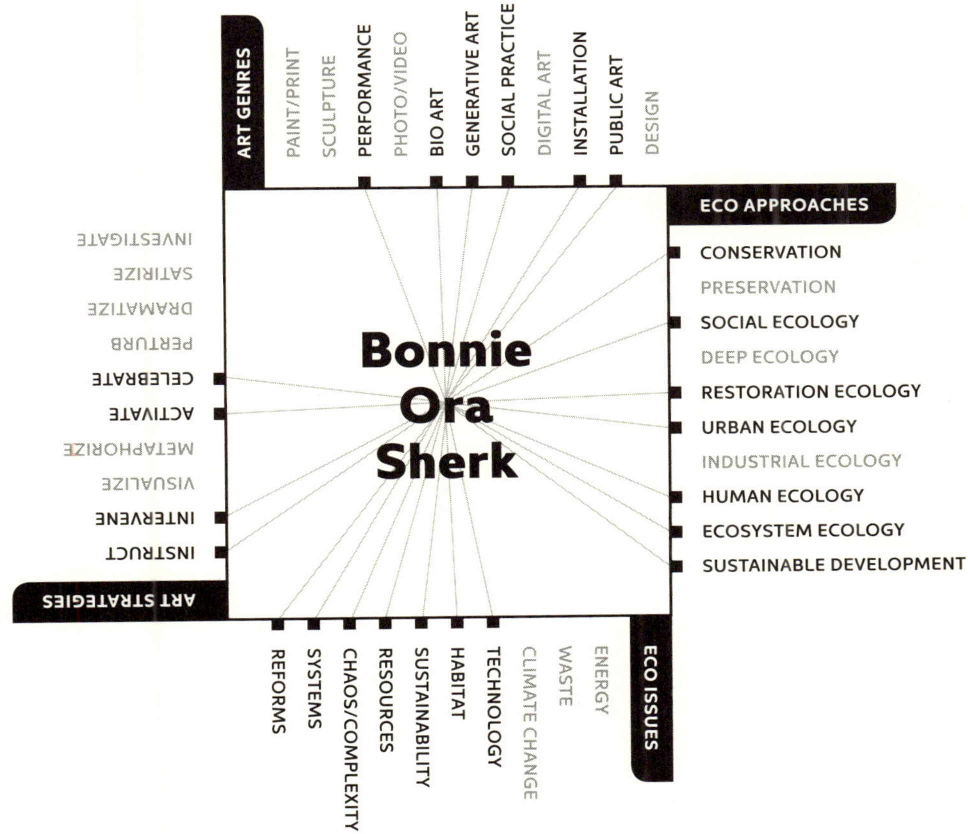

Urban Oasis

Born Massachusetts, USA

IMAGINE A SINGLE DELICATE FLOWER growing in the midst of a massive, roaring, industrialized landscape. Bonnie Sherk notes, "It was this incredible contrast that was very much a part of me, and I was fascinated by this image. I would literally conjure it up at night, and dream it."[1]

Instead of fading in the manner of most childhood dreams and fantasies, fascination with this image intensified as Sherk matured. At first she treated it as a metaphor. The fantasy flower was a poignant symbol for entire populations of plants, trees, insects, and animals plagued by industrial, commercial, and domestic intrusions into their habitats. Then Sherk and the musician Jack Wickert launched an ambitious, multifaceted art project to help the defenseless metaphoric flower blossom into a vibrant experimental community and agricultural center. Sherk named it *Crossroads Community (The Farm)* (1974–1980). She was its founding director/president.

The location Sherk chose to establish *The Farm* was not a tranquil, rural setting but a six-and-a-half acre tract of cement adjacent to abandoned warehouses that was barren except for heaps of debris. It was situated in the midst of clamorous, exhaust-spewing cars, buses, and trucks speeding along the elaborate maze of the Army Street–freeway interchange in the heart of San Francisco. The landscapes in this region had become macadam-scapes, leveled and paved to accommodate the velocity of motorized vehicles and the foundations of urban structures.

Sherk imagined this degraded habitat as a multicultural, interspecies, ecological, neighborhood oasis. Two forms of the diversity she sought were already in place—three underground creeks converged on the derelict site, and four distinct neighborhoods bordered it. According to Sherk, this vibrant mix of waterways and disparate people made it "a magnet site of invisible energy."[2] This energy was augmented by introducing animals, plants, programs, and infrastructures. Their plan was well timed and well placed. The freeway interchange had just been completed, and public money was available for the acquisition of open space and the establishment of new parks. Sherk explains, "I saw the total integration as a new art form: a triptych (human/plant/animal) within the context of a counter-pointed diptych (farm/freeway: technological/non-mechanized)."[3]

Over the next seven years Sherk's ambitious aspirations were gradually realized. A broad array of life enhancements was launched: garden, farm, park, school without walls, alternative art space, performance space, community center, environmental education center, kitchen, library, and more. Sherk describes the process of establishing this new integrated art form: "I thought of it as a performance piece; I was creating the performance of being." She goes on to explain, "The ultimate performance is being a total human being. . . . Within this performance I performed multiple roles. I was the administrator, politician, strategist, teacher, cook, designer, gardener, etc. In a sense, everyone who participated was also a performer."[4]

The social experimentation conducted at *The Farm* was integral to the idealism that roiled through San Francisco in the '70s. It was as sweeping a rejection of the repressive institutions as the San Francisco Mime Troupe's "guerrilla theatre," the Artists Liberation Front's demands for artists' rights, the San Francisco Diggers' defiance of market practices, and the Black Panther Party for Self Defense's uprisings. However, *The Farm* did not contribute to the extremist strategies that turned San Francisco into a hotbed of radicalism. Instead, it pursued its progressive agenda according to mainstream requirements, gently insinuating its radical utopianism into the established cultural framework. *The Farm* was registered as an official nonprofit organization, submitted annual reports to the IRS, was run by a board of directors, and earned grant moneys from such authorized agencies as the National Endowment for the Arts, California Arts Council, and foundations. Other income was earned by renting spaces for concerts and events.

Four years before *The Farm* got underway, Sherk established her connection to the site by creating an uplifting artwork on a downtrodden urban site. *Sitting Still No. 1* (1970) was a performance of great intensity but minimal action. Sherk put on a formal gown and sat in an old stuffed armchair exactly where she found it—in a heap of garbage strewn in a flooded empty lot beside the Army Street Circle interchange that was under construction at the time.

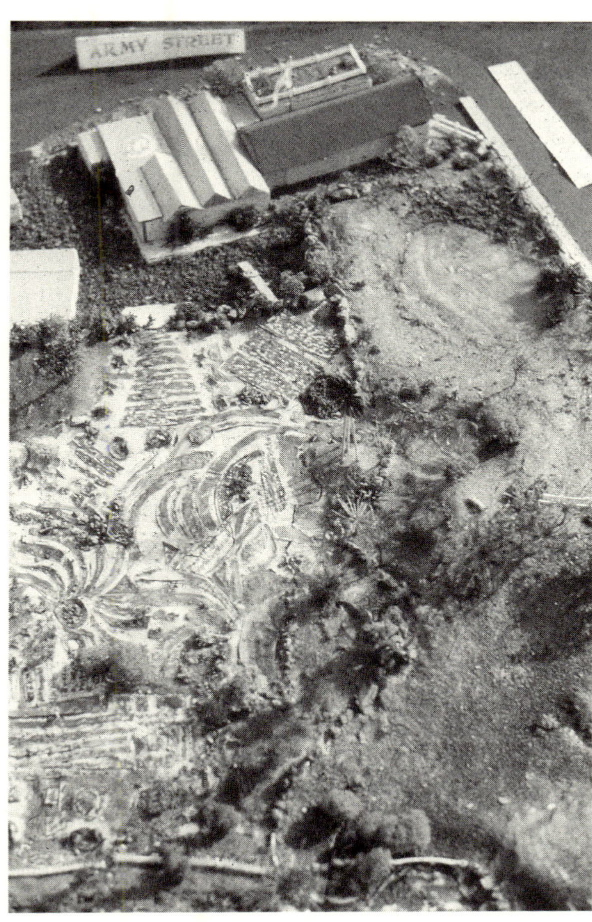

Bonnie Ora Sherk | Crossroads Community (The Farm) | Model (view south) | 1975–76 Mixed media | Dimensions: 3′ × 5′

PHOTO: BONNIE ORA SHERK / COURTESY BONNIE ORA SHERK

Sherk describes being inspired by "a potential audience" that consisted of people creeping along in the traffic slowed by the highway construction.[5] Her performance involved simply sitting and occasionally making eye contact with the drivers as they passed.

Sherk places great significance on the mysterious force that drew her to this location because while performing *Sitting Still*, she faced the northernmost frame of the Islais Creek Watershed, where *The Farm* would later be established. This watershed has continued to inspire many subsequent artworks. "I feel I am on this path, being in my alignment. There is a spiritual power and energy that is inherent to the work, including precognitions of work that were to become part of my future. . . . I really believe it was the universe guiding me."[6]

The commingling among humans and diverse living species at *The Farm* was also anticipated in an earlier work. *Living in the Forest—Demonstrations of Aktin Logic, Balance, Compromise, Devotion, Etc. (A,B,C,D,E)* (1973) is the elaborate title of an equally elaborate installation at the de Saisset Museum at Santa Clara University in California. It consisted of a six-week experiment to facilitate interspecies communications. These communications were enhanced by the interplanetary alignments suggested by feng shui, a Chinese system that seeks to gain positive energies from a site's location and its surroundings. A rat, chickens, male and female rabbits, doves, a pig all occupied the museum "forest." This menagerie's physical features, behaviors, and evidence of their native intelligences performed the functions of paint, brush, and manual dexterity in conventional art works. No bars or cages separated the animals from each other or from the museum visitors. They roamed freely within the environment, seeking places to eat, groom, sleep, etc. Sherk explains that the animals were "both performers and beings."[7]

Each week one section of a transplanted forest was opened, giving human and nonhuman participants access to it. Sherk documented the dramas that ensued with sound recordings, video, and photography and by writing about the events that ensued on the gallery walls. For example, Sherk titled one event "Pigme Demonstrating Double Imposition—Destruction: the pig digging up the tree roots counterpointed with the humans who cut the tree roots for the Christmas holiday."[8] Another event was titled "The Lady Doe Makes a Warren for Her Family—Birth: a litter of rabbits is born in the safest place in the installation the mother rabbit could find to create an underground nest—in the bottom of tree with no roots."[9]

The Farm earned its reputation as a pioneering eco artwork by greatly expanding the opportunities for humans to interact with diverse animal species. It was neither a zoo, nor park, nor farm—the conventional locations where animals reside and plants grow. Nor was it a school—the typical place people learn about these life-forms; nor was it a bureaucratic organization—the normal structure designed to carry out these functions. Its digressions from these cultural conventions steered it in a direction that many subsequent public artworks emulated.

Not a zoo Zoos are the urban norm for such concentrations of animals. While more than seventy animals made their homes on the site beneath the freeway, *The Farm* did not resemble a zoo because no animals were isolated in cages or otherwise barricaded from visitors. Sherk named her comprehensive social experiment "The Raw Egg Animal Theatre" (TREAT). Ducks, geese, chickens, rabbits, sheep, and other species "performed," which meant that their normal behaviors were observed by urban residents who had few opportunities to hear a rooster crow, or see rabbits tend their young, or pet a lamb. In this manner, the concept of a community of interacting organisms expanded to include people and animals.

Not a park Likewise, *The Farm* expanded urbanites' enjoyment of the bucolic setting beyond the conventional park. Instead of limiting experience to passive contemplation and recreation, visitors to *The Farm* actively engaged in its use and maintenance. Through "interactive learning" and "integrated community programs," people at the farm touched, tended, and communed with the many plants and animals that occupied the site.

Not a farm The standard meaning of *farm* did not define this community artwork either, because the people who dug, planted, and harvested were acrobats, actors, activists, poets, children, old folks, and even punk band members from MDC, Tragic Mulatto, Polkacide, and DOA. Everyone participated in tending gardens and caring for the animals. People even planted special gardens to grow food for the chickens, rabbits, and other animals. Tending to their needs fostered a nurturing alliance that demonstrated the codependence between humans and the nonhuman species in their diets. In addition to enjoying fresh eggs, fruits, and vegetables, these urban laborers were introduced to sensual and functional contact with their foods.

Not a school *The Farm*'s progressive educational philosophy united disciplines that typical schools separate. The humanities, sciences, education, art, agriculture, and social sciences

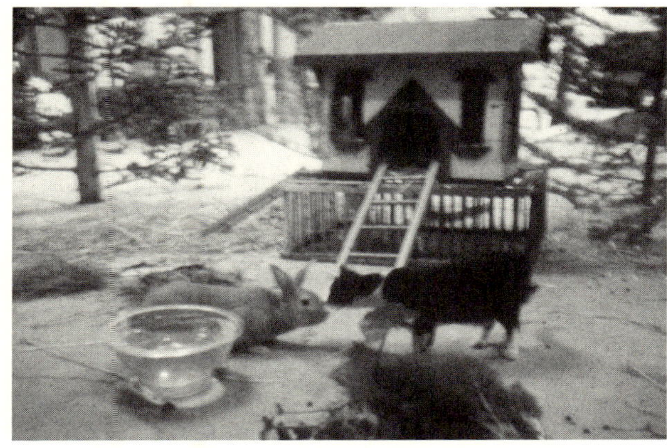

Bonnie Ora Sherk | Crossroads Community (The Farm) | Scene from the Raw Egg and Animal Theatre (TREAT) | 1976

PHOTO: BONNIE ORA SHERK / COURTESY BONNIE ORA SHERK

merged with research, planning, design, implementation, use, maintenance, and management. The garden as a living laboratory served as the hub for these diverse disciplines. Garden-based learning is an instructional strategy that utilizes a garden as a teaching tool. Sherk explains that *The Farm* approached education as "an ecological system."[10] Students from over seventy-five public schools participated on a regular basis. The children's learning program was one of five in the state of California funded as an Alternative Education Program.

Not an organization *The Farm* transformed the standard bureaucratic structure of institutions by including the public in multiple phases of its functioning, including decision making. Sherk explains the many benefits that derive from distributing work and diversifying roles: "It is from these rich processes that significant solutions can be found which will help to heal misunderstandings and prejudices among people, flawed educational systems, as well as solve serious problems of misuse, neglect and abuse of the environment."[11] In regard to *The Farm*, this disorganizational structure helped resolve the separations and inequalities existing among and between humans and nonhuman species.

The grand scale and holistic design of the experiment was envisioned when the project was first conceived. Sherk recalls, "It was an epiphany. I could see it in full flower. So I set to work to implement the vision. You can look at the drawings that I made in 1974."[12] What they present is a detailed layout of the entire site. Neatly typed at the outer edges are the names of the crossroads that gave the project its Crossroads Community name. Areas within these boundaries are allocated for a school, theater, barn, and roof garden. Tiny drawn figures interact with miniature chickens, cows, and sheep in the midst of fruit-laden trees and patches of cabbages, zucchinis, and strawberries. The drawings envisioned uncovering natural resources of the earth, like the water that flows from beneath, and recycling the concrete, which covered the land, to create meadows, gardens, and ponds. The vision was complete—a bleak urban lot converted into a flourishing promised land.

Six years after Sherk left *The Farm* to pursue other projects, an official eviction notice was issued. Sherk explains that this tiny grassroots society was a threat to the authority of government institution, even if this threat was merely symbolic. Furthermore, the owner of the property saw income-earning potential that *The Farm* was not satisfying. In 1981 the municipality began construction of a conventional park on the site, although *The Farm*'s influence persists. There are community gardens, and live/work studios are available to artists to rent.

Sherk looks back on this bold experiment and comments, "The bad news is that the planet is falling apart. The good news is that it is forcing people to think holistically. When I started, people didn't want to think holistically and did not think of art in this way. . . . Art is really the most powerful transformational methodology available to human beings. I'm not talking about formal design. I'm talking about art that has infinite manifestations of integrated elements and forms. It is when all parts are integrated systemically that it gains its power and greatness."[13]

Pioneering Contribution to Eco Art ***The Farm*** **established an autonomous zone of action that far exceeded the alternative art spaces that were being established at the time. Attending to the problems of the urban environment as an art practice was one noteworthy innovation. Another was including nonhumans within its definition of a city community. In this manner its site-specific features model an ecologically based society in which biological and cultural systems are fully integrated. Sherk identifies the ultimate significance of these accomplishments by saying that** ***The Farm*** **"had to do with the theory and practice of art as a tool for cultural transformation and human survival."[14] Over the succeeding decades, the implications and opportunities provided by this inclusive vision have continued to expand. Sherk's subsequent artistic activities include the establishment of community learning environments—called** ***A Living Library & Think Park*****—in public parks, school yards, civic centers, and urban wastelands around the United States. Each branch is developed with local resources and integrated with community programs to cultivate and vitalize human and nonhuman populations, as well as all nonliving resources—economic, technological, and ecological.**

NOTES

1 Bonnie Sherk quoted in "Between the Diaspora and the Crinoline: An Interview with Bonnie Sherk" by Linda Frye Burnham, *High Performance Magazine*, Fall 1981. Accessed through CommunityArtsNetwork.com (2002). http://www.communityarts.net/readingroom/archivefiles/2002/09/between_the_dia.php.

2 Ibid.

3 Ibid.

4 Bonnie Sherk interview with the author, March 12, 2010

5 Ibid.

6 Ibid.

7 Bonnie Sherk correspondence with the author, October 9, 2010.

8 Ibid.

9 Ibid. Bonnie Sherk interview with the author, March 12, 2010.

10 Bonnie Sherk, A Living Library: A Global Ecological Network of Diversity and Commonality," *UN Chronicle* online. http://www.un.org/Pubs/chronicle/2006/webArticles/121806_lib.htm.

11 Bonnie Sherk interview with the author, March 12, 2010.

12 Bonnie Sherk correspondence with the author, October 8, 2010.

13 Bonnie Sherk quoted in "Between the Diaspora and the Crinoline: An Interview with Bonnie Sherk" by Linda Frye Burnham, *High Performance Magazine*, Fall 1981. Accessed through CommunityArtsNetwork.com (2002). http://www.communityarts.net/readingroom/archivefiles/2002/09/between_the_dia.php.

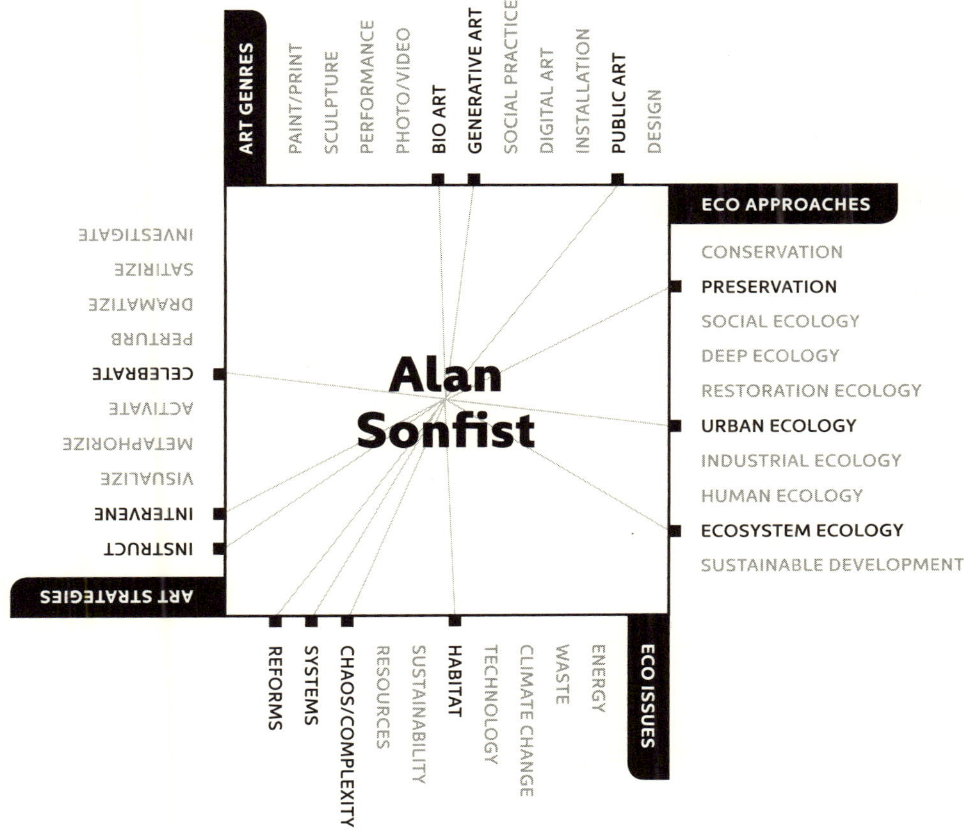

Preservation of Living Systems

Born 1946, Bronx, New York, USA

IMAGINE A CARTOON OF TARZAN that exaggerates the bulk of his muscles, the skimpiness of his loincloth, and the wildness of his tresses. Instead of swinging gracefully among the limbs in the canopy of a dense forest, he races across a desolate landscape that consists of nothing but tree stumps, the remains of a clearcut forest. His arms are spread wide. His hair is streaming. He is screaming, "Aaaaaeeeeh, aaaaaaeeeeh, aheeeeaaaa!" This is the cry of a preservationist.

Other preservationists who advocate for forests devise mischievous tactics to prevent the wholesale felling of trees for timber. They may wrap their arms around tree trunks in a defiant embrace intended to silence loggers' saws (tree huggers) or drive spikes into tree trunks to damage chainsaws (ecoterrorists). In 1978 Alan Sonfist chose a less confrontational path by replicating an entire forest on a vacant lot in Manhattan as it existed before European settlement. This time-warping, trailblazing artwork reestablished a historic condition that preceded the development, commercialization, and construction that ensued throughout the intervening years. Named *Greenwich Village Time Landscape* (1978–ongoing), this artwork resembles a riddle in which a forest is created in the *present* by reconstructing a *past* condition that generates its own *future*.

Time Landscape was created by transforming a 45′ x 200′ litter-strewn lot between Houston Street and La Guardia Place in downtown New York City into a snippet of Manhattan Island as it would have appeared to Dutch settlers disembarking from ships as they arrived in the New World. Sonfist meticulously studied Sixteenth-Century Dutch surveyors' maps, diaries, and logging records, as well as consulting with botanists and historians, to replicate three types of presettlement forest botanicals: wild flowers and grasses like Virginia creeper, dandelion, thistles, and goldenrod; young trees and shrubs like bittersweet, blackberries, sumacs, and wild roses; and mature trees like oak and hickory.

Sonfist's pursuit of accuracy also led him to represent the entire cycle of growth and decay within healthy forest ecosystems. He installed dead botanical specimens along with seedlings. Historic exactness also propelled him to acquire topsoil for his constructed landscape from excavations in a part of Manhattan that had been undisturbed since it was paved by early settlers. In this manner the botanical descendants of four-hundred-year-old soil microbes were incorporated into the site that was now characterized by human residents hustling along concrete sidewalks amid the din of traffic. Passersby wound Manhattan's clock backwards by observing the species of trees that native populations hollowed for canoes, early Dutch settlers carved into wheel spokes, and both burned for cooking, light, and warmth.

The artwork has its own impressive history. Sonfist conceived of *Time Landscape* in Manhattan in 1965, but it was not until 1978 that construction began. It required thirteen years to persuade city planners and bureaucrats to approve construction of an art installation on a valuable piece of real estate in the heart of Manhattan. They had to be convinced that botanical and cultural histories were more important than the tax revenues they would forgo and the municipal responsibilities they would undertake if the project proceeded. Furthermore, funds had to be raised. This hurdle was overcome when the National Endowment for the Arts, businesses, government departments, and several New York banks all contributed to the project.

Isolating and protecting a snippet of forest contributes multiple services to the urban environment. Besides uplifting the spirits of passersby, it replenishes soil, freshens city air, provides nesting for birds, creates habitats for many organisms, conducts carbon sequestration, purifies water, prevents erosion, and so forth. Sonfist notes that the work is also a vivid reminder that when Native Americans and Europeans chose to settle here, "they didn't come because of the concrete walkways."[1] A bronze plaque enumerates the enticements that attracted them to the island: "The surrounding neighborhood that is now known as Greenwich Village was once a marshland dotted with sandy hills that the Canarsie Indians called the *Sapokanica*. . . . The trout-filled Minetta brook ran to the west and made the area a favorite spot for fishing and duck hunting. Over the course of three and a half centuries, agricultural, residential, commercial, institutional, and industrial development replaced the natural

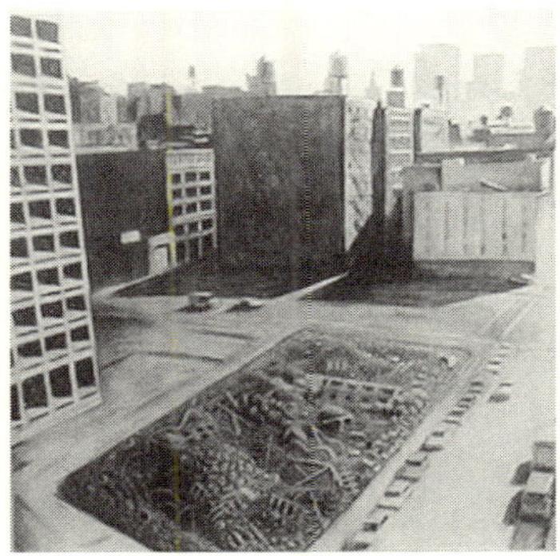
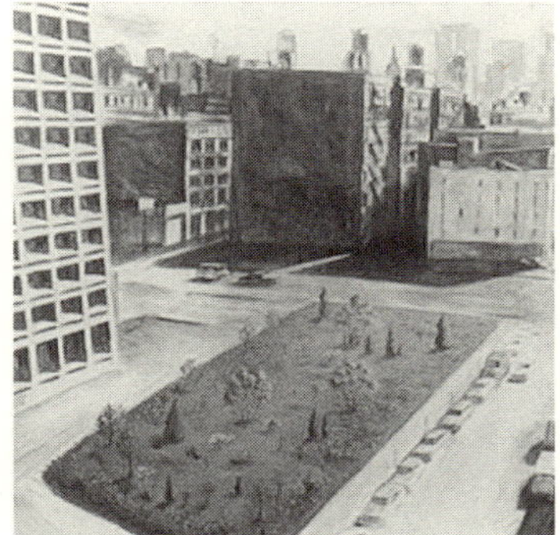
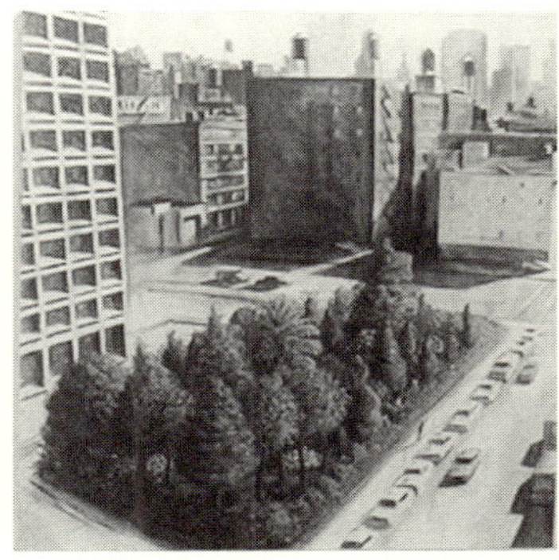

Alan Sonfist | Greenwich Village Time Landscape | 1965 Mixed media triptych | Three panels, 4′ × 4′ each

COURTESY ALAN SONFIST.COM STUDIO

marshland with an urban landscape. . . . This forested plot invites city dwellers, including insects, birds, people, and other animals, to experience a bygone Manhattan."

Sonfist describes himself as "a visual and ecological archeologist."[2] The visual component of his self-identification identifies him as an artist. He is an archeologist because he attempts to discover and disclose the material remains of an era that has ceased to exist. But instead of excavating evidence of bygone civilizations, he recreates past botanical communities. He is an ecological archeologist because his re-created wilderness is a living artifact from the Earth's valued legacy. This type of archeology is commonly referred to as "preservationism." Preservationists tend to believe that humans have an ethical commitment to preserve and protect surviving remnants of the past from the encroachments of agriculture, industry, recreation, and other forms of human occupation. All such activities are viewed as intrusive. For this reason, humans are typically exiled from sites preservationists choose to protect. *Time Landscape* manifests this belief by asserting that the ideal forest is a wilderness ecosystem, not a capital resource that provides humans with timber and opportunities for recreation.

In 1998 Sonfist received a rare honor for any living artist. The New York City Landmarks Preservation Commission awarded the artwork landmark status, bestowing the same legal protection against alteration or demolition that protects the Statue of Liberty. According to the terms of the agreement, the site will maintain the artist's preservationist vision. It will not be maintained like a park. Leaf litter should not be collected. Plants will not be trimmed. Grass will not be mowed. Birds, insects, and small animals will enjoy free access, but a tall iron fence will exclude people. There will be no picnicking, sunbathing, strolling, or picking wild mushrooms from this forest.

These strictures do not mean that the community won't benefit from the artwork. A forest reserve in the midst of a teeming metropolis is, according to Sonfist, "a public monument honoring the history of natural phenomena of a city. It demonstrates how cities can rediscover their natural identity by planning to reconstitute a section of their original natural environment within its present urban context."[3]

Sonfist referred to this and other similar projects as "tree museums." At the same time he was developing his living monument to an old-growth forest, the renowned singer Joni

Mitchell was also imagining a tree museum. Her lyrics to "Big Yellow Taxi" evoke the growing menace to forests by development:

They took all the trees
And put 'em in a tree museum
And they charged the people
A dollar and a half just to see 'em.
Don't it always seem to go
That you don't know what you've got
Till it's gone.
They paved paradise
And put up a parking lot."[4]

Unlike conventional museums, Sonfist's tree museum does not preserve dead artifacts. The collection of the museum named *Time Landscape* sprouts, lives, dies, and evolves. It welcomes all the components of dynamic ecosystems that conventional museums banish: daylight, moisture, wind, temperature, competition, and evolution. These conditions allow life-forms to enact their inherent defenses for survival in response to changing conditions. Sonfist explains, "The land is constantly evolving. I am choosing a moment in that time with the idea that these landscapes will still be evolving. I don't place a glass bubble over them."[5] For this reason the contract with the municipality ensures *Time Landscape* will conduct its own maintenance. Sonfist comments, "In all of my sculptural environments, maintenance and liability are internal components of the artwork. The plants are indigenous, and the formations follow the natural, historic growth."[6]

In actuality, the precolonial forest is struggling to survive assaults that the surrounding metal fence has not been able to prevent. Bare soil, not verdure, exists on the side of the forest that faces away from the street. Plants and critters have succumbed to assaults by bus fumes, concrete paving, acid rain, sewers that divert water, buildings that cast long shadows, and subways that rattle among their roots. Sonfist's willingness to adhere to his vision even if it means sacrificing visual appeal is apparent in the following statement: "My concern is to show the struggles within nature, which in reality make for a true natural system. One would observe, within each of my environmental sculptures, the struggle of life and death, as well as the human interaction in a historical time forest."[7] At the same time, the no-care prescription has not quite been fulfilled. Annual flowers have been planted on the side of the forest that is most visible to pedestrians and car passengers. This section of the forest affirms the public's preference for cultivated versions of nature despite the artist's intention to display the untamed, untended, and unimproved aspects of a wilderness.

The work's cultural and artistic significance have not been compromised even as changes in the work's physical conditions have shifted its meaning. Soon after its planting, *Time Landscape* served as a reminder that the city was once a thriving wilderness and marsh. Now it chronicles the stresses imposed by contemporary lifestyles. Still, Sonfist notes the positive effect of his work on the city as well as urban and suburban centers throughout the world. "The *Time Landscape* has become a living laboratory of how a historical landscape planting can be successful in a city. . . . The Parks Department has set up an Urban Forestry department as an outcome of my artwork. The public schools as well as the universities use it actively as an ecological laboratory of the success of historical plants in the city. I have been contacted by developers in working with them in creating natural habitats for their buildings as well. The success of the project has grown, as other artists and architects have been inspired by my work and are doing similar projects. My goal is to create an ancient forest for every major urban and suburban area in the world."[8]

Over the succeeding decades Sonfist has received invitations to fulfill this ambition from distinguished cultural institutions around the world. One particularly thought-provoking example, *Time Enclosures of the Southeast* (1979), consists of five time capsules shaped into two-foot cubes. Each is fabricated out of a different metal: stainless steel, COR-TEN steel, brass, copper, aluminum. The capsules were fabricated with double sides to ensure strength. Then moisture was removed to protect the seeds that Sonfist inserted within them. These seeds represent all the known forest botanicals in the southeastern United States. Because the metals that form the capsules deteriorate at different rates, the containers afford five opportunities for such forests to survive threats that cannot be anticipated. The least stable will break down and release its seeds in a hundred years. The most stable will discharge its seeds in five hundred years. Instead of preserving the past for current generations, this work preserves the present for future generations.

Sonfist sums up preservationist goals and protocols by commenting, "As we preserve our architectural heritage, we have to preserve our natural heritage. . . . You can't just pay attention to human heritage. Preserving gives us an ecological understanding of ourselves. If we don't pay attention to our environmental history, we will destroy ourselves."[9]

Pioneering Contribution to Eco Art **Elevating the importance of ecosystems, dramatizing their vulnerabilities, and safeguarding their continuity confront eco artists with two alternatives. They can focus on either humans or ecosystems. The human-centered approach involves intensifying peoples' interactions with the animate and inanimate components of a site. The ecosystem-centered approach that Sonfist helped inaugurate treats ecosystems as refuges. As such, they have been given physical and legal barriers to prevent human interactions. Sonfist's efforts are accurately described as "living museums" because they isolate objects of value, safeguard them, and present them to the public for observation only. He extends this metaphor by noting that museum attention is an indicator of cultural esteem. He notes, "Things that are important to cultures are collected by museums."[10]**

NOTES

1 Alan Sonfist interview with the author, January 20, 2005.

2 Alan Sonfist, *Nature: The End of Art—Environmental Landscapes* (Florence, Italy: Gli Ori, 2004), 15.

3 Alan Sonfist, "Rediscovering the Natural Identity of Cities: A Proposal for a Pilot Project to Demonstrate How Urban Land Can Be Re-Created to Its Original Natural Condition."

4 Joni Mitchell, "Big Yellow Taxi," *Ladies of the Canyon* album (New York, Burbank: Warner Music Group, 1970).

5 Alan Sonfist interview with the author, January 20, 2005.

6 Alan Sonfist interview with Christopher Chambers, "The Business of Art: The Earthwork as a Commodity—Discussion with Seminal Environmental Artist Alan Sonfist." http://www.worldofartmagazine.com/WoA7/7woa_Chambers.htm.

7 Alan Sonfist interview conducted by Robert Rosenblum in *Alan Sonfist 1969–1989*, Hillwood Art Museum (New York: Long Island University,1990), 8.

8 Alan Sonfist correspondence with the author, October 3, 2010.

9 Alan Sonfist interview with the author, January 20, 2005.

10 Ibid.

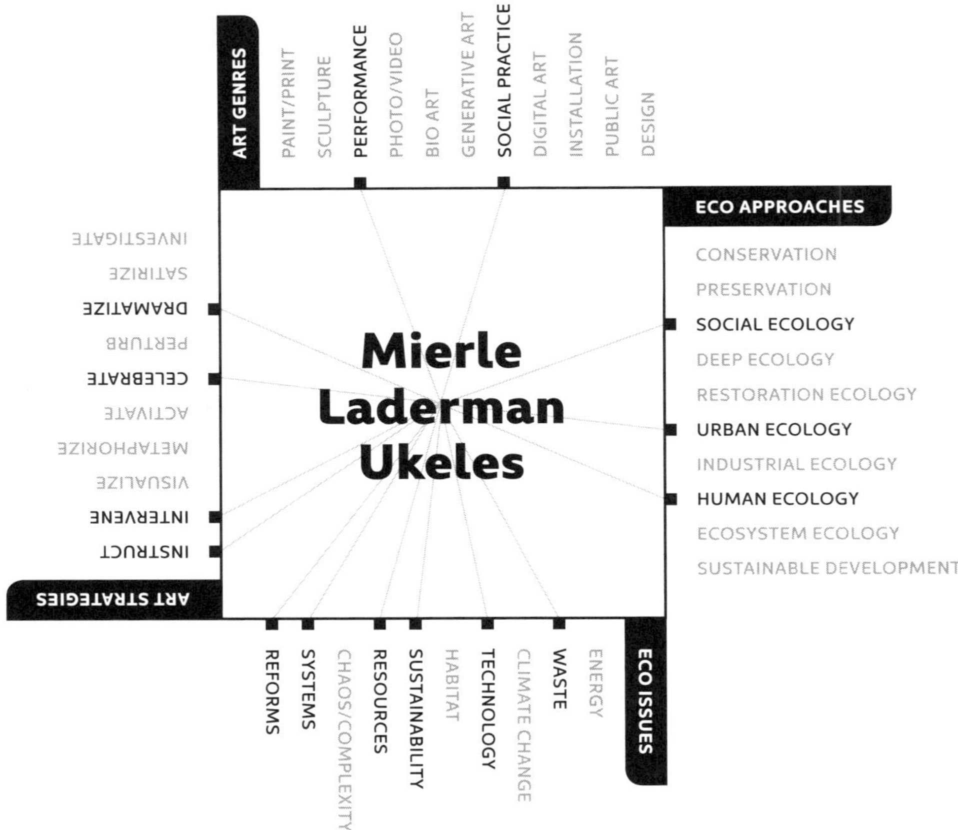

Honoring Maintenance

Born 1939, Colorado, USA

IMAGINE A MONUMENT that weighs a billion tons, measures 2.9 billion cubic feet, and occupies 995 acres. These are the dimensions of the Fresh Kills landfill, an enduring monument that memorializes a massive scale of material disposal that was created, without intention, by the 8½ million residents of New York City. Located across from New York Harbor in Staten Island, it is situated in an estuary that provided habitats for many forms of wildlife. Fifty years of dumping have produced four mounds of discards that range in height from 90 feet to 225 feet! It is the world's largest landfill. While manufacturers and businessmen might interpret the enormity of New Yorkers' discards as evidence of profitable marketing, environmentalists tend to view it as an open-air crime lab. Besides providing forensic evidence of reckless consumer extravagance, the Fresh Kills poses a triple environmental jeopardy because it is situated in a salt marsh, subject to tides, and unlined.

Across the industrialized world, people are anxiously trying to figure out how to reduce, or at least manage, the onslaught of urban waste, an unsavory mixture of biodegradable and nonbiodegradable, benign and polluting substances.

The current waste management crisis is likely to escalate as urban populations around the globe increase from 3.3 billion to 6.4 billion between 2007 and 2050, as projected by a United Nations report.[1] The predicament has engendered a new term, a new discipline, and a new art form. The term *Homo urbanus* has been proposed as an alternative to *Homo sapiens*, since contemporary humans are more accurately described as "city dwellers" than "wise." Urban ecology is the study of urban concentrations; it is devoted to improving the odds against ecosystems that are being trammeled each day by the cities built upon them. "Sanitation art" applies urban ecology to *Homo urbanus*, a species that squanders material products, sending twelve thousand tons of its wastes to landfills like the Fresh Kills every day, and then disrespects the individuals who manage this refuse for them.

Ukeles acknowledges that the production of waste is an inherent aspect of functioning systems. Indeed, maintaining the health of any unit requires the removal of waste generated during energy-producing activities. This fact applies equally to cells, organisms, households, and metropolises. In all these instances, if wastes accumulate, they are toxic—and eventually lethal—to the system. The same detoxifying functions performed by kidneys, intestines, and lungs are repeated by transfer stations, sanitation trucks, and landfills. Ukeles's "back half of life"[2] efforts engaged the unprecedented glut of New York City's garbage. She comments, "We (Americans) use a huge percentage of the world's resources. . . . So we make that big of a mess, but we also use that much of the world's resources. Right. That's dumb. There's something really, not just dumb, but really wrong, really wrong in that equation."[3]

Ukeles explains her artistic decision to address the wanton use and careless rejection of material goods: "I consciously put myself in a position to deal with some of the hardest issues in our society: What to do with our garbage, how might we transform a place that's completely poisoned and degraded by our own waste, how might these places become available to us again? Placing myself in the sanitation department, where these questions never go away, is a way for me to keep myself in the real. If our dreams can be expressed in material form, then I want to place myself where the material is completely degraded. I want to deal with the landfill. That's the center of reality; that's where I try to locate my work."[4]

Ukeles's concern for the urban environment was matched by her commitment to the workers who clean and sanitize it. She comments, "This is 1968, there was no valuing of 'maintenance' in Western Culture. The trajectory was: make something new, always move forward. Capitalism is like that. The people who were taking care and keeping the wheels of society turning were mute, and I didn't like it!"[5]

Thus Ukeles invented a form of art-making that enabled her to serve as spokesperson for the city's maintenance workers who were regularly scorned and belittled, a tendency she calls "a stunning transcultural lobotomy of humanity."[6] Her experience as a mother prepared her to be an advocate for sanitation workers because maintenance is a consuming aspect of childrearing—and because mothers are not granted esteem for their profession either. Ukeles stated, "I am an artist. I am a woman. I am a wife. I am a mother. (Random order.) I do

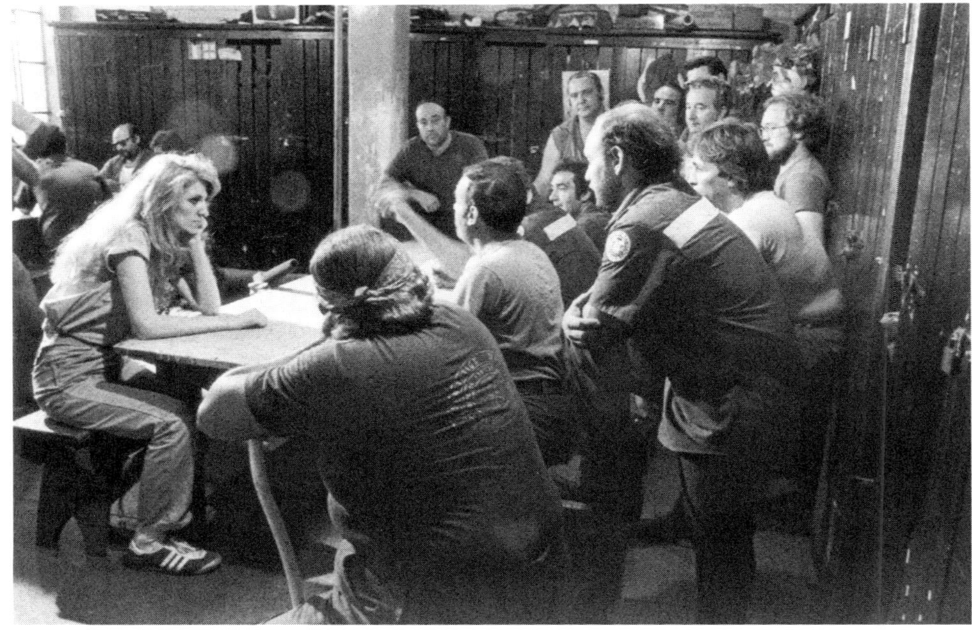

(above) Mierle Laderman Ukeles | Touch Sanitation | 1979–80 Performance, Fresh Kills Landfill | Sitting at a table with workers of the New York City Department of Sanitation

COURTESY RONALD FELDMAN FINE ARTS, NEW YORK

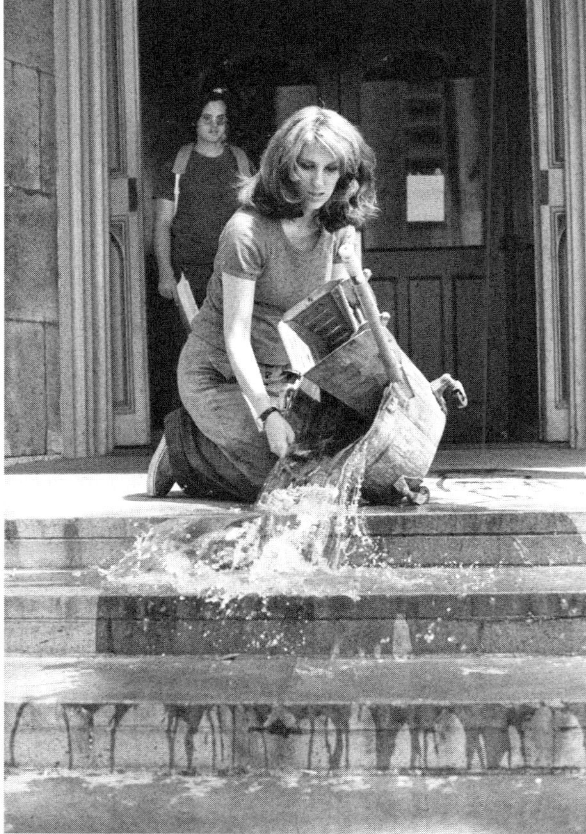

(right) Mierle Laderman Ukeles | Hartford Wash: Washing Tracks | 1973 | Maintenance, outside, part of Maintenance Art Performance Series, 1973–74 Performance, Wadsworth Atheneum, Hartford, Connecticut

COURTESY RONALD FELDMAN FINE ARTS, NEW YORK

a hell of a lot of washing, cleaning, cooking, renewing, supporting, preserving, etc. Also, (up to now separately) I 'do' Art. Now I will simply do these everyday things, and flush them up to consciousness, exhibit them, as Art."[7]

When Ukeles undertook her maintenance art project, every borough of New York except Manhattan had its own landfill. Ukeles explored them all, approaching them as urban earthworks or "inner city outer spaces."[8] "Inner city" indicates that the landfills were either within or directly facing the city where the garbage originated. "Outer space" indicates that people rarely considered the leachate, methane, polluted air, contaminated water, and other aftereffects of household and commercial garbage.

In order to usher this new kind of art into the cultural discourse, Ukeles composed *Manifesto! Maintenance Art* in 1969. The section entitled "Development and Maintenance" encapsulates her concerns by posing a provocative question: "After the revolution, who's going to pick up the garbage on Monday morning?" The text acknowledges the value of creativity but bestows comparable value on maintenance because it is required to "keep the dust off the pure individual creation; preserve the new; sustain the change; protect progress; defend and prolong the advance; renew the excitement; repeat the flight."[9]

The manifesto includes a proposal for an art exhibition composed of personal housekeeping chores, interviews with maintenance professionals, and a delivery each day of a truckload of items in need of cleansing: the contents of a sanitation truck, grimy Hudson River water, polluted air, and ravaged soil. During the exhibition, all these nasty substances would be cleaned and purified by the artist and professionals, expanding the museum's normal function by adding the rehabilitation of refuse. Ultimately, its status as a shrine where people encounter the culture's most cherished treasures would be respected. If cleanliness is a sign of godliness, creating cleanliness is certainly eligible for consideration as an inspired artistic act. "The museum becomes this crucible of transformation, almost like a temple . . . like some sort of ritual place where the impure comes in, various procedures, magical procedures or scientific or whatever are done and then these basic elements are sent back out to the city purified so life is improved."[10]

Ukeles integrated her art practice into the city's waste processing unit when, in 1976, she was accepted as an unsalaried artist in residence with the New York City Department of Sanitation. Her office/studio in DSNY headquarters became a center of advocacy for sanitation workers. Ukeles recalls that funding cuts and layoffs coincided with a major blizzard. Together they interrupted garbage collection. Garbage froze and accumulated on street corners. The public was outraged at the sanitation department. Ukeles, who had an insider's perspective on the situation, witnessed the workers' determined efforts to keep the streets clear of garbage. She became indignant. Her first impulse was to incite the workers, goading them "to burn an image of interdependence into the public's eye."[11] Instead, she launched a landmark work of art entitled *Touch Sanitation* (1979–80) to highlight the indispensable contribution of maintenance workers to urban life. Ukeles toured all five boroughs of New York City, working days and nights for eleven months. The piece was not complete until she had shaken the hands of over 8,500 sanitation employees. Handshakes are symbolic gestures that convey greeting, express gratitude, indicate agreement. Face to face, one by one, Ukeles said to each worker, "Thank you for keeping New York City alive."

The public learned about Ukeles's performance in galleries where she exhibited photographs of the hand-shaking ritual and shared stories about the indignities and humiliations the workers suffered. At the conclusion of the performance Ukeles received two unusual commendations that confirmed that her artistic ambition was being respected. She was made honorary deputy commissioner of sanitation as well as honorary teamster member of Local 831, United Sanitationmen's Association.

Ukeles likened garbage collectors to health providers. This change in stature was indicated by reference to them as "sanmen" (sanitation workers), not "garbage men." She concludes, "The design of garbage should become the great public design of our age. I am talking about the whole picture: recycling facilities, transfer stations, trucks, landfills, receptacles, water treatment plants, rivers. They will be the giant clocks and thermometers of our age that tell the time and the health of the air, the earth, and the water. They will be utterly ambitious—our public cathedrals. For if we are to survive, they will be our symbols for survival."[12]

Pioneering Contribution to Eco Art Capitalist manufacturers typically concentrate on production and consumption. Their customers tend to focus on personal needs and wants. The by-products of production and consumption are not normally factored into business models, marketing strategies, or commodity purchases. It required an artist, Mierle Ukeles, to usher the "back half of life" into the public's consciousness. Specifically, she shielded the urban environment and maintenance workers from degradation by publicly and performatively investing them both with dignity. But her more comprehensive contribution involved restraining art's alliance with consumer culture. Instead of consuming resources to create new objects for consumption, Ukeles manages wastes responsibly.

NOTES

1 Department of Economic and Social Affairs: Population Division, "World Urbanization Prospects: The 2007 Revision," United Nations. http://www.un.org/esa/population/publications/wup2007/2007wup.htm.

2 Mierle Laderman Ukeles / MATRIX 137, Wadsworth Atheneum (Hartford, Connecticut: 1998) 2. http://www.wadsworthatheneum.org/pdfs/Matrix%20137.pdf.

3 Mierle Laderman Ukeles interview coordinated by Erin Salazar for the Bronx Museum (Spring/Summer 2006). http://www.feldmangallery.com/media/ukeles/general%20press/2006_ukeles_tgc-bx%20museum.pdf.

4 Mierle Laderman Ukeles, "Manifesto for Maintenance: A Conversation with Mierle Laderman Ukeles" by Bartholomew Ryan, *Art in America*, March 20, 2009. http://www.artinamericamagazine.com/news-opinion/conversations/2009-03-20/draft-mierle-interview/.

5 Ibid.

6 Mierle Laderman Ukeles quoted in "The Manifest Disharmony of Ephemeral Culture," From *Virgin Land to Disney World: Nature and Its Discontents in the USA of Yesterday and Today*, by Megan C. McShane, edited by Bernd Herzogenrath (Critical Studies: Ingentaconnect), 353.

7 Mierle Ukeles (1969) quoted on Greenmuseum.org. http://greenmuseum.org/c/aen/Issues/ukeles.php.

8 Mierle Laderman Ukeles, "Time Travel in Public Landscapes," *Landviews.org*, Online Journal of Landscape, Art & Design, Summer 2003. http://www.landviews.org/la2003/time-mlu.html.

9 Mierle Laderman Ukeles: *Manifesto for Maintenance Art*, proposal for an exhibition by Mierle Laderman Ukeles (1969). http://www.feldmangallery.com/media/pdfs/Ukeles_MANIFESTO.pdf.

10 Mierle Laderman Ukeles interview coordinated by Erin Salazar for the Bronx Museum (Spring/Summer 2006). http://www.feldmangallery.com/media/ukeles/general%20press/2006_ukeles_tgc-bx%20museum.pdf.

11 Mierle Laderman Ukeles / MATRIX 137, Wadsworth Atheneum (Hartford, Connecticut: 1998), 7. http://www.wadsworthatheneum.org/pdfs/Matrix%20137.pdf.

12 Mierle Laderman Ukeles quoted in "People Who Are Making a Difference," Rotten Truth (About Garbage), *Environmental Action Magazine*, July–August 1991. http://www.astc.org/exhibitions/rotten/ukeles.htm.

Twenty-First-Century Eco Art Explorers

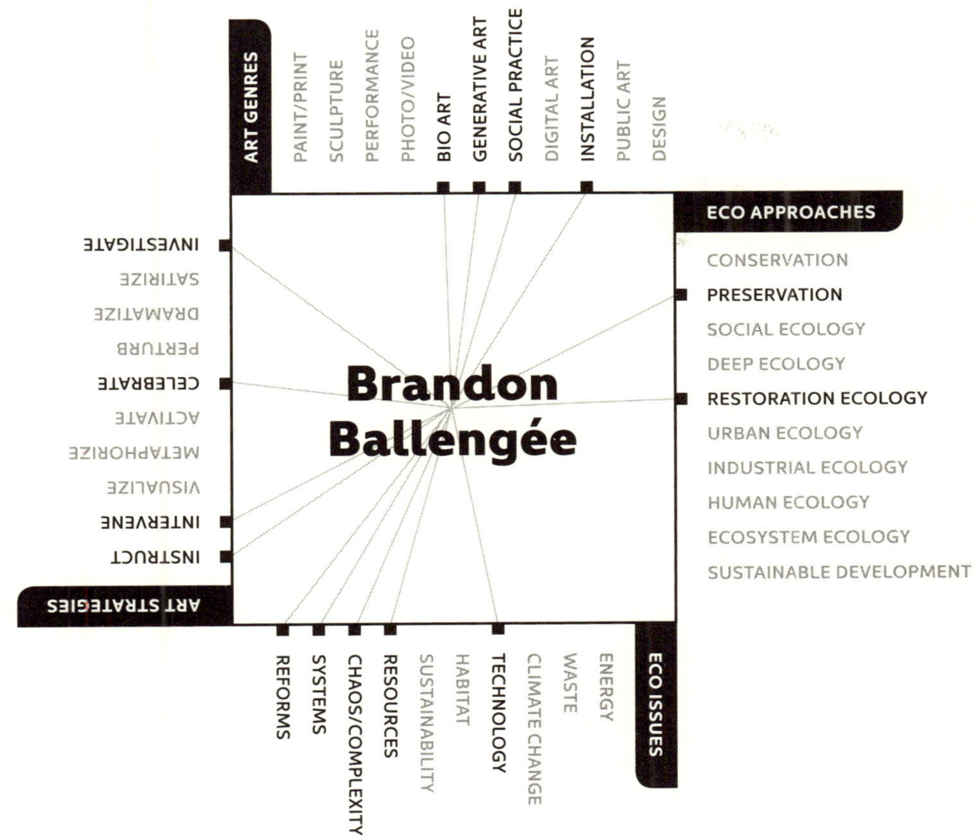

Species Reclamation

Born 1974, Ohio, USA

WHEN WILLIAM S. BURROUGHS, a star poet of the beat generation in the 1950s, wrote, "All serious and dedicated artists attempt the miraculous: to create life,"[1] he was speaking metaphorically. For Burroughs, "life" applied to any creation that possessed an animated spirit. His statement might also describe those who create lifelike experiences via virtual reality technologies. Brandon Ballengée is a bio artist who practices an even more radical interpretation of Burroughs's dictum. He takes it literally. Ballengée replaces metaphors and digital simulations with actual living cells.

Ironically, it is extinction that provides the impetus for his bold, life-creating art practice. Ballengée solves this contradiction by ap-

Brandon Ballengée | Species Reclamation Via Non-Linear Genetic Timeline: An Attempted Hymenochirus curtipes Model Induced by Controlled Breeding | "Generation 1 Through 6 Hind Limb Variations" | 1998–2006 Mixed media including live Hymenochirus genus frogs selectively bred by the artist | Dimensions: variable

COURTESY BRANDON BALLENGÉE AND NOWHERE GALLERY, MILAN

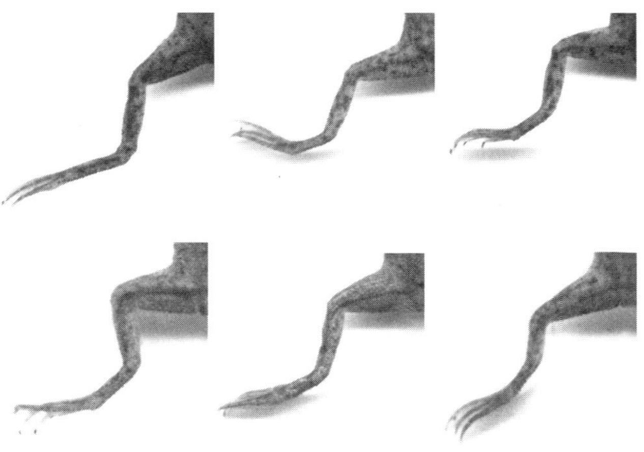

proaching extinction as an opportunity for resurrection, reversing the theory of evolution as an irreversible linear progression. In one significant project he re-created a population of frogs that appears to have vanished from Earth's genetic stock. In order to accomplish this, he devised a studio practice that consists of breeding the amphibians backwards to recover the lost species. His success transcends the realm of biology. It also uplifts the human spirit by offering reassuring evidence that extinctions are not necessarily terminal events. Ballengée demonstrates that we humans possess the capacity to actually reverse the extinctions we may be guilty of causing.

Species Reclamation via Non-Linear Genetic Timeline: An Attempted Hymenochirus curtipes *Model Induced by Controlled Breeding* (1998–2006) is the confounding title of the project that is, simultaneously, a scientific experiment, a population of living organisms, and a work of art. The title stresses the bio side of Ballengée's bio art activities. He helped decipher it for artists, word by word:

Species A species is a group of living organisms that is capable of reproducing with each other.

Reclamation *Reclamation* typically refers to the rehabilitation of disturbed lands, making them suitable for habitation or cultivation. Ballengée applies the term to disturbed amphibian populations, making them capable of surviving and reproducing. He then expands the extent of *reclamation* by making the audacious assertion that reclamation strategies are not limited to endangered species; they can also reclaim species of organisms that have become extinct.

Nonlinear Nonlinear responses are characterized by outputs that are not directly proportional to their inputs. Because they have multiple dimensions and are not predictable, they cannot be represented by straight lines on a graph. Ballengée uses the term *nonlinear* to describe genetic timelines.

Genetic timeline The timeline of discoveries related to genetics typically begins in 1859 when Charles Darwin published *On the Origin of Species by Means of Natural Selection, or the Preservation of Favored Races in the Struggle for Life* and proceeds to our pres-

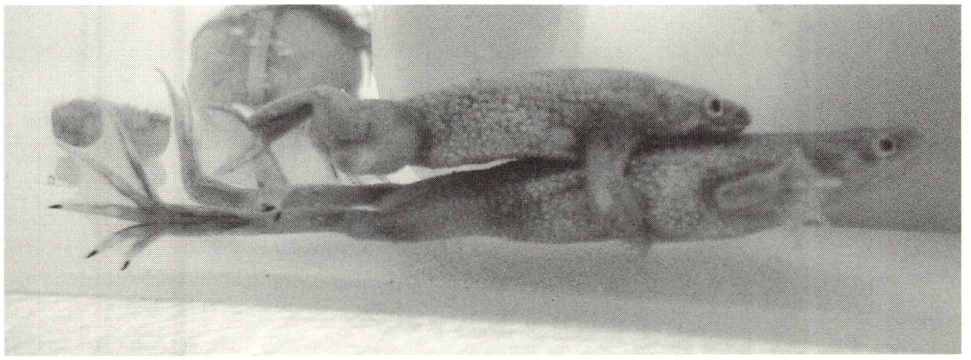

Brandon Ballengée | Species Reclamation Via Non-Linear Genetic Timeline: An Attempted Hymenochirus Curtipes Model Induced By Controlled Breeding | "Generation 2 Adults in Amplexus (mating)" | 1998–2006 Mixed media including live Hymenochirus genus frogs selectively bred by the artist | Dimensions: variable

COURTESY BRANDON BALLENGÉE AND NOWHERE GALLERY, MILAN

ent understanding of the human genome. Ballengée, however, uses the term to refer to an evolutionary process whereby ancestral species gradually diversify over the course of many generations until they form a new species. This process accounts for the millions of branches on Earth's tree of life. Ballengée demonstrates that this genetic timeline is nonlinear by breeding manifold generations of *Hymenochirus curtipes* frogs.

Hymenochirus curtipes *H. curtipes* frogs belong to the family of dwarf African clawed frogs that are indigenous to the Congo. While they appear to have disappeared from their native habitats, their descendants are thriving in bedrooms and playrooms in England, the United States, and elsewhere because the retail pet industry has been breeding these tiny frogs as an aquarium species since the 1960s. Originally, Ballengée acquired *H. curtipes* frogs for a deformed frog project. He comments, "The animals I was receiving differed from the ones described in early literature and the ones I observed as specimens from one hundred years ago in natural history museums. The more I ordered, the more I realized it was not the same frog. All the frogs I received were laboratory bred, never wild. I questioned: Where is the original? Did it go extinct?"[2]

These questions are unanswered because although the frog's native habitat in the Congo is one of the most biodiverse regions on Earth, it is also one of the least researched. Answers are further complicated because populations of frogs in this region are being decimated by slash-and-burn clearing of forests, increased logging, and rampant development.[3] Amphibians are declining at an unprecedented rate worldwide. One-third of the 6,285 known species are currently at risk of extinction.[4] This trend is worrisome to Ballengée: "Some of the species that are showing up as declining have been around 250 billion years or more, and yet something that we are doing now is wiping them out. Consciously or not, we are engineering life on this planet."[5]

Attempted This is a pivotal word in the title because the artwork it identifies was undertaken as a nonlinear experiment that generates unpredictable results. The word reveals that the attempt was more crucial than achieving a desired outcome. Furthermore, it announces that Ballengée did not relegate his studio process to private preparations. He named the work at its inception because procedures are crucial to his art project.

Controlled breeding The process of selecting mating partners in order to cultivate a particular trait in their offspring is called controlled breeding. This technique has produced high-yielding milk cows, champion dog litters, speedy horses, double ruffled orchids, blunt-ended carrots that don't tear their packaging, and so on. Ballengée's efforts to advance the long history of controlled breeding coincide with current efforts by scientists to re-create the extinct aurochs portrayed in cave paintings, the quagga that is an extinct subspecies of the zebra, and the giant Galápagos tortoise made famous by Charles Darwin.

The tedious task of controlling genetic outcomes can be greatly accelerated by adopting high-tech laboratory interventions. But Ballengée prefers the time-honored and time-consuming methods of introducing a potent adult male to a fertile adult female, relying on his own eyes for observation, simple tools for measurement, and his hands for production. Although his goal exists at the forefront of contemporary scientific explorations, his means of accomplishing this goal would be recognizable to the early humans who discovered how to manage such goal-oriented reproduction. Like them, he concedes to the organisms' physical limitations and inherent tempos. It takes eight to twelve weeks for tadpoles to grow into mature frogs. Reverse breeding the frogs from the pet store variety back to their wild state required four years.

Ballengée describes his bio art process:

> I began by making a Characteristic Code of hundred-year-old specimens from natural history museums. These traits were all different from the frogs in the pet trade where there has been a lot of interbreeding. As my frogs developed from tadpoles into adults, snout and hind limbs and particular textures of skin appeared. I examined the ones that died by clearing and staining.[6] With each generation of frogs I got a certain number with the characteristics I was looking for. . . . At the peak I had over a thousand frogs, most were tadpoles. Out of each generation, there would always be extra that I gave to schools or neighbors. I made adoption certificates for everyone who took a frog.[7]

Although Ballengée shares tools and processes with research biologists, he conveys the results of his experimentations as an artist. Even his process activates the artist's quest for harmonious form, color, texture, and size.[8] These aesthetic elements are products of the methodical breeding of frogs that gradually differentiate themselves. He affirms these connections by stating, "There is a constant mental feedback loop for me between the art making and scientific inquiry—neither could happen without the other. The art is an expression derived from the experience with animals in nature. Scientific methods and standards are rigorously followed while conducting primary research biological studies and questions are answered through experimentation. The creation happens from the seemingly divergent techniques informing one another."[9] He asserts, "Each generation of living forms is stylistically different just as each individual animal is unique and should be viewed simultaneously as a living creature and a work of art."[10]

Ballengée's project was initiated in response to reports that flooded the media at the turn of the century, chronicling scientists snipping, inserting, and rearranging genetic material. Headlines announced the first genetically engineered food, the first use of genetically engineered bovine growth hormone, the first transgenic animal, the first cloned animal, the first genetically altered animal. The scientific community was proclaiming that they held the promise of a glorious future: made-to-order organisms would make agriculture sustainable, eliminate world hunger, cure disease, and even remove environmental contamination. Ballengée doubted these reports. "I wanted to challenge the ideas put forth by scientists and the media at the time. They were all claiming that these advances were simply the next normal stages of evolution, that genetics was a one-way street. They were too confident. They use the Earth as an open experiment."[11] Backward breeding undermines such confidence by demonstrating that life is neither as plastic nor as manageable as the scientists were asserting. It highlights both the capricious nature of life's nonlinear course and the possibility of overcoming such hurdles to recover lost species.

All bio artists confront the challenge of exhibiting a living artwork in a museum, since the conditions that support living artworks also support the fungi, bacteria, and molds that are banished from museums because they damage typical artworks. Ballengée's solution entailed displaying six different generations of frogs in ten aquarium tanks. The tanks were installed in a row that showed how the frogs regressed toward the wild version. Although the tanks were arranged in a linear fashion, museum goers could not miss the nonlinearity of the physical changes that occurred in fits and starts. A computer animation and digital prints documenting Ballengée's breeding process were installed beside the tanks.

Ballengée deflects the criticism that bio artists manipulate living entities for art's sake by stating, "What I liked most about the exhibition is that the frogs seemed very comfortable being on view. The frogs would swim up, interact with their caregivers. They did not show signs of stress. One of the venues scheduled the feedings as a performance so that the public could watch. My biggest concern was making certain that each venue could take care of frogs after I left. They had to know how to feed them and how to change the water, and set the temperature."[12]

Ballengée assigned museum staff members the task of maintaining adult frogs, but not of breeding them, although breeding was both the subject of the artwork and the means to create it. He explains, "This seemed too dangerous for the frogs and too complicated for caregivers. The eggs are tiny, about the size of a poppy seed. Tadpoles are just three millimeters long when they hatch. They swim to the top of the water and look for live food. Their food is barely visible. At first they are fed parameciums that are super tiny. Then they progress to microscopic zooplankton. Once they become adults, they eat baby brine shrimp eggs. These exceptionally tiny frogs are hard to raise."[13]

The dismantling of an exhibition of bio artworks also presents ethical and practical challenges, since living art can't be placed in storage. Ballengée rejected the option of releasing a lost species into the wild, although this romantic dramatization of a biological feat must have been tempting. However, this artistic impulse was restrained by his scientist persona: "We don't know if the artist-bred species can survive in the wild. Two, we don't know if the original wild *H.c.*'s can survive in today's changed habitats. Three, even if they were raised in sterile conditions, they can carry fungus, bacteria, viruses that endanger other populations."[14] Thus, Ballengée returned the frogs to his studio where he cared for them until their normal life spans were spent.

The death of the last survivor of this experiment occurred in 2009, but the event did not mark the second extinction for *H. curtipides*. Ballengée had proved that it is possible to re-create the species. This form of species longevity manifests the remarkable malleability of life that includes birth and death, evolution and extinction. In order to assure the conceptual endurance of the work, Ballengée plans to create a database of declining amphibian populations around the world. It will be paired with wiki technology to allow nonscientists to participate in amphibian research. He comments, "Working and communicating with diverse groups is vital to my creative process. It allows the works to function as site-specific not only in geographic terms, but also culturally. This intellectual exchange also permits the work to grow in novel directions guided by group ideas instead of a solitary artist's hand—like organisms evolving to changing environmental stimuli."[15]

Ballengée concludes by recalling his childhood fascination with animals. He lived near a stream that emptied into a marsh teeming with life. He recalls, "I would spend hours every day catching and drawing salamanders, diverse species of fish, box turtles, and other fantastic creatures. Nature was my refuge and classroom. When I was a teenager, the largest forest trees were cut and sold to a lumber company. Today, the only remaining forest is a seven-acre island surrounded by housing subdivisions. Most of the stream runs through pipes. The wildlife is most visible as roadkill."[16] Ballengée deals with this loss by attempting to reverse it. He notes that by conducting primary biological research fused with his art practice, "the Earth, once again, became [his] studio."[17]

NOTES

1 Brandon Ballengée quoted in "A Brief History of Art Involving DNA" by George Gessert, *Art Papers*, vol. 20, no. 5 (September–October 1996), 25.

2 Brandon Ballengée interview with the author, November 11, 2010.

3 Brandon Ballengée, "Species Reclamation via a Non-Linear Genetic Timeline: An Attempted *Hymenochirus Curtipes* Model Induced by Controlled Breeding." (1999–2000). http://www.disk-o.com/malamp/species.html.

4 Richard Black, "Global hunt begins for 'extinct' species of frogs," BBC News: Science and Environment, August 8, 2010. http://www.bbc.co.uk/news/science-environment-10859989.

5 Brandon Ballengée interview with the author, December 2, 2010.

6 "Clearing and staining" renders the soft parts of the specimens almost transparent in order to study the development of their morphologies. Blue stain reveals cartilage. Red stain shows calcified tissue.

7 Brandon Ballengée interview with author, December 2, 2010.

8 Brandon Ballengée, "Malamp UK, Brandon Ballengée, 2007 (The Arts Catalyst)" posted by artscat on YouTube, August 3, 2008. http://www.youtube.com/watch?v=Ca1AiJEolgE.

9 Brandon Ballengée, "Understanding How Scientific Ideas Function in the Cultural Realm," posted (20:53:01) on Visual Culture and Evolution: An Online Discussion, April 13, 2011. http://vcande.blogspot.com/2010/04/411-understanding-how-scientific-ideas.html.

10 Brandon Ballengée interview with the author, November 20, 2010.

11 Ibid.

12 Brandon Ballengée interview with author, December 2, 2010.

13 Ibid.

14 Ibid.

15 Brandon Ballengée, "Small Universe" interview by John K. Grande, originally published in *Dialogues in Diversity* (2007). Accessed though http://ecologicalart.org/branbal.html.

16 Brandon Ballengée interview with the author, December 2, 2010.

17 Brandon Ballengée, "Small Universe" interview by John K. Grande, originally published in *Dialogues in Diversity* (2007). Accessed though http://ecologicalart.org/branbal.html.

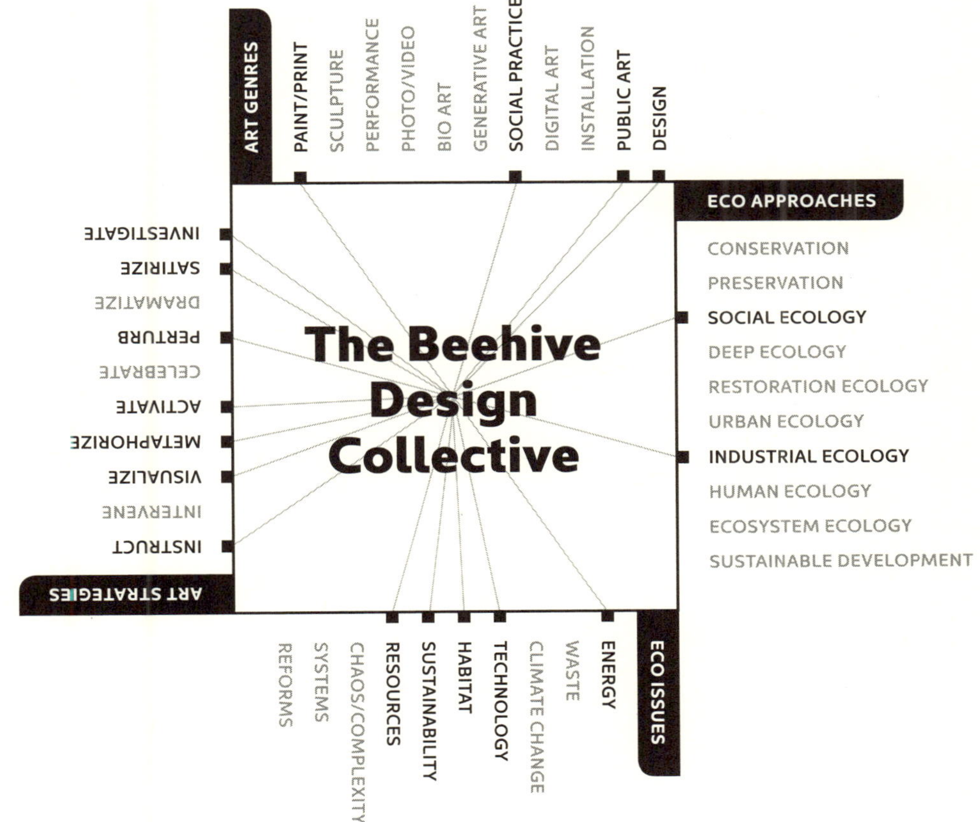

The True Cost of Coal

Group founded 2000, Maine, USA

THE CONTEMPORARY ENVIRONMENT may be more accurately described as a "mediascape" than a landscape because images that have been printed and duplicated now infiltrate highways, paper towels, menus, labels, publications, seat covers, little league fields, beach towels, and almost every other surface in the contemporary environment. The Beehive Collective is demonstrating that the potential of this popular medium of communication has not yet been exhausted. They even expanded the use of the print medium in fine art. Print as a fine art practice is commonly associated with authenticating signatures, small editions, archival papers, and hefty prices. The activist artists who comprise the Beehive Design Collec-

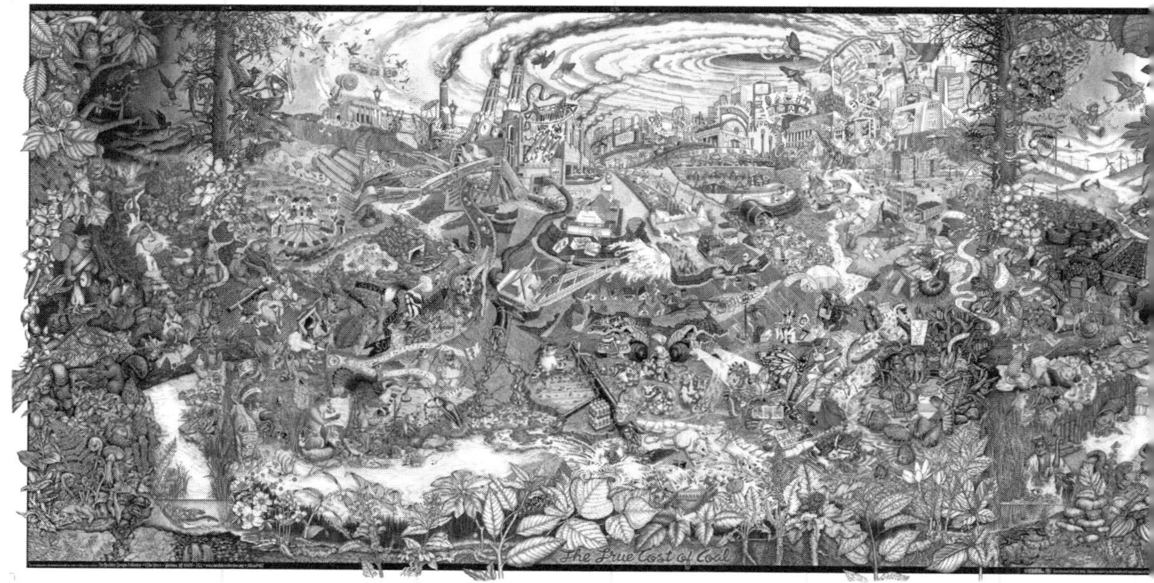

The Beehive Design Collective | The True Cost of Coal | 2008–2010
Pencil and ink wash on paper | 4′3″ × 8′6″

COURTESY BEEHIVE COLLECTIVE

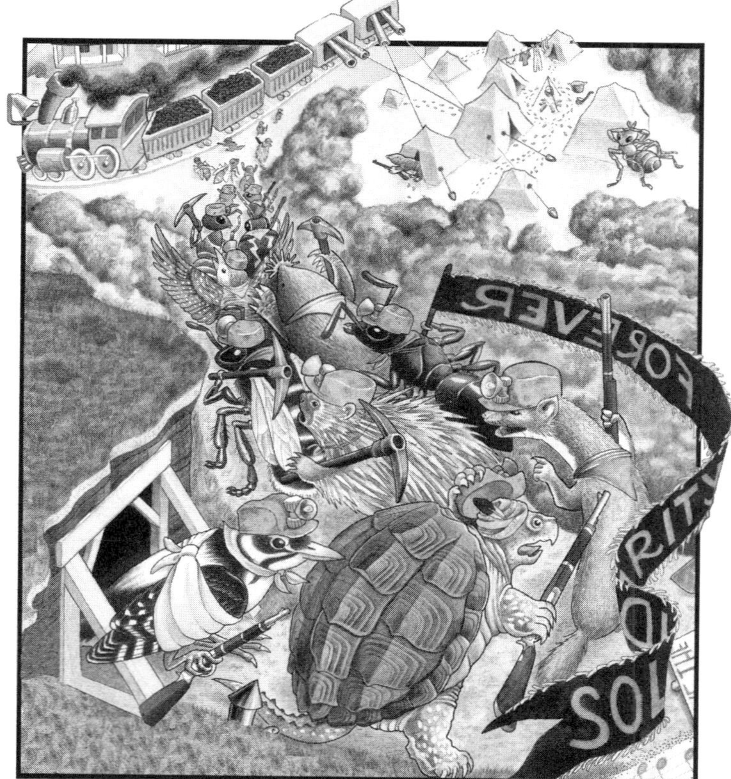

The Beehive Design Collective | The True Cost of Coal: Mountaintop Removal Detail - Solidarity Forever | 2008–2010 Pencil and ink wash on paper | Dimensions: 4′3″ × 8′6″

COURTESY BEEHIVE COLLECTIVE

tive reverse these conventions; they create public-domain images to encourage duplication in multiple formats for use as educational and protest-organizing tools.

The Bees fulfill the attributes of their namesake by maximizing teamwork and productivity. Although they are based in Maine, members continually travel as a decentralized "swarm" in search of new prospects—not pollen-laden flowers, but problem-laden sites where they "cross-pollinate the grassroots."[1] The artists explain that they discovered an opportune example in the Appalachian Mountains, which have been exploited as a "resource-extraction colony within the US."[2] This incursion is being waged by energy corporations and government bodies that are "continuing to show the extent of their violence and greed as they push their extractive agendas in the 'New Coal Rush.'"[3]

The True Cost of Coal (launched 2008, printed 2010) is an elaborate exposition of coal's role in satisfying humanity's ravenous appetite for cheap power, "a practice which blasts mountains into moonscapes to fuel the ever-growing global demand for electricity."[4] Instead of generalizing the coal industry's assaults on the environment, the graphic zeros in on Appalachia, where rampant mountaintop removal is devastating entire watersheds. The artists cite an incriminating fact that incites them—it is reported that five hundred mountains in the region have been blasted into oblivion.[5] The Bees dare to "expose the deceptions of clean coal technologies"[6] by interrogating the status quo. "What would it mean to think of power not in terms of domination and control and military might, but in terms of our ability to contribute to our communities and provide enough for everyone without sacrificing any place to wholesale destruction and toxification? With over 50% of all electricity consumed in the US coming from coal, the graphic implicates all of us in the destruction of the mountains while demanding system change—not just light bulb change!—to honor and protect the mountains."[7]

The True Cost of Coal represents the culmination of two years of intensive research in which the Bees traveled throughout the Appalachian region to gather first-person accounts of those directly affected by coal mining. Residents shared memories of the pristine landscape and local cultural traditions that were being destroyed, of past union struggles and defensive acts of civil disobedience, of current health issues and environmental contaminations. Furthermore, as the Bees toured the area, they conducted on-site research into the remarkable, irreplaceable diversity of the temperate forests enveloping Appalachia's surviving mountains. These observations were supplemented by interviews with botanists and entomologists. In order to affirm the biological treasures that are being threatened and destroyed, the graphic provides faithful renderings of over a hundred plant and animal species native to the Appalachian region and threatened by mountain detonations.

The graphic contrasts these natural assets with illustrations of the brutal events that occurred in the region. The history of the Appalachians is marred by the passage of thousands of Native Americans who were forcibly removed from their homelands in the 1830s. Their harrowing exodus is now known as "the Trail of Tears" because so many died from exposure, disease, and starvation along the way. The region also bears the stain of the Battle of Blair Mountain, which occurred in 1921 when over ten thousand miners staged a bloody insurrection against coal operators to protest their exploitation and demand the right to unionize. *The True Cost of Coal* chronicles how this violent history is being perpetuated by corporate coal giants.

In the graphic, the sorrowful fate of the mountains is portrayed as colossal machines gnawing at the landscape and dumping their loads into the valleys where pristine streams once flowed. They enact ecological havoc on communities downwind and downstream of coal-burning power plants. Plumes of exhaust spew into the atmosphere. Runoff poisons the water. Garbage chokes cities. Meanwhile anti–coal mining activists parachute in to protest the despoliation and help those organizing the frontline communities on the ground. All these roles are assigned to animals and insects whose characteristics augment each situation by contributing metaphoric significance. Hares wear parachutes. Porcupines carry pickaxes. Turtles are armed with guns. Helmeted frogs load dynamite. Clocks, dials, smokestacks, hoses, machinery, flames, weapons—all seen from acute angles in deep space—form a dense panorama of narrative detailing. Unlike typical posters that simplify their content to provide easy access, the Bees' graphics demand sustained scrutiny. Only then can the viewer discern that each narrative is strategically mapped to convey its connections to ecological destruction and social injustice, energy use and energy generation, the past and present. The work progresses in sections toward an optimistic outcome: Story of the Land, Industrialization, Mountaintop Removal, Resistance, and Regeneration.

The narrative is infused with a moral fervor that extends beyond corporate giants disfiguring Appalachia for profit. It also confronts viewers with the environmental cost of their own electricity-dependent lifestyles. The Bees intend this reaction, stating, "*The True Cost of Coal* will challenge all of us who casually flip on a light switch to examine our own connections to mountain top removal—and to think about what we can do to stop it from within our own communities."[8]

Because print techniques allow for the production of multiple originals, print is ideally suited to such an ambitious mission. For this reason, completing the imagery is not the culmination of the Bees' socially committed art practice. They devote as much creative energy to designing a campaign that capitalizes on the print's multiplier potential. It is apparent in their pre- and postproduction schemes:

Preproduction "Cross-fertilizing" is accomplished because decisions are made by consensus, "as horizontal and non hierarchically as possible,"[9] among the four to six artists who comprise the core members of the collective. These "worker bees" collaborate with part-time, autonomous "pollinator" artists whose skills as researchers, documenters, and layout artists are laminated into the production process. Grassroots groups, local activists, and ordinary folks are invited to protest the indignities that afflict them by contributing the content and critiquing the imagery as it is being produced. The Bees explain, "Cross-pollination is our core mission at the Beehive. Collaboration is at every stage of our work. Our collaborators offer advice and advocate for our role in the work they are involved in. In exchange we supply them with much-needed graphic material in many different forms and have a unique presence at their events."[10] In all these ways the artists engage the principles of sharing that are inherent to the print medium but are rarely utilized. The Bees explain, "We seek to take the 'who made that!?' and 'how much does it cost!?' out of our creative endeavors by anonymously functioning as word-to-image translators of the information we convey."[11]

In terms of the practical conditions of collaboration, income is earned through the distribution of posters that are offered on a sliding scale. The nonprofit project is also supported by speaking fees. No one gets paid, but room and board expenses are covered for core members. Otherwise, everyone is a volunteer.

Production The Bees exploit the power of images to cross boundaries of language, age, education, and learning styles. They draw the story of the coal industry's invasion of Appalachia in a cartoonish manner to ensure broad appeal. This teaming imagery receives a verbal boost from signs integrated into the drawings. They announce, "No jobs on a dead planet." "Clean coal is a dirty lie." "Community power!"

The Bees illustrate their riveting narrative the old-fashioned way—with pen and ink on paper. The tasks are divided among the members. Some do line work while others do shading. Some will work on the flora and others on the fauna that is interspersed through the graphic. Each section, therefore, represents the composite contributions of several artists. Images of individual scenes are then compiled and interwoven into one monumental 8′ x 4′ panorama. The mural is printed on fabric to make it portable.

Another expression of the collective's ecological concerns is its relationship with the Sustainable Green Printing Partnership, a nonprofit organization dedicated to reducing the environmental impact and promoting the social responsibility of the print and graphic communication industry.[12] The Bees explain, "Traditional methods of printing large format graphics involves the use of toxic and polluting processes, consumes large amounts of raw materials, water and energy, and results in items that eventually end up in the world's landfills. In the case of vinyl products, these waste items will continue to pollute the environment for hundreds of years."[13] However, the Beehive Design Collective's environmental commitment extends far beyond a baseline material obligation.

Postproduction The Bees' creative ingenuity is apparent in the postproduction phases of their graphic enterprise. These efforts optimize the impact of their public indictments of capital environmental offenders and defenses of environmental victims. They encourage limitless duplication of their graphic narratives. These images are released into the world via a creative commons license "with the hope that they will self-replicate, and take on life of their own"[14] seeding confidence and indignation.

Both the artists and the artworks circulate. These itinerant artists roll up their portable mural and travel to fairs, protest rallies, schools, and other places to deliver "picture-lectures" interweaving anecdotes and personal stories into chronicles of environmental abuse and social injustice. They also travel to support grassroots organizations whose grievances need to be amplified if they are going to be recognized.

The graphic imagery tours without the Bees too. In addition to the reproducing technologies that define the print medium, propagation is expanded exponentially by utilizing multiple print formats. Material related to *The True Cost of Coal* exists in the following formats:

- Publicity fliers fit on standard 11" x 17" paper and are printed in black and white to facilitate replication.
- Posters reproduce the entire mural. They are 60" x 31" and come folded to coincide with the mural's five thematic sections.
- A narrative booklet explains the images presented in the mural.
- Banners are designed for public presentations and workshops.
- Patches illustrate details of the mural, such as rainwater harvesting (bees collecting water in flowers) and regeneration (a salamander planting reeds in a stream).
- Clip art is available on a CD-ROM that is packed with anti-copyright art and narratives for any nonprofit use.

Posters and patches are exchanged for money, which the Bees refer to as "donations" not "sales." The group's commitment to broad, print-inspired dissemination schemes is apparent in their sliding scale of price options: $10, $15, or $20 for a paper poster, and $3, $4, or $5 for a patch. The Bees explain, "We do this because we want everyone to have access to our materials, regardless of their financial situation."[15]

Their campaign toolkit might be considered the culmination of *The True Cost of Coal*. It contains educational materials intended to catalyze community action. Tyler Bee refers to it as an "activist's cheat sheet."[16]

The Bees have tackled issues as diverse as biotechnology, corporate globalization, agriculture, and colonialism. They summarize their practice by stating, "All of our work is anonymous and anti-copyright for free use as popular education tools. We are working to dispel the tradition of activism that is based on books, experts, speeches, and 'hoarding knowledge,' by creating communication methods that are more holistic, accessible and invite participation . . . inspiring action, instead of passive listening or absorbing."[17]

NOTES

1 Beehive Design Collective, "The Beehive's Mission," Beehive Collective page on Wiser Earth: The Social Network for Sustainability. http://www.wiserearth.org/organization/view/6351671c5622dboeb2532d9042beofef.

2 Beehive Design Collective, "The True Cost of Coal." http://www.beehivecollective.org/english/coal.htm.

3 Ibid.

4 Beehive Design Collective, *The True Cost of Coal*, "Narrative Graphics." http://www.beehivecollective.org/english/store/POSTERS_LARGE.htm.

5 Sam Schild, "Beehive Design Collective Shares Stories of Activists," *Daily Vidette* (Illinois State University), April 24, 2009. http://www.videtteonline.com/index.php?option=com_content&view=article&id=27538:beehive-design-collective-share-stories-of-activists&catid=69:featuresarchive&Itemid=54.

6 Beehive Design Collective, "Workshop Listings." http://www.beehivecollective.org/english/workshops.htm#MTR.

7 Beehive Design Collective, "Press Kit." http://www.beehivecollective.org/RESOURCES/COAL%20Press%20Kit_Final.pdf.

8 Beehive Design Collective, *The True Cost of Coal*, "Narrative Graphics." http://www.beehivecollective.org/english/store/POSTERS_LARGE.htm.

9 Sam Schild, "Beehive Design Collective Shares Stories of Activists," *Daily Vidette* (Illinois State University), April 24, 2009. http://www.videtteonline.com/index.php?option=com_content&view=article&id=27538:beehive-design-collective-share-stories-of-activists&catid=69:featuresarchive&Itemid=54.

10 Beehive Design Collective, "Graphics Campaigns." http://www.beehivecollective.org/english/graphics_campaigns.htm.

11 Beehive Design Collective, "The Beehive's Mission," Beehive Collective page on Wiser Earth: The Social Network for Sustainability. http://www.wiserearth.org/organization/view/6351671c5622dboeb2532d9042beofef.

12 "About SGP," Sustainable Green Printing Partnership (SGP). https://www.sgppartnership.org/index.php?PageID=2.

13 Beehive Design Collective, "Sustainable Signage." http://banners.beehivecollective.org/.

14 Beehive Design Collective, "The Beehive's Mission," Beehive Collective page on Wiser Earth: The Social Network for Sustainability. http://www.wiserearth.org/organization/view/6351671c5622dboeb2532d9042beofef.

15 Beehive Design Collective, prices as listed on the webstore. http://www.beehivecollective.org/english/store_gate.htm.

16 Sam Schild, "Beehive Design Collective Shares Stories of Activists," *Daily Vidette* (Illinois State University), April 24, 2009. http://www.videtteonline.com/index.php?option=com_content&view=article&id=27538:beehive-design-collective-share-stories-of-activists&catid=69:featuresarchive&Itemid=54.

17 Beehive Design Collective, "About Beehive Collective Design," Beehive Design Collective Press Kit, 3. http://www.beehivecollective.org/PDF/Beehive-PressKit.pdf.

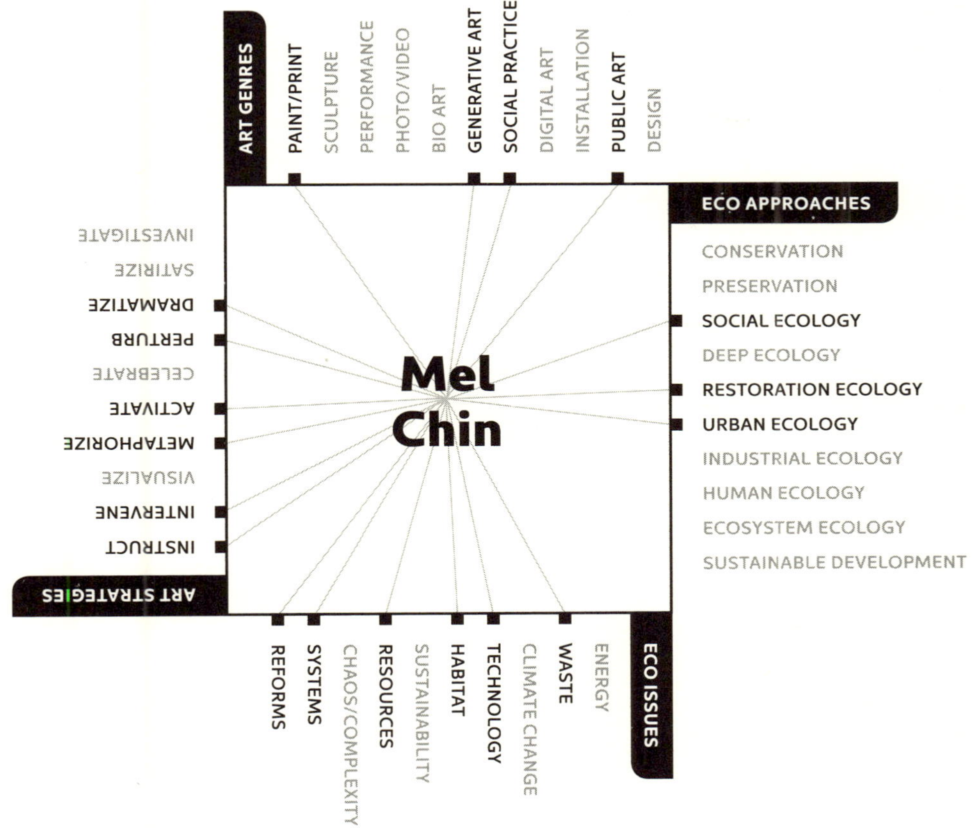

Soil Remediation

Born 1951, Texas, USA

OPERATION PAYDIRT (2006–ongoing) is a $300 million art project that depends upon the participation of three million artists and will, according to artist Mel Chin's plans, occupy 350 square miles. Chin hopes to reap major dividends from this grandiose undertaking. However, the profit margins he seeks are not calculated in terms of personal profit or fame; they are measured according to benefits to the health and well-being of impoverished children, a goal he plans to achieve by detoxifying the soils in their neighborhoods.

Chin first chose contaminated soil as his sculptural medium when he successfully applied an innovative remediation process developed by the botanist Rufus Chaney to a toxic state Superfund site known as the Pig's Eye Landfill near St. Paul, Minnesota. *Revival Field* (1991) is acknowledged as a landmark bioremediation artwork because it used plants to withdraw heavy metals from contaminated soil instead of relying on front-end loaders, fossil fuels, and high-tech fixes. The Minnesota version of *Revival Field* lasted from 1991 to 1993. At the time, this landfill was so contaminated with the waste from incinerated sewage sludge that it was illegal for anyone to be on the site.[1] Chin and his assistants received forty hours of training to learn how to respond in a hazardous materials incident before they began efforts to detoxify a sixty-square-foot section of this unpicturesque 250-acre site that was marred by mounds of garbage along Pig's Eye Lake, smoke billowing from burning tires, and trash floating along the shore of the Mississippi River. Chin explains how he merged art and science to accomplish a feat that professional bureaucracies had failed to accomplish, "We live in a world of pollution with heavy metals saturating the soil, where there is no solution to that. If that (pollution) could be carved away, and life could return to that soil, with a diverse and ecologically balanced life, then that is a wonderful sculpture. I think there is a profound aesthetic in there and it's really simple. But we have to create the chisels and we have to create the tools and we have to isolate the problem: identify where the block of pollution is, so we can carve it away. It became very clear to me that (*Revival Field*) would be a sculptural project worth engaging in."[2]

Such projects resemble vast receptacles into which Chin's many talents funnel and thrive. He is an artist, visionary, pragmatist, entrepreneur, healer, and activist. To accomplish *Operation Paydirt*, he is amplifying his faculties by collaborating with consultants, researchers, site managers, publicists, funding officers, web designers, environmental scientists, artists, landscape architects, educators, and schoolchildren who are contributing to his current soil remediation work of art. But before it was launched, Chin conducted a prolonged search for an inspiration that would facilitate the recovery of New Orleans.

Chin conceived of *Operation Paydirt* when he was invited to develop an art project in the wake of Hurricane Katrina.[3] He describes surveying the shattered remnants of a city that had been ravished by gale-force winds, torrential rains, and a surge of floodwaters the levies failed to contain. "I was in the Ninth Ward, and I was overwhelmed. There was no more water, but I was flooded with an emotional and psychological response that was uncommon for me as a creative person."[4] Art must have seemed futile in this hurricane-ravaged context. The public was already saturated with the media's images of Katrina ripping through the region with apocalyptic fury. These images had unleashed historic outpourings of sympathy, generosity, and aid. Chin goes on to explain, "When I got here I was not even remotely prepared for the level of devastation I encountered. Even months later, I felt a sense of inadequacy. It was like, how do you do something on this scale? I became obsessed, coming back again and again, to try to come up with a project of equivalent magnitude."[5]

Eventually, Chin focused on a "disaster before the disaster."[6] For decades toxins had been accumulating in New Orleans soils, making it one of the worst lead-contaminated cities in the entire nation. There were eighty-six thousand city lots laced with up to six times the lead concentrations that the EPA permits for play areas.[7] Thirty to fifty percent of the inner city's children were afflicted with lead poisoning. A lead hazard translates into a societal crisis because childhood lead poisoning is the single greatest predictor of childhood disciplinary problems, juvenile crimes, and adult violence. New Orleans ranked among the most violent cities in the country.[8] Chin noted that neighborhoods with the highest crime rates also had the highest concentrations of lead. Yet this blight was neglected. Unlike Katrina,

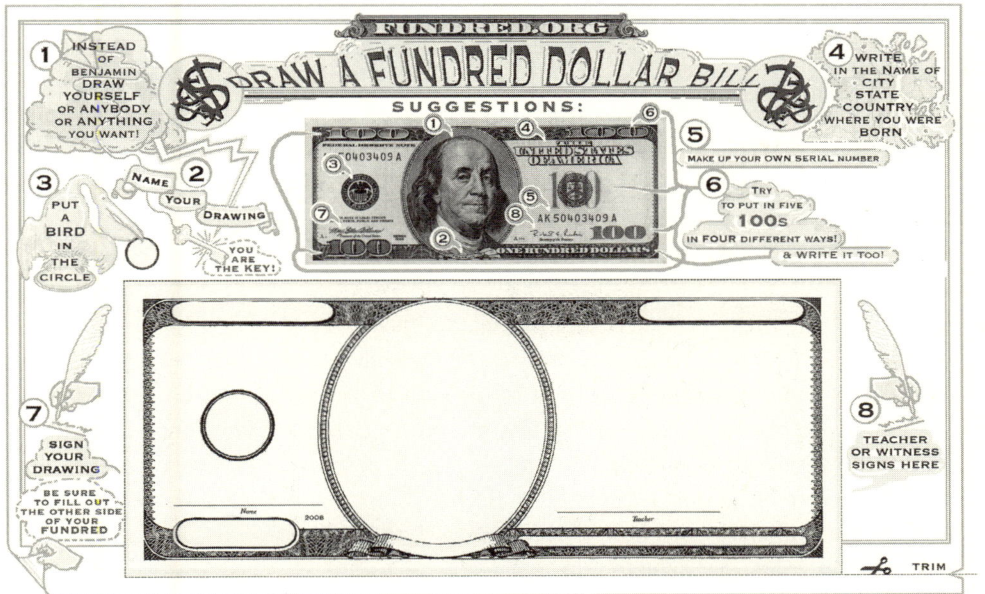

Mel Chin | Operation Paydirt / Fundred Dollar Bill Project | 2006–ongoing Fundred half page template | Printed document | Dimensions: 5½" × 8½"

PHOTO: *OPERATION PAYDIRT / FUNDRED DOLLAR BILL PROJECT* / COURTESY *OPERATION PAYDIRT / FUNDRED DOLLAR BILL PROJECT*

lead poisoning does not generate riveting tales of heroism and alarming images of disaster. Particles of almost imperceptible dust from lead-based paints and car exhaust in soil, along with the lack of observable symptoms of lead poisoning, fail to activate the public's outrage, sympathy, or protest. Furthermore, those who are most afflicted with lead poisoning are impoverished children who are the least able to petition in their own defense. Detoxifying the soils on a citywide scale required an ambassador to negotiate on their behalf, a leader to mobilize supporters, and a problem solver to discover a practical remediation strategy.

Chin volunteered for all these positions. He initiated this effort by contacting Howard Mielke, a toxicologist and urban environmental expert at Tulane/Xavier Center for Bioenvironmental Research in New Orleans. In 2004 Mielke had conducted a small but successful pilot project to remove the immediate risk to children from lead-contaminated soil.

Mielke told Chin that 30 percent of the population of the inner city was lead poisoned before the storm hit. Then he translated that statistic into learning disabilities, poverty, and violence. Chin recalls, "It shocked me. I remember telling him I was upset and asked him how much it would cost to solve this problem, and he said it would take around $300 million dollars. Of course, when you're a renegade artist sometimes $300 dollars is a lot of money, but I didn't blink."[9] Instead of blinking, Chin set about raising the funds to remediate the soil of the entire city of New Orleans.

Mielke's approach was more economical than conventional "dig and dump" methods that required removing and replacing the contaminated soil, a hopelessly expensive procedure. However, Mielke's method offered only a temporary fix. So Chin solicited Dr. Andrew Hunt to develop a more permanent solution. Hunt's innovative scheme is a "treat, lock, cover" method that utilizes calcium phosphate, a by-product of the local fishing industry, to neutralize the lead to tolerable levels. Then uncontaminated soil is brought in. His innovative method introduced a workable protocol for lead neutralization in urban residential soils everywhere.

Chin launched the project in the spirit of optimism by naming it *Operation Paydirt,* a slang term used by prospectors during the American gold rush of the Nineteenth Century who exclaimed "Pay dirt!" when they struck gold. Chin's title suggests that every speck of detoxified soil in New Orleans hit "pay dirt." Then Chin began formulating a strategy to raise this staggering sum of money. "I thought that if a child's mind, future and imagination were going to be compromised by this well documented agent called lead, it was important to have their voice out there, out front. They need to be the ones to deliver the message. I decided to design a project that would be a catalyst for that to happen."[10] Thus, the *Fundred Dollar Bill Project* was initiated to fulfill *Operation Paydirt*'s hopeful mission.

The project recruits children from across the nation to create a work of art by completing templates designed by Chin. The template takes the form of an actual-size US $100 bill. Chin removed Benjamin Franklin's face from the front and Independence Hall from the back to make room for children to personalize bills with their drawings and add their own symbols. Chin carefully calculated this cooperative effort. If $100 bills are drawn by three million children, they are symbolically equivalent to the $300,000,000 needed to remediate New Orleans's soils.

Gathering children's art may challenge some people's definition of a professional art practice, but it confirms Chin's faith in "the participatory power of art as a driving force for public awareness, dialogue, and action."[11] He offers the following explanation to skeptics who ask about his artistic contribution to this artwork. What he created and shaped was an "understanding of the problem and consequently finding the poetic answer to it, a very pragmatic answer which can be accomplished."[12] Combining a pragmatic goal with the imagination, elegance, and emotional appeal of poetic symbols exemplifies the special tactics Chin deploys to propel the *Fundred* project into actuality.

The practical task of collecting three million Fundred dollar bills from across the country could have been accomplished via parcel post or an ordinary pickup truck. Instead, Chin evoked a metaphor of significance and value by retrofitting a classic 1977 armored Brinks truck with bulletproof glass. The truck began its first nationwide tour in November 2009 by traveling 18,000 miles as it zigzagged across the country to pick up Fundred dollar bills from 117 schools that served as collection points from the surrounding areas.

Chin also summoned a poetic answer to another pragmatic problem—the need to establish a headquarters for the *Fundred* project. His solution highlighted the severity of the project's mission by locating it in St. Roch, a New Orleans neighborhood where some of the nation's highest concentrations of lead in residential soil are found.[13] Then he gave the headquarters where the bills were stored a poetic name—*Safehouse* (2008)—to assure residents whose plight had been ignored that their security was finally being addressed. Next, Chin added a sculptural component to convey the social significance. He replaced the door on the front facade of this humble dwelling with an enormous, thousand-pound, circular vault mounted on huge silver hinges. The disproportionate scale between the vault door and the modest house functioned like a billboard to broadcast the fact that it contained a treasured cache. Chin explains the new measure of value this poetic metaphor introduced: "What's valuable is another generation not being raised in conditions that compromise the capacities of a child at birth. And that's what *Fundred* and *Safehouse* represent."[14]

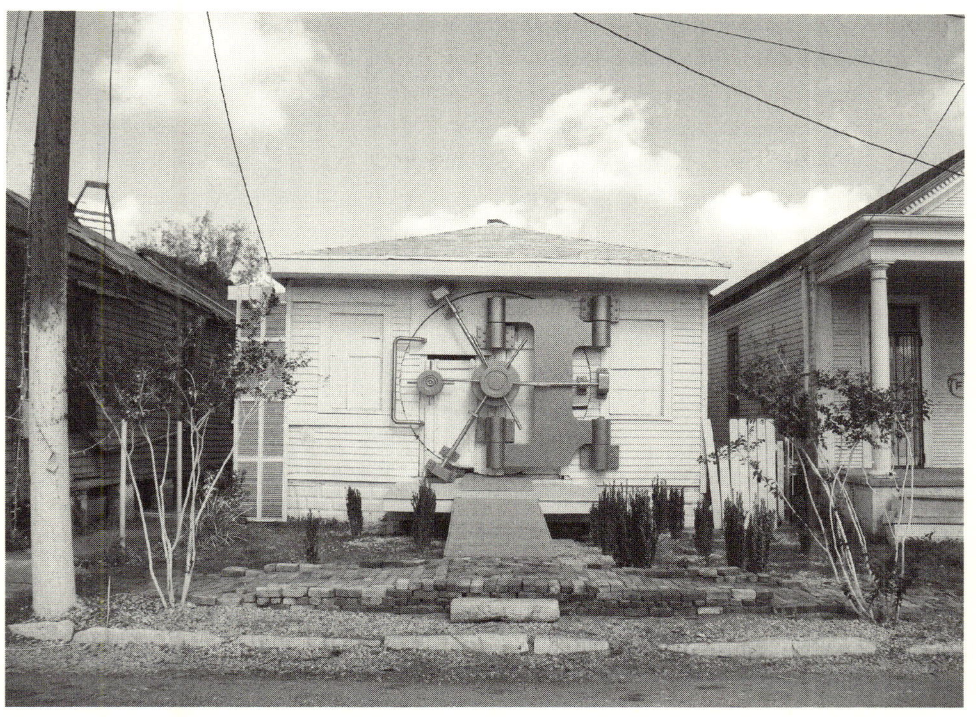

Mel Chin | Safehouse, a house transformed into a bank vault | Operation Paydirt / Fundred Dollar Bill Project | 2008 Exterior: existing house, stainless steel, steel, wood, plywood, Gatorboard, lead-encapsulation paint, automotive body and paint finishes | Interior: storage of hand-drawn Fundred Dollar Bills

PHOTO: MEL CHIN / COURTESY MEL CHIN

Fundred's success in protecting the children also depends upon rallying the support of voting-age citizens representing art, science, health, education, environment, and social activism. Chin addresses this need by providing a tutorial for enlisting their support on the *Operation Paydirt* website. One document is titled "Team Tips for Working with the Media"; it includes advice about "pitching," "working the phones," and "greeting the press." In order to assure that these PR outreach strategies convey accurate information, the site also provides a fact sheet detailing horrific statistics about lead-contaminated soil. Most significantly, it contains a one-page summary and map of the correlations between levels of lead in soil, in blood, and in student achievement in New Orleans.

Instead of acting as commander in chief of this ambitious endeavor, Chin has adopted the modest role of facilitator of locally focused engagements. He designs exhibitions of *Fundred* in museums and art spaces nationally. Behind the scenes he negotiates the protocol and process to advance scientific implementation and provide evidence of responsible data. Chin even offered the remediation protocol to EPA Region 9 Emergency Response and demonstrated its effectiveness to HUD employees, New Orleans Health Department, New Orleans Childhood Lead Poisoning Prevention Program, and the Center for Bioenvironmental Research. "I can't pull off *Operation Paydirt* alone, and that's the point. . . . This project is less and less about me, and more about how I need to create this opportunity for engagement and need someone else to follow it."[15] He explains his artistic process by stating, "I want to move out of the spotlight so people can see the true artists, those who choose to volunteer their 'Fundred' dollar bills. All I did was to provide a format that allows for this and I am honored to deliver their work."[16]

The project's dramatic climax will occur when the Fundred Dollar Brink truck pulls up in front of Congress in Washington, DC, to deliver an estimated seven thousand pounds of hand-drawn cash, the poetic equivalents of write-in ballots demanding soil remediation for New Orleans. The guards will request an exchange of $300,000,000 of art currency for $300,000,000 of US Treasury bills to pay for the health and safety of the children of New Orleans. Chin hopes it will serve as symbolic "collateral" with legislators and government agencies who will use the gift as a new kind of "stimulus package."[17] Since enacting these demands requires moving beyond symbolism to implementation, the guards will also deliver verifiable scientific solutions to lead in soils and a detailed program to conduct the cleanup.

Chin hopes that his project will prove that soil remediation can be accomplished in a citywide context. The make-believe currency provides a standard of multiple cultural values Chin hopes to make real with this work of art. He explains, "*Operation Paydirt* is about the delivery of so many things—of the imagination of children and the delivery of their art to request an even exchange, of money and services from Congress, and of the delivery of a solution to a terrible toxic problem. And it's also about the delivery of a city that can help deliver other cities from a similar fate."[18] *Operation Paydirt* is ultimately intended to serve as a model for Cleveland, Providence, Detroit, and Chicago, other post-industrial cities with severe lead contamination. Whether or not this project ultimately remediates New Orleans's tainted soil, its cultural success as an instrument of conscience raising is already ensured. The work is earning distinction as a cultural landmark by informing and activating millions of citizens. In addition, all three million dollars drawn by American children is being offered to the Smithsonian/Hirshhorn Museum of Art in Washington, DC. In all these ways the *Operation Paydirt/Fundred Dollar Bill* project provides a model for tackling large-scale environmental problems that combines pragmatism and poetry.

NOTES

1 "Phytoremediation," Case Studies, Design Integration for Sustainable Landscape Construction, University of Washington Department of Landscape Architecture. http://courses.be.washington.edu/LARCH/433/Phyto/Case.htm.

2 Revival Field, Art21.org. http://www.pbs.org/art21/artists/chin/clip2.html.

3 Transforma Projects brought arts people from all over the country to New Orleans six months after Hurrican Katrina to come up with a response to the tragedy. http://www.transformaprojects.org/.

4 Mel Chin interview with Kelly Schindler, "All About Fundred," Art21.org, March 21, 2008. http://blog.art21.org/2008/03/21/all-about-fundred-interview-with-mel-chin-part-1/.

5 D. Eric Bookhardt, "Mel Chin's Operation Paydirt Aims to Get the Lead Out of New Orleans' Inner City Neighborhoods," *Art Papers*, January/February 2009.

6 Jan Cohen-Cruz, "Art in Rebuilding Community: The Transforma Project in New Orleans," Community Art Network. http://www.communityarts.net/readingroom/archivefiles/2007/06/art_in_rebuildi.php.

7 Pam Radtke Russell, *Art Imitates Remediation As First Step in City Cleanup* (The McGraw-Hill Companies, January 7, 2009). http://www.theburnscompanies.com/documents/ENR_KatrinaCleanup_10709.pdf.

8 "A New Kind of Stimulus Package: Children Leveraging Art for Money for Change in New Orleans," Arts USA. http://serve.artsusa.org/blog/entry/a-new-kind-of-stimulus-package-children-leveraging-art-for-money-for-change/.

9 D. Eric Bookhardt, "Mel Chin's Operation Paydirt Aims to Get the Lead Out of New Orleans' Inner City Neighborhoods," *Art Papers*, January/February 2009.

10 Ibid.

11 Mel Chin, www.fundred.org.

12 Mel Chin quoted in "New Orleans: The Rescue City—Mel Chin and the Poetics of Pragmatism," by Dr. Simeon Hunter, *Art Voices*, October, 2009.

http://www.fundred.org/downloads/Art_Voices_Issue21_2009.pdf.

13 Mollie Day, "Heavy Metal: New Orleans Is One of the Most Lead-Polluted Cities in the United States, Placing Thousands of Children in Danger of Poisoning. Can Art Alter the Outcome?" *Gambit*, Best of New Orleans, January 5, 2001. http://www.bestofneworleans.com/gambit/heavy-metal/Content?oid=1255562.

14 D. Eric Bookhardt, "Mel Chin's Operation Paydirt Aims to Get the Lead Out of New Orleans' Inner City Neighborhoods," *Art Papers*, January/February 2009.

15 Mel Chin interview with Jeffry Cudlin, *Sculpture Magazine* (March 2010), 37.

16 Mel Chin quoted in "New Orleans The Rescue City—Mel Chin and the Poetics of Pragmatism," by Dr. Simeon Hunter, *Art Voices*, October, 2009. http://www.fundred.org/downloads/Art_Voices_Issue21_2009.pdf.

17 "Fundred Talking Points." http://www.fundred.org/downloads/Fundred_Talking_Points.pdf.

18 D. Eric Bookhardt, "Mel Chin's Operation Paydirt Aims to Get the Lead Out of New Orleans' Inner City Neighborhoods," *Art Papers*, January/February 2009.

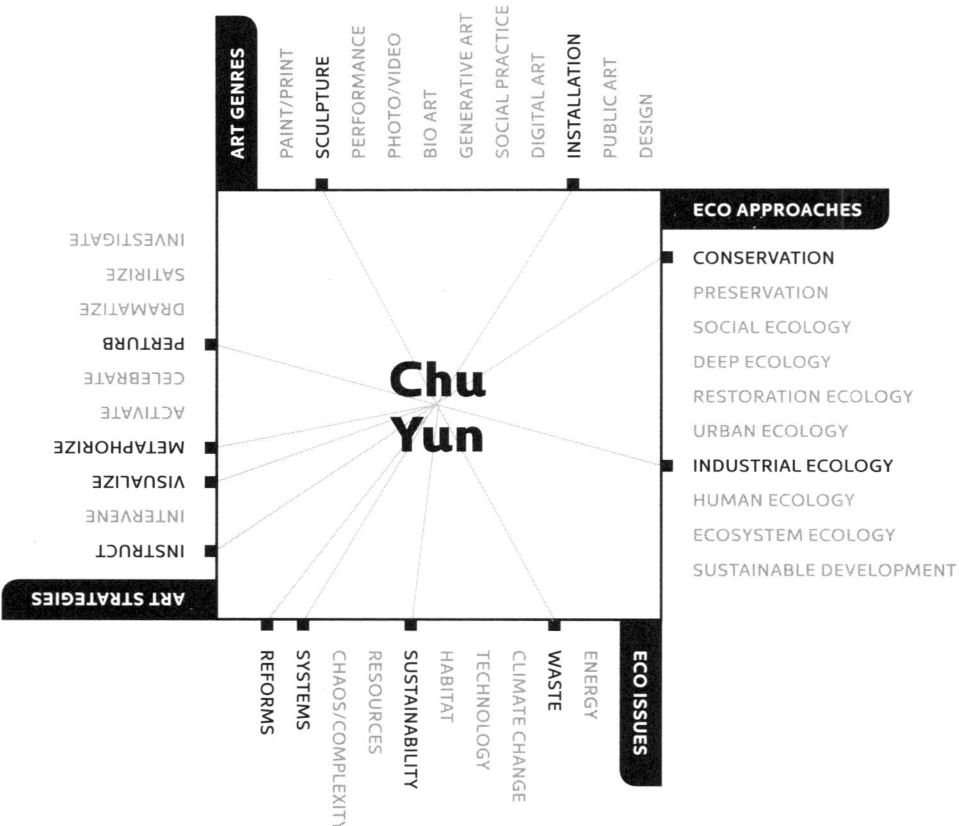

Planned Obsolescence

Born 1977, Jiangxi, China

IMAGINE STANDING ON A MOUNTAINTOP on a clear, moonless night gazing at a panorama of stars piercing the night sky with blinking dots of red, blue, green, white, orange, and yellow. Chu Yun's installation *Constellation No. 3* (2006) elicits this dazzling optical impression. But as viewers' eyes become accustomed to the darkness of the gallery, they discover that the sources of the mysterious lights are closer to home. Each is a standard indicator light mounted to a water cooler, DVD player, fan, computer, MP3 player, washing machine, phone, fax, cassette recorder, or one of countless other electronic gadgets that enhance the lives of post-industrial folks.

Another work by Chu is a soap piece that cements viewers to

the banalities of this world with as much fervor as *Constellation* transports them into a celestial realm. Officially titled *Who Has Stolen Our Bodies?* (2008), this humble sculptural assemblage consists of seventeen used bars of soap. Their sizes and shapes are surprisingly uniform, and their colors offer a harmonious range of soft pastel tones. Chu placed them on a low white pedestal in a scattered arrangement that formally corresponds to stars in the sky.

Divergent as these works are, they share two characteristics that are key to Chu's distinctive art practice. Both present objects that are so common that their appearance and cultural significance are rarely acknowledged. Chu explains his strategy: "What changes us are not necessarily those things of which we are overtly conscious about, or even the things that we are able to remember. I think we are more liable to being unconsciously changed by things we cannot easily observe, and that these things change us even more quickly and drastically."[1]

While these items in their normal contexts might have a subliminal effect, as installations in art museums, they cease being objects of everyday use and become symbols of contemporary cultural patterns. The items Chu selected from landfill glut are as emblematic of cultural mores as horseshoes and quill pens once were. Because both works of art are material castoffs, they reveal today's rampant wastefulness.

Chu acquired some of the electronic appliances and gadgets from the surplus of electronics that were discarded. Others found their way to the secondhand market for consumer goods. In both instances, they were classified as unwanted despite the fact that their blinking indicator lights prove that they were still capable of functioning. Regarding the remnants of used bars of soap, Chu rescued these from his friends' and acquaintances' waste bins; they became garbage even though they were still capable of lathering their owners. Chu intervened at the end of these objects' appointed periods of usefulness. The appliances were no longer emblems of sophisticated engineering, and the soaps had ceased being desirable toiletries. To consumers, they had become nonobjects, merely worthless clutter. Even the visual pleasure they conveyed was unwelcome. Indeed, the enchanting visual experiences offered by blinking lights and pastel soaps are intriguing contrasts to the searing critique of current market policies they deliver. The appliances indicate "planned obsolescence." The soap signals "planned waste." Both policies shorten a commodity's life to promote sales and profits for their manufacturers.

Scrutiny of *Constellation* is instantaneous, stimulated by the installation's visual beauty. Analysis, however, is not initiated until viewers recognize that this beauty emits from devices and appliances culled from today's commodity-driven market system. While the accumulation may at first seem like a ridiculously comic exaggeration of peoples' lives, in fact versions of these items appear on inventories of many of their personal belongings. Chu encourages viewers' self-identification by arranging the items on shelves and tabletops just as they would appear in their workplaces or homes until they get relegated to closets, garages, and basements where unwanted electronic products are stashed, or discarded. The array presents evidence of the profusion of commodity temptations and the ability of middle- and upper-class consumers to indulge them.

The environmental subtext conveyed by *Constellation* is encapsulated in the term *planned obsolescence*. According to Brooks Stevens, the American industrial designer who originated the phrase, it means "instilling in the buyer the desire to own something a little newer, a little better, a little sooner than is necessary."[2] In industrial design, *planned obso-*

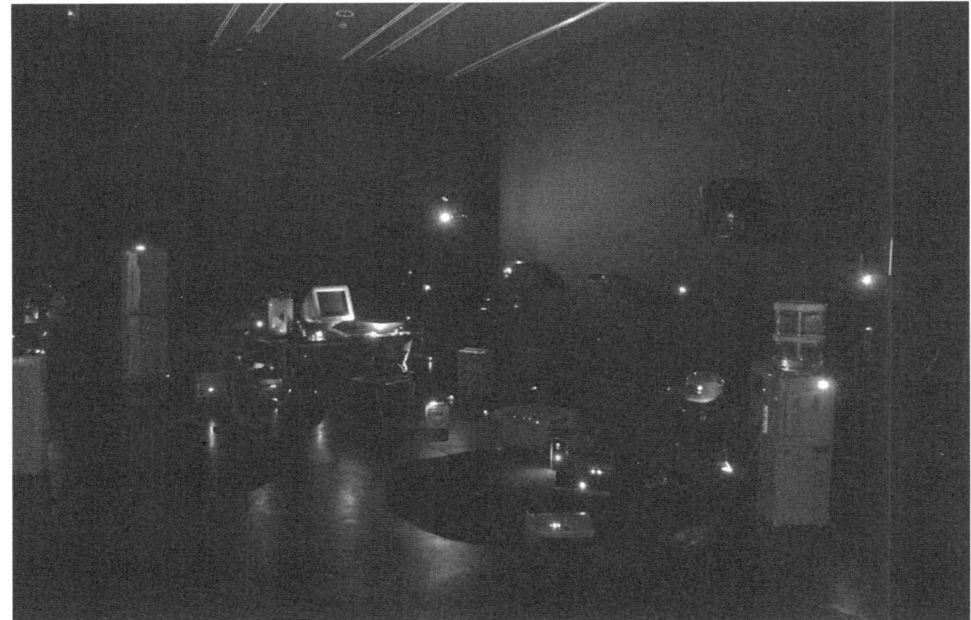

Chu Yun | Constellation No. 3 | 2009 Households appliances | Dimensions: variable | Exhibition view at Breaking Forecast: 8 Key Figures of China's New Generation Artists, UCCA, Beijing, China

COURTESY ARTIST AND VITAMIN CREATIVE SPACE, GUANGZHOU, CHINA

lescence implies the policy of designing a product according to a predetermined expiration date set by manufacturers. The policy boosts sales because items that become obsolete or malfunction require the purchase of replacements. Engineers hired to serve a planned-obsolescence agenda strive to devise feeble products instead of durable ones. Breakdowns are timed. Repair is costly. Termination is expedient. Replacement is enjoyable.

The ecological subtext offered by *Constellation* involves two divergent preludes to becoming refuse or debris. One is a result of the manufacturing policy of planned obsolescence. The other derives from the biological processes of death and decay. Living entities are born with built-in obsolescence programs that limit their life spans. However, they are also hardwired to postpone this inevitability as long as possible. Organisms gasp for air, defend their turf, retreat from danger, compete for food, and so forth. Neglecting one's needs, desiring weakness, and committing suicide are aberrations within biological realms, but they are norms among the electronics that Chu selects as his artistic medium.

Chu Yun takes none of the attributes of the free market for granted. While his contemporaries in the West were being bombarded with commercials promoting consumption and personal satisfaction, he was growing up in China being inculcated with state doctrines that mandated thrift and collective values. Now his homeland is rushing to become digitized, commodified, gadget-ized, capital-ized, and media-ized. Thus in China, *Constellation* is likely to evoke gadget cravings, while in the United States and Europe where the public is well stocked, this work is more likely to stir misgivings about seasonal upgrades and other marketing enticements.

The electronic abundance that Chu highlights is a testimony to the unprecedented productivity of industrialized factory production. However, supporters of environmental and

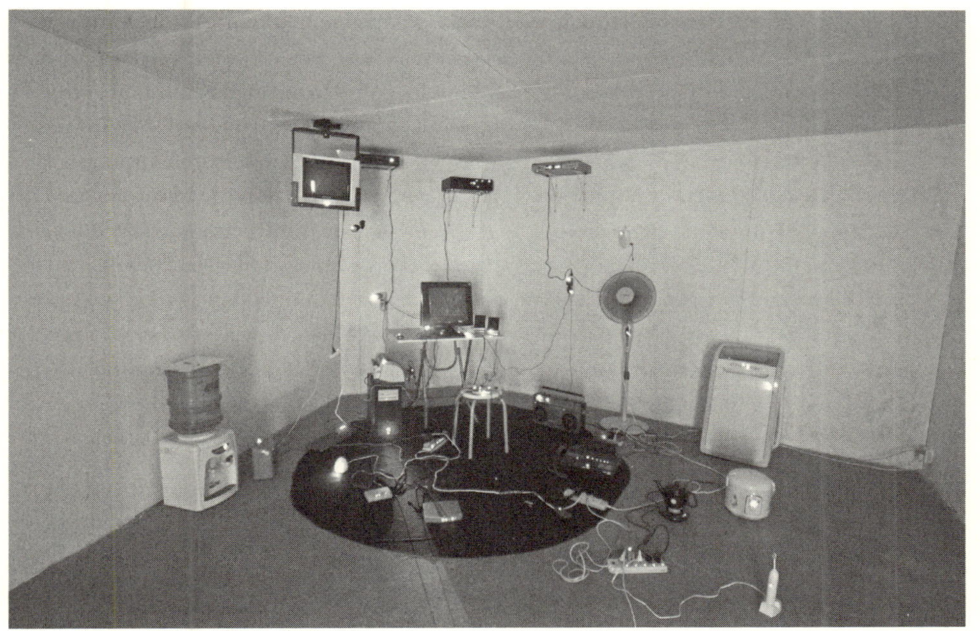

Chu Yun | Constellation No. 3 | 2009 Household appliances | Dimensions: variable | Exhibition view at Breaking Forecast: 8 Key Figures of China's New Generation Artists, UCCA, Beijing, China

COURTESY ARTIST AND VITAMIN CREATIVE SPACE, GUANGZHOU, CHINA

humanitarian causes often relate the word *electronic* to wasteful extravagance, not desirable abundance. They cite the fifty million metric tons of unwanted computers, entertainment devices, mobile phones, television sets, refrigerators, iPods, cell phones, media players, web browsers, GPSs, Bluetooths, and so forth that are generated worldwide every year[3] and known collectively as e-waste. It is difficult to identify a management option that would satisfy environmentalists. Recycling is problematic because reclaiming valuable components is complicated and costly. Up to sixty different elements can be found in a single electronic device. Some of these elements are benign and some are hazardous; some are efficient to recycle and some are not; some are rare and others are abundant. The problem of separating and sorting is aggravated by the trend toward miniaturization that makes disassembly difficult. It is far easier to toss the gadgets into the trash. Indeed, 80 to 85 percent of electronic trash goes directly into landfills and incinerators, where it can leach into water, soils, and the atmosphere, posing significant risks to environmental and human health.[4] Dangers involved in salvaging obsolete electronics include carcinogens and neurotoxins released into the air when equipment is burned to melt plastics and metals that are low in value. Furthermore, men, women, and children who are employed to extract metals, toners, and plastics from electronic waste or repair the devices are in constant contact with mercury, lead, cadmium, PVCs, brominated flame retardants, and hexavalent chromium. New manufacture of electronic gadgets is not a reasonable solution either. Producing a single computer and a single monitor, for example, consumes 530 pounds of fossil fuels, 48 pounds of chemicals, and 1.5 tons of water.[5]

Constellation evokes the sublime to visualize such disheartening statistics. The installation exposes our culture's joyride with gizmos and gadgets, not stars and planets. Likewise, the pitiful and puny soaps in *Who Has Stolen Our Bodies?* still embody the appeals that have been engineered into them. These colors, scents, and textures are irrelevant to their function but essential to their marketability. The fact that both works are so appealing testifies to the challenge of extending the lives of products, eliminating their frills, and reducing consumption.

Chu is known for shutting down his studio for periods of time. In 1999, for example, his disappearance from the art scene was so abrupt that rumors circulated about his untimely death. In actuality, he had joined the labor force in the Pearl River Delta producing outsourced goods. For two years Chu immersed himself in the drudgery of ordinary employment and dormitory living. When he reemerged, he brought with him the deep, if ironic, appreciation for the common material ingredients of contemporary life. Another such occasion occurred in Beijing in 2007 just after he had begun to enjoy critical acclaim. Chu stopped making work, apparently because he felt oppressed by the cultural hype, spectacle, and extravagance spurred by China's Olympic game festivities. These life experiences manifest the refined elegance of Chu's oppositional stance. He is never confrontational. He is always ingratiating.

NOTES

1 Chu Yun, "Portikus," from interview with curator Hu Fang (October 16–November 15, 2009). http://www.e-flux.com/shows/view/7284.

2 "Industrial Strength Design: How Brooks Stevens Shaped Your World," *Milwaukee Art Museum Biography*. Retrieved 2008-03-08.

3 United Nations Environment Programme (UNEP), "Basel Conference Addresses Electronic Wastes Challenge." (November 27, 2006). http://www.unep.org/Documents.Multilingual/Default.asp?DocumentID=485&ArticleID=5431&l=en.

4 "Statistics on the Management of Used and End-of-Life Electronics," US Environmental Protection Agency. http://www.epa.gov/epawaste/conserve/materials/ecycling/manage.htm.

5 Facts and Figures. http://www.reciclemos.net/docs/pdf%20ingles/Facts%20and%20figures.pdf.

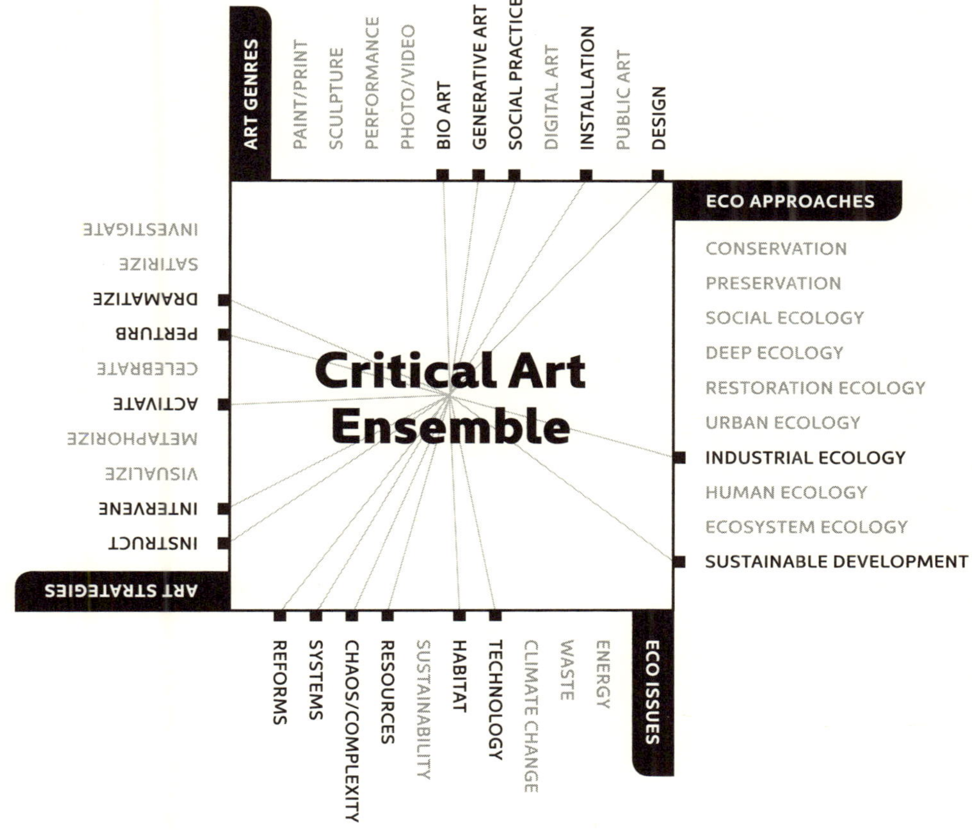

Contestational Biology

Group founded 1987, Tallahassee, Florida

IT WASN'T UNTIL THE END OF THE EXHIBITION titled *Molecular Invasion* (2002) that visitors to the Corcoran Gallery of Art in Washington, DC, discovered whether Critical Art Ensemble's bio art experiment would be a success. Even the artists did not know until then. Prior to the climactic spraying of corn, soy, and canola plants, the exhibition consisted of seedlings maturing under grow lights in neatly arranged, stylishly designed planters. Accompanying material informed visitors that some of the crops were genetically modified and that a control group was not genetically manipulated. The artists intended to sabotage the protections provided by the genetic modifications. Thus, a few days before the closing of the exhibition,

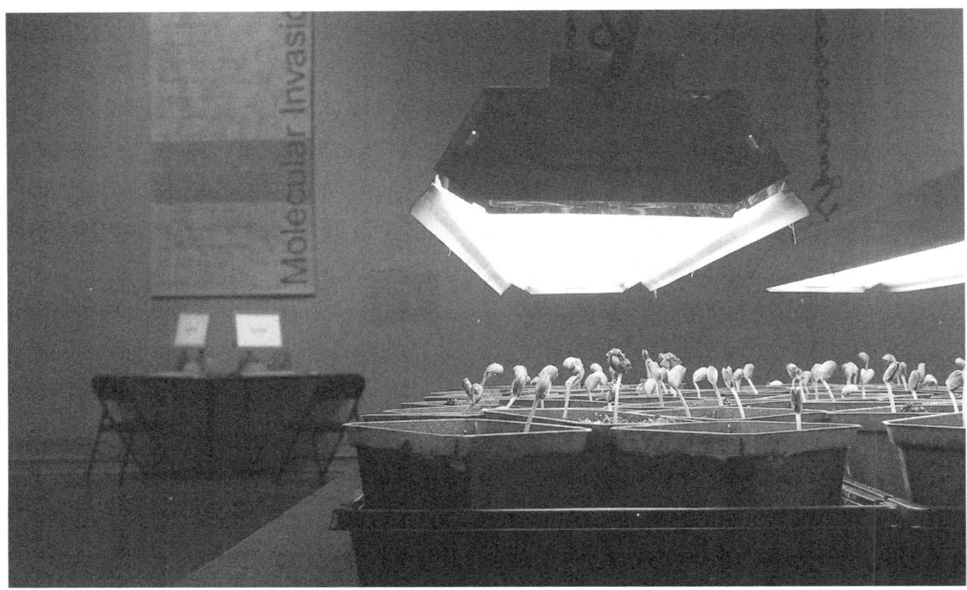

Critical Art Ensemble | With Beatriz da Costa, Claire Pentecost, and students from the Corcoran School of Art | Molecular Invasion | 2002 Installation view at the Corcoran, Washington, DC | Participatory science-theater work | Genetically modified canola, corn, and soy plants, co-enzyme from vitamin B-6, Roundup, planters, grow lights | Dimensions: variable

PHOTO: CRITICAL ART ENSEMBLE / COURTESY CRITICAL ART ENSEMBLE

the members of this renowned collective conducted a carefully planned intervention by spraying both groups of plants with the herbicide Roundup.

Roundup is a powerful herbicide manufactured by Monsanto that inhibits a specific enzyme that plants require to grow. After a single treatment, unwelcome plants are guaranteed to die in a few days. But there is one exception. Monsanto manufactures it. These "Roundup Ready" crops are genetically modified to produce a resistant enzyme that withstands Roundup's lethal effect. Thus Roundup Ready crops survive while all competing weeds surrounding them are decimated.

Critical Art Ensemble (CAE)[1] is a collective of tactical media practitioners with various specializations including computer graphics, web design, film/video, photography, text art, book art, and performance. The group in 2002 consisted of Steve Kurtz, Steve Barnes, Hope Kurtz, and Beverley Schlee. To produce *Molecular Invasion*, they collaborated with designer/photographer Melissa Mechler, artist Claire Pentecost, scientist Mustafa Unlu, artist Beatriz da Costa, and students from the Corcoran's bachelor of fine arts program to test whether it was possible to reverse the effects of the genetic modifications of canola, corn, and soy seeds that were being aggressively marketed worldwide.

The artists began by transforming the museum into a nursery, and the nursery into a rebel laboratory. GMO and natural seedlings were allowed to grow normally. Near the end of the exhibition, when the plants were fully grown, a nontoxic chemical disrupter, PLP,[2] was applied to the GMO crops. The action was aimed at eradicating the protection against the herbicide that had been methodically engineered into their biology. A few days later, CAE tested whether this defense worked by spraying all the plants with Roundup. Then everyone waited. Would the GMO plants survive, or would they succumb to the herbicide despite

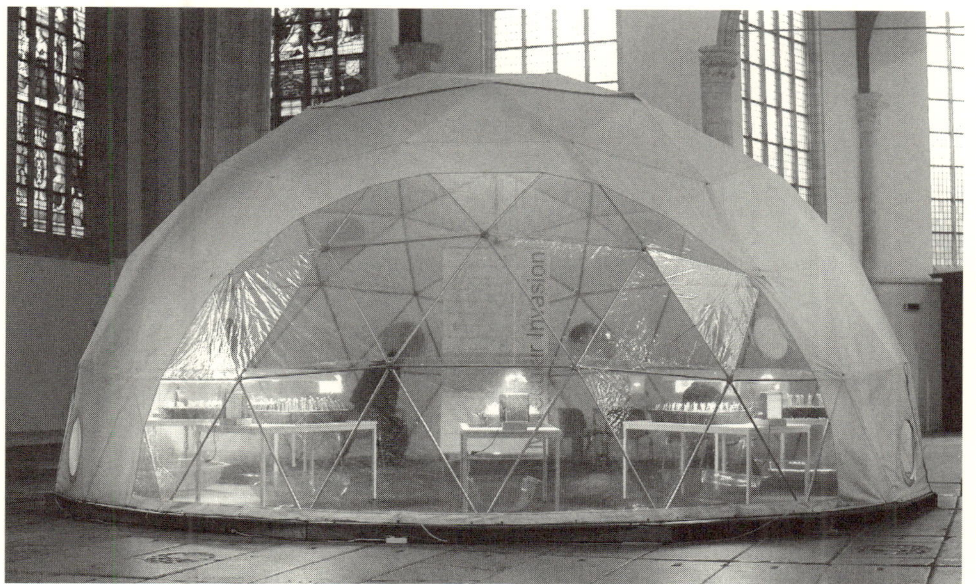

Critical Art Ensemble | With Beatriz da Costa and Claire Pentecost | Molecular Invasion | 2002
World Information Organization installation in Amsterdam (detail) | Dimensions: variable
PHOTO: CRITICAL ART ENSEMBLE / COURTESY CRITICAL ART ENSEMBLE

their high-tech protections? The rogue molecular biology experiment was declared a great success when all the plants died, even those that were genetically fortified! Besides demonstrating that genetic manipulations can be overcome, it proved that a few indignant artists are capable of undermining the calculated manipulations of a corporate giant.

When CAE explains that its goal is "to discover and create products for resource management that are harmonious with the ecosystems in which they function,"[3] it may seem they are referring to an art practice that is as benign as gardening. However, CAE prefers the term contestational biology to emphasize the group's subversive intention—undermining the corporate underpinnings of genetic manipulations that challenge such harmonious management. Steven Kurtz, one of the group's founding members, clarifies the target of their dissident actions when he comments, "We do protest the system. . . . We do not categorically condemn genetic modification."[4] The system CAE protests is pancapitalist policy, which "fuels, strengthens, and expands the profit machine"[5] by attempting to consolidate and control the world's food supply. Traditional methods of contestation seemed too puny to accomplish this imposing multinational corporate challenge. The artists asked themselves, "How can the new molecular/biochemical front be directly engaged as a means to disrupt profits? This is an area that is completely undertheorized, and is the subject matter of contestational biology."[6]

In an interview, Kurtz explained that GM seeds for Roundup Ready crops are a product of advanced science research coalescing with strong profit motives. The single corporate entity that serves to benefit from their production is responsible for testing them. As a result, claims made by the corporation and reinforced by its media agents are not responsibly critiqued before they are marketed. The artists trace this problem to the fact that GMO corporations capitalize on the authority that science wields to promote their self-serving agendas. "Science has slowly but surely become a key myth maker within society, thus defining for the general population the structure and dynamics of the cosmos and the origins and makings of life, or, in other words, defining nature itself."[7]

CAE acknowledges that the short-run benefits of GMOs enable farmers to easily eliminate weeds without harming their crops. Such efficiencies translate into lower consumer prices. However, CAE also produced a book, *Food for a Hungry World*,[8] to satirize corporate promises about efficiency. To display the ludicrous aspects of such economies, the group published recipes comparing "easy recombinant dishes created with the new GE foods"[9] with those made from organic ingredients. One recipe is titled "Antibiotic Bananas with Hershey's Chocolate Syrup." The genetically engineered cost is $ .81. The organic cost is $2.09. Kurtz explains that their intention was to include "the most sickening recipes and illustrations thereof we could come up with. That food is horrible. However, we were also making fun of foodie culture that is so out of touch with what working people are facing in regard to food options. In this area of work, CAE liked neither the greens nor the corporatists."[10]

Still, the artists reserve the majority of their ire for the worrisome unknowns associated with genetically altered foods. "No long-term studies have been done on new types of crops and creatures, and could not be, because the technology is too new. One would hope that the producers of such products would want to err on the side of caution and wait a few decades before releasing genetically modified organisms so that proper long-term testing could be done, but for the most part it is too late now."[11] In the absence of such studies, fears mount that genetically engineered foods—in combination with the intensive use of herbicides associated with cultivating GM crops—lower nutritional value, increase antibiotic resistance and allergic reactions, contaminate ordinary crops, harm wildlife, and promote the spread of super weeds and pesticide-resistant insects. Because CAE is not content to denounce this "capital-driven technocracy,"[12] it mounts two counteroffensives. On the one hand, it attempts to impose "inertia" upon industries that rush products to market. On the other, it conducts public experiments on these products to strip the industry of its immunity from democratic review.

Like most citizen uprisings, CAE's opposition depends upon cunning, not might. The collective rejects flagrant acts of sabotage like burning test sites for new product lines of GMOs. Such actions would brand the artists as criminals and earn the corporations sympathy as victims of attack. They also discarded the notion of destroying genetically modified organisms. Because they are claimed by corporations as private property, and since capitalism values property so highly, "one can only expect the strongest types of denunciation and response to its destruction."[13] In addition, farmers and workers involved in the GMO industry were exempted from their dissident operations: "From the corporate perspective, workers are expendable and there is a large enough reserve labor army to fill the ranks, so this would have no effect other than making a working family miserable."[14]

In the end, CAE's strategy involves deploying "fuzzy biological sabotage." CAE's *sabotage* refers to nonaggressive actions that embolden the public to challenge corporate and scientific authorities. For *Molecular Invasion*, they simply demystified the scientific process. *Fuzzy* refers to choosing contexts where regulations are blurred and therefore less risky. While these tactical efforts are designed to encourage amateurs to resist centers of power, they are guided by three military attack principles:[15]

Focus the attack on the weakest link in the system. CAE discovered a crack in the defense of corporate/science mergers. Steve Kurtz explains, "Whenever a product is patented, including GMOs, all the information surrounding it is placed in the public domain. Scientists and the public can take that information and investigate it, replicate experiments, and publish their results."[16]

Form accurate targeting systems to avoid collateral damage. CAE might have expected full-scale corporate retaliation when they violated Monsanto's license restriction on the GM products. Indeed, Monsanto did send its lawyers to the exhibition, who took pictures and waved cease-and-desist letters. But, Kurtz explains, "It was a false show, just a bluff. Were they going to sue us for license violation for using ten dollars' worth of seeds? Also, the museum that hosted the show would need to be sued. Monsanto's public relations image is not good. We knew they would want to avoid the nightmare publicity if they sued a venerable art institution that was part of the Smithsonian. That is one reason we launched the project at the Corcoran. It provided an umbrella of legitimacy. Just try to get us now! It was like having superman protecting you."[17] Then Kurtz added wistfully, "Actually, we would have been interested to see what would happen if we went to court."[18]

Use the minimum amount of force necessary to accomplish an objective. By reading a published article, CAE discovered that affecting GMO modifications did not require technically advanced genetic manipulation on a molecular level, or expensive laboratory equipment, or advanced degrees in science. The article described a biochemical intervention on a cellular level that disrupts the herbicide inhibitor in the gene of the modified Monsanto plant. It was surprisingly easy to acquire the chemical that deactivated the advanced genetic protection. It was vitamin B-6, which can be purchased at any vitamin store. Thus, the process was simple enough and safe enough for artists to carry out in a gallery setting before a large public of witnesses.

Mininum force also enabled the artists to acquire the patented seeds for their art work. They did not convince proprietors of seed stores in the Midwest to violate their contract with Monsanto and sell this licensed product to unlicensed artists. Kurtz reports that the shopkeepers refused their request but suggested an alternative. "They whispered that bags break and we might find some spilled seeds in the bottom of their trash bins."[19]

In sum, Kurtz explains the radical aspects of CAE's intervention by stating, "What was innovative was not the chemical process. The way we used it was innovative. We made the plant's strength its weakness. We used the process for political reasons. There was no bio hacking in 2002 when we did this piece. Applying amateur garage research to art in the public sphere was innovative at the time. . . . We wanted to start huge networks of politicized hackers in biology, not just electronics."[20]

As this work demonstrates, CAE's practice has two distinct prongs. The public receives training to become GMO industry watchdogs capable of undermining the corporations' immunity from scrutiny. Besides simple GMO experiments conducted in gallery settings in real time and without known outcomes, CAE deploys "tactical media kits" that consist of books that are disseminated free on the group's website, critical writing, and performance, film/video, and photography. These accessible models of risk assessment enable the public to evaluate the risks of GM organisms, as well as the promises of GM producers. CAE terms this kind of art "participatory science-theater work."[21] Kurtz notes, "Half our project is building our relationship with the audience."[22]

Corporations, on the other hand, are targets of insubordinate actions designed to "stir up internal institutional paranoia, or they can be used to divert attention toward useless activities."[23] Kurtz admits, "We always thought of this work as a demonstration. There is no way artists can interrupt the giant colossus of Monsanto. The only way for that to happen is if large networks form. We did foment public attention."[24]

Kurtz is pensive about the years 1997–2004 when CAE worked in biotechnology. "*Molecular Invasion* will be one of those touchstone pieces when it comes to bio hacking for political purposes. It was prophetic. No one listened to us at the time. Now . . . biotechnology in food production is big news. Local and federal governments are involved. When stuff gets mainstreamed, it doesn't need us. We are cultural researchers—we look into things that people aren't paying attention to. Now this cause is working on its own volition. We have made ourselves obsolete. We worked ourselves out of a job."[25]

This chapter concludes with a warning from Kurtz: "Even when you don't do anything illegal, if you are going to be a provocateur, you had better expect trouble."[26] This sentiment ceased being hypothetical on May 11, 2004, following the sudden death of Kurtz's wife of congestive heart failure. When the police were called to investigate, they discovered some suspicious biological material that was, in actuality, harmless bacteria cultures Kurtz was planning to use for a project about the public health impact of germ warfare. The FBI was summoned. It promptly invoked the US Patriot Act and seized Kurtz's car, equipment, computer hard drive, books, writings, correspondence, art projects, even his cat and his wife's body. Kurtz was arrested on suspicion of bioterrorism. The charge shifted from bioterrorism to mail and wire fraud after the sequestered materials proved to be harmless. The ordeal lasted four years. In the end he was vindicated. This is a somber confirmation of the group's mission—to reveal and challenge the authoritarian underpinnings of pancapitalism.

NOTES

1 Critical Art Ensemble was founded by Steve Kurtz, Steve Barnes, and Dorian Burr in 1987. Other members have included Hope Kurtz (Kurtz's late wife), Claudia Bucher, George Barker, Ricardo Dominguez, and Bev Schlee.
2 Vitamin B-6 exists in different forms. One of those forms is pyridoxal 5'-phosphate (PLP). It serves as a cofactor in many enzyme reactions.
3 "Where Is Critical Art Ensemble," Artnet Questionnaire, Artnet.com (March 21, 2007). http://www.artnet.com/magazineus/features/quest/quest3-20-07_detail.asp?picnum=4.
4 Steve Kurtz correspondence with the author, July 8, 2011.
5 Critical Art Ensemble, *The Molecular Invasion*, 7. http://www.critical-art.net/books/molecular/intro.pdf.
6 Ibid, 10.
7 Ibid, 40.
8 Critical Art Ensemble, *Betty Crocker 3000 Presents Food for a Hungry World* (Phoenix, AZ: Critical Art Ensemble, 2008–2009).
9 Critical Art Ensemble, *The Molecular Invasion*. http://www.critical-art.net/books/molecular/intro.pdf.
10 Steve Kurtz correspondence with the author, July 8, 2011.
11 Critical Art Ensemble, "Fuzzy Biological Sabotage." http://www.critical-art.net/Molecular Invasion.html.
12 Ibid.
13 Ibid.
14 Ibid.
15 Ibid.
16 Steve Kurtz interview with the author, June 3, 2011.
17 Ibid.
18 Ibid.
19 Ibid.
20 Ibid.
21 Critical Art Ensemble, "Fuzzy Biological Sabotage." http://www.critical-art.net/Molecular Invasion.html.
22 Steve Kurtz interview with the author, June 3, 2011.
23 Critical Art Ensemble, "Fuzzy Biological Sabotage." http://www.critical-art.net/Molecular Invasion.html.
24 Steve Kurtz interview with the author, June 3, 2011.
25 Ibid.
26 Ibid.

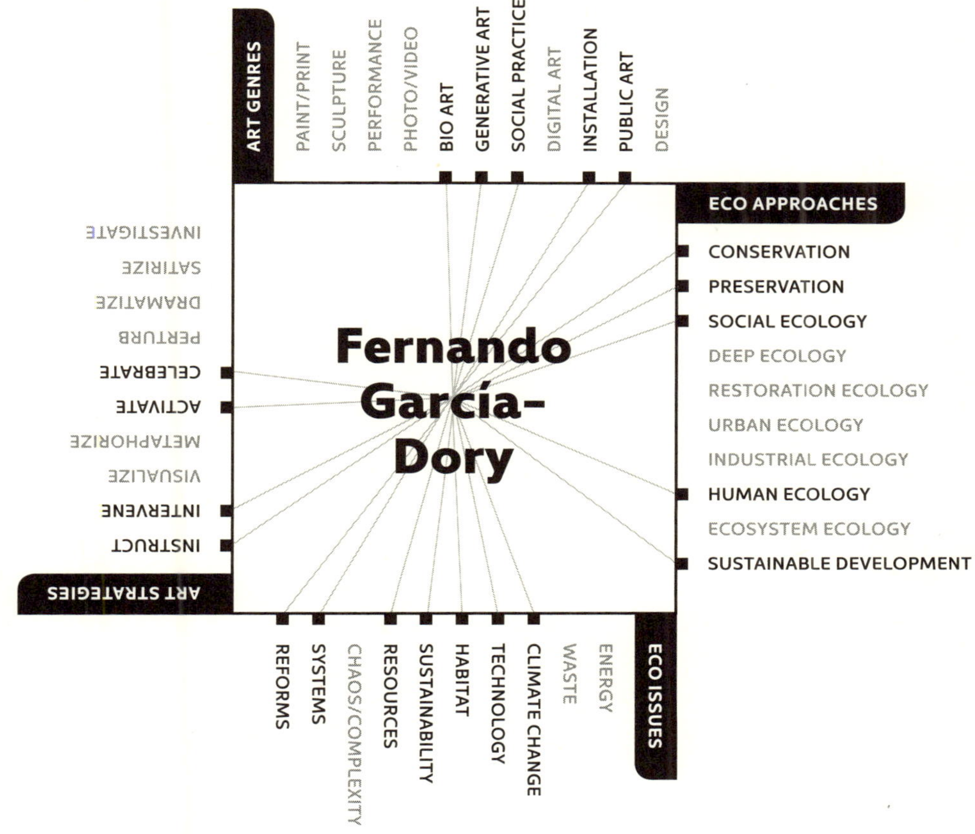

Neo-Pastoralism

Born 1978, Madrid, Spain

THE WORD *PASTORALISM* conjures enchanting images of shepherds quietly tending herds of livestock within majestic mountain terrains under expansive blue skies. The term is associated with pleasures that have become rare in recent times—innocence, tranquility, and rustic charm. An excerpt from Christopher Marlowe's poem "The Passionate Shepherd to His Love" (1599) offers a classic evocation of the idyllic life of the shepherd living in harmony with nature:

> Come live with me and be my Love,
> And we will all the pleasures prove

That hills and valleys, dale and field,
And all the craggy mountains yield.
There will we sit upon the rocks
And see the shepherds feed their flocks,
By shallow rivers, to whose falls
Melodious birds sing madrigals.[1]

Pastoral settings have long served as antidotes to stressful environments. They have inspired music, poetry, and painting dating back to Hellenistic Greece. The artist Fernando García-Dory notes that the clamor of contemporary urban environments and the harsh and hurried lifestyles of their residents are augmenting the appeal of pastoralism. As allure escalates, actual pastoralists are declining. In Spain, for example, the active population working in agriculture has plummeted. In 1960, 42 percent of the population was engaged in agricultural work; by 2007, the percentage fell to just 6.5 percent. In the past fifteen years, over a million peasants abandoned the countryside and relocated in the cities. Of those who remained, many shifted from traditional subsistence agriculture to market-driven farming.[2] This scenario is particularly problematic for shepherds. Common lands that were available to them for grazing for six thousand years are being claimed for national parks.[3] Furthermore, laws have been passed that prevent the shepherds from managing the area's natural resources, such as regenerating pasture grasses with controlled burns, as they have done successfully for millennia.

These disturbing statistics are masked by charades that transform surviving pastoral regions into tourist attractions. García-Dory observes wryly, "The rural tends to be artificially maintained or reproduced as the picturesque, virtuous primal state for the urban-dweller's weekend retreat."[4] Outrageous tactics are being considered to overcome the shortage of actual pastoral communities in northern Spain, where García-Dory's family farm is located. One city council in the Catalonian Pyrenees actually planned to contract actors to perform rural activities like mowing the hay, in order to offer tourists a more animated experience of rural landscapes. In fact, the craving for the countryside is so popular that national park guards now patrol the areas where shepherds once roamed freely. Their uniformed presence is needed to maintain order among the two million tourists who visit the region every year. Ironically, these visitors who crave contact with artisans crafting local resources regularly consume industrial products in urban settings that compete with the shepherds' products. García-Dory describes this pseudopastoral experience observing that they are "driven to a building with an artificial forest and cardboard goats."[5]

García-Dory is updating the long tradition of pastoral art by dedicating his practice to salvaging and reinvigorating the vestiges of pastoral lifestyle in northern Spain. His dual studies in fine art and rural sociology prepared him for a career as a "neo-pastoralist." The *neo* demonstrates that his motive has little to do with nostalgia or reprieves for urban clamor. Instead, García-Dory approaches waning pastoralism as an ecologist approaches an endangered species, even applying strategies devised by ecologists to prevent extinction: help the species propagate, bolster defenses of the threatened entity, and create a hospitable habitat to enable the entity to prosper.

Propagation García-Dory attempts to propagate pastoralists through the establishment of a Shepherds School, which officially commenced in 2007. The staff for the school consists of seven shepherds, four shepherd-teachers, and one artist. The student body is limited to

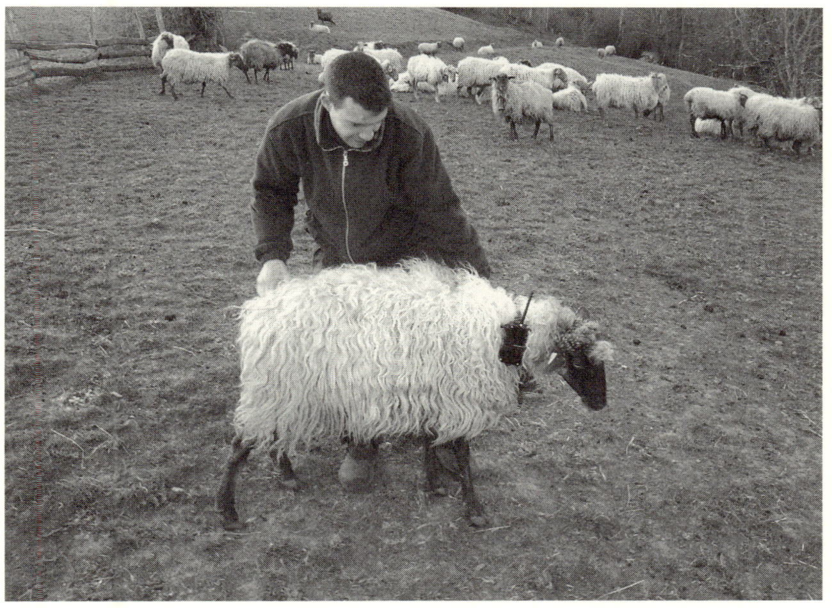

Fernando García-Dory | In collaboration with Stewart Breck, Research Wildlife Biologist—National Wildlife Research Center Yellowstone / Eugenio Sillero ISOM & Dpto. Ingeniería Electrónica—E.T.S.I. de Telecomunicación / Dorian Moore / National Park of Picos de Europa / Laboral Centro de Arte / Libellium | Bionic Sheep | 2006–ongoing

COURTESY FERNANDO GARCÍA-DORY

four pupils at a time. The application procedure involves a February deadline. Prospective students are interviewed and tested over the course of a weekend. The shepherds choose who to accept. Students attend the school free of charge and have even received stipends of approximately $750 per month, provided through a grant from the Spanish national parks service. The campus facilities consist of four cheese-making ateliers and three shepherds' huts that have been rebuilt from ancient ruins. These facilities are available for the collective use of all shepherds, free of charge, to help preserve the productive capacity of the mountain pastures and their pastoral lifestyles.

The contrived romanticism and Disneyfication of the countryside is purged from the school's curriculum. Instead of leisurely communion with rocks, sky, animals, and fire, each student lives with one shepherd for five months. The rigorous curriculum during the first month focuses on the study of mountain ecology, European farming policies, cheese-making techniques, veterinary skills, animal management and physiology, and shepherding culture. Then the students accompany their mentors into the mountains where they remain throughout the summer and autumn months. There they learn how to shear, slaughter, milk, breed, and skin animals. They also rebuild mountain huts and make cheese. All the while they study the topography of the region so that they become so familiar with its contours and conditions that they can construct mental maps detailing the availability of water, the abundance of forage, and the accessibility of pathways for their flocks at different times of the year and in different weather conditions. García-Dory demonstrates he is a neo-pastoralist with an ecological perspective when he uses contemporary terminology to describe the unstructured oral transmission of this traditional knowledge as "variables of time, space and movement in non-linear system dynamics."[6] Through such unsentimental moves, the Shepherds School becomes a bold experiment in art as social ecology with a pragmatic mission.

The course ends in September with a graduation ceremony. García-Dory comments that in addition to a tired body and rough hands, graduates earn the opportunity to commit to a pastoral lifestyle. To García-Dory, this moment means "facing the ideal, the utopia."[7] Those who choose to remain continue to receive advice and support from the shepherd community. Despite these advantages, few of the one hundred graduates are pursuing shepherding.

Bolster defenses García-Dory fortifies the shepherds' ability to adapt to a changed environment by encouraging the students who receive instruction via traditional oral transmissions to teach the shepherds to use advanced communication technologies. García-Dory describes this mutual mentoring as "communication from the young person—who comes from the city, from the university, from a techno party or an art school—to the shepherd. And communication from the shepherd to the hopeful, yearning, sometimes wishful pupil."[8]

Another defensive measure against an age-old vulnerability is addressed in an art project entitled *Bionic Sheep* (2006 and ongoing). In this case García-Dory is collaborating with an electronics engineer, wildlife biologists, shepherds, representatives of the national park, and others to develop a high-tech replacement for the bell that, for millennia, has been hung around the necks of sheep to ward off wolves and other predators but does not eliminate the problem. The portable system being designed by these experts is fueled by a small solar plate and emits ultrasound waves in a frequency that repels wolves and coyotes but is inaudible to sheep and shepherds. The multipurpose device is also equipped with a GPS to monitor the location of large flocks in steep mountain passes. The device emits short message service (SMS) to the shepherd's personal digital assistant (PDA). Several prototypes of *Bionic Sheep* have been developed. Once the system is perfected, García-Dory plans to offer it, without license restrictions, so that it can be reproduced freely to maximize its defensive benefits.

Create hospitable habitats García-Dory's initiative to create an environment conducive to the pastoral lifestyle laid the groundwork for protective legislation. *The PASTOR (Shepherd) Project* (2004) established an alliance among dispersed shepherds so that their combined voices magnified their protest. García-Dory assembled thirty shepherds from the northern Spanish Pyrenees to share their grievances and compose a manifesto. The manifesto protested their lack of access to education, inadequate health care, and instances when indigenous nomadic communities were excluded from decisions affecting the marketing of their products and the control of their lands. While the goal was preservation of the shepherding culture and the Picos de Europa mountain range, nostalgia was banished from its agenda. Instead of attempting to preserve traditional credos, it acknowledged that securing the continuity of pastoral ways depended upon gaining access to new technologies that could improve shepherds' living standards and augment their productivity.

Since public opinion is essential to constructing a supportive habitat, García-Dory presented the shepherds' cause to audiences. He used the commission provided by the LABoral, an art center in Gijon, Spain, to bring the shepherds themselves into the exhibition space. *Museum's Pastoral: A Meeting of the Federation of Shepherds* (2009) consisted of "installing" members of the Spanish Shepherds Federation (FEP) in the museum. The shepherds "exhibited" their concerns by conducting discussions in front of visitors whose

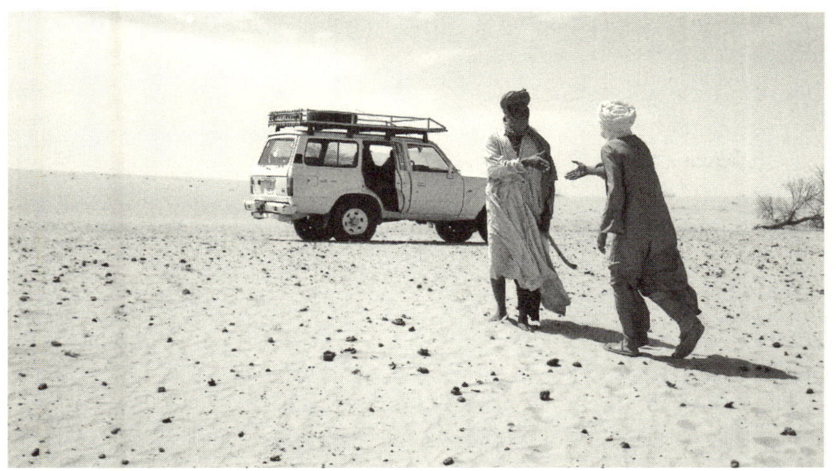

Fernando García-Dory | World Gathering of Nomadic Peoples | 2007 Two hundred representatives of nomadic communities from all over the world | Segovia, Spain

COURTESY FERNANDO GARCÍA-DORY

romanticized ideas about pastoralism vanished because their art experience consisted of observing shepherds describing the actualities of their existence. Besides stimulating public concern, another positive outcome of this art strategy occurred when the shepherds were granted a position on the advisory board of the Ministry of Farming."[9]

There was a conventional sculptural component to this project as well. García-Dory fabricated an open-sided wooden structure he named *The Assemblies Module* to "frame" the shepherds. It was built of wood reclaimed from an artwork by Rirkrit Tiravanija, who is renowned for fostering convivial social gatherings.

Rallying support for the document that was generated by the Spanish shepherds provided an opportunity to unite shepherds who live isolated lives in dispersed regions. García-Dory expanded this challenge by convincing dozens of Spanish shepherds to attend *World Gathering of Nomadic Peoples*, an assembly of nomadic and transhumant pastoralists that he instigated in Segovia, Spain, in 2007. During this event, over two hundred pastoral representatives from forty different countries in Africa, America, Asia, and Europe gathered to explore possible solutions to the problems faced by nomadic and transhumant herders around the world. García-Dory describes the incongruous way shepherds were shepherded to the convention site: "It was only by means of hypersonic flights, in mediated visas, internet instant messaging, and communication mainly in English—all the conditions that characterize the 'rich nomads' of today . . . that the 'poor nomads' could get together and challenge the Arcadian activity, or for them, the daily routine of the slow, silent, outdoor company of a grazing flock."[10]

Members of this global alliance were introduced to Spain's six-thousand-year-old pastoral culture when García-Dory took advantage of the fact that the conference dates coincided with the annual migration of flocks in Spain. He convinced the Spanish herders to cross the city with their animals as they made their way on the "royal shepherd road" to winter pastures. García-Dory explains that the action accomplished a double mission. As a defensive move, it deepened the roots of the pastoral lifestyle within a postmodern world: "Our first commitment as migratory pastoralists is to organize ourselves and to defend our rights. We must rely first on ourselves and our own rich capacities and traditions to ensure our own survival."[11] As an offensive tactic, it attempted to expand pastoral influence: "Our knowledge and experience must be valued and shared with the world."[12] The event highlighted the eight-hundred-year-old legislation in Spain that guarantees the movements of mobile herds across the entire country—over seventy-five thousand miles of roads traversing more than a million acres of open land. In this manner a tiny population living on the far periphery of mainstream culture gained its voice.

García-Dory's defense of pastoralism is not limited to his personal Spanish heritage. He is intent on demonstrating that its strategies are not historic throwbacks but viable means to reverse the perilous decline of the Earth's productive capacities. He describes his artistic interests as a "Re-Modern operation, or Retro-Modern, insofar as it means taking a step back to address present situations and future possibilities."[13] Shepherd lifestyles, some of the oldest in all human history, have changed little, but the needs of world populations have changed a great deal. García-Dory mentions peak oil, food scarcities, the desertification of the countryside, and climate change. Pastoralism could help resolve these contemporary issues:

- **Pragmatically,** migratory pastoralism offers an adaptive production strategy that could help ensure the economic survival of world populations because it is productive within marginal areas where intensive, technologically sophisticated means of cultivation are not possible. Thus pastoralism offers an environmentally sustainable model of agro-food production.
- **Socially,** pastoral food production demonstrates how sustainable and ethical codes of behavior naturally emerge from practical adaptations to specific environmental conditions.
- **Psychologically,** shepherding is an age-old occupation that satisfies a desire to live in tune with the seasons, in partnership with animals, in service to the planet.

In sum, García-Dory's collective environmental art projects align the accelerated pace of the communications in our technosphere with the leisurely wandering of the shepherd through a pasture with his flock. In this manner his art celebrates a human lifestyle option that is ultimately unified with its nonhuman environment. García-Dory explains that it "transcends the limits of established perceptions and expands the present to re-invent the future."[14] It may be too soon to determine whether these projects are reinventing any future, but García-Dory takes some credit when he reports that Spain's ministries of the environment and culture recently launched a program in support of rural life.[15] Perhaps these bureaucrats are adopting this artist's poetic vision of the future: "The last citizens might live in the mountains, might care for sheep, know the flowers, recognize the birdsong, understand the path and tribulations of the beasts."[16]

NOTES

1 Christopher Marlowe, "Passionate Shepherd to His Love" (1599), the complete poem. http://www.bartleby.com/106/5.html.

2 Iberia Nature by Nick Lloyd. http://www.iberianature.com/directory/farming-in-spain/.

3 "WAMIP: World Alliance of Mobile Indigenous Peoples." http://www.wamip.org/index.php?option=com_content&view=article&id=56%3

A-cenesta-in-brief&catid=2&Itemid=94&lang=en.

4 Fernando García-Dory, "Arts and Agroecology, or How Can Culture and Creativity Be Tools to Preserve A Living Rural World." Unpublished essay.

5 Fernando García-Dory, "A Shepherds School." http://fernandogarciadory.com/index.php?/projects/a-microkingdom-of-utopia-shepherds-school/.

6 Fernando García-Dory, "Razing Arcadia and Shepherding amongst the Ruins." Unpublished essay.

7 Fernando García-Dory, "A Shepherds School." http://fernandogarciadory.com/index.php?/projects/a-microkingdom-of-utopia-shepherds-school/.

8 Fernando García-Dory, "Razing Arcadia and Shepherding amongst the Ruins." Unpublished essay.

9 Beneath the Bureaucracy, the Beach: A Conversation between Fernando García-Dory and Chris Fite-Wassilak. http://www.growgnome.com/Downloads/F2-p24-29.pdf.

10 Fernando García-Dory, "Razing Arcadia and Shepherding amongst the Ruins." Unpublished essay.

11 "WAMIP: World Alliance of Mobile Indigenous Peoples." http://www.wamip.org/index.php?option=com_content&view=article&id=56%3A-cenesta-in-brief&catid=2&Itemid=94&lang=en.

12 Ibid.

13 Fernando García-Dory, "Razing Arcadia and Shepherding amongst the Ruins." Unpublished essay.

14 Fernando García-Dory, "Arts and Agroecology, or How Can Culture and Creativity Be Tools to Preserve a Living Rural World." Unpublished essay.

15 Alexander McSpadden, "The Urban Orchard: On City Farming & Avant Garden," Urban Rural, *DAMn°* magazine no. 26. www.newschool.edu/WorkArea/DownloadAsset.aspx?id=58175.

16 Fernando García-Dory, "RAZING ARCADIA and Shepherding amongst the Ruins," Unpublished essay.

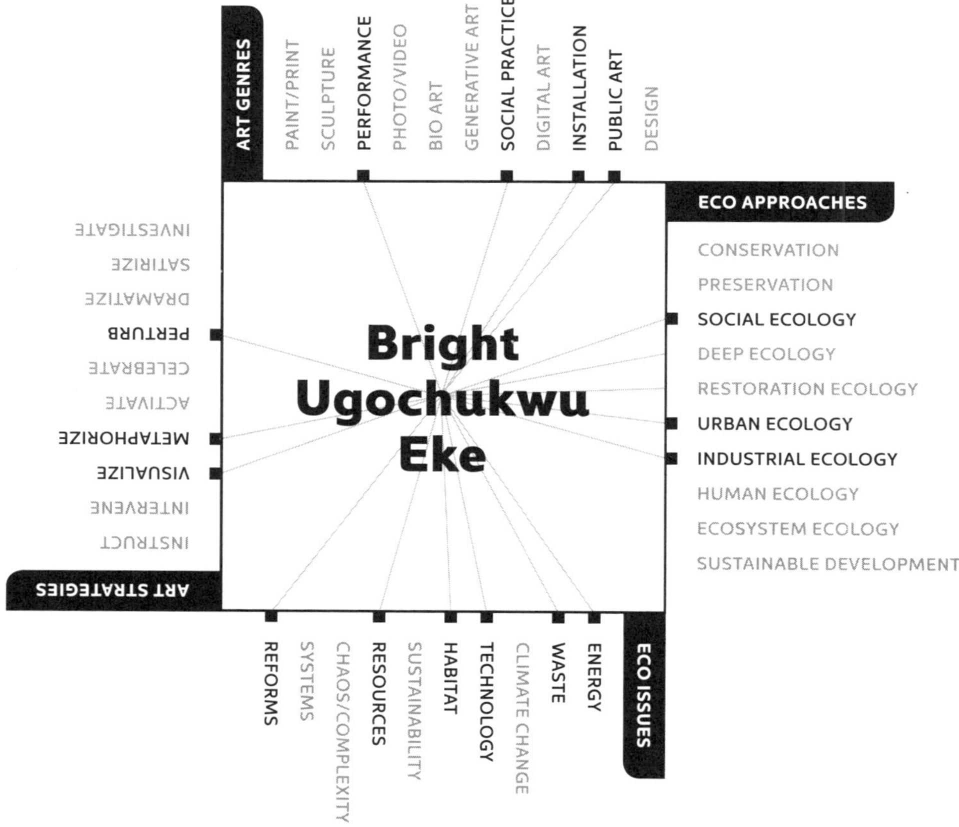

Acid Rain Check

Born 1976, Nsukka, Nigeria

WATER HAS A COMPLEX PERSONALITY. On the one hand, it is gregarious, continually absorbing, dissolving, and transporting other materials. On the other hand, it is meddlesome, actively seeping into the tiniest crevices and permeating the greatest expanses of the atmosphere. Most significantly, water is essential to life. However, in many regions of the globe, humans, plants, animals, insects, and bacteria with access to water are at risk. According to a UNESCO report, "Water-related diseases are among the most common causes of illness and death, affecting mainly the poor in developing countries. They kill more than 5 million people every year, more than ten times the number killed in wars. The diseases can be divided into four categories: water-borne, water-based, water-related, and water-scarce diseases."[1]

The Nigerian artist Bright Ugochukwu Eke laments the wholesale corruption of much of the planet's waters that is endangering life and sabotaging water's time-honored role as an embodiment of life, birth, and renewal. He asks, "How do we understand ourselves? I thought of a common language in nature. Water is a precious natural medium/resource with a universal language. It occupies the largest part of the earth, but has been disrespected, polluted, and contaminated with the advent of industrialization. It has been forced to lose its spirituality and purity."[2]

Eke sought a way to translate his lament into the language of art. He weighed the possibility of incorporating defiled water as his medium against representing it symbolically. He explains his dilemma: "All the actions of water pose problems to man and society. How can my expressive engagement deal with these problems? So in trying to come to terms with some of these questions, I have to think of what man has done to water, what water has done to man. That led me to question the relationship between man and the environment. I see water as a water medium with a water language. I thought it would be necessary to use water as a metaphor to articulate my ideas about man's relationships. I'm using a small part to talk about a whole phenomenon, of which one is acid rain."[3]

Eke narrowed the aperture of his perception and attended to a single location (his homeland, Nigeria), a single water hazard (acid rain), a single jeopardy (contaminated drinking water), a single culprit (petroleum refineries), and a single indicator of the problem (packaged potable water). In this manner he focused on one of water's distinguishing attributes—its ability to dissolve both bases and acids. As a "universal solvent," water does not discriminate between substances that are safe and those that are toxic. As a result, when water molecules in the air dissolve effluents from factories, waste treatment plants, automobiles, fertilizers, pesticides, and so forth, they fall back to earth as acid rain. Acid particulates in rainwater cause deforestation, taint soils, poison animals, cause respiratory and skin diseases, and destabilize river and lake ecosystems so that they can no longer support biological diversity. Most alarmingly, they poison drinking water. Potable water amounts to less than a percent of the Earth's total water store.[4] Contamination is causing these supplies to shrink at the same time that swelling populations and the industrialization of emerging economies is increasing demand.

A personal experience in Port Harcourt, a major industrial center in Nigeria, provides evidence of this regrettable state of affairs. Eke explains, "I was working outside in the rain. In two days I discovered skin irritation from toxic chemicals that go into the atmosphere from the industry. The emissions from the industry come down when it rains. I was not surprised, as Port Harcourt has a lot of industries, especially in manufacturing and the oil production. Then I came to think about not just myself but the people who live around the area. What about the aquatic life? What about the vegetation?"[5]

Eke had this experience in the delta of the Niger River in Nigeria, which is blessed with abundant freshwaters that support one of the highest concentrations of biodiversity on the planet. Yet these waters are now among the most contaminated, due in large measure to the fact that the region is also rich in oil. Since 1958, the petroleum industry has accounted for more than 90 percent of the nation's total export.[6] In Nigeria, productivity and contamination are linked because the country does not have a pollution control policy. There is nothing to prevent oil companies from spilling oil, which pollutes groundwater, and burning natural gas flares, which fills the atmosphere with pollutants. Acid rain is so severe that the longevity of the corrugated iron sheets used for roofing in most Nigerian villages has decreased from twenty years to five.[7]

Runoff from petroleum processing and petrochemical plants dumps tons of toxic wastes into nearby waters. This problem is compounded because few regions in Nigeria have pipe-borne water that is treated. As a result, even the very poor must purchase drinking water. Throughout Nigeria, thousands of water vendors push heavy water carts around the rutted streets to sell water at a cost to consumers of approximately $480 per year, a sum that is far greater than the cost of water in advanced countries.[8] But even these waters may not be safe. Some water vendors sell surface water from scummy rivulets that may contain sewage. Others drill boreholes that, in areas of mining and oil-drilling activities, often produce water that is contaminated.

In Nigeria, both surface water and borehole water is packaged in cheap plastic bags called sachets. A disconcerting paradox emerges from these containers because the manufacture and purchase of these bags is caused by the petroleum industry's negligence, but they are made of petroleum-based plastic! As a result, drinking packaged water intensifies the demand for petroleum. This increases petroleum production and exacerbates acid rain and groundwater contamination, generally worsening the conditions that require water to be packaged.

Eke identifies yet another aspect of this troubling scenario: "The problem is that people buy the water in plastic bags and after use they throw them away and they become litter in the environment. You find plastic bags all over the place."[9] Besides being unsightly, discarded plastic bags pose a serious peril to wildlife that is enduring because most plastic bags take centuries to biodegrade. Even when they photo-degrade, toxic particles linger, mix with the soil, and enter the food chain.

The proliferation of discarded sachet bags provided Eke with a compelling vehicle for conveying Nigeria's water crisis through art. *Shields* (2005/2006) is an installation constructed out of thousands of sachet water bags that Eke and assistants gathered from the littered streets. The bags appear in the installation in their soiled states so that viewers can discern their squalid history and the environmental perils they pose. The "shields" in the title indicate the need to protect the body against rain that is now associated with hazards instead of health. Eke explains, "Now we need something that stops the same water from going in. So I picked up some plastic water bags and made out of these raincoats and umbrellas."[10]

The rain gear was fabricated by tearing the sachet bags open and laying them flat so they could be ironed together along the edges. The large sheets of plastic were then cut to size and assembled into raincoats and umbrellas. The coats and umbrellas in *Shields* are long, hooded, unfitted, and unembellished. Stripped down in this manner, they announce to viewers that the reason for their existence is exclusively functional. They reference emergency survival gear, not fashion or commerce.

Eke conveyed that the toxic effects of rainwater impinge on the entire community by fabricating enough gear to completely fill the exhibition space—120 coats and 60 umbrellas. When the work premiered in Senegal, the raincoats were suspended from the ceiling and hung on the walls of the gallery, and the umbrellas were scattered on the floor. *Shields* has assumed different configurations in shows in Nigeria, Germany, Algiers, and Greece. Eke added a community component in Lagos by involving local residents in the labor-intensive process of fabricating the coats and umbrellas. He explains, "My idea is about the connec-

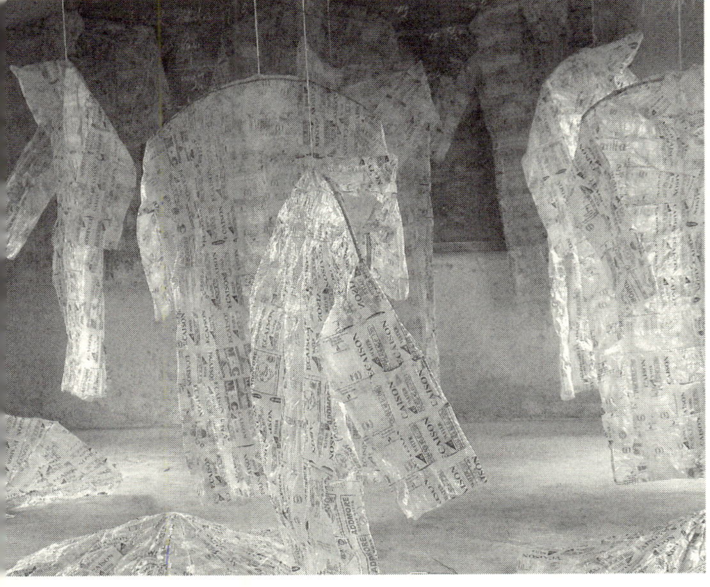

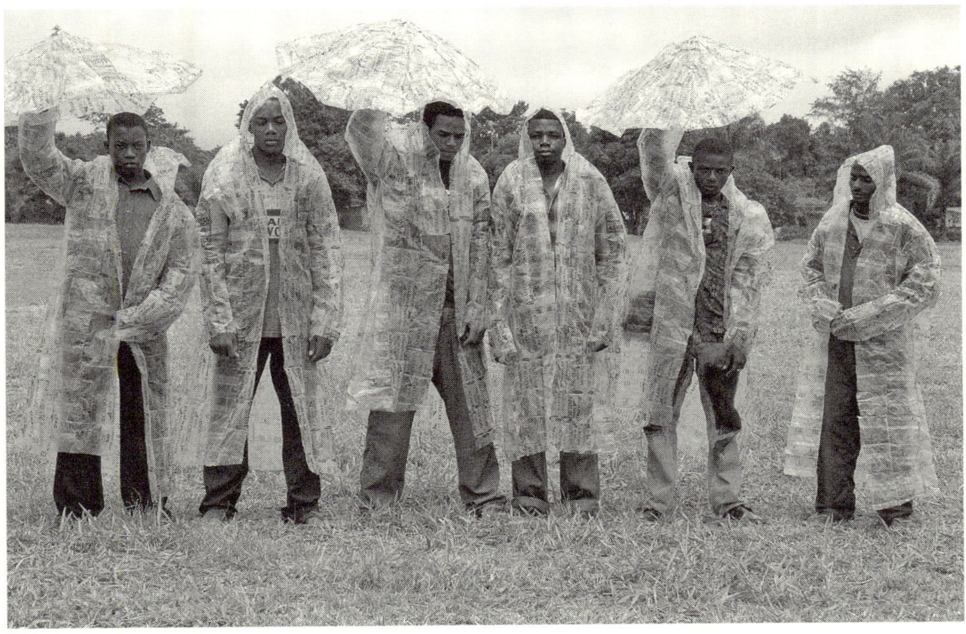

(left) Bright Ugochukwu Eke | Shields (installation) | 2005–2006 Thousands of used and discarded plastic water sachets | Dimensions: variable

PHOTO: BRIGHT UGOCHUKWU EKE / COURTESY BRIGHT UGOCHUKWU EKE

(below) Bright Ugochukwu Eke | Shields | 2005–2006 Parade/performance | Dimensions: variable

PHOTO: BRIGHT UGOCHUKWU EKE / COURTESY BRIGHT UGOCHUKWU EKE

tion with people, the societies/cultures, and the environment, how one affects the other. So I will not feel fulfilled even when I can do the work all alone."[11] Community members paraded through the streets wearing the coats and holding the umbrellas, a public demonstration of the blighted state of the source of life on Earth.

For Eke, packaged water, raincoats, umbrellas are all symbols of the barriers contemporary humans erect to protect themselves from their surroundings. He ponders such issues by commenting, "We have continued to produce and consume a lot of toxic and dangerous chemicals that cause the deterioration of the Earth: water and air pollution, deforestation, acid rain, endangered species etc. simply because we do not care. I just wonder why it is in the nature of man to be ruthless, and I am afraid he does not seem to be scared of this impending ecologic crisis."[12]

Eke poses three questions on his blog: "Who am i? Who is the Other? Where is the meeting point?"[13] His answers are implied by breaking two rules of written English. First, he uses the lower case to write the word *I*, which diminishes the significance of the individual. Then he capitalizes the word *other*, which augments the stature of other humans, other species, and other forms of matter. *I* has not always been capitalized in the English language. Significantly, capitalization emerged at the same time as capitalism—when Britain and the United States became world powers in the eighteenth and nineteenth centuries. Like the capital *I*, the economic construction of capitalism endorses private ownership, private investments, private property, and private profits. While the comforts and conveniences generated by these systems are enjoyed by many, Eke directs attention to the stresses and risks they also engender. He comments, "It is high time we changed our notion of 'Modernist individual freedom', which only meant freedom from community, freedom from obligation to the world, and freedom from relatedness."[14] Eke offers a poignant confirmation of the ethics of ecocentrism, the belief that suppressing the dominant self can avert many environmental calamities and social inequities.

Eke sums up his artistic enterprise by noting how water reestablishes bonds between individuals, cultural traditions, community, resources, and habitats: "Water is a universal medium. It's common to everybody, no matter who or where you are. Whatever I do with water is what every other person does with it in every part of the world. The most interesting part is that we are bound or connected by [water.]"[15]

NOTES

1 Benedict Okereke, "Nigerians' Forced Romance with Boreholes: Associated Hazards," nigeria villagesquare.com. http://www.nigeriavillage square.com/articles/benedict-okereke/nigerians -forced-romance-with-boreholes-and-their -waters-associated-hazards-starting-from.html.

2 Bright Ugochukwu Eke, "Artist's Statement 2" (October 29, 2008). http://u-bright.blogspot .com/search?updated-max=2008-12-08T08 %3A43%3A00-08%3A00&max-results=7.

3 "Bright Ugochukwu Eke: Presentation," posted on YouTube by ubrek2, November 15, 2009. http:// www.youtube.com/user/ubrek2.

4 Matt Murphy, "Global Water Cycle & Supplies." http://academic.evergreen.edu/g/grossmaz/ murphymw/

5 Bright Ugochukwu Eke telephone interview with the author, March 30, 2010.

6 Jonas E. Okeagu, et al., "Environmental and Social Impact of Petroleum and Natural Gas Exploitation in Nigeria," *Journal of Third World Studies*, Spring 2006, 3.

7 Ibid.

8 Andrew Walker, "The Water Vendors of Nigeria," BBC News (Abuja, Nigeria: February 5, 2009). http://news.bbc.co.uk/2/hi/science/ nature/7867202.stm.

9 "Bright Ugochukwu Eke: Presentation," posted by on YouTube by ubrek2, November 15, 2009. http://www.youtube.com/user/ubrek2.

10 Ibid.

11 "Fluid Connections, Bright Ugochukwu Eke: by Celeyce Matthews, delivered in a graduate seminar on modern African art at San Jose State University" (May 13, 2009). http://u-bright .blogspot.com/2009/05/bright-ugochukwu-eke -fluid-connections.html.

12 Bright Ugochukwu Eke, "Artist's Statement" (November 2, 2007). http://u-bright.blogspot .com/search?updated-max=2008-09-29T08 %3A55%3A00-07%3A00&max-results=7.

13 Ibid.

14 Bright Ugochukwu Eke, "Artist's Statement 2" (October 29, 2008). http://u-bright.blogspot .com/search?updated-max=2008-12-08T08% 3A43%3A00-08%3A00&max-results=7.

15 "Fluid Connections, Bright Ugochukwu Eke: by Celeyce Matthews, delivered in a graduate seminar on modern African art at San Jose State University" (May 13, 2009). http://u-bright.blog spot.com/2009/05/bright-ugochukwu-eke-fluid -connections.html.

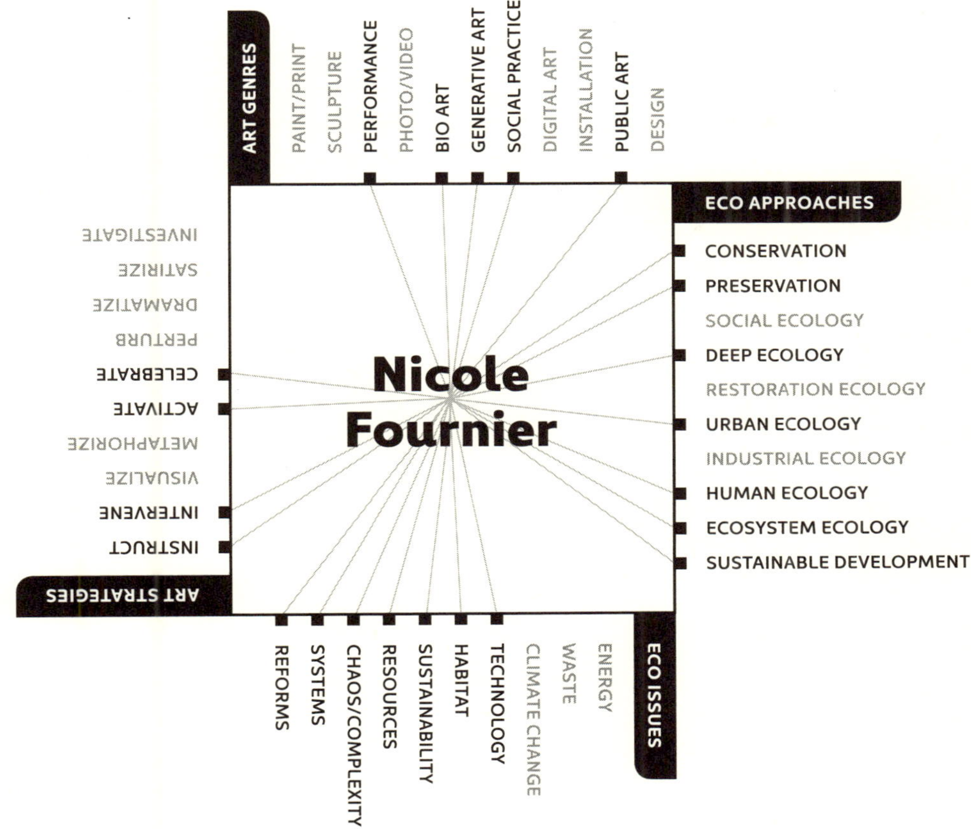

Poly Agriculture

Born 1966, Montreal, Canada

IF YOU WERE INVITED TO A PICNIC by Nicole Fournier as part of her *Live Dining Project*, she might suggest that you meet her in the parking lot behind the mall. This unlikely setting is where the preparation and the eating would transpire. It is also where your luncheon ingredients would be acquired. The menu might consist of edible weeds harvested from the cracks of the asphalt. "Live dining" describes Fournier's visual/conceptual/performance-based art practice that reformulates peoples' relationships to food by substituting the local participatory poly-agriculture system (polyculture) for the global corporate mono-agriculture system (monoculture) that dominates food production today. She applies this principle to cultivating, acquiring, preparing, and ingesting edibles.

Polyculture allows multiple crops to coexist in the same space at the same time. Monoculture, on the other hand, produces large expanses of a single crop, a scheme conceived for the expedience of turbines, tractors, and plows, not for the well-being of the species living in that habitat or its soils and waters. Fournier differentiates these cultivation strategies by referring to the former as "growing" and the latter as "production." Growing, she says, encourages an organism's natural assimilation of nutriments, the "aesthetics of care that seeks to foster life systems."[1] Production, on the other hand, means "one plant is grown (let's say all corn, all potato, all green peppers) in a big, big field with lots of inputs (synthetic fertilizers and pesticides), which are introduced to guarantee lots of food that does not get destroyed by insects and boosting up the land with synthetic chemicals to make those veggies fat and pretty."[2]

Industrial procedures and engineering manipulations are so prevalent within today's food industry that they dominate the production of "fresh" fruits and vegetables that fill produce bins in markets, as well as processed foods concocted in factories with synthesized ingredients. Both categories of edibles are engineered, mass-produced, prepackaged, and far-flung. Fournier is an outspoken critic of industrialized food production. She is particularly critical of monoculture that boosts yields and profits but reduces biodiversity and sustainability. She laments "the effects fat and pretty veggies have on killing the soil, and life in the soil, and the pollution those extra inputs are doing to the planet (oceans, gulfs, rivers, land, and atmosphere)."[3]

Gathering her ample skills as an artist/polyagriculturist/activist/feminist/herbalist/gardener, Fournier revises food practices, from foods' points of origin in the earth to their destination in the mouths of eaters. Her "live dining" art practice cultivates foods that are eaten, land where the food is produced, and people who eat it. She describes this special kind of dining as "an adjective as well as a concept that is adaptable and can be applied to different contexts—urban, suburban, or rural, as well as public or private, to bring attention to our relationships to agriculture, food security, and look at notions of controlled and wild nature, utility and nonutility. The project changes according to the context."[4]

One such context is Place Benoit, a rundown neighborhood in Montreal where low-rent apartment blocks have housed a succession of immigrants from Africa, the West Indies, India, Ukraine, Italy, South America, and Mexico since the 1950s. In the past five years it has become a forgotten ghetto where single mothers and their children struggle against drugs, crime, and unemployment.

Issiaka Sanou, an urban agronomist, was hired to construct a community garden in the Place Benoit neighborhood as part of his job as director of a Quartier 21 city project. The project honors Montreal's commitment to urban revitalization reflecting *Earth Summit Agenda 21*. This United Nations plan, created at the 1992 Earth Summit in Rio de Janeiro, promotes low-cost/high-impact interventions. It strives to reduce the environmental impact of urban lifestyles, increase the quality of life of its residents, and vitalize the local economy.[5]

When Fournier joined the project in the fall of 2010, Sanou had almost finalized his design and construction of raised beds for planting in an area of asphalt enclosed by three brick walls. The open side of this urban garden faced the neglected parking lot of an industrial park. When Fournier looked in that direction, she did not perceive urban blight. Instead, the abundance of weeds that were growing in the tiny spaces between the buildings and the

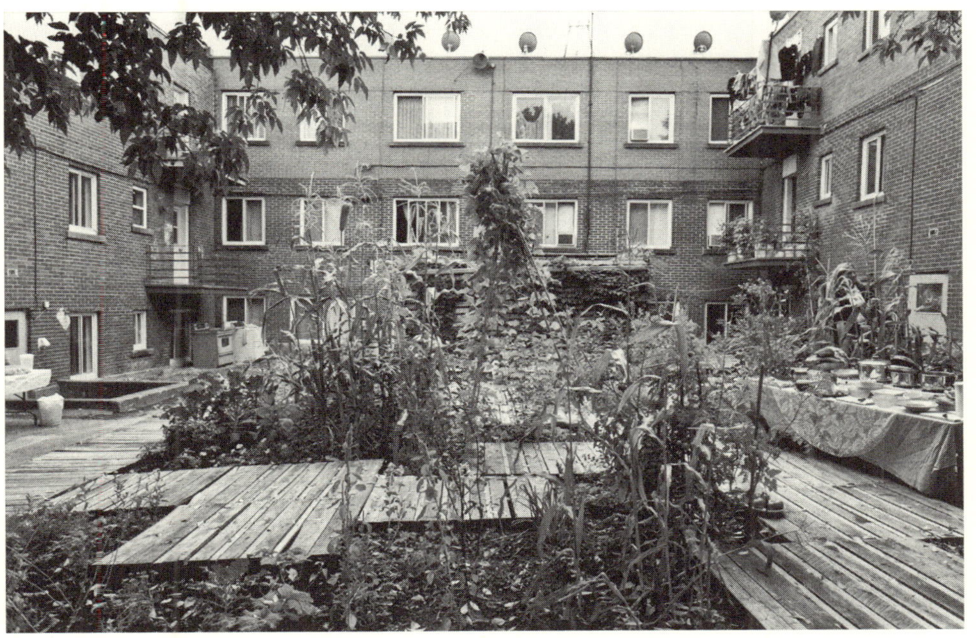

Nicole Fournier | Kiwi Box Live Dining | 2010 Place Benoit community, St. Laurent borough of Montreal / RUI Hodge-Place Benoit | Quartier 21 project, city of Montreal | Installation, performance, ecovention

PHOTO: LUC BOURGEOIS / COURTESY NICOLE FOURNER

asphalt offered an ideal live dining opportunity. "The building was falling apart. The asphalt was breaking apart. Nature was taking over."[6]

The Kiwi Box is the name Sanou chose for the project because his garden was intended to grow a single crop—kiwi. When Fournier joined the project, a more elaborate agenda unfolded. First it expanded from monoculture to polyculture cultivation of multiple farm crops. Then Fournier added three preindustrial strategies for acquiring food: foraging, diverse polyculturing, and rewilding. While industrialized monocultures typically debilitate soils and pollute groundwater, these primeval methods conduct a host of vitalizing functions. They build soil, diversify habitats, produce ecotones, and increase biodiversity.

Foraging Foraging, the direct procurement of edible plants from the wild, was humanity's sole means of acquiring plant matter for all but the last ten thousand years. It is a reminder that growing the ingredients for meals in a garden is not the only alternative to acquiring them by shopping. While foraging requires just a few simple tools, what is essential to this practice is extensive knowledge. Skilled foragers amass information otherwise found in farmers' almanacs, botanical catalogs, horticultural manuals, and wildlife surveys. The ethnographer Richard Lee corrected the long-held assumption that foragers lived desperate lives at the mercy of nature's whims. He demonstrated that an entire community can be fed by 60 percent of adults foraging only fifteen hours a week![7] This is because the practice proceeds directly to harvesting and bypasses such laborious tasks as planting, weeding, and watering.

In September 2010, Fournier introduced impoverished urban residents in Place Benoit to this efficient means of acquiring food. Community members joined her to search out robust and nutritious specimens of wild plants, guaranteed to be pesticide-free, in vacant lots and cracks in sidewalks. She taught them how to identify and utilize weeds that are typically eradicated with herbicides or yanked out by the roots. The participants then learned how to conduct harvesting as a mindful practice intent on preserving the plants' abilities to thrive and reproduce. Dandelions, for example, survive harvesting if the flowers and leaves are picked, but not their stems. Fournier explains, "Beneficial weeds grow all around us. Foraging lets the wildness be."[8]

Diverse polyculture cultivation Fournier allocated space in the garden for multiple vegetables. Then she added flowers and herbs, even mixing perennials and annuals. But her commitment to polyculture diversity was not fulfilled until she included "enemy" plant species in her cultivation efforts by sowing or transplanting edible weeds. Fournier's digression from conventional gardening protocols escalated into a betrayal when she decided to invite weeds with no known nutritional or medicinal uses into the garden. She defends the policy by stating that even those that are poisons to us are important "for ecosystem maintenance, for greening spaces, for human global food security."[9] However, the Quartier 21 project's mission to maximize food output and develop the community's food security required that only edible weeds were included in the *Kiwi Box Live Dining* project.

Minimal effort is required to reap benefits from these weeds because they thrive without human caregivers. Fournier explains, "Agriculture needs us to control the planting, and manage and care for the growth. Weeds have adapted to the environment and do not need to be cared for."[10] Thus, like foraging, cultivating weeds requires minimal human labor.

Since weeds for the *Kiwi Box Live Dining* project could not be purchased from nurseries, Fournier foraged for those she had cultivated in her own yard and sold them to the *Kiwi Project* organizers. She comments, "The city bought the wild plants at a very good price—from my garden. I have become a mini wildlife nursery because no nursery provides them." She reports that most of her stock of weeds came from the compost she acquired from a farmer. He warned her that it was laden with weed seeds. He was surprised when she replied, "That is just what I want."[11]

Rewilding Fournier's maverick version of greening cities ultimately involves leaving space for wild things to grow according to their own inclinations. Not all the wild species given this latitude are plants. Fournier hopes that mice, squirrels, pigeons, insects, birds will make their homes in the garden as well, since animals are essential to self-perpetuating life systems.

Rewilding charges humans with the uncomfortable task of suspending their judgment, suppressing their taste, and repressing their desire to control outcomes. In this way, the practice of letting things go merges preservation ecology that eliminates human interventions, restoration ecology that allows indigenous life-forms to repopulate a site, and deep ecology that promotes interconnectedness with living forms, including those that are wild. Fournier notes that in all these ways, rewilding reintroduces elements missing from contemporary lifestyles. "Civilization is about control, controlling, managing, designing every aspect of human made environments, including plant and tree growth, and measuring, and monitoring scientifically with our inventions in technology, all aspects of human-environment relationships. There is no wildness left (hardly) in the city. Even urban agriculture, a wonderful and important initiative, is about control (no weeds please)."[12]

Fournier's definition of *diversity* is radical. It means mixing plants and animals, weeds and cultivars, wildness and management. Humans, too, are included in Fournier's nurturing

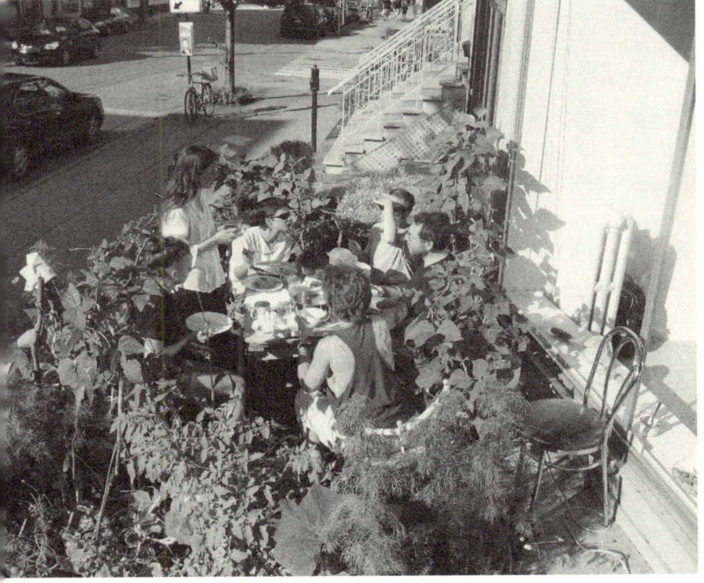

(left) Nicole Fournier | Next to Sidewalk Live Dining | May–September 2007 Galerie d'Articule | Montreal, Quebec, Canada | Installation/performance with Mile End community

PHOTO: ESME TERRY / COURTESY NICOLE FOURNIER

(below) Nicole Fournier | Urban Wild Field Live Dining | October 2007 Mile End, Montreal, Quebec, Canada | Collaborated with Artivistic 2007, Un.Occupied Spaces, and passersby | Installation, performance, ecovention

PHOTO: KAREN ELAINE SPENCER / COURTESY NICOLE FOURNIER

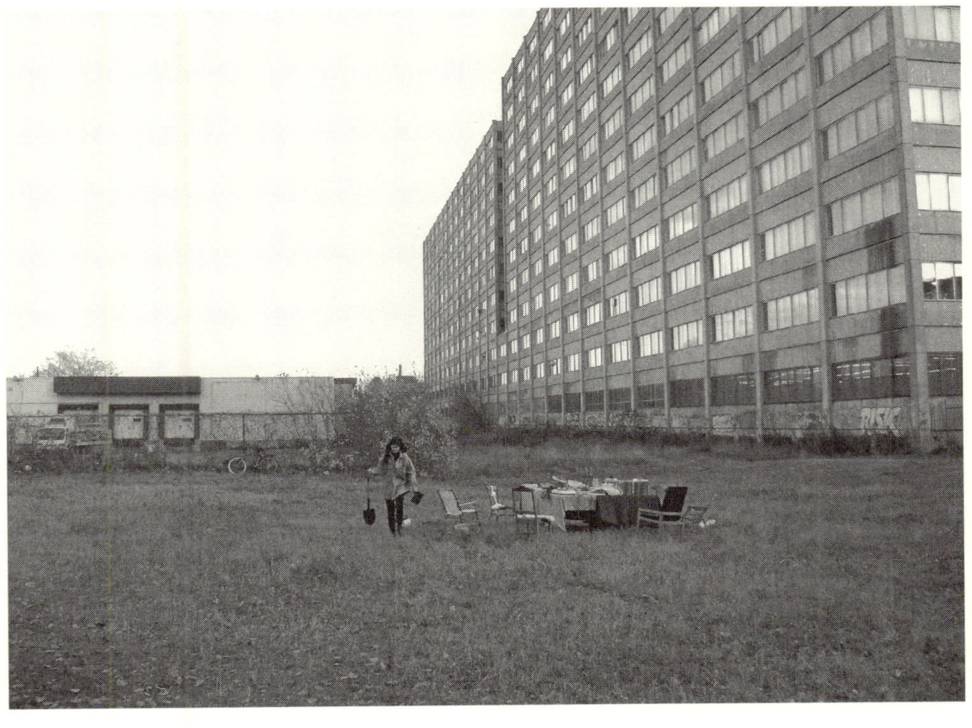

of diverse life-forms. The *Kiwi Box Live Dining* integrates Benoit residents in all these cultivating and garnering processes. They are also engaged in preparing the food and eating it. To connect people to the sources of their foods, these culminating events occur outdoors. Tables and chairs are placed in the same earth where the foods grow. Fournier describes it as the "touching of our physical organic environment, in the site of food growth, while dining, which includes touch, proximity, intimacy in exchange and production."[13] In this way she adds sensual and metaphoric significance to the act of eating.

Fournier refers to these dining events as "a way to celebrate the creation of this green space for people, plant biodiversity and ecosystem development."[14] The public celebrates by picking and chopping lemon balm, dandelion, shepherd's purse, sow thistle, burdock and by transforming these ingredients into nourishing meals that they eat and offer friends. The meal that was served at the inauguration of the *Kiwi Box* project consisted of nettle soup and carrot soup seasoned with onions, yarrow, and basil and salads made of tomato, lettuce, evening primrose flowers and leaves, and yarrow.

People who have not participated in a *Live Dining* event frequently ask Fournier why she goes to so much trouble to produce a simple meal. However, people who have participated experience the rewards of being connected to the sources of their food. She comments, "There are no words for this. It is a visceral experience. They get it once they have that experience of doing everything in one place. That's when their feeling of awe comes."[15]

The awe generated by munching on the leaves of a dandelion you discovered and plucked also carries a political payback and ethical rewards. Live dining not only undermines the authority of industry; this radical version of agriculture has the capacity to alleviate poverty and ill health. Fournier explains *Live Dining* as an activist's pursuit: "Who controls production and who has the power to determine what we're eating? Citizens' interests become controlled and limited by ignoring or discrediting plants as a valuable solution for health. Biodiversity and food security raises a person's sense of accountability to the practice of eating in everyday life."[16]

NOTES

1 "Live Dining, Nicole Fournier," Visualeyez 2007 (May 28, 2007). http://visualeyez2007.blogspot.com/2007/05/live-dining-nicole-fournier.html.

2 Nicole Fournier telephone interview with author, March 31, 2011.

3 Ibid.

4 Ibid.

5 The Agenda 21 mission matched the mission Fournier formulated when she established InTerreArt. The organization's goal is to realize "art practices which include non-disciplines and disciplines in arts, sciences, traditional ecological knowledge, environmental, health, and social services, as art." http://interreart.blogspot.com/.

6 Nicole Fournier telephone interview with author, March 31, 2011.

7 Dennis O'Neil, "Foraging" (updated October 30, 2006). http://anthro.palomar.edu/subsistence/sub_2.htm.

8 Nicole Fournier, "Edible Plants Growing in Urban Cracks Wednesday, May 23rd, 2007," Live Dining de Nicole Fournier. http://livedining.blogspot.com/2007_05_25_archive.html.

9 "Industrial Park Live Dining, 2009–2011." http://industrialparklivedining.blogspot.com/2009/06/industrial-park-live-dining-2009-update.html.

10 Dennis O'Neil, "Foraging" (updated October 30, 2006). http://anthro.palomar.edu/subsistence/sub_2.htm.

11 Nicole Fournier telephone interview with author, March 31, 2011.

12 "Industrial Park Live Dining, 2009–2011." http://industrialparklivedining.blogspot.com/2009/06/industrial-park-live-dining-2009-update.html.

13 Background to Live Dining 2002 and 2004. http://livedining.blogspot.com/2007_06_20_archive.html.

14 "Industrial Park Live Dining, 2009–2011." http://industrialparklivedining.blogspot.com/2009/06/industrial-park-live-dining-2009-update.html.

15 Nicole Fournier telephone interview with author, March 31, 2011.

16 Ibid.

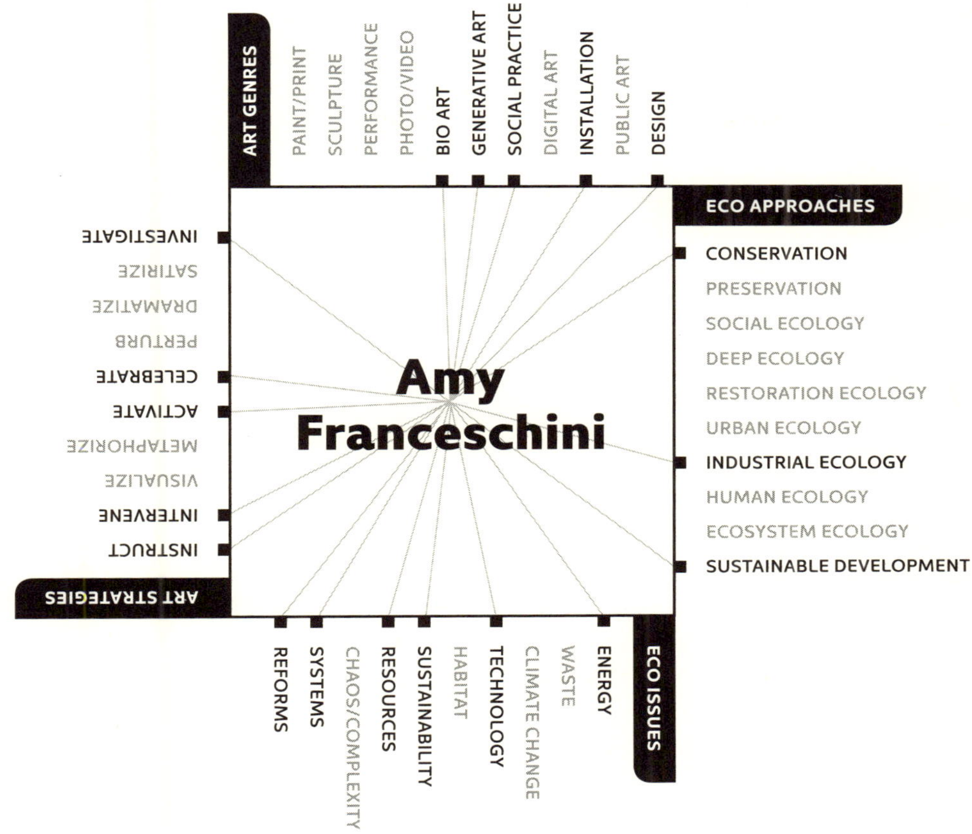

Do-It-Yourself Energy Generation

Born 1970, California, USA

CREATING A WORLD POWERED BY WATER seems like a fairy tale. If this enchanted fable actually came true, energy for human use would be infinite and everlasting and produce zero polluting emissions. In fact, the renowned originator of science fiction, Jules Verne (1828–1905), conjured such a vision when he wrote *Mysterious Island*. In this novel a shipwrecked engineer consoles the survivors by announcing that once they run out of coal, they can use water as their energy source. Presumably Verne's fictional engineer knew how to extract hydrogen from the surrounding ocean waters.

Many of Verne's outlandish speculations have become realities. His uncanny prescience may be repeated regarding water as a source of power to fuel contemporary lifestyles if environmental scientist Jonathan Meuser and the artist Amy Franceschini succeed in their collaboration. Together they created *DIY Algae/Hydrogen Bioreactor Kit* (2004) that tests the reality quotient of Verne's fantasy. Franceschini describes the mammoth implications of their experiment by stating, "Taking energy in light and turning it into a usable form would dismantle the whole social economic energy pyramid that exists now. We have the ability to do that."[1]

Meuser supplied the technical knowledge regarding capturing the carbon-free energy source. Franceschini invested his research with cultural significance. Simply relocating Meuser's experiment—removing it from a secluded science laboratory and positioning it in the public forum of an art gallery—helped incite a "social economic energy" revolution. Thus, while Meuser was demonstrating the scientific feasibility of Verne's theory, Franceschini was empowering ordinary folks to cancel their contracts with the centralized and polluting energy industry and become independent producers of a nonpolluting alternative. The art museum, a place where boundary-defying speculation is welcome, provided an ideal context to demonstrate do-it-yourself energy technology.

Domestic energy production may seem radical today, but energy generation for the homestead and the workplace occurred on-site until the introduction of coal that powered the Industrial Revolution. For all prior millennia, people relied on animals for muscle power, wood for heat, tallow for light, water for milling, wind for grinding, etc. All these energy sources are local and renewable. Once coal, oil, and uranium began to dominate energy production, extraction and processing moved far from the homestead and workplace. Environmentalists are kept very busy calculating the environmentally and socially detrimental effects of mining, manufacturing, and use. In addition, coal, oil, and uranium are finite.

The frenzied pursuit of alternative energy sources that are sustainable is predicated on the expectation that world consumption of marketed energy will increase from 421 quadrillion Btus in 2003 to 722 quadrillion Btus in 2030.[2] Such statistics are driving a contingent of researchers to the limits of the material world in search of an energy panacea. They are experimenting with solar energy, wind power, hydroelectric power, geothermal heat, biomass fuels, and tides. No item on this list is a perfect remedy, not even solar panels. Franceschini notes, "A great deal of energy is used to produce them, and they can't be recycled. After 40 years they become waste ridden with heavy metals."[3] Instead, she is a fervent advocate for a relatively new approach. She explains, "We will have to be creative and work together to find new ways to harvest energy from wind and sun and ALGAE!!"[4] She capitalized word *algae* to indicate that her energy quest focuses on hydrogen derived from water that is processed by algae. The process exploits the ability of some algae's enzymes to perform a remarkable deed. They can split water molecules when they absorb solar energy.

Hydrogen fuel cell technologies are prominent on the alternative energy horizon. The gas is colorless and odorless and liberates large amounts of energy per unit weight in combustion. Because the only by-product of hydrogen combustion is water vapor, hydrogen eliminates the direct production of exhaust gases that lead to smog and global warming. Furthermore, once it is compressed, it can be easily converted to electricity by fuel cells. These benefits, however, are counterbalanced by the fact that hydrogen is not found in a pure state in the environment. Since it cannot be mined, it must be produced. One means to create hydrogen is to split water molecules into two hydrogen atoms and one oxygen atom. However, the fossil fuels that are commonly used to execute this split consume more nonrenewable energy than the renewable energy they produce. Franceschini hopes to fulfill

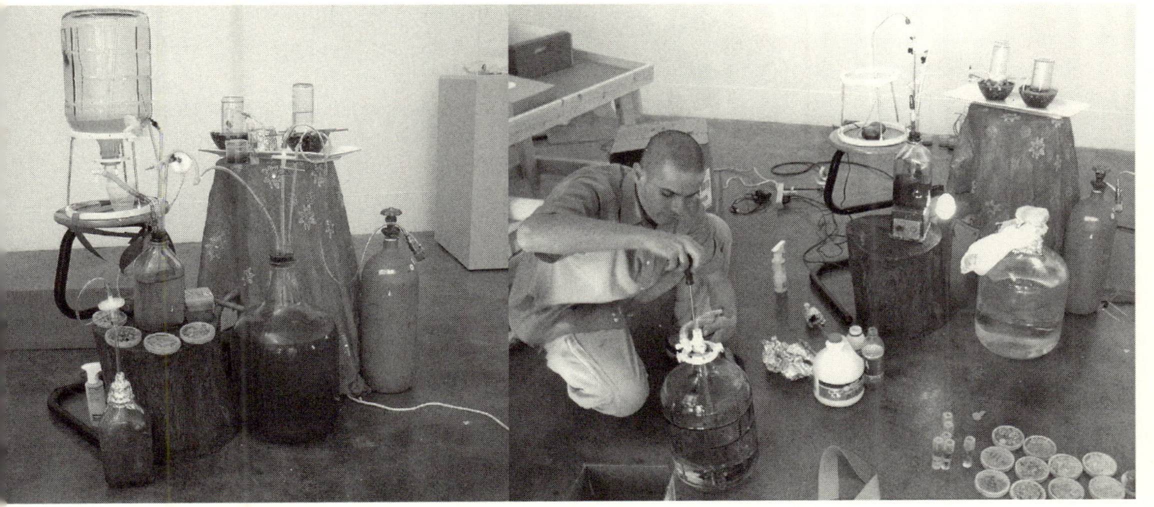

Amy Franceschini | With Jonathan Meuser | Futurefarmers | DIY Algae/Hydrogen Bioreactor Kit | 2004 Installation view | Water, algae, oxygen, anaerobic tank, sterilized nutrient tank, tree stump, tablecloth, glass vials, and assorted materials | Dimensions: 5′ × 4′ × 3′

PHOTO: AMY FRANCESCHINI / COURTESY FUTUREFARMERS

humanity's goal of achieving nonpolluting energy production from water by enlisting tiny green algae.

Theoretically, this scheme would allow virtually unlimited energy production because it relies on Earth's two most plentiful resources—water and sunlight. However, two hurdles must first be overcome. A technical hurdle is imposed by the known species of light-dependent green algae. They do not convert 10 percent of the available solar energy, the minimum figure if water is to be split efficiently. A psychological hurdle is imposed by the horrific ferocity of hydrogen. In the public's consciousness, hydrogen is envisioned as bombs detonating huge mushroom clouds that discharge lethal torrents of radioactive mud. Furthermore, hydrogen is implicated in the infamous explosions of the *Hindenburg* passenger airship in 1937 and the Space Shuttle *Challenger* in 1986. Meuser set about engineering a solution to the technical obstacle. Franceschini devoted herself to the psychological one. She explains their shared mission: "Our challenge was asking people to become active energy producers. We hoped people would consider backyard hydrogen production as a possible solution to current energy woes. We wanted to give them a sense of independence, to help them believe that they do not have to be dependent on multinational companies."[5]

These challenges guided the preparation of *DIY Algae/Hydrogen Bioreactor Kit*, an installation exhibited in the art museum at Pacific University in 2004. Meuser engineered the green algae's functions for hydrogen production by depriving the algae of oxygen. This stimulated the algae's cells to split water molecules in an effort to access the water's oxygen. At the same time, Franceschini calmed people's anxieties by joining the expressive capacities of art to the technical constraints of science. She notes, "Art offers a visual language that breaks down boundaries between disciplines."[6]

The requirements for biological hydrogen production by photosynthetic microorganisms are surprisingly unterrifying. Only a simple solar reactor, such as a transparent closed box, is required. The reassuring aspects of this process determined Franceschini's strategy: "I

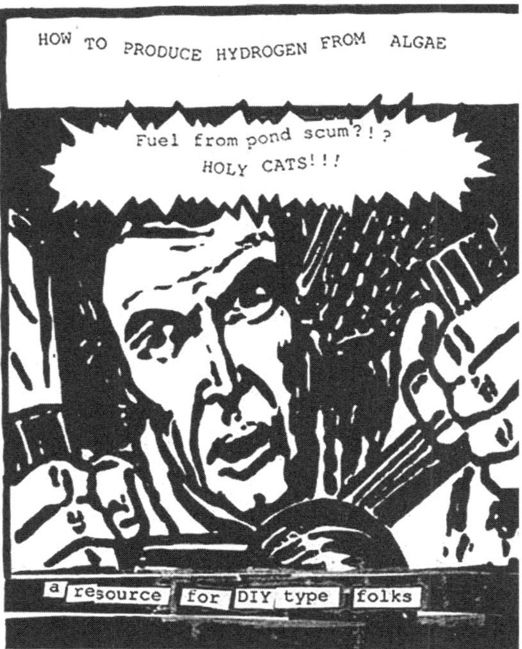

Amy Franceschini, Jonathan Meuser, and Zachary Smith | Futurefarmers | How to Produce Hydrogen from Algae: A Resource for DIY Type Folks | 2006
Online publication
COURTESY FUTUREFARMERS

created a formal constellation that invited viewers to reflect on what might otherwise seem intimidating."[7] One cunning scheme involved scaling the hydrogen conversion mechanism down to the unintimidating size of a back yard gazebo (5′ x 4′ x 3′). Then, by exposing the water containers, tubing, and lights, Franceschini showed that algae are living organisms that require only light and water to survive, thus growing them is as agreeable as gardening. In addition, she made the process seem more homey than industrial by choosing ordinary bottles, glasses, tubes, and lights to construct the device. Franceschini notes, "These off-the-shelf objects are not high-tech in any way. They invite people to cross the threshold of sustainable possibilities."[8]

Franceschini cleaned and arranged these inexpensive items in an attractive composition. Then she reinforced all these observable signs of ease and confidence with a verbal maneuver: "I inserted the word *kit* in the title in order to evoke the ethos that surrounds DIY culture. Kits emphasize the work's connection with hobbies and other pleasurable pursuits. Amateur practice is not about monetary profit. It is about excitement, skill, sharing, and discovery."[9] Meuser made his aesthetic contribution by adding a yellow flowered table cloth, to enhance the work's domestic appeal, and a tree stump to evoke the pleasant association with nature.

A handicraft approach to a task that is generally performed by professionals on an industrial scale is risky. The artist comments, "Art is like science. We are operating on an island of knowledge. The most exciting place to be is on the edges of that island bordering the Sea of the Unknown. If you know what you are doing, your job is over."[10]

Even the success of this experiment does not guarantee a desirable outcome. Franceschini says, "I am apprehensive about the industrial applications of this seemingly simple science. If the process is used for large-scale, commercial applications, it will require an amping up, which in turn will require a biological engineering that I currently do not support."[11] Scale is a serious issue. She and Meuser calculated that a forty-square-foot pond of algae could produce enough hydrogen to drive a car two hundred miles. This means that a hundred-square-mile area would be needed to produce enough hydrogen to power the entire electrical needs of the United States. They note that this figure may seem large, but more area is currently paved as roads.

The close of the exhibition did not end the art project. The innovative use of photosynthetic microorganisms expanded from demonstration to investigation after Franceschini and Meuser received a flood of emails from people wanting to help test the potential of this utopian scheme for energy production. The collaborators responded by producing a downloadable PDF that provides instructions for participation in this credible experiment. Once again, art aligned with science when Franceschini and Meuser decided that instead of publishing a technical manual, they would create a document that resembled a punk rock zine. Franceschini's vivid illustrations and the lively layout are designed to mobilize a hydrogen technology research team composed of amateurs who are testing the hydrogen-producing capabilities of thousands of algae species—a monumental task.

The feasibility of amateur experimentation inspired Meuser, Franceschini, and artist Michael Swaine to enlist high school students to contribute to this certified scientific pursuit. Together with the support of the National Renewable Energy Lab and the Museum of Modern Art in Manhattan, they created the *Lunchbox Laboratory* (2008),[12] a prototype of a laboratory kit for testing algae strains. The kit contains algae samples, custom-designed glass beakers, an LED light source, an embedded pressure sensor to control the light, and a bioreactor. The plan is to mass-produce *Lunchbox Laboratories* and distribute them across the country so that thousands of students can contribute to the research regarding alternative energy futures. Franceschini comments, "I love the idea that the user has complete control over a piece or space, so much so that he/she becomes the author, and that the artist is more of a facilitator."[13]

Franceschini could hardly have envisioned growing algae when she founded Futurefarmers in 1995, an art and design collective that invites multidisciplinary artists to collaborate on new work. At that time the term was autobiographical. It was a way to look to the future by acknowledging her paradoxical past—her organic-gardening mother and her pesticide-farming father. She comments, "To this day, I am still interested in food production, distribution, and consumption. But I still do not live on a farm. I believe a farm is a state of being rather than a physical place. It is a road to cultivating my consciousness and others. I started Futurefarmers because I wanted to work with people and use this platform of collaboration to learn and foster relationships."[14] Thus her maxim, art as a catalyst for change, exceeds energy production. She hopes that the *DIY Algae/Hydrogen Bioreactor Kit* reverses "the perceived separation between humans and nature."[15] She concludes, "Much of my work is about balance."[16]

NOTES

1 Amy Franceschini telephone interview with the author, January 9, 2007. Biophotolysis is the action of light on a biological system that results in the dissociation of a substrate, usually water, to produce hydrogen.

2 International Energy Outlook, 2006, Energy Information Administration, US Department of Energy. http://www.fypower.org/pdf/EIA_Intl EnergyOutlook%282006%29.pdf.

3 Amy Franceschini telephone interview with the author, January 9, 2007.

4 Alex Pasternack, "Futurefarming: An interview

with Amy Franceschini," *Present! One: An Ob-Literary Experiment in Unusual Things*. http://presentzine.blogspot.com/2004/08/future farming-interview-with-amy.html.

5 Amy Franceschini telephone interview with the author, January 9, 2007.

6 Ibid.

7 Ibid.

8 Ibid.

9 Ibid.

10 Amy Franceschini correspondence with the author, March, 2011.

11 Ibid.

12 Lunchbox Laboratory is a collaboration between Futurefarmers and the biological sciences team at the National Renewable Energy Laboratory (NREL). The NREL is the only federal laboratory dedicated to the research, development, commercialization, and deployment of renewable energy and energy efficiency technologies.

13 Amy Franceschini telephone interview with the author, January 9, 2007.

14 Ibid.

15 "GIZMODO Gallery: Amy Franceschini," March 3, 2006. GIZMODO. http://us.gizmodo.com/gadgets/gizmodo-gallery/gizmodo-gallery-amy-franceschini-157897.php.

16 Ibid.

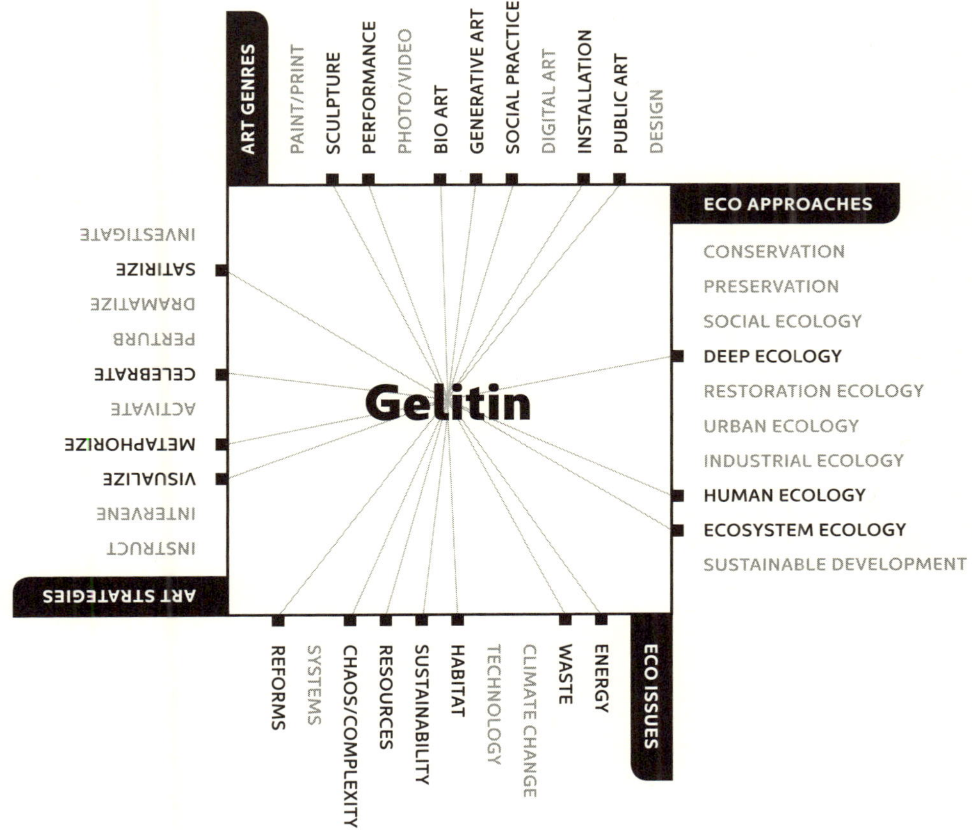

One with Nature

Group formed in 1993
Ali Janka born 1971, Mistelbach, Austria
Florian Reither born 1967, Salzburg, Austria
Tobias Urban born 1968, Munich, Germany
Wolfgang Gantner born 1970, Austria

THE SPIRITUAL PRACTICE that inspired a soap company in Ohio to choose the name "One with Nature" also inspired the four-artist Austrian collaborative group, Gelitin, to create *Klunk Garden* (2009), a large sculpture unveiled in Tokyo that resembles a Japanese rock garden. The motto "one with nature" also provided the impetus for the massive sculpture they created on a pristine mountaintop in the Alps entitled *Hase (Rabbit)* (2005–2025). These works represent the complementary poles of "oneness," a desire to attain harmonious union with a greater power. *Klunk Garden* applied this pursuit to a spiritual quest. *Hase* applied it to the physical realm. In both cases the conventional aspects of sculpture are toppled from their pedestals. These works incorporate living matter or materials that are either grown or scavenged. Furthermore, they embrace temporal progressions to accommodate mental and physical transformations. Thus, they resemble events more than objects or installations. Pooling the multidisciplinary imaginations of artist Ali Janka, political scientist Wolfgang Gantner, engineer Florian Reither, and artist Tobias Urban accounts for these digressions.

As offered by the company One with Nature, the timeless state of spiritual enlightenment can be achieved with soap and water. Their customers can purchase it online when they pay $3.47 for Dead Sea Mud Soap and Rose Petal Soap. In contrast, the path to enlightenment offered by *Klunk Garden* honors meditation, the primary tenet of Zen Buddhism, which is not available for purchase. The name *Zen* derives from the Sanskrit word *dhyana*, which means *meditation*. This process of prolonged introspection was familiar to the audience who visited this installation at the Tomio Koyama Gallery, Tokyo, Japan. However, they quickly discovered that the version of meditation that *Klunk Garden* offered was not designed to enlighten, ennoble, and uplift them. In fact, it was more impudent than reverential, confirming Gelitin's reputation for delivering its uplifting messages in the form of raunchy humor. In this work, the group parodies hallowed meditation practices by brandishing their naked posteriors. The four artists in this Viennese art collective first met at a summer camp in 1978, an ideal launching pad for their mischievous path to enlightenment.

The path of the visitors' journey in this installation originates on the ground floor of the gallery. From there they proceed up a rickety set of stairs that is cobbled together with wooden scraps. Then, at the highest point, the path continues across a precarious, railless bridge that terminates at an opening cut high up the gallery wall. The elevation of their bodies parodies the elevation of a mystic experience visitors are seeking. This threshold marks the halfway point in Gelitin's crash course in the attainment of extraordinary awareness. The comparable process undertaken by actual Zen practitioners consumes decades, with no assurance of success.

When viewers step through this portal, they look down onto a pristine Zen garden meticulously constructed by the artists on a raised platform. All the traditional qualities are faithfully re-created—sand raked into neat patterns that resemble rippling water, rounded solid forms that are distributed to suggest mountains, refined composition that unifies these symbols of Earth's elemental components. It even retains the rock garden's traditional purpose. Gelitin made just one alteration to the tradition. In place of inert stone, they substituted their own naked buttocks, along with other rock-resembling body parts such as naked backs, knees, hips, thighs, and even the top of one hairy head. These wiggly, goose-bumped versions of rocks protruded through holes cut precisely to their shapes. The rest of the artists' bodies lay beneath the garden, visible to exiting visitors. The artists literally became one with the landscape.

While *Klunk Garden* can be enjoyed as a parody of Zen Buddhism, it also visualizes a fundamental tenet of deep ecology. This philosophy's primary principles were set forth by the Norwegian philosopher Arne Naess (1937–2004). Naess coined two terms to clarify opposing ways that humans interface with the nonhuman realm: *shallow ecology* relies upon practical information and technical skills; *deep ecology* cultivates metaphysical affinities with nonhuman entities and the nonliving components of habitats. Deep ecologists

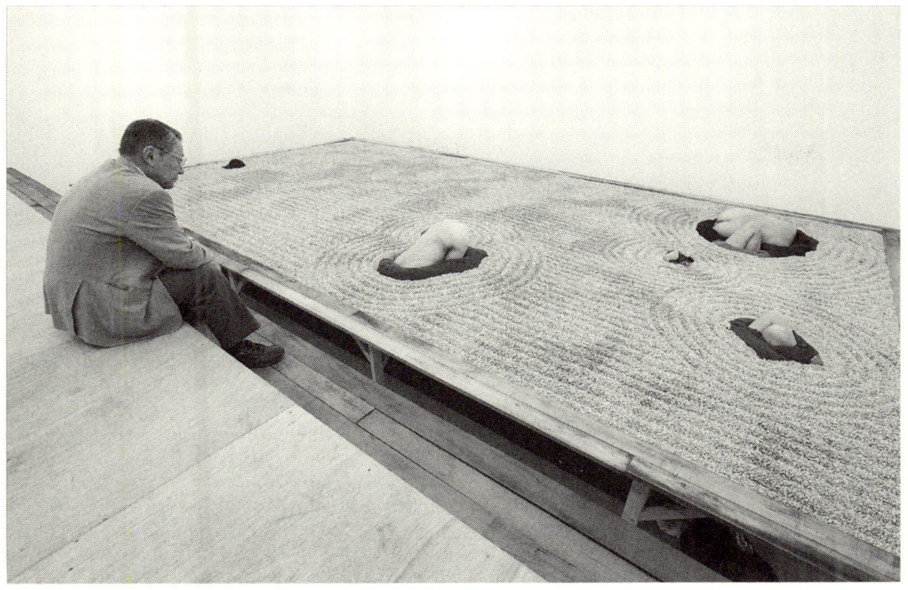

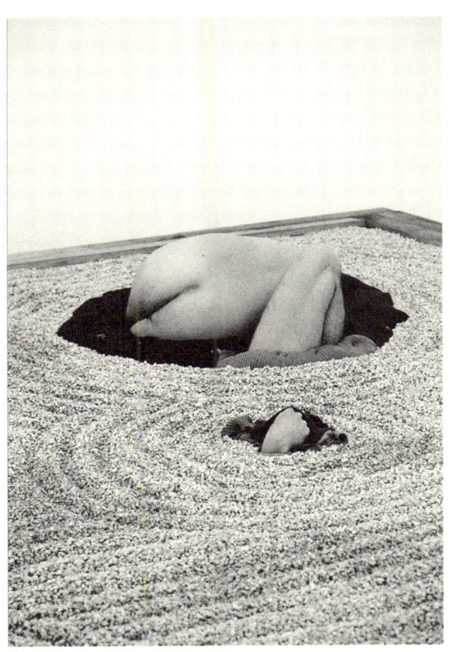

(above) Gelitin | Ali Janka, Florian Reither, Tobias Urban, and Wolfgang Gantner | Klunk Garden | 2009 Installation view, Tomio Koyama Gallery, Tokyo, Japan | Wooden platform, sand, rocks, artists' bodies

PHOTO: KEI OKANO / COURTESY GELITIN STUDIO AND GREENE NAFTALI, NEW YORK

(left) Gelitin | Ali Janka, Florian Reither, Tobias Urban, and Wolfgang Gantner | Klunk Garden (detail) | 2009 Installation view, Tomio Koyama Gallery, Tokyo, Japan | Wooden platform, sand, rocks, artists' bodies

PHOTO: KEI OKANO / COURTESY GELITIN STUDIO AND GREENE NAFTALI, NEW YORK

assert that ecological reform depends on dissolving the discrete I and reimagining the self as indistinguishable from the surrounding world. Thus, they seek ways to shift human consciousness from "being outside of nature" to "being in nature." *Klunk Garden* interpreted this mandate literally. Their satiric "re-earthing" process, designed to expand awareness, was conducted bottoms up.

While the search for oneness remains an elusive spiritual goal, environmentalists are achieving a physical form of re-earthing by recycling such forms of matter as car tires, motherboards, water bottles, spent nuclear fuel, and corpses as a certain path to ensuring a

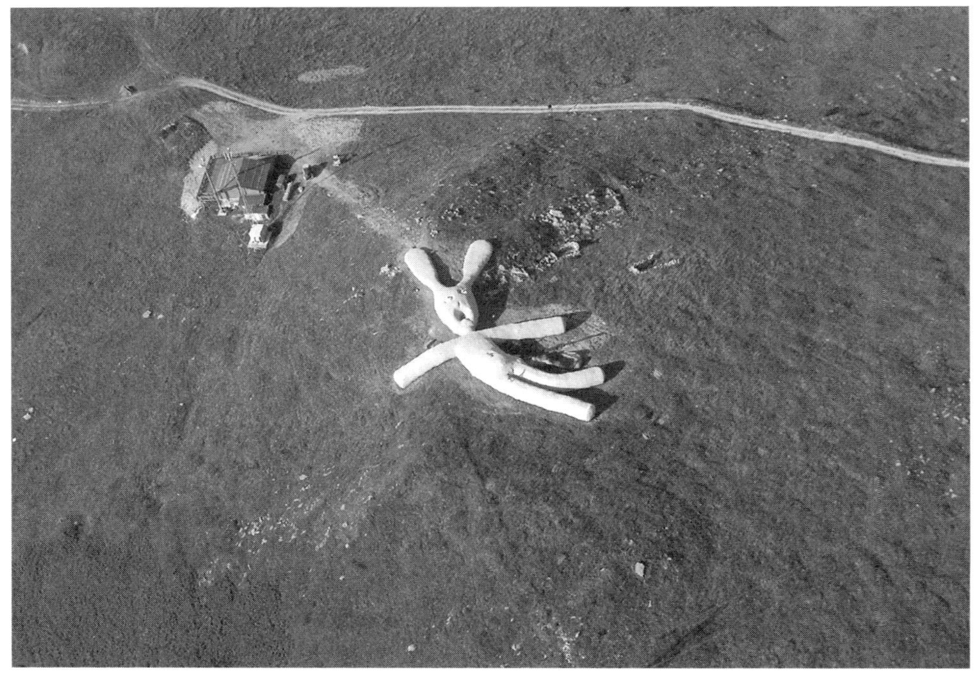

Gelitin | Ali Janka, Florian Reither, Tobias Urban, and Wolfgang Gantner | Hase (Rabbit) | 2005–2025 Installation view, Artesina, Italy, 2005 | Wool fabric and straw | Dimensions: 200′ × 20′

vital and resplendent environment in the future. Through recycling, molecules remain productive within the dynamic systems of the Earth. Such oneness with nature actually unifies rocks and clouds and rain and wind and plants and humans. The process occurs molecularly. *Hase* is a pink Gulliver-sized rabbit that Gelitin constructed to demonstrate the environmentalists' path to material oneness.

This massive artwork manifests Gelitin's assertion that it is "against everything prepared and easy and available if you just pay money and consume—like television."[1] Tobias Urban, one of the four members of Gelitin, explains that they applied this principle to their choice of setting: "The site has to be remote. Visitors can't go by car; they must walk to it. There is no view from the village; it can be seen only by being there. They must take time. It is not easy. They must do something."[2] After an extensive search, Gelitin located a mountain that fit this description. Visitors to *Hase* undertake a forty-five-minute trek on foot from Artesina, Italy, the nearest village. The gorgeous alpine vista does not prepare them for the sight they behold when they arrive—a gigantic stuffed pink rabbit with a last-gasp expression on its anguished face. It lays face to the sky in the manner of a sacrificial offering. Its arms are spread wide and both legs flop on the downward slope. Its position is not the only indicator that the rabbit is suffering from mortal wounds. The animal's stuffed entrails spill out of its body cavity and sprawl across the ground. Why the sprawling guts? The artists explain, "Rabbit entrails are lively. If it didn't have intestines it would be just a puppet or doll. Intestines make it more engaging and vital and emotional for the viewer. As soon as you think there is not just cotton inside, that something is on verge of dying, this is not just an enlarged doll from childhood."[3] Such vitality makes the rabbit's death all the more compelling. It looks like a victim of some lunatic cult.

If sacrificial acts are scaled according to the level of adversity they are intended to prevent, *Hase* is an emblem of global catastrophe. The rabbit is so huge, it is impossible to view it in its entirety except from a distant mountain top or a helicopter. Its belly adds twenty feet to the height of the mountain upon which it rests, and its intestines rise as outcroppings on the terrain. The sculpture exists to be climbed upon, although satellite images are compelling. Thus, the rabbit's open mouth and the lumpy guts are experienced as gaping hollows that visitors descend and rising mounds that they scale.

The artwork does not merely represent a stuffed pink rabbit in the throes of death. It is actually decomposing. Gelitin has converted this embodiment of *cute* and *endearing* into a real rotting corpse by offering it to the elements as a grand recycling gesture. Such experiences of nature are rarely presented on the Nature Channel or by nature photography and wilderness documentaries. They typically ignore the unphotogenic appearance of decomposition, a process essential to the existence of the photogenic plants, animals, and habitats they prefer. The artists, however, acknowledge decay when they describe the experience of visiting the rotting rabbit joyfully: "Happy you feel as you climb up along its ears, almost falling into its cavernous mouth, to the belly-summit and look out over the pink woolen landscape of the rabbit's body, a country dropped from the sky; ears and limbs sneaking into the distance; from its side flowing heart, liver and intestines. Happily in love you step down the decaying corpse, through the wound, now small like a maggot, over woolen kidney and bowel. Happy you leave like the larva that gets its wings from an innocent carcass at the roadside. Such is the happiness which made this rabbit."[4]

Opportunities for such exuberance will intensify in the coming years as *Hase* undergoes the slow process of decomposing. Gelitin developed two strategies to ensure that this process proceeds without interference. The strategy designed to foster physical decomposition was satisfied by intentionally selecting straw as stuffing, an unstable material that biodegrades when it is exposed to sun, rain, wind, microbes, wild critters, and human visitors.

Strategizing also entailed convincing the local populace not to interfere with the sculpture as it rotted into foul brown mess over the course of many years. Gelitin overcame this psychological challenge by acquiring all one hundred tons of straw from local farmers. Then the artists enlisted dozens of local women to perform the daunting task of knitting the yarn, acquired from a manufacturer's overrun, into panels that were then sewn together on site as the rabbit's fur. Villagers thereby became personally invested in the artwork that may be unsightly in the short run but is designed to vanish into the landscape, leaving behind nothing but a more fertile, more diverse, and more beautiful site. Farmers and knitters pledged that the artwork would not be disturbed over a period of twenty years as it "became one with the environment."

Urban reports that thus far the villagers have honored their commitment. "Vandals don't want to harm the rabbit. People know it was done for them. It is not for sale, not for tourists, not for opportunity, and not a logo for any company. There are no souvenirs, no postcards, no T-shirts."[5]

Nonhumans are already profiting from the work. Plants and animals are sheltered and fed by the rabbit's decay, a process that began before the last stitch was knotted. Maggots, bacteria, and fungi burrow into the cavities to enjoy a molecular feast. Grass sprouts in the fertile medium these organisms are manufacturing. Urban explains, "The rabbit is feeding a lot of other kinds of life. There are already mushrooms and grass growing out of it. And there is lots of this yellow thing appearing. It looks like the doll vomited. I saw birds nesting. Cows want to lie down on the straw. The straw is radiating warmth as it decays. This is appealing to animals in winter. It is creating niches that protect animals from the wind. It stores moisture between the legs. It makes all these animals feel like home."[6] In all these ways the sculpture replenishes the Earth.

When asked what experience the rabbit is intended to induce, Urban replied, "We want people to see what they have not seen before. . . . Death and deterioration are not so important. They are just a part of life. I don't think of positive or negative. Everything is both. Some things stay for just awhile. The Earth takes over. It is not necessary to remove them. People are touched by this."[7]

This quaint narrative does not provide a complete picture of the process by which *Hase* was created. In addition to elderly women knitters and local farmers, the artists hired a brigade of professional contributors. An international crew of thirty-five worked for seven weeks to construct the rabbit. They also teamed up with a public relations team, production manager, production assistant/interpreter, caterers, driver, architect, and designer. The list ends with an impressive catalog of supporting galleries and funders.

In sum, Gelitin utilizes the expressive freedom of art to help overcome failings to achieve flip sides of "oneness." In one instance, an installation of serene beauty satirizes the oneness with nature that both Zen and deep ecology espouse. In the other instance, a sculpture that looks disgusting and smells bad invites people to frolic as they acknowledge that decay means life-affirming renewal. These impudent means serve an earnest environmental goal—to assert the role of human attitudes in setting our planet's course.

NOTES

1 Tobias Urban interview with the author, November 30, 2005.
2 Ibid.
3 Ibid.
4 Mackenzie Frere, "Gelitin: Hase/Rabbit/Coniglio," posted on artclothtext.com, December 9, 2010. http://www.artclothtext.com/?p=1956.
5 Tobias Urban interview with the author, November 30, 2005.
6 Ibid.
7 Ibid.

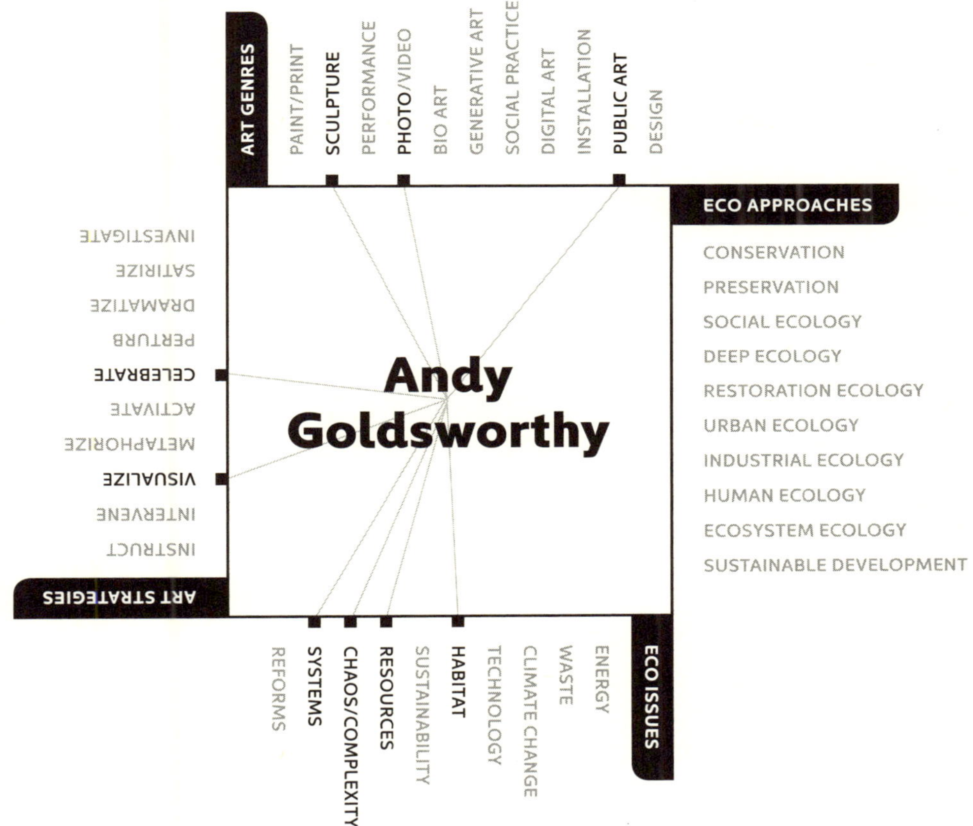

Anthropocentric/ Ecocentric Beauty

Born 1956, Cheshire, England

IT IS THROUGH the time-honored association of beauty and nature that Goldsworthy has earned his acclaim among art lovers as well as legions of people who rarely engage with contemporary art. The sensual rapture his works evoke is apparent in the following quotes:

> Goldsworthy opens our eyes and all of our senses to the beauty and the multiple enchantments of the natural world that we so often take for granted.[1]

> His work whispers to us of winds streaming off mountains, of shoots and branches, the transience of beauty in nature.[2]

Using nature as his canvas, the artist creates works of transcendent beauty.[3]

The work inspires me to embrace each moment of beauty for the time that we have it and to make the ordinary . . . extraordinary![4]

If beauty were merely skin deep, it would not inspire the bliss expressed in these quotes, or the perennial production of treatises, poetry, and song. They attest to the fact that beauty assumes divergent forms. This formal morphing evolves in tandem with each culture's defining features. This fluidity provides the opportunity for beauty to display another remarkable attribute; even though it is always manifested as a temporary construction, it consistently embodies a culture's most esteemed values. Beauty, therefore, may appear differently, but it represents each culture's conception of ultimate delight and unsurpassable merit.

Goldsworthy is extending the historic narrative of beauty by disclosing two sets of values regarding relationships between humans and ecosystems. One body of work epitomizes anthropocentric beauty; it reinforces contemporary systems of production and organization that assert control over nonhuman entities, materials, and conditions. The other manifests ecocentric beauty; it is consistent with protecting and enhancing ecosystem functions, not commanding them. While Goldsworthy's popularity springs from the conservative nature of the former, his lasting legacy may ultimately be traced to the vanguard aspects of the latter.

In creating his anthropocentric artworks, Goldsworthy greatly expands the role of craft and manual dexterity in art. Instead of limiting his creative engagement to observation, representation, and interpretation, he activates tactile interactions with the physical actualities afforded by each site. Goldsworthy explains, "Looking, touching, material, place and form are all inseparable from the resulting work. . . . I need the shock of touch, the resistance of place, materials and weather, the earth as my source."[5] The desire for intimacy with nature's substances and forces during the creative process has led Goldsworthy to reconfigure art production accordingly:

Studio Instead of the confined space of an indoor studio, Goldsworthy's creative acts are conducted in forests, along shorelines, beside streams, within fields, and in many other pristine outdoor settings.

Medium Instead of applying a manufactured product like paint or pastel to a manufactured surface such as canvas, Goldsworthy produces form, color, and texture by assembling actual twigs, ice, petals, snow, leaves, and stones that he then arranges. He leaves these scavenged materials on-site after they have served their purposes as mediums for a work of art.

Tools Instead of purchasing ready-made tools like brushes, chisels, binders, and adhesives, Goldsworthy collects his resources on-site. His sculptures are carved and/or assembled with feathers, thorns, reeds, water, and sometimes the artist's own saliva.

Creative process Instead of the free expression of artistic will made possible by the steady-state predictability of an indoor studio, Goldsworthy contends with the variability of climate, season, and weather. The actual construction of an artwork is dependent upon whether the day is breezy or calm, rainy or dry, sunny or cloudy, below or above freezing, etc.

The site determines the work in all ways but one. Form is the noteworthy exception, and it is the distinguishing feature of Goldsworthy's work. These forms are not discovered; they are conceptualized and fabricated. Collecting, trimming, arranging, and joining these forms

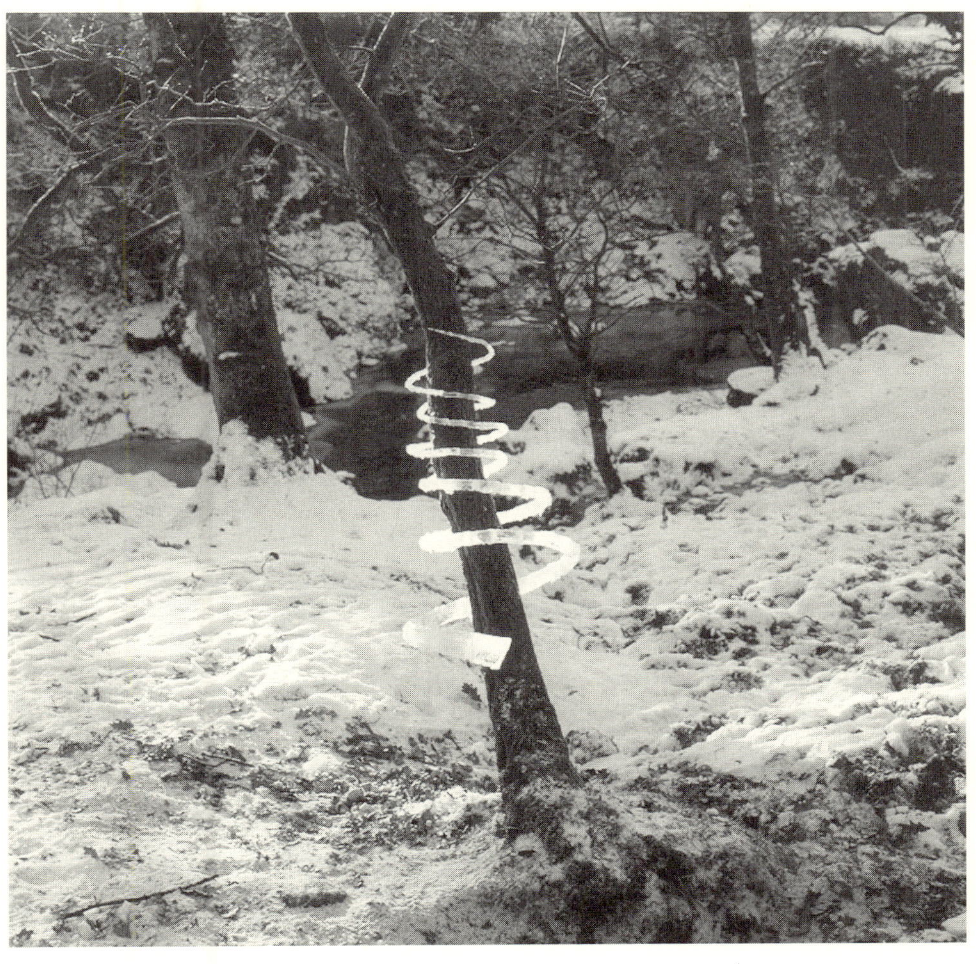

Andy Goldsworthy | Soul of a Tree | December 28, 1995 Reconstructed icicles / around a tree / finished this afternoon / catching the sunlight | Glen Marlin Falls, Dumfriesshire | Icicles and saliva

manifest the artist's personal inventiveness, not the site's inherent functions. This formal control accounts for Goldsworthy's acclaim as a master of anthropocentric beauty.

Soul of a Tree provides a compelling example of Goldsworthy's formal independence. It consists of a curvilinear icicle that spirals around the trunk of a tree with a ballerina's grace and elegance. To accomplish this implausible shape, Goldsworthy exploited the normal interactions between water and temperature that produce icicles, but he defied the forming influence of gravity. Instead of allowing the drips to accumulate, he intentionally melted the tips of straight stalks of ice and prodded them into the slim serpentine spiral as ice adhered to ice when the tips refroze. Through this meticulous process, a spiral was formed around the trunk of a tree, creating a gorgeous apparition that could never exist without human intervention. Although spirals factor prominently in nature's vocabulary of forms, they are never configured in this manner. In other works Goldsworthy applies his aesthetic sorcery to petals, grass, and leaves to create elegant multicolored geometries. Or he may stack stones in precarious and determinate alignments that wind, erosion, or flowing water could never have created.

Goldsworthy's artistic process is imbued with drama. First he accomplishes a virtuosic feat of manipulation by arranging unstable elements in precarious patterns within ever-shifting environs. Icicles defy gravity. Fallen leaves assume an unattainably tidy form. Stones perform acrobatic feats of balance. Then there is the urgent race against time to capture each achievement in a photograph. The constructions must last just long enough to pose for the artist's camera. Within seconds after the shutter is snapped, the materials typically collapse, shrivel, scatter, melt, or tumble, reverting to their status as ordinary leaves, ice, and rocks. It is Goldsworthy's ordering efforts that make them intelligible as works of art, however briefly, until they are reclaimed by forces more persistent and powerful. That is why Goldsworthy says he creates "as if trying to hold on to some kind of stability against a backdrop that was really in turmoil."[6] That turmoil is the dynamism of life. It is the flux of weather. It is the course of evolution.

Photographs are essential to Goldsworthy's project. He envisions the camera angle while he is originating the form, anticipating a work's appearance as a static, two-dimensional construct even as he handles three-dimensional objects in four dimensions, including time. These picture-perfect images appear in lavishly illustrated coffee-table books that are widely distributed. The artist comments, "Each work grows, stays, decays—integral parts of a cycle which the photograph shows at its height, marking the moment when the work is most alive. There is intensity about a work at its peak that I hope is expressed in the image."[7]

Browsing through books of Goldsworthy's acclaimed photographs reveal that he is a master of anthropocentric beauty. To create these photographs, Goldsworthy tames the wildness out of leaves, ice, and stones to form mathematically precise abstractions like a spiral, circle, or line. The multitudes who delight in a Goldsworthy photograph confirm culturally entrenched anthropocentric preferences: tidiness, not nature's messiness; unity, not nature's diversity; simplicity, not nature's multiplicity; clarity, not nature's complexity; appearance, not nature's functions. Goldsworthy confirms, "My art is unmistakably the work of a person. I would not want it otherwise."[8]

From an environmental perspective, the allure of Goldsworthy's refinements aligns with the belief that nature is a resource to be manipulated by humans for humans. It is this assumption that can lead humans to generate the "unbeautiful" conditions that currently beset the planet. Goldsworthy has developed another body of work that conveys ecocentric beauty consistent with the dynamic forces that maintain the vitality of ecosystems. *Snowballs in Summer* (2000) embodies these divided loyalties. The exhibition officially opened on June 21, the longest day of the year. However, the sculptures were formed six months earlier because they required winter cold for forming and summer heat for melting. The sculptures took the form of thirteen snowballs that weighed between one and two tons each. They survived the vagaries of weather between their formation and their debut in a huge cold storage locker at Galloway Frozen Foods.

The snowballs assumed their ecocentric roles after they were transported by truck from the site of their creation in rural Scotland to the site of their display in urban London. In the predawn hours on Midsummer's Eve, Goldsworthy and a team of assistants scurried behind the truck and a forklift to distribute the frozen sculptures around the one square mile of London's financial district. Thus far, the work was anthropocentric.

The sculptures shifted into an ecocentric mode when the snowballs began to interact with the materials, conditions, and forces in their midst. Goldsworthy prepared for the artwork's second act by completing the distribution process before dawn. His deadline was de-

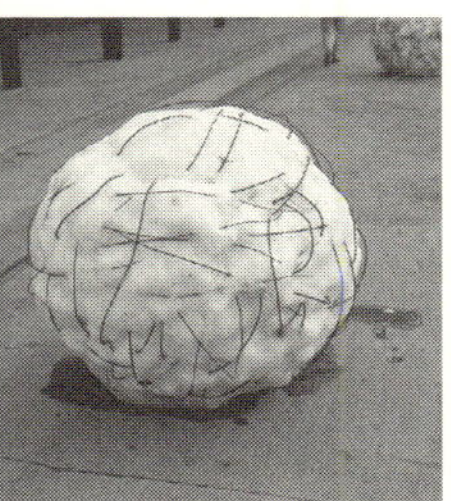 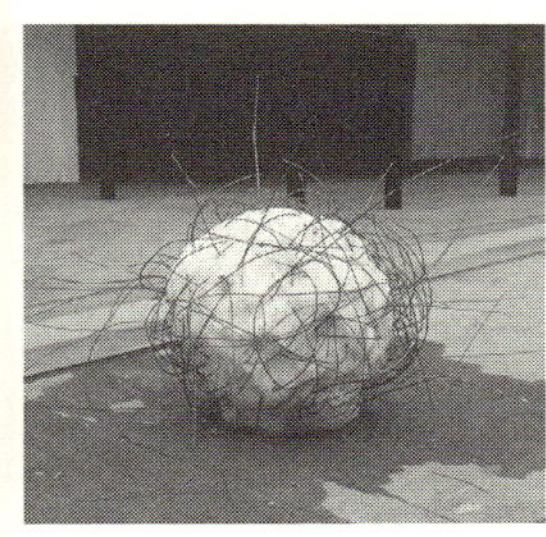 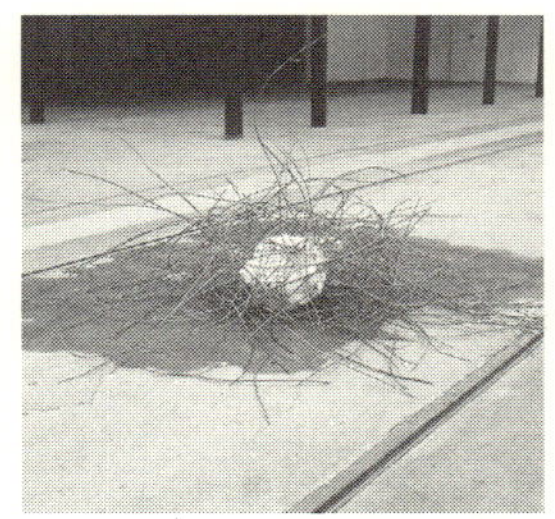 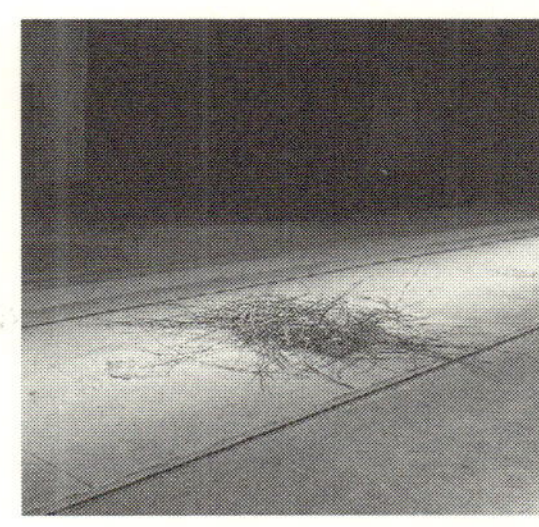

Andy Goldsworthy | Snowballs in Summer / Glasgow version/ Chalk | 1988–89 Snow and dogwood branches | Suite of four C-prints, 27½" × 77½" each

termined by a desire to heighten the drama of the commuters' encounters with the previous winter's snow melting under the summer sun. He calculated that by their lunchtime breaks, enough snow would have melted to reveal the bits of sheep's wool, crow feathers, chestnut seeds, ash seeds, Scots pine cones, elderberries, barley, metal, barbed wire, branches, chalk, pebbles, and cow hair that he had inserted as he formed the balls months before. By the evening commute home, these fragments would begin to drop. Gradually more would fall. The first items to fall lay in pools of melting ice, but after three to five days all that remained were bits of solid matter fallen in disarray on the sidewalks.

During the forming half of the creative process in Scotland, Goldsworthy enacted his feat-oriented, race-against-time art process. He explains, "There is always a sense of working against time and temperature. I feel such a sense of relief when the often dripping snowballs are put into the cold store and start freezing."[9] However, he relinquished his control during the melting half in London. That is when Goldsworthy yielded carving responsibilities to such uncontrollable conditions as temperature, shadow pattern, cloud cover, and wind. He also exposed the sculptures to the public's whims and impulses. In this manner *Snowballs* allowed the dynamic components of the site to factor into his artwork. He confirms this ecocentric perspective by commenting, "Time, change and fluidity in all things, not just snow, is the subject of the snowball project."[10]

Snowballs unites two divergent systems. One is composed of commuters preoccupied with affairs of finance, whose schedules are detailed by employer-employee contracts and whose activities are conducted indoors in mechanically controlled conditions. The other system consists of nonhuman conditions commuters easily neglect—the phase changes of water, temperature, season, wind, and sun made evident by the sculptures' melting, collapsing, sloughing, and evaporating. Goldsworthy explains, "I am interested in the dialogue between two time flows. A snowball melting amongst the river of people that flow through a city. . . . This is the audience the snowballs are aimed at and whose daily rhythms are in counterpoint to those of the snowball."[11] The audience makes these expanded connections because, unlike photographic records of situations that occurred in the past in a distant location, *Snowballs in Summer* enables people to make actual ecocentric connections with invisible forces and systems that exist in their midst.

The materials packed into the balls offer compelling cultural narratives. Goldsworthy explains the crumpled barbed wire in one snowball: "Both city and countryside are defined by boundaries and fences, which seem threatening from the outside yet secure from within. The barbed wire snowball will become protected as the wire is revealed during the melt.

The weaker and more vulnerable the snowball becomes, the stronger its defenses will be. Then, inevitably, the snow will be gone, leaving a pile of barbed wire without a purpose—just as I found it, rotting in coils at the edge of a field."[12]

Another snowball integrates with Smithfield Market, where meat has been sold since the twelfth century. It contains long red hair from highland cows. Goldsworthy comments that this snowball "will show something of the animal not usually seen—a reminder that these bits of meat are life. This is not a vegetarian stance, but a recognition of the animal, the land upon which it grew and the farmer who reared it."[13]

Other snowballs contain seeds that are released as the snow melts. Goldsworthy notes that urban seeding "could be seen as a hopeless attempt at growth in a built-up environment. For me it is an expression of nature's tenacious ability to re-colonize a city—to find cracks and openings into which a plant can throw down a root."[14]

Thus, while *Soul of a Tree* offers an experience that is exclusively visual and recognizably beautiful, *Snowballs in Summer* celebrates the entirety of ecosystem functions that may not conform to visual beauty but are examples of transformations that are ecologically beautiful because they are vital to maintaining ecosystem functions. Such beauty is not invented. It is discovered.

In sum, *anthropocentric beauty* privileges appearance, serves humans, manages materials and conditions; *ecocentric beauty* considers the welfare of all forms of life, enhances ecosystem functions, and involves responsive interactions. As a result, dynamic processes cease to be seen as obstacles to overcome, resources to consume, or conditions to control. Goldsworthy epitomizes this dichotomy.

NOTES

1 Frederic and Mary Ann Brussat, film review of *Rivers and Tides: Andy Goldsworthy Working with Time*. http://www.spiritualityandpractice.com/films/films.php?id=9214.

2 Joanna Pitman, "Andy Goldsworthy at YSP," *Times* online, March 26, 2007. http://entertainment.timesonline.co.uk/tol/arts_and_entertainment/visual_arts/article1567140.ece.

3 Arthur Lubow, "35 Who Made a Difference: Andy Goldsworthy," *Smithsonian Magazine*, November 2005. http://www.smithsonianmagazine.com/issues/2005/november/goldsworthy.php.

4 Stefan Beyst, "Andy Goldsworthy: The Beauty of Creation" (June 2002). http://d-sites.net/english/goldsworthy.htm.

5 Becky Mengel Freund, "Andy Goldsworthy," Web Design for Raymond Walters College. http://www.rwc.uc.edu/artcomm/web/w2005_2006/maria_Goldsworthy/philosophy.html.

6 "Mother Nature's Son," *Telegraph Magazine*, December 5, 2004. http://www.theage.com.au/news/Arts/Mother-natures-son/2004/12/04/1101923382384.html.

7 Holly Holmes and Emily Busse, "What Is Art? What Is an Artist?" Department of Art History, Sweet Briar College. http://www.arthistory.sbc.edu/artartists/photoandy.html.

8 Richard Mabey, "Andy Goldsworthy's Ecological Art," *Guardian Unlimited*, March 31, 2007. www.arts.guardian.co.uk/art/visualart/story/0,,2046697,00.html.

9 Andy Goldsworthy talks to Conrad Bodman, Curator at the Barbican Centre in London. This interview was produced by the Barbican to mark Goldsworthy's "Snowballs in Summer" project. Copyright Andy Goldsworthy 2000.

10 Ibid.

11 Ibid.

12 Ibid.

13 Ibid.

14 Ibid.

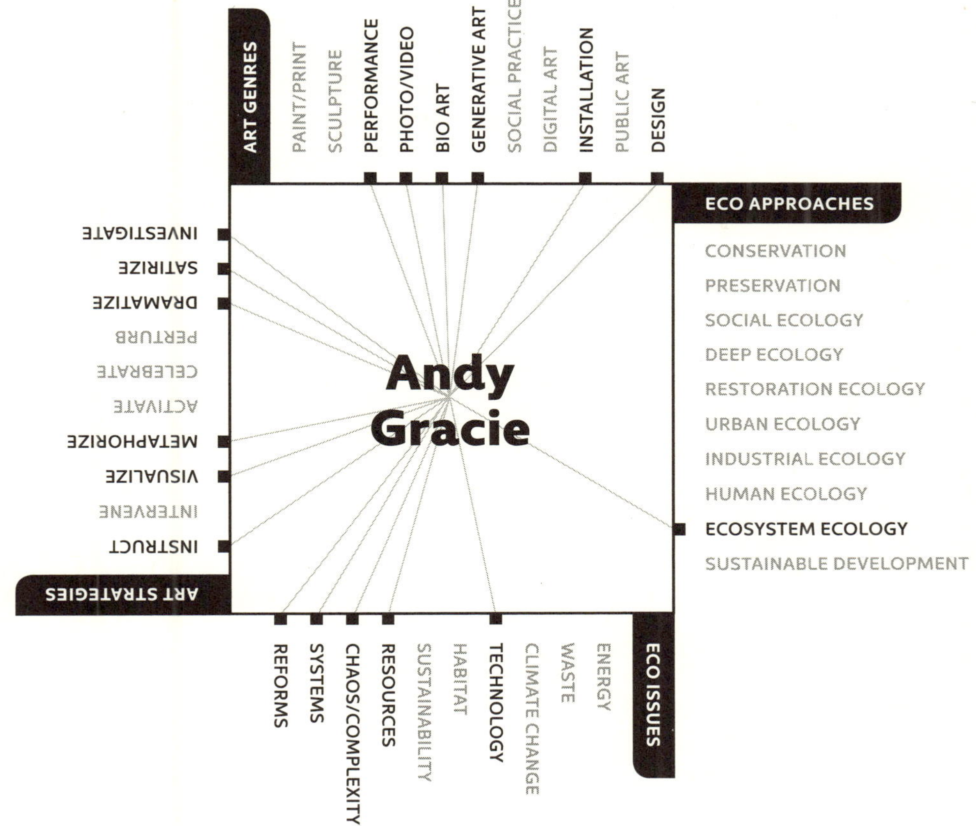

Bioelectronics

Born 1967, London, England

BIOELECTRONICS is a paradigm-shifting discipline that is positioned at the interface between biology and electrical engineering, with chemistry and physics included as well. Advocates have faith that integrating biology and electronics promises such desirable outcomes as advances in health care, a cleaner environment, and enhanced national security. Critics fear that this intensification of technology's role in human experience will divert people from natural systems and further alienate them from the planet's functional, aesthetic, ethical, and spiritual endowments. Andy Gracie's bioelectronic art practice provides the occasion to contemplate these dual outcomes. He comments, "Whatever our stance on these

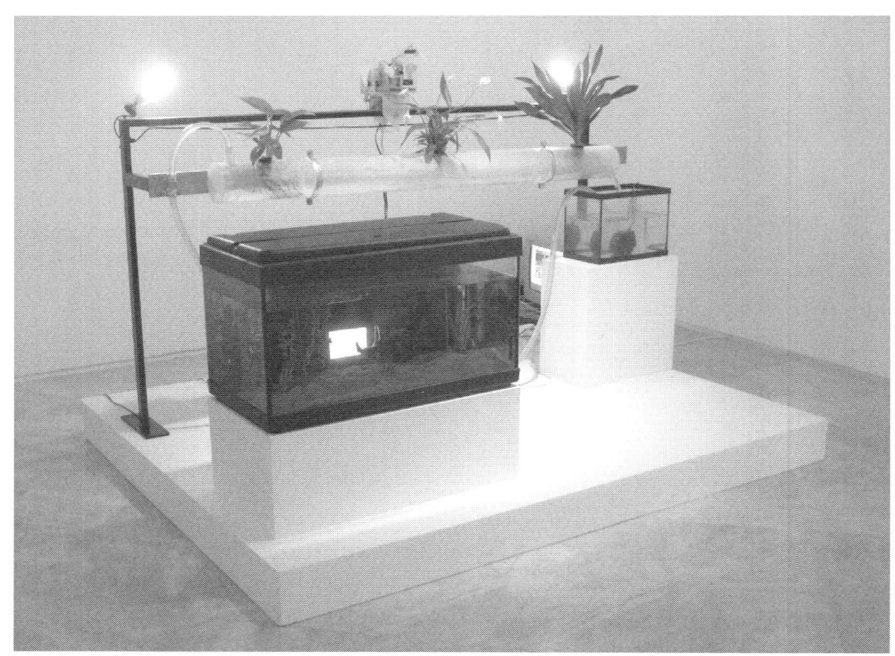

Andy Gracie | fish, plant, rack | 2004 Mixed media installation | Dimensions: 6.5′ × 4.9′ × 4.9′ approx

PHOTO: ANDY GRACIE / COURTESY ANDY GRACIE

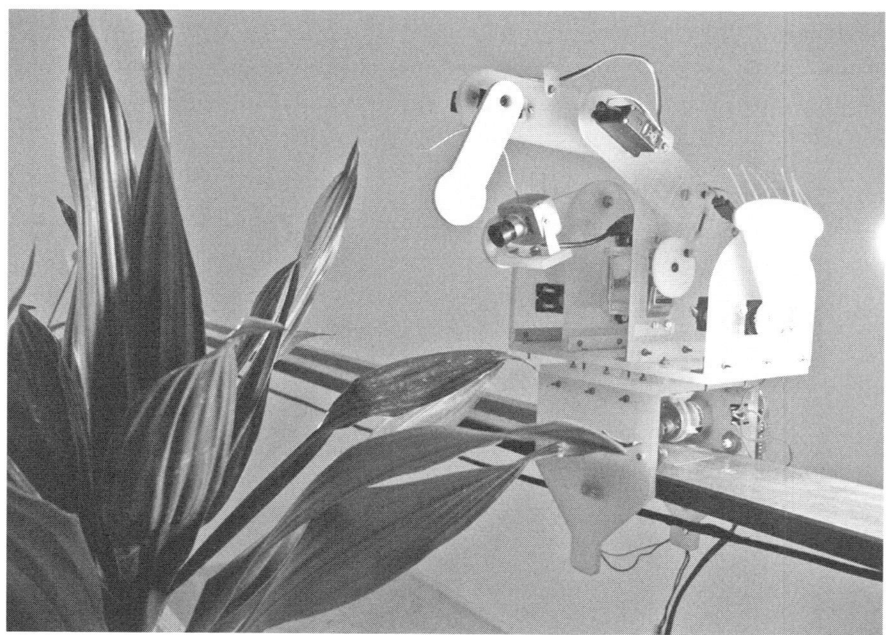

Andy Gracie | fish, plant, rack (detail) | 2004 Mixed media installation | Dimensions: 6.5′ × 4.9′ × 4.9′ approx

PHOTO: ANDY GRACIE / COURTESY ANDY GRACIE

questions though, it is relatively easy to imagine a 'natural' appearing environment which is in fact completely separate from nature and maintained via technological means. The home hydroponic system is the simple end of the scale, the future multistory industrial farm is the other."[1]

Gracie presents the escalating contest between the natural and the unnatural by merging biological systems that existed long before humans began playing a role in Earth's history with electronic systems that epitomize advancements recently engineered by humans. By linking these disparate systems together into a composite whole, Gracie explores the mystifying domain of human possibility. Humanity's future and the future of the planet may be determined, in large measure, by their interdependence.

By attempting to establish a communications network that links a living organic entity and a synthetic electronic device, the installation entitled *fish, plant, rack* (2004) delves into the revolutionizing promises of bioelectronics. Technically, the system of relationships Gracie creates combines biology and biochemical interactions with electronic signal detection, processing, and analysis. He delivers these technically daunting specifications to viewers in an enchanting and amusing manner that resembles a comic burlesque more than a solemn prognostication or a scholarly dissertation. This amusement is formulated out of the bizarre cast of characters that populate and activate his bioelectronics installation:

Fish An elephant nose fish occupies an aquarium that is prominently displayed in the installation. Its extended lower jaw explains how it got its name. This species is semiblind and emits small electrical pulses from an organ located inside the nose in order to navigate, hunt, and communicate. The pulsations change depending on the fish's mental and physical state.

Plants Three varieties of common indoor plants are growing hydroponically in a single clear tube that is filled with nutrient solution. This rack hangs high and horizontally between two grow lights.

Robot A small robot sits on a horizontal bar that is installed just above the rack containing the plant's hydroponic solution. The robot's lightweight construction consists of a white polycarbonate body, a low-geared DC motor, four standard servo motors, and an onboard micro video camera. All these "organs" and "nerves" are exposed. It also has a microcontroller mounted on its back to receive AI instructions that it must interpret in order to act.

The daunting premise posed by *fish, plant, rack* is that a coherent communication network can be accomplished when aquatic, botanical, and electronic systems interact. By escalating the handicaps, Gracie predisposes the system to resemble a ludicrous burlesque, not a utopian hope for the future. The convoluted nature of the communication trail optimizes the possibility of communication breakdowns. It proceeds along the following trajectory:

Fish to robot The fish's electrical pulses take the form of clicks and pauses. As such, they resemble the binary code of zeros and ones. Using the artificial intelligence system known as DharmAi,[2] the robot hears the incoming stream of audible pulses from the fish. This activates the robot's artificial intelligence program, enabling it to interpret the emerging patterns and densities. These clicks are amplified so that humans can listen in to the fish's transmissions in real time. They comprise a processed generative soundscape.

Robot to plants When the robot is first turned on, all it has is an operating system and a set of possibilities, much like any other computer. As information is received from the fish, these possibilities and capacities are unlocked and recombined to form new capacities. Thus, the robot is not a slavish automaton. Gracie complicates its contribution to this bioelectronics communication system by endowing the robot with choices. For instance, it has the ability to vary its regimens for dispensing nutrients to the plants, discharge its own vibrations and frequencies, and even modify its own behavioral codes. Since the process by which the robot "learns" how to process the hidden language within the fish's signals is gradual, its behavioral responses are refined over the course of the exhibition.

Gracie explains that the robot does not actually care for the plants, although it contrives strategies for interacting with the plants using touch, vibration, and sound. "The robot's actions refer to experiments carried out in the '60s and '70s where plants were found to respond to noise and vibration. The conclusions pointed towards a correlation between the growth of plant cells and various frequencies. This research is described in Peter Tompkins and Christopher Bird's book *The Secret Life of Plants*."[3]

Expressing "feelings" through motions and sound and light signals is another capacity bequeathed to the robot. Gracie qualifies this capacity by commenting, "I think the emotions and feelings I mention are more metaphorical than literal. For example, there is a sense of agitation if the fish is not sending much information, where the way in which the robot moves could be seen as impatient or frustrated, or even bored. Likewise if it is receiving a lot of information it will appear more excited. The speed at which it moves and the expressivity of the 'wing' and 'arm' movements, as well as the speed and frequencies of the sound, suggest these feelings."[4]

Plants to fish The fish observes the results of its instructions via a tiny screen that is fixed to the outside of its tank. These live-feed images are transmitted from a video camera mounted on the robot. They display the plants' conditions and growth.

The convoluted trail of communication can be summarized as follows: environmental conditions trigger responses in a fish that emits electrical impulses that become audible clicks that are transformed into electronic data that generate actions that affects botanical growth that is recorded by a camera and sent as electronic data to be projected as video images visible to the fish. Gracie says, "It's a bit like a game of Chinese whispers in that you never know what is going to come out the other end. These kind of works exhibit forms of closed system feedback loop that are very common in ecological, biological and social systems."[5] The work's message is clear. Predictable outcomes in all these categories are unlikely.

As Gracie indicates, obstacles to meaningful communications are inherent to nature's systems. Unintentional interdependencies are apparent in pine trees, for example, which happen to produce needles so that bluebirds can build nests; nor do frogs lay eggs expressly to feed other aquatic animals. By the same token, pine trees and frogs cannot be blamed for withholding these resources any more than the fish and robot could be blamed for neglecting the plants in Gracie's installation. Conscious intention is not the operational principle that runs most of the planet's systems.

However, the long history of life on Earth demonstrates that functionality can be accomplished by relationships that lack conscious communications. The round-robin transfer of information ensues, although there is no intentional transmission from the semiblind aquatic sender, nor conscious understanding by the sighted robotic recipient. The fact that the plants survive under the robot's care is evidence that the system functions, but it hardly conveys a triumph of efficient design. Gracie makes certain that the viewer gets the point of this drama. Despite the sophistication of its program, the robot often flails as if trying to figure out how to interpret the patterns and densities of clicks, implying that the fate of the hydroponic plants is being determined more by happenstance than design.

Gracie expands on the unplanned and unforeseen character of natural systems by adding a reasonably intelligent robot. He defines this hybrid ecology as "the 'next nature' or 'post nature.'"[6] In order for communication to transpire within a postnatural system, both artificial and natural intelligences must relinquish their normal modes of operation and discover a common ground between them. They must enter, he declares, a "third state."[7]

Humans are absent from the routing of information in the artwork's third-state communication system. Their roles occur behind the scenes as they provide nutrient solution for the plants, food for the fish, electricity for the pump and lights, software for the robot, and so on. This is an artistic intentional maneuver to evoke "a meditation on ecosystems which are completely isolated from any kind of fundamentally natural or human influence or interference."[8] In this manner, the piece envisions a third state that is anticipated by smart technologies that are currently managing manufacture, banking, voting, tax reporting, surgery, surveillance, entertainment, leisure, and transport. The next frontiers of occupation are thinking and creativity.

Gracie adopts the earnest demeanor of an environmentalist when he considers postnatural realities, "With the continuous introduction of man-made products into the natural environment such as genetically modified plants and animals and the gradual convergence of nature and technology through biomimetics, biorobotics and cybernetics, it is worthwhile to explore the adaptive reactions of animals to these disruptions of their ecosystems and the possibility of new data types suggested by nature/machine interactions. Our aim with this work is to provoke thought about how new technologies are changing the way both humans and nature live and evolve, and how many vital processes that shape the world around us are adapting to accommodate new bioartificial ecosystems."[9]

The imminent emergence of a technologized environment leads Gracie to conclude by posing a wry dilemma: "The logical—or maybe not so logical—extension of this line of thinking leads us to scenarios of how we will be able to get what we need from nature once we have fully removed ourselves from it."[10]

NOTES

1 Andy Gracie, "2000 to 2010 . . . Research, Narratives and Practice . . . An Overview," October 2010. http://www.hostprods.net/text/20002010/.

2 The design of DharmAi was by Brian Lee Dae Yung for this project.

3 Andy Gracie e-mail correspondence with the author, January 6, 2011.

4 Ibid.

5 Andy Gracie, "Interview with Andy Gracie" by Regine, *We Make Money Not Art*, October 18, 2006. http://www.we-make-money-not-art.com/archives/2006/10/whats-your-back.php.

6 Andy Gracie, "Tightening the Loop: From Machine-Nature Communication Towards Symbiosis," by Andy Gracie and Brian Lee Yung Rowe, Siteseerx (2002). http://citeseerx.ist.psu.edu/viewdoc/summary?doi=10.1.1.103.1085.

7 Ibid.

8 Andy Gracie, "2000 to 2010 . . . Research, Narratives and Practice . . . An Overview," October 2010. http://www.hostprods.net/text/20002010/.

9 http://hostprods.net/rsc/Tightening_Loop.pdf.

10 Andy Gracie, "2000 to 2010 . . . Research, Narratives and Practice . . . An Overview," October 2010. http://www.hostprods.net/text/20002010/.

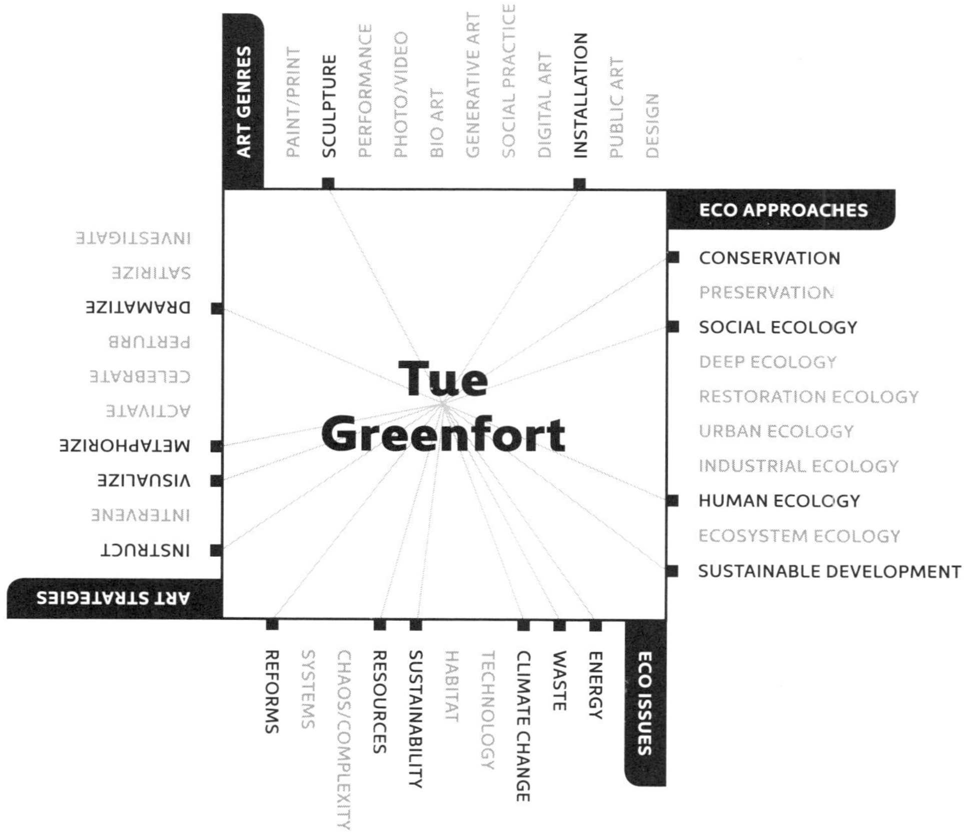

Salvation through Conservation

Born 1973, Holbaek, Denmark

TUE GREENFORT IS NO LIGHTWEIGHT ARTIST, but he may qualify for the title of featherweight champion of contemporary art because his minimal artworks are models of artistic restraint. He produces droplet-scaled artworks for a splash-starved art world, commenting, "My attempted perception of the total biosphere begins with the small experiences of nature and extends outwards. I believe that whatever we might recognize, be it a bird or a small plant, we still do not have a clue about what it actually means. This is nature. It represents this complex relationship between belonging and the unknown. Behind this understanding lies—for me—the belief that we humans do not play an important role in the bigger picture, that there is no meaning to our existence. We are not here with a special mission, which would give our existence a reason."[1]

An example of his stripped-down manner of delivering a hefty dose of environmental guilt is provided by a work entitled *Exceeding 2 Degrees* (2007). The installation links a worldwide concern about global warming to a national context in the United Arab Emirates. To create this work, Greenfort convinced the Sharjah Art Museum to adjust its air-conditioning thermostat by two degrees, making it slightly warmer than normal. The intervention was dramatized by the museum's location in a country known for its scorching climate (temperatures can reach 130 degrees Fahrenheit), its abundant energy resources (the UAE possesses enormous oil and natural gas reserves), and ironically, its mounting energy deficiencies (despite its abundance of resources, supplies of electricity lag behind rapid domestic and commercial development).[2]

At the time the work was shown, references to "two degrees" were appearing so frequently in the news that they became a slogan of impending climate calamity. These two words consolidated the findings of a 700-page report issued by the Stern Review, *The Economics of Climate Change* (2006). The report announced that 2 degrees Celsius (3.6 degrees Fahrenheit) was the dreaded temperature change that would trigger global catastrophe. It projected that worldwide emissions would need to be cut to at least 25 percent below current levels to avoid this rise in temperature. The report was presented as an urgent call for worldwide economic, political, and consumer reform. Greenfort made certain that visitors understood this reference by adding a few pages from the report to the installation "as a clear reference to the title and to the overall concept behind the project."[3] Greenfort's initiative not only dramatized the truth of these warnings, it manifested the ease of complying with them.

Minimal material investment was required to complete this work. It consisted of a meteorological instrument called a thermo hygrograph, coffee table, glass, human hair, plastic membrane, climate diagram, certificate, and map, plus photography. Yet these nominal expenditures of material were offset by major negotiations with the conservation staff at the Sharjah Museum. The conservators protested that even this modest rise in temperature could endanger the valuable artworks in their collection. Concern over the sensitivity of the artifacts was aggravated by the fear of upsetting the owner of the collection and the museum's major supporter. HH Sheikh Dr. Sultan bin Mohammed Al Qasimi was also a member of the Supreme Council of the UAE and ruler of Sharjah. Ultimately, permission was granted to include this work in an exhibition that seems to have anticipated such conflicts. Its title was "Still Life: Art, Ecology and the Politics of Change."

Greenfort utilized four strategies to make the barely perceptible temperature shift noticeable to museum visitors. Each element highlighted the consumption of fossil fuels and the critical need for conservation:

- The wide passageways within the museum were draped with huge sheets of foil polyethylene, a thin transparent plastic. The plastic was installed with slack so that it billowed out when the air-conditioning was active and it sagged when it was not, conferring a powerful visible presence to invisible air. It also dramatized peoples' demands for energy-consuming comforts.
- A thermo hygrograph was placed on a decoratively carved wooden coffee table. The device continually measured and recorded the temperature and

humidity in the gallery. The artist's own hair was inserted as the active element responding to the fluctuating conditions. The thermo hygrograph documented the activity of the AC system in the gallery while a paper plotter reported how much electricity was being saved by resetting the dial on the thermostat.

- The elaborately carved table on which the thermo hygrograph was placed was itself installed on a white pedestal. By presenting the table in the manner of a sculpture, viewers were notified of its relationship to the theme of this installation—energy use and climate change. Labels provided the explanation. They announced that the wood for the table grew in Malaysia, was shipped to Japan for fabrication, and then arrived halfway around the globe in Dubai. Yet despite its global travels, it was very inexpensive. By pairing high environmental investments and low sticker cost, the table embodied the convoluted economic model common in industrialized nations and its problematic effects on climate.
- Wall texts conveyed straightforward information about the themes implied by the other elements in the installation. They took the form of notated diagrams from the thermo hygrograph, assembly instructions from the mass-produced coffee table, the signed agreement from the museum to increase the temperature by two degrees Celsius, photographs of the museum's air-conditioning system, and a lengthy quote from *The Economics of Climate Change: The Stern Review*. In all, the installation served as a call to action to increase energy efficiency and reduce energy demand.

Greenfort capitalized on the fact that reducing energy use also reduced the museum's energy costs by introducing another conservation measure into this installation. He stipulated that the museum donate the dollars that were saved from their energy bill to the environmental organization Nepenthes, to purchase rain forest for preservation in Ecuador.

In sum, this installation functions like an equation in which the two degrees represents a global warming problem on one side and a global warming solution on the other. The problem relates incremental temperature change to catastrophic consequences; this side of the equation asserts the necessity for initiating reforms. The solution side of the equation relates this barely perceptible two-degree difference to remedial measures; it demonstrates that conserving energy is an achievable goal if individuals, corporations, and government agencies share the responsibility.

Where does Greenfort's project fit within the history of contemporary art? Despite his extreme frugality of means, it cannot be described by the term *dematerialization* that was introduced in the seminal text *Six Years: The Dematerialization of the Art Object from 1966 to 1972*. In that context, authors Lucy Lippard and John Chandler define dematerialized art as "an ultra-conceptual art that emphasizes the thinking process almost exclusively."[4] *Exceeding 2 Degrees* is not "dematerialized," because it does not divert attention from the tangible object to the intangible concept; in fact, the work is emphatically rooted in the material environment. Nor can Greenfort's work be described as "immaterial." The term sometimes describes performance art, which is immaterial because it is an ephemeral event. It is also applied to computer art that is immaterial because it is based upon digitized data.

Greenfort's efforts may best be described as "eco materialization" because they economize on the material components of art production. The guiding principle of sustainability

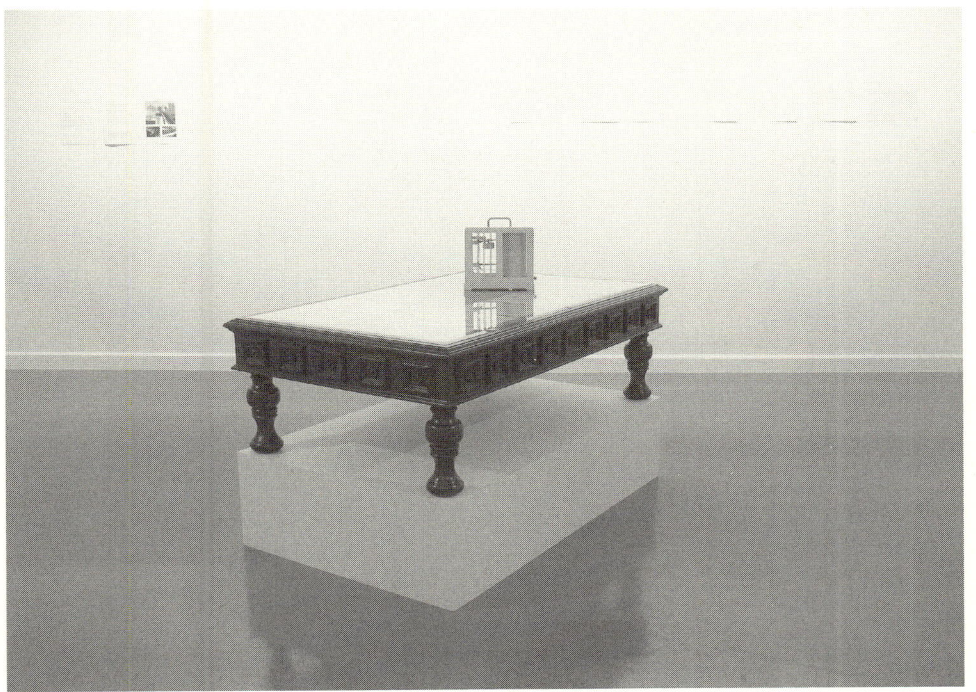

Tue Greenfort | Exceeding 2 Degrees | 2007 Thermo hygrograph (meteorological instrument), coffee table, Malaysian rubber wood, glass, human hair, plastic membrane, Stern Report quotes, A4 photocopy, photography, climate diagram, certificate, map | Exhibition view: Still Life: Art, Ecology and the Politics of Change, Sharjah Biennial 8, Sharjah, United Arab Emirates | Dimensions: variable

PHOTO: TUE GREENFORT / COURTESY JOHANN KÖNIG, BERLIN

is to reduce the quantity of energy and materials required to serve a function. Greenfort explains how he applies this maxim: "I would point out that my work still follows the old codes of 'conceptualism' and 'dematerialization,' though not by ignoring or compromising the object and the material but by reflecting its physicality and belonging to the notion of place and resource/energy flow. This links strongly to the scientific use and exploration of the ecosystem as such."[5]

PET-Flasche (2008) provides a vivid example of eco materialization. This sculpture consists of a single, shriveled plastic water bottle that looks as grisly and as pitiable as a shrunken skull. Greenfort made the sculpture by emptying the mineral water from a standard 1½ liter PET mineral water bottle, melting it in an oven, and then refilling it with tap water to its greatly reduced capacity—merely a half liter. The shrunken bottle reveals as much about industrialized societies around the globe as shrunken heads reveal about indigenous cultures in the Amazon basin. Both are trophies of violent acts that are rewarded with status and wealth. In this instance, the violence is committed by the producers and consumers of bottled water. As the title indicates, the bottle (*flasche* in German) was created with PET (polyethylene terephthalate), a substance with a schizoid personality. On the one hand, PET is a wonder material that combines functionality and recyclability. It is strong, lightweight, and cheap and can be melted and reshaped when it is subjected to heat. Greenfort introduced the unsavory aspects of PET's personality by posting the diseconomies associated with drinking bottled water in the exhibition. "Producing 1 kilogram of PET plastic requires

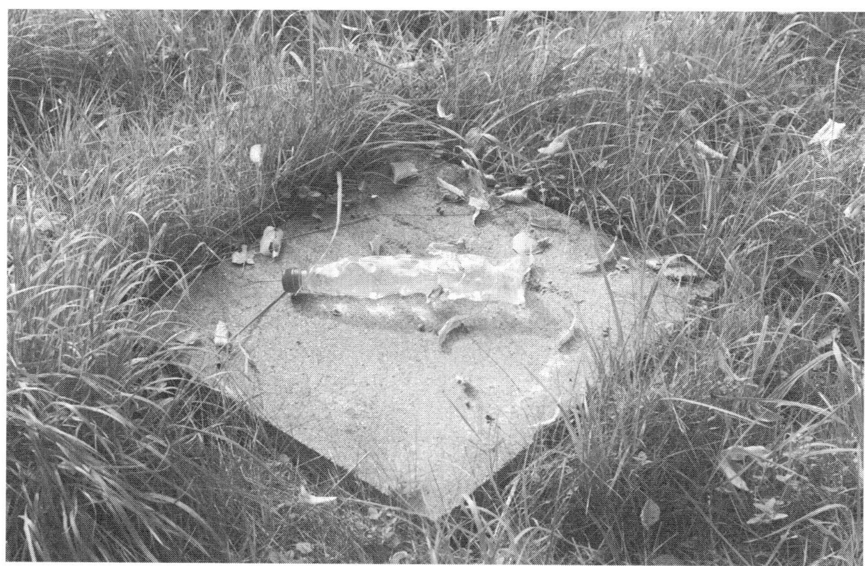

Tue Greenfort | PET-Flasche | 2008 PET water bottle, Braunschweig tap water, groundwater | Exhibition view: Linear Deflection, Kunstverein Braunschweig, Germany | Dimensions: variable

PHOTO: ALEXIS ZAVIOLOFF / COURTESY JOHANN KÖNIG, BERLIN

17.5 kilograms of water and results in air emissions of 40 grams of hydrocarbons, 25 grams of sulphur oxides, 18 grams of carbon monoxide, 20 grams of nitrogen oxides, and 2.3 kilograms of carbon dioxide. In terms of water use alone, much more is consumed in making the bottles than will ever go into them."[6]

Although recycling of water bottles diverts materials from landfills and incineration, Greenfort's isolated bottle suggests the disquieting truth that recycling does not provide a sustainable solution for PET products. Inefficiencies are associated with fossil fuels burned during transport to markets, handling plastic waste, packaging that consumes more water to produce than the package can hold, and costs of recycling that exceed costs of virgin plastic.[7] These facts become much more disquieting when they are accompanied by a withered and wasted emblem of consumer culture. It demonstrates that Greenfort's contribution to the debate regarding PET packaging is to add the evocative and ethical implications of the rigorous and scientific data.

A progressive reduction of material inputs and expansion of ethical stances distinguishes Greenfort's career. He explains,

> I started out as a painter. But this was before I became aware of different artists' practices that directly took up environmental questions and ecological issues. I came back to my real interest in the idea and understanding of the natural world. I was interested in these issues before my time as an art student, when I birded a lot, studied butterflies and was a member of several environmentalist groups. . . . Watching nature programs on TV by the likes of Jacques Cousteau in the 80s was certainly influential for me. They usually had a very pessimistic moral message along the lines of: "if you don't want these beautiful animals to become extinct in your lifetime then we'd better change our way of living," and this didn't go unnoticed with me.[8]

Greenfort first imagined becoming a fearless Greenpeace warrior fighting against nuclear power plants and whalers. "But over time I think these adventurous organizations ceded to more basic desires. The romantic ideals of riding the waves and fighting evil industries became compromised as the picture became more complex."[9] He shifted from bombast to restraint because the complexity he discerned requires quietude for observation and deliberation. Greenfort shares the perception that he discovered in this quiet space and that guides his practice: "I observe nature as an external phenomenon . . . call it a habitat or a certain environment—where other organisms are present beside me. It's a form of mirroring and it's important for me to turn to the other forms of life that exist alongside human life."[10]

NOTES

1 Tue Greenfort interview with Zoe Gray, *Tue Greenfort: Photosynthesis.* (The Netherlands: Witte de With Gallery, 2006).

2 US Energy Information Center. http://www.eia.doe.gov/cabs/UAE/Background.html.

3 Tue Greenfort correspondence with the author, October 20, 2010.

4 Lucy Lippard, *Six Years: The Dematerialization of the Art Object from 1966 to 1972* (London, Berkeley: University of California Press, 1997), 42.

5 Tue Greenfort correspondence with the author, October 20, 2010.

6 Paul McRandle, "Behind the Scenes: Bottled Water," *State of the World, 2004* (Worldwatch Institute publication, 2004), 86.

7 http://www.ecologycenter.org/ptf/misconceptions.html.

8 Tue Greenfort quoted in "Max Andrews: Weirdy Beardy," *Wonderland* no. 2 (January 2006). http://johannkoenig.de/inc/02_art_texts_popup.php?publication_id=99.

9 Ibid.

10 Ibid.

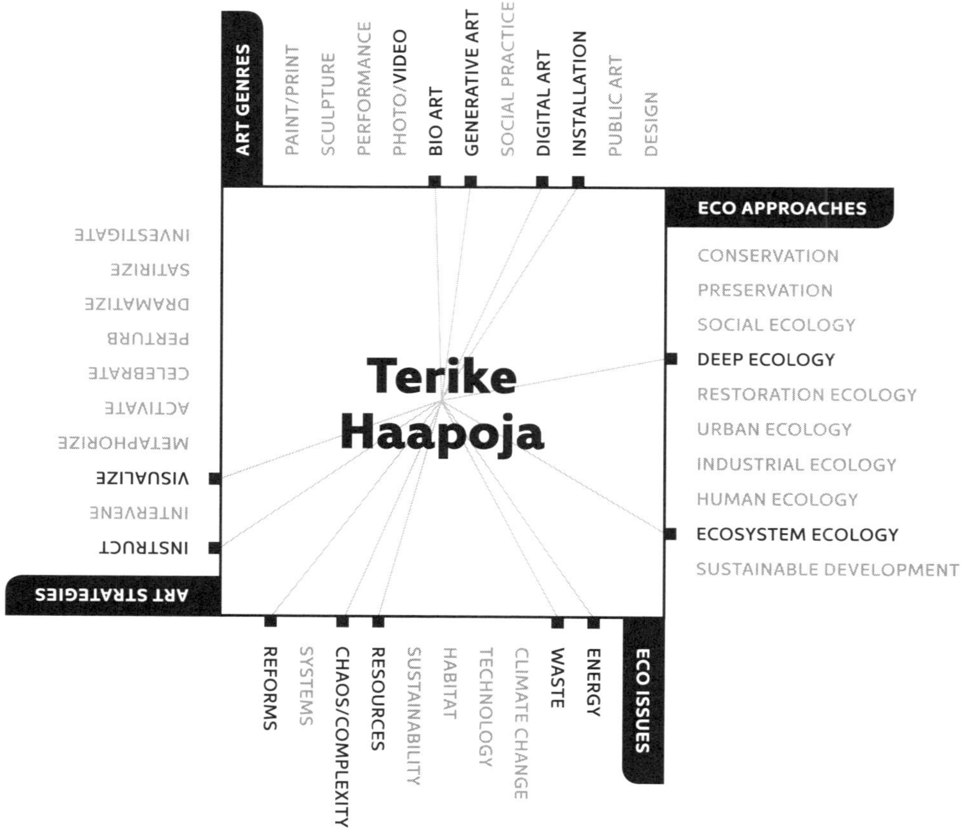

Cross-Species Affinity

Born 1974, Helsinki, Finland

"I **EXPERIENCE SPACES**. I am always more interested in what is happening around me. I explore otherness."[1]

In this statement, Terike Haapoja implies that she sheds self-expression, self-assertion, and self-consciousness from her art. By presenting herself in terms of her surroundings and the varied populations that occupy them, this Finnish artist replaces these unilateral aspects of conventional art with multilateral perspectives of eco art. Things normally identified as separate from the self, different from the self, or as context for the self are her primary focus. The specific events and entities she presents are distinguished in two ways. First, the human body's sensory apparatus cannot discern them. Second, they are the events that are commonly thought of as repulsive. The second refers to death and decay; the first, to the multitudes of microorganisms that inhabit our bodies.

Haapoja relies on sophisticated scientific tools to generate visually alluring images of these outcasts from common experience. She notes, "I have always been interested in the relationship between the spectator/audience and the environment. That is how I became involved in new technologies that were derived from science. Each new optical device allows us to gain knowledge of the micro and macro scales of nature. They form relationships with nature. I am not as interested in the image as I am in these new relationships. My work is not about representation, and it is not about framing preconditions. Every physical process is an emergence of consciousness or subjectivity or experience of life. Expanding perception is the role of art. That is what I seek when I work with scientific tools to create art."[2]

Sources of estrangement from the "other" were replaced with opportunities to form affinities in the six installations that comprised "Closed Circuit–Open Duration" (2008), an exhibition that first opened at the Gallery Forum Box in Helsinki. This affinity was facilitated by architectural spaces, platforms, and passages providing places for visitors to pause, observe, listen, and interact. Each installation gently unhinged viewers' self-orientations and connected them to an expanded ecocentered otherness. The title suggests the merging of a closed-circuit path of currents that flow among organisms and open-duration processes that sustain the lives of individuals and species. In order to realize these interactions in sound, light, and movement, the installations incorporate tools utilized in environmental research, as well as digital and analogical technologies.

Succession (2008), a work included in the "Closed Circuit–Open Duration" exhibition, introduces ecocentric interactions between humans and nonhumans. These nonhumans are not the typical species, such as garden plants and pets. Instead, the work features trillions of invisible bacteria and parasites. They are shown in this single-channel video projection reproducing, struggling to stay alive, and dying. This life/death scenario cannot be classified as another's drama, because the bacteria were harvested from Haapoja's own body when she rubbed her face with a canvas about 8" x 9". She then recorded the invisible creatures until the last one died nine days later. The video, edited into a four-minute loop, provides irrefutable evidence that the *self* consists of multitudes of microscopic species. It affirms that existence depends upon coexistence. It is, therefore, folly to think of ourselves as autonomous individuals. Haapoja comments, "This work can be considered a portrait because bacteria are part of us. It is called *Succession* because that is the word used by microbiologists to describe the cultivation of microbes. This work shows different colonies of bacteria emerging. They grow and fade. We are not individuals, but communities of species."[3] Haapoja's self-portrait, therefore, is presented in terms of the organisms that her body hosts. Some of the microbes that live in and on her body cause disease. Others are essential for her well-being. Both kinds derive nourishment from her cells and fluids. They depend upon her warmth.

Haapoja goes on to explain why she uses a circular format when projecting the nine-day drama of microbe populations perishing: "I chose a moon shape for my human microbiome project because only 1 percent of the species in our bodies is known. What is interesting is the reason we don't know more. Most species can't survive outside of the habitat we provide. This is a metaphor of unknown-ness! The video looks like an old NASA film because the human body is like a new discovery."[4] Haapoja suggests that after mapping the human genome, the next great feat of science might entail mapping humanity's microbiome. That

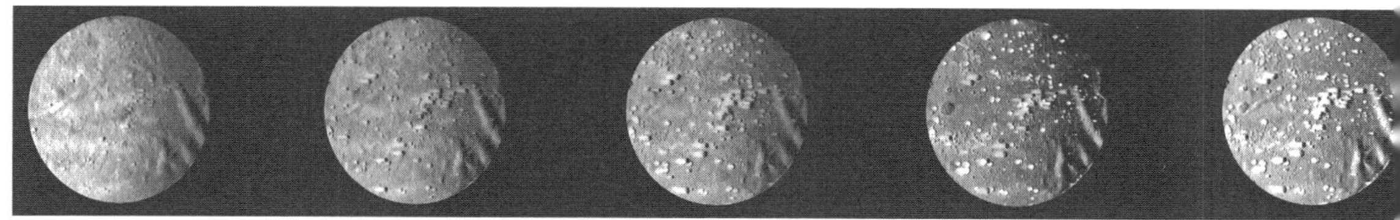

Terike Haapoja | Succession | 2008 Still from one-channel video installation of facial bacteria developing and dying | Duration: four minutes, loop | Projection size: variable
COURTESY TERIKE HAAPOJA

less than 1 percent of species living in a human body are identified is why she refers to the inhabitants of our bodies as a "wilderness."[5]

Dialogue (2008), another work in the "Closed Circuit–Open Duration" exhibition, provides an opportunity for museum visitors to help sustain the live trees that grow through a platform in the installation. A bench is installed nearby as an invitation for visitors to sit and initiate the process of giving a gift to the trees simply by whistling. When they do, a carbon dioxide sensor placed in front of the bench is activated and turns on three spotlights that are focused on the trees' branches. This light initiates the photosynthesis process in the leaves, showing museum visitors that they are feeding the trees the carbon dioxide they require simply by exhaling. Because this exchange of carbon dioxide is invisible, Haapoja provides an audible verification of the viewers' contributions. This is accomplished with sound-generating devices adapted from forest ecology for measuring photosynthesis. They are hung on the trees' branches. As a result the trees seem to answer the whistling of humans by whistling back. Otherness dissolves into oneness as this whistling call-and-response ensues between humans and the trees.

Haapoja explains her intentions by stating, "The interaction between species is thus physical, as we are practically parts of the same metabolism. I wanted to address the relations of human and nonhuman world in a playful tone, by suggesting that the interaction with human breathing, technology, and photosynthesis could be understood as a dialogue, not as a mere reaction, but as communication."[6] *Dialogue* thereby demonstrates that since carbon dioxide is the product of multidirectional interactions, there is no *other*. As we breathe out, we release carbon dioxide into the atmosphere. Photosynthetic organisms fix the carbon dioxide and release oxygen, enabling us to survive.

Haapoja explains her work in terms of inquiries into persistent issues that seem to baffle philosophers and pragmatists: "When does a living 'thing' become a 'being' and not an object? What kind of change in perception has to occur before we understand this experience as a dialogue? This raises a huge ethical dimension within the environmental movement and animal rights."[7] In other words, Haapoja traces the possibility of environmental reform to recognition that the nonhumans that support us also depend upon us.

Community (2007) is a video installation that presents death as an event that is both physical and emotional. It transforms the grisly spectacle of decaying corpses into five visually beautiful video projections. Each projection is accompanied by five-channel sound that documents the gradual cooling of an animal corpse, a process that commences immediately after an organism takes its last breath. Spectators observe life-size videos of the cooling of a dead horse, a calf, a cat, a bird, and a dog. Instead of being projected like paintings onto gallery walls, the videos are projected like spotlights on the floor. Spatially, they appear to

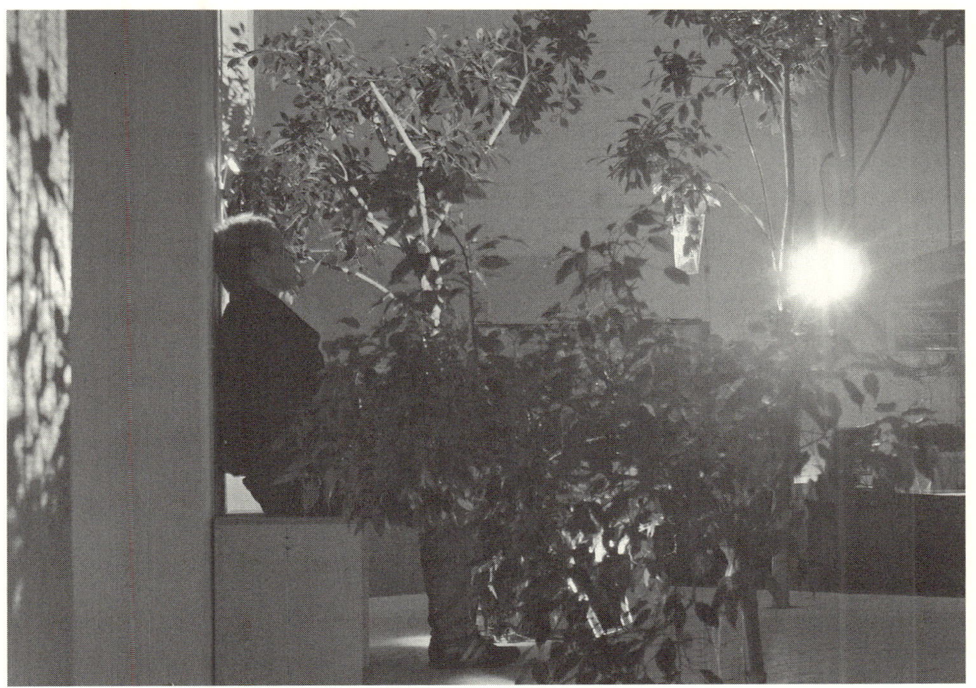

Terike Haapoja | Dialogue | 2008 Interactive installation | Live trees, electronics, sound, light, carbon dioxide sensors, breathing | Dimensions: variable | Programming: Aleksi Pihkanen, Gregoire Rousseau

COURTESY TERIKE HAAPOJA

have succumbed to gravity, like real corpses. In this way, *Community* evokes the emotional charge of real-life encounters with death.

The videos were created by replacing a normal camera that is light sensitive with an infrared camera that is heat sensitive. During the process of losing heat, the image of the animal slowly vanishes. This postdeath scenario is not a predictable process. The rate of cooling is different in different parts of the body, and it varies depending upon the size of animal and the ambient temperature in the environment. The process was so slow for the larger animals that these videos were condensed in time. The decay of the smaller animals proceeds in real time. No animals were sacrificed to create this work of art. Each was scheduled to be euthanized by veterinarians.

These videos manage to be disquieting despite the proliferation of images of death and mayhem in popular culture and the media, perhaps because evidence of the unraveling of the orderly form of an organism into a disorganized array of molecules is rarely included in media representations of death. The fading of each animal in the videos manifests the merging of Haapoja's ecological and artistic interest in "gradually disappearing." She explains, "As we die, the difference between us and our surroundings vanish. We give away the energy needed for sustaining life, we lose the coherent form of our body, and finally, we become dust."[8] Haapoja refers to the dust phase as a "horizon we cannot see beyond,"[9] commenting, "For us, death is a significant point of no return. In physical reality there is no end. As we die we disappear and get organized again. This piece is a delicate reminder that the human community is based on the deaths of other species."[10] *Community* testifies to the fact

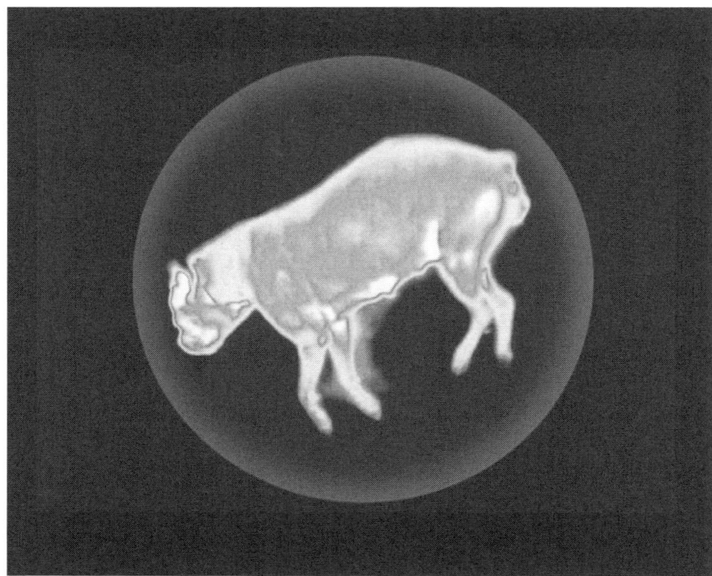

Terike Haapoja | Community | 2007 Still from one of five videos in five-channel video installation, five-channel sound, plywood | Durations: two to five hours | Sound design: Petteri Mård

COURTESY TERIKE HAAPOJA

that each birth is a product of organisms that have been dying for 4.5 billion years. Likewise, our death will support populations far into the distant future. Singularity and independence are relinquished as viewers bear witness to the mysterious aftermath of death and the universe of mutual dependencies.

Haapoja explains that she diverged from the artistic norms she learned as a student because, "I was frustrated dealing with dead subjects in dead museum spaces that were so detached from what is really happening in the world. I needed to return to real time and substance."[11] Thus, she reminds viewers that microbes are our saviors and decomposition is a blessed event. We are immersed in continuums that make ego-conscious isolation a fallacy and confirm that eco-conscious equivalence is our reality.

NOTES

1 Terike Haapoja interview with the author, July 13, 2010.

2 Ibid.

3 Terike Haapoja interview with the author, July 13, 2010. This definition of *succession* differs from that used by ecologists, which refers to the reoccupation of a piece of land after a severe disturbance—a lava flow, landslide, fire, logging, etc. An orderly succession of life-forms takes place as each prepares the habitat for the next occupants.

4 Terike Haapoja interview with the author, July 13, 2010.

5 "SELF-PORTRAIT" (December 2011). http://www.terikehaapoja.net/exhibitions/selfpotraits.htm.

6 Terike Haapoja interview with the author, July 13, 2010.

7 Ibid.

8 Ibid.

9 Ibid.

10 Ibid.

11 Ibid.

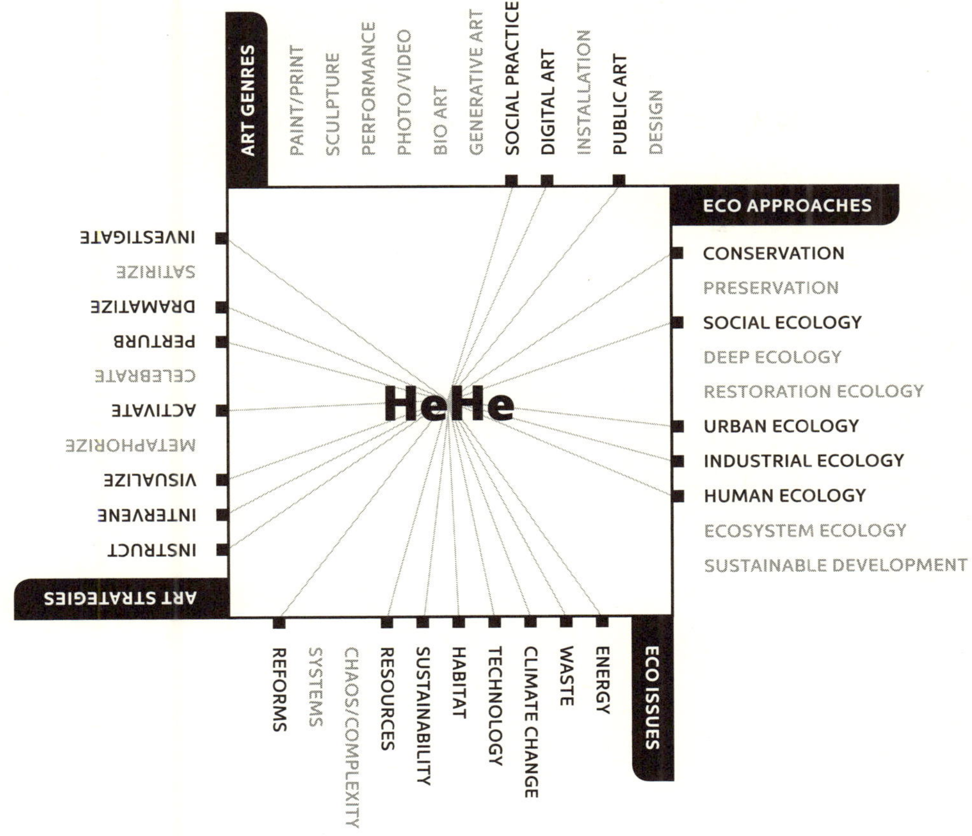

Air Pollutants

Helen Evans born 1972, Welwyn Garden City, United Kingdom
Heiko Hansen born 1970, Pinneberg, Germany

LIKE ANY CLOUD IN ANY SKY, the cloud featured in *Nuage Vert* (2008) by HeHe continually morphed as it was swept by ambient winds. Nonetheless, the residents of Helsinki might have mistaken it for the ominous arrival of a mysterious UFO because this cloud remained outlined by a brilliant green neon light even as it shifted and billowed. In actuality, its earthbound source was easily observed. This ghastly but gorgeous cloud emitted from the towering chimney of the Salmisaari coal-fired power plant. The physical dimension of the Salmisaari site made it difficult to miss. While its underground coal storage tunnels descend over four hundred feet

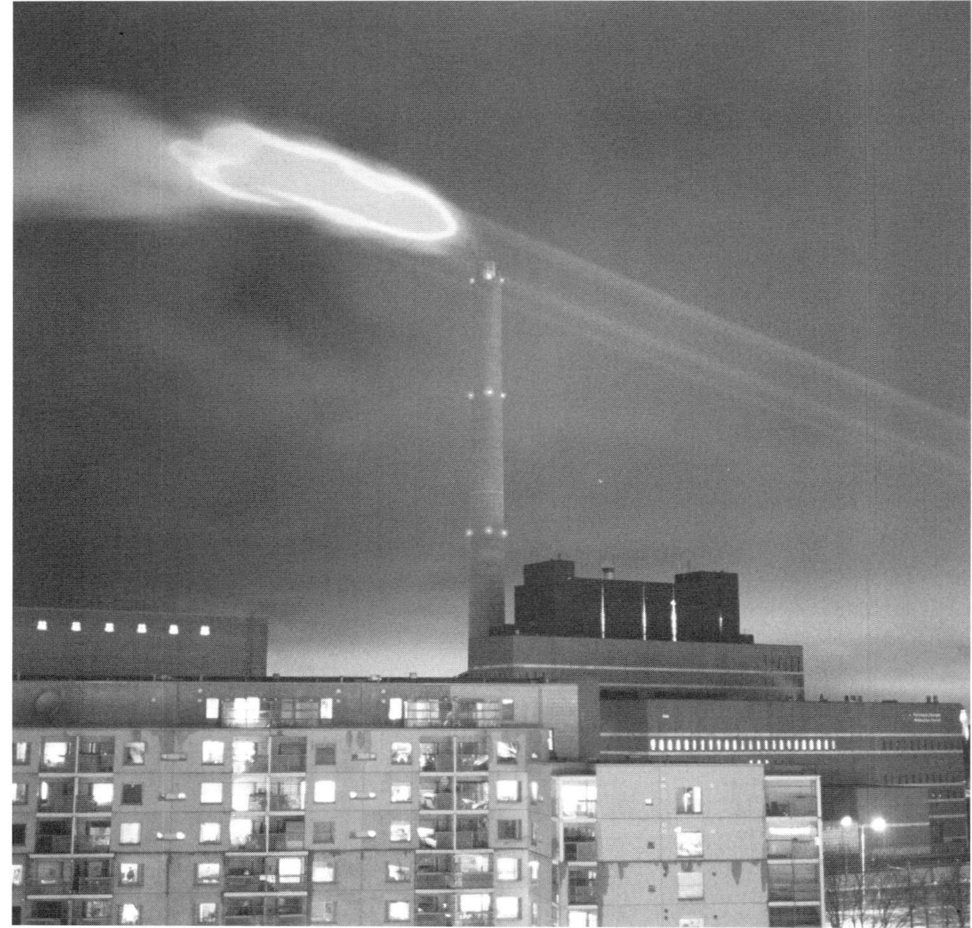

HeHe: Helen Evans and Heiko Hansen | Nuage Vert | 2008 Public light installation showing cloud of vapor emissions produced by a power plant in Helsinki outlined by a laser beam

PHOTO: HEHE / COURTESY HEIKO HANSEN AND HELEN EVANS

below sea level, its chimney towers five hundred feet over the capitol of Finland. The two artists responsible for transforming the night sky are known collectively as HeHe, named for its members Helen Evans and Heiko Hansen.

The cloud acquired this eerie coloration by serving as the projection surface for a fluorescent laser animation that the artists beamed at it. This technical feat was accomplished by aiming a video camera at the chimney emissions while a laser continually drew its fluctuating contour. This contour was then projected back onto the cloud. The light show ran every night between February 22 and 29, 2008.

Though the Salmisaari plant had been modernized to reduce emissions, energy use had not diminished, because the benefits of efficient production were offset by increased energy consumption. According to Evans and Hansen, "Electricity just flows freely, like a wild river, only monitored on an individual basis."[1] HeHe realized that only a communal conservation effort could improve the city's air quality. Thus, they designed *Nuage Vert* to function as a massive power meter. Normally, power meters are tucked away in dark recesses of houses, where they calculate energy consumption of individual households. HeHe's meter, in contrast, functioned like a high-tech smoke signal that made the energy use of the entire city visible all the way up to the lower atmosphere. Because the work monitored instant-by-instant energy consumption, anyone who owned an electric device that was plugged in at the time contributed to the production of this unnatural cloud. As the artists note wryly, "the cloud belongs to us all."[2] Thus, as the citizens gasped in astonishment, they likely inhaled contaminated air they themselves helped produce.

Nuage Vert is part of an ongoing series of artworks by HeHe that stream information in real time, thus the title "Pollstream" (pollution + streaming). Evans and Hansen explain that the term refers to "a series of interactive environments in which members of the audience are in a process of monitoring localized pollution at the very same time that they produce it. The audience is required to conceptualize themselves as responsible collectively and individually for their emissions."[3] The artists explain that the consumer default position is disengagement, either relying on others to clear up the mess or becoming lost in globalized pollution data. Both undermine consumer reform. "Pollstream, using visual, kinetic and sonic technologies, undermines these typical disengagement defenses by speeding up the normal time it takes for our actions in and on the environment to have consequences. Across a number of projects, a sense of constant rather than delayed feedback is created."[4]

Air pollution is the target of this manifesto-like declaration. Each work within the Pollstream series features a reason why contemporary associations with air focus on soot, smog, ozone depletions, sulfur dioxide emissions, greenhouse gases, radon, molds, and pathogens. The contrast to air's former associations with transcendent purity is revealed in the roots of many common words. For example, the Sanskrit word for *atmosphere* identifies air as the zone of the soul. Likewise the Latin word for *spirit* means gust of wind.[5] Within these cultures, each inhale was infused with a sacred cosmic force. This discrepancy can be explained by noting that air's chemistry is as easily infused with salt spray as with asbestos fibers, clover pollen as with coal ash. For this reason, air is the litmus for the precise combination of substances and conditions that comprise each ecosystem each second.

Nuage Vert was conceived one night in 2003 while the artists were living in a house where a domestic waste incinerator offered the view out the living room window. Instead of fretting over the burning of accumulations of discards, the artists enjoyed the pastoral scene of billowing clouds that filled the sky night and day. Then, one fateful night, their attitudes abruptly shifted. "The wind changed direction and the cloud headed in the direction of home. This terrifying change led to an investigation about the utilitarian function of the 'cloud factory', and the sociological dimension of the project began to unfold."[6]

The artists extrapolated their personal experience, expanded its significance, and applied it to the community's effects on air quality, explaining, "In the past decade new buzz words have entered into media discourse and everyday language: ecological visualizations, carbon offsets, eco footprints, food miles etc. These abstractions signify our attempts to quantify individual responsibility and to find ways of facing up to the very real challenges of climate change, and the exploitation of finite natural resources. *Nuage Vert* is based on the idea that public forms can embody an ecological project, materializing environmental issues so that they become a subject within our collective daily lives. . . . A city scale light installation onto the ultimate icon of industrial pollution, alerts the public, generates discussion and can persuade people to change patterns of consumption."[7]

HeHe did not rely on a single light show to fulfill this ambitious agenda. It took three years to prepare for the finale. Much of that time was spent enlisting environmental activ-

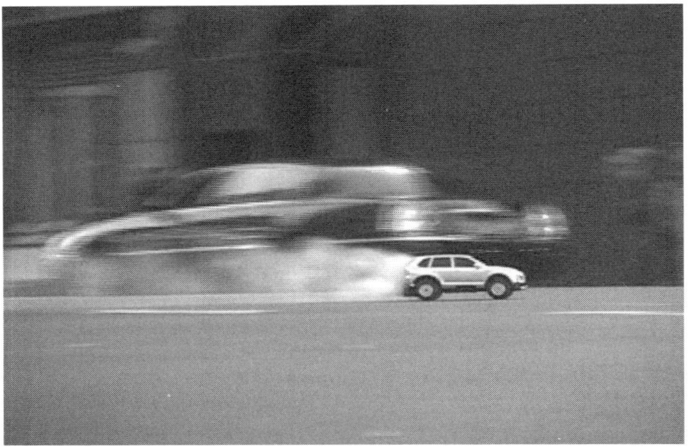

Hehe: Helen Evans and Heiko Hansen | Toy Emissions (My friends all drive Porsches) | 2007 Video still of toy car equipped with smoke bombs giving off yellow, pink, green, blue, or purple smoke | Duration: 3:08 minutes streaming

COURTESY HEIKO HANSEN AND HELEN EVANS

ists and a governmental think tank to help convince the owners and managers of Helsinki Energy to provide information about energy consumption by local residents. Meanwhile, HeHe was busy creating multiple educational programs. They recruited cultural management students to broadcast the "umbilical connection between the local actions and the vapor."[8] The students created slogans such as "Aurora borealis in Helsinki?" that were printed on flyers and posters. Schoolchildren and members of community organizations distributed this information to four thousand households. Throughout this period the technicality of the laser projection was being designed in collaboration with the Laser Physics Department at Helsinki Technical University, the Computer Science Department at the University of Illinois, and a medical laser company. Preparation also included consulting with Devalence, a Parisian design group that developed a communication strategy to ensure that the event was reported by local and national press. This partial list of participants omits the many culture, science, industry, and environment organizations that participated. The contributors underscored the efforts of the artists, whose own research is so rigorous they have published scientific papers, held research positions in informatics laboratories, and taught in graduate and undergraduate design and media programs.[9]

The immediate result of this concerted effort was apparent during a special "unplug event" that occurred between 7 and 8 PM on February 29, 2008, when four thousand local residents reduced their energy consumption by 800 kilovolt amperes (kVA). Citizens were rewarded with a greatly enlarged cloud spectacle, which is explained by the fact that vapor increases with reduced use because the unused energy cannot be stored. However, the event's more enduring accomplishment was to demonstrate that complex energy calculations can be made understandable to consumers. *Nuage Vert* was the first time an invisible digital infrastructure measuring local electricity consumption had been made public and visible.[10] HeHe summarizes this project by stating, "Over the Helsinki skyline, awareness of climate change and the burning of our limited natural resources came back home—and it looked pretty cosmic."[11]

Nuage Vert highlights two uses of energy that are sources of air pollutants in urban areas—electricity and heat. Another major source is the personal automobile. Driving a private car is often cited as a typical citizen's most polluting daily activity.[12] Emissions from individual cars posed a particular artistic challenge to HeHe because there is no iconic image, like a smokestack, of air pollution from car exhaust. Thus, Hansen and Evans invented one—a remote-controlled model of a luxury sport utility vehicle. *Toy Emissions (My friends all drive Porsches)* (2007) was a street event performed by a tiny toy car that the artists sent barreling through the streets of New York in the midst of actual cars, buses, taxis, trucks, pedestrians, and ambulances. All the while it belched great plumes of colored smoke from its miniature tailpipe. The exaggerated emission spewing from the two-inch engine was more than a "hehe" laugh. It also referred to "hehe" tattletaling by assigning guilt to everyone who drives.

Pollstream projects also address a form of urban air pollution that is neither chemical nor particulate. *Bruit Rose (Pink Noise)* (April 2004 to September 2005) refers to sound that contains random noise across all sound frequencies. While *pink noise* conveys the soothing resonance of ocean waves, HeHe applied the term to a location decisively deficient in calming sounds—a busy urban thoroughfare in Paris. The work occupied an actual light box meant to relay advertising messages. Hehe retained its public communication function but altered its content. In this instance, the light-emitting panels visualized the noise of traffic, pedestrians, and general urban clamor. Thus, instead of selling a product, the work's animated visual surface "essentially advertises the existence of noise pollution."[13]

HeHe designs spectacles to communicate that air is not a passive mix of gases. The cumulative effects of each person's slightest polluting acts are responsible for the compromised state of the air we breathe, which explains why the artists refer to the Pollstream series as "an intervention in environmental ethics."[14]

NOTES

1 Helen Evans, "Nuage Vert," *Cluster Magazine*, issue 07, Transmitting Architecture (Torino: May 2008). http://hehe.org.free.fr/hehe/texte/nv/index.html.

2 Ibid.

3 "HeHe—Pollstream (Champs d'ozone and Nuage Vert)." http://www.greenmuseum.org/c/aer/projects/pollstream/index.htm.

4 Ibid.

5 David Abram, "The Air Aware: Mind and Mood on a Breathing Planet," *Orion Magazine*, September/October 2009. http://www.orionmagazine.org/index.php/articles/article/4935/.

6 Helen Evans, "Nuage Vert," *Cluster Magazine*, issue 07, Transmitting Architecture (Torino: May 2008). http://hehe.org.free.fr/hehe/texte/nv/index.html.

7 Ibid.

8 Ibid.

9 Hansen and Evans have taught at the Interaction Design Institute Ivrea in Italy, the National School of Industrial Design (Les Ateliers) in Paris, and the University of Amsterdam. They have worked with researchers in informatics laboratories such as Fraunhofer Institute in Bonn, Germany, and the National Institute for Research in Informatics and Automatics in France.

10 Helen Evans, "Nuage Vert," *Cluster Magazine*, issue 07, Transmitting Architecture (Torino: May 2008). http://hehe.org.free.fr/hehe/texte/nv/index.html.

11 Karl Fabricius, "Mysterious Green Haze Over Helenski," *Environmental Graffiti*. http://www.environmentalgraffiti.com/featured/mysterious-green-haze-aover-helsinki/8636.

12 US Environmental Protection Agency, Office of Mobile Sources, *Automobile Emissions: An Overview*, EPA 400-F-92-007 (August 1994). http://www.epa.gov/oms/consumer/05-autos.pdf.

13 HeHe, "surface 02, HeHe.org: Pollstream." http://www.v2.nl/events/surface-02-hehe.org-pollstream.

14 "HeHe—Pollstream (Champs d'ozone and Nuage Vert)." http://www.greenmuseum.org/c/aer/projects/pollstream/index.htm.

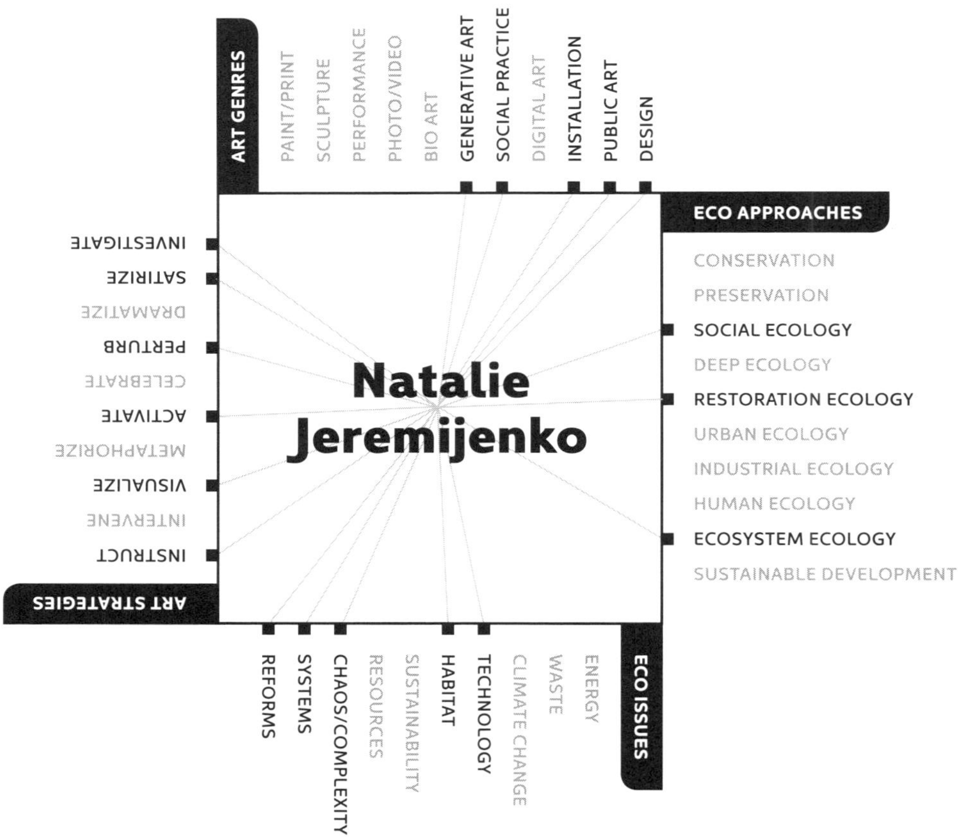

Citizen Ecologists

Born 1966, Mackay, Australia

MOST JOURNALISTIC REPORTS about Natalie Jeremijenko, a high-profile techno-artist, begin with a description of her Rollerblade skills, her venture as a rock concert impresario, her experience growing up with nine siblings, her oddball attire, the names for her three children that are both very strange and very long. Typically they then explain that her preparation for an art career involved earning remarkable credentials as a scientist. Jeremijenko holds a bachelor's degree in biochemistry and physics, a master's degree in English, an all-but-dissertation PhD in neuroscience, another all-but-dissertation PhD in mechanical engineering, and a complete PhD in computer science and electrical engineering. In 1994 she was hired as a consultant research scientist in the renowned Silicon Valley lab at the Xerox Palo Alto Research Center. Eventually, these reports relay how she is channeling this expansive training into artworks that invite the lay audience to participate in scientific environmental investigations that are shaping the present and could determine the future of the planet.

Jeremijenko explains, "The art world is a very prissy little thing over in the corner, while the major cultural forces are being determined by techno science."[1] The alternative she has developed involves collaborative research-based art projects for which there are no prerequisites, even though they test the limits of scientific inquiry and vanguard art. "Grassroots tool for monitoring the environment"[2] is the way she describes her efforts to combine the technical forces of science with the public outreach made possible through art. The result is a radical departure from the isolation of biotechnical studies conducted in laboratories by professionals employed by major institutions. It is, simultaneously, a major digression from painting traditions that utilize brushes and easels and from sculpture crafted with chisels and modeling tools. In order to intensify the audience's scrutiny and creative engagement with local conditions, participants are rewarded with exposure to the wondrous complexity of the material environment.

OneTree(s) (1998–ongoing), for example, is a bold exploration of two hotly contested arenas of scientific investigation. One half of this doubleheader confronts the nature/nurture debate associated with such esteemed evolutionary biologists as Edward O. Wilson, Richard Dawkins, Richard Lewontin, and Stephen Jay Gould. Their attempts to determine the relative importance of inherited qualities (nature) versus environmental conditions (nurture) have unleashed a hornet's nest of moral proclamations and political debates regarding the significance of humanity's impact on the environment. In this work the public helps test whether nature minimizes human responsibility more or less than nurture maximizes it.

The other half of this artwork applies this heated discourse to cloning, a process of making exact copies of organic life, which fascinates scientists and nonscientists alike. Jeremijenko refers to the fantastic claims attached to cloning technologies as *speculative hype* that begs the public to "be struck in dumb awe at the complicated marvels."[3] Nonetheless, she designed an experiment that utilized the attention-grabbing power of cloning to materialize the nature/nurture debate. Furthermore, she optimized public engagement in this daunting and obscure topic by enabling nonscientists to act as observers and analyzers of this cloning experiment. Through direct experience, she hoped they would be better equipped to form independent conclusions about the importance of nurturing the environment, as opposed to letting it go to "nature."

A century-old paradox walnut tree with a circumference of about thirty feet contributed its juvenile (undifferentiated) tissue to produce the clones used in this work of art.[4] Jeremijenko acquired one thousand genetically identical seedlings of the tree and named her project *One Tree(s)*, a shorthand way of saying that a single tree is also a plural tree if its genetic structure is duplicated through cloning. These clones were propagated in a laboratory under sterilized environmental conditions. They were then exhibited as sprouts in the controlled museum environment within the Yerba Buena Center for the Arts in San Francisco.

The punch line of this complex project became immediately apparent because the little trees were not at all identical, despite their genetic sameness and the consistent conditions in which they sprouted and grew. Their individuality revealed that even such minor environmental differences as the distance from air-conditioning ducts, heating vents, lighting fixtures, and carbon dioxide–emitting observers produce microclimates that are distinct enough to vary growth patterns. Each variation disproved the assertion that cloning homogenizes life and that living forms are predetermined by genetic inevitability. At the same time, they testified to the all-powerful role of environmental factors, amplifying warnings against carelessness and neglect. Jeremijenko comments that her aim was "to demonstrate the irreducible complexity of genetic information. . . . This seems incredibly critical to the sensible discussion of genetic technologies within the public sphere. It was an effort to simply demonstrate how much genes *don't* explain. This unknown part is what is at stake."[5]

For four years, as the seedlings were growing into saplings, Jeremijenko was busy identifying locations in the San Francisco Bay Area where the trees might be planted and negotiating for permissions with parks managers, private property owners, school officials, public transport representatives, a performing arts center director, and rail administrators. She asked them to allow pairs of cloned trees to be planted on their properties and grow undisturbed until they fully individuated—approximately fifty years.

It was imperative to plant the trees in pairs in order for citizen scientists to conduct on-site comparisons that would enable them to discern the individualized growth patterns of the genetically identical tree twins. Conveniently, the donor tree was named a *paradox* long before it was recruited by Jeremijenko to demonstrate the biological paradox—that sameness can coexist with difference.

The sites were carefully chosen by Jeremijenko. They had to be close enough to allow for comparative inspections but different enough to demonstrate the environmental impact on the trees' developments. One form of dissimilarity involved habitat; it demonstrated that the condition of soil, air, and water was an important factor. Another difference was cultural; it revealed that the wealthy and poorer neighborhoods also affected the health and vitality of the trees. Another factor was accessibility so that both trajectories of meaning could reach a broad public. Jeremijenko explains, "The diversity of local conditions in the Bay Area is not captured by environmental variation alone, dramatic as it is. In addition to radically different microclimates, the Bay Area has highly Balkanized social contexts. The biological sameness of the trees will render both the environmental and social differences to which they are exposed. The trees will become evidence, witness, and mediator of these differences."[6] In fact, the artwork provided conclusive evidence that trees are less healthy in low-rent than high-rent districts.

Because participants in *One Tree(s)* learned that every tree's uniqueness is a gauge of its environment, without ever registering for an academic degree, they became monitors of life's sensitivity to wind, humidity, light, soil conditions, particulate matter, carbon dioxide levels, contaminants, water sources, shadows, paving, topographies, and so forth. This process is not an end in itself. It primes the participants to become vigilant stewards of their own behaviors, and informed critics of others' actions.

Jeremijenko explains that *One Tree(s)* "demonstrates that this complex multi-parameter phenomena of growth can be understood in many ways, can sustain many interpretations and can be 'read' from the material phenomena itself, not as a pre-interpreted digested data packet, not delivered by an expert, not wrapped in the incontestable authority of science. It facilitates and instruments a more active understanding of information, not as complete, accurate and factual, but interpretable, partial and incomplete. The evidence being more persuasive and somehow more precise for this understanding of its partiality."[7]

In another project titled *Feral Robotic Dogs* (2005–ongoing), engineering students at Yale University became Jeremijenko's collaborators when they enrolled for a course that

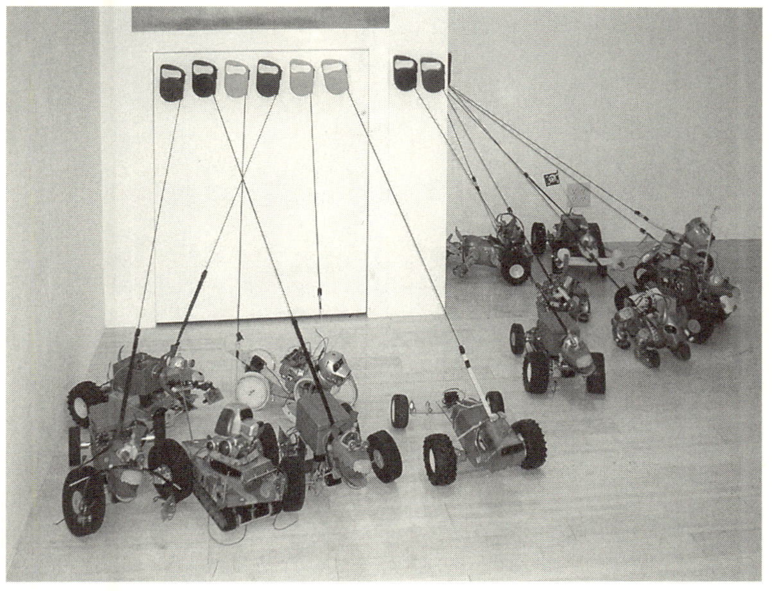

Natalie Jeremijenko | Feral Robotic Dogs | 2005–ongoing Toy robot, chemical sensors, open-source robotics, microprocessor hardware

COURTESY NATALIE JEREMIJENKO AND POSTMASTERS GALLERY, NEW YORK

she taught with the peculiar title "Mechanical Engineering 386, Feral Robotics: Information Technology in the Wild." Jeremijenko comments, "Many people complain that engineers are very narrow in their focus. . . . This class not only poses technical challenges but involves the students in real social and political problems as well. They are rethinking the role of technology in society."[8]

The artwork started out as endearing robot puppies, inexpensive toys available for sale online. The toys were crudely programmed to scurry along flat surfaces, bark the national anthem, and perform silly dances. Jeremijenko assigned her students the task of upgrading them by installing on their noses sensors programmed to sniff out toxic waste products and by changing their circuitry to allow them to move along uneven terrain. These new and improved robo-dogs were then unleashed to roam freely in industrial sites that had been officially declared decontaminated and in brownfield sites designated "safe for redevelopment."

If these official declarations and designations were accurate, the "feralized" dogs prowled around aimlessly. But if their newly installed sensors detected lingering contamination, they scurried to the offending hot spots, where their sniffing actions announced the presence of vapors from lead, arsenic, ozone, and other toxic substances lurking beneath the surface. In this way these toys acted as undercover agents gathering and transmitting subversive evidence of the chemical contamination in their midst. Ironically, the chemicals they sniffed were the same as those used to manufacture these high-tech toys: "These dogs are kind of sniffing their own bums,"[9] notes Jeremijenko.

On one occasion, witnesses responded with nervous giggles and worried frowns as these four-legged surveillance patrols sniffed, swarmed, and clustered at locations on a defunct Con Edison plant along the Bronx River. This was no ordinary art experience. Instead of focusing on the dogs as sculptures, the public's attention was directed to the invisible and

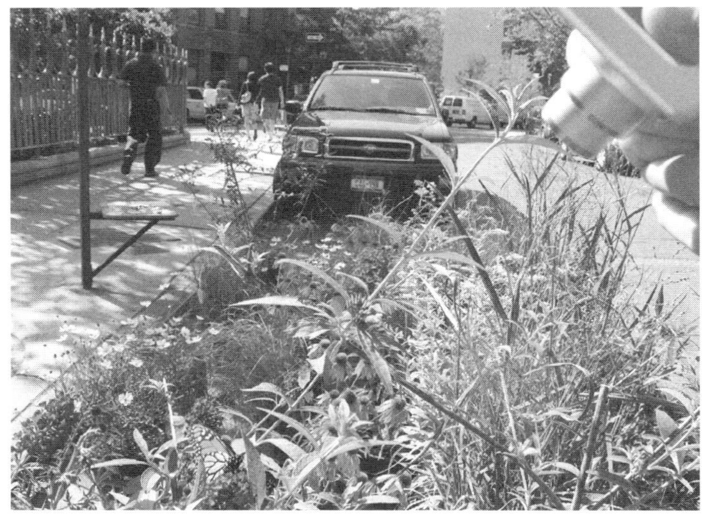

Natalie Jeremijenko | No PARK | 2008 Low-growth mosses and grasses
COURTESY NATALIE JEREMIJENKO AND POSTMASTERS GALLERY, NEW YORK

unrecognized hazards in areas that authorities had declared safe. Jeremijenko explains, "It's necessary to have such devices to ground the information in something comprehensible, because the EPA, satellite images, GIS, they're not publicly legible. Even though they're publicly accessible, they're not an active part of public discourse by any means."[10]

In order to maximize the size of the canine pack, Jeremijenko has posted instructions for altering toy dogs as open-source software. Furthermore, toy conversion workshops have occurred in many locations.[11]

Agency is the word Jeremijenko frequently utilizes to describe the mission of the xDesign Environmental Health Clinic she established at New York University in 2008. The clinic's mission is to remedy illnesses that afflict the environment. The medical metaphor links the health of an individual with the health of the environmental commons. As such, it encourages the public to actively seek and implement "cures." Visitors to the clinic are referred to as "impatients" because they are impatient to find remedies for the ailing planet. The "treatments" the clinic dispenses entail "referrals" to environmental agencies and non-profits, and "prescriptions" that detail interventions—all targeted at the particular concerns of the individuals who visit. An example is an environmental malady that is common to many urban settings—degraded water quality, over-taxed sewage treatment centers, and polluted storm drainage. The art prescription it generated is titled *No PARK* because the remedy is located in the no parking zones that are reserved for emergency vehicles throughout city streets, and because these rarely used sites are replaced with mini parks. The *No PARK* prescription calls for removing the concrete and asphalt along the curb and planting the area with mosses and low growing grasses. It recommends durable species that will recover from the occasional compression by fire engines and ambulances. *No PARK* parks not only transform areas of bleak asphalt into verdant foliage, they activate a remedial strategy by providing the permeability needed to capture oily runoff from road surfaces, dilute uric acid deposited by city dogs, reduce puddles, and absorb contaminants that would otherwise seep into estuaries.

In sum, while science is stitched into many eco art practices, most artists initiate such collaborations to compensate for their lack of familiarity with rigorous laboratory experiments, simulation technologies, and statistical analysis. As a trained scientist, Jeremijenko reverses this pattern. Instead of seeking rigor, she capitalizes on the liberating privileges of being an artist. Jerimijenko also tampers with conventional definitions of science, explaining, "What we've missed is the idea that science is not the singular expertise. . . . But it comes back to the question of who participates and how. How can individuals, without a master's or PhD in environmental science or boundary layer physics, and without having published a peer-reviewed paper, have access to material evidence, or permission to ask questions and to draw on the facts?"[12] She demonstrates how by inventing alternatives to the controlled tests and laboratory sterility that comprise her colleagues' professional methodologies. Then she uses wit and humor to reach beyond readers of specialized, peer review journals. Her works demonstrate that amateur scientists can dispel the myth that there exists a simple chain of causality that enables professional biological research to deliver reliable information. In conclusion, Jeremijenko pronounces a definitive inquiry of the current era: "Moral authority of environmentalism has been centered around what you cannot do. Turn off the lights, use less gas, use less paper, ring your hands, do not touch, leave no trace. . . . What about what you can do?"[13]

NOTES

1 Kevin Berger, "The Artist as Mad Scientist," Salon, June 22, 2006. http://www.salon.com/entertainment/feature/2006/06/22/natalie/index.html.

2 Zahid Sardar, "Society's Signposts: Natalie Jeremijenko's Trees Aren't Simply Decorative—They Can Be Read Like a Social Register," sfgate.com, October 23, 2004. http://articles.sfgate.com/2004-10-23/home-and-garden/17450657_1_planting-trees-clones.

3 Natalie Jeremijenko, "A Response to the Paradise Now Exhibition." http://mrl.nyu.edu/~nat/investnow/response.html.

4 The paradox walnut is the offspring of a native black walnut tree (*Juglans hindsii*) fertilized by an English walnut (*Juglans regia*). It is more vigorous and larger than either of its parents. In the Nineteenth Century it was named by Luther Burbank as a paradox because, in addition to its beauty and vigor, it generated fast-growing hardwood that does not bear fruit. Burbank did not anticipate its advantages within the urban context. The paradox walnut does not produce pollen, does not drop nuts, does not pull up pavement or underground pipes. For these reasons this clone is being commercially produced by the Burchell Nursery, which is supporting the *One Tree(s)* project. It is also being studied in the Walnut Improvement Program at UC Davis.

5 Natalie Jeremijenko, "A Response to the Paradise Now Exhibition." http://mrl.nyu.edu/~nat/investnow/response.html.

6 http://www.nyu.edu/projects/xdesign/onetrees/ecosystems/index.html.

7 Ibid.

8 David Case, "An Engineer for the Avant-Garde: Natalie Jeremijenko Makes Robotic Dogs, Remote-Controlled Geese, Genetically Identical Trees—and Social Commentary. It's Art, All Right. But Is It Engineering?" *Yale Alumni Magazine*, March/April 2004. http://www.yalealumnimagazine.com/issues/2004_03/jeremijenko.html.

9 Natalie Jeremijenko quoted by Quinn Norton in "Robots with a Nose for Trouble," the *Guardian*, March 20, 2004. http://www.guardian.co.uk/technology/2005/oct/20/hacking.internetcrime.

10 Emily Gertz, "Natalie Jeremijenko: The World-Changing Interview by Emily Gertz," World-Changing, October 22, 2004. http://www.worldchanging.com/archives/001450.html.

11 "Feral Robot Dogs," posted by Phillip Torrone on *Make: Technology on Your Time*, at 5:48 PM, March 26, 2005. http://blog.makezine.com/archive/2005/03/feral_robotic_dogs.html.

12 Natalie Jeremijenko, "The Aesthetic Activist on Altering Participation in Scientific Discourse" (December 19, 2006). http://seedmagazine.com/content/article/natalie_jeremijenko_lawrence_krauss/.

13 Natalie Jeremijenko, "The Aesthetic Activist Gives a Tour of Her Pigeon Paradise" (December 20, 2006). http://seedmagazine.com/content/article/revolutionary_minds_natalie_jeremijenko/.

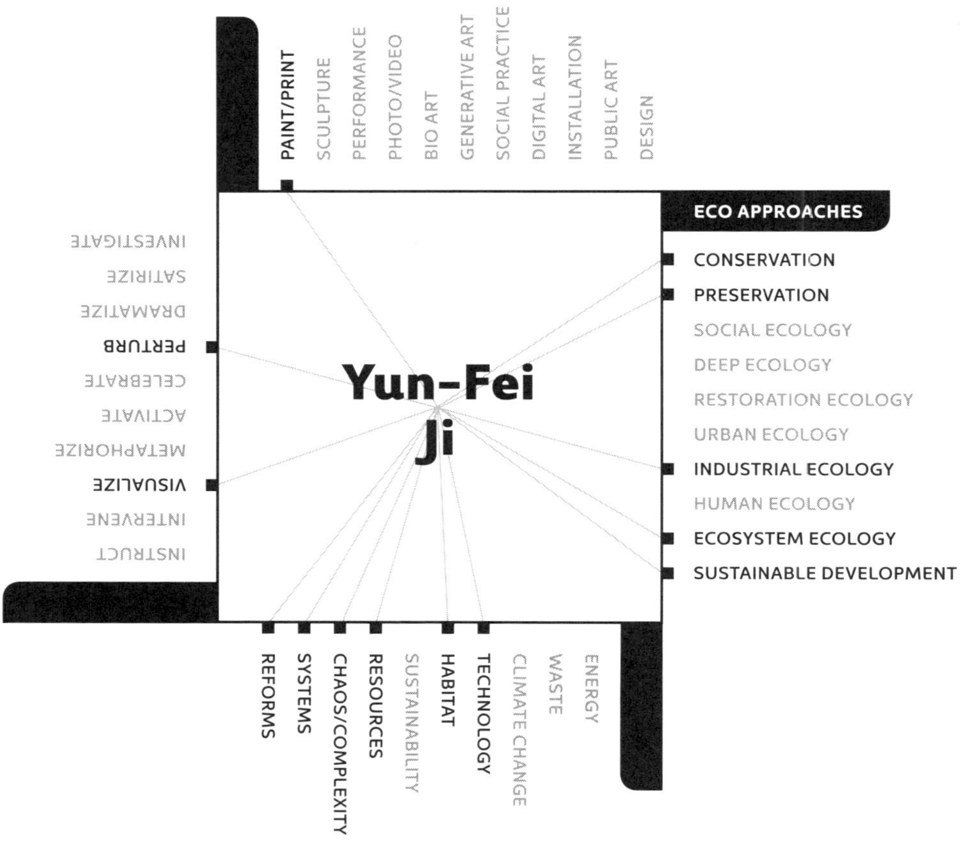

Failings of an Engineering Triumph

Born 1963, Beijing, China

WHEN YOU SEE that the people have been treated badly, you can be sure that nature is being treated even worse. When you defend one, you defend the other."[1] This declaration by Yun-Fei Ji was also expressed with brushstrokes that chronicle the sorrowful plight of 1.5 million Chinese. This number represents entire populations of three cities, 140 towns, and 1,350 villages that have been expelled from their homes and their homelands to make room for the largest, and potentially the most destructive, hydroelectric dam in the world. The Three Gorges Dam was designed to boost China's mad-dash race to catch up with power-consuming industrialized nations. Yet recently, even Chinese officials have ceased boasting about this technological venture. The dam has inundated the habitats of countless species of mammals, amphibians, birds, and plants, along with myriad sites of archeological treasures and family legacies. In addition, concern grows about the people who have not been evicted but whose homesteads surround the 370-mile-long reservoir. Despite the 350 billion cubic feet of rock and earth imported to construct this massive structure, this population now lives in jeopardy of landslides, waterborne diseases, fish die-offs, and water contamination from the submergence of hundreds of factories, mines, and waste dumps. Ji painted *Migrants of the Three Gorges Dam*, a ten-foot-long narrative scroll, to document the hardship to these people and their lands.

Beyond feeling sympathy for the victims of the Three Gorges Dam, Ji perceives the project as an affront to the beliefs that guided the Chinese people for thousands of years. It held that nature was the source of wisdom, the "mother of all things." By balancing the yin and the yang, it ensured eternal renewal. Ji decries the fact that this mediating balance sheet has been overtaken by abuses committed in the name of progress: "I want to develop a new set of metaphors, a new way of looking to reflect the condition on the ground today. We do not see nature as something nurturing as in tradition. Scholars used nature as a way to purify themselves. They learned cosmic law from meditating on nature. But today, our way to nature is cut off. We see nature as something to yield profit and exploit. It is a place to dump garbage we don't want."[2]

Ji's indignation is bolstered by verifiable information and historic facts about the nation where he spent the first twenty-six years of his life. He states, "My job is to see the reality clearly. That is why I travel and research. That is part of my work."[3] This statement may seem unremarkable in countries that encourage independent research, but in China during the Cultural Revolution, it was a punishable offense. Even as a student, Ji questioned what he learned in school because it excluded the rich traditions of folktales, religious beliefs, and cultural achievements he learned about from his elders. "When I came to the States later, I became more aware that I was lied to in China. You can't get true information by going to school in China because the history is rewritten. I wanted to find out what really happened. Through my art project, I'm trying to understand."[4]

Ji's research is less an academic pursuit than a journey of discovery. One of his first discoveries was that China's rush to industrialize followed its defeat during the Opium Wars. Until then, China isolated itself, believing it was so superior there was nothing to gain by interacting with "barbarians." Ji remarks that through this humiliating war "China gained the knowledge that you have to be modern so you are not beaten down. The goal was to catch up with England in fifteen years and US in twenty. Its traditional belief systems, Confucius and Taoism, had to be pushed aside to create this new China. The Maoist Revolution was radical. It meant smashing the old to meet these high goals. This includes building a major dam on the Yangtze River."[5]

Because Ji felt the Chinese people were being robbed of traditions rooted in intimate interactions with the soils, waters, plants, and animals in order to pursue progress and profit, he visited surviving remnants of agriculture lifestyles in China's ancestral lands. That is when he discovered disturbing evidence of forced relocations of masses of people into hastily constructed cities hundreds of miles away. The relentless churning of factories, not the seasons, suddenly determined the rhythms of these peoples' lives. *Migrants from the Three Gorges Dam* documents these discoveries and their ethical and emotional fallouts. "Chemical companies dump their pollution into poorer areas. People can't see the sun. The sky

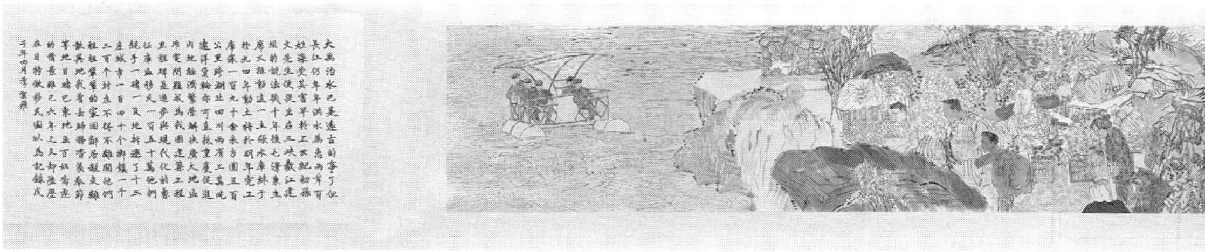

Yun-Fei Ji | Migrants of the Three Gorges Dam | 2009 Hand-printed watercolor wood block mounted on paper and silk | Dimensions: 15⅞" × 10' 3¾"

PHOTO: WADE AARON / CREDIT: © YUN-FEI JI / COURTESY JAMES COHAN GALLERY, NEW YORK/SHANGHAI

is a perpetual gray. They can't even breathe the air. In the village where my grandmother lived, they built a mine up the mountain where rivers were fast and self-cleaning. Now rivers become static. Rich fertilizers from agriculture cause algae blooms. The new geological environment creates mudslides. Now the people can't get water and the fish die."[6]

These social and environmental concerns are embedded in Ji's art medium, format, style, and technique. His artistic choices defy the broad policy of suppression during the Cultural Revolution that had not only crushed ancient cultural traditions; it landed fiercely upon modern art. Social realism was the one permissible form of artistic expression when Ji was a student. Thus centuries of Buddhist art and decades of vanguard art were both missing from his education.

Ji began the project by traveling, creating drawings, and then assembling them to construct scenes of stragglers, scavengers, and ghosts occupying lands slated for the flooding. These composite drawings formed the basis of the painting's narrative, which reads from right to left in the manner of traditional Chinese scrolls. *Migrants from the Three Gorges Dam* was also reproduced as an artist's book by the renowned Rongbaozhai ("Studio of Glorious Treasures") that was once part of Beijing's imperial enclave in the Forbidden City. The book version of the painting also takes the form of a scroll. The printed imagery was produced in the traditional manner with over five hundred hand-carved, pear wood blocks.

The opening image presents trees, branches, and mountains. It would constitute a delightful landscape except for the inclusion of a tractor—an ominous sign of impending changes. The final scene consists of five uniformed soldiers seated in rows on a raft patrolling a vast expanse of water, presumably the dammed Yangtze River. Their postures convey authority for maintaining order. The scenes in between portray masses of people among a clamorous disarray of carts, bicycles, and trucks heaped with bundles of belongings and furniture. They are dejected but calm, seemingly resigned to a fate they cannot defy. Two men wearing Western-style suits appear in one chilling scene. Their heads are covered with cloth hoods, like those that are placed on criminals just before hanging or execution, suggesting that the actions of these Western investors are comparable to crimes that are capital offenses. A monstrous rat also makes an appearance. According to Ji, its bloated belly, long snout, grizzly fur, and beady eyes resemble corrupt Chinese officials who prosper as others suffer. This grotesque figure towers over the people who appear to have grown accustomed to its presence in their lives.

Scene after scene evokes the current loss of land and its wildlife, of ways of life and connections to ancestors—all casualties of modernization. In order to resuscitate homeland

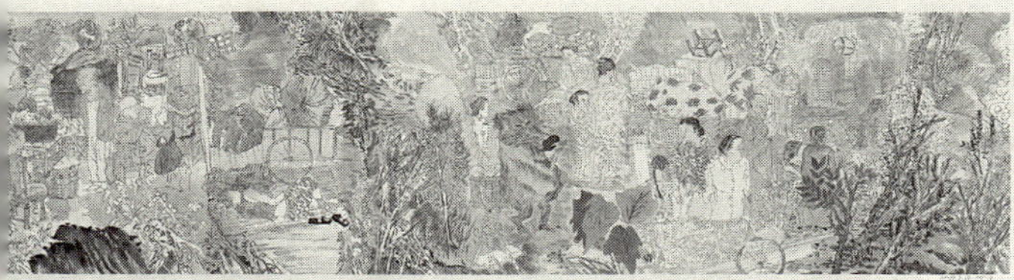

traditions, Ji emulates the elegance of the golden age of Sung landscape painting a thousand years ago. But instead of sublime transcendence, Ji's version presents a searing indictment of the current government's ruthless policies and actions.

Calligraphy is one way Ji revives a threatened tradition. It appears in the areas beyond the pictorial component of the *Migrants* scroll. However, instead of presenting an inspirational poem, as is the custom, Ji's calligraphy enumerates China's longstanding ambitions to tame the Yangtze River and the regrettable outcomes of these efforts.

The hand-painted scroll format connects *Migrants* to the five-thousand-year history of Chinese art. Ji explains, "I learned scientifically correct anatomy and one/two/three-point perspective. When I went to see old art in China, I discovered a different way that was not backed by scientific knowledge; it was backed by tradition. The artist was moving, not standing in a fixed place. That way is closer to experience. Things gradually unfold while we are walking, looking, and seeing."[7] This compositional device perfectly suited a painted portrayal of the plight of an estimated 1.9 million people and hundreds of miles of land. Scenes merge, overlap, and stack.

Techniques used to render these scenes with brush and pigment provided another entry into China's cultural legacy. Ji comments, "The process of applying ink with the flexible hair of the brush is an elaborate culture. Minute differences have ritual clarity." The particularities of each kind of stroke used to depict the migrants are as expressive as the subjects they convey, and as the words that denote them—*withered, moist, gathering, dismissing, serious, free, young, old, quiet, busy, vigorous,* and *charming.*[8] "When you study traditional Chinese painting," Ji recalls, "you learn that even a simple horizontal line is made with the image of a layered horizontal cloud formation in mind. A dot should be like a suspended rock about to roll down the hill."[9] Ji uses the word *meditate* to explain that the painting process goes beyond thinking and copying. He says, "It brings real life experience into painting. The energy is alive."[10]

Ji's material choices affirm that ancient cultures were more sustainable than their modern replacements. They are all indigenous to the Chinese mainland. Inks and pigments, for example, derive from local minerals and vegetables. The mulberry and rice papers were made in the traditional manner from local trees. They were mounted on silk woven from native silkworms. Native sheep, fox, goat, wolf, and horse provided the hair for his brushes.

Ji summarizes the challenging cultural assignment he has chosen by stating, "To serve the country means bringing knowledge into human relationships. Poetry and art have to change. They have lost their sources of inspiration. We can still go to surviving pristine

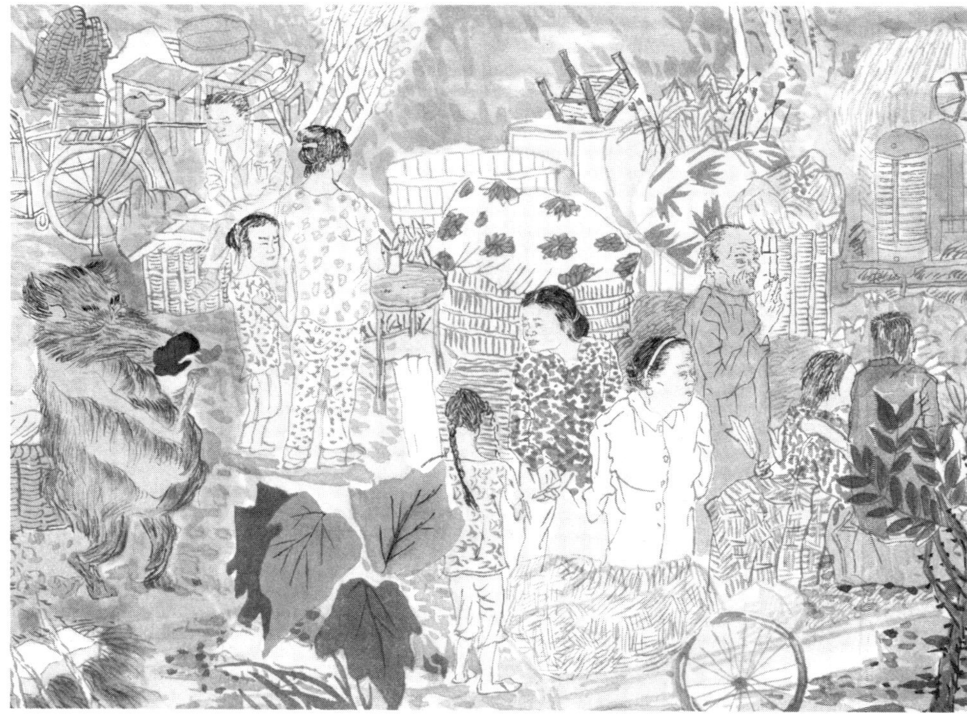

Yun-Fei Ji | Migrants of the Three Gorges Dam | 2009 Detail. Hand-printed watercolor wood block mounted on paper and silk | Dimensions: 13⅞" × 10′ 3¼"

mountains, but we have to face the problems today. As artists, we need to find new metaphors to address these problems. My *The Three Gorges* scroll is a meditation on a ruin. That is our legacy."[11]

NOTES

1 Yun-Fei Ji interview with the author, April 7, 2010.
2 Ibid.
3 Ibid.
4 Ibid.
5 Ibid.
6 Ibid.
7 Ibid.
8 "Chinese Painting," Orientalgiftshop.com, http://www.orientalgiftsshop.com/seo/55/1/chinese_painting.htm.
9 Yun-Fei Ji, "Artist Yun-Fei Ji on How He Paints," *The Observer*, September 20, 2009. http://www.guardian.co.uk/artanddesign/2009/sep/20/guide-painting-yun-fei-ji.
10 Ibid.
11 Yun-Fei Ji interview with the author April 7, 2010.

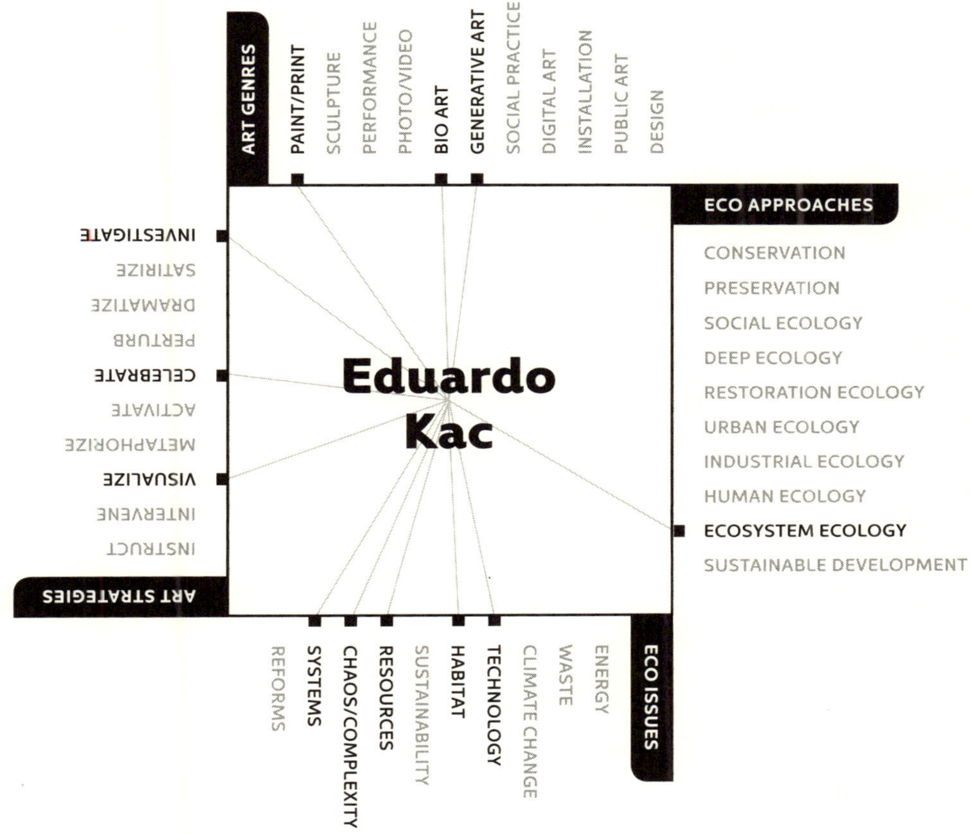

Painting with Life

Born 1962, Rio de Janeiro, Brazil

EDUARDO KAC's boundary-defying "biotopes" might baffle members of both of the following art audiences—those who delight in painting as an act of placing pigment on a surface, and those who prefer innovative alternatives to painting traditions. The artist himself does not know how to categorize these works. He explained that they pose the same kind of problem that emerged in the 1830s when art critics, collectors, historians, and curators struggled to comprehend the ultramodern form of representation known then as photography.[1] The debate regarding photography's place in art required a new art vocabulary, new cultural principles, and new criteria of artistic merit. Kac's biotopes pose a similar challenge.

A biotope (*bio* = "life"; *topos* = "place") is a uniform environment occupied by a specific community of plants and animals. Unlike habitats, biotopes are small and can be managed. Aquariums and rooftop gardens are examples of constructed biotopes. Kac's biotopes are shallow, transparent, 19" x 23" rectangular boxes that he populates with communities of live microorganisms that are too small to be seen by the naked eye. The borders of the boxes are permeable so that three kinds of interactions can occur between the microbial populations inhabiting the biotopes and their surroundings: the organisms respond to the environment's temperature, humidity, airflow, light levels, etc.; they relate to each other by competing for food and space and dealing with the ongoing production of wastes; they interact with people feeding, installing, transporting, and viewing the artwork who alter biotope conditions by generating warmth, shadows, and humidity and by releasing populations of microorganisms when they breathe, sneeze, or cough.

Are these framed living pictures the most recent addition to painting's ongoing evolution? Or do they constitute a new genre of eco art-making unrelated to painting? Kac contributes to the debate when he announces his intention to "challenge the notion that the artwork must be centered on the 'author' and that it must be materially stable, as is common in painting and sculpture."[2] The quandaries posed by biotopes arise from all three ways of studying painting.

Painting as process In order to produce biotopes, Kac's studio is configured into a room-size incubator. Living microbes replace a liquid medium to convey the artwork's visual elements. Stirring the cells of millions of microorganisms into a nutrient-rich liquid replaces squeezing paint from commercially manufactured tubes. Constructing a shallow plastic case to limit the range of microorganisms takes the place of stretching a frame to establish the parameters of the paint. Kac paints this slurry onto the back wall of the plastic case, where it appears as an undifferentiated field of black because the microorganisms have no color until they are active.

At this stage Kac halts work until there is an exhibition opportunity. When this occurs, the biotopes are transitioned from states of suspended animation into active living systems. This process requires three to five months of continual management of light levels, temperature, and feeding to create a vital habitat. The bacteria that benefit from the particularities of this regimen begin migrating, reproducing, consuming resources, and releasing waste products. Most significantly, they produce pigments as they harvest light energy. Gradually, each type of organism contributes its own color, shape, texture, and pattern. Through their growth the biotopes acquire the visual components of a conventional painting. Compositions emerge when, for example, aerobic populations within the biotope migrate to the top to access oxygen from outside while anaerobic organisms settle in the lower regions where air is absent. At exhibition time, the biotopes look as comfortable in a museum setting as any conventionally painted abstraction.

Kac is not just a passive bystander. He collaborates with the bacteria to create certain compositions. Instead of a brush, however, he uses a long feeder tube and electric lights to encourage growth along specific paths and patterns. He explains, "The initial composition is not random. I can encourage forms. It is like a garden. I steer the behavior. I set the conditions. The organisms adapt."[3] Nonetheless, they continue to respond to surrounding conditions after they are released from his artistic operations. The image, therefore, gradually diverges from his composition. Although the same slurry is used for all the biotopes,

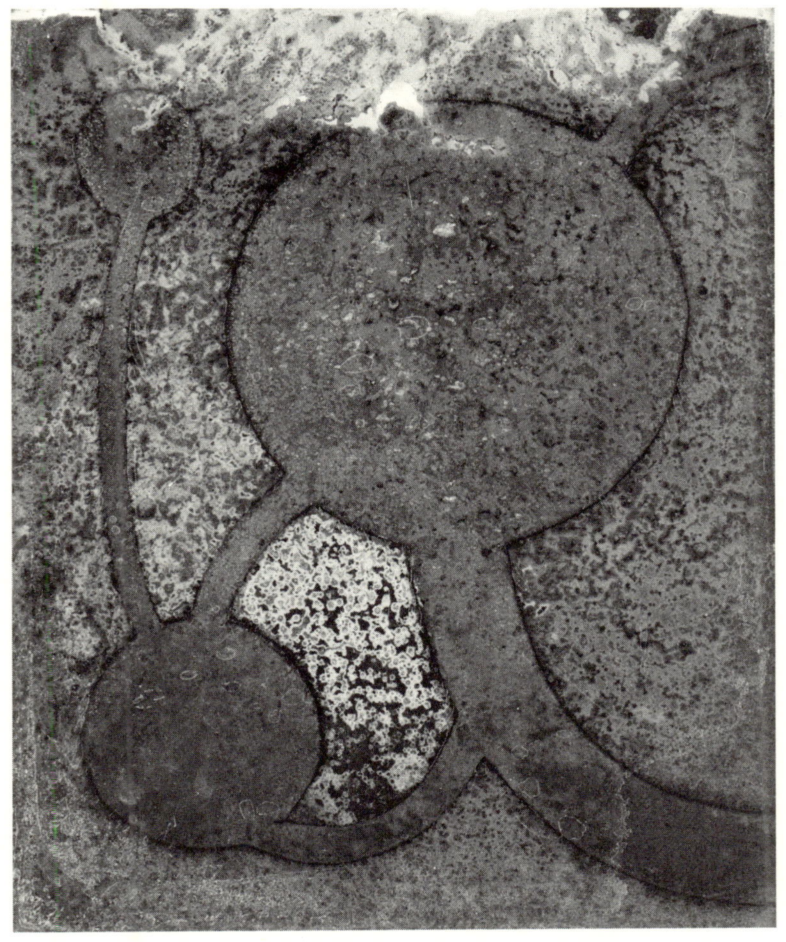

Eduardo Kac | Apsides (from the "Specimen of Secrecy about Marvelous Discoveries" series) | 2006 Biotope of thousands of microscopic beings living in a medium of earth, water, and other materials | Dimensions: 19″ × 23″

PHOTO: HAUPT AND BINDER / COURTESY EDUARDO KAC

each generates a distinctive appearance because each is subjected to unique conditions. Kac honors their individuality by granting each its own name: *Hullabaloo, Oblivion, Theorem, Apsides, Clairvoyance, Odissey, Doohickey*. Then he credits the surprise factor by naming the biotope series, *Specimen of Secrecy about Marvelous Discoveries*. He comments, "Their future is totally unknown."[4]

Kac likens the period during which he oversees the microbes' activation to the biotope's gestation. The opening of an exhibition is its birth. Like all living entities, the populations inhabiting the biotopes undergo conditioning, mutation, adaptation, and evolution. Kac explains that a biotope's "presence and overall behavior is that of a new entity that is at once an artwork and a new living being. It is with this bio-ambiguity that it manifests itself."[5]

Kac explains his artistic role by asserting, "I'm not indifferent to the experience of a viewer, but I'm not interested in decorative elements either. I don't deliberately please or upset the viewer. The sensibility I'm looking for is not the result of vision. It hinges on a dialogical interaction. It is like your phone, your computer. Each has an ergonomic interface. This requires strategies as well as design."[6]

Painting as object Biotopes, like paintings, are objects that are hung on walls to be viewed frontally. Visually, they share left/right and up/down orientations, positive/negative and angular/curvilinear shapes, light/dark and warm/cool colors. Furthermore, neither paintings nor biotopes are merely physical products. Paintings are not just summations of dabs of paint; their appearance reflects the artist's will, talent, and sensitivities. Likewise, biotopes are not only collections of cells; besides revealing the health of each micropopulation, they provide visual evidence of the dynamic flux between a habitat and the forms of life that occupy it. Thus, the creative process is not confined in an artist's studio. The ongoing process of destruction and creation occurs in full view of the audience.

A profound difference in the regimens of physical care emerges from the difference between inert and living art. Traditional paintings require no-touch, no-exposure, no-risk protocols. They are isolated from surrounding conditions so that their fixed surface compositions endure. In contrast, biotopes demand integration. Kac explains: "Like a pet, it will keep company and will produce more colors in response to the care it receives. Like a plant, it will respond to light. . . . Like an animal, it is multi cellular, has a fixed bodily structure and is singular. What is the biotope? It is its plural ontological condition that makes it unique."[7] As such, biotopes participate in "biological time," a term Kac uses as contrast with the frozen time of painting. He comments, "Each 'image' seen at a given time is but a moment in the evolution of the work, an ephemeral snapshot of the biotope metabolic state, a scopic interface for human intimacy."[8]

Painting as communication When Kac states, "I think that artists must have a sense of being uncomfortable, of investigating, of asking questions, of experimenting, or taking risks,"[9] he is reiterating a sentiment that is expressed by an undeviating succession of artists who discard one set of conventions as more timely forms, principles, and mediums emerge. Biotopes may earn a place is this historical accounting. One reason is that integrating microbial life cycles into planning, processing, and producing regimens is core to current ecological considerations. Biotopes, therefore, are artistic applications of this broadscale change in consciousness. Furthermore, Kac notes that biotopes echo the broader cultural contexts by noting, "When you look at stable three-dimensional works of art, the stability in these works seems to resist the fluctuation, the flow, the instability we experience in our thought processes, in our environment, in world politics, in our lives. I'm trying to acknowledge that instability and build it in the work itself."[10] Kac provides a third justification for the renegade introduction of biotopes into the tradition of painting when he speaks about "I-it" conventions that dictate the audience's interactions with conventional paintings. By this he means that encounters between a viewer (I) and an artwork (it) permit viewers to observe, empathize, imagine, and criticize but cannot affect the works of art. He comments, "I really distrust the idea of communication when it comes from one end and it goes towards the other end, with no opportunity for the other person to participate. . . . I am interested in proposing alternatives to the unidirectionality of the system of art."[11] Kac's alternative is a multilateral, networked system that shares the organizational patterns that prevail in electronic technologies, ecological processes, and global communication systems. "With the globalization of the economy and the expansion of networks, connectivity has become near-ubiquitous, where before, unidirectional discourse—as in painting or single-channel video—was predominant. My work responds to this characteristic of contemporary life."[12]

Thus, by incorporating microbial life cycles into art, Kac materializes the dynamic instability and multidirectionality that are currently infiltrating intellectual discourse, reformulating human expectations, and redefining lived experience.

NOTES

1 Eduardo Kac interview with the author, October 23, 2010.

2 Eduardo Kac, "Beyond the Screen: New Directions in Interactive Art," *Veredas*, Ano. 3, No.32 (Rio de Janeiro, 1998). http://www.ekac.org/new interactive.html.

3 Eduardo Kac interview with the author, October 23, 2010.

4 Ibid.

5 Eduardo Kac, "Specimen of Secrecy about Marvelous Discoveries," Instituto Valenciano de Arte Moderno (IVAM) Eduardo Kac Exhibition catalog (Valencia: IVAM, 2007). http://www.ekac.org/specimen_text.html.

6 Eduardo Kac interview with the author, October 23, 2010.

7 Eduardo Kac, "Specimen of Secrecy about Marvelous Discoveries," Instituto Valenciano de Arte Moderno (IVAM) Eduardo Kac Exhibition catalog (Valencia: IVAM, 2007). http://www.ekac.org/specimen_text.html.

8 Ibid.

9 Simone Osthoff, "Eduardo Kac: The Aesthetics of Dialogue" (1994). http://www.ekac.org/intervcomp94.html.

10 Ibid.

11 Simone Osthoff, "Eduardo Kac: The Aesthetics of Dialogue" (1994). http://www.ekac.org/intervcomp94.html.

12 Eduardo Kac interview by Daniele Perra, "Eduardo Kac: Interview," *Thema Celeste* (Milan), no. 81 (July–September 2000), 76–81. http://www.ekac.org/tema.html.

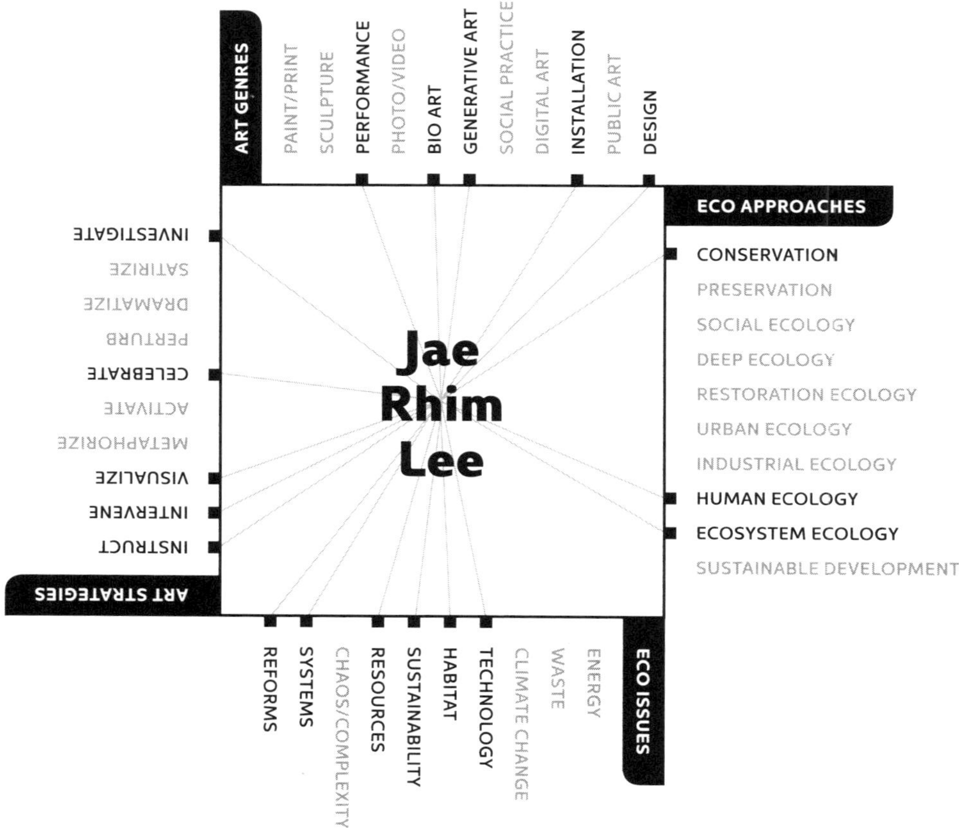

Cultivating the Human Body

Born 1975, Kwangju, South Korea

THE WORD *IMPACT*, when referring to humanity's interactions with the environment, typically conjures a list of misdemeanors that suggests humans are menaces to the Earth, mindlessly sacking its precious storehouse of resources and inflicting ecosystems with maladies they are ill equipped to overcome. Regrettably, the chronicle of human history frequently verifies this scenario. Environmental calamities are known to have been committed by the ancient Persians, Greeks, Romans, Vikings in Greenland, Mayans in Central America, Native Americans in the Southwest, Polynesians on Pacific islands, Chinese, Sumerians, and others. Jae Rhim Lee's art practice is doubly daring. First, she halts this entrenched pattern. Then she reverses humanity's rampage by supplying the Earth with resources that vitalize its systems. To accomplish this task, she relies on substances that are typically considered foul and unhygienic—urine and corpses. Lee applies this remedial scheme to herself by disassociating her urine and her eventual corpse from protocols of flushing, burying, and burning. Instead, she engages them as beneficial bequests to the future. In fact, because everyone urinates and everyone dies, all people are capable of contributing to such acts of Earthly salvation no matter what their income, education, age, or political affiliation.

Lee's engagement with urine began when she discovered that although urine can be damaging to plants if it contains high concentrations of inorganic salts such as sodium chloride, its potential to benefit can be optimized through diet. Meat eaters, for example, produce acidic urine, while vegetarians produce urine that is alkaline. By devising a diet to provide plants with optimal proportions of chemicals and minerals, Lee enhances healthful nutrient cycles. Her perfected urine is an actual plant-vitalizing substance. It is also her work of art. She explains, "In April 2006 I sent my urine to a floriculture lab and learned that it contained all the nutrients required for plant growth, just not in the optimal concentrations. Using diet-planning software, I developed and followed a vegan diet that transformed my urine into a more ideal nutrient solution for plants. . . . I ate lots of spinach, tofu, and nuts; collected and processed my urine; grew napa cabbages hydroponically with the urine, made kimchi from the napa cabbages, and served the kimchi to the public."[1]

N=1=NPK=KIMCHI=N (2006) is a mobile living unit Lee designed as an art installation to conduct her urine-optimizing scheme before the public. The unit combines the appearance of a sterile operating room, a living space, and a garden. It consists of a kitchen table and a foam bed cut in the shape of Lee's body as she lies on her side. It is also equipped with a urinal, urine processing system, napa cabbage growing in a liquid nutrient solution, and sprouted cabbage seedlings. After the unit gets installed in a gallery, she moves in and demonstrates to viewers how to nourish plants with the waste substance of her own body.

The puzzling title Lee composed for this work, *N=1=NPK=KIMCHI=N,* requires some mental calisthenics to decipher. Lee provides guidance:

- NPK stands for nitrogen (N), phosphorus (P), and potassium (K), the primary macronutrients required by plants. All three elements are found in peoples' urine.
- The first N and the last N in the title refer to narcissism, a word derived from the Greek myth of Narkissos who fell in love with his own reflection. Psychoanalysts adopted the myth to examine self-centeredness. Within this discipline extreme narcissism is considered essential in the development of children but pathological when it lingers beyond puberty. Moderate narcissism, however, is a fundamental survival instinct because it strengthens the will to stay alive. Lee combines this psychoanalytic interpretation with an ecological mission when she states, "I elaborate on the intimate affiliation between the narcissistic self and the planet proposed by N=1=NPK=KIMCHI=N."[2]
- N=1 also refers to a notation used in scientific experiments. "N = x" indicates the number of subjects in any given study. N=1 indicates that in this experiment there was just one subject, the artist.
- Kimchi is a traditional Korean dish made from fermented napa cabbage. Millions of people who may never have tasted it know about it because the main

character in the popular television series Chowder has a pet named Kimchi. It appears as a brown-colored gas that smells bad and talks in a belching manner. While this comic caricature reflects the disagreeable side effects of eating kimchi, Koreans prefer to emphasize its healthful properties. The editors of Health magazine agree. They included it on a short list entitled "World's Healthiest Foods."[3]

Thus, the two *N*s that bracket this formula denote the fruition of Lee's accommodating proposition. Moderate narcissism enables an affiliation to develop between the physical body and the ecosystem that "ensures the psychological well-being and survival of both person and planet."[4]

This self-perpetuating system reflects Lee's exhaustive studies of leading scholars such as Christopher Leach, Theodore Roszak, Ernest Becker, Abraham Maslow, and others. Their composite writings comprise a dismal portrait of contemporary society degrading the environment and its populations suffering from the ill effects. Pathological narcissism is the strategy many people develop to cope with the resulting despair and destabilizing insecurity. Lee, herself, says she suffers in this manner. She confesses that in addition to physical pain and exhaustion, she is afflicted by "alienation from the natural world."[5] The personal act of crafting urine to enhance plant fertility bolsters the individual against the ill effects of estrangement from life processes. Lee explains, "In a time of mounting threat and destruction, the self also needs an offensive strategy, one that heals the core of the psyche."[6]

But the benefits of the simple act of producing nourishing cabbage extend far beyond the individual. It has the potential to enhance large-scale agricultural productivity, food security, and sewage processing. Lee explains, "In this relationship, self-seeking, and the needs of the plants and the larger ecosystems are closely tied, thus offering an expanded construction of self."[7]

In a second series of works, Lee's pursuit of environmental reciprocity extends beyond excreting to include dying. She notes, "Death is the eventual distribution of the body into the earth via decay—the ultimate formlessness, weightlessness of the body."[8] Thus, she is already planning to optimize the ecosystem enhancements her corpse will provide, although the Earth will have to wait until she dies to receive them. Once she is dead, this art performance will proceed indefinitely as generations of the microorganisms she nurtured reproduce. This explains the artwork's title, *N=1=0=Infinity* (2008–present).

For the moment, the work consists of *The Infinity Burial Suit*. This fitted body suit is fabricated out of black organic fabric and embroidered with thread that has been inoculated with Infinity Mushroom mycelia.[9] Lee is working with mycologists to develop this new hybrid mushroom's functions. It will enhance her body's contribution to the vitality of her burial site by facilitating the decomposition of her body, remediating industrial toxins in the soil, and encouraging new plant growth. The mushroom will also help her avoid the possibility that her body will contaminate her burial site; according to the US Centers for Disease Control and Prevention, pollutants are lodged in the bodies of 93 percent of people age six and older. Because corpses are storehouses for dangerous chemicals that are released into the ground when burial occurs, and into the atmosphere when they are cremated, Lee is training the Infinity Mushroom to detoxify her accumulated pollutants. The research process involves feeding shitake and oyster mushrooms with the artist's own body tissues and excretions—her skin, hair, nails, blood, bone, fat, tears, urine, feces, and sweat.

The swirling embroidery pattern on the suit is not just visual embellishment; it mimics the growth and migration of mycelia. Fins extend from the suit into the surrounding environment. Wicks uptake a solution of processed and sterilized urine that provides ammonia and nitrate, necessary nutrients for mushroom growth. Then, to ensure this efficient passage of her corpse into the soil, Lee created *Infinity Spore Mass Slurry*, a reverse embalming fluid that speeds decomposition of the body. She plans to market the product to funeral directors when it is perfected. In all these ways Lee accelerates the process of dismantling the molecules that comprise her living body so they can break down as compost and then commence their eternal (hence "infinity") cycling. Lee expresses her utopian vision of death by stating, "Today I'm confronting my own mortality and developing a post-apocalyptic, urban eco-burial system that is no/low-cost, carries a zero carbon and ecological footprint, and uses urban industrial waste and psychoactive and medicinal mushrooms for soil remediation and human consumption."[10]

Ultimately, Lee hopes her work will serve individuals who lack soul-fulfilling connections with life processes, which is a fundamental requirement for environmental stewardship. This involves perceiving life in physical terms—urinating, dying, decaying. Her culture-shifting projects present the body, living and dead, as a beneficial offering to the future of life on Earth. She summarizes her bold artistic mission by stating, "I synthesize concepts of the self-body, narcissism, death, and ecology to arrive at a methodology for the long-term preservation of the self and the planet."[11]

NOTES

1 "In May, 2006, I sent urine to Floriculture lab and followed a customized vegan diet designed to transform my urine into an ideal nutrient solution for plants. I diluted my urine with water and added ground soybeans, which contain urease, the enzyme which converts urea into ammonia. I also added nitrosomas bacteria to activate the nitrogen cycle, which converts ammonia into nitrate, the form of nitrogen required by plants. I then sterilized the solution and pumped it into a hydroponic napa cabbage garden." Jae Rhim Lee, thesis for the Master of Science in Visual Studies, submitted to the Department of Architecture at the Massachusetts Institute of Technology (2006), 1. http://dspace.mit.edu/bitstream/handle/1721.1/37269/86109832.pdf?sequence=1.

2 Ibid., 1.

3 "World's Healthiest Foods," Health.com, February 1, 2008. http://www.health.com/health/article/0,,20410299,00.html.

4 Jae Rhim Lee, thesis for the Master of Science in Visual Studies, submitted to the Department of Architecture at the Massachusetts Institute of Technology (2006), 22. http://dspace.mit.edu/bitstream/handle/1721.1/37269/86109832.pdf?sequence=1.

5 Ibid, 19.

6 Ibid, 21.

7 Ibid, 22.

8 Ibid, 32.

9 "Designing a Mushroom Death Suit," Alison George interviews Jae Rhim Lee, in CultureLab, *New Scientist*, July 20, 2011. http://www.newscientist.com/blogs/culturelab/2011/07/designing-a-mushroom-death-suit.html. Lee is considering an improvement by using gelatin as a second skin that would dissolve and provide start-up ingredients for mushroom growth.

10 "Jae Rhim Lee, Lecturer (2007–2009)." http://mit.edu/vap/people/faculty/faculty_lee.html.

11 Jae Rhim Lee, thesis for the Master of Science in Visual Studies, submitted to the Department of Architecture at the Massachusetts Institute of Technology (2006), 1. http://dspace.mit.edu/bitstream/handle/1721.1/37269/86109832.pdf?sequence=1.

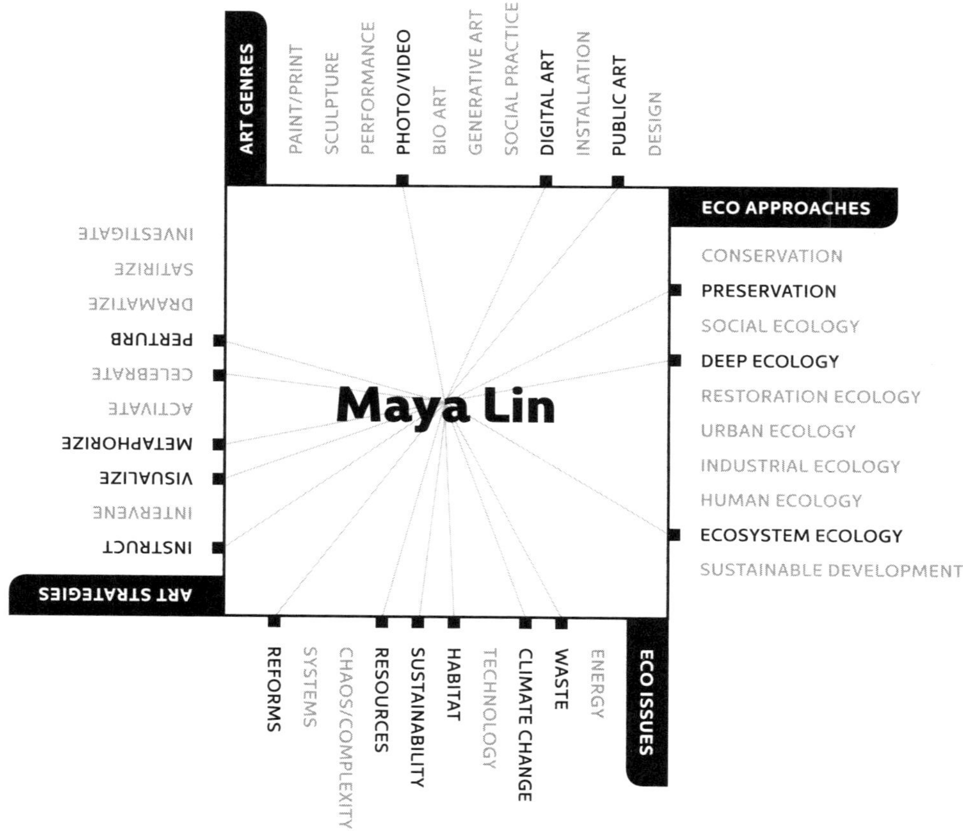

The Sixth Extinction

Born 1959, Athens, Ohio

THE ONLY DISTINGUISHING FEATURE of the four flights of stairs I climbed to meet with Maya Lin was their length. This was the first indication that my destination was a work space, not a showroom to display the accomplishments of this internationally recognized architect/designer/artist whose acclaim was launched in 1981 when she designed the Vietnam Memorial in Washington, DC. The unmarked and unlocked metal door was the second indicator. It opened into a large space with banks of computers and diligently working employees. Lin occupied an area cordoned off from the rest. I found her there, pencil in hand, pouring over the 3″ x 5″ note cards spread out on a table. Without looking up she waved for me to take a seat opposite her. This low-tech station was the headquarters for a technologically sophisticated project entitled *What Is Missing?* (2009–ongoing). This formidable artwork/memorial is archiving current peoples' memories of past environmental conditions for future generations.

The area devoted to this project is packed with evidence of what is missing from the planet. Cases are crammed with books chronicling environmental losses. Shelves are piled with notes examining symptoms of Earth's current maladies. A metal frame holds rows of hanging files reporting recent additions to the list of "missings" from the Earth's species, resources, and circumstances. The bound materials piled on the windowsill are mock-ups for books detailing conditions and entities that have become memories. Less visible was Lin's extensive collections of historic maps, computer visualizations, satellite photos, radar and sonar images, drawings, models, audio recordings, quotations, and personal recollections gathered from scientists, conservationists, journalists, activists, artists, NGOs, and citizens. Lin is consolidating this sweeping and ever-expanding collection into a multidimensional portrait of a planet in crisis.

The ponderous roll of drums, taps, and eulogies are cultural conventions that mark the end of a day and the death of an individual. No custom has yet been devised to commemorate extinctions of entire species and the demise of entire ecosystems across the globe. The grief associated with these losses carries ominous projections because they are occurring at an accelerating rate. Lin's work of art is being created within the context of the "Sixth Extinction," the latest in Earth's long history and the first in which responsibility for wreaking global havoc is assigned, at least in part, to humans. Lin comments, "*What Is Missing?* will make us aware of the enormous loss of species that is presently occurring. Chronicling not just the extinction of specific species, it will focus equal attention on the threatened habitats and ecosystems that are vital to other species' survival."[1]

Likewise, fountains, arches, and sculptures comprise a long tradition of memorials, but these too seem inadequate to observe the impairments, afflictions, and depletions that currently encompass the globe. In order to accommodate this mammoth theme, Lin reinvented the memorial as an expandable, multifaceted system, not a grandiose monument that is fixed in time and space. The work is an assemblage of historic evidence, scientific facts, and personal memories presented as sculptures, books, and interactive websites. These formats utilize sound, text, and image and are presented at art museums, at science institutions, and as applications for laptops and portable media. It is not difficult to understand why Lin declares, "*What Is Missing?* is my last monument, but it will occupy me for the rest of my life."[2] The work is being created to galvanize the public into action, whether that means initiating new behaviors that benefit Earth's populations or halting actions that threaten them.

Lin inaugurated *What Is Missing?* on Earth Day in 2009 at the California Academy of Sciences in San Francisco. A year later *What Is Missing?* morphed into three short DVDs. The 2011 version is an online site, Whatismissing.net. Lin plans to update the work annually every Earth Day. This chapter focuses on the DVD version in 2010. It was projected as a billboard visible to the teeming pedestrians who jam the streets in Times Square, New York City.[3] Running once each hour for three weeks, it appeared in the midst of gigantic advertisements for Swatch, Pepsi, Foot Locker, and Toys"R"Us. One by one, the video discloses twelve examples of loss. Some enumerate mournful finalities. Others feature species that may soon vanish from Earth's rosters of living forms. Still others disclose the sounds and sights that will no longer enrich the Earth when these species are gone. The detrimental conditions that threaten them provide causes for these unfortunate effects. Lin parcels these installments in slow measured increments. Casual skimming is not an option. Viewers are given time to consider their "landscape amnesia," which Lin defines as "the notion that we don't know what is missing if we have forgotten what was there."[4] Such amnesia is particularly pronounced in New York City, where this artwork premiered.

The DVD introduces this thought-provoking content with a cricket/frog/songbird chorus. This beguiling musical greeting is remote from the urban clamor of Times Square. Then letters appear against a blank, black screen, gradually forming words. A question mark is added. Gradually viewers decipher "What Is Missing?" This question remains fixed on the screen throughout the video as a haunting reminder of the work's memorial status. Answers to this question come into view as each new sequence begins. Here too, viewers must decode the meaning. Images are blurred. Sounds are muffled. Each triad of sound, word, and image gradually clarifies, fades, and is replaced. The oscillation between appearing and disappearing seems tenuous. Each of the twelve sequences confirms the fragility of existence:

1. **"What Is Missing? The Scale of Species"** is the first entry on this troublesome list of missing items. These words are accompanied by a thunderous gurgle and the sight of a single large stingray performing arabesques against an expanse of blue water.

   Lin's consideration of scale did not include the largest endangered or extinct species. This distinction is held by blue whales. Nor did Lin select a small species like the bee, whose dwindling populations in China, Brazil, North America, and Europe are alarming environmentalists. She chose stingrays, a medium-size aquatic species about the size of humans. Perhaps the scale that Lin was measuring focused on stamina, grace, and beauty. Stingrays, whose current protection status is "threatened," have long graced the Earth with these forms of excellence.

2. **"What Is Missing? The Abundance of Species"** is represented by a herd of elk grazing contently on an open plain.

   Elk migrated to North America about a hundred thousand years ago, crossing the Bering land bridge from what is now Russia. At the time European settlers arrived, the continent's population is estimated to have been 10 million animals. Now, two of the six known subspecies are extinct. The remaining species have dwindled to a total estimated population of 960,000.[5] Although elk are not yet missing for the Earth's populations, they will survive only if their evolution keeps pace with the current rates of extinctions and if conservation efforts to protect and rehabilitate their lands succeed.

3. **"What Is Missing? The Longevity of Species"** is presented as a towering evergreen tree with a massive trunk that the camera pans from base to crest.

   This single tree represents all the species on the planet whose longevity is threatened by such age-old assaults as asteroids and lightning and such recent forms of abuse as nuclear waste, paving, mountaintop mining, and mono agriculture. Even geneticists are adding causes of premature death by tinkering with the DNA of trees to hasten their growth and thereby boost their productivity.[6] Nonetheless, Lin's choice is poignant because trees, which produce a new ring each year, are natural markers of the passage of time.

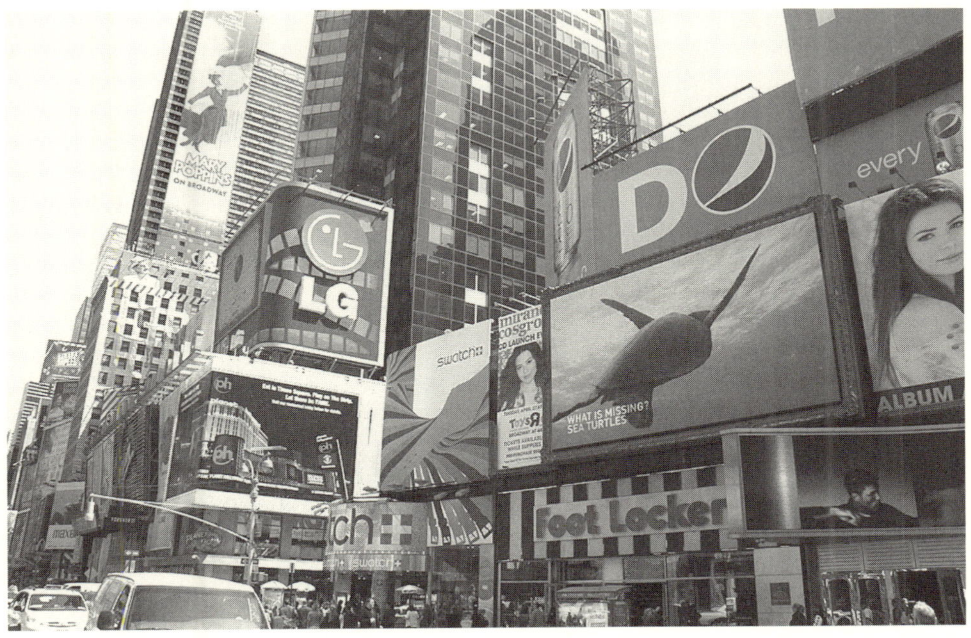

Maya Lin | What Is Missing? | 2009–present With support of the Cornell Lab of Ornithology | Multi-sited memorial | MTV / Creative Time 44½ Billboard April 15–30, 2010

PHOTO: CORNELL LAB OF ORNITHOLOGY / COURTESY CORNELL LAB OF ORNITHOLOGY AND MAYA LIN STUDIO

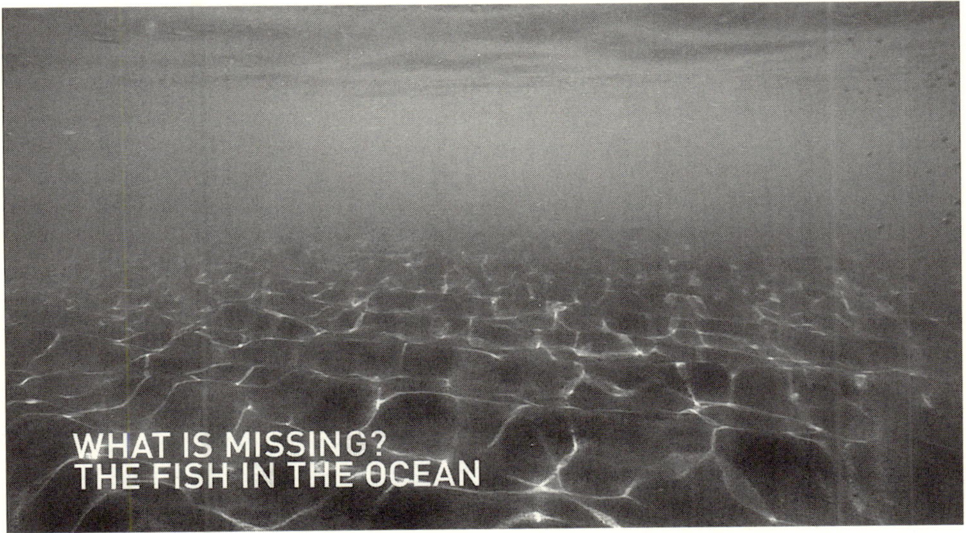

Maya Lin | What Is Missing? The Fish in the Ocean | 2009–present With support of the Cornell Lab of Ornithology | Multi-sited memorial | MTV / Creative Time 44½ Billboard April 15–30, 2010

PHOTO: CORNELL LAB OF ORNITHOLOGY / COURTESY CORNELL LAB OF ORNITHOLOGY AND MAYA LIN STUDIO

Lin amplifies her theme of longevity by presenting a pine tree, a common symbol of immortality. In many cultures, ancient pine trees are revered as embodiments of fitness that prolongs life.

4. **"What Is Missing? Animal Migrations"** is embodied by giant cranes flying across the screen with determined squawks and flapping wings.

   Humans travel roadways, highways, parkways, expressways, freeways, and beltways. Yet these congested "ways" rarely evoke the awe associated with mass migrations of monarch butterflies, wildebeests, arctic terns, caribou, leatherback turtles, and salamanders. These nonhuman beings also travel on "ways." Flyways are required for migrating birds, bats, and insects. Waterways allow aquatic animals to conduct seasonal breeding and rearing. Pathways enable land animals to cross mountains, rivers, and tracks of land. These travelers depend upon open corridors of undeveloped habitat to supply their needs en route. By hampering migrations, such common components of the contemporary landscape as dams, skyscrapers, and airports are adding species to "What is missing?" lists. Because migrating animals can't go partway, if something is in their way, they pass away.

5. **"What Is Missing? Bird Songs"** shows a close-up of a common wren twittering softly as it clings to a swaying reed.

   Dawn choruses of warbles, tweets, and chirps are marvels of nature. But musical splendor is incidental to the main reason why birds sing, which is to communicate with potential mates, rivals, and predators. Just as rap music echoes the sounds of the ghetto and yodels model the Swiss mountains, birdsong is shaped by its environment. Forest-dwelling birds emit constant short signals because sounds bounce off trees. Species that make their home on the plains tend to buzz. Those that live near loud running water produce high-frequency calls.[7] All these habitats will be diminished if birds cease to sing.

6. **"What Is Missing? The Ability of Animals to Hear and See Under Water"** is represented by a mother humpback whale and her baby swimming in circles. They are filmed in close-up so that viewers of the video, like the underwater animals, cannot see where they are going.

   Undersea racket is a product of icebreaker ships, dredging boats, oil-drilling rigs, sonic oil exploration, and dynamite explosions from construction and demolition projects. Fish must contend with approximately 130 supertankers at sea at any given time. Each generates 187 decibels of low-frequency sound, as deafening as some military artillery explosions. The loudest new noisemaker in the ocean is the US Navy's low-frequency sonar. The Natural Resources Defense Council, an environmental watchdog group, estimates that this form of sonar tops the list of noise polluters by emitting about 240 decibels of noise![8]

7. **"What Is Missing? The Oxygen in the Ocean"** is depicted by dead fish, too numerous to count, drifting in murky waters.

   Thousands of square miles of ocean have been depleted of oxygen that supports aquatic life. The spread of these "dead zones" is a looming environmental crisis caused, significantly, by industrial agriculture. Large-scale farming douses fields with fertilizers. When these fertilizers seep into waterways, they get flushed into the sea, where they spur the growth of algae. Populations of bacteria escalate as they feast on the algae. They use up the oxygen, which causes other organisms in their aquatic neighborhood to suffocate.[9] Thus, boosting food production on land can shrink food production in water.

8. **"What Is Missing? Mountain Tops"** shows a dynamite explosion blasting off a mountain peak, followed by images of hurled boulders and tumbling debris. The thirty-second sequence on the DVD encapsulates a multiphased volley of violent acts. The initial action in mountaintop removal for mining involves scraping away trees, topsoil, understory growth as well as all wildlife that cannot move out of the way. Then explosives are detonated that can blast eight hundred feet off mountaintops and unleash a storm of "fly rock." Next, huge shovels gouge into the loosened debris. Trucks haul millions of tons away or push the waste into adjacent valleys.[10]

9. **"What Is Missing? Clean Water"** is introduced by the peaceful sound of lapping, the only pleasant component of the litter-strewn waterway that comes into view. Five facts about water provide a snapshot of the current global drinking-water crisis: twenty percent of freshwater fish species have been pushed to the edge of extinction from contaminated water;[11] half the world's five hundred major rivers are seriously depleted or polluted;[12] there are more than three hundred thousand contaminated groundwater sites in the United States alone;[13] roughly one-sixth of the world's population does not have access to safe drinking water;[14] the water we drink today is the same water the dinosaurs drank—there is no new water.[15]

10. **"What Is Missing? Rivers That Run Freely to the Sea"** provides an aerial view of a circuitous river flowing through a magnificent rust-red landscape.

    Rivers that meander through valleys create seasonal floodplains and connect headwater lakes and shallow wetlands and creeks with the oceans. They are often viewed by engineers as flaws that can be improved by deepening, straightening, widening, blocking, and draining. By the end of the twentieth century, fifty thousand dams choked more than half of the Earth's major rivers,[16] preventing some from reaching the sea. These massive engineering programs were designed to generate electricity, supply drinking water for people, serve the needs of industry, control floods, and facilitate navigation. However, they are often accompanied by grave watershed disturbances.

11. **"What Is Missing? Clean Air"** is represented by the clamor of traffic in a mauve-colored, smog-laden city.

    In the United States, the Environmental Protection Agency publishes a daily Air Quality Index. The service was not instituted to boast about the quality of the country's air but to warn against levels of carbon monoxide, nitrogen dioxide, lead, ozone, particulate matter, and sulfur dioxide in the air.[17] Air pollution from motor vehicles, power plants, airplanes, smelters, factories, and other components of contemporary lifestyles ruins vacations, causes serious health problems, and contributes to acid rain formation that decimates fish, erodes buildings, and damages farm crops.

12. **"What Is Missing? Visibility of the Stars"** is depicted by a huge metropolis where electrical lights are outcompeting starlight.

    Light pollution rarely appears on lists of environmental threats. However, there is increasing evidence that illumination from street fixtures, lighthouses, oil rigs, airports, and high-rises profoundly affects the mating, resting, feeding, and migration patterns of wildlife. Humans are not immune to its impact. Our internal clockworks also evolved to function according to the natural oscillation of light on Earth.[18]

These scenes augment the challenges that commence this DVD: Can we humans balance our needs with the needs of the planet? Can we imagine rearranging the lights? Can we learn to share the planet?

This DVD is the memorial component of this sprawling enterprise. Other components provide guidance and inspiration to reverse the relentless stripping of species, conditions, and qualities from the planet. Lin concludes, "The goal of *What Is Missing?* is to not just make us aware of these losses but to give us direction and hope for what can be done to help. *What Is Missing?* will provide an overview of what is being done throughout the world in terms of conservation and habitat protection. It will give viewers a glimpse of our global environment, taking people to different places, highlighting specific groups and showing the progress that is being made in the critical areas in which they work."[19]

NOTES

1 "What's Missing?" http://www.mayalin.com/.
2 Maya Lin interview with the author, December 10, 2010.
3 Creative Time Video: April 15–April 30, 2010. The videos ran on MTV HD Screen in Times Square. Each lasted three to five minutes.
4 Maya Lin interview with the author, December 10, 2010.
5 "Information on Elk." http://www.planet-pets.com/plntelk.htm.
6 Hugh Warwick, "The Next GM Threat: Frankenstein Forests," *The Ecologist*, vol. 29, no. 4 (July 1999). http://www.theecologist.info/page17.html.
7 Gareth Huw Davies, "Bird Songs," PBS.org. http://www.pbs.org/lifeofbirds/songs/index.html.
8 "Sources of Noise," University of California Santa Cruz. http://scicom.ucsc.edu/SciNotes/9601/OceanNoise/Noises.html.
9 Carl Zimmer, "A Looming Oxygen Crisis and Its Impact on the World's Oceans," *Yale Environment 360*, August, 5, 2010. http://e360.yale.edu/content/feature.msp?id=2301.
10 "What Is Mountain Top Removal Mining," Mountain Justice.org. http://mountainjustice.org/facts/steps.php.
11 "The Facts about the Global Drinking Water Crisis," Blue Planet Network. http://blueplanetnetwork.org/water/facts.
12 Ibid.
13 Ibid.
14 Ibid.
15 Ibid.
16 "About Dams," International Rivers. http://www.internationalrivers.org/node/287.
17 "Air Quality Index (AQI): A Guide to Air Quality and your Health," AirNow.gov. http://www.airnow.gov/index.cfm?action=aqibasics.aqi.
18 "Light Pollution," Urban Astronomer. http://www.urban-astronomer.com/articles/astronomy-101/light-pollution.
19 "Mission Statement." http://whatismissing.net/#/home/about_the_project.

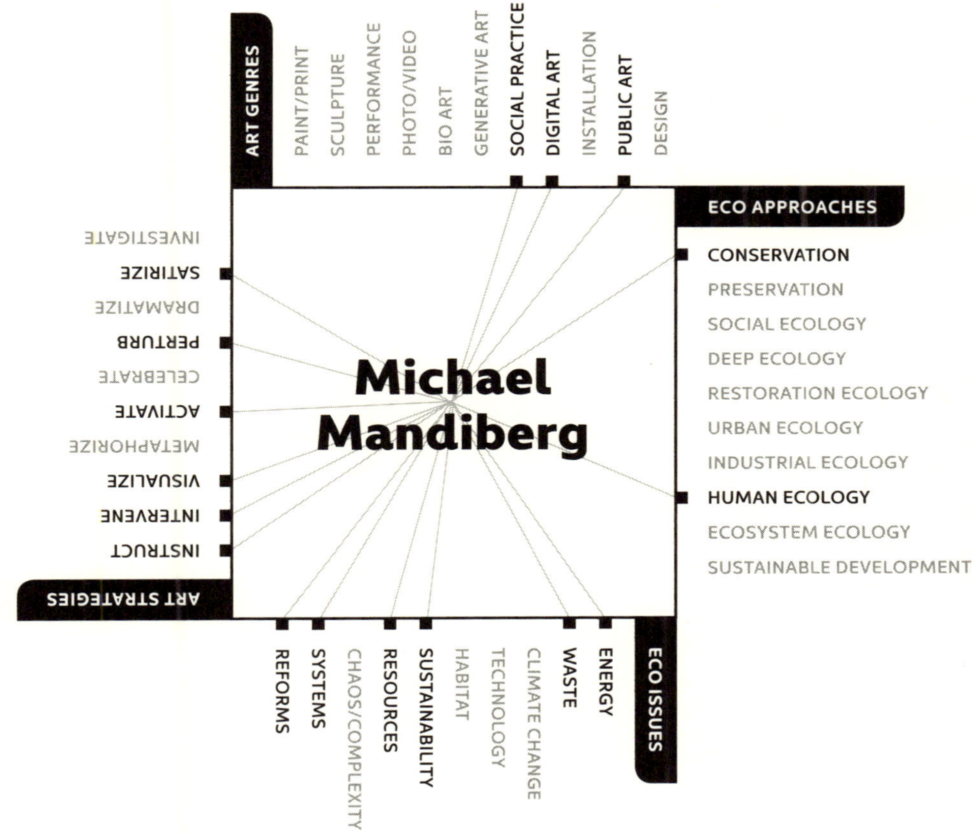

Tactical Media Campaign

Born 1977, Michigan, USA

CONTEMPORARY CIVILIZATION has transformed many of the sensual complexities of lived experience into data. Spaces that were once occupied by smells, temperatures, weight, and mass have been relinquishing these attributes as they are claimed by the immaterial realm of digital forms and networks. Likewise, these experiences disengage from geography, climate, and topography when they take up residence in cyberspace. The Internet is changing the nature of human experience because it is where more and more people shop, bank, socialize, play, work, research, communicate, daydream, laugh, seek enlightenment, give advice, and receive news. Cyberspace may be the equivalent of the great cathedrals of the medieval period where the masses congregated for prayer, commerce, culture, community, information, and excitement. Art throughout that era was created for, situated within, and inspired by these places of worship. The cathedral was as integral to life as art was integral to the cathedral. Because of this connection, an affinity prevailed between medieval artists and their audiences. Common folk understood art's symbols, resonated with its aesthetics, complied with its messages, and appreciated its techniques. In a similar manner, the Internet has become a near universal tool for communication today. Artists creating their work with electronic hardware and software utilize the tools and imagery that are more intrinsic to their cultural context than painting and drawing. Like their medieval predecessors, they enjoy rapport with their viewers and benefit from presenting their work in a venue where the masses are already converging. Michael Mandiberg is one of many contemporary artists who utilize the web to communicate the core issues of the day. His message is not to warn of eternal damnation in hell, but to warn of environmental collapse on Earth.

While Mandiberg's mass of red hair and electrifying expression might suggest that he would exploit the graphic extravaganzas that computer technologies allow, his creative interventions introduce statistics culled from the glut of available data aimed at promoting consumer restraint. His appearance is confirmed by his wily strategy that involves graphically simplifying and organizing these facts and then insinuating them into point-of-purchase sales on line. This renegade conservation scheme factors environmental costs into price tags just as consumers are about to click "Complete Purchase."

Real Costs (2007), for example, inserts emissions data into travel-related e-commerce websites.[1] This artwork manifests Mandiberg's calculated approach to engaging the web as an instrument of social change. As someone is booking a flight online, a user interface presents guilt-inducing evidence of the carbon dioxide emissions their planned trip will generate. The first version of *Real Costs* added this information to twenty-five airfare websites, including Orbitz.com, United.com, and Delta.com. A Firefox plug-in that had previously been downloaded into users' browsers enabled this consciousness-raising function. The code was activated when a web page for booking reservations was accessed.

This work appropriates mass media strategies that reverse the one-way flow of communication and power. Furthermore, it parallels situationism, an international political and artistic movement of the 1950s and 1960s that criticized consumer society for alienating people and turning their lives into meaningless pursuits of commodities. Mandiberg describes his work as an "interventionist" art project: "I created something inside of an existing context which changes the viewers' understandings of that context. In this case, I inserted a bit of HTML code back into airplane website pages making it work inside of those contexts, and making people aware of the result of what they are about to do. Is it subversive? I'm definitely aiming at surprise. People forget they have installed the software. It makes them think about their roles as consumers. Even if they installed it, they forget that when they go to book their next ticket. Boom! Surprise! Oh right!"[2]

Consumers who acquire Mandiberg's software encounter four cunning scenarios for insinuating unwelcome data into the normal websites of the airlines:

- A graph with bold red bars displays the carbon dioxide emitted from four alternative forms of transportation for the planned trip: plane, car, bus, train. The car portion is personalized so that those calculations are derived from

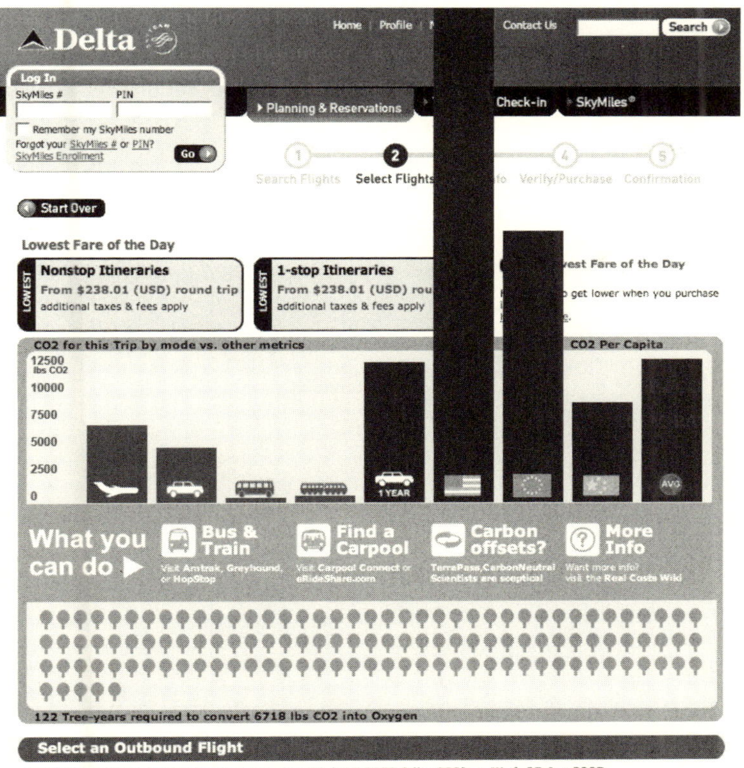

Select an Outbound Flight

New York-Kennedy, NY (JFK) to Los Angeles, CA (LAX 3359.2 lbs CO2) on Wed, 25 Apr 2007

Different city or date? Search by schedule?

Narrow your results by checking or unchecking the boxes below.
Stops Nonstop Itineraries 1-stop Itineraries

Click the column headings to sort your results. Displaying **15** of **15** flights

Departs	Arrives	Stops	Travel Time	Flights & Cabin (Class)		Price per Passenger (USD) Round trip
Nonstop						
7:00am JFK	10:11am **LAX 3359.2 lbs CO2**	Nonstop	6 hr 11 min	Delta 1025 Boeing 757	Coach (T) **View Seats**	LOWEST From **$238.01** round trip + $20.80 Taxes/Fees = $258.81 Select
8:40am JFK	11:49am **LAX 3359.2 lbs CO2**	Nonstop	6 hr 09 min	Delta 1459 Boeing 757	Coach (T) **View Seats**	LOWEST From **$238.01** round trip + $20.80 Taxes/Fees = $258.81 Select
11:45am JFK	2:48pm **LAX 3359.2 lbs CO2**	Nonstop	6 hr 03 min	Delta 1841 Boeing 757	Coach (T) **View Seats**	LOWEST From **$238.01** round trip + $20.80 Taxes/Fees = $258.81 Select
4:40pm JFK	8:04pm **LAX 3359.2 lbs CO2**	Nonstop	6 hr 24 min	Delta 83 Boeing 757	Coach (T) **View Seats**	LOWEST From **$238.01** round trip + $20.80 Taxes/Fees = $258.81 Select
7:00pm JFK	10:37pm **LAX 3359.2 lbs CO2**	Nonstop	6 hr 37 min	Delta 133 Boeing 757	Coach (T) **View Seats**	LOWEST From **$238.01** round trip + $20.80 Taxes/Fees = $258.81 Select
1-stop						
6:00am JFK	10:50am **LAX 3359.2 lbs CO2**	1-stop Cincinnati (58 min layover)	7 hr 50 min	Delta 5089 CRJ 700 operated by Comair Delta 1692 Boeing 757	Coach (T) **View Seats** Coach (T) **View Seats**	LOWEST From **$238.01** round trip + $41.60 Taxes/Fees = $279.61 Select

Michael Mandiberg | Real Costs (screenshot on Delta.com) | 2007–ongoing
Firefox plug-in that inserts emissions data into travel-related e-commerce websites | Software art / Internet art

IMAGE URL: WWW.FLICKR.COM/PHOTOS/THEREDPROJECT/6334978263 / COURTESY CC BY-SA MICHAEL MANDIBERG

the specific make and model of the consumer's car. This information appears overlaid on the MapQuest site.

- The graph then charts carbon dioxide emissions per capita from a rotating selection of the world's most populated countries. The bars of travelers from countries where residents are frequent flyers soar off the top of the chart. It nudges viewers to place their self-serving intentions into the context of national averages.
- A pictogram visualizes how many trees are required to convert the amount of carbon dioxide emitted by the trip back into oxygen. In other words, instead of calculating the cost of a trip in terms of dollars, Mandiberg computes the trip in terms of "tree years." The round trip from Los Angeles to New York on Continental Airlines, for example, would require seventy tree years to convert one person's carbon footprint back into oxygen.
- Three energy-saving alternatives are presented just after these unsettling data are read and viewers are primed for reform. A click of the mouse links to the websites of Greyhound and Amtrak. Another click connects to car pool sites. A third is linked to carbon offset sites. And just to make certain that the viewer gets the point, raw data about the quantities and ill effects of carbon dioxide emissions are available as a grand finale.

A second component of *Real Costs* consists of Mandiberg's open invitation to the public to contribute to the creative construction, design, and data included in the presentation. The site is set up as a wiki to facilitate the public's ability to edit the interlinked web pages. Programming-savvy viewers can access and alter the workings of the open-source code.

Both wiki contributors and travelers manifest the crafting skills that support Mandiberg's tactical media artworks. His extensive knowledge of software tools, data collection, user engagement, simulation, visualization, and databases enables him to parody official web sites. Mandiberg compares these skills to knitting and sewing. He explains, "In order for something to be a parody, it has to mimic what it is referencing, but be different. My parody is not ironic. I am giving information the user wouldn't get on a regular mapping site. It's a really subtle balance to prove you know the rules as you are breaking them. I need to know how to write code before I can break rules about writing code. It is the same with any medium. You have to know its tenets, strategies, and belief systems."[3]

Fortified with these skills, Mandiberg's site is doubly dynamic. First, the travel data it provides change as prices change. Second, the structure and appearance of the site change as visitors participate in collaborative creation. These active components will be expanded in the future. Mandiberg plans to infiltrate websites that provide car directions, car rentals, and shipping, to "make legible the invisible."[4] He explains, "It comes down to a design-focused question: How do you present information in the clearest way possible? I don't mean 'designing' in terms of surface, but 'designing' of the clarity of communication."[5]

This challenge produced another impish energy-use consciousness-raising web project. *Oil Standard* (2006)[6] is directed at Standard Oil, the largest oil refiner in the world and one of the first multinational corporations. It, too, is a plug-in for the Firefox web browser. By reversing the company's name to read "oil standard," the work invites comparison with the "gold standard," evoking the controlling power of oil in establishing the stability of today's global markets. Mandiberg suggests that providing for a country's security has shifted away

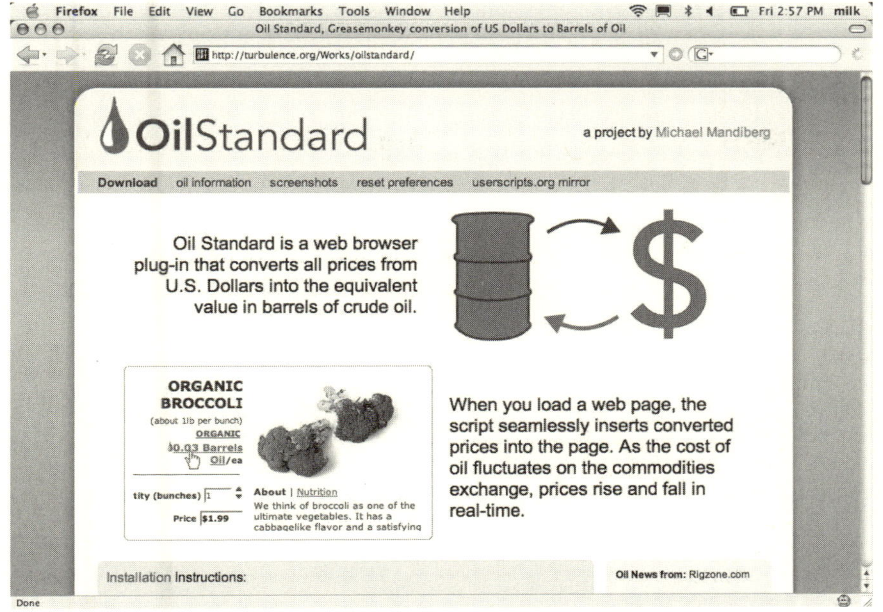

Michael Mandiberg | Oil Standard (screenshot) | 2006 Web browser plug-in that converts prices from US dollars into equivalent value in barrels of crude oil | Software art / Internet art

IMAGE URL: WWW.FLICKR.COM/PHOTOS/THEREDPROJECT/6335779034 / COURTESY MICHAEL MANDIBERG

from gold—a precious element that has been stockpiled since ancient times to maintain the value of nations' currencies—to crude oil.

In order to visualize this shift, *Oil Standard* calculates costs of common consumer purchases in terms of barrels of crude oil instead of dollar costs. When the consumer loads a web page, converted prices are automatically inserted onto the page. Rising and falling prices for real goods are synchronized with real-time fluctuations in the cost of oil on the commodities exchange. One example from the 2006 screen shot and video documentation is the Apple 4G iPod Nano Black that appears as an overlay on an Amazon.com web page. With sardonic humor, the site emulates Amazon's discount policy by crossing out the original cost (4.01 barrels) and replacing it with a bargain price (3.85 barrels). Mandiberg explains his intentions by stating, "*Oil Standard* synthesized my interest in hacktivism and Internet art, sustainable economics, and information design to create an art piece that opened up a dialogue about oil, economics, and the environment."[7]

Oil Standard also recalculates the cost of organically grown broccoli being sold on FreshDirect.com into oil units. Then it adds this sum, .03 barrels of oil, to the website's "Your Cart" section. Likewise, this intervention adds parentheses to the multiple, mega dollar references in the *Wall Street Journal*'s front page; each parenthesis contains the dollar equivalents in oil. Another example is the intervention on personal banking statements on the Chase Bank site; the user can click on any purchase and receive its instantaneous conversion into the oil standard. In all these ways *Oil Standard* demonstrates that the petroleum story is not a one-liner about fuel. Petroleum is a primary component of tires, asphalt, soaps, detergents, solvents, drugs, explosives, paints, epoxy resins, flooring, insulation, plastics, and so forth.

Since raw data may not be sufficient to reform buying habits for all these products, Mandiberg injects a metaphorical "oil booster" into his artwork; this additive takes the form of oil industry headlines from RSS feeds announcing the dire consequences of oil dependence. One example states, "Alaska Oil Spill Is Environmental Catastrophe," while another warns, "Iraq Threatens to Use Oil in Nuke Standoff." In this manner energy-related news stories cease seeming remote from peoples' daily lives. *Oil Standard* assigns global significance to personal consumption at the same time that it demonstrates how global fluctuations of the price of oil affect personal finances.

The website for *Oil Standard* is packed with information that is presented without distracting bells and whistles. In fact, the site offers a textbook sampling of graphic devices. For example, a list compares population with consumption of energy resources. A column bar graph shows how crude oil is used. A bar graph compares oil consumption in different countries. A line graph estimates timetables for the exhaustion of oil reserves. A directory presents recent news stories related to oil.

When asked how these projects function as art, Mandiberg replied, "The information is more prominent than the work's identity as 'art.' There is something pleasurable about pushing that boundary. I really like working at the edge of art, where something is perceived as other than art. It can access audiences that are not looking for an art experience. My work shows up in a lot of different places—business and environmental blogs and the *New York Times* business section."[8]

Mandiberg maintains that his projects accomplish the same social function as Michelangelo's or Monet's paintings. "The role of the artist is to show the world to the world, whether it is three-point perspective, or an impressionist painting, or a photograph. Art reveals something to the viewer. I take data that is already there and bring it into a context that makes it clear in a personal way. Saying 'millions of tons of carbon dioxide' means nothing to people. As raw data, it means nothing to me because it is not something I can fathom. There is a whole tradition of art as social and political commentary. I'm making my commentary through utility. My hope is that consumer change will drive citizen change, and that in turn will drive corporate change and governmental change."[9]

Mandiberg admits it is difficult to test the effectiveness of his interventions. He concludes, "When you are attempting to enact massive change, you aren't going to achieve this yourself. You are part of a social movement, one of many voices. There will be no revolution."[10]

NOTES

1 Michael Mandiberg, Concept, Programming, Aesthetics; P. Timon McPhearson, PhD, Ecological Advisor, The New School University; Carlo Montagnino, Junior Programmer; Evan Moran, Designer.

2 Michael Mandiberg interview with the author, April 15, 2010.

3 Ibid.

4 Ibid.

5 Ibid.

6 Oil Standard is a 2006 commission of New Radio and Performing Arts, Inc., (aka Ether-Ore) for its Turbulence website. It was made possible with funding from the Jerome Foundation and New York City Department of Cultural Affairs.

7 "A Case Study of the Real Costs," posted by admin, January 7, 2011. http://www.mandiberg.com/2011/01/07/a-case-study-of-the-real-costs/.

8 Michael Mandiberg interview with the author, April 15, 2010.

9 Ibid.

10 Ibid.

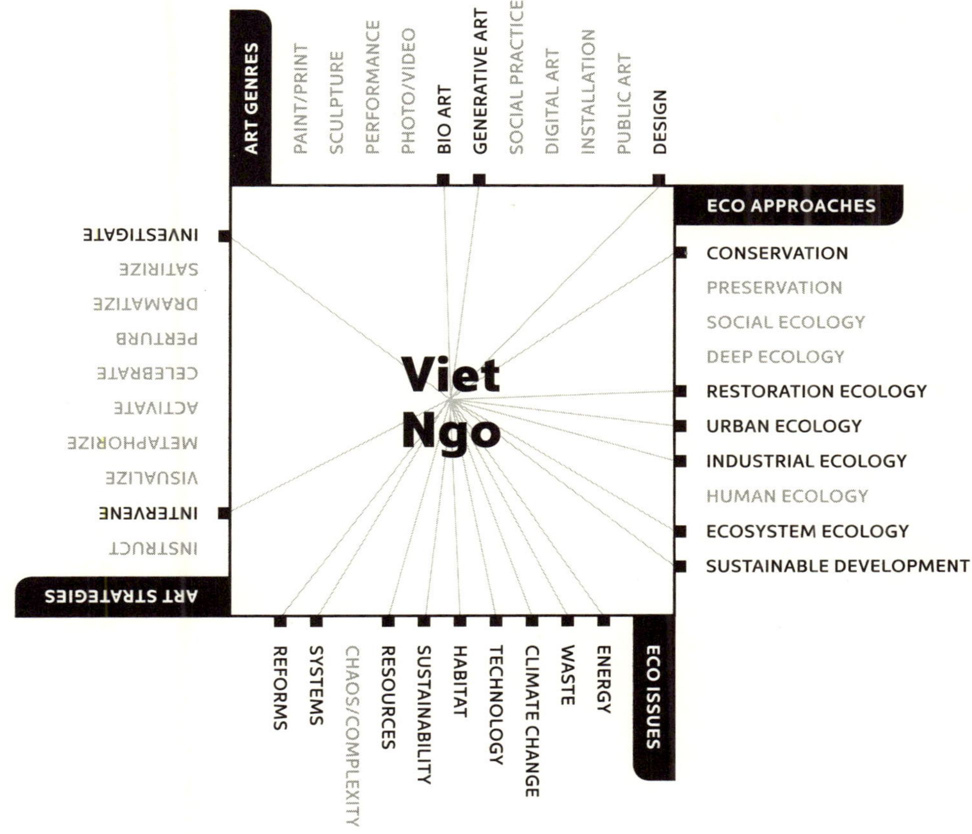

Corporate-Scale Eco Art

Born 1952, Vietnam

"**WE HUMANS** are like little brats. We go make a mess without thinking of the consequences. But the brats we were fifty years ago are growing up. When we see our mess, we become more responsible. We made a mess because of ignorance, not because we are mean. Now we are learning. . . . At the end of the day, no one wants to live on Earth where we can't breathe or drink the water. It is against our nature to do that. This change is incremental. It takes time. But a long-system view shows that we are making positive progress. Doomsday attitudes are not good. I believe we humans can be a good virus, not a plague."[1]

This optimistic assessment that humans are capable of correcting the predicaments they created was expressed by Viet Ngo. Ngo does not just declare this belief; he proves it by inventing strategies that divert the destructive momentum of contemporary civilization. Site-specific schemes characterize many worthwhile eco art restoration projects; they are undertaken by artists who make long-term commitments to a particular location such as a threatened cranberry bog. Not Ngo. The entire Earth's deteriorated waters, soils, and air establish the scope of the massive challenge Ngo assigned himself. He demonstrates that obstacles are opportunities for innovative design.

Ngo's biography is replete with examples of such accomplishments. He arrived in the United States from Vietnam in 1970 without knowing English. Nonetheless, he managed to support his seven younger siblings in South Vietnam while taking up to forty credits a semester. He graduated from the University of Minnesota in just two years.

Ngo's primary interest was art, but he also studied engineering as an undergraduate because the Vietnamese government didn't support education in studio art. After graduation he produced a series of extremely large sculptures, but it did not satisfy his desire to improve environmental conditions across the globe. To overcome this problem, Ngo decided to continue his training as a civil engineer, but he quickly discovered that the strictness of engineering protocols stifled the innovative strategies and aesthetic designs he envisioned as an artist. His goal was to combine the rigor of engineering with the liberties of art.

Since there was no context that could accommodate this composite profession, Ngo created one. Energized by the opportunities for individual accomplishment he discovered in America, he added a third profession to his resume. Ngo became an entrepreneur and founded Lemna International in 1983 with a microbiology student named Del Hogan. They state their mission: "We are experts in selecting the most suitable and sustainable technologies to meet local conditions and satisfy local needs."[2] Ngo is Lemna International's president and CEO.

Merging art, engineering, and entrepreneurship immediately yielded an innovative raw sewage treatment technology. The system that the company pioneered and patented employs small floating aquatic plants called lemna to treat waste by absorbing and neutralizing pollutants in the water. It offers multiple advantages. The system is easily installed, competitively priced, and low maintenance. It is also odorless because the floating plants seal the pond and thereby prevent odors from escaping. Additionally, it avoids the costly process of removing sludge, because the only by-product of this raw sewage treatment is an effluent that is safe to discharge into nearby rivers and lakes or use in irrigation. This saves money because sewage treatment can occur on-site. Occasional harvesting of the plants yields a nutrient-rich compost material that can be applied directly to fields as a soil amendment. A final benefit of lemna plants is their high concentrations of proteins, making them a food source for animals and, potentially, humans.

Ngo and his colleagues installed the system they imagined in Devils Lake, North Dakota, in 1990. This groundbreaking engineering project also manifests Ngo's sculptural training. The wastewater facility exists as a large-scale environmental artwork composed of nine serpentine channels resembling snakes slithering across the fifty-acre site. Since then, the company has steadily invented new state-of-the-art technologies to produce state-of-technology art. Company reports announce that Lemna International has designed and built more than three hundred projects in sixteen countries and currently has more than $2.5 billion in projects under development.

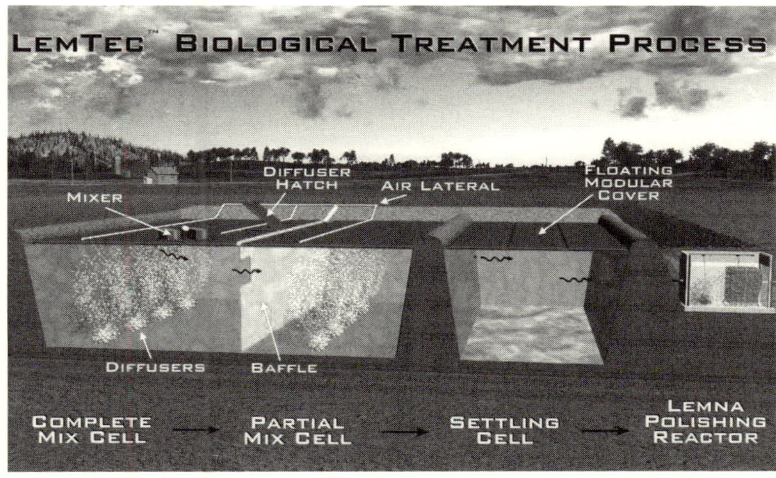

Viet Ngo | LemTec Biological Treatment Process Diagram; Launch Base Test Plan | 2011–present

PHOTO: LEMNA CORPORATION / COURTESY LEMNA CORPORATION

Ngo's credentials as an artist, engineer, and entrepreneur have their counterparts in Lemna's far-ranging tasks, far-sighted time frames, and far-flung environmental concerns. Each specific project is approached holistically. They all are undertaken with consideration of transforming waste into useful compounds, reforestation, creating greenbelts for cities, promoting ecotourism, and nurturing endangered fauna and flora. These considerations are applied to the following initiatives that appear in the Lemna International portfolio:

- **Energy services** include the design and construction of hydropower plants, thermal power plants, combined-cycle gas power plants, and combined heat and power plants. The focus is on alternative, green, renewable, and clean energies. The company also designs waste-to-energy facilities that produce renewable energy from biomass, municipal solid waste, and forest wastes. In addition, it promotes wind, solar, geothermal, hydrogen, and other innovative processes for energy generation.
- **Oil and gas services** include full-scale engineering and construction for exploration and production, onshore and offshore. The company has developed unique patented technologies for safe treatment of wastes generated through these processes.
- **Transportation services** focus on providing clean and efficient solutions to urban transportation problems. The company's light-rail transit and its bus rapid transit utilize a patented technology developed by Lemna. In addition, Lemna designs and constructs roads, bridges, and crossings that respond to local conditions and use local resources.
- **Waste treatment strategies** combine biological, mechanical, and chemical processes to recover and recycle the valuable components of solid waste, compost organic waste, safely dispose of hazardous chemical wastes, and incinerate waste to produce electricity and heat. Its facilities are equipped with groundbreaking pollution control systems.
- **Infrastructure services** involve design and implementation of housing, schools, and commercial developments that feature solar power, energy efficiency, on-site waste treatment, and the use of green buffer zones.

- **Water services** treat wastewater discharge, restore contaminated lakes, treat landfill leachate, and clean up contaminated shorelines and lakes.

Such broadscale innovations for achieving sustainable management of the environment are typically conducted by civil engineers, CEOs, and environmentalists. Ngo takes particular pleasure in assigning this success to art. "Art is not just an embellishment at the end of a big project. It is not like action painting. Artists offer a more philosophical approach that other professions don't see. Artists create excitement. They show us that this project is thrilling. Artists are also practitioners. Art has to change with the environment. It has to call attention to things. It has to evolve into something that works. Art is not just about beauty. It services people."[3]

Being in service to people reverses the aggressive, profit-seeking competitiveness that characterizes much of the corporate sector. Ngo's gentle demeanor is apparent when he comments, "Environmental problems span different continents since what we are doing in one place affects other places. Since our problems are global, we must make more friends. It is no longer possible to be a loner artist. Now artists need teams. The nature of art making is changing. It has to evolve to be part of other disciplines. When partners share the same aspirations, we cannot help but be positive. Art is powerful when it is being useful."[4]

Ngo compares the functional aspects of contemporary eco art to the Renaissance, when art provided "a bridge to God; it created social order, it provided belief in higher things. Today, art is functional too, but instead of wearing frocks and painting the Sistine Chapel, we wear blue jeans and work with local city councils to eliminate pollution in our waters."[5]

This does not mean that Ngo ignores aesthetics. "Beauty creates value and gives excitement that becomes inherent in the entire enterprise. . . . It makes people happy when things are well done and are attractive. Decoration is important, but it needs depth that comes from being imbued with values beyond decoration. Artists need to infuse decoration with the thought processes of people and their needs and the environment. It is a human duty not to tolerate ugliness in the world."[6]

Ngo's optimism supports his ambition; his ambition accounts for his accomplishments; his accomplishments confirm his optimism. He offers these concluding remarks for artists: "The time we are in is a good time for art to manifest itself as a great part of life. We enjoy the freedom that our forebears didn't have. . . . Artists can reach out a lot further than before. Our power is more, not less. The belief that we can change things is the source of our power. Pessimists work alone. By linking we get each other's power. All the necessary tools to make Earth a beautiful place are in our hands right now. There is knowledge, technologies, practices, resources. The only interferences are politics and distrust. We lack togetherness as a race, a species. Cooperation and collaboration are the engines that make this world better. If there are enough of us, working long enough, spreading out enough, eventually we will have good impact. We can clean up the environment and make it into an Eden."[7]

NOTES

1 Viet Ngo interview with the author, October 8, 2006.
2 Ibid.
3 Ibid.
4 Ibid.
5 Ibid.
6 Ibid.
7 Ibid.

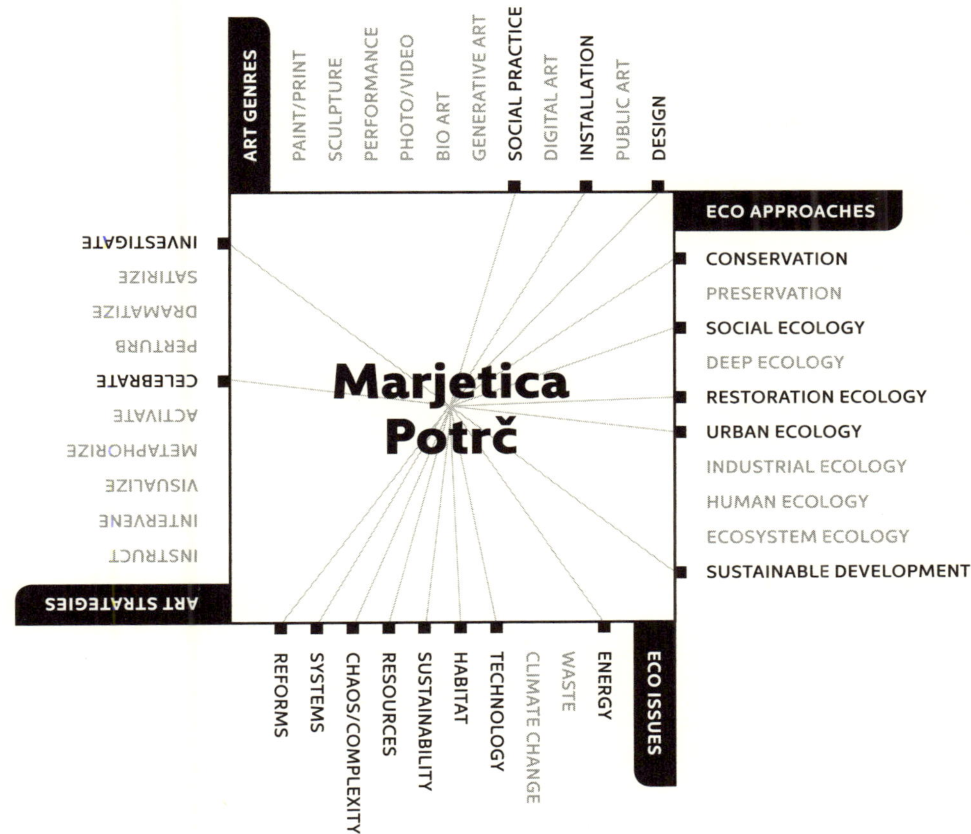

DIY Renewal for Slums and Condos

Born 1953, in Ljubljana, Slovenia

MANIFESTATIONS of the do-it-yourself movement have roared through US culture with roller coaster speed. While DIY always refers to self-expression and self-reliance, the course it has charted in the United States has been erratic:

> **1950s:** Postwar DIY meant self-conducted home improvement and car repair undertaken in the name of cost-saving economies.
>
> **1960s:** Hippie DIY involved bread baking, leather crafting, zine publishing, yurt building, and herbal

medicine making produced in communal living units and sold in cooperative outlets.

1970s and 1980s: Punk DIY was antiestablishment, anticapitalist, anti–mass production, and anti–conspicuous consumerism.

1990s: Grunge DIY involved low-budget alternatives to the glam scene that was being hyped by the mainstream media.

2000s: Martha Stewart DIY introduced homemakers to hands-on craft activities for entertaining and decorating. At the same time, "do-it-yourself" advocates shifted to "do-it-ourselves." These DIY advocates band together to establish community-supported agriculture, farmers markets, slow food consortiums, eco villages, and local currencies.

Marjetica Potrč's contribution to this ongoing DIY excursion is best appreciated by considering the cultural context in which it originated. She was born and educated in Slovenia, where a "do it for the state" economic and political system prevailed until the 1990s. According to the mandates of Soviet-style socialism, it was the state's responsibility, not the people's, to provide the basic needs of the citizens. DIY self-expression and DIY self-reliance were viewed as traitorous acts frequently punished by authoritarian dictators and secret police.

Reaction against suppression of self-responsibility provided the ideal impetus to apply DIY strategies to seemingly insurmountable economic and social problems associated with slums. Potrč explains why: "Today, there is not much Arcadian landscape left for us to ponder. Instead, we find ourselves trying to understand how we as individuals can define our existence against the urban terrain of the megalopolis."[1] Statistics confirm her choice of subject. *The State of the World's Cities 2010–2011*, a report published by the UN, predicts that slum-dwelling populations could climb to two billion over the next thirty years.[2] According to the UN's description of a slum, all these people will be afflicted with insufficient safe water, inadequate access to sanitation, poor structural quality of housing, overcrowding, and insecurity.[3] These dire conditions pose a double jeopardy because they are harmful to residents and to habitats. Supporting growing urban populations in a sustainable manner is the focus of Potrč's DIY art practice.

Potrč travels extensively to discover how slum dwellers currently cope with deficiencies and figure out how to tackle the problems they can't attend to. She has visited shantytowns, barrios, slums, ghettos, and favelas in South Africa, Ireland, Slovenia, Brazil, Venezuela, and Puerto Rico to search for resourceful DIY strategies that apply to slum conditions. Because she maintains that "the main problems in the barrios are not buildings but infrastructure,"[4] her DIY efforts focus on helping slum dwellers attain and maintain their own sanitation, sewage, and electricity. She has no use for a studio, since her artistic inquiries are conducted on-site and her exhibitions consist of artifacts she encounters in the slums and delivers to museums and galleries.

Potrč noted one significant form of abundance that impoverished urban populations enjoy, that their more wealthy neighbors lack. They have bountiful opportunities for DIY practices, which is due, ironically, to municipal neglect and governmental incompetence.

Duncan Village in South Africa provides one compelling case study of crowded and squalid conditions that engaged Potrč's artistic attentions. In the late 1980s during the apartheid era, thousands of Africans flocked to Duncan Village. Shacks sprung up every-

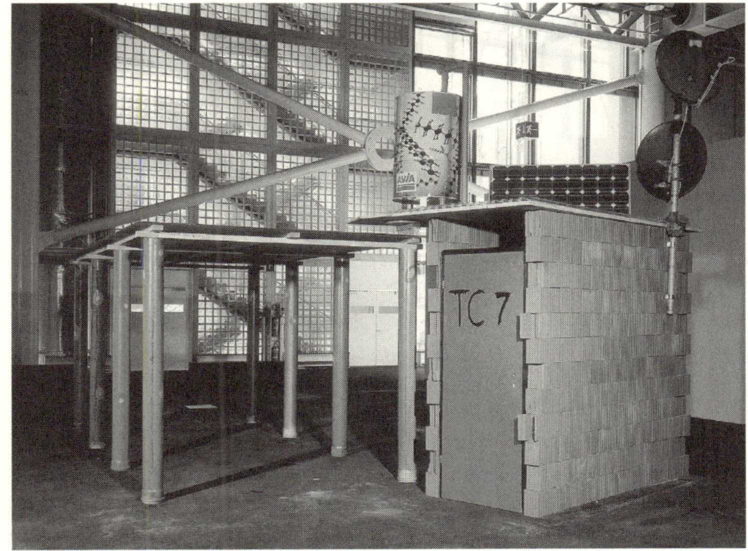

Marjetica Potrč | Duncan Village Core Unit | 2003, third installation Art Fair Basel, Basel, Switzerland | Building materials, energy, communication, and water supply in infrastructure | Service core unit 8′6″ × 5′3″ × 6′10″

PHOTO: ROBERT OGRAJENSEK
COURTESY MARJETICA POTRČ AND GALERIE NORDENHAKE, BERLIN/STOCKHOLM

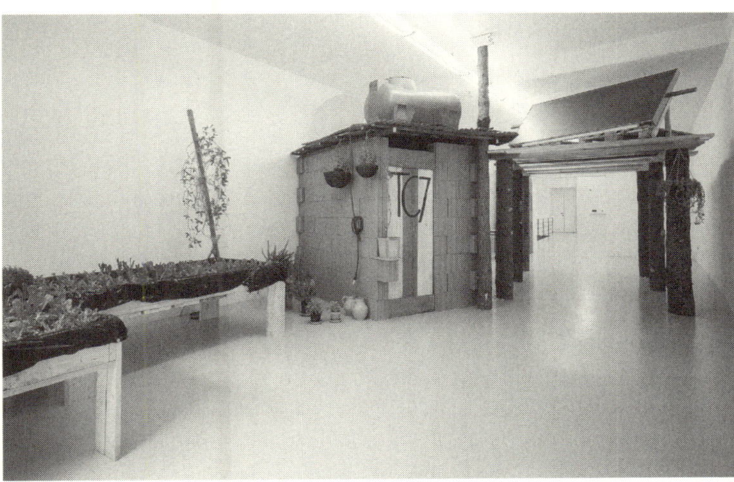

Marjetica Potrč | Duncan Village Core Unit | 2003, fourth installation Galerie Museum ar/ge kunst, Bolzano, Italy | Building materials, energy, communication, and water supply in infrastructure, and vegetable garden | Service core unit 8′6″ × 5′3″ × 6′10″

PHOTO: MARTIN PARDATSCHER
COURTESY MARJETICA POTRČ

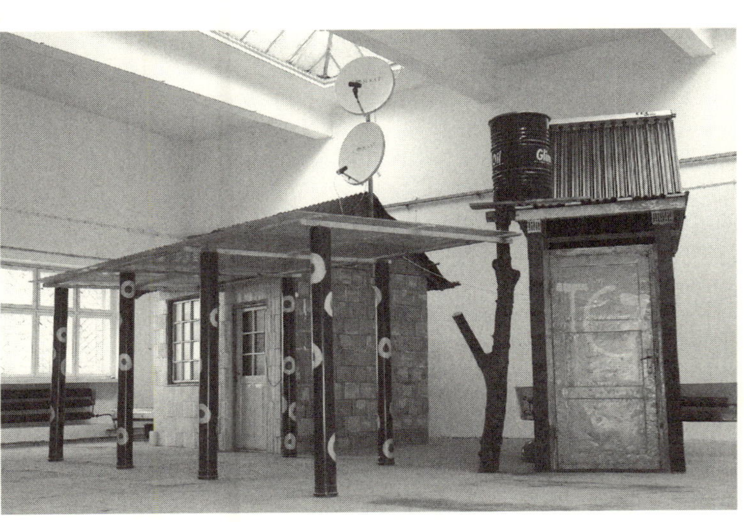

Marjetica Potrč | Duncan Village Core Unit | 2004, fifth installation 1st Lodz Biennial, Lodz, Poland | Building materials, energy, communication and water supply in infrastructure, and vegetable garden | Service core unit 8′6″ × 5′3″ × 6′10″

PHOTO: MARJETICA POTRČ AND GALERIE NORDENHAKE, BERLINSTOCKHOLM / COURTESY 1ST LODZ BIENNIAL

where, cluttering public spaces, playgrounds, and even the backyards of municipal buildings. In this densely packed village lacking in sanitation, mortality rates of children and cases of tuberculosis soared.[5] The apartheid state attempted to correct these mounting problems by forcibly relocating the village residents to mass suburban housing in a township outside of the village. This well-meaning plan backfired. Instead of being grateful for more spacious and sanitary conditions, the villagers resented being moved to housing they viewed as drab and alienating. They missed the haphazard clustering that allowed them to form the closely knit communities they customarily relied upon for cultural, social, and economic support.

When Potrč visited Duncan Village in 2002, she discovered evidence of a progressive housing scheme that respected the way of life of the residents. The new policy permitted residents to build their own shacks in locations they chose. Construction occurred around core units provided by the municipality. These mass-produced, prefab units were equipped with high-tech infrastructure solutions like photovoltaic panels for independent energy generation, as well as satellite dishes for access to communications. They also contained low-tech infrastructure for strategies like rainwater harvesting for water collection. In addition, they were outfitted with a toilet, sink, and stove and a secure enclosure to store valuable belongings. Walls, windows, and doors, however, were not provided. These architectural elements remained the responsibility of the occupants, who were accustomed to cobbling their own shelters with materials they scavenged.

The promising solutions provided by core units not only fulfill the DIY pursuit of self-reliance; the environmental efficiencies that result are manifold. Core units avoid the costly and disruptive processes involved in connecting gerrymandered slum communities to centralized utility systems; they tend to be safer, more reliable, and less costly than centralized systems because they are monitored and managed by their owners; they depend upon local resources like sunlight and rain, not fossil fuels as municipal utilities commonly do.

Potrč presents these tokens of her travels in museums, exhibiting each "case study" as a full-scale reconstruction of the makeshift dwelling. She goes to great lengths to avoid presenting them as formal sculptures. Her creative contribution to each art installation is not aesthetic. Referring to herself as a conceptual artist, she invents strategies to preserve the egalitarian opportunities and generative processes that characterize shanty dwellings. Thus, Potrč's eco art practice showcases the resourceful infrastructure initiative as well as the aesthetic and material inventiveness of the individuals who design and fabricate the walls and roof of their homes. For example, *Duncan Village Core Unit* (2002–2003) was exhibited in five museums, in five countries, in five different manners.[6] Potrč perpetuated the DIY transformation that characterizes its slum origin by assigning the museums' curators the task of completing the core units at their sites. The instructions Potrč provided regarding the construction were so general that the curators could not avoid being self-expressive. They were told to "use concrete blocks or their equivalent" and "paint the structure in a local, happy color."[7] As a result, the same unit and the same instructions generated a different artwork at each location, ensuring that the idiosyncratic nature of decision making in shantytowns was maintained. Through these means the humble buildings Potrč features celebrate a new social contract where personal expression filters throughout a legitimized and bureaucratized society and becomes apparent in the uniqueness of each dwelling. Potrč explains, "The erosion of traditional barriers to creation marks the onset of the DIY future, when everyone is a potential designer (or architect, or engineer, or author) of integrated experiences."[8]

Potrč reinforces this democratic message by stating, "I don't need to control the production. I don't have to be there to build the work and to agonize over materials or colors. If a team decides to put up a core unit, they take care of all these decisions themselves. The core unit has a life of its own. It changes and grows or disappears. . . . There is nothing wrong with letting a situation take over. A dialogue is always more productive than a monologue."[9]

With or without core units, shantytowns are hubs for DIY construction and design. Potrč celebrates these liberties, noting that modernist design is not merely a style; it is "a way to represent the authority and power of the state."[10] Wealthier urban dwellers might envy the expressive outlets enjoyed by their poorer counterparts. Owners of condos and renters of apartments relinquish self-reliance because they are dependent on municipalities and corporations to supply their material needs, generate their energy, manage their wastes, and design their dwellings. Furthermore, they sacrifice the public display of their tastes and creativity by occupying architecture that utilizes standardized construction materials that arrive from places the occupants have never visited, are chosen by architects they do not know, and are formed into generic living and working spaces they must accommodate. Shanties are playful, populist, spontaneous, and personal. Their DIY design conventions might resuscitate urban experiences of the wealthy.

Thus, core units reverse the stultifying anonymity of middle- and upper-class neighborhoods by fulfilling the twin components of the DIY ethic. One is self-reliance, associated with independent infrastructure facilities. The other is self-expression, activated by individual design decisions. People at all ends of the social spectrum might take heed when Potrč states, "The present time is about self-reliance, individual initiative, and small-scale projects,"[11] qualities that naturally prevail in slum neighborhoods.

In sum, rather than returning from her travels into downtrodden neighborhoods around the world with a message of misery and gloom, Potrč highlights the adaptive strategies she discovers during her forays. Whereas others may envision the need for a bulldozer, she discovers hope and pragmatic possibilities that not only aid the socially and economically unprivileged; they benefit privileged museumgoers as well. Derelict structures are presented as model ecological living spaces and works of art. Potrč explains, "I believe that the structures produced by these communities convey the aesthetic and political power of today's society simply by the manner in which they were made."[12] Potrč's art thereby affirms her belief that in the future, states will be founded on survival strategies that are optimized by local knowledge, spontaneity, and flexibility.[13] By featuring Duncan Village, Potrč coaxes into public consciousness three virtues derived from an area ridden with crime, congestion, squalor, and disease: DIY self-expressiveness, DIY self-reliance, and DIY sustainability.

NOTES

1 Marjetica Potrč, "There Is Strength in Movement," *Marjetica Potrč: Next Stop, Kiosk* (Ljubljana: Moderna galerija, 2003), 110.

2 David Kay, "Shack Settlement Planning: Duncan Village, South Africa." http://www.lulu.com/items/volume_62/1728000/1728641/1/print/1728641.pdf.

3 Ibid.

4 Michael Rush, *Marjetica Potrč: Urgent Architecture* (Lake Worth, FL: Palm Beach Institute of Contemporary Art, 2004), 11.

5 David Kay, "Shack Settlement Planning: Duncan Village, South Africa." http://www.lulu.com/items/volume_62/1728000/1728641/1/print/1728641.pdf.

6 Through a Sequence of Space, Nordenhake Gallery, Berlin, 2002. PARA > SITES: Who is

moving the global city?, Badischer Kunstverein, Karlsruhe, 2003. Art Unlimited, Art Fair Basel, Basel, Switzerland, 2003. Urban Strategies, ar/ge kunst Galerie Museum, Bolzano, Italy, 2003. 1st Lodz Biennial, Lodz, Poland, 2004

7 Marjetica Potrč: Institut Valencia d'Art Modern 22-V/7-IX (Valencia: IVAM, 2003), 36.

8 Ibid.

9 Marjetica Potrč, Kunstlerhaus Bethanien (Berlin: Philip Morris Kunstforderung, 2001), 40.

10 Marjetica Potrč, "There Is Strength in Movement," *Marjetica Potrč: Next Stop, Kiosk* (Ljubljana: Moderna galerija, 2003), 106.

11 Marjetica Potrč, "Five Ways to Urban Independence," a conversation with Hans Ulrich Obrist, *Marjetica Potrč: Next Stop, Kiosk* (Ljubljana: Moderna galerija, 2003).

12 Ibid.

13 Marjetica Potrč, "Future Talk Now with Marjetica Potrč," a videotaped discussion at The New School. http://fora.tv/2007/11/01/Future_Talk_Now_with_Marjetica_Potrč.

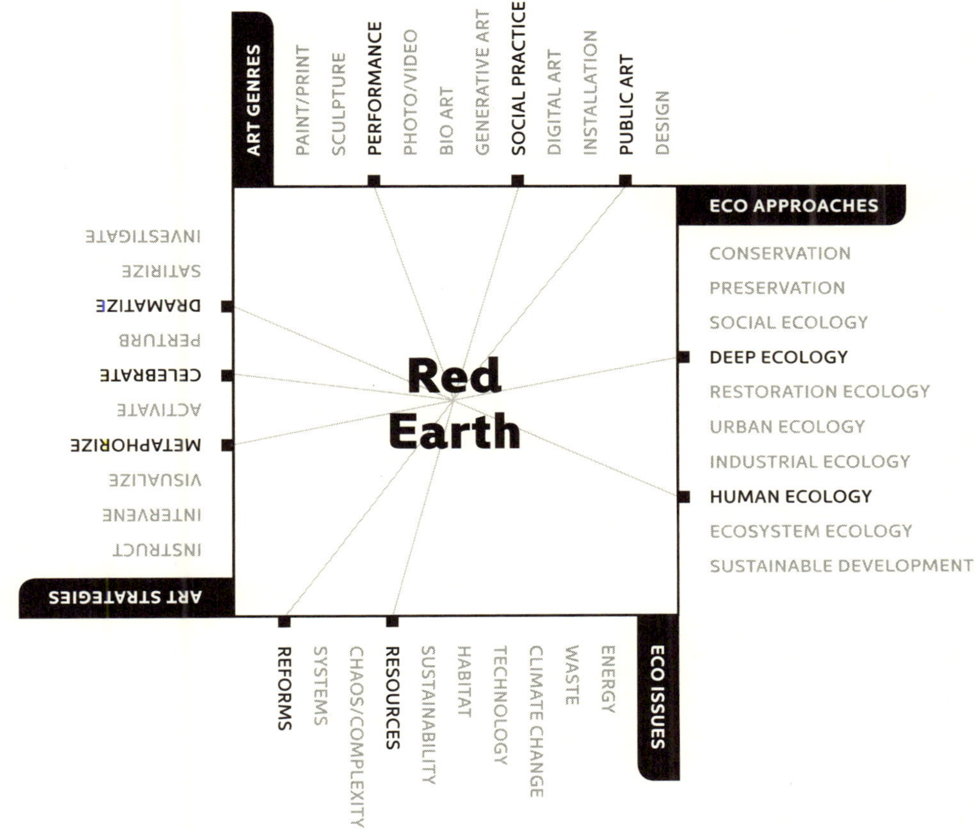

Deep Time

Caitlin Easterby born 1963, Bedford, England
Simon Pascoe born 1960, Newport, South Wales

A CHILLY RAIN fell on September 23, 2007, the day *Enclosure* was scheduled to take place. This outdoor "performance journey"[1] was part of the Inside Out Festival in Great Britain. Festival organizers approached Caitlin Easterby and Simon Pascoe, known collectively as Red Earth, and proposed postponing the event due to the inclement weather. Easterby and Pascoe explained that human comfort and convenience were irrelevant to this work of art. *Enclosure* was timed to coincide with sunset on the autumn equinox, the exact time on one of the two days in the year when the Earth is poised in temporal symmetry between day and night. "The artists explain the equinox is a moment of balance and equilibrium, a fragile stillness before the pendulum of the year swings again. *Enclosure* marked this point of convergence: day with night, summer with winter, life with death. We were intent on carrying out our ritual regardless of weather and the presence of the public."[2] Twenty-five horn players, ten flag bearers, and nearly seven hundred people braved the rain that September evening to embark on "a symbolic journey that walked a boundary between time and space, reactivating this landscape, reconnecting with both the land and with the people who shaped it."[3]

A single photograph served as my introduction to this work of art. It depicted a figure whose contorted body seemed gripped by a spasm that might have been caused by torment or rapture. His right hand was clenched behind him, while his left hung limply over his chest. He wore only boots and a loincloth. The rest of his flesh was caked with mud, and his dark hair hung in long wet strands. Although the vision that appeared behind his tightly shut eyes remains a mystery, and the sounds emitting from his gaping mouth cannot be heard, the figure in this photograph seems to emerge from the primordial history of the earth upon which he stood.

The figure stood upon the majestic geological region in southern England that is configured out of chalk and flint that were formed in gradual increments over the course of millions of years. Overlaid upon this geological record is compelling evidence of humanity's history. The "enclosure" that gives this artwork its name dates back over five thousand years. That is when Neolithic humans dug a pair of long trenches on a hilltop that is now known as Hambledon Hill. Later they extended the earthworks to create the largest Neolithic causewayed enclosure in Europe.[4] This imposing Neolithic earthen complex, extending over an irregularly shaped chalk hilltop in Dorset, England, contains shards of the earliest pottery made in England. Archeologists speculate that the entire thirty-acre earthwork was constructed with rudimentary tools like deer antler picks, wooden spades, and shovels made from animal shoulder blades. Remarkably, its configuration remains visible despite centuries of disturbances by ploughs and recent disturbances by bulldozers. The part of the site where the event took place was a causewayed enclosure consisting of an earthen passageway providing access between ringed mounds.

The historic construction of this grand earthwork coincided with a host of remarkable innovations that continue to define civilization: agriculture, pottery, chiefdoms, roads, forest clearing, ceremony, trade, etc. The actual artifacts unearthed here suggest that the enclosures served as mortuary chambers for the ritual disposal of the dead. Great repositories of human skulls, bones, and the skeletons of crouched infants have been found, along with pottery and tools. Evidence of an Iron Age hill fort, erected between 750 and 400 BC, augments the site's notable past. It is an elaborate complex consisting of earthen stockades, ditches, and terraces that follow the contours of the hill.

Conducting research into this elaborate geological and archeological history may seem alien to the visceral art experience that these preparations ultimately engendered. Pascoe explains, "For *Enclosure*, we studied past ecologies, ethnographic distribution, different cultures, mythologies, ethnographic behavior, and tribal systems. We read textbooks on archeology. We learned lots of factual things about the site, the lifestyle, and the conscicusness of the peoples who lived thousands of years ago. But this was not like an academic program. We wanted that information, but we didn't want to be bound by it. We also looked deeply into the place. We made at least twenty visits to the site, which was two hundred miles from

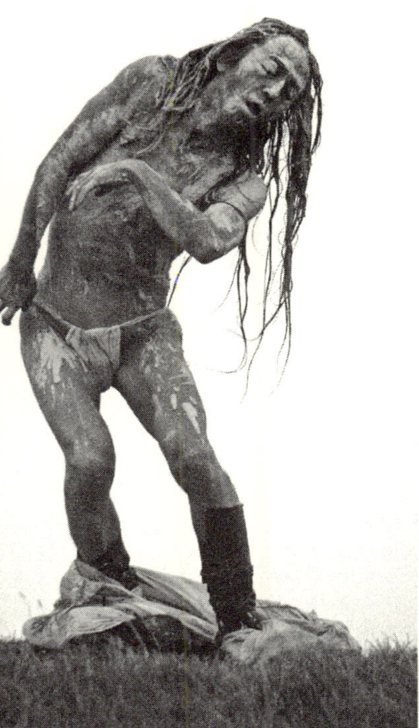

(left) Red Earth | Caitlin Easterby and Simon Pascoe | With Atsushi Takenouchi, Mark Anderson, and Ansuman Biswas | Enclosure (Atsushi Takenouchi) | September 23, 2007 Hambledon Hill, England | Two-hour, site-specific, multimedia performance, sound installation, pyrotechnics

PHOTO: TONY GILL / COURTESY RED EARTH

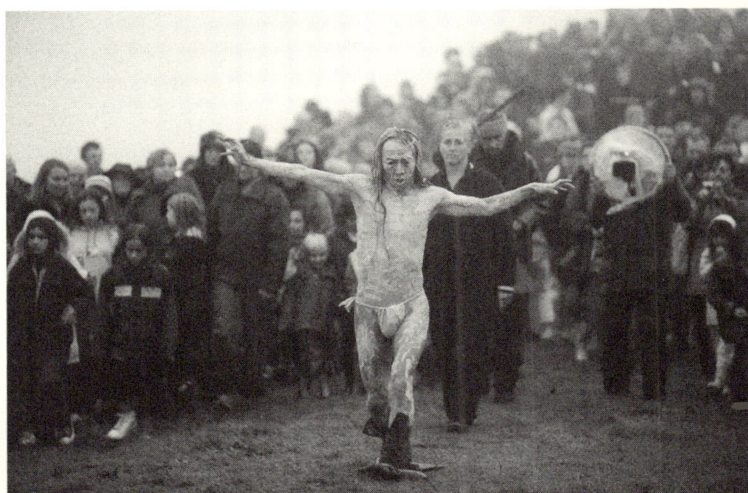

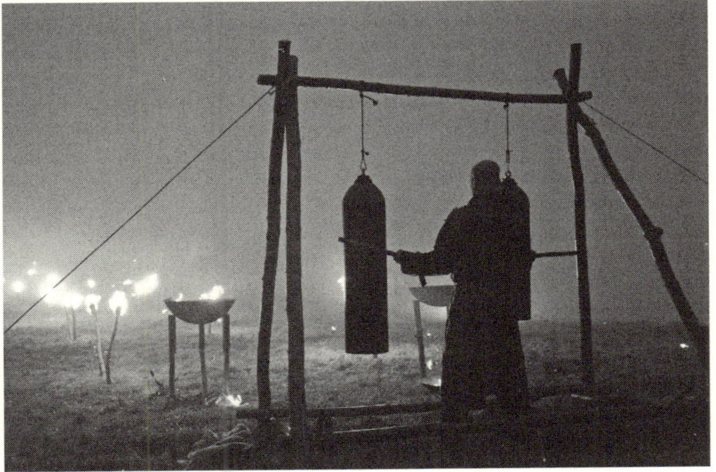

(above right) Red Earth | Caitlin Easterby and Simon Pascoe | With Mark Anderson, Ansuman Biswas, Chloe Dear, Sax Impey, David Statham, Rick Wilson, Karen Wimhurst, Atsushi Takenouchi, and other horn players, flag bearers, volunteers, and stewards | Enclosure (Ansuman Biswas playing bells as Atsushi departs across the star field) | September 23, 2007 Hambledon Hill, England | Two-hour, site-specific, multimedia performance, sound installation, pyrotechnics

PHOTO: TONY GILL / COURTESY RED EARTH

(above) Red Earth | Caitlin Easterby and Simon Pascoe | With Mark Anderson, Ansuman Biswas, Chloe Dear, Sax Impey, David Statham, Rick Wilson, Karen Wimhurst, Atsushi Takenouchi, and other horn players, flag bearers, volunteers, and stewards | Enclosure (Atsushi leading audience) | September 23, 2007 Hambledon Hill, England | Two-hour, site-specific, multimedia performance, sound installation, pyrotechnics

PHOTO: ROY RILEY / COURTESY RED EARTH

where we live. It helped us develop our intuitive response to the place. The site is high. It is an obvious place to make connections with the sacred."[5]

The artists' research included controversial studies indicating that the capacity for religious experience is hardwired into the neurology of the human brain.[6] This means that experiencing the divine is integral to being human. According to the theory, this inherent spirituality receded as the components of civilization that demanded logical accountings developed, but it still dominated the lives of the premodern humans who constructed the site for *Enclosure*. If true, these humans perceived everything as part of an all-encompassing sacredness—rocks, rain, animals, winds, sun, and flowers. Red Earth reached back to our Neolithic heritage to help reawaken this dormant neurological function and recapture reverence for the planet we inhabit. This is the essence of today's deep ecology movement. Pascoe explains Red Earth's belief that the gods survive, to this day, within the subliminal corners of the modern mind: "The idea of 'god' can be contained within our own minds and spirits. We are connected with everything. How can we not be? I am one of those people who is a closet animist. I believe everything has energy, essence, and spirit. The idea of inside and outside is irrelevant. Our work is about identification with land. The land has consciousness. It is not a thinking thing, but it is a responsive thing."[7]

Pascoe and Easterby pay tribute to this primeval tradition by drawing from a treasure trove of spiritual practices that are associated with the Neolithic period. They factored into their work the possibilities for prayer, trance, ritual, and divination that were available in Neolithic society on this particular site five thousand years ago—offerings of earth and water, horns, drums, fire, body painting, endurance. Pascoe explains that *Enclosure* evolved by asking, "Could we get any closer to the Neolithic mindset through an emotive and experiential encounter with a very specific time in a very specific landscape? Could we cross an impermeable boundary and reconnect with both the land and with the people who shaped it?"[8] Thus, they imagined the causeways, banks, and trenches as avenues for ceremonial processions and locations for ritual enactments. Most importantly, they imagined the role of the setting sun on the autumn equinox.

At the same time, Red Earth insists, "We are artists, not archeologists. We do not try to achieve a reenactment of Neolithic ritual. Ours is a contemporary art event that is informed by the resonant past of ancient history. As artists, we decide what to do. Ours is a ritualized action, but it is not in any way a relic from the past. Our intention is to create response to landscape and site. This was not a virgin piece of landscape. The past gives it a resonance. This may have been the first time in 2,300 years that people en masse stood on Hambledon Hill on the equinox."[9]

Enclosure commenced as a procession of horn players and hundreds of people set out through the drizzle over the rough Dorset terrain, across its chalk escarpments, up the steep incline of Hambledon Hill. They arrived at the Iron Age fort half an hour later. Their destination was a woven branch gateway that had been constructed by the artists. It overlooked an open field that was once the site of Neolithic excarnation.[10] Massive white flags were planted, and guardians were stationed at the gateway to announce that this passage marked an exodus from familiar territories and an entrance into a mysterious realm. Participants sounding hunting horns, post horns, trombones, and clarinets played a simple melodic sequence of repeated phrases to usher them into a transcendent state of being. Pascoe explains, "Sound is a way of transposing your consciousness from the mundane to a slightly altered state of being. Sound resonates with body attunements. It is powerful. It affects people's subconscious emotions."[11]

A strange figure approached as the assemblage proceeded along this high spine of the earth toward the Neolithic remains.[12] His thin body was draped in pale fabric, and his face was framed by long tangled strands of dark hair. Moving extremely slowly, the Japanese artist Atsushi Takenouchi led the audience to the first of the Iron Age defenses, then he disappeared from sight only to reappear bound by a white cord that suggested an umbilical cord or sacrificial rope. He was led toward the central Neolithic burial mound that dominates the top of the hill. Spinning gongs and metal saw blades created a dark, humming soundscape as the figure crossed the mound and reached a bridge. Pascoe explains that the bridge was "creating a space between past and future, summer and winter, day and night, life and death."[13] Suspended on the bridge, the figure seemed to relinquish his human status and hover between earth and sky, exempt from the force of gravity and the passage of solar time. In actuality, he arrived at the precise moment of sunset. Atsushi poured white chalk milk over his body, an element of the land upon which he stood. He turned white, like an emissary from the realm of the spirits. Then, moving at a quick pace, he led the people to the final open space as the day's light waned. When they arrived, they encountered attendants moving across the field igniting small fires, as if to transform this patch of earth into a field of stars. Then, to the sound of heavy bells, the apparition figure made his way along a path of fire as forty flares arranged just below the crest of the hill were ignited by a single detonation. He disappeared, entering what Pascoe describes as "the non-here, that which is not substantial—the mythical realm."[14]

What happened next? Pascoe recalls, "The people didn't applaud. They didn't go and say, 'That was nice.' This was an experience. Hard, cold, powerful, unforgettable. They were allowed to enter a liminal world, scraping away what they always see so they could see something else, something *other*. Many people have never been there before."[15] The place they visited was a mythic realm only perceivable to their "primitive/subconscious minds." It transformed mundane time, flesh, and earth into eternity, spirit, and rapture.

Pascoe explains that this event was different from familiar art forms and from ordinary life experience. "Our work is not theater. Theater presents a play. A story is being told to you. Ours is about taking people into a special space. And it is not like an installation that viewers walk around. Here they are IN the landscape. And this was not just an ordinary walk. No one walks up here at dusk in the rain. They were more than witnesses to what was happening. It was misty, rainy. This was like a fairy realm. We needed to do very little. Our work was to enhance the atmosphere. The work is much about being there."[16]

Enclosure offered a reprieve to urbanized, technology-dependent, media-saturated people who are distracted from the living, geological, and celestial systems that once served as sources of human reverence. By awakening fundamental forms of fulfillment provided by flame, water, earth, sunlight, starlight, shadow, smoke, wind, rain, and rock, such rituals help curb the pandemic of "nature-deficit disorders."[17]

The Norwegian philosopher Arne Naess (1937–2004) coined the term *deep ecology* to refer to body/mind immersions imbued with such elemental affinities. Deep ecologists believe that "re-earthing" experiences, like those evoked by *Enclosure*, induce respectful behaviors toward the environment because the Earth is seen as sacred. Naess comments, "If reality is experienced by the Ecological Self, our behavior naturally and beautifully follows norms of strict environmental ethics."[18]

In other works Red Earth applies this quasi-mystical environmental approach to coastal erosion and climate change. Pascoe states, "There is an environmental argument for doing this work. Deep green activism is connected to indigenous tribes and animistic societies. Those societies developed personal relationships with the landscape and its elements. The people identified with plants and animals as 'people' in a landscape connecting all in a matrix of consciousness. Theirs was a living relationship, built on necessity, not just respect. It was a question of survival. This is a relationship modern society has lost. By means of our arrogance and consequential domination of nature, we are distanced from our landscapes and the sort of spiritual reciprocity they can inspire. The performance is payback to nature for what nature has given us."[19]

Pascoe does not ignore a less salutary lesson offered by the Neolithic era. By developing agriculture and mining, the Neolithic people introduced humanity's penchant for abusing nature. He concludes, "The Neolithic was the beginning of the decline. Hunter/gatherer societies were the natural climax of the human race. This is when humans were on top. Since then we have been trying to dominate. Something went wrong. We have become the Cains of the world as opposed to the Abels."[20]

NOTES

1 "Enclosure September 23rd, 2007." http://www.redearth.co.uk/enclosuretext.html.

2 Ibid.

3 Ibid.

4 "Iron-Age Hillfort," September 28, 2010. http://www.roman-britain.org/celtic/hambledon_hill.htm.

5 Simon Pascoe interview with the author, December 12, 2010.

6 David Lewis-Williams and David Pearce, *Inside the Neolithic Mind: Consciousness, Cosmos and the Realm of Gods* (London: Thames & Hudson, 2005).

7 Simon Pascoe interview with the author, December 12, 2010.

8 Simon Pascoe, "Enclosure: awakening the Neolithic mind: Performance as ritual across a mythographic landscape." http://sites.google.com/site/tag07york/performance.

9 Simon Pascoe interview with the author, December 12, 2010.

10 Excarnation, as explained by Pascoe, is the process whereby people who have died are dismembered and their parts are laid about for birds to eat. It is a way to show that the spirit leaves body.

11 Simon Pascoe interview with the author, December 12, 2010.

12 The apparition is Atsushi Takenouchi (born 1962), a Japanese dancer who has developed a form of Butoh movement drawn directly from the earth's energy. He is dedicated to the principle that dance can awaken primeval memories of being a tree, grass, animal, wind, soil, fire, or water. Takenouchi explains, "I've got my body from the earth. I've got my life from the sun and the moon, my parents, my friends and my love. Then I'll return the gifts to the universe. I'll return them to others through dancing body and soul" (http://www.resonant-wave.net/atsushi.htm). As such, he shares Red Earth's goal of mending severed relationships between humans and the Earth.

13 Simon Pascoe correspondence with the author, February 22, 2011.

14 Simon Pascoe interview with the author, December 12, 2010.

15 Ibid.

16 Ibid.

17 Richard Louv, *Last Child in the Woods: Saving Our Children from Nature-Deficit Disorder* (Algonquin: 2005).

18 Arne Naess quoted in John Seed, "The Ecological Self," *Earth Light Library*. http://www.earthlight.org/2005/essay53_johnseed.html.

19 Simon Pascoe interview with the author, December 12, 2010.

20 Ibid.

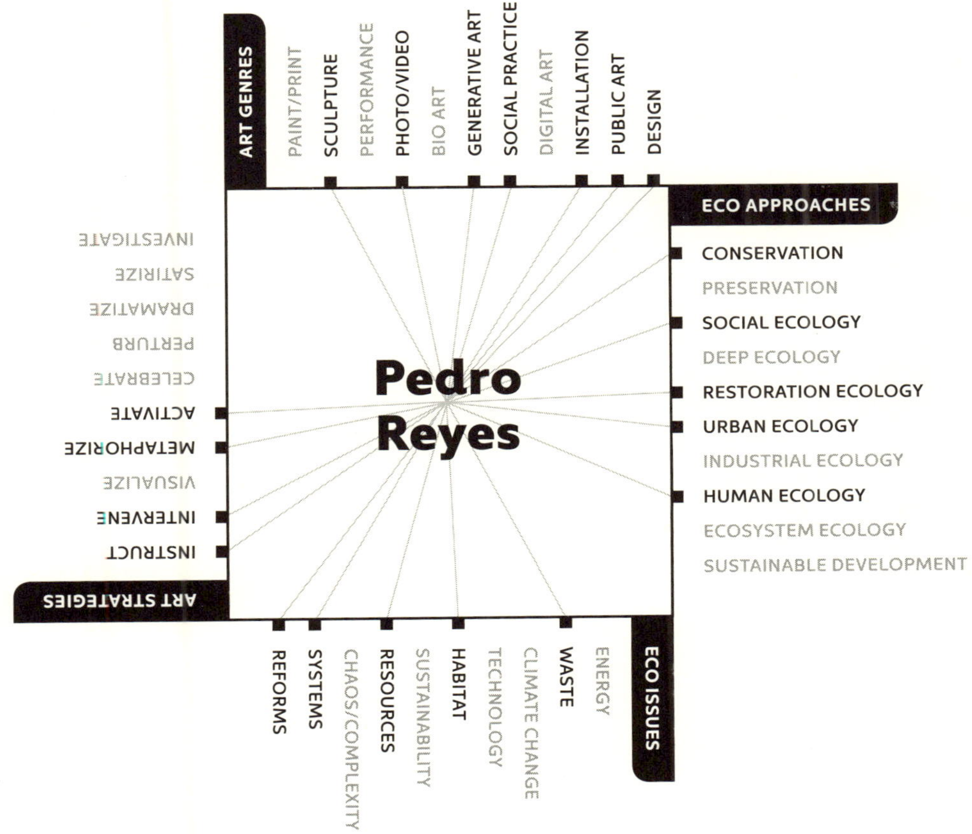

Pistols into Spades

Born 1972, Mexico City, Mexico

ECO ART CONNOISSEURS, like wine connoisseurs, are not content to know the ingredients of a product and its final embodiment. They also evaluate the way the product was generated, processed, and presented to the public. Similarly, art connoisseurs will be rewarded by Pedro Reyes's sculptural edition of shovels. These shovels are beautifully burnished and elegantly shaped. Beyond that, they not only maintain their digging function, they also serve by reducing urban violence and protecting forest ecosystems. Reyes explains, "There is a design element, which is an expression of my personal style in the tools themselves. But this is as important as the social design embedded in the process."[1]

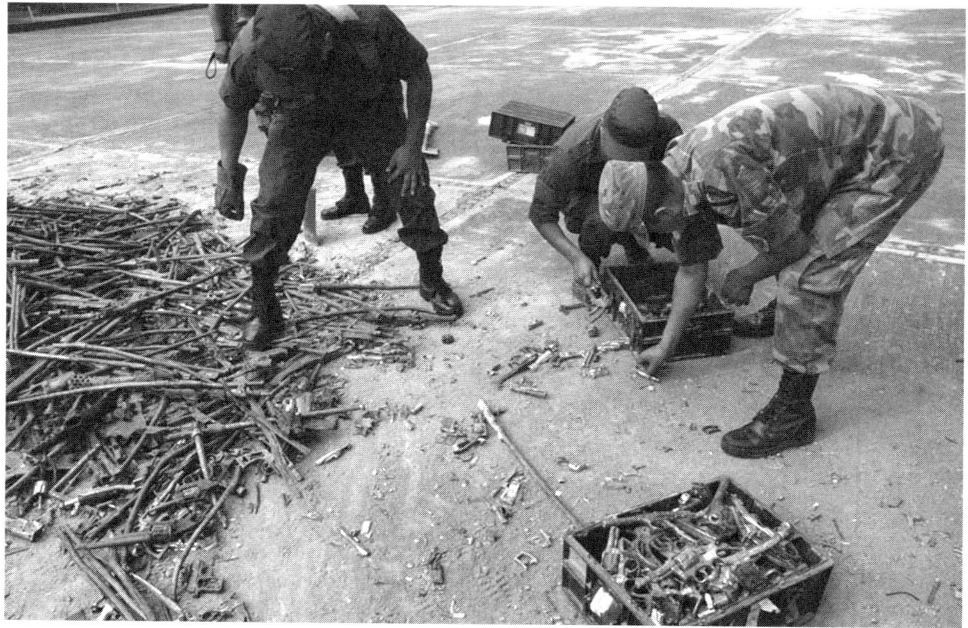

Pedro Reyes | Palas por Pistolas | 2008 Soldiers collecting weapons voluntarily donated by the population of Culiacán, Mexico

COURTESY PEDRO REYES

Ad usum is the term Reyes uses to define his socially and environmentally constructive art practice. "I think you can make a division when it comes to form and function. There is art and there are applied arts, which are functional objects that have a special degree of craftsmanship. But there should be a third category for an art *ad usum*, an art *to be used*. . . . The piece or the artwork operates as a tool, a device or a tactic."[2]

When, in 2008, Reyes was commissioned to create an artwork at the Botanical Garden in Culiacán in northern Mexico, he discovered that the city commissioning the artwork had the most handgun deaths in all of Mexico. This social crisis was matched by an environmental crisis. Mexico has one of the fastest rates of deforestation in the world, second only to Brazil.[3]

Reyes applied the ad usum principle to address these grim statistics by tracing them to their common source—rampant drug trafficking that lay at the intersection of these stubborn predicaments. Supplying the arsenals of drug dealers explained the glut of guns in the city. Planting marijuana and opium for a ready market in the United States explained the thousands of acres of forests that were being clear-cut. As drugs moved northward into the United States, guns traveled southward into Mexico. Reyes explains, "We may send drugs to the US, but they don't kill us as fast as guns. This is all connected to unregulated market in the United States. All the guns are smuggled into Mexico. This is the biggest threat to democracy and economy and well-being of everyone. The idea for this artwork was to connect guns to deforestation—to turn an agent of death into an agent of life."[4]

Slowing the illegal trafficking of guns and drugs has evaded the efforts of elected politicians, armed soldiers, and professional law enforcement officers on both sides of the border. Attempts at reforestation have also failed. Seventy percent of the trees replanted by the Mexican government have died. But these failures did not deter Reyes from applying ad usum to these stubborn problems. Inspired by the biblical phrase "to beat swords into plowshares,"[5] he set about converting weapons of violence into tools for remediation. His concept involves a sequence of causes and effects. If trees were planted on lands currently growing narcotic plants, the availability of drugs would be reduced. If drug use lessened, the need for gun trafficking would also shrink. Reyes's methodology is also marked by a chain of events: planting trees required shovels. Shovels required metal. Acquiring the metal was crafted into an opportunity to address gun violence. Reyes invited citizens to turn in their firearms so the metal could be melted down for shovels. As an inducement, they received coupons that could be cashed in at Coppels, a well-known chain of appliance stores that sells refrigerators, computers, and other domestic products.

Behind the scenes, there was the negotiation with the owner of Coppels, an art collector who served on the board of the host museum. This wealthy businessman was as essential to Reyes's remedial social agenda as drug dealers and gun runners. "I wanted to use a collector, not as a client who acquires finished work but as a coproducer of social change. Rather than purchase artwork, they purchased a social good. They were excited about it."[6]

As a social artwork, Reyes's sculptural process involved constructing social responsibility while chipping away at hostility, danger, destruction, pollution, and erosion. He comments, "It's like a transmutation of metal motivated by the social design embedded in the process of removing the weapons from circulation—like agents of death turned into agents of life."[7]

It required five years of effort to develop *Palas por Pistolas (Pistols into Spades)*. The engraving on the handle of each shovel announces the success of Reyes's initiative as an equation: "1527 weapons destroyed, 1527 shovels made, 1527 trees to plant."

While *Pistols* engaged problems on the street and across the land, the museum installation was an important component of the project. Shiny new garden shovels hung in a single row along a wall in the gallery where the work was exhibited. They were accompanied by five video monitors that ran continuously to communicate the far-reaching ad usum strategies Reyes employed in the production of the art shovels.

Video #1 documented how citizens were informed about the gun-surrender program. Reyes enlisted the cooperation of a local television station to produce a series of thirty-second television and radio spots that were inserted into normal media programming by replacing commercials. They ran for a month and a half. The dramatizations utilized a concept of modeling behavior,[8] a social learning strategy in which a new behavior is learned by observing it in others. Reyes chose to emulate soap operas so this lesson would be accessible to television viewers. One spot features a father looking in his son's closet. He finds a gun and says, "I don't want my son to be a murderer." The next scene is set in the city hall where the father is handing the gun to a friendly woman who thanks him politely. Reyes explains, "The TV spots make people comfortable. They trigger psychological dynamics within the family nucleus because women are very important as catalysts for this process. Women would tell their husbands, 'Let's trade this gun for a fridge.' We had to make clear that there would be no questions asked. The important thing was to collect as many weapons as possible. We would assume the gun was your grandfather's weapon."[9]

Video #2 documented how the guns were reprocessed. Reyes estimates that 40 percent of the weapons collected were automatics of military caliber. To assure people that the guns would not filter back into circulation, Reyes convinced the military to serve as gun collectors. Then he recruited teenagers, those most likely to be lured into the lucrative gun

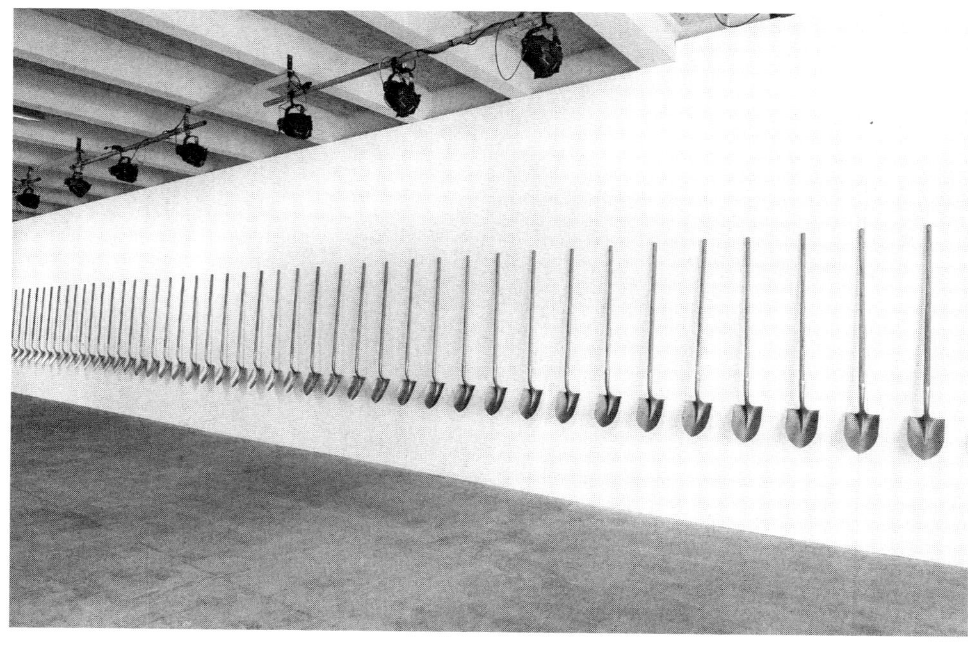

Pedro Reyes | Palas por Pistolas | 2008 Fifty shovels made from metal recovered from 1,527 destroyed weapons voluntarily donated by the population of Culiacán, Mexico
COURTESY PEDRO REYES

and drug trafficking industries, to dismantle the weapons. Instead of perpetuating violence, they helped initiate social reform.

Videos #3 and #4 displayed the foundry melting the metal from the weapons and the factory forming the metal into shovels. Reyes accomplished the manufacturing component of his project by convincing the owner of Truper, Mexico's leading company in the manufacture and distribution of tools, to suspend normal factory production, incur the costs of manufacturing the art shovels, and temporarily sacrifice his profits. Reyes factors the manufacturer's cooperation into the artwork too. "The key thing about ecology is not the relationship between man and environment. It is the psychological forces that lead to change in attitudes and habits that are selfish everyday behaviors. People are looking for opportunities to be generous to the world. There exists a reservoir of time and money if there is an opportunity that people find interesting and that has a degree of effect."[10]

Video #5 presented the art shovels contributing to reforestation and the development of sustainable behaviors. Reyes provides a shovel to anyone who will use it to plant a tree anywhere. In exchange, they can keep his shovel. Participants receive a certificate that is an official recognition of their good deed and formalizes their commitment to care for the tree they planted. This strategy teaches people to nurture and protect a valuable resource they might otherwise neglect or destroy. If a museum serves as host, the tree is introduced into the museum collection whereby the conservation department diverts its professional caregiving from inert objects to living entities. At the time of this writing, trees planted with these special shovels were growing in thirty different cities around the world. Reyes estimates at least fifteen hundred trees have been planted, three thousand people have participated in this project, and 99 percent of them were not aware that they were participating in an

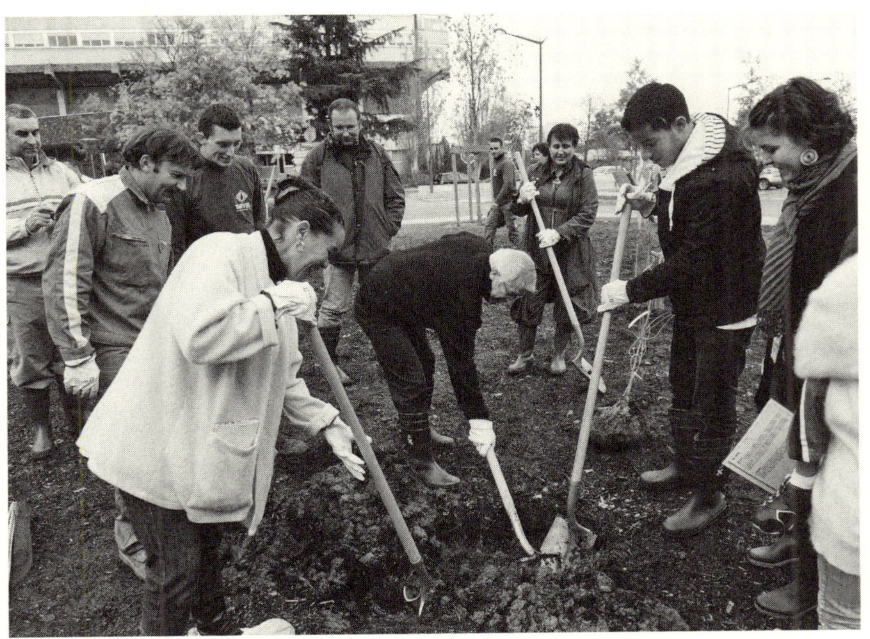

Pedro Reyes | Palas por Pistolas, installation view | 2008 Tree planting with shovels from melted collected guns. Jardin Botanico de Culiacán.

PHOTO: BALISE ADILON / COURTESY PEDRO REYES

artwork. Reyes thinks of it this way: "People have been exposed to violence in their neighborhoods and in the media. Planting a tree has a positive effect. It is a sign that reversal is possible. We can turn death into life."[11]

Reyes credits Antanas Mockus for showing him how to package projects so that they appeal to a broad and diverse public. Mockus, the eccentric former mayor of Bogota, Colombia, is renowned for inventing innovative schemes that successfully solve nagging municipal problems. He addressed the problem of jaywalking, for example, by hiring mimes to poke fun at the people who might otherwise receive a fine. Reyes comments, "Mockus taught me to use creativity in the social and political field, but not as a way of protest. He is a modern Gandhi. It is fine that some people make protest. It creates awareness. But I am most interested in creating new regenerative driving forces. Resistance means you are using energy to oppose an existing force. I want to use energy to create a new driving force."[12]

Because this driving energy is pooled from the contributions of so many sponsors, it far exceeds the artist's individual capabilities. Reyes is pleased to announce that he is not involved in the choices of trees that are planted, who will plant them, or where they will be planted. He explains, "The idea is to provide an operations manual so that anyone can replicate the project. It is like a franchise. The project will work best the less I'm needed to be involved."[13]

Reyes is strategically crafting ways to maximize this franchise effect. Besides gallery exhibitions and online postings, his project exists as a story that he hopes will become lodged in a culture like a myth, be transmitted by the populace through oral storytelling, and convey accessible guidance like a parable. He comments, "Taking these guns out of circulation actually saves a few lives, but the real purpose of the piece is to add a story to the world so in the neighboring cities they will say, 'In Culiacán they did that.'"[14] Reyes insists, "Adding stories to the world is a peaceful weapon for change."[15]

NOTES

1 Pedro Reyes quoted in "Pedro Reyes," by Titiana Cuevas, *BOMB* 94 (Winter 2005–2006). http://bombsite.com/issues/94/articles/2779.
2 Ibid.
3 Nick Miles, "Mexico's 'Devastating' Forest Loss," *BBC News World Addition*, March 4, 2002.
4 Pedro Reyes interview with the author, May 10, 2010.
5 "They will beat their swords into plowshares and their spears into pruning hooks. Nation will not take up sword against nation, nor will they train for war anymore." Isaiah 2:4 and Micah 4:3.
6 Pedro Reyes interview with the author, May 6, 2010.
7 Pedro Reyes in "Building New Topias, a Conversation with Pedro Reyes," by Carolee Thea, *Sculpture* vol. 28, no. 5 (June 2009), 52.
8 "Modeling behavior" is associated with the distinguished sociologist Albert Bandura (1925).
9 Pedro Reyes interview with the author, May 6, 2010.
10 Ibid.
11 Ibid.
12 Ibid.
13 Ibid.
14 Pedro Reyes quoted in "Pedro Reyes," by Titiana Cuevas, *BOMB* 94 (Winter 2005–2006). http://bombsite.com/issues/94/articles/2779.
15 Ibid.

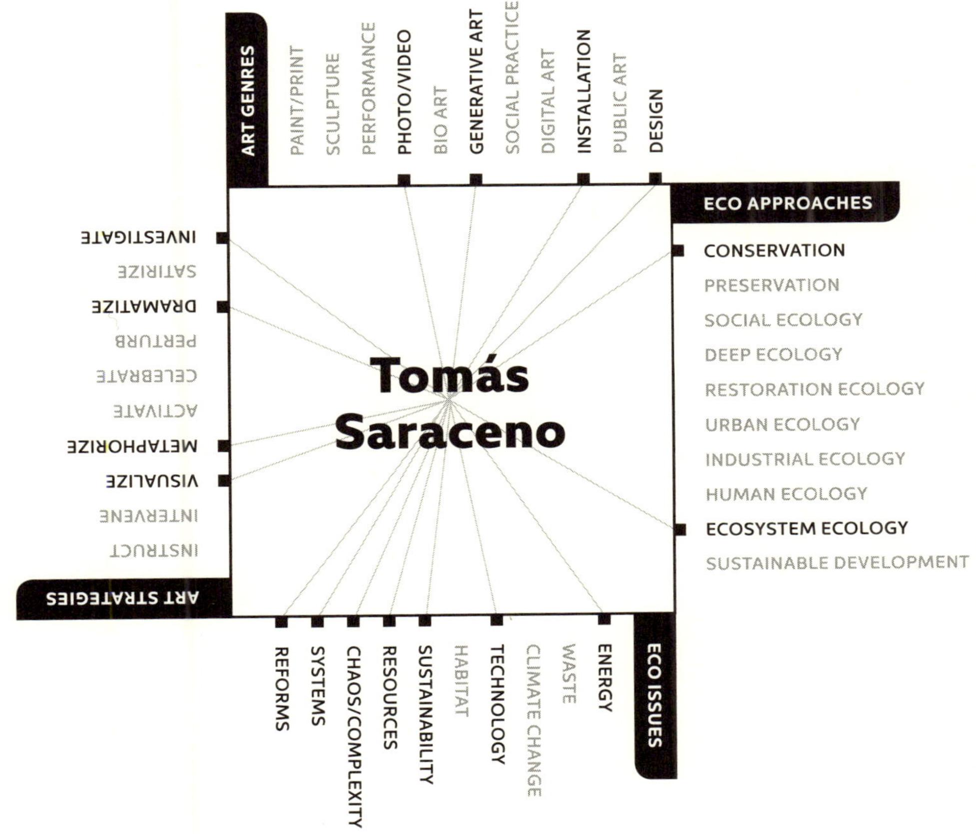

Sun/Wind/Flower Power

Born 1973, Tucuman, Argentina

ONE OF MANY WAYS that photographers adopt the label *eco* is by capitalizing on the ability of their imagery to inspire environmental advocacy and provoke environmental protest. These visualizations can arouse reverence for pristine wildernesses, or indignation regarding industrial wastelands, or compassion for endangered species, and so forth. Photographer Peter Dombrovskis's persuasive images of Tasmania's wild places, for example, were instrumental in defeating plans to dam the Franklin River for a hydroelectric power plant.

However, even photographers who aim their cameras at graduations and weddings can join the environmental movement by applying sustainable criteria to their materials and their processes. They plant trees to offset their carbon footprints, use DVD proofing in place of paper proofs, reuse packing materials, choose paper with recycled content, avoid toxic chemicals, patronize environmentally responsible manufacturers, and so forth. Photographers can even formalize their commitment to sustainability by inviting an independent third-party audit of their practices in the hope of becoming a Certified Green Photographer.[1] For some artists, photographic considerations of ecosystems have led them to such innovative alternatives as creating tonal images on lawns by controlling the photosynthesis of grass, or creating a new type of photographic image by allowing microbes to conduct their normal life activities on film.

Tomás Saraceno expanded these eco-photographic options. Although he still employs standard photographic components such as focus, aperture, shutter speed, metering, and filters, he departs from tradition by inviting nonhuman forces to dictate how his camera operates and what images it records. The results provide evidence of the formative roles that environmental conditions can play in such human-centered activities as taking photographs.

Girasol (Turning Sun) (2009) is the product of an inventive photographic process in which the sun fuels the camera and the wind determines exposure, framing, and shutter speed. As a result, representatives of three mighty forces that shape the Earth converged to create this artwork, which premiered at the Walker Art Center in Minneapolis, Minnesota: chemical power is exemplified by the sun; mechanical power is embodied by the wind; and humanity's intellectual power is represented by the ingenious use of chemistry and mechanics.

An isolated flower serves as the hub where these forces convene. What kind of flower did Saraceno choose to play this key role? The rose is too fragile. The daisy is too common. The dandelion is too stubborn. The flower that was just right was the sunflower. Standing high in the garden, radiating yellow flares, it not only resembles the almighty sun, it is genetically programmed to follow the sun as it sweeps the sky each day from east at dawn to west at dusk. Botanists refer to this sun-tracking action as heliotropism (*helio* = sun; *tropism* = automatic response).

Saraceno recruits these wide-ranging forces as his nonhuman collaborators in creating a series of time-lapse photographic images of the sun. By attaching a tiny still camera to the flower's head, he becomes as dependent upon the sunflower to direct the filming of *Girasol* as the sunflower is dependent upon the sun to dictate its movements. The camera does not record what the photographer is looking at. Instead, it registers what the flower "sees" as its "face" rotates in pursuit of the sun.

Furthermore, instead of activating the camera when he decides an image is picture worthy, Saraceno enlists flowing air to press the shutter for him. A large wind turbine mounted on the museum terrace creates the electricity that powers the camera's shutter.[2] When the day is windy, many pictures are taken. When the air is still, no pictures are taken. When there are gusts, the tempo is erratic. These pictures are delivered to a computer laptop installed in the gallery. It, too, is powered by the wind turbine. Because all these elements are visible to museumgoers through a window in the gallery, they easily discern that the footage on the computer is a product of the force and frequency of the wind blowing outside and does not reflect the subjective editing style of the artist.

In all these ways the sun, the wind, and the flower are liberated from their roles as compliant art mediums and processes. They attain full-partner status that grants them creative powers. Saraceno sacrifices his artistic will, but he achieves a form of parity with nonhuman forces that is more than a personal dividend. It earns Saraceno's photographic process the

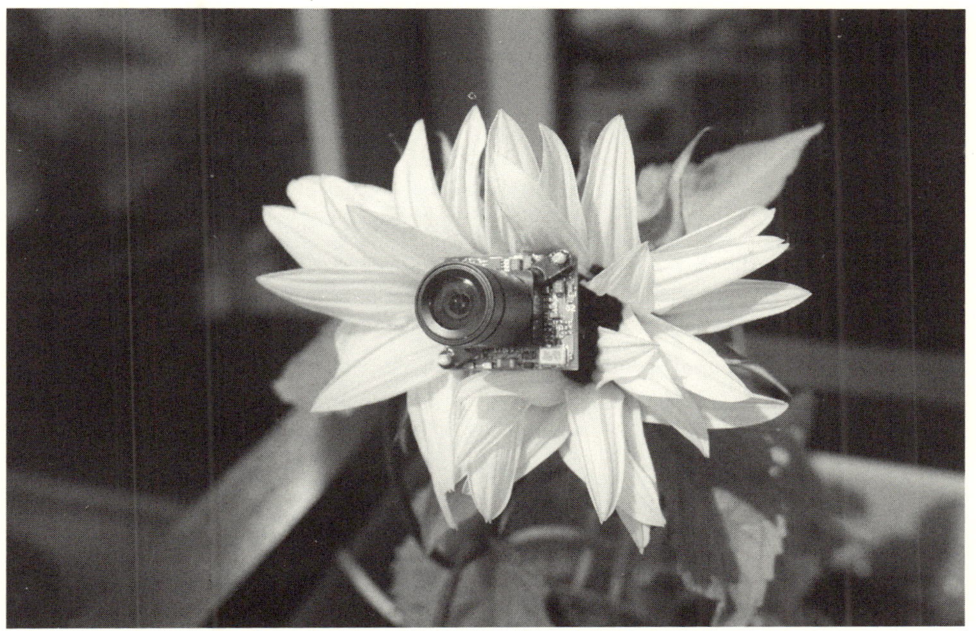

Tomás Saraceno | Girasol (Turning Sun) | 2009 Installation from Walker Art Center
COURTESY TOMÁS SARACENO AND TANYA BONAKDAR GALLERY, NEW YORK

status of model for a culture-wide reform of human behaviors. His "attempt to re-establish new concepts of synergy"[3] is a core entry on environmentalists' playlists. Synergy suggests that cooperative mergers are preferable to competitive contests. Saraceno provides a vivid description of this principle: "I try to see an ecosystem working. Everything is codependent. You rely on everything. You are imbedded in cycles. In this work, you can rethink your relationship with human beings, animals, plants, and the planet. We must stay flexible."[4]

Sun and wind are ideal candidates to model a culture-wide enrichment of synergetic relationships, because neither can be owned, so cooperating with them is available to anyone. Furthermore, since they exist in limitless supplies, they can serve everyone simultaneously. Finally, because they cross geopolitical borders without regard for passports, visas, tariffs, border patrols, and other limits to passage, they are available everywhere. Thus, Saraceno's partnerships with the sun and the wind are not merely novel photographic techniques. They present the territory of the sky as a supranational free space with untapped potential to serve human needs without commandeering the planet's assets. *Girasol* bolsters the argument for these alternative energy sources.

Each deviation from photographic norms that this work introduces brings it into closer alignment with the dynamic interdependencies that prevail in ecosystems:

- The intervals in conventional time-lapse photography are regular and predetermined; the intervals between still images in *Girasol* are irregular and unpredictable.
- Conventional cameras are merely light gauges; the camera used in *Girasol* also functions like a weather vane and hourglass.

- Photographic imagery is typically a record of a past time and distant place; *Girasol*'s images are dynamically generated on-site, in real time.
- Traditional photographs register material appearances; *Girasol* also provides a record of immaterial forces such as wind.
- Humans dictate the aesthetics of a conventional photograph; surrounding nonhuman conditions control the picture taking in *Girasol*.

Saraceno traces the origin of his inspiration for this work to a quaint recollection from his childhood. "When I was a kid, I had a telescope. The first thing the instructions said was, 'Don't point at the sun. It will burn your eyes.' The sun became the forbidden star, exactly what you should not look at. Well, I thought looking at the sun might be interesting. Relying on the wind allowed me to watch the impossible."[5]

Initially Saraceno planned to fulfill his childhood desire by using the sunflower and turbine to produce a video in which the sun remained fixed in the middle of the screen from sunrise to sunset. He quickly discovered that this vision was easy to imagine but impossible to achieve. The uninterrupted image of the sun would have required a perfectly cloudless day (so the sun would always be visible), breezes moving with undeviating velocity (to produce a continuous sequence of picture taking), and wind that maintained a minimum velocity of twenty-four frames per minute (to make still images appear to be moving). Since these conditions are unachievable on Earth, the imagery that viewers see is as confounding as the gusts that activate the picture taking and the lulls that leave the screen blank.

The erratic conditions of the atmosphere are not the only reasons why Saraceno's original vision failed to materialize. Others supply ample material for a farce about the trials and tribulations of being an eco artist. Saraceno is candid when he reports the comedy of hurdles he encountered:

- The computer's uptake capacity was overwhelmed on windy days by the torrent of images it received. It could neither process nor store them all.
- Winds had to be brisk for the turbine to function. Gentle breezes did not charge the battery.
- The camera got so hot on sunny days that it burned the sunflower and ceased working.
- The camera that was attached to the sunflower shook in the wind so it no longer was aimed at the sun.
- The sunflower was relocated inside the gallery to avoid the heat and wind problems, but this prevented it from responding to the sun because polarized glass that filters ultraviolet light was used on the museum windows.
- When the sunflower was returned outside, the head hardly moved because its heliotropic response was stunted while it was being raised inside.

These problems turned out to be valuable because Saraceno ultimately concluded that the unintended imagery was far more captivating than the steady-state picture he anticipated. He explains, "I've made two or three attempts to create what I was wishing for, what I was demanding. This work challenged my flexibility of mind. Because I was disappointed, it opened up new possibilities. This work is about learning, the process of thinking and looking. The difference between what I wish and what was the result allows me to see something completely new and different. I want to see something. It comes out different. There is beauty in accepting change."[6]

Saraceno applies this surprise factor to audiences as well. The unpredictability of the resulting image commands attention, evokes mystery, stimulates curiosity. He sums up the work's significance by commenting, "Expanding the process of perception sets a critical attitude into motion that considers and reconsiders, reinterprets, decodes your position, reverses the reality, reverses the world."[7]

NOTES

1 "What Is a 'Green Photographer'?" The Green Photographer (Fun Photo Guys, 2006–2011). http://thegreenphotographer.net/.
2 The artwork was located on the terrace of the Walker Art Center in Minnesota where it premiered.
3 Tomás Saraceno interview with Stefano Boeri and Hans Ulrich Obrist, January 30, 2006.
4 Tomás Saraceno interview with the author, November 15, 2010.
5 Ibid.
6 Ibid.
7 Tomás Saraceno, "Conversation with Pinksummer and Luca Cerizza," October 1, 2004. http://www.pinksummer.com/pink2/exb/sar/exb001en.htm.

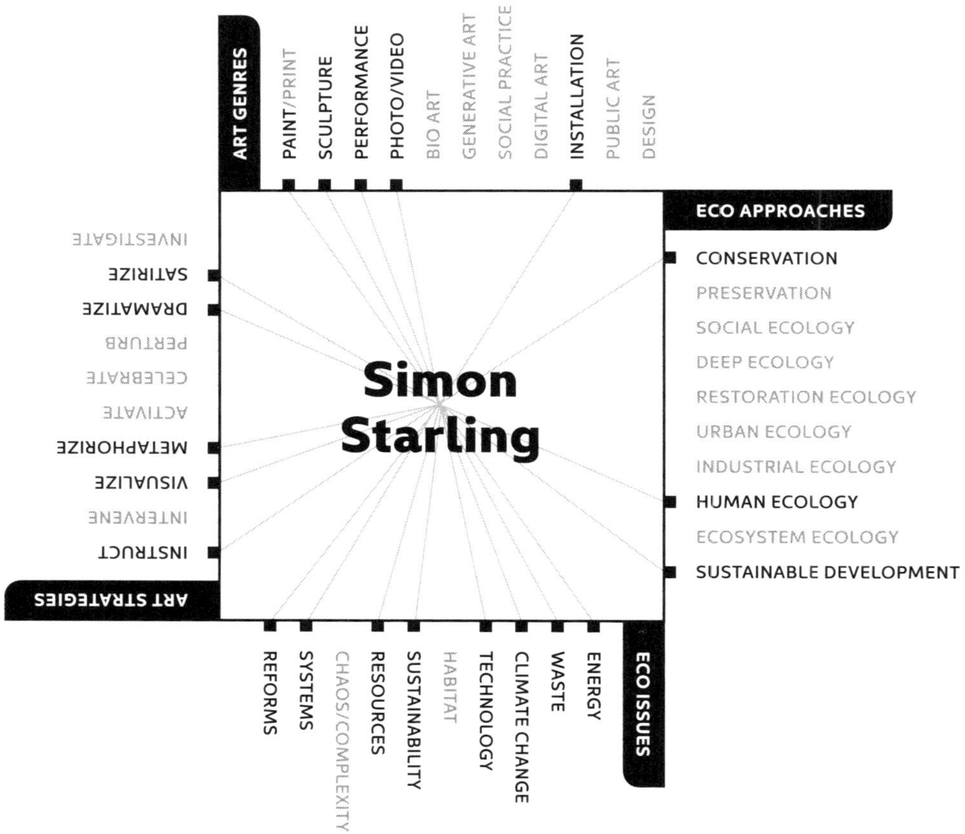

Energy Foibles and Follies

Born 1967, Epsom, UK

WHILE THE HOLY GRAIL has been envisioned in numerous ways over the course of history, it always represents an era's most elusive and most tantalizing goal. Embarking on a quest for the Holy Grail is, therefore, a heroic venture that is more often associated with quests than achievements. Such lofty pursuits often earn the elevated status of legends.

What is the Twenty-First-Century version of the Holy Grail? What goal is so improbable that it seems magical and mysterious? One candidate is the quest for a source of energy that is capable of fueling the needs and desires of soaring human populations in a sustainable and affordable manner. This is the quest of a global cast of scientists, engineers, technicians, physicists, chemists, astronomers, and biologists all striving to materialize the illusory energy elixir.

Entries in the catalog of alternatives for fossil fuels are as familiar as the hurdles that accompany them: solar collectors and wind turbines occupy large tracts of land; hydroelectric plants destroy free-flowing rivers and the bottomland in river valleys; harvesting biomass can cause deforestation and soil degradation; processing and burning biomass can pollute water and air; manufacturing photovoltaic cells utilizes toxic substances; natural gas can pollute groundwater; spent nuclear fuel from nuclear power plants is a radioactive hazard; producing ethanol consumes nearly as much energy as it generates.[1]

Simon Starling is not among the contemporary artists who have joined the energy crusade. He has claimed a ringside seat to observe and critique its frenetic explorations. He then designs eccentric situations that highlight energy follies, dramatizes conservation shortcomings, and contributes energy-expending processes he conducts with his body in order to avoid energy-consuming processes conducted with fossil fuels. In these works, the human body is offered as an untapped source of energy generation.

Starling discloses an energy folly that is as comical as it is instructive in *Kakteenhaus (Cactus House)* (2002). The installation represents the climax of a chronicle that began when Starling picked a cactus from the hot dry desert in Spain and transported it in his beat-up red Volvo to a cold and wet northern European climate where it was installed in the Temporäre Kunsthalle in Berlin. The entire exhibition space was transformed into a greenhouse. Its sole function was to warm the single, scrawny, displaced, prickly cactus.

A wall text revealed the unfolding of the work's story line to visitors. Called a "recipe" by Starling, it tracks the coordinates of his expedition. "A Cereus cactus found growing at Texas Hollywood Film Studio in the Tabernas Desert, Andalucia, and transported 133 miles to Frankfurt in a Volvo 240 Estate."

Only part of Starling's Volvo was parked outside the gallery. The engine still started from inside the car, but the engine itself was running inside the gallery. Its gasoline tubes, water pipes, exhaust pipe, and electrical wiring had all been extended eighty-five feet like horizontal smokestacks so that they reached from the car outside to the engine inside. The exhaust and supply pipes discharged enough heat in the gallery to raise the indoor temperatures to 32 degrees Celsius, the ideal temperature for the desert cactus. Starling comments, "Internal combustion engines produce a lot of heat that they don't use."[2]

That statement is truer than car manufacturers would like to admit. It is estimated that automobile engines convert only 20 percent of their combusted gasoline into kinetic energy; 80 percent is released as heat.[3] Thus the life-saving heat for the cactus was provided by the life-threatening waste of petroleum combustion by people. Starling dramatized this rampant inefficiency by putting the wasted energy of the automobile to work in a manner that visitors could observe and feel. The contrast between the superb efficiency of a cactus and the clumsy inefficiencies of technology is both droll and insightful. At the same time, Starling created an accessible metaphor for the warming of the globe that is commonly believed to be a product of carbon dioxide emissions from burning fossil fuels.

As in all his work, Starling has created a chain of relationships, not a finite object. He typically elaborates on the energy flows he is highlighting as they pass through natural and cultural systems, explaining, "I'm very interested in eco-systems in a broad sense, whereby we can talk about nature, but we can also talk about culture, and history and sociology. Ecosystems are just systems of connection."[4] Thus, besides comparing the efficiency and endurance of the automobile and the cactus, Starling added the following narratives:

- Previous to the cactus's transport for this work of art, its ancestors were relocated to the Tabernas to make the Spanish desert appear like the deserts in Mexico and the US Southwest. They were transplanted so the region could serve as a setting for the filming of Western movies,[5] which explains why the work's recipe referred to a "Cereus cactus found growing at Texas Hollywood Film Studio in the Tabernas."
- Global warming is believed to be the cause of the Tabernas Desert's rapid expansion.[6] This work dramatizes the urgent need to reduce carbon dioxide emissions.
- Industrial agricultural installations for growing tropical vegetables, fruits, and flowers now occupy 158,000 acres of the Tabernas Desert. The crops are sustained in this barren region by elaborate artesian wells and irrigation systems that deplete underground aquifers and disperse chemical fertilizers.[7]

Shedboatshed (Mobile Architecture No. 2) (2005) is another caper, but this one serves as a model of economy, not waste. The inspiration came to Starling as he was bicycling along the Rhine River near the Swiss town of Schweizerhalle, contemplating a way to incorporate the river in his upcoming exhibition downriver in Basel.[8] Along the way he came across a decrepit, unpainted wooden shed. He introduced himself to the owners and expressed his desire to convert their shed into a boat for an art exhibition. His plan was to then load the remains of the shed onto the boat and paddle approximately seven miles down the Rhine to Basel. There he would dismantle the boat and rebuild it as a shed that would be installed at the Museum für Gegenwartskunst.

Starling recalls, "I was looking for something that I could use for a river-based project and, being lucky, I found it. The shed even had a paddle attached! And the owners were really happy with what I wanted to do. What I'm doing is just adding another layer to its history. It used to be a guard hut on the Swiss border."[9] Starling learned that the paddle was used on boats called *weidlings*, so that was the type of boat he constructed. It was about thirty feet long and resembled a gondola.

This journey in a handmade vessel required more than courage. It also entailed detailed planning, knowledge of construction, and substantial outlays of effort—both mental and physical. Starling's personal energy expenditures challenged the extravagant expenditures of energy being made worldwide through industrial mass production. By pitting sweat and calories against coal and petroleum, *Shedboatshed* fortifies the moral principle that production should maximize sustainability instead of maximizing productivity. Starling confirms this by stating that his efforts were "an attempt to make an artwork which is very ergonomic and easy on the environment."[10]

Ergonomics maximizes productivity by reducing the worker's fatigue and discomfort. Starling's reference to the applied science of ergonomics seems to be transferred, from reducing a strenuous human process to reducing stress on the planet. Indeed, the total energy invested to produce and install this work of art was a fraction of conventional costs of conducting art protocols. Using handheld tools, reusing local neglected materials as his sculp-

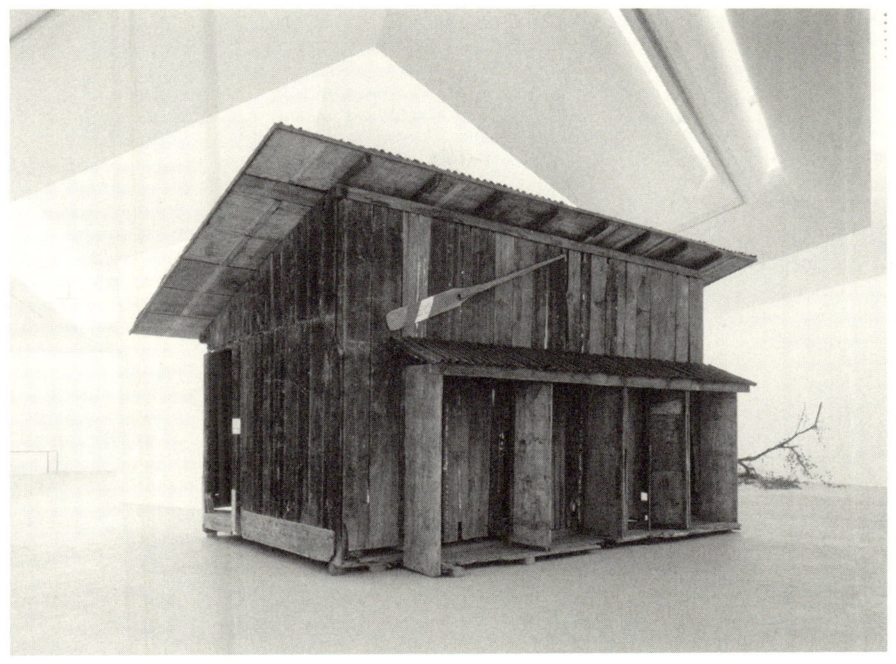

Simon Starling | **Shedboatshed (Mobile Architecture No. 2)** | **2005**

COURTESY SIMON STARLING AND CASEY KAPLAN, NEW YORK

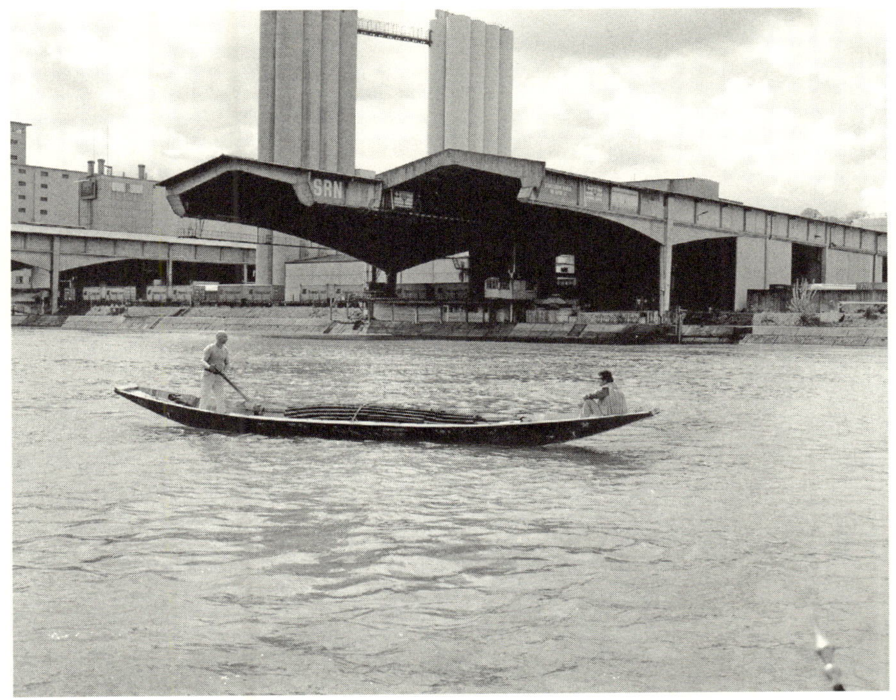

Simon Starling | **Shedboatshed (Mobile Architecture No. 2)** | **2005**

COURTESY SIMON STARLING AND CASEY KAPLAN, NEW YORK

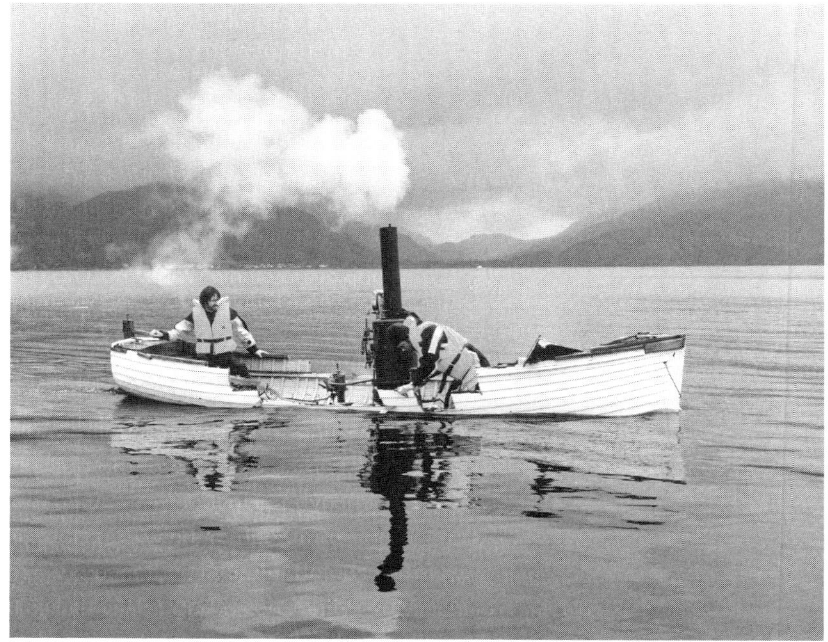

Simon Starling | Autoxylopyrocycloboros | 2006 Thirty-eight color transparencies, Götschmann slide projector, flight case | Slide dimensions: 2.4" x 2.75"

COURTESY SIMON STARLING AND CASEY KAPLAN, NEW YORK

tural medium, and attending to the crating, transport, fabrication, and installation in one operation, Starling accomplished an impressive feat of conservation. Despite his exertions, Starling seems to have been refreshed by the process. To him, the labor is about "slowing things down, about trying to retard this incredible speed at which we live".[11]

Investing in a laborious process that entailed dismantling, constructing, then dismantling the construction and reconstructing it may seem pointless, if not incredibly ludicrous. But it is this elaborate effort that conveys the work's compelling message. Starling made certain that museumgoers would discern this process. He comments, "If you step up into the shed you'll start to see the cuts, the marks of the boat-building process. Also you'll discover lying on the floor a pile of cotton caulking which was used to fill the boards to keep the water out. There's also some steel brackets we used to keep the ribs in place."[12] He then comments, "You can read its history in its scars."[13]

The third example of Starling's explorations is directed at the energy required to mine raw material for commodities that are manufactured, packaged, and transported to global markets. *One Ton* (2005) applies this wasteful scenario to platinum, a precious metal that endows fine art photographs with their delicate tones and extraordinary permanence. The massive amount of platinum ore required to produce one platinum print provides the theme of *One Ton*. The number of 20" x 24" photographic prints in this installation was determined by how many prints could be produced by the output of refined platinum from an entire ton of platinum ore. It yielded only five prints!

The platinum mine where the platinum was acquired to produce these images originated is the subject of these photographs. Starling chose an aerial perspective to convey the enormity of strip-mine operations that transformed the landscape into a gaping barren pit.

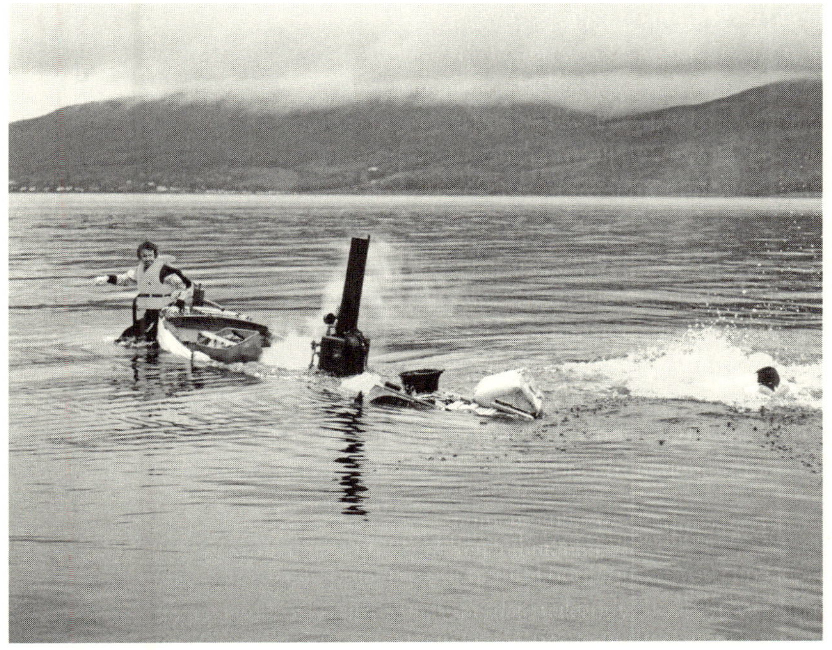

Simon Starling | Autoxylopyrocycloboros | 2006 Thirty-eight color transparencies, Götschmann slide projector, flight case | Slide dimensions: 2.4″ × 2.75″

The identical image is repeated in all five prints to direct attention to quantity—the meager payoff from an immensely destructive practice. These strategies generate visual evidence of the dire environmental and human toll wrought by open cast platinum mining.

As in his other projects, the work's meaning is embedded in the process used to produce it. Starling ensured that his effort was proportionate to the environmental consequences of platinum mining by journeying halfway around the world from his studio in Scotland to visit the platinum mine in South Africa. This strenuous, time-consuming, and costly pilgrimage was in total contradiction to the normal means of acquisition—purchasing the product from a local commercial outlet. While it was unnecessary materially, the trip was essential thematically. It exposed the far-flung, energy-guzzling supply routes that contemporary consumers do not see, and therefore rarely consider.

Autoxylopyrocycloboros[14] (2006) stages another burlesque of energy gluttony. In order to demonstrate the consequences of squandering finite supplies of fossil fuels, Starling and a partner rode across a Scottish lake in a twenty-two-foot-long wooden boat that had already accumulated an elaborate history. The boat's original steam engine had been converted to run on diesel power. Then it had sunk and been refloated. Starling outfitted it again for steam. Like all steamboats, this one required continual feeding of fuel. Unlike most steamboats, the fuel for this one was supplied by the boat itself. As the boat chugged along, Starling steered as his mate gradually dismantled the boat to feed its boiler. Photographs document the two artists setting out in their bright orange life vests in full anticipation of the vessel sinking. Eventually it did, and as it descended it left in its wake a vivid metaphor for the destiny of a society dependent upon finite supplies of fossil fuels.

One final example completes this survey of Starling's elaborate art labors undertaken to critique society's actual and potential energy practices. *Tabernas Desert Run* (2004) is a museum installation that consists of a bicycle and a large and beautifully rendered watercolor of a cactus. These disparate objects are connected by another Starling journey. This time the artist traveled forty-one miles across the Tabernas Desert in Spain on the bicycle featured in this installation. The bike was outfitted with an improvised electric motor that ran on hydrogen from a fuel cell. Fuel cell vehicles have the potential to significantly reduce dependence on foreign oil and lower harmful emissions. While these vehicles are in the early stages of development, Starling's small-scale excursion indicates their large-scale potential. To manifest the success of his journey to museumgoers, he collected the only waste product from hydrogen combustion—water—and used this waste product to liquefy the paints to create the delicate painting of the Tabernas Desert cactus. Thus, Starling provided a model of ultimate efficiency by relying on renewable energy and then using its harmless by-product.

Whether working on a photograph, a sculpture, or an installation, Starling creates active exchanges of energy. The elemental forms of kinetic energy he musters by doing work serve as the basis for his comparisons with the complex sources of energy that fuel contemporary production. On the one hand, Starling applies this materiality to the production and display of art. On the other, he applies it to our bodies, manifesting that we are energy-driven machines that run on food fuel and are capable of performing work. These insights add a dimension to the meaning of the "law of conservation of energy." They not only confirm that energy changes from one form to another, they demonstrate that "conservation of energy" can also mean saving energy.

NOTES

1 John Holdren, "Solar and Other Renewable Energy Sources," *The Encyclopedia of the Environment*, edited by Ruth Eblen and William Eblen (New York: Houghton Mifflin, 1994), 660–61.

2 Montse Badia, *Interview with Simon Starling*, Espai 13—Fundació Joan Miró, Barcelona, posted on YouTube by MontseBadia, December 24, 2008. http://www.youtube.com/watch?v=kwhkG6npudo.

3 "Next Presentation of the Cold External Combustion Engine," Air Car Factories S.A. http://www.aircarfactories.com/important-notice.html.

4 Montse Badia, *Interview with Simon Starling*, Espai 13—Fundació Joan Miró, Barcelona, posted on YouTube by MontseBadia, December 24, 2008. http://www.youtube.com/watch?v=kwhkG6npudo.

5 Simon Starling, "Talks about Kakteenhaus (2002)," Art Forum, May 2003.

6 "The fight against desertification," posted on Technology for Life, September 9, 2007. http://technology4life.wordpress.com/2007/09/09/the-fight-against-desertification/.

7 Ibid.

8 Simon Starling, *Cuttings (Supplement)*, Kunstmuseum Basel, Museum für Gegenwartskunst, Basel, Switzerland, June 11–August 7, 2005.

9 Simon Starling, "I Got a Lovely Poem from a Lady in St Albans about Sheds," an interview with Stuart Jeffries, the *Guardian*, December 6, 2005. http://www.guardian.co.uk/artanddesign/2005/dec/07/art.turnerprize2005.

10 "Is It a Shed? Is It a Row Boat? No, It's Art!" AFP, The Times. http://www.designtaxi.com/news.php?id=1572.

11 Ibid.

12 Simon Starling in "Turner Prize 2005," Tate Britain (October 18, 2005–January 22, 2006). http://www.tate.org.uk/britain/turnerprize/2005/transcript_simonstarling.htm.

13 Simon Starling interviewed by Ross Birrell, *Art and Research* vol. 1, no. 1 (Winter 2006–2007). http://www.artandresearch.org.uk/v1n1/starling3.html.

14 Autoxylopyrocycloboros: auto = automatic; xylo = wood; pyro = fire, heat; cycl = bicycle, motorcycle, tricycle; oboros (ouroboros) = ancient symbol depicting a serpent eating its own tail, representing the eternal return.

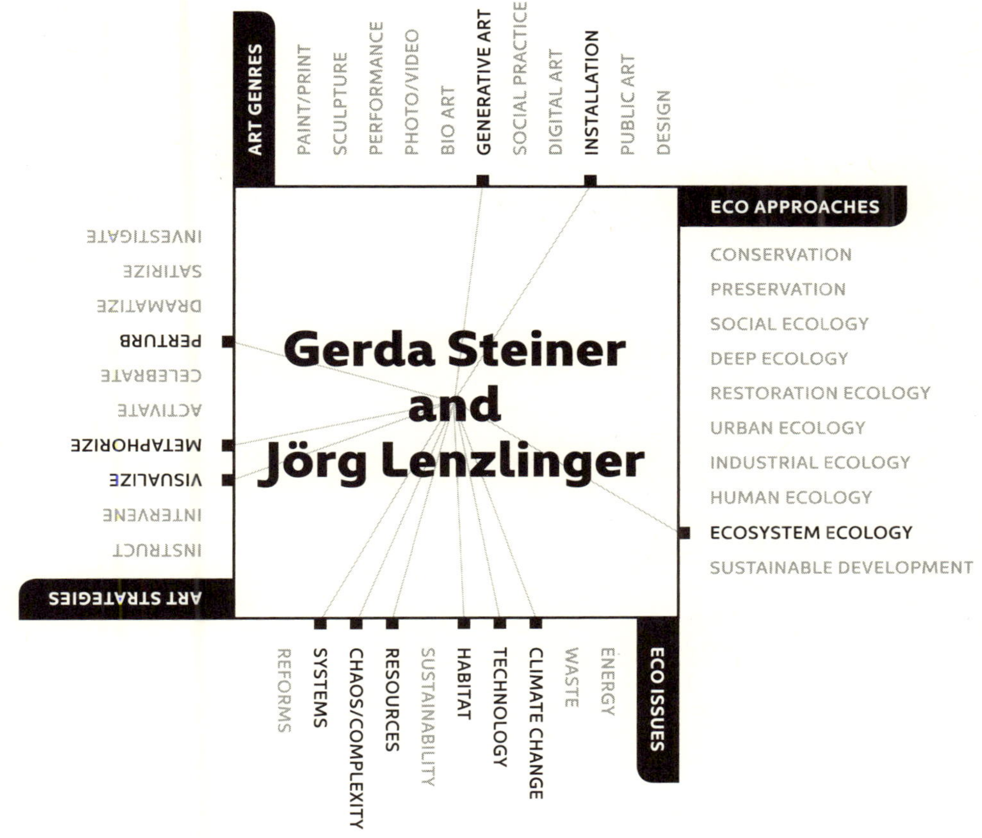

Twin Perils—Excess and Scarcity

Gerda Steiner born 1964, Ettiswil, Switzerland
Jörg Lenzlinger born 1967, Uster, Switzerland

A GOOGLE SEARCH of "Gerda Steiner / Jörg Lenzlinger" is rewarded by a deluge of postings by bloggers who have been dazzled by the visual wonderlands the artists construct, especially those that function like giant living systems that conduct nutritional cycles via a network of tangled tubes and cables that circulate among and around the public. They are created collaboratively by Gerda Steiner, who is known for room-size wall paintings, and Jörg Lenzlinger, who uses crystallization as his artistic process.

To create *O Escrito (The Office)* (2007), an example of an installation that grows, the artists arranged dozens of office cubicles in

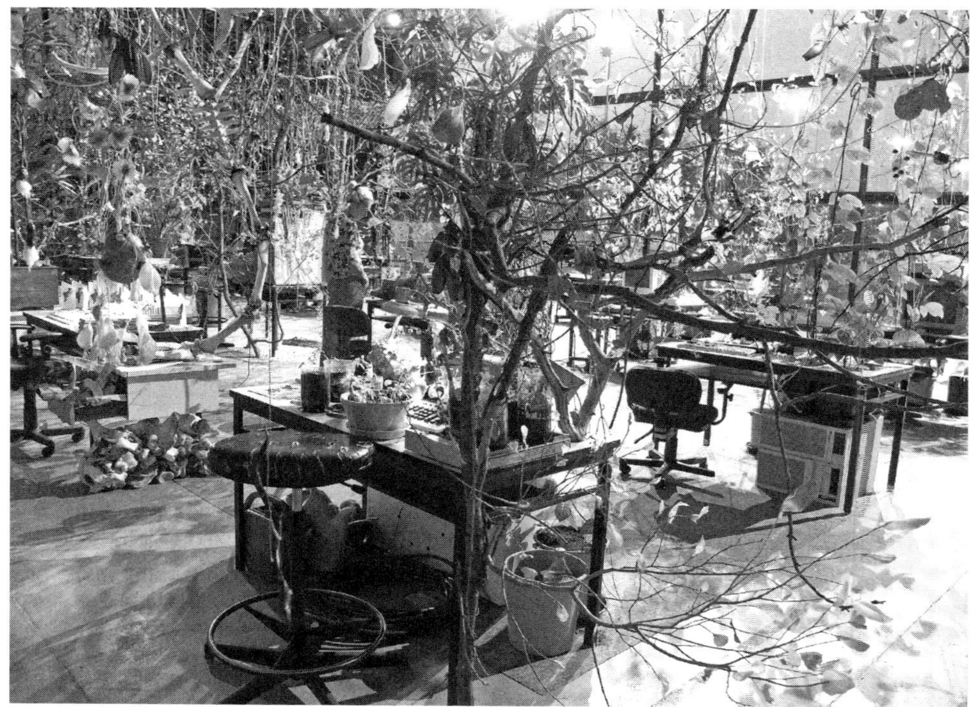

Gerda Steiner and Jörg Lenzlinger | O Escrito (The Office) | 2007 CCBB Brasilia | Mixed media installation | Office furniture, office equipment, office supplies, fertilizer, fertilizer crystals, cables, dead branches, artificial plants and flowers, real plants and flowers

PHOTO: GERDA STEINER AND JÖRG LENZLINGER / COURTESY GERDA STEINER AND JÖRG LENZLINGER

neat rows in a vast, glass-enclosed atrium in the administrative center of Brazil. The walls of the offices were omitted, but a complete inventory of office fixtures and furniture was included: desks, chairs, wastebaskets, telephones, computers, filing cabinets, snacks, plants, fire extinguishers, flip charts, keyboards, printers, and scanners. At the onset of the exhibition, the space was as sterile and orderly as any corporate workplace. However, as the exhibition proceeded, this embodiment of humanity's predilection for orderly management was overtaken by an unpredictable invasion of sprouts, germinations, and blossoms whose uncanny growth was spurred by relentless forced tube feedings of a garish fluorescent pink power drink.

Although all these blossoms were growing, most were not alive. The nonliving blooms were crystals whose exuberant patterns developed as they transmuted from a liquid to a solid. The sensitivity of crystals to fluctuating environmental conditions accounts for their astonishing variety, while the nutrient they engorged accounts for the r proliferation. Steiner and Lenzlinger set up this generative system and then watched as a profusion of shapes resembling bells, spheres, stars, and saucers lavishly embellished with ruffles, spikes, branches, and fringes emerged. The glaring presence of the nutrient solution directed visitors' attention to the unnatural source of the gorgeous surrounding—synthetic urea fertilizer. The artists explain, "Urea (nitrogen fertilizer) is the base of the modern industrialized agriculture. It is worldwide used in megatons to blow up the crops. . . . It is a question whether this fertility is a blessing or a curse."[1] Both alternatives are possible. As a blessing, synthetic nitrogen fertilizer created a "green revolution" that is responsible for feeding almost half the people on the Earth today.[2] As a curse, synthetic fertilizer depletes soil and guzzles natural gas, coal, and water during production, and its runoff causes severe water pollution.

Steiner and Lenzlinger expand their interrogation of contemporary agricultural technologies by choosing salt as the catalyst for their flourishing crystal formations. Salinization is caused by the accumulation of salt in water and soil, typically from irrigation for crops and excessive applications of fertilizers. It is a grave environmental problem worldwide because it chokes vegetation, kills fish, and renders water useless for irrigation and drinking. Ironically, the crusting that is a sign of this environmental blight is also responsible for the beautiful crystal formations in the installation. By cramming a vast space with artificially induced abundance, the artists evoke the contest between attraction and repulsion that applies to reliance on damaging synthetic strategies to boost production, whether in agriculture, in business, or in art. The installation asks, Does industrially manufactured abundance produce a garden of delights or a little shop of horrors?

There was so much creeping and blooming going on in the *O Escrito* installation that these eruptions threatened to overtake the tidy predictability of white-collar work. Consider the cultural metaphors at stake here: nine-to-five predictability within a predetermined structure versus a self-generating system that is hypersensitive, prolific, and engenders its own outcomes. In this work of art, the office ceases to be the upholder of commerce, government, professionalism, contracts, authority, and organization.

The Water Hole (2008–2009) applies this critique of contemporary human interventions to the Upper Yarra Dam, which was constructed to remedy the seriously dwindling water supplies around Melbourne, Australia. Whereas *O Escrito* poses the predicament of industrially induced abundance, *The Water Hole* evokes the crisis of scarcity, the consequence of overgrazing, climate change, and general squandering of water resources. The artists provide a vivid accounting of the distressing scene they observed when they visited Australia: "The dammed water shoots down a thick pipe into the thirsty, booming city below, branching off into millions of smaller pipes until it is swallowed up in wash basins, showers and bathtubs—the urban water holes. Between the ferns and the dripping car wash sponge there lies a dried out landscape. The people of the city barricade themselves in little rooms, mostly alone, to celebrate the urban rituals of the water hole, after which the water is always dirtier than it was before. It is time to turn this situation around."[3]

Evidence of the severity of this water shortage accumulates as visitors move from station to station within the meandering installation. The first sign that this journey will be ominous is that an essential component of the living trees that form the entrance tunnel is missing. There are no leaves. They are replaced by silver foil that is supported by the trees' branches. When the foil ripples, it creates the distinctive sound of rustling leaves. This obviously synthetic substitute for natural foliage is a certain indicator of habitat malfunction. At the end of this passageway the space opens to accommodate a chaotic heap of bottles, buckets, funnels, toilets, wash basins, shower caps, drainage pipes, umbrellas, and bathtubs. The entire collection of water-related items is grievously dry. A disorderly clutter of contemporary bric-a-brac dangles from strings and lies scattered about. The artists' description of a single detail conveys the abnormality of the situation: "Alongside the farting beans, hairy mobile phone spiders hatch from mutating eggs and play with the bones that are scattered around."[4]

Liquid appears in only two locations within this parched landscape. A pool of waste mo-

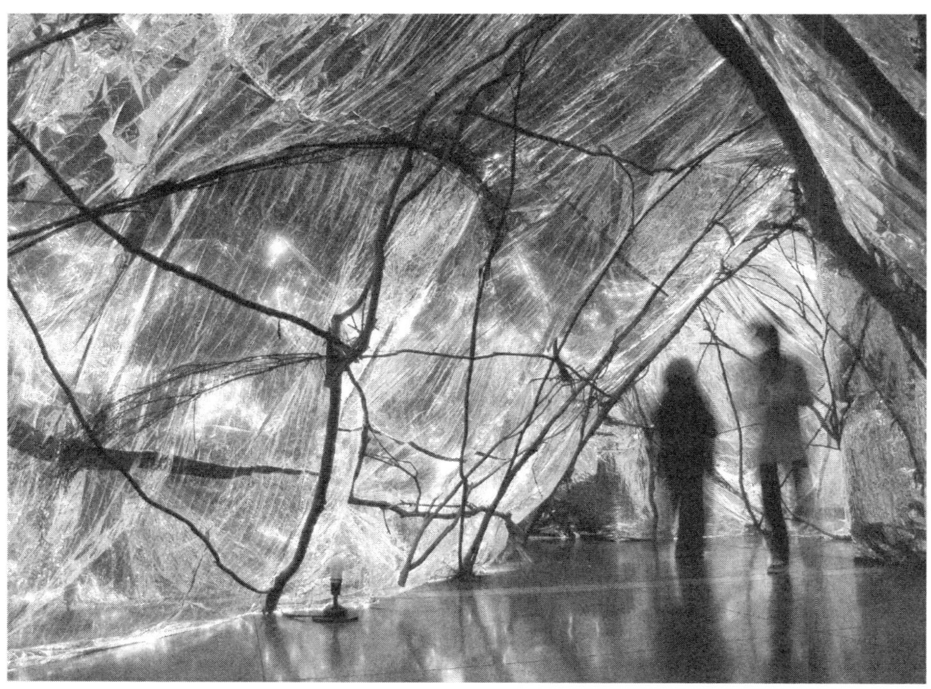

Gerda Steiner and Jörg Lenzlinger | The Water Hole (entrance) | 2008 Mixed media installation

PHOTO: GERDA STEINER AND JÖRG LENZLINGER / COURTESY GERDA STEINER AND JÖRG LENZLINGER

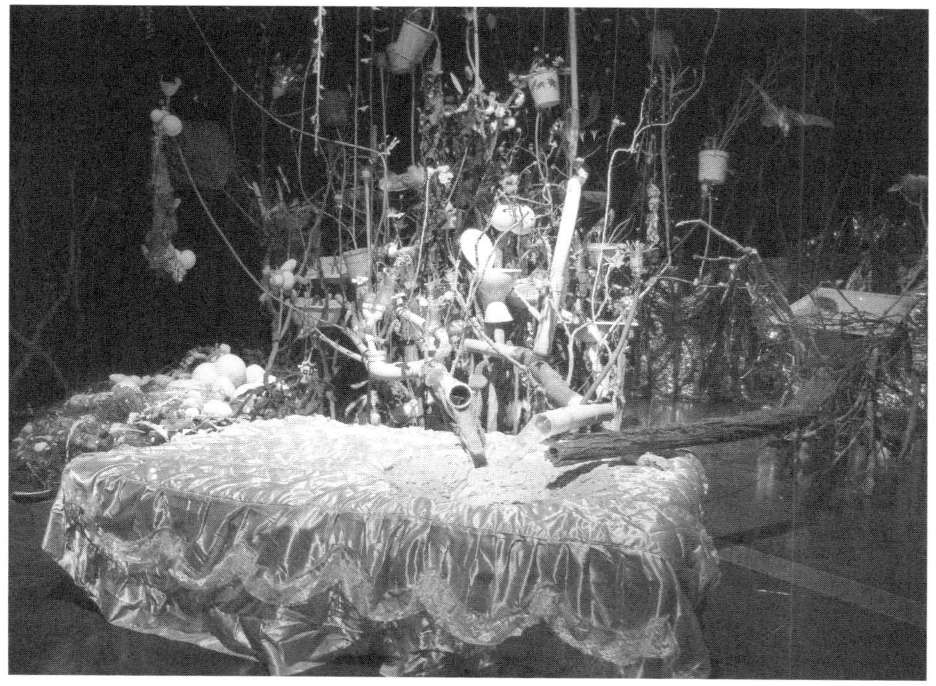

Gerda Steiner and Jörg Lenzlinger | The Water Hole (mattress detail) | 2008 Mixed media installation

PHOTO: GERDA STEINER AND JÖRG LENZLINGER / COURTESY GERDA STEINER AND JÖRG LENZLINGER

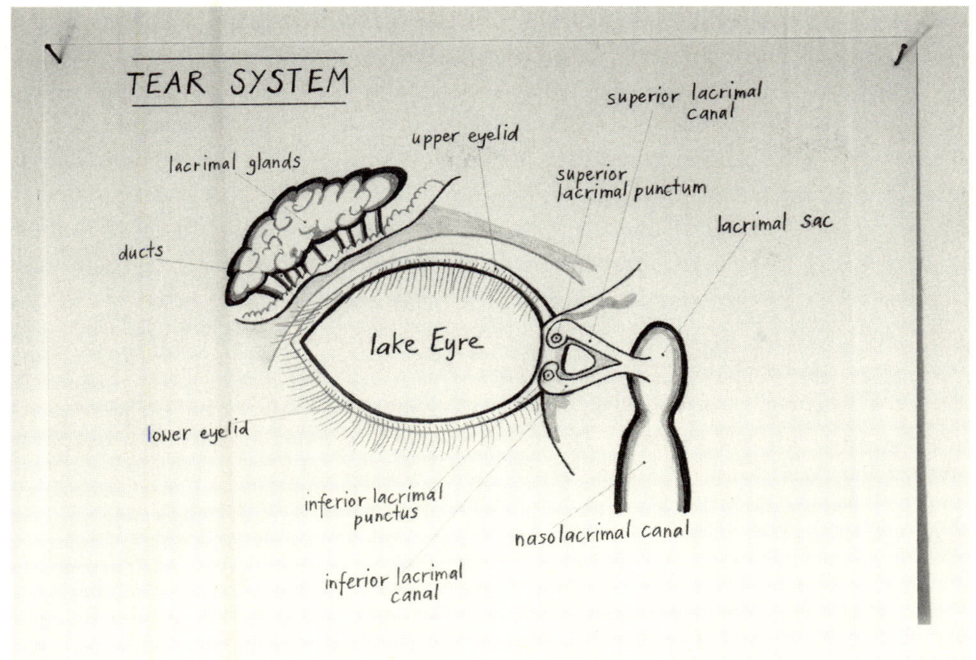

Gerda Steiner and Jörg Lenzlinger | The Water Hole (drawing) | 2008 Drawing from mixed media installation

PHOTO: GERDA STEINER AND JÖRG LENZLINGER / COURTESY GERDA STEINER AND JÖRG LENZLINGER

tor oil is a reminder of the disruptive role of petroleum in manufacture, during use, and at disposal. Its rainbow-colored swirls are disconcertingly beautiful. Its distressing counterpart is a water hole that is represented by a mud-splattered depression in an old worn mattress. It appears as a miniaturized version of a half empty dam in a barren landscape. This pitiful reservoir receives emergency drips from a medical pouch hung high overhead. Steiner and Lenzlinger provide a vivid explanation for this component of *The Water Hole*: "The network of pipes links all the urban water holes and is ready to channel the eagerly awaited rain into the clay pit which lies on the golden bed."[5]

Visitors are then directed to a dark area where windows look out onto the tower of dry water implements and the water hole they have just passed through. Binoculars are provided, allowing people to "gain perspective" on these recent experiences. A water dispenser in this area offers visitors a refreshing drink as they contemplate the probability of water deprivation. Steiner and Lenzlinger refer to this station as an "observation room" because it provides "the opportunity to study your own species and your behavior in a reversed environment."[6]

The next stations present opportunities for visitors to lie on water beds and watch videos of rain and spurting water. They contribute emotional resonance to its absence in other parts of the installation. This bleak, drought-ridden journey culminates at the end of a narrow corridor where a desk is installed. Glass tubes, vials, flasks, candles, and a microscope are laid out on it. A sign announces their intended use. This is a "Desalination plant for tears." All the equipment needed to conduct the desalinization process is provided. There is even a diagram illustrating how to use these items. It describes a "tear system." The artists offer a wry conclusion: "And if the rain truly never comes again, we can still drink our tears."[7]

Thematically, *O Escrito* and *The Water Hole* explore crucial environmental themes. But do these ambitious installations qualify as eco art in terms of their physical and material presence? Regarding *O Escrito*, the artists worked with local art students to fabricate fantasy fruits, insects, and plants from garbage. They also collected thorns, real insects, and coins. All the office furniture and equipment came from the storage of the Banco do Brasil in Brazil. The used paper was collected from the local paper dump. The creeping plants were raised in advance by a gardener. The dry branches were collected from a park nearby. The bones were found on a trip to the country. The artificial flowers were recycled from a previous installation. The synthetic fertilizer was bought at the farmer supply store.

What became of these materials after the installation was dismantled? The office items went back to the Banco do Brasil. The plants were returned to the gardener. Most of the other materials were reused for an exhibition in Rio de Janeiro. The crystals were dissolved so they could regrow in the Rio installation. A similar scenario of gleaning, scavenging, and borrowing explains the material gathering and dispersing for *The Water Hole*.

Works such as *O Escrito* and *The Water Hole* demonstrate that an installation is not merely a painting without a frame, or a sculpture without a pedestal. Installation accommodates artists, like Steiner and Lenzlinger, whose interests are sprawling, whose content develops through time, whose art engages multiple senses, and whose aesthetics are enveloping.

NOTES

1 Gerda Steiner and Jörg Lenzlinger, "The Found and Lost Grotto of Saint," Artpace, San Antonio (2006). http://www.steinerlenzlinger.ch/eye_the-lostfoundgrotto.html.

2 Erisman et al., "How a Century of Ammonia Synthesis Changed the World," *Nature Geoscience* October 2008. http://www.physics.ohio-state.edu/~wilkins/energy/Resources/Essays/ngeo325.pdf.xpdf.

3 Gerda Steiner and Jörg Lenzlinger, *The Water Hole, ACCA, Melbourne, 2008*. http //www.steinerlenzlinger.ch/eye_waterhole.html.

4 Ibid.

5 Ibid.

6 Ibid.

7 Ibid.

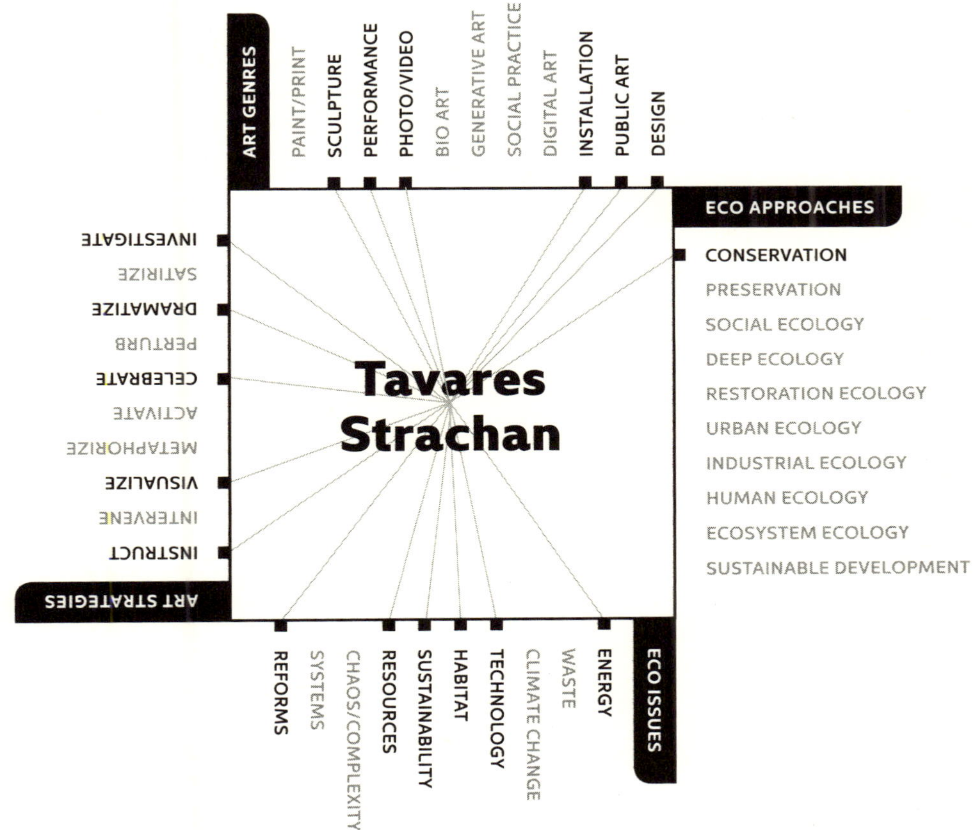

Prepping for Global Warming

Born in 1979, Nassau, Bahamas

TAVARES STRACHAN gave the schoolchildren in the Bahamas an experience they are not likely to ever forget. It was sent to them via FedEx from its point of origin three thousand miles away. On July 27, 2006, at the peak of tropical summer, a 4.5 ton block of Arctic ice arrived at the Aubrey Sayle Primary School, which Strachan attended as a child. The ice was transferred from its insulated traveling crate to a hermetically sealed, glass-sided freezer. The energy to prevent the ice from melting was generated, remarkably, by harnessing the blazing tropical sun. Strachan dramatized the remarkable potential of solar energy to address problems arising from global warming by displaying the sun's ability to maintain frigid arctic conditions in the tropics.

In order to ensure that this artifact from the top of the globe was not merely an exotic curiosity to the children who had never seen ice or snow, Strachan revived the local storytelling tradition he recalled from his childhood.

> I remember, growing up on the island, there were stories told by the older people in the community, and the stories would be about things that had happened which were not written down. . . . There was a combination of storytelling and physical movement that described actions and activities that had happened in the past; myth about the blue holes in Nassau, myths about animals that live on different islands that no one has actually seen but everyone has a lot of information about. . . . At a certain point you start to understand how some of the stories could be real, how some could morph into myth, and how the hyper-real and the real merge so you don't know the difference between the two. That's why the ice is an interesting material for me.[1]

For seven months prior to the arrival of the ice, Strachan primed the children for their first encounter with polar ice by visiting local schools and reciting tales of global warming and climate change. Through these narratives he introduced the children to the geographic, meteorological, and social repercussions they might expect in their lifetimes. He also reenacted his expedition to the Arctic Circle, describing how he searched for a frozen river and then extracted and transported the multiton chunk they would eventually see. Most essentially, Strachan invoked the sun's almighty power by assigning it the preposterous job of maintaining frigid conditions in the sultry tropics, a prospect that seems as uncanny as the myths and legends his elders had told to him. In this manner, the children received a triple dose of encouragements: the artist proved that great deeds can be accomplished by someone who was once a Bahamian child like themselves, that humans can craft ingenious solutions to problems that seem insurmountable, and that the sun is a powerful ally in these endeavors. When the youngsters finally gazed upon this frozen anomaly, they were fully prepared to perceive evidence of the potential of solar energy to aid them in surviving the challenges that global warming could inflict in their lifetimes. This theme is embodied in the work's title, *The Distance Between What We Have and What We Want* (2006).

Despite the apparent earnestness of Strachan's action, the word *absurd* appears frequently in writings about his work.[2] The artist provides ample opportunities to use it, admitting that he is "preoccupied with the notion of the impossible."[3] He even invokes the term *hyperextension*[4] to acknowledge the absurdity of the expanse traveled by the artist and the ice, the vulnerability and weight of the ice, the investment in fabricating a container for shipment and a freezer for display. All these aspects of the artwork transcend conventional definitions of *reasonable* and even *extreme* and can easily appear absurdly excessive. Because of this, Strachan subjects himself to criticism from environmentalists who demand prudent use of material and energy inputs.

Strachan defends his practice by noting that a hyperextended action is required to convey the illogical fact that the star responsible for tropical heat can also create polar cold. He notes, "Any raw experiment produces some waste. You have to define *waste*. In a classic experiment, there is a goal, an apparatus, and by-products. A lot of art making is a waste of materials and time because it is experimental. I admire waste once the stakes are high enough. The desire and goal is more important than anything else. The material is an in-

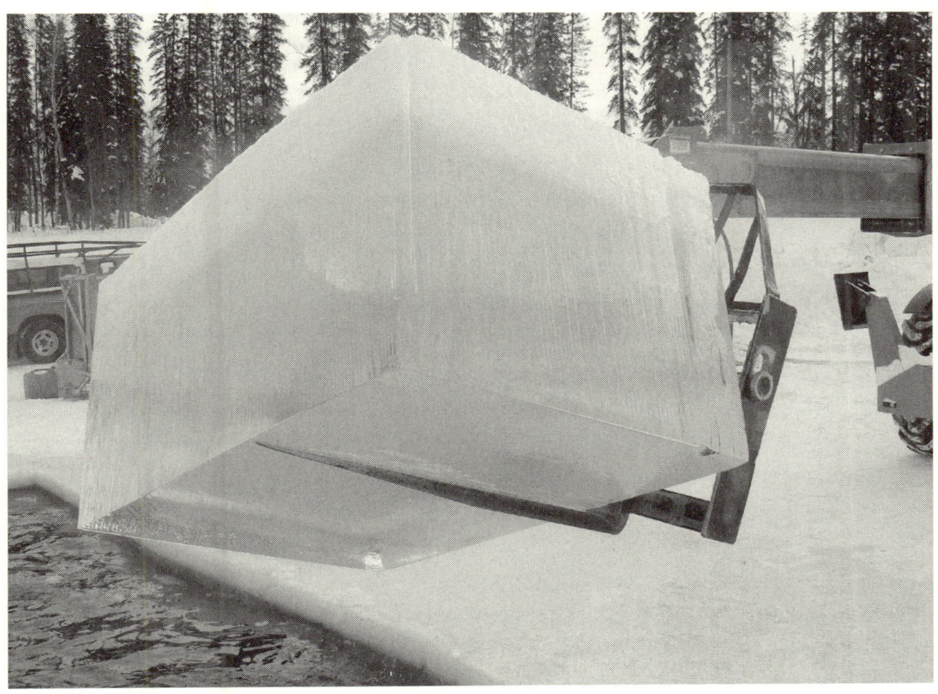

Tavares Strachan | The Distance Between What We Have and What We Want—Arctic ice project | 2004–2006 "Ice Walk," 2004, digital C-print, edition of 5 | Dimensions: 20" × 30"

PHOTO: CHRIS HOOVER / COURTESY TAVARES STRACHAN AND PIEROGI GALLERY, NEW YORK

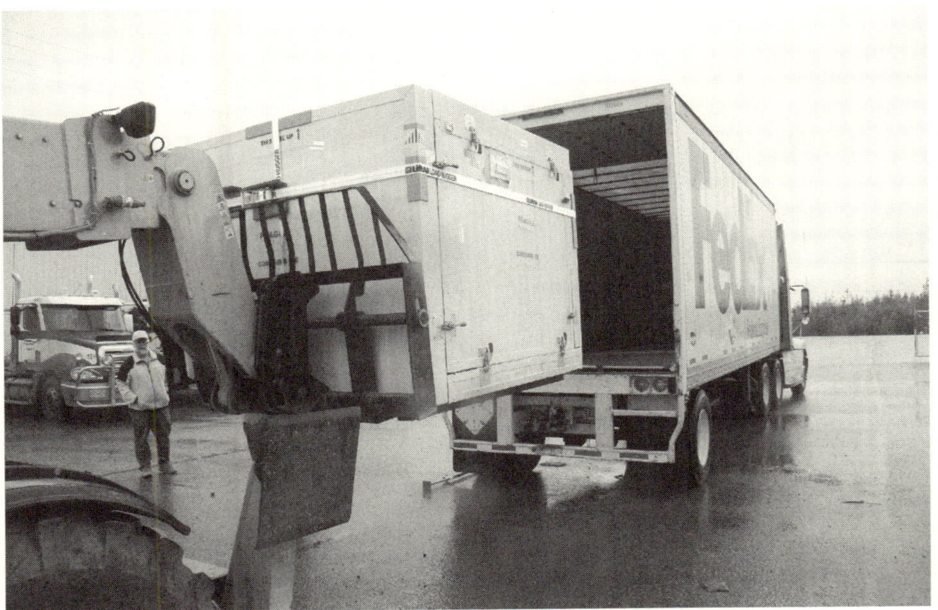

Tavares Strachan | The Distance Between What We Have and What We Want—Arctic Ice Project | 2004–2006 Ice block in transit, 2004

PHOTO: CHRISTOPHE THOMPSON / COURTESY TAVARES STRACHAN AND PIEROGI GALLERY, NEW YORK

nocent bystander of your work. Unusable results are not waste. They are part of the input. We must redefine *waste*. It is all alchemical. Two thousand years ago, the word *waste* didn't exist. Waste is an apocalyptic concept."[5]

The second justification for his extravagance is psychological. The comment "being passive is failure"[6] reveals that Strachan's heroic display of confidence, determination, and courage are essential components of the artwork dedicated to countering the planet's bleak prospects. Thus, besides commemorating the power of solar energy, *The Distance Between* transmits the power of humans to overcome obstacles. Conveying this inspiring message to Bahamian children explains why Strachan installed a flag commemorating Matthew Henson beside the freezer. Henson is an African American explorer who was part of the team that discovered the North Pole. He serves as an inspiring model of heroic achievement.

Strachan changed the flags that accompanied the sculpture when the work was moved to Miami Beach in Florida, as part of the Miami Basel Art Fair, and then to the Brooklyn Museum in New York. In these venues there was one flag that represented Mount McKinley, which is known for its ferocious winds and massive ice-clad peaks that register below-zero temperatures. A second flag represented the Bahamas, whose warm waters and lush foliage are as congenial as Mount McKinley is hostile. In order to dramatize these contrasting regions of the globe, the artist added two fans. One made the Mount McKinley flag flap fiercely. The other caused the Bahamian flag to rustle gently.

The work embodies the interconnectedness of a globe where melting polar ice caps endanger equatorial islands thousands of miles away by raising ocean waters. Climatologists note with alarm that many of these connections do not resemble the simple linking of hands; instead, they ignite at each juncture. Such amplifications of change occur, for example, when the white ice in the Arctic Sea, which reflects the sun's energy and reduces global warming, melts and is replaced by dark water, which absorbs the sun's energy and increases global warming. It is the ice's displacement that highlights the Earth's interdependencies and its associated vulnerabilities.

Thus, the intrepid heroism of the artist/explorer is contrasted with the pathetic victimization of the ice. Dislocated from its normal habitat and ill adapted to its new location, it can only survive if it remains on twenty-four-hour technological "life support" within a steel and glass chamber. As an artwork, the precarious existence of one chunk of ice warns of entire glaciers succumbing to the heedless behaviors of people across the globe. It portends dependence upon "hyperextended" technologies to redeem us from our imprudent deeds. The ice chunk is, simultaneously, a wonder of nature, a strange anomaly, a holy relic, an alarming warning, and a pitiful refugee.

In actuality, contrasting conclusions can be drawn from research studying the potential of solar energy to resolve humanity's challenges. The basic drawback is that generating power from photovoltaic panels costs more than four times as much as coal, and more than twice as much as wind power.[7] Furthermore, the manufacture of photovoltaic cells often requires hazardous materials such as arsenic and cadmium. The limitations of solar take an ironic twist when it is applied to *The Distance Between*. The mission could not have been accomplished without the fossil fuels to power the airplane that transported both the artist to the Arctic and the ice block to the Bahamas, as well as the tools and machines that manufactured the solar panels, the generator, and the freezer. To date, the ice chunk has survived five years in exile from its homeland. It is touring to museums in the United States and Canada as an ambassador negotiating the destiny of solar power.

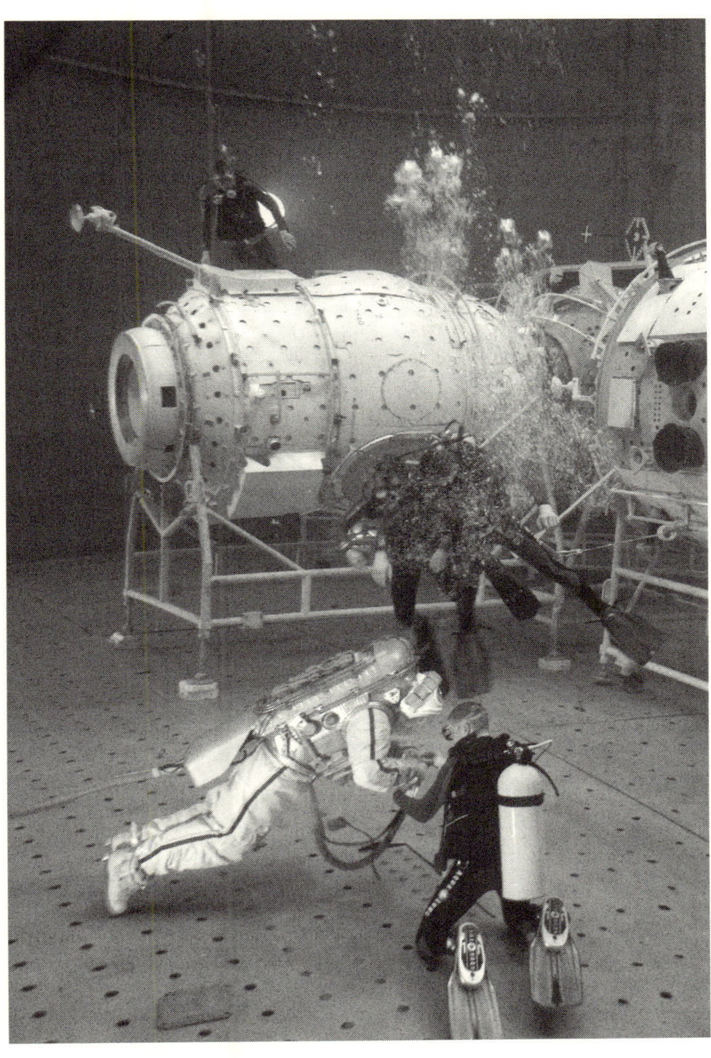

Tavares Strachan | Orthostatic Tolerance: It Might Not Be Such a Bad Idea if I Never Went Home | 2010 The Plunge, digital C-print, edition of 5 | Dimensions: 30" × 20"

PHOTO: GARRETT LYNN / COURTESY TAVARES STRACHAN AND PIEROGI GALLERY, NEW YORK

Strachan's faith in humanity's ability to accommodate impending disruptions of the Earth's systems seems secure. He notes, "As I experienced the freeze of the arctic and survived, the freezer will use heat as a part of its (the ice's) survival. Here, alternate levels of opposites ascribe resilience, as human ability is paralleled by technological adaptation."[8]

In a multiphased work of art entitled *Orthostatic Tolerance: It Might Not Be Such a Bad Idea if I Never Went Home* (2007–ongoing), Strachan engaged his own body in his exploration of adaptability to extremely inhospitable environments. Just as the chunk of Arctic ice tested the limits of Arctic glaciers, he tested the limits of the human body to survive in alien gravity conditions. Orthostatic tolerance is a measure of the body's ability to endure gravitational stress. Strachan prepared for this work of art by testing his orthostatic tolerance during a residency at MIT's Sea Grant College Program's Autonomous Underwater Vehicle Laboratory that involved riding a spinning g-force test bed. While g-tolerance can be developed to some degree through training, it can be severely damaging to organs and connective tissues. When the work was displayed at the MIT List Visual Arts Center in 2010, photos and video showed Strachan riding on the g-force test bed.

Next Strachan pursued orthostatic tolerance training at the Yuri Gagarin Russian State Science Research Cosmonauts Training Center outside Moscow. There he experienced zero g-force, synonymous with weightlessness. In this instance he paralleled the ice block's total dependence upon technology as a lifeline. Documentation of this experience shows him wearing a space suit and climbing around a spacecraft submerged in a giant water tank. Thus Strachan trained to endure perilous environments at both orthostatic limits—the g-force test bed by increasing g-force, and the cosmonaut training by reducing g-force. Both instances manifest "hyperextended" exploits that distinguish Strachan's art career.

In sum, Strachan's proactive stance indicates that he expects major disruptions in world climate and that he believes humanity can avert disaster through adaptation strategies. With crises pending, it may be that our era is ripe for heroic ventures into uncertain physical and technological realms. Strachan describes his bold artistic course: "As an explorer, I engage in systems of energy that never begin or end."[9]

NOTES

1 Tavares Strachan interview with the author, May 11, 2007.

2 Four examples: http://artfever.blogspot.com/2006/12/where-are-we-tavares-strachan.html; http://www.yaledailynews.com/Article.aspx?ArticleID=31542; http://www.boston.com/ae/theater_arts/articles/2010/05/28/tavares_strachan_explores_boundaries_of_sea_and_space_in_list_visual_arts_center_show/; http://gregcookland.com/journal/2010/07/05/tavares-strachan/.

3 Tavares Strachan interview with the author, May 11, 2007.

4 Tavares Strachan, "Conversation with Tavares Strachan and Susan Swenson," San Francisco, November 11, 2006, in *The Distance Between What We Have and What We Want* (New York: Pierogi Gallery and Ronald Feldman Fine Arts, 2006.

5 Tavares Strachan interview with the author, May 11, 2007.

6 Ibid.

7 "Solar Energy," *The New York Times* (updated January 10, 2011). http://www.nytimes.com/info/solar-energy/.

8 Tavares Strachan, "Conversation with Tavares Strachan and Susan Swenson," San Francisco, November 11, 2006 in *The Distance Between What We Have and What We Want* (New York: Pierogi Gallery and Ronald Feldman Fine Arts, 2006.

9 Tavares Strachan, "Proposal for *The Orthostatic Tolerance* 2007." http://grandarts.com/downloads/TavaresPressRelease.pdf.

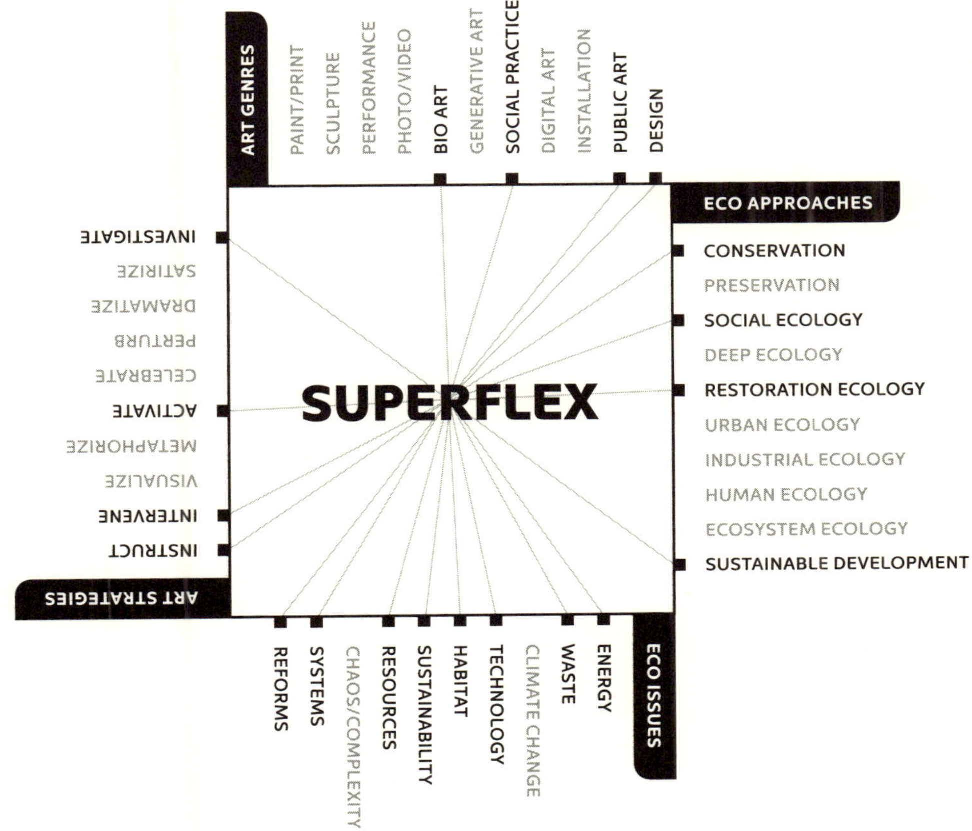

Toolbox for Social Justice

Group formed 1993
Jakob Fenger born 1968, Odder, Denmark
Rasmus Nielsen born 1969, Denmark
Bjørnstjerne Christiansen born 1969, Denmark

IT IS NOT ALWAYS ADMIRABLE TO BE SUPER. While you might be super fine, a superstar, or a superpower, you might also be supercilious, superficial, and superfluous. Alternatively, you could be a member of SUPERFLEX, a three-artist collaborative group whose name reveals its intention to remain "super flexible" about the collaborators, mediums, topics, locations, and forms of interaction it chooses to engage. It is strict, however, regarding its social mission. SUPERFLEX empowers those who are powerless. In both projects presented in this chapter, SUPERFLEX supports people who were suffering from corporate takeover. One instance restrains corporate abuse. The other reverses corporate neglect. The first entails generating economic opportunity and democratic representation. The other demands inventing, marketing, and distributing a self-empowering product. Both strategies enhance the well-being of human populations and the resilience of their ecosystems.

By resisting the power of supersized businesses, the group's renegade tactics activate a recent addition to the progressive integration of art and life that was initiated in the early years of the twentieth century. Basically the art/life interface evolved from collage (constructed out of flat found materials and observed like a painting) to assemblage (composed of three-dimensional found objects and/or constructed elements and observed like a sculpture) to installation (a three-dimensional art environment that the audience enters) to happenings and performance art (events incorporating space and time that replace objects). SUPERFLEX exemplifies social practice art by adding functional engagement to the activities that actually sustain human populations and their habitats in space and time.

An example of the group's pragmatic problem-solving art involved poor guaraná farmers in the Brazilian Amazon. Guaraná is a berry native to the Amazon basin, where it has long been cultivated as a caffeine-packed, energy-boosting drink. Multinational corporations like Pepsi and Coca-Cola infiltrated the locale in the late 1990s to win back the market shares they were losing to guaraná drinkers. Their manipulations caused the price the farmers received for their product to plummet from $25 per kilo to $4 per kilo in just four years.

Jakob Fenger, a member of SUPERFLEX, recalls, "In 2001 we were in Brazil. Somehow, by accident, we ran into farmers who told us about their struggle. The farmers were angry not only because the price for guaraná was dropping but because the corporations were stealing their identity by using their city, Maués, in their advertisements. The guaraná plant is so deeply ingrained in the culture of the region that its arrival on Earth is the subject of an elaborate myth among the Guarani tribe. In it, the guaraná plant is honored with divine origin."[1]

International beverage companies were more interested in profits than divinity and cultural heritage. Coca-Cola, for example, invested millions to boost the output of berries. Their tactics included genetically altering the plant to increase productivity.[2] Profitability also led these companies to disrupt the family-based guaraná agricultural practice despite the fact that its sustainable methods had preserved the rain forest ecosystem and the people occupying it for centuries.[3] Family-based processing of the guaraná seeds could not compete with industrial mass production of the carbonated guaraná soft drinks.

Guaraná Power (2003 and ongoing) was launched when the artists conspired with the farmers to devise a counterattack. The artists contributed the motivation and the start-up money they raised through their art world contacts. The farmers contributed knowledge of traditional agricultural techniques. Together they hatched a mischievous plan to recoup the farmers' lost wages and their stolen identity and to correct the power imbalance between local guaraná farmers and corporate giants. Their strategy involved establishing an independent soda bottling plant and then copying the sophisticated marketing methods and the logo the corporations devised to promote their competing beverage. Fenger comments, "When we came back to Denmark, we found that the big corporations were selling the Brazilian drink in cafes. So we copied everything they did to promote their drink. They sponsored a concert; we sponsored a concert. They produced a T-shirt; we did the same. It comes down to a struggle of identity."[4]

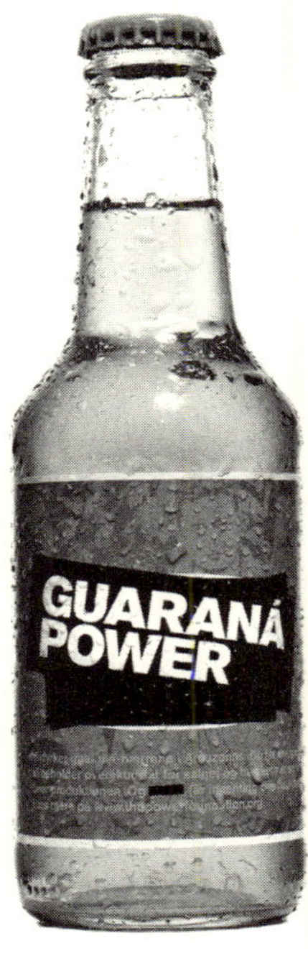

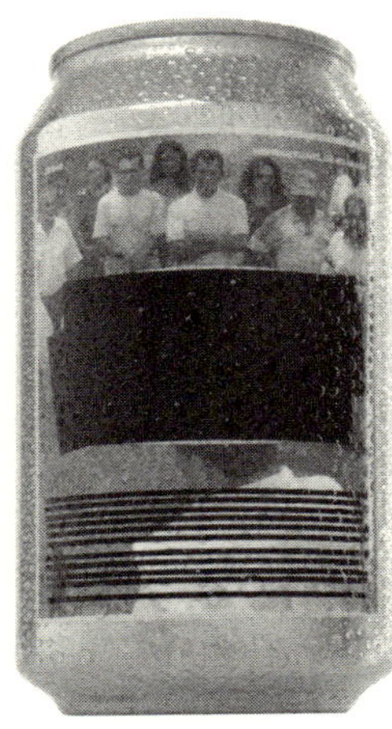

(far left) SUPERFLEX | Rasmus Nielsen, Jakob Fenger, and Bjørnstjerne Christiansen | Guaraná Power (bottle) | 2003–present Soft drink made of guaraná, a caffeine-rich berry

COURTESY SUPERFLEX AND THE PETER BLUM GALLERY, NEW YORK

(left) SUPERFLEX | Rasmus Nielsen, Jakob Fenger, and Bjørnstjerne Christiansen | Guaraná Power (can) | 2003–present Soft drink made of guaraná, a caffeine-rich berry

COURTESY SUPERFLEX AND THE PETER BLUM GALLERY, NEW YORK

Even the design of the corporate advertisement for the beverage was appropriated, but the content and imagery were altered to market the beverage's appeal as a product manufactured by small family farms, not a corporate giant. For example, the anonymous model and the anonymous text used by the corporation were replaced by an indigenous guaraná farmer who was identified by his real name, profession, and location. He mocked corporate sales tactics by relaying a fantastic story that greatly exaggerated the benefits of his product. The *Guaraná Power* text on the advertisement read, "A cowboy at a farm. This cowboy was trying to catch a bull but didn't know how to do it. Meanwhile the bull starts running towards him. The cowboy quickly opens a bottle of Guaraná Power and drinks it. When the bull is about to poke him the cowboy grabs the bull by the horns and throws it on the ground. All because he drank Guaraná Power. It's really delicious."

Fenger sums up the riveting series of events that ensued from their joint campaign: "The farmers were fed up with the company using their identity for this other soft drink. We stole it back. Then the corporation sued us. We showed that if we could not use their logo, they couldn't use the name of the farmers' city."[5] In the end, the farmers succumbed to corporate pressure by designing a new logo. However, they retained their defiant stance by exposing this example of corporate bullying. This tactic involved the insolent act of slapping the new drink sticker directly over the corporate label in a manner that deliberately revealed that a label switch had occurred, thereby exposing an act of corporate intimidation.

While the advertisement promises that Guaraná Power invigorates the people who drink it, SUPERFLEX also ensures that *Guaraná Power* vitalizes farmers, local economies, and ecosystems. The artists admit that this lofty goal is not yet fully accomplished. The corporations are growing stronger through mergers. Still, the farmers are doing better because the price for the guaraná berries has gone up. Fenger says modestly, "We don't know if we can take some of the credit."[6]

Guaraná Power provides one example of the manner in which SUPERFLEX produces opportunities for others to be creative and assertive, which is why the group refers to its art output not as objects, which embody past actions and past accomplishment, but as tools that improve conditions and inspire creativity. Thus SUPERFLEX's tools do not resemble a band saw that is used according to step-by-step instructions to fill a specific task. The group's special tool kit is designed to establish "conditions for the production of new ways of thinking, acting, speaking and imagining."[7] As described in a 295-page book produced by the artists,[8] the tools facilitate three phases of creative processes that the artists identify according to their signature color scheme.[9] They manifest how far SUPERFLEX digresses from art that is materially and temporally finite:

1. White phase: Research. Set up budget, time schedule, vision, and design strategy.
2. Orange phase: Innovate. Experiment with different ideas. Test them.
3. Black phase: Production. Implementation. Plan further development.

These tools provided electrical energy to poor rural communities around the equator in a project entitled *SUPERGAS* (1996–ongoing). Because the villages exist beyond the reach of the energy grid, people depend upon firewood to supply their energy. This depletes forests, causing erosion and exhausting soils. SUPERFLEX's flexible thinking revealed the connection between the environmental degradation and the human poverty that is rampant throughout the region. The artists recognized that villagers are both agents and victims of deforestation, poverty, and poor health. SUPERFLEX comments, "The fact that the main energy supply is firewood can be seen as a lack of innovation instead of just a lack of firewood. . . . *SUPERGAS* addresses this problem."[10]

SUPERGAS is the creative solution that emerged from applying SUPERFLEX tools to this problem. It is a simple biogas unit the artists designed and are constructing in collaboration with Danish and African engineers. Their goal was to confer energy self-sufficiency on poor families—enough energy to meet their cooking and illumination requirements. The units rely upon renewable and nonpolluting sources of energy derived from animal dung, human waste, and sunlight. This alternative energy supply provides numerous benefits. Erosion decreases because trees are allowed to root; water contamination diminishes because human and animal wastes are managed as productive resources; food production increases due to the super potent compost produced by the biogas plants; health improves.

The unit that they developed is small (it can be transported on a bicycle), manageable (it can be installed on site), and inexpensive (prices range from US$100 to US$1,700). The product was launched in Tanzania and subsequently expanded into Cambodia, Thailand, and Zanzibar.

The pragmatic components of this project introduce innovative variations on standard business models:

- Organization: SUPERFLEX reverses the energy industry's top-down, centrally-owned-and-operated standard by allocating ownership, management, and output of the energy-producing mechanisms directly to the individual households. This organizational scheme shifts power from corporations and financiers to the people.
- Social service: SUPERFLEX rejects charity, believing that self-help schemes are more likely to succeed if their owners pay for them. Commerce empow-

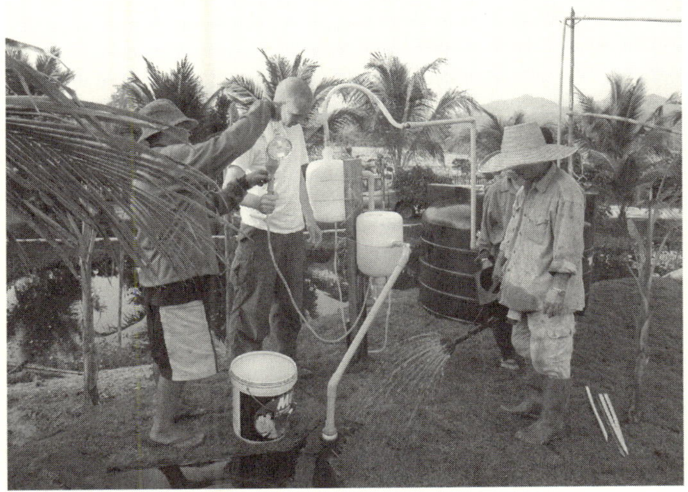

SUPERFLEX | Rasmus Nielsen, Jakob Fenger, and Bjørnstjerne Christiansen with Jan Mallan | SUPERGAS | 1996–present
Installation photo from "The Land" in Chaing Mai, Thailand | Biogas system running on organic materials | Dimensions: variable

PHOTO: SUPERFLEX / COURTESY SUPERFLEX AND PETER BLUM GALLERY, NEW YORK

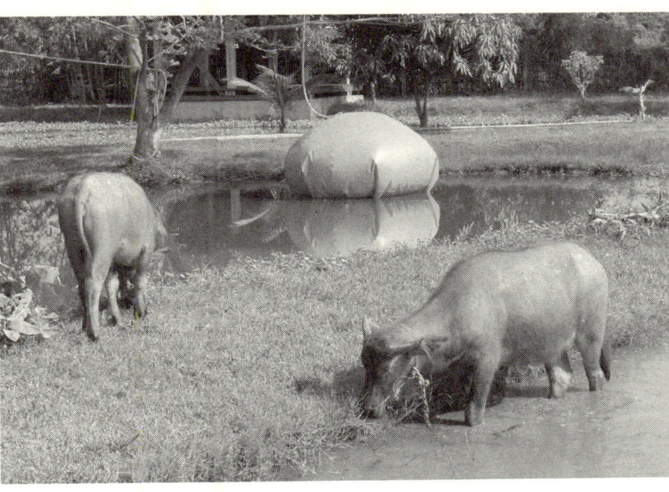

SUPERFLEX | Rasmus Nielsen, Jakob Fenger, and Bjørnstjerne Christiansen with Jan Mallan | SUPERGAS | 1996–present
Installation photo from "The Land" in Chaing Mai, Thailand | Biogas system running on organic materials | Dimensions: variable

PHOTO: SUPERFLEX / COURTESY SUPERFLEX AND PETER BLUM GALLERY, NEW YORK

ers people more than gifts. SUPERFLEX compares acquiring a biogas unit to "a Western family buying a car."[11]

- Economics: SUPERGAS works as an actual business designed to mass-produce user-friendly biogas units. Funds were raised by selling shares in the company. SUPERFLEX also invited Surude (Sustainable Rural Development) to participate in the project. This Tanzanian NGO stimulates the economies of undeveloped countries through the use of renewable natural resources.

Art asserted itself into these pragmatic considerations by replacing "art for art's sake" with "art as a service industry." Then it added the project's aesthetic and psychological components:

- Marketing: Biogas units fulfill the unglamorous functions of a furnace, oil tank, septic tank, and sewage treatment plant all at once. SUPERFLEX gave these disagreeable apparatuses commercial appeal by painting each unit a dazzlingly bright orange color, emblazoning it with a stylish logo, and encouraging customers to install the units conspicuously in the front of their homes as status symbols. Nielsen explains, "We like the fact that although these are basically shit containers, there's an aesthetic element. It can be low-scale cheap technology, but it doesn't have to look like shit."[12]

- Psychology: Superflexible thinking was required to win the trust of villagers who were naturally suspicious of foreigners. Thus, SUPERFLEX had to distinguish themselves from corporate executives motivated by self-interest, tourists interested in entertainment, and government bureaucrats who are often corrupt. The artists accomplished this by wearing clothes that no executive, tourist, or bureaucrat would wear. They dressed in trustworthy khaki shorts and light-green shirts. Photographs of them introducing themselves to villagers are included in all the gallery installations of this work.
- Promotion: In order to inform villagers of the benefits offered by the biogas units, the artists discarded technical manuals and adopted simple cartoons. One depicts four recognizable villagers gathered in front of a cabin, speaking to each other in the local manner. The man who appears to be the leader announces, "My friends, this is a new century of science and technology. I'm no longer using firewood. I'm using bio-gas."[13]

At the time of this writing, SUPERFLEX was revising the energy-producing unit by basing it on the "IKEA model." Fenger explains, "Do-it-yourself is too hard. Customers are lazy. They want to buy something that already works. We want an 'IKEA' version of energy production. It must be easy to install, easy to use, and affordable."[14]

In all its projects SUPERFLEX channels power from entrepreneurs to consumers, from governments to citizens, and from corporations to workers. Nobody hired them to perform these deeds. They may not receive payment for their efforts. In some cases, they pay to pursue the projects by raising donations, attracting investors, or selling products. In addition, they frequently fund their projects with money from museum commissions, which essentially means that museums invest in them. Furthermore, the profit they seek accrues to the people. These atypical means yield unorthodox results—they aid two unambiguous losers to corporate incursions worldwide: impoverished people recoup control over their lives, and the habitats they occupy are revitalized.

NOTES

1 Jakob Fenger interview with the author, September 17, 2010.
2 Ian E. DeMello, "Guarana Geographic Indicator," TED Case Studies No.780, 2005. http://www1.american.edu/ted/guarana.htm.
3 Ibid.
4 Jakob Fenger interview with the author, September 17, 2010.
5 Ibid.
6 Ibid.
7 Doris Berger, et al., "Introduction," *The SUPERFLEX/Tools Book* (Cologne: Walther Konig, 2002).
8 Doris Berger, et al., *The SUPERFLEX/Tools Book* (Cologne: Walther Konig, 2002).
9 Working Agreement Between Rooseum and SUPERDESIGN. *The SUPERFLEX/Tools Book*, (Cologne: Walther Konig, 2002), 126.
10 SUPERFLEX, "Invitation," SUPERFLEX/Tools/Supergas. http://www.SUPERFLEX.net/tools/supergas/invitation.shtml.
11 Åsa Nacking (Louisiana Museum, Denmark), "An Exchange between Åsa Nacking and SUPERFLEX," 1998. http://superflex.net/texts/an_exchange_between_aasa_nacking_and_superflex/.
12 Glenn Sumi, "SUPERFLEX," *NOW* vol. 24, no. 4 (September 23–29, 2004). http://www.nowtoronto.com/issues/2004-09-23/cover_story.php.
13 Doris Berger, et al., *The SUPERFLEX/Tools Book* (Cologne: Walther Konig, 2002), 24.
14 Jakob Fenger interview with the author, September 17, 2010.

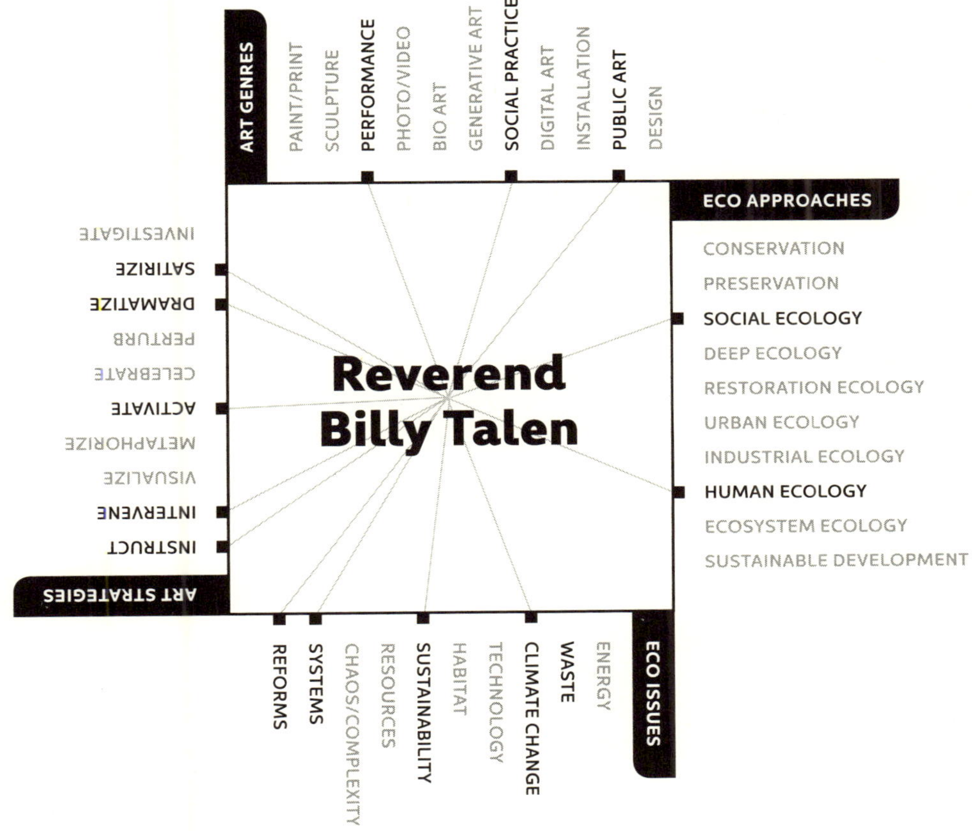

Stop Shopping Gospel

Born 1950, Rochester, Minnesota

WHILE BIOLOGISTS refer to instinctive desires and aversions as *tropisms,* psychologists note that humanity's built-in tropisms can be supplemented with add-ons as we mature. Our impressionable minds are fertile territory for the implantation of new desires that promise us a healthy heart, a satisfying snack, firm abs, stylish shoes, sexual prowess, vacation adventures, and protections against back pain, basement mold, halitosis, dry skin, yellow teeth, constipation, and credit problems. Thus shopping is the accepted means to conduct these diverse seeking and averting behaviors in today's consumer societies.

Billy Talen decries culturally sanctioned shopping compulsions,

"Like crack cocaine or membership in the National Rifle Association, shopping is an annihilating addiction that must be slowed down to be stopped, or flooded with new and different light. . . . The research phase is over. How many times do we have to hear that 7 percent of the world's population is taking a third of the world's resources? How many neighborhoods need to be malled? When will our foreign policy be violent enough to turn our heads?"[1]

Talen assumes the persona of the Reverend Billy, devoting his talents as a performance artist to save human souls and secure ecosystem health by battling against the scourge of rampant material stockpiling and discarding. As a self-appointed evangelical, he evokes the fervor of a Baptist preacher and the authority of religious doctrine to break consumer addictions to shopping. Talen established a church whose name proclaims its holy mission. The *Church of Stop Shopping* is where he delivers exuberant sermons that admonish parishioners to "back away from that silly little product on the shelf"[2] and save their souls.

These high-spirited pronouncements are punctuated with exclamations of "Hallelujah!" and "Praise be to God!" and "Amen!" Invariably, as Talen's zeal builds, sweat trickles down his radiant face, soaking the ecclesiastical collar he wears with his polyester leisure suit. Meanwhile his Elvis-like pompadour hair bops across his forehead as he gazes upward to invoke heaven and scowls downward to evoke hell.

Talen augments his supplications and admonishments with the surging gospel harmonies of the Stop Shopping Choir. Golden-robed members comprise a cross-cultural array of born-again, stop-shopping converts, enabling every member of the audience/congregation to identify with at least one born-again saver. The singers make no attempt to contain the joys of unmaterialism. They don't merely raise their voices on high. They jump. They cheer. They wave their hands. The audience typically joins them.

The contagion of Talen's vision of paradise—an idyllic setting untainted by credit card debt, two-income households, and sidewalks heaped with black plastic garbage bags—is delivered at the epicenters of conspicuous consumption where shopping sinners congregate. Although Reverend Billy sometimes preaches in museums, theaters, and universities, he and his band of faithful followers spread the word most effectively at Starbucks, the Disney Store, GAP, Walmart, Barnes & Noble, and Nike. Talen explains:

> We try many strategies. Enacting a purchase in a formal church ritual on Sunday or acting out a comic version of being born again might help those parishioners when they are cornered in Temptation Mall. Sweatshops are truly shocking, and I've seen the sheer force of the information stop a shopper. We make dramas, we sing and shout, and chain ourselves to Mickey Mouse. We are desperate to access the bright and unclaimed space that the corporations must desperately hide.[3]

Talen initiated his crusade in 1996 by presenting solo performance-artist events preaching against consumerism on the sidewalks of Times Square. Now his performances include a forty-person choir and a five-person band. Together they have produced two CDs, three documentary films (*Preacher with an Unknown God, Reverend Billy and the Church of Stop Shopping,* and *What Would Jesus Buy?*), two books (*What Should I Do if Reverend Billy Is in My Store* and *What Would Jesus Buy?*), and eight 28-minute television shows (*The Last Televangelist*). Talen has been a guest on *The Today Show, CBS Evening News, Nightline,* Fox News, Al-Jazeera, *Glenn Beck, Hannity & Colmes, Democracy Now,* NPR's *All Things Considered* and *Marketplace, The Geraldo Rivera Show,* CNN, *The Tavis Smiley Show,* the BBC World Service, BBC 1, and more.

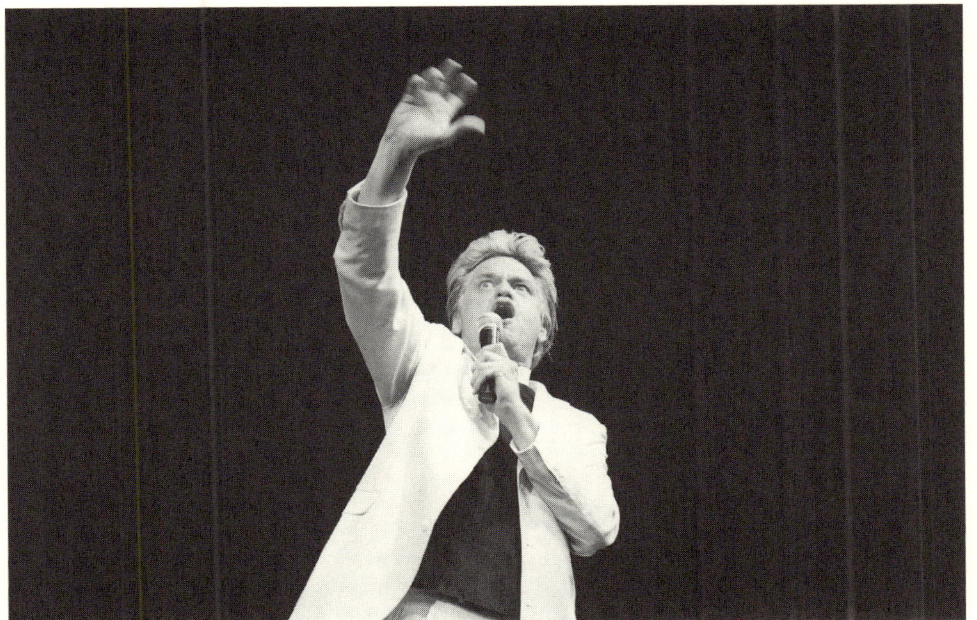

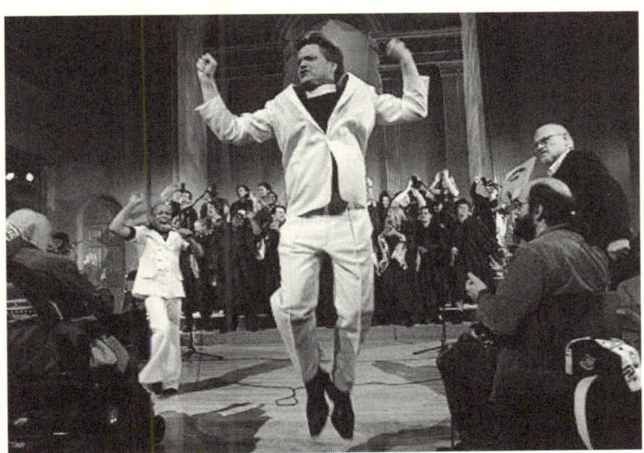

Reverend Billy Talen | Church of Earthalujah | June 19, 2011

PHOTO: ALVARO CORZO / COURTESY REVEREND BILLY TALEN

Reverend Billy Talen | Church of Stop Shopping | March 2005 St. Mark's Church, New York

COURTESY REVEREND BILLY TALEN

The Church of Stop Shopping is particularly known for staging in-store "spat theater" in which choir members pose as customers and pretend to argue about the ethics of consumption. On one occasion a choir member shouted sarcastically, "We need more Starbucks; one on every corner, one in every home, one in every mind!! Give the shareholders their value!!! Expand!!! Expand!!"[4] Another time the choir spent an entire day at a Walmart store defying consumer norms by pushing empty shopping carts up and down the aisles. The church also orchestrates revival meetings in malls to proclaim the joys of nonconsumerism and to advocate for a new national holiday—Buy Nothing Day. All of these events typically culminate in the choir's spirited rendition of the "Stop Shopping! Stop Shopping!" hymn.[5]

Experiencing Reverend Billy in theater settings is no less culturally sacrilegious. The choir typically goes among the people in the audience, shaming them by placing duct tape over their Nike swooshes, Levi's tags, and other evidence of conspicuous consumerism. At the end of his preaching the Reverend sometimes beckons the entire audience to follow him to a corporate outpost, like a local Chevron station, to protest its desecration of the environment and the exploitation of workers. In all these ways the people are sanctified with a reverse-merchandising theology.

Exorcisms, however, may top the list of culturally subversive actions by the *Church of Stop Shopping*. They are conducted upon such iconic symbols of sinful consumption as cash registers and credit cards. On one occasion, the Reverend placed a sleek new Sunbeam toaster on an altar. It was as enticing as a Mercedes coupe. Talen reports that a young man named Jonah walked up and willingly submitted to the rite of exorcism to release him from his addiction to shiny new appliances. The Reverend's essay "Shopper, Repent!"[6] is a vivid account of this event. It also provides a sampling of the persuasive techniques employed by the *Church of Stop Shopping*, which include, ironically, the same techniques used by advertisers, public relations specialists, politicians, religious leaders, educators, and other influence-peddlers. Talen summons them to promote an odd product—consumer restraint. The following quotes are revealing:

- **Modeling the success of the product:** "As Jonah reached for the product we prayed hard. The choir hummed and the deacons moved forward to lay hands on the craven consumer as the devil pulled the young man's begging fingers toward the toaster. . . . But wait! Jonah's hand hesitated, and then pulling out of that force field, it flew back and wavered there in the air. Jonah stared, in shock, at his released fingers."
- **Displaying the emotional rewards of accepting the product:** "Then he (Jonah) ran around the church as if proving to a Pentecostal TV audience that now he could walk. Held aloft by the preacher, his hand was shaking with new freedom, unburdened. The Stop Shopping Gospel Choir was swaying with the power of a receiptless God-Goddess that surpasseth all valuation. The object looked cheated, cuckolded. Finally the Sunbeam deluxe toaster was just fucking junk."
- **Presenting warnings associated with use of the product:** "Not buying is a brave thing to do. At first it may induce vertigo, identity weirdness, and a desire for an unwanted pregnancy, but most often a new believer will have an abnormal kitsch-acquisition fit. The first response to the break in buying may be a huge sucking sound in your hands—you want to buy something, anything. You are headed for a relapse, a spree."
- **Proclaiming status gained from the product:** "In the Church of Stop Shopping we believe that buying is not nearly as interesting as not-buying. When you back away from the purchase, the product may look up at you with wanton eyes, but it will slump quickly back onto the shelf and sit there trying to get a life. The product needs you more than you need it—remember that."
- **Assuring that the product avoids something undesirable:** "Those who organize defenses against the Unknown (such as religious fundamentalists and consumer fundamentalists) foment numbness, hatred, and war. Unfortunately, they have perfected their imitation of ordinary living, and that comes to us as the comforting ghost gesture of shopping."

In 2004 this radical posture took the form of an improvised theater piece at the Northridge, California, Starbucks. As a result, Talen spent forty hours in jail because a jury found him guilty of trespassing with intent to interfere with business. Later, he was legally enjoined from coming within 250 yards of any of the 1,500 Starbucks stores in the state of California. The injunction reads, "The defendant shall not annoy, harass, strike, threaten, sexually assault, batter, stalk, destroy personal property of, or otherwise disturb the peace of the . . . Starbucks Corporation." Evidently it is illegal to not shop in America.

Talen did not drop the Reverend persona when he ran for mayor of New York City on the Green Party ticket in 2010. Hurdles were significant since success required appealing to voters who make purchases to express affection (gifts), honor national holidays (sales), construct memories (souvenirs), and compensate for disappointments (self-gifting).

The environment, because it bears the brunt of manufacture, consumption, and disposal, is treated to his thoughtful commentary. Sarcasm is absent when he states,

> Climate change is the impetus for the most basic aspect of our work: that shopping can no longer be a way of life. The physical systems of the earth cannot support a consumer-based, distribution economy for all its inhabitants; we as individuals cannot wait for big government solutions or technological advances. We must practice sustainable consumption in our everyday lives and dedicate ourselves to spreading the skills and resources to others for as long as it takes. . . . We maintain that consuming less is the single most effective and immediate step an individual can take toward halting the climate crisis.[7]

Talen discarded histrionics to offer some encouraging words to artists: "This is an exciting time for the arts. It is as if the world is insisting that the arts take their responsibility in the community and the nation and the world. There was a time when the arts could simply hide behind their art forms and their prestigious institutions—not now. We have an emergency that is graphically visited on our senses every day."[8]

In December 2010, the Reverend sent an email to the author, updating his mission because high unemployment was preventing consumerism. He said, "The name of the enterprise was changed at the beginning of the recession (or Shopocalypse) to The Church of Life After Shopping, and the choir is now the Life After Shopping Gospel Choir. We're looking for that promised land after the consumerism ends."[9]

This chapter concludes with the Reverend's advice that applies universally: "Make love so energetically that you stop buying things. It is difficult to swipe a credit card while experiencing an orgasm."[10]

NOTES

1 Rev. Billy Talen, "Shopper, Repent!" *The Society of Mutual Autopsy.* http://www.somareview.com/revbilly.cfm.

2 Rev. Billy Talen, "AHN Interview: Bill Talen, Artist and Activist," Arts and Healing Network, February 2004. http://www.artheals.org/news_2005/apr05.html.

3 Rev. Billy Talen, "Shopper, Repent!" *The Society of Mutual Autopsy.* http://www.somareview.com/revbilly.cfm.

4 Rev. Billy Talen, "Reverend Billy's Starbucks Invasion," INeedCoffee.com. http://www.ineedcoffee.com/02/revbilly/?page=2.

5 These events have been created in collaboration with Savitri D, who is referred to as the director of the performances.

6 Rev. Billy Talen, "Shopper, Repent!" *The Society of Mutual Autopsy.* http://www.somareview.com/revbilly.cfm.

7 "About Us," Reverend Billy—the Church of Stop Shopping. http://www.revbilly.com/about-us.

8 Rev. Billy Talen, "AHN Interview: Bill Talen, Artist and Activist," Arts and Healing Network, February 2004. http://www.artheals.org/news_2005/apr05.html.

9 Rev. Billy Talen e-mail to the author, December 4, 2010.

10 Ibid.

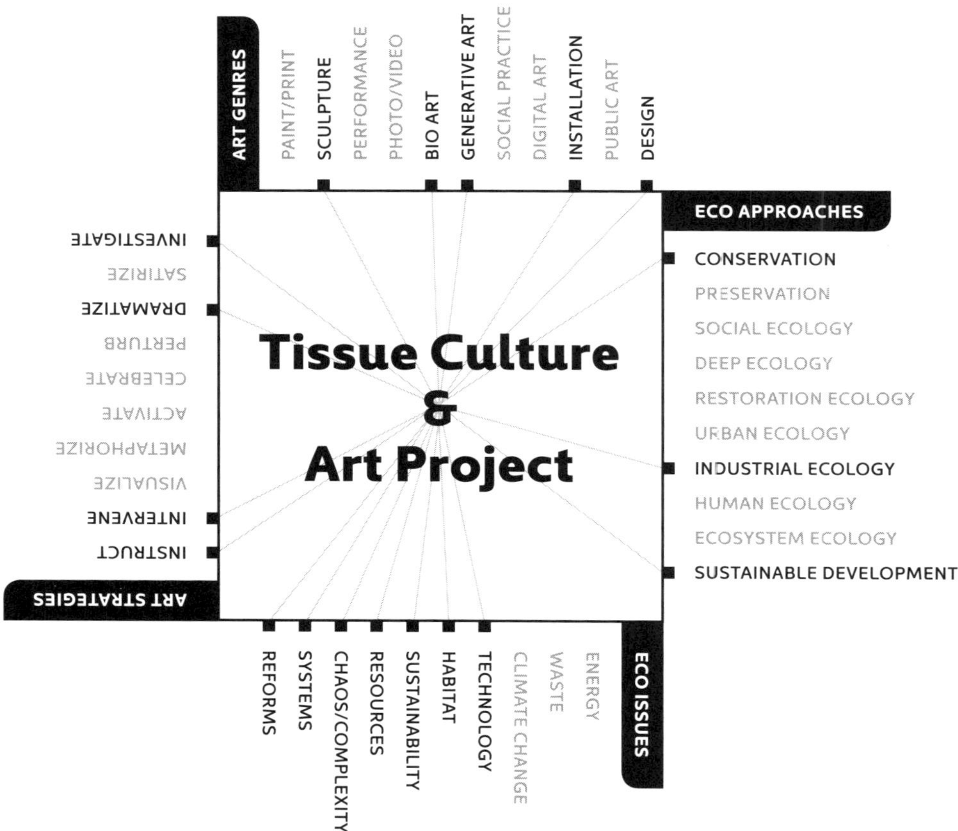

Victimless Leather and Meat

Oron Catts born 1967, Helsinki, Finland
Ionat Zurr born 1970, London, England

"**MUSEUM KILLS LIVE EXHIBIT**" appeared as a headline in the *New York Times*.[1] The accompanying story described a dubious work of art installed at the Museum of Modern Art in Manhattan that consisted of living cells extracted from a mouse. Until the decision was made to terminate them, the cells were kept alive in an incubator and fed a regimen of nutrients. However, as one curator explains, "The cells were multiplying so fast that the incubator was beginning to clog."[2] Thus, the nutrients were withdrawn so the cells would starve to death.

Oron Catts and Ionat Zurr anticipated a different outcome. The artwork was designed to produce a very special kind of leather. Instead of being tanned, cut, and sewn, this leather would grow directly from a culture of mouse stem cells that gradually multiplied, forming a layer of tissue that would resemble leather. The biodegradable polymer structure on which the mouse cells reproduced was shaped like a tiny coat. The cells and the framework were situated inside a bioreactor that acted as a surrogate for the living body. The artists named this artwork *Victimless Leather* (2008) because no animal would be slaughtered to acquire the leather to make this coat. If it had grown to completion, the tiny coat would have been the perfect size for the donor mouse to wear.

While *Victimless Leather* was motivated by the desire to devise a nonviolent, nonwasteful, and nonexploitative alternative to raising and killing animals, it embroiled the curators in an ethical predicament surrounding the murder of a work of art. Pulling the plug was not included in their curatorial training. The controversy that ensued facilitated the artists' mission by drawing attention to the material components of clothing. This garment was not made of a chemically contrived substance like nylon, polyester, and GORE-TEX, nor was it a by-product of living organisms like silk, cotton, and linen. The artists referred to it as "semi-living." It was living because it grew but only semi-living because it could exist only in a petri dish and it demanded constant high-tech caregiving.

While fabricating leather garments in this manner may seem like a flight of the imagination, Catts and Zurr pursue such projects within the rigorous settings of scientific laboratories. After adopting the name Tissue Culture & Art Project (TC&A) in 1996, they founded SymbioticA, the first bio art research laboratory dedicated to artistic investigation of all aspects of life sciences and biomedical technologies. Currently SymbioticA hosts TC&A's research projects as well as those being conducted by over seventy other research residents. This art studio/lab is situated in the School of Anatomy and Human Biology at the University of Western Australia in Perth. It is jointly funded by the University of Western Australia and the Government of Western Australia's Department of Culture and the Arts. SymbioticA welcomes undergraduate and postgraduate students, artists, and scholars from all disciplines to join its interdisciplinary research teams.

Tissue culturing is prominent in SymbioticA's research portfolio. The artists describe this adventuresome frontier with the fervor of a bio art manifesto: "Artists must immerse themselves in the dialectics of new knowledge and technologies. They must adopt not just a representational approach but what we refer to as 'wet engagement.' Hence, artists researching and exploring the role of biotechnology in society can and should engage with the actual technologies and get their hands wet and dirty."[3] Wet biology is distinguished from scientific experimentation that relies upon simulations and computer analysis. Thus, there is nothing metaphorical or illusory about this artistic enterprise. Research involving wet biology practices places the artists in the midst of one of the most fiercely contested issues of our time.

Although this work of art needed to be terminated like a dreaded Frankenstein, Catts and Zurr do not view the project as a failure. Within the scientific context, the experiment yielded valuable information about tissue cultivation. Within the art context, the discussion generated by shutting down the exhibit drew attention to the cultural significance of *Victimless Leather*. The implications extend far beyond fashion because they are relevant to all forms of manufacturing. The artists explain, "Changing the culture of production from manufacturing to growing . . . could reduce the environmental problems associated with the process of manufacturing. The relationships that consumers will form with these semi-living products will be different from the relationships they have with inanimate products.

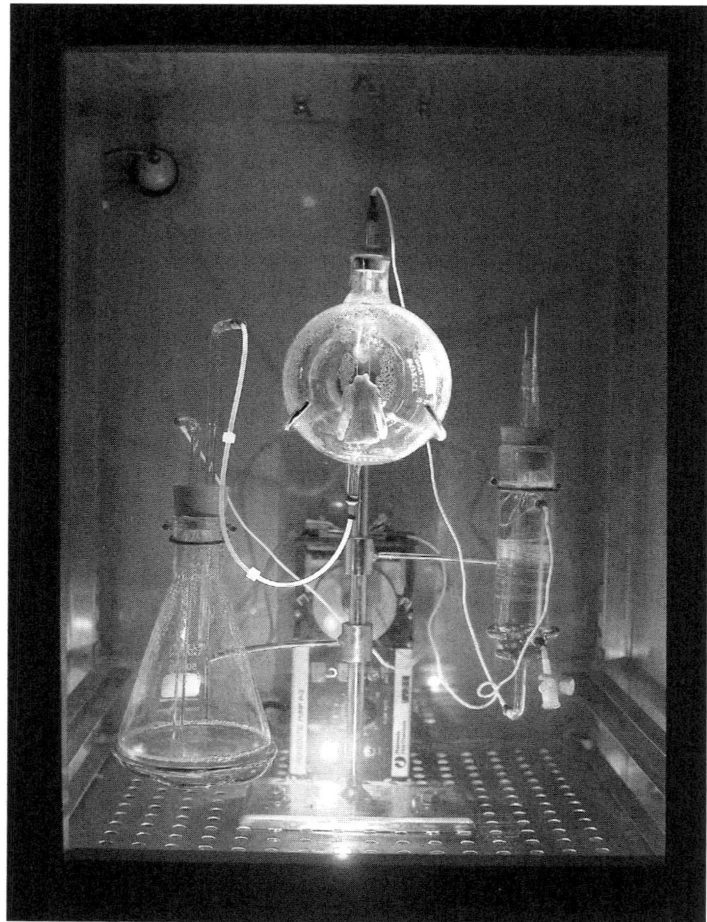

Tissue Culture & Art Project | Oron Catts and Ionat Zurr | Victimless Leather | 2004 Prototype of a stitchless jacket grown in a technosc entific body | Biodegradable polymer connective, bone cells, custom-made perfusion pump

COURTESY THE TISSUE CULTURE & ART PROJECT

This can reduce the amount of waste; moving from a throw away culture into a more caring one."[4] Thus, the moral impact of victimless leather is not confined to clothing. The ethical implications of all resource use by humans, whether or not they are living, and whether or not they are manipulated, are foregrounded. The artists assert that the "actualized possibility of wearing 'leather' without killing an animal is offered as a starting point for cultural discussion."[5] Zurr notes that logic was often missing from these discussions: "People were disturbed by our ethics of using living cells to grow living fabric, while the use of leather obtained from animals seems to be accepted without any concern for the well-being of the animals from which the skin has been removed."[6]

Besides producing leather, tissue culturing can replace meat production, an even more essential resource provided by animals and one that is laden with ethical and ecological dilemmas. In order to understand the severity of problems associated with meat production, consider that the human population on Earth is currently estimated at seven billion. While this number may seem staggering, it is meager compared with the fifty-six billion land animals currently being reared and slaughtered for human consumption annually.[7]

This lopsided equation equals an environmental calamity. Farm animals impose the same drains and strains on ecosystems as people because they consume food and water, require shelter and transportation, and produce solid, liquid, and gaseous wastes.[8] Vast quantities of energy are consumed to plow, irrigate, harvest, mill, and ship their food, remove their waste, and transport their bodies. Furthermore, fences that confine livestock obstruct the ability of wildlife to forage, migrate, and mate; hooves trample vegetation and compact the soil; grazing can ravish indigenous plants. The ultimate absurdity, however, involves the following statistic: it takes up to sixteen pounds of grain[9] and five thousand gallons of water[10] to produce one pound of meat. How will eight billion hungry people satisfy their protein requirements in the near future? Only two solutions seem viable. Either people learn to eat low on the food chain by concentrating on vegetables, or they consume "victimless meat."

Disembodied Cuisine (2003) is a work by TC&A that tackled the problem of raising meat "on the hoof" by taking biopsies of living tissue from the muscle of living frogs. The frogs' cells were inserted into a fully functioning tissue culture laboratory that the artists installed as part of the "L'art Biotec" exhibition in Nantes, France. The "micro-gravity bioreactor" was outfitted with a sterile hood, incubator, microscope, and a sophisticated monitoring system that simulates the conditions of the body of the frog from which the cells and tissue were derived. The installation was, in other words, an artificial womb containing a nutrient medium to keep the cells alive and multiplying.

The meat produced in this artwork progressed directly from frog cells to edible frog steak, bypassing the tedious development from a frog embryo, to tadpole, to an adult with

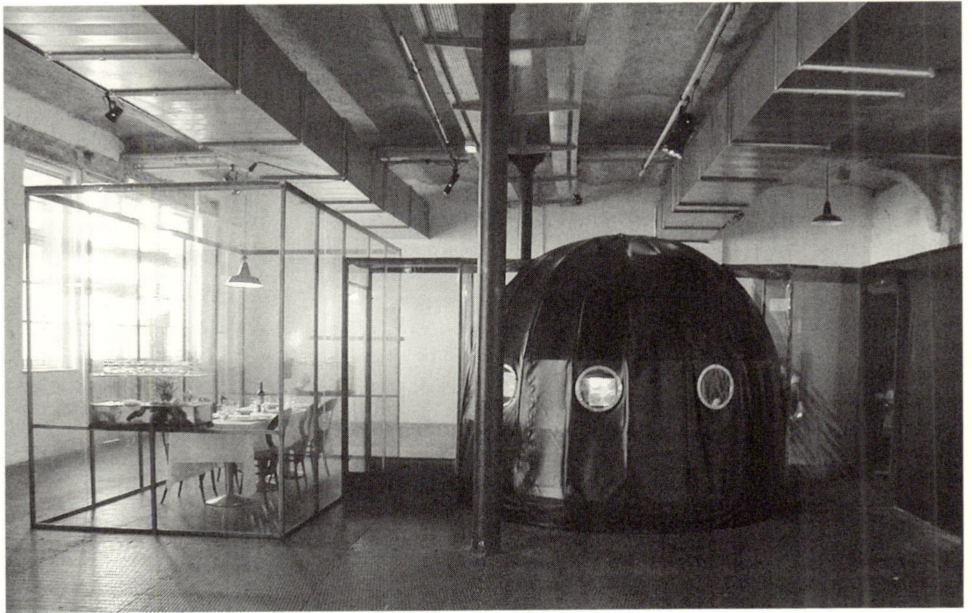

Tissue Culture & Art Project | Oron Catts and Ionat Zurr with Guy Ben-Ary | Disembodied Cuisine installation | 2003 Mixed media | Dimensions: variable | Duration of exhibition: three months

PHOTO: AXEL HEISE / COURTESY THE TISSUE CULTURE & ART PROJECT

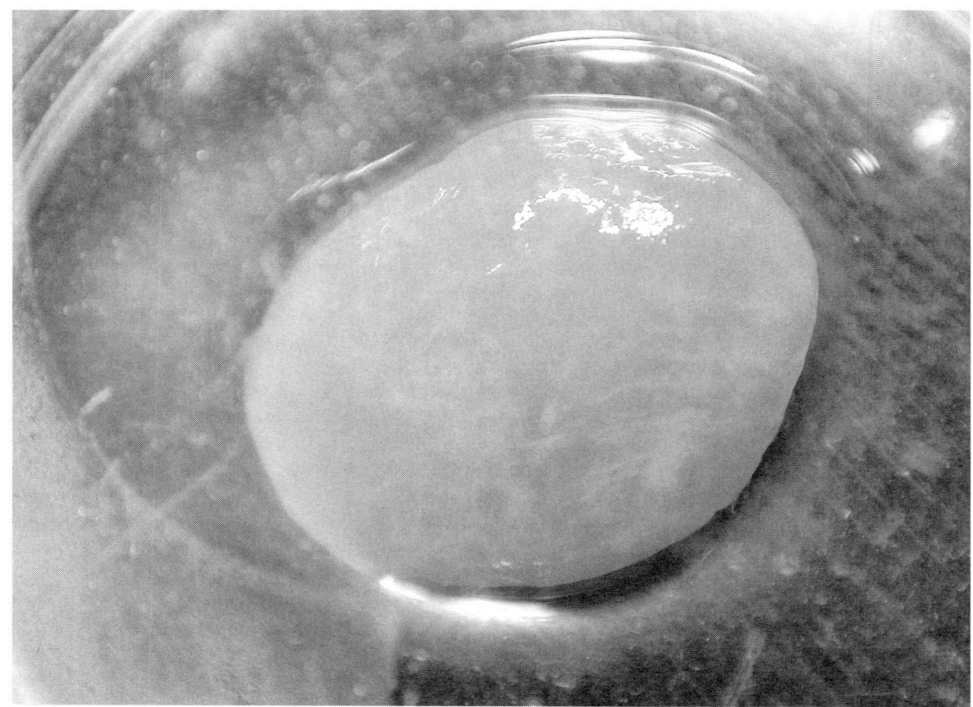

Tissue Culture & Art Project | Oron Catts and Ionat Zurr | Untitled (from the Semi-Living Steak Project) | 2000–2001 Tissue Engineering and Organ Fabrication Laboratory, MGH, Harvard Medical School | Prenatal sheep skeletal muscle, degradable PGA polymer scaffold, and a bioreactor | Dimensions: 1.2″ × 1.2″ × .12″ approx

PHOTO: IONAT ZURR / COURTESY THE TISSUE CULTURE & ART PROJECT

meaty thighs. This abridged production scheme was observable to gallery visitors and to the donor frogs that occupied a terrarium located beside the bioreactor in the installation. It provided them a ringside view of their progeny gestating to become their caregivers' dinner.

TC&A formalized the maintenance procedures by naming them. The "Feeding Ritual" highlighted the total dependency of these living entities. The "Killing Ritual" demonstrated their extreme fragility because it was accomplished simply by removing the semi-living sculpture from its sterile environment and touching it. The normal colonies of fungi and bacteria that exist on human hands were lethal to the culture. The artists explain how disruptive this is to traditional communications by humans with nonhumans: "By the most obvious or 'natural' act of human nurturing, through caressing, we kill communities of cells which are stripped from their host body and immune system. When interacting with semi-living entities, humans must learn to translate their limited understandings and perceptions towards a different set of instincts of a different living system."[11]

The Killing Ritual marked the sculpture's death, but it did not mark the conclusion of this artwork. It proceeded toward its intended culmination when the artists marinated the frog steak in Calvados overnight. It was then fried in honey and garlic, both rich sources of natural antibacterial agents. Then, for the first time in all human history, the artists, two curators, the chef, and six volunteers feasted on semi-living frog steak. The rest of us did not miss a culinary delight. The gastronomic experience failed because, according to the artists, it "lacked the texture of a steak (for that we would need to 'exercise' the muscle tissue in culture)."[12] The artists are hoping to make their steak less mushy by introducing a strict physical conditioning regimen for their sedentary steaks. The second reason it failed proved equally distasteful: "Unfortunately, as the growth period was too short, much of the polymer did not degrade and the steak had the texture of jellied fabric."[13]

Despite the shortcomings, TC&A was approached by an animal welfare organization with a request to grow semi-living steaks from human cells. The artists explain, "The group's director asked for a feast based on a steak grown from her own flesh."[14]

The economy test also fell short of optimistic projections. Ten grams of meat grew in the lab during the three-month period of the exhibition. The artists estimate that the frog steak cost $650 per gram. Nonetheless, they defend the project. Referring to the research for this project that began in 2000 in a highly reputable scientific setting—the Tissue Engineering and Organ Fabrication Laboratory at Harvard Medical School—Catts and Zurr comment, "The artist has the license to imagine, to fantasize and to exhibit unrealistic expectations of science and technology. . . . In the case of artists, who are also research fellows at the same laboratory in Harvard, these presumed separate realms of science/fact versus art/imagination can fuse into each other in the eyes of the wider community."[15]

This merger with science subjects art to new realms of moral responsibility. Regarding their artistic process, TC&A acknowledges the irony that the medium they used to keep the frog tissues alive contains fetal calf serum. Because a pregnant cow was killed in order to extract the fetal serum, a fetal calf and its mother were unavoidable victims of the "victimless" meat experiment.[16] The artists also acknowledge an ethical jeopardy introduced by their in vitro enterprise. "By creating a new class of Semi-Being, which is dependent on us and our technology for survival, we are also creating a new class for exploitation. As part of the TC&A project, we explore the ironies involved in the promise of a Victimless Utopia."[17]

Catts and Zurr drive process art to its logical extreme by establishing a goal-oriented practice, pursuing that goal in public venues where the process contributes the thematic, aesthetic, and material components of an artwork, and then welcoming any and all outcomes. They explain, "Our intention is not to provide yet another consumer product but rather to raise questions about our exploitation of other living beings. We see our role as artists as one in which we are providing a tangible example of possible futures, and research the potential effects of these new forms on our cultural perceptions of life. It is not our role to provide people with goods for their daily use. We would like our work to be seen in this cultural context, and not in a commercial context."[18]

NOTES

1 John Schwartz, "Museum Kills Live Exhibit," Science Times, *New York Times*, May 13, 2008.

2 Ibid.

3 Ionat Zurr and Oron Catts, "Big Pigs, Small Wings: On Genohype and Artistic Autonomy," Culture Machine vol. 7 (2005). http://www.culturemachine.net/index.php/cm/rt/printerFriendly/30/37.

4 "Oron Catts and Ionat Zurr—Perth, The Tissue Culture & Art Project," ANAT. http://serendipity.anat.org.au/residencies/ORON-IONAT.htm.

5 "Trans-Evolution: Examining Bio Art," CEPA Gallery: The Art of Photography. http://www.cepagallery.org/exhibitions/trans_evolution/cattszurr.html.

6 Ionat Zurr quoted in "Jacket Grows from Living Tissue" by Lakshmi Sandhana, *Wired*, October 12, 2004. http://www.wired.com/science/discoveries/news/2004/10/65248.

7 Gowri Koneswaran and Danielle Nierenberg, "Global Farm Animal Production and Global Warming: Impacting and Mitigating Climate

Change," *Environmental Health Perspectives*, January 27, 2008. http://www.ncbi.nlm.nih.gov/pmc/articles/PMC2367646/.

8 Stephan Leckle, "How Meat-Centered Eating Patterns Affect Food Security and the Environment: International Development Research Centre." http://www.idrc.ca/cp/ev-30610-201-1-DO_TOPIC.html.

9 John Robbins, *Diet for a New America* (Walpole, NH: Stillpoint, 1987), 298.

10 Ibid, 367.

11 Ionat Zurr and Oron Catts, "Are the Semi-Living semi-Good or semi-Evil?" http://www.tca.uwa.edu.au/publication/AretheSemi-Livingsemi-Goodorsemi-Evil.pdf.

12 Oron Catts and Ionat Zurr, "Ingestion/Disembodied Cuisine," *Cabinet Magazine* online, issue 16 (Winter 2004–2005). http://www.cabinetmagazine.org/issues/16/catts.php.

13 Ibid.

14 Ibid.

15 Ionat Zurr and Oron Catts, "Big Pigs, Small Wings: On Genohype and Artistic Autonomy," Culture Machine vol. 7 (2005). http://www.culturemachine.net/index.php/cm/rt/printerFriendly/30/37.

16 Oron Catts and Ionat Zurr. "The Ethics of Experiential Engagement with the Manipulation of Life," in *Tactical Biopolitics Art, Activism, and Technoscience*, edited by Beatriz da Costa and Kavita Philip (Cambridge, MA: MIT Press, 2008), 143–157.

17 Oron Catts and Ionat Zurr, "Model for Artistic Engagement with the Life Sciences: The Embedded Irony," article sent to the author by the artists.

18 Oron Catts and Ionat Zurr, "Semi-Living Food: Disembodied Cuisine," *Genetologic Research*, July 11, 2007, 19:19. http://www.enoughroomforspace.org/research_blog_posts/blog/page:12/researchBlogId:4.

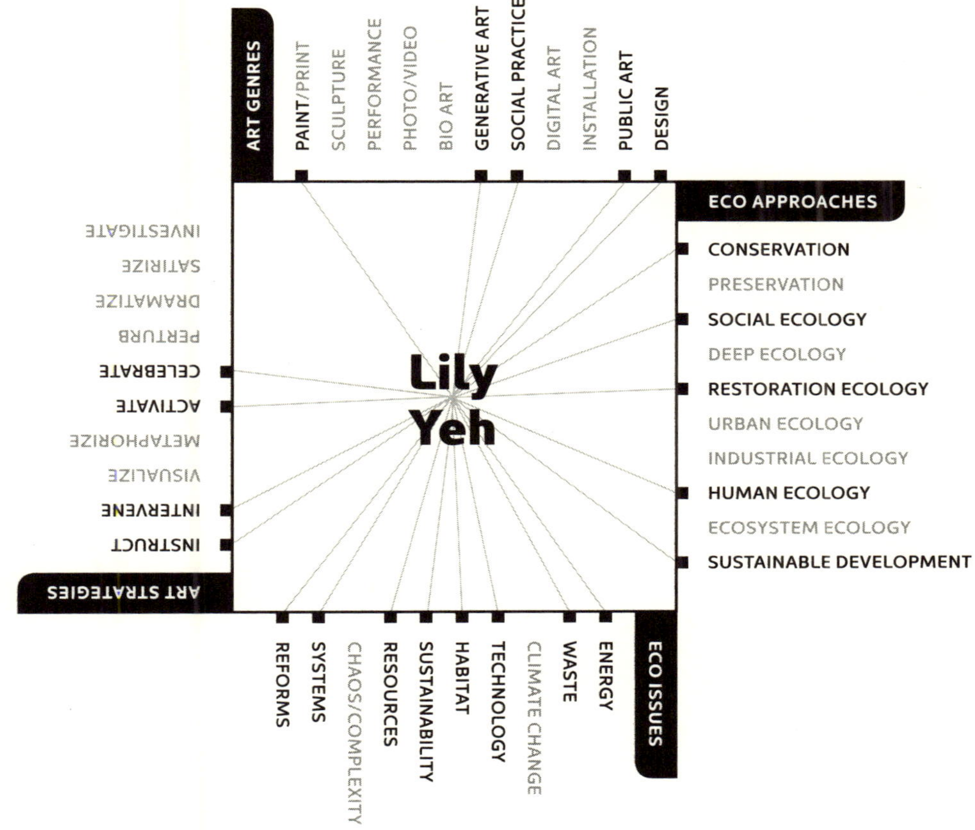

Holistic Healing and Renewal

Born 1941, Kueizhou, China

IN THE RELIGIONS OF SUB-SAHARAN AFRICA, death does not end the life of an individual. The deceased become ancestors and continue to participate in the lives of their families and within their communities. If a burial is not properly performed, the dead person may become a wandering ghost capable of endangering those who remain alive. As a result, dread accompanies sorrow each time someone dies.[1]

Imagine the emotional anguish of the survivors of the hundred-day rampage of killing when over eight hundred thousand Tutsis in Rwanda were methodically and brutally massacred by state-supported extremists. Many were hacked to death by their

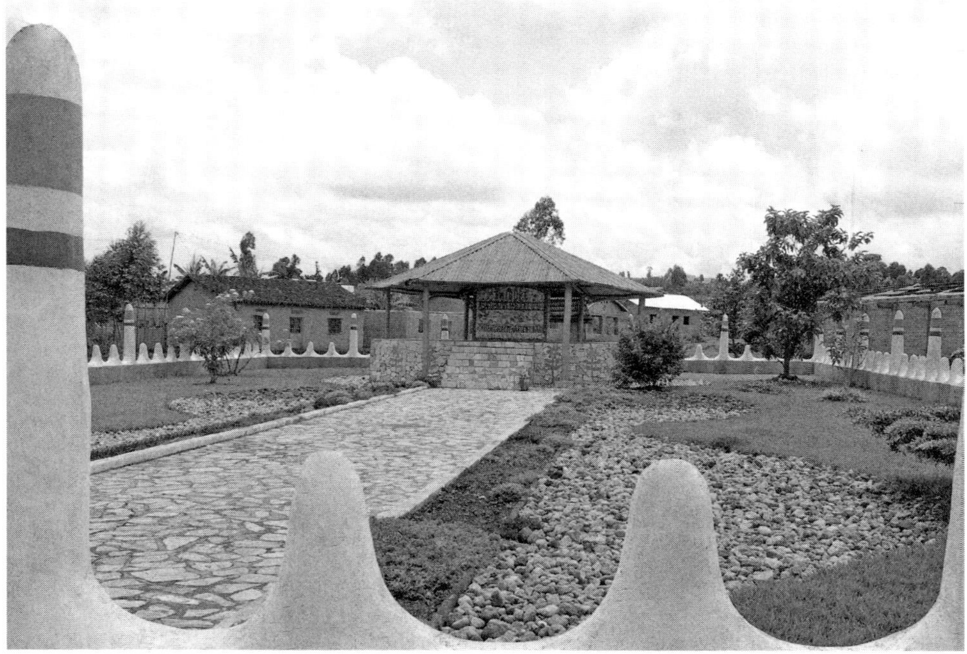

Lily Yeh | Rwanda Healing Project | The Rugerero Genocide Memorial | 2005–2007 Designed by Lily Yeh, built under the auspices of Barefoot Artists Inc. | Constructed by China Road and Bridge Construction Company | Rugerero sector, Rubavu district, Rwanda

COURTESY LILY YEH

Hutu neighbors wielding machetes and farm tools. When the artist Lily Yeh journeyed to Rwanda in 2004, ten years after these brutal acts of genocide, she discovered that the deceased still had not been buried according to custom. A crude unmarked structure served as the mass grave. Consequently, the survivors were not only displaced, orphaned, widowed, disabled, penniless, grieving, vulnerable, and frightened, they were constantly haunted by the ghosts of their ancestors. Yeh understood that they could not attend to their own futures until they satisfied their duties to their ancestors. She pledged to help them by launching the *Rwanda Healing Project* (2004–ongoing) to restore the spirit of a people paralyzed by their memories. Yeh, a petite woman who hardly tips the scale at 100 pounds, was qualified for this massive mission because she had already developed comparable public art projects in derelict neighborhoods in Pennsylvania, Ghana, Kenya, Ecuador, China, Ivory Coast, and the Republic of Georgia. Her nickname, warrior angel, is well earned.

Yeh learned about the plight of the Rwandans at a conference where Jean Bosco Musana Rukirande, who worked for the Red Cross, described the dismal state of the region. Yeh recalls, "My heart was moved. If my loved ones were buried there, I wouldn't find healing in my heart. I want to bring beauty to a memorial. Beauty gives dignity. Beauty heals."[2]

Yeh arrived in Rugerero Survivors Village, a grim settlement built by the Rwandan government in 1997–98 to house the poorest and most vulnerable refugees who had fled to escape the genocide. The average daily income of the villagers at the time was less than $1 per day.[3] Infrastructure was in disrepair. The economic system had collapsed. Traditional semi-subsistence agriculture was decimated. The land had ceased to be productive. How-

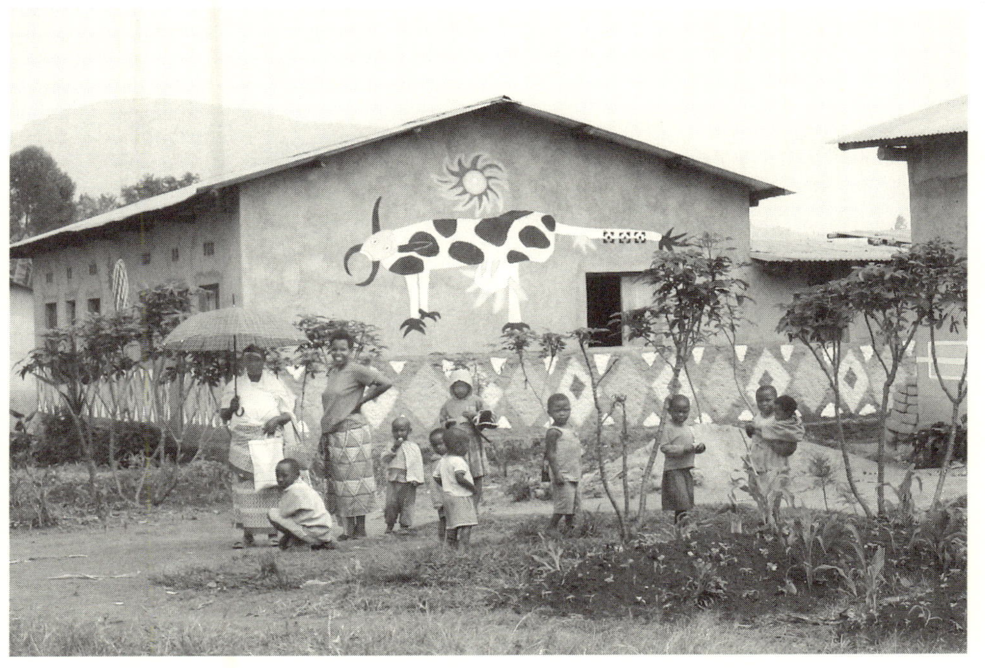

Lily Yeh | Barefoot Artists Inc. | Rwanda Healing Project | 2006 The Cow Abundant with Milk mural | Rugerero Survivors Village, Rwanda | Image developed from a child's drawing, painted with the help of adult villagers

PHOTO: LILY YEH / COURTESY LILY YEH

ever, Yeh did not focus on the dejection and the squalor. She credits her Chinese heritage for instilling the yin and the yang: "It is the shady and the sunny side of a mountain or an object. . . . When I see the brokenness, poverty and crime in inner cities, I also see the enormous potential and readiness for transformation and rebirth. When I see deficits, I see resources on the other side of the coin."[4]

Yeh envisioned a splendid genocide memorial created by hundreds of local children and adults. She exclaims, "Bringing the community together to make beauty can be compared to an ecosystem. Imagination is the fertilizer. Once it is activated, nothing remains the same. Fertilizer enables procreation. It produces deep roots. This provides the power of growth. . . . This is the process of human ecology."[5] Two strategies of sustainable reform emerged as the *Rwanda Healing Project* responded to the multiplicity of problems endemic to this village. One focused on the construction of the *Genocide Memorial Park* dedicated to the past by honoring those who lost their lives during the ordeals. The other fostered hope for the future among the residents in the Survivors Village so that positive change could occur.

Yeh returned to Rugerero in 2005 with several volunteers to initiate "an organic creative process. I call it living social art."[6] They brought an affordable plan for the memorial. The villagers, however, were not satisfied. They wanted an elaborate sunken tomb chamber to house the bones of their loved ones. Yeh explains her dilemma: "I didn't have funds so I asked the villagers to do the construction, but they refused. They told me that this structure was for their loved ones. It had to be perfect. They demanded a professional construction team."[7] Yeh responded by interpreting the problem as an opportunity to develop a skill among the unemployable. Instead of hiring a construction company to do the work, she asked it to send representatives to direct the local workers while she trained villagers to convert her drawings into glittering mosaics that would embellish the walls of the memorial. The sparkling visual surface not only enlivened the architectural space; it contributed symbolically by creating something whole out of shattered parts. In this manner the mosaic embodied the healing function of the memorial.

Yeh soon discovered that her ignorance of local customs produced three additional reasons to adjust her original design. The flower motif was removed to make the memorial appear more somber. The villagers replaced the flowers with phrases they wrote expressing their grief. In addition, purple was added to the all-white structure because it is Rwanda's national color of mourning. Finally, the undulating form Yeh proposed was eliminated because the villagers interpreted it as a snake, the term they used for their marauders, not the mountains Yeh had intended.

On April 5, 2007, thousands of people gathered for the *Genocide Memorial* dedication. They formed a long procession down the stately promenade that lead to the enclosed tomb containing the bones of hundreds of genocide victims. The sunken chamber is painted a solemn blue-green, while the tops of the promenade walls are painted bright white and purple, and the tomb enclosure is brilliant turquoise. A raised portion is embellished with colorful mosaics. On that day the care of the memorial was officially transferred to the local government. The people celebrated with song, drumming, dance, and bouquets of flowers wrapped with purple ribbons.

Yeh founded a nonprofit arts organization, Barefoot Artists Inc., in 2003 to tackle the village's equally urgent social and environmental problems. The organization introduces expert volunteers who train local people to provide for themselves and their neighbors. Yeh chose the term *barefoot* because removing one's shoes is a formal act of humility in cultures around the world. Furthermore, the term indicates the extreme poverty of the people the organization hopes to invigorate. Its mission is to utilize the transformative power of art to convert faltering communities and ecosystems into ones that are thriving.

Yeh began by taking advantage of children's natural appetites for the action, color, life, excitement that art could introduce into their dreary lives. Some of the youngsters' drawings were enlarged as murals to enliven the gray walls of the existing buildings. Gradually, the village began to come to life. Adults were invited to illustrate their stories too, although many scoffed at this tiny foreigner with crazy ideas. Yeh explains, "I work with kids first to gain the trust of the adults. Then they begin to trust me with their stories."[8]

They also trusted her with their wishes. Yeh was approached by some young women who were orphaned as children during the genocide and were now bearing children they could not support. They were uneducated and unskilled and wanted to learn to sew. What transpired took two parallel courses. One trajectory was launched in 2007 when Barefoot Artists hired a sewing teacher and provided twelve young women with sewing machines, which they were allowed to keep after graduation eighteen months later. This program has been repeated three times. In addition to sewing classes, the women were taught skills of living that would make the investment in their skill sustainable. They learned about co-operative business models, nutrition, HIV prevention, and more. Yeh describes the role of art in their holistic learning experience by recalling her early encounters with the women: "Deep sadness crossed the women's faces as they travelled into the darkness of their memories. They needed to prepare to enter their grief. For weeks, the women held hands. They prayed and sang together to prepare. Slowly they began to draw."[9] At first they made crude stick figures. The figures had no arms. They were covered in blood. They saw only black. Slowly color appeared. Yeh exclaims with relish, "Now they cannot stop singing, dancing, drumming. They have changed. Art makes their transformation visible."[10]

At first, the women drew to release their grief, but gradually they began to express their hopes. Motorcycles, computers, and lots of goats appeared in their artworks. In order to demonstrate that dreams can come true, Barefoot Artists raised a modest $2,000. The money was spent to give goats to half of the families in the Survivors Village. The goats were not gifts, which meant they could not be slaughtered for a one-time feast. They belonged to the entire community and were intended for procreation and sharing. Thus, it was not due to lack of funds that only half the villagers received a goat. The investment was designed to establish communal bonds among the uprooted villagers and to generate a source of sustainable wealth that would also benefit the ecosystem. The first births occurred in 2009. The event was celebrated with a grand goat-sharing ceremony. Yeh explains, "They began to see that working together, they could control their futures. Hope provides a climate for investment."[11]

Yeh notes that many NGOs work with needy communities, but their projects often fail because they give people money or resources, but not appreciation and knowledge of how to make those gifts multiply. Yeh's "organic methodology" involves investing in the psychological infrastructure of the people as well as the physical infrastructure of the village. She comments, "Instead of challenging the established system, Barefoot Artists finds new ways to reduce the suffering of people. It is a creative solution. I generate goodwill and joy and sense of hope so people can envision the future. I never have a set program. Usually a program is launched because it is requested by residents. That way they have a sense of ownership. That is why I call my art a living monument."[12] The following projects initiated by Barefoot Artists reveal its holistic healing philosophy. In each instance needs are satisfied by providing locals with opportunities for self-sufficiency gained through entrepreneurial ventures initiated by locals and supported by a healthy population. Benefits also accrue to the region's soils, air, water, fauna, and flora.

Water and sanitation All one hundred families in the Survivors Village relied on two faucets to supply their water needs. Because this service was unreliable, residents were often required to take an hour-long walk to the Sebya River, where the water was contaminated with disease-producing organisms. This predicament persisted despite the fact that rainfall arrived predictably in the region through two rainy seasons a year. At the same time, the rudimentary sanitation systems were in disrepair, leaving sewage dangerously exposed. Yeh intervened. By applying living social art[13] to the situation, she transformed a problem into an opportunity for skill building by inviting volunteers to teach community members how to construct latrine buildings and to harvest rainwater. In addition, a contracted engineer from the company that supplied the water tanks taught villagers how to install its systems. Ultimately, the nonprofit organization Engineers Without Borders partnered with Barefoot Artists to train villagers to restore and build ventilated sanitation facilities. A skilled labor force and sanitary facilities appeared throughout the village, eliminating a major source of pollution.

Employment One example of an employment scheme initiated by Barefoot Artists is the Basket Weaving Cooperative that was formed in response to a request by twenty elderly women. They wanted to learn how to harvest, beat, scrape, wash, and weave yucca leaves in the way that was once practiced by their ancestors but had lapsed. Children were encouraged to draw what they observed. In the process, they too learned to utilize this local resource according to a sustainable tradition.

Energy Rugerero was off the power grid and needed an energy source. Instead of receiving imported photovoltaic modules, survivors were taught how to construct them with materials that could be acquired in local markets. Yeh is pleased to report that people who live without a table, chair, or mattress now have energy to sew and weave long into the night.[14]

Finance Barefoot Artists raised funds through donations and joined with local authorities to sponsor a Micro Lending Program. It enables extremely impoverished people with neither savings nor credit opportunities nor loan contacts to initiate self-employment.

Physical health In 2006, Thomas Jefferson University medical students, two faculty members, and a public health nursing student joined Barefoot Artists to assist a population suffering from sanitation problems, poor nutrition, and AIDS. They not only treated patients, they worked with villagers to produce public health murals demonstrating food preparation, infant care, and water purification. They even staged interactive performances in which hygiene-related practices are enacted.

In addition, Barefoot Artists helped ensure the success of all of these initiatives by instilling hope through empowerment initiatives, trauma therapy, and family planning. Art making contributed to these healing strategies. Survivors shared their stories and aspirations through painting, photography, dance, and video. Colorful murals now adorn many grim dwellings. Parades celebrate villagers' accomplishments. Barefoot Artists documents these imaginative creations in books and films to inform distant audiences about Rwanda's harrowing history and its promising future. These publications also generate funds that help make the Barefoot Artists association sustainable.

Yeh may have lacked the expertise of city planners, social workers, construction contractors, and community developers who typically conduct sustainable community revitalization. However, she offered assets that these professionals typical lack. "I was well equipped with the artist's skills of improvisation, invention, and spontaneous action. In particular, I knew the power of action."[15] For Yeh, art is not so much about visualizing form and color. It is creativivity applied to traumatized communities. She notes, "To me, the Survivors Village and the *Genocide Memorial* are living art forms because they are being used. Some activities are related to art, others to social action. I do not make distinctions."[16]

Yeh concludes by asking, "What can I do to reduce suffering? As an artist I share the joy of creating together with people. How to help? By observing what is needed and what is possible. That is organic creativity."[17] She cites six steps that optimize sustainable outcomes: heed your calling, meet a guide, use your skill and training, plant seeds (create), always return, and support the project.

NOTES

1 "African Religions," *Encyclopedia of Death and Dying*. http://www.deathreference.com/A-Bi/African-Religions.html#ixzz1OvcwcYGk.

2 Lily Yeh interview with the author, July 28, 2011.

3 Setting Up a Solar Cottage Industry in Rwanda, Africa. http://www.mainesolar.org/Rwanda09.pdf.

4 Lily Yeh, "Americans Who Tell the Truth." http://www.americanswhotellthetruth.org/pgs/portraits/Lily_Yeh.php.

5 Lily Yeh, Bioneers conference lecture, San Rafael, California, October 2009.

6 Lily Yeh interview with the author, July 28, 2011.

7 Ibid.

8 Ibid.

9 Lily Yeh interview with the author, October 19, 2009.

10 Ibid.

11 Ibid.

12 Lily Yeh interview with the author, July 28, 2011.

13 Ibid.

14 Setting Up a Solar Cottage Industry in Rwanda, Africa. http://www.mainesolar.org/Rwanda09.pdf.

15 Bill Moskin and Jill Jackson, *Warrior Angel: The Work of Lily Yeh—October 21, 2004*, 1. http://www.barefootartists.org/Lilys_Warrior_Angel_11_2.pdf.

16 Lily Yeh interview with the author, July 28, 2011.

17 Ibid.

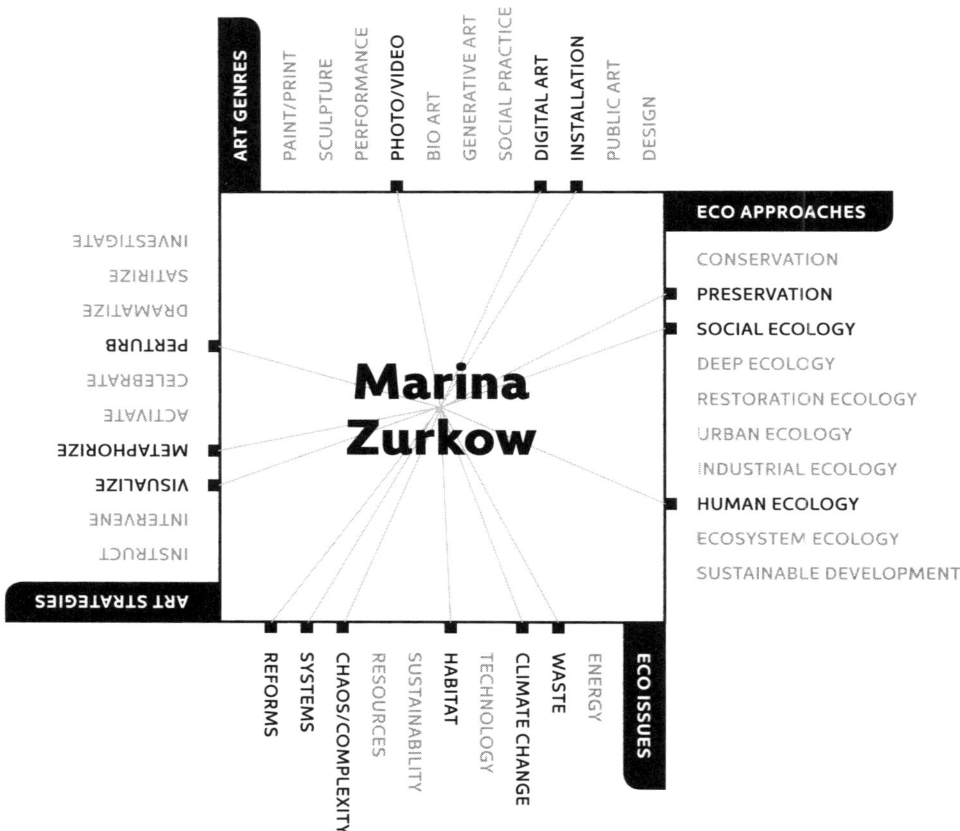

Turf Wars and Global Warming

Born 1962, New York, USA

"BE WORRIED. BE VERY WORRIED."[1] This headline was attached to a story on CNN.com in 2006 reporting on the globe's rising temperature. Journalists worldwide were providing accounts explaining the causes for the fever. Marina Zurkow did not only take note of the evidence. She also scrutinized the media and the powerful role of images in delivering this worrisome message. In response she created a suite of animated video works that present the water-logged apocalypse anticipated by current media channels. Zurkow explains, "I place climate change in a bigger context. I'm interested in our relationship with the environment and the assumption about stasis.

We seem to prefer a dumb known to an intelligent unknown. My strategy, in part, is to help myself and others tolerate this discomfort."[2]

Zurkow encapsulates these complex issues in her film *The Poster Children* (2007), a nine-minute animation loop.[3] Formally, it combines two traditions of visual storytelling—the thousand-year-old Chinese scroll painting and the hundred-year-old cartoon tradition. Thematically, however, it shatters the uplifting tales conveyed by ancient scrolls and the childlike innocence of her animation sources. *Poster Children* reveals the harrowing prospects of global warming.

The video is set in the Arctic landscape. Although it is often described as the last pristine refuge on Earth, here the Arctic is depicted as an all-encompassing sea dotted with meager icebergs and ominous heaps of floating, discarded televisions, VCRs, computers, and other electronic waste. An endless expanse of pastel blue water fills the screen from top to bottom throughout the duration of the film. A large white bear is balanced precariously on one shard, the meager remnant of a former ice floe. Other shards of ice float by. The bear is as endearing as a stuffed teddy. Two scenes lead the viewer to surmise that this charming creature is unaware of its peril. In one scene it enjoys a swim while the sun blazing overhead is heating its Earthly habitat. In another scene the bear encounters two children, a boy and a girl who are drawn in the manner of early Twentieth-Century cartoons. Although they are naked and stand on cloudlike forms, they cannot be mistaken for innocent cherubs, because both wield pistols. Their relentless shooting is conducted as listlessly as if they were blowing bubbles. It is the bear that represents innocence in this context. It behaves coyly before the girl, who is aiming her gun directly at it.

Suddenly, the narrative shifts and the bear's status as victim is reversed. The animal appears digging its teeth into some prey, perhaps the child. The blood that stains its mouth is the only red element in the midst of a blue, white, pink, and black landscape. The color red warns of impending danger.

Zurkow orchestrates a suite of powerful symbols: guns as signs of human violence, children as emblems of innocence, nudity as the hallmark of vulnerability, polar bears as embodiments of nature's threatened wonders, the Arctic as representative of wilderness, the relentless sun as an ominous projection of the Earth's warming. They converge in a context that Zurkow describes as "an animated Arctic dystopia."[4]

By stating "the images define territorial wars,"[5] Zurkow identifies her concern that entire populations will be forced, through desperation, to defend the bits of turf that have not yet submerged. This theme is conveyed in this work by two animated gun-toting children with their bare feet planted firmly on chunks of floating ice. In fact, seven countries have already claimed major sectors of Antarctica.[6] Some are clamoring for control of the vast wealth of oil and gas believed to lie beneath the Arctic sea beds. Others are eagerly anticipating the melting ice and the opening of shipping channels.

Zurkow interprets the global warming saga through the lens of three news stories that riveted citizens in nations around the world at the time she was creating this work of art. The images that ignited the fiercely emotional responses to these events serve as Zurkow's visual and thematic sources. They include controversy surrounding a photograph of two polar bears apparently stranded on a small iceberg, the birth of polar bear twins in a Berlin zoo, and the massacre of students at Virginia Tech. By exploiting the compact, narrative capacity of cartoon animation, Zurkow condenses these complicated media news stories into

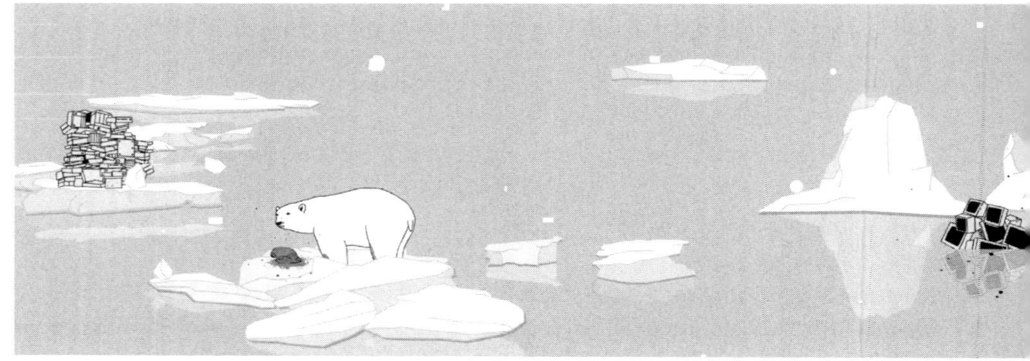

Marina Zurkow | The Poster Children | 2007 Duration: nine-minute loop | Medium: animation | Dimensions: variable

a lucid fine art account of environmental warming. "This use of animation invites viewers to suspend disbelief because they relate to animation by opening up like a child. Animation becomes a great place to have nonthreatening discourse about dark subject matter. Cartoons invite viewers to 'read' material that is not easy to accept, to present a moral code, to make the connections. Others who share my concerns offer a more scientific discourse."[7]

The heart-wrenching photograph of two polar bears balanced precariously on what appears to be a floating chunk of ice melting into the Arctic Ocean was the centerpiece of Al Gore's award-winning film *An Inconvenient Truth* (2006). An enlarged version of the image appeared behind him as he lamented the plight of the polar bears to arouse the public's concern about global warming. "Their habitat is melting . . . beautiful animals, literally being forced off the planet. They're in trouble, got nowhere else to go."[8] This mage of jeopardy invigorated the campaign in the United States to place the polar bear on the endangered species list, and it kindled resistance from the petroleum industry that was clamoring to drill in the region. However, it also provided fodder for skeptics who doubt the dire consequences of climate change. This ironic reversal came about when it was revealed that the iceberg in the photograph was melting because of normal summer temperatures, not global warming, and the animals were close to shore, not imperiled. Nonetheless, the emblematic role of this image was already lodged in the public's consciousness of global warming.

The emotional fervor surrounding polar bears was heightened further when news broke that on December 5, 2006, a polar bear gave birth to twins in a Berlin zoo. This rare event generated a volley of media attention that escalated when the death of one of the twins was reported, then escalated again when the mother bear rejected her frail cub that had been named Knut, and a third time when the zoo appointed a human surrogate to sleep with the cub and provide feedings every two hours. YouTube videos and photographs of the adorable cub, not much bigger than a snowball, whirled throughout the media, along with Knut toys, Knut media specials, Knut DVDs, Knut books, all popularly referred to as Knutmania. Zurkow reports that this story factored into *Poster Children* as well.

The third news story that contributed to this work of art dramatized humanity's capacity for brutality, a theme Zurkow relates to climate change. On April 16, 2007, a horrific massacre occurred at Virginia Tech when a crazed student named Cho Seung-Hui massacred

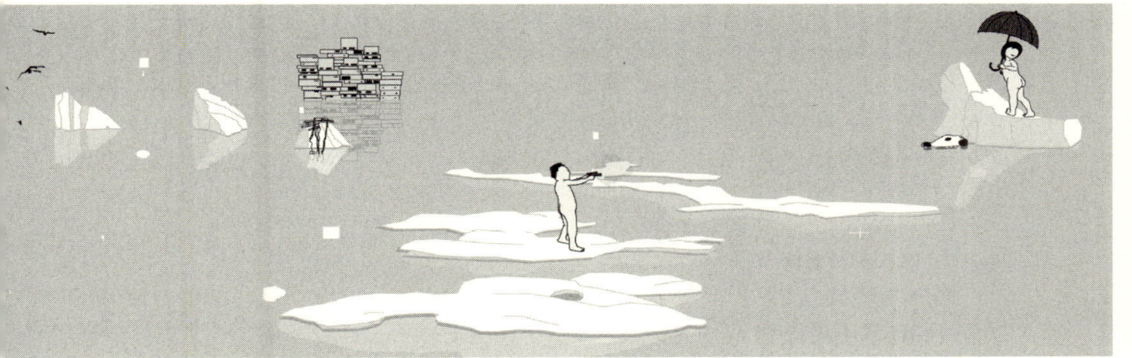

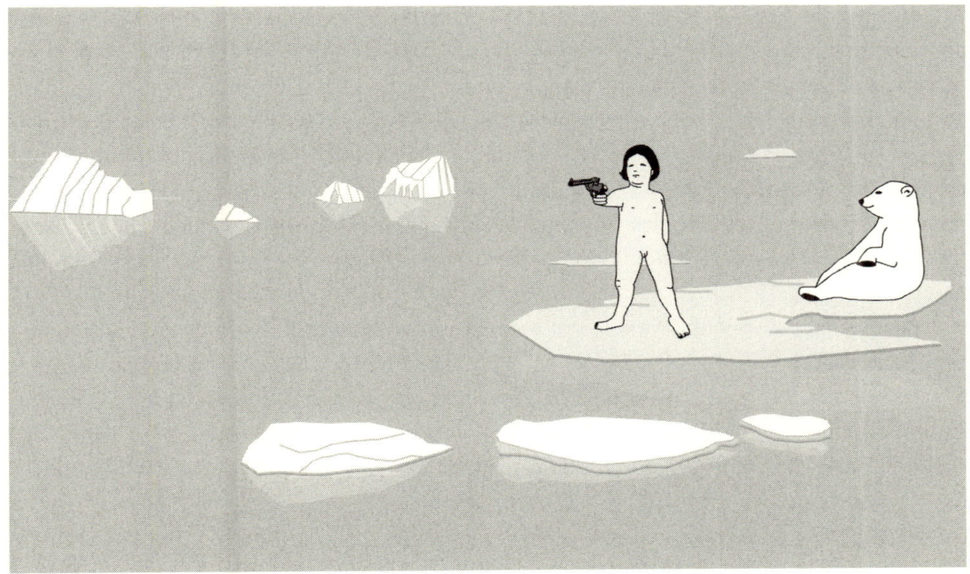

Marina Zurkow | The Poster Children (detail) | 2007 Duration: nine-minute loop | Medium: animation | Dimensions: variable

thirty-two people, wounded many others, then took his own life. The incident was reported to be the deadliest peacetime shooting by a single gunman in United States history.

Zurkow expounded on the deviant nature of this horrific event by addressing the issue of children possessing guns. This particularly incendiary spin-off claimed fanatics among those who supported the right to self-defense and those who protested the aggression. Zurkow explains the role of the Virginia Tech disaster in her depiction of global warming: "I was interested in this shooting in part because the killer was not white (or pink), and I began to research 'kids with guns' online. My search procured a dazzling array of videos on YouTube, many of proud parents teaching their young sons and daughters how to shoot firearms. These pink children became my source material for the rotoscoped characters in *The Poster Children*."[9] The story provided a compelling example of the senseless, large-scale, destructive acts by humans that also aggravate climate change.

Zurkow took advantage of the fact that these news stories ignited emotional responses to endemic social problems. Her title, *Poster Children,* refers to children with deformities or diseases who are used by charities to solicit donations by evoking sympathy. The children, polar bears, and even the Arctic depicted in the video serve in this manner. They are presented as entities in desperate circumstances. Rescue comes to mind. The children represent humanity as victims and aggressors. The polar bears represent species of all kinds that are threatened and belligerent. The Arctic stands in for surviving wildernesses and endangered habitats the world over. Referring to the work's title, Zurkow explains that her subjects are "allowed a break from their ideological duties as mercenary images-for-hire."[10] She enlists them to reveal the unwelcome complexities of the global warming debate. This unsentimental approach reveals an "anti-Eden"[11] where rising waters confuse old notions of victim and culprit.

In order to create this animation, Zurkow downloaded YouTube footage and stock images on the Internet. She explains, "Every image was taken from the Internet. It is the primary place where we get our visual information, where we find what is popular, where we learn about the world."[12] She then undertook the laborious task of rotoscoping, a process of tracing over live-action film, frame by frame, using a stylus and a tablet. Next she sequenced the hand-drawn images into an animated film. The jittery movements of the figures are distinct from computer graphics. Repeating short sequences make the figures appear eerily machinelike. Eliminating a soundtrack, so familiar in animation, directs attention to the animated painting.

Zurkow sums up with a query, not a conclusion. Regarding the relationship between bears and children, "Each is the poster child for a distinct social issue, and both are natural enemies. Are they a danger to each other, or mutual protectors in a new world, ordered by extreme and reconfiguring environments of the North Pole and the Internet?"[13] Like the rising waters themselves, these issues confound and overwhelm. Perhaps the film's perpetually looping sequence confirms the futility of finding ready answers.

NOTES

1 "Be Worried, Be Very Worried," CNN.com, March 26, 2006. http://articles.cnn.com/2006-03-26/us/coverstory_1_cubic-miles-greenland-ice-sheet-global-warming?_s=PM:US.

2 Marina Zurkow interview with the author, April 21, 2010.

3 Zurkow has created 3-, 6-, and 9-minute versions of *The Poster Children* in single and multiple channel formats that are presented in galleries as customized, multiscreen computer pieces. They are all looped and silent.

4 Marina Zurkow, "Gender on Ice Gallery: Artist's statement." http://www.barnard.edu/sfonline/ice/gallery/zurkow.htm.

5 Marina Zurkow interview with the author, April 21, 2010.

6 France, Chile, Argentina, Australia, United Kingdom, Norway, New Zealand.

7 Marina Zurkow interview with the author, April 21, 2010.

8 Marina Zurkow quoted in "How the Environmental Extremists Manipulate the Masses" by Carole "CJ" Williams, NewsWithViews.com, January 26, 2008. http://www.newswithviews.com/Williams/carole7.htm.

9 Marina Zurkow, "Gender on Ice Gallery: Artist's statement." http://barnard.edu/sfonline/ice/gallery/zurkow.htm.

10 Ibid.

11 Ibid.

12 Marina Zurkow interview with the author, April 21, 2010.

13 Marina Zurkow, "Gender on Ice Gallery: Artist's statement." http://barnard.edu/sfonline/ice/gallery/zurkow.htm.

The Future

THE HISTORY OF CIVILIZATION is chronicled as a narrative of yearning and striving, not satisfaction and contentment. The contemporary era may be the first time in all of human history when abundance and luxury are not confined to stories that involve magic cauldrons, mysterious horns of plenty, and mighty dragons. However, the result of actualized abundance for ordinary people may surprise previous generations of strivers. It suggests that while human minds and bodies are certainly not well served by want, they may fare better under conditions of scarceness than profusion.

The rampant spread of obesity suggests that the human body didn't evolve to deal with an abundance of cheap fats and sugars, or laborsaving devices, or motorized transportation. Even the human mind may not cope well with riches.[1] The Digital and Information Age we now occupy can produce an "information overload" that can cause disorientation and lack of responsiveness at worst, confusion over the validity of content and the risk of misinformation at best. A recent study entitled "The Joys and Dilemmas of Wealth"[2] reveals that many wealthy people suffer from isolation, overwork, and lack of confidence. Much of the planet's soils, water, minerals, and biota are faltering as well. The technological and scientific achievements responsible for fulfilling the material fantasies of our ancestors also seem to be responsible for jeopardizing the well-being of our posterity. It is ironic that many grave environmental problems are products of achieving success and progress, as these terms are popularly conceived. At the same time, the masses at the opposite end of the income scale are also taxing the environment because their survival often depends upon overgrazing, overcropping, and overlogging. These factors intensify as world populations of humans soar. The Earth supported 2.3 billion people in 1950 and 6 billion in 2000 and will have to support 9 billion people by the year 2050, according to projections by the US Census Bureau. The physical conditions of human populations parallel the conditions of their environments. Health risks in developed countries stem from stressful living, environmental pollution, overeating, drug use, alcoholism, and violence, while the greatest threats to health in undeveloped countries are overcrowding, poor water quality, disease-carrying insects and vertebrates, and inadequate food, housing, and sanitation.

These predicaments are not the only factors that may motivate someone to become an eco artist. Many other factors can be gleaned from the Earth's wondrous uniqueness. Of the planets that may orbit the estimated hundred pentillion stars that are visible through today's telescopes, Earth is the only known planet with living organisms. Four statistical miracles constitute the explanation:

- Earth's temperatures fall precisely within the range at which the chemical and physical processes that are the basis of biological functions perform best.
- Earth's atmosphere both shields it from excessive ultraviolet radiation, pre-

venting it from becoming a raging inferno like Venus, and holds in heat, preventing it from becoming a frozen wasteland like Mars.

- Seventy percent of Earth's surface is covered by water. Liquid water is the basis for all life.
- One percent of the solar energy striking plants on Earth is converted into chemical energy, yet that is sufficient to supply all the energy needed by all the animals on the planet, and all the stores of wood, coal, and petroleum.

Wonders as well as horrors stimulate humanity's search for its proper niche among millions of species that share the Earth's resources. The artists included in this book have devoted their curiosity, inventiveness, and energy to this task. They are summoning the persuasive powers of art to rally an environmental crusade. In doing so, they comprise a citizens' army of defenders against the harm humans are inflicting upon their planet. Their work is far from complete.

The strength and effectiveness of the varied schemes of environmentalism, as a work in process, are still in their trial stages; the signs announcing, "Wanted—Creative Problem Solvers and Persuasive Strategists" remain posted throughout the world. A special entreaty might be made to artists because problem solving and persuasion are two qualities that have always been used to measure art's excellence and to explain its significance. Because innovative eco art explorations are still burgeoning around the globe, this book's finale is not a conclusion. It is a springboard to the future.

NOTES

1 John Tierney, "Use Energy, Get Rich and Save the Planet," *New York Times*, April 20, 2009. "As their wealth grows, people consume more energy, but they move to more efficient and cleaner sources—from wood to coal and oil, and then to natural gas and nuclear power, progressively emitting less carbon per unit of energy."

2 Ibid.

Addendum

A QUESTIONNAIRE *occupies the last pages of this volume because this book was conceived of as a training site for future eco art enactments. The multiplicity of eco art approaches represented in it reveals that no authority exists to define the single best course. Thus, choosing among the options provided may help you construct your actual, potential, and desired role as an artist and environmental advocate.*

PERSONAL SURVEY—WHAT DO I BELIEVE?

The Earth is

Mysterious / banal / frightening / boring / beautiful / intimidating / pitiful / other

The Earth is my

Refuge / responsibility / frustration / pleasure / liability / storehouse / shame / wonder / companion / master / slave / other

When I envision my environment, I imagine

Pure air, clean water, blossoms, trees, rainbows, butterflies/
Germs, rotting carcasses, blight, weeds, mold, mutants, slime/
Clear-cut forests, strip-mining, landfills, toxic waste dumps, oil spills, smog/
Dams, highways, industrial parks, high-rise buildings, nuclear reactors, pipelines/
Parks, zoos, aquariums, planetariums, botanical gardens, game farms, theme parks/
Residential homes, yards, driveways, barbecues, air-conditioners, lawns/
Shopping malls, e-commerce, brand names, advertisements, credit cards/
Web sites, blogs, instant messaging, iPods, e-mails, YouTube, MySpace/
Other

The interactions that sustain my life are based upon

My physical strength / my intelligence / other people's physical strength / other people's intelligence / people I know personally / people I don't know personally / animals / machines / electronic technologies / other

The invisible part of the environment I consciously pay attention to consists of

Forms of matter such as molecules / electromagnetic fields, ultrasonic waves, infrared waves, radio waves / conditions such as air pressure, wind, temperature, humidity / spirits that reside in land, rocks, water, plants, animals / the souls of the deceased / humanity's past / other

The aspects of my environment that I am least familiar with are

People / institutions / electronics / mechanics / pets / farm animals / pests / wild animals / ornamental plants / utilitarian plants / weeds / microbes / stone / soil / water / air / wilderness / suburbia / cities / the products of human manufacture / media / astronomical entities / forms of energy / gods, angels, other superhuman beings / other

The state of the planet today is
Robust / thriving / stable / evolving in a logical progression / unstable / evolving in an unpredictable manner / gradually deteriorating / about to collapse / other

The factors that most influence my opinions about the state of the planet are
Personal observations / routine experiences / exceptional experiences / research / academic study / the arts / religious teachings / media fictions / nostalgic recollections / instinct / imagination / other

The people who most impact the place where I live are
Myself / family / ancestors / friends / professional colleagues / neighbors / offspring / corporate managers / government officials / religious leaders / financial authorities / media stars / artists / educators / healers / scientists / manufacturers / farmers / engineers / other

In the future I anticipate
Life as we know it will continue/
Current endangered sites will be reinvigorated/
New species will evolve and populate the Earth/
World peace and sustainability will prevail/
New problems will arise and accelerate the demise of the planet/
Homo sapiens will become extinct but other life-forms will survive/
Worldwide extinctions will end life on Earth/
Other

Suggestions for Further Research

TWENTIETH-CENTURY ECO ART PIONEERS

Ant Farm

Lewallen, Constance M., and Steve Seid, *Ant Farm 1968–1978*. Berkeley: University of California Press, Berkeley Art Museum, Pacific Film Archive, 2004.

Radical Nature: Art and Architecture for a Changing Planet 1969–2009. New York: Koenig Books, 2009. Distribution outside Europe by Distributed Art Publishers.

Scott, Herbert, and Felicity Dale Elliston, *Living Archive 7: Ant Farm: Allegorical Time Warp: The Media Fallout of July 21, 1969*. New York: Actar, 2008.

Herbert Bayer

Bauhaus, 1919–1928. Edited by Herbert Bayer, Walter Gropius, and Ise Gropius. New York: Museum of Modern Art, 1975, 1938.

Bayer, Herbert, *Herbert Bayer: Painter, Designer, Architect*. New York: Reinhold, 1967.

Cohen, Arthur Allen, *Herbert Bayer: The Complete Work*. Cambridge, MA: MIT Press, 1984.

Joseph Beuys

Adams, David, "Joseph Beuys: Pioneer of a Radical Ecology," *Art Journal* (of the College Art Association), Summer 1992.

Borer, Alain, *The Essential Joseph Beuys*. Edited by Lothar Schirmer. Cambridge, MA: MIT Press, 1997.

Joseph Beuys, Mapping the Legacy. Edited by Gene Ray, with essays by Lukas Beckmann and others. New York: Distributed Art Publishers and Sarasota, FL: John and Mable Ringling Museum of Art, 2001.

Joseph Beuys: The Reader. Edited and translated by Claudia Mesch and Viola Michely, with a foreword by Arthur C. Danto and additional translation by Nickolas Decarlo, Kayvan Rouhani, and Heidi Zimmerman. Cambridge, MA: MIT Press, 2007.

Tisdall, Caroline, *Joseph Beuys*. New York: Solomon R. Guggenheim Museum, 1979.

Hans Haacke

Bourdieu, Pierre, *Free Exchange: Pierre Bourdieu and Hans Haacke*. Stanford, CA: Stanford University Press, 1995.

Grasskamp, Walter, Molly Nesbit, and Jon Bird, *Hans Haacke*. London: Phaidon, 2004.

Haacke, Hans, *Hans Haacke*. Eindhoven: Stedelijk Van Abbemuseum and London: Tate Gallery, 1984.

Hans Haacke for Real: Works 1959–2006. Edited by Matthias Flügge and Robert Fleck for the Akademie der Künste, Berlin, and the Deichtorhallen Hamburg; translated by Hans Haacke and Steven Lindberg. Düsseldorf: Richter, 2006.

Helen and Newton Harrison

Harrison, Helen Mayer, and Newton Harrison, *Casting a Green Net: Can It Be We Are Seeing a Dragon?* Catalog for Artranspennine98, 1998. Copyright 1999 Helen Mayer Harrison and Newton Harrison.

Harrison, Helen Mayer, and Newton Harrison, *From There to Here: Peninsula Europe: The High Grounds*. Berlin: Reschke & Steffens, 2001.

Harrison, Helen Mayer, and Newton Harrison, *Meditations on the Condition of the Sacramento River, the Delta and the Bays at San Francisco, a Discourse*. http://174.132.159.222/~hstudio/wp-content/uploads/2011/03/sacmedog.pdf.

Friedensreich Hundertwasser

Hundertwasser, Friedensreich, *Hundertwasser Architecture: For a More Human Architecture in Harmony with Nature*. English translation by Philip Mattson. Cologne, New York: Taschen, 1997.

Restany, Pierre, and Friedensreich Hundertwasser, *Hundertwasser*. Translation by All Global Solutions International. New York: Parkstone Press International, 2010.

Restany, Pierre, *Hundertwasser: The Painter-King with the 5 Skins: The Power of Art*. Cologne: Taschen Art Album, 2004.

Allan Kaprow

Buchloh, B.H.D., and Judith F. Rodenbeck, *Experiments in the Everyday: Allan Kaprow and Robert Watts, Events, Objects, Documents*. With an essay by Robert E. Haywood and interviews by Larry Miller and Sidney Simon. New York: Columbia University and Miriam and Ira D. Wallach Art Gallery, 1999.

Kelley, Jeff, *Childsplay: The Art of Allan Kaprow*. With a foreword by David Antin. Berkeley: University of California Press, 2004.

Kaprow, Allan, *Essays on the Blurring of Art and Life*. Edited by Jeff Kelley. Berkeley: University of California Press, 1996, 1993.

Meyer-Hermann, Eva, Andrew Perchuk, and Stephanie Rosenthal, *Allan Kaprow: Art . . . as Life*. Los Angeles: Getty Research Institute, Museum of Contemporary Art, 2008.

Frans Krajcberg

Filho, Joao Merelles, "The Meeting of Franz Krajcberg and Thiago de Mello," *(o)eco Amazonia*, May 1, 2011. http://www.oecoamazonia.com/en/articles/9-artigos/199-o-encontro-de-frans-krajcberg-e-thiago-de-mello-.

Kaplan, Leon, "Frans Krajcberg Brazil's Eco Sculptor," *ARTFOCUS* 67 (Toronto), vol. 7, no. 3 (Fall 1999).

Restany, Pierre, "The Rio Negro Manifesto." http://www.frans-krajcberg.com/fkmanifeste english.html.

Mario Merz

Beccaria, Marcella, and Carolyn Christov-Bakargiev, *Mario Merz: The Monograph*. Turin: Fondazione Merz, 2005.

Celant, Germano, *Mario Merz*. New York: Solomon R. Guggenheim Museum, 1989.

Mario Merz: Disegni. Edited by Dieter Schwarz. Turin: Fondazione Merz, 2010.

Carolee Schneemann

Schneemann, Carolee, *Carolee Schneemann: Up to and Including Her Limits*. New York: New Museum of Contemporary Art, 1996.

Schneemann, Carolee, *Imaging Her Erotics: Essays, Interviews, Projects*. Cambridge, MA, London: MIT Press, 2003.

Schneemann, Carolee, *More Than Meat Joy: Complete Performance Works and Selected Writings*. Edited by Bruce McPherson. New Paltz, NY: Documentext, 1979.

Stiles, Kristine, and Carolee Schneemann, *Correspondence Course: An Epistolary History of Carolee Schneemann and Her Circle*. Durham, NC: Duke University Press Books, 2010.

Bonnie Ora Sherk

Burnham, Linda Frye, and Bonnie Sherk, "Between the Diaspora and the Crinoline: An Interview with Bonnie Sherk," *High Performance Magazine*, Fall 1981.

Cohn, Terri, "A Living Library, Celebrating 30 Years," *ARTWEEK*, vol. 31, issue 12 (December 2000).

Sherk, Bonnie, "A Living Library: A Global Ecological Network of Diversity of Commonality," *UN Chronicle* online, December 20, 2006. http://www.alivinglibrary.org/UN_article.pdf.

Alan Sonfist

Sonfist, Alan, *Autobiography of Alan Sonfist: A Self-Presentation by Alan Sonfist*. Ithaca, NY: Herbert F. Johnson Museum of Art, Cornell University, 1975.

Sonfist, Alan, *Nature, the End of Art: Environmental Landscapes*. With an introductory interview with the artist by Robert Rosenblum and essays by Wolfgang Becker. New York: Distributed Art Publishers and London: Thames & Hudson, 2004.

Weintraub, Linda, *Environmentalities: Twenty-Two Approaches to Eco-Art*. Rhinebeck, NY: Artnow Publications, 2007.

Mierle Laderman Ukeles

Finkelpearl,Tom, *Dialogues in Public Art*. Cambridge, MA: MIT Press, 2000, pp. 295–322.

Liss, Andrea, *Feminist Art and the Maternal*. Minneapolis: University of Minnesota Press, 2009, pp. 43–67.

Ryan, Bartholomew, "Manifesto for Maintenance: A Conversation with Mierle Laderman Ukeles." artinamerica.com, March 30, 2009. http://www.artinamericamagazine.com/news-opinion/conversations/2009-03-20/draft-mierle-interview/.

Salazar, Erin, "Mierle Laderman Ukeles: Interview," *TGC*, Spring/Summer 2006: 14–21.

TWENTY-FIRST-CENTURY ECO ART EXPLORERS

Brandon Ballengée

Ballangée, Brandon, "The Origins and Application of Artificial Selection," *Biomediale* anthology. Kaliningrad, Russia: National Center for Contemporary Art, 2004.

Grande, John K., "Bio-Art with Brandon Ballengée" (interview), *Dialogues in Diversity: Art from Marginal to Mainstream*. Pari, Italy: Pari Publishing, 2007.

Weintraub, Linda, *Environmentalities: Twenty-Two Approaches to Eco-Art*. Rhinebeck, NY: Artnow Publications, 2007, pp. 21–28.

Beehive Design Collective

Beehive Design Collective. http://www.beehivecollective.org/.

Spencer, Keith, "The True Cost of Coal (and Urban Condos): A Poststructuralist Critique of the Beehive," November 27, 2010. http://criticaldispenser.wordpress.com/2010/10/03/truecostofcoal/.

Tan, Berny, "Poster as Pollination," *The Visual and Critical Studies Blog*, School of Visual Arts, December 8, 2010. http://visualandcriticalstudies.wordpress.com/2011/02/02/berny-tans-essay-on-the-beehive-design-collective/.

Mel Chin

Art: 21, Art in the Twenty-First Century. Produced by Susan Sollins and Suan Dowling. Distributed by PBS Home Video, Harry N. Abrams, 2004.

Chin, Mel, *Do Not Ask Me.* Houston, TX: Station Museum of Contemporary Art, 2011.

Inescapable Histories: Mel Chin. Catalog for touring exhibition by ExhibitsUSA, curators Benito Huerta and Lucy R. Lippard, Mid-America Arts Alliance, 1996.

Weintraub, Linda, *Art on the Edge and Over: Searching for Art's Meanings in Contemporary Society.* Litchfield, CT: Art Insights, 1996.

Chu Yun

Tinari, Philip, "Openings: Chu Yun (March 1, 2009)," *Artforum*, March 2009. http://philtinari.com/writing/openings-chu-yun/.

Critical Art Ensemble

Critical Art Ensemble, *Electronic Civil Disobedience: And Other Unpopular Ideas.* New York: Autonomedia, 2004.

Critical Art Ensemble, *Flesh Machine: Cyborgs, Designer Babies, and New Eugenic Consciousness.* New York: Autonomedia, 1998.

Critical Art Ensemble, *The Molecular Invasion.* New York: Autonomedia, 2003.

Critical Art Ensemble, *The Electronic Disturbance.* Los Angeles: Semiotexte, 2004.

Fernando García-Dory

"Beneath the Bureaucracy, the Beach: A Conversation between Fernando García-Dory and Chris Fite-Wassilak," *Art Papers.* http://www.growgnome.com/Downloads/F2-p24-29.pdf.

García-Dory, Fernando, "A Shepherds School as a Micro Kingdom of Utopia," *Common, Collection of Minds*, issue 2, 2010.

Bright Ugochukwu Eke

Bright Ugochukwu Eke, *Eco-Scope Blog.* http://u-bright.blogspot.com/.

Bright Ugochukwu Eke, written email interview by Celeyce Matthews (California, April 25, 2009). *Eco-Scope Blog.* http://u-bright.blogspot.com/.

"Bright Ugochukwu Eke," *Eco-Scope Blog*, May 13, 2009. http://u-bright.blogspot.com/2009/05/bright-ugochukwu-eke-fluid-connections.html.

Nicole Fournier

Fournier, Nicole, "Industrial Park Live Dining, 2009–2011." http://industrialparklivedining.blogspot.com/.

Fournier, Nicole, "InTerreArt." http://livedining.blogspot.com/2007/05/edible-plants-growing-in.html.

Fournier, Nicole, "Live Dining, Nicole Fournier," *Visualeyez*, Latitude 53, May 28, 2007. http://visualeyez2007.blogspot.com/2007/05/live-dining-nicole-fournier.html.

Amy Franceschini

Brucker-Cohen, Jonah, "GIZMODO Gallery: Amy Franceschini." Interview/article. http://us.gizmodo.com/gadgets/gizmodo-gallery/gizmodo-gallery-amy-franceschini-157897.php "Amy Franceschini".

Franceschini, Amy, and Daniel Tucker, *Farm Together Now: A Portrait of People, Places, and Ideas for a New Food Movement*. Photographs by Anne Hamersky, foreword by Mark Bittman. San Francisco: Chronicle Books, 2010.

Futurefarmers. http://www.futurefarmers.com/2007site/about.html.

Gelitin

Gantner, Wofgang, *Gelatin's ACB*. Cologne: Walther Konig and New York: Distributed Art Publishers, 2008.

Lachmayer, Herbert, "Inspiring Decadence," *Parkett* 79, 2007: 165–168.

Van den Bergh, *All Together Now: Gelitin—Partners in Crime*. Exhibition catalog. Antwerp: Tim Van Laere Gallery, 2011.

Andy Goldsworthy

Donovan, Molly, and Tina Fiske, *The Andy Goldsworthy Project*. New York: Thames & Hudson and Washington, DC: National Gallery of Art, 2010.

Goldsworthy, Andy, *Andy Goldsworthy: A Collaboration with Nature*. New York: H.H. Abrams, 1990.

Goldsworthy, Andy, *Hand to Earth: Andy Goldsworthy Sculpture, 1976–1990*. Edited by Terry Friedman. New York: H.H. Abrams, 1993.

Andy Gracie

Gracie, Andy, "2000 to 2010 . . . Research, Narratives and Practice . . . An Overview," Hostprods, October 2010. http://www.hostprods.net/text/20002010/.

Regine, "Interview with Andy Gracie," *We Make Money Not Art*, October 18, 2006. http://www.we-make-money-not-art.com/archives/2006/10/whats-your-back.php.

Whitelaw, Mitchell, "Andy Gracie: Symbiotic Circuits," *Pylon*, December 2006. http://pylon.tv/andy_gracie_symbiotic_circuits.pdf.

Tue Greenfort

Eichler, Dominic, "Making Do," Frieze Magazine, issue 108 (June–August 2007).

Tue Greenfort. Featuring essays (in German and English) by Maria Mühle and Jesper Hoffmeyer and an interview with the artist by Zoë Gray. Rotterdam: Witte de With Center for Contemporary Art and New York: Lukas & Sternberg, 2006.

Wagner, Hilke, Klaus Topfer, and Tue Greenfort, *Tue Greenfort: Linear Deflection*. Cologne: Walther Konig, 2009.

Terike Haapoja

Haapoja, Terike, *Closed Circuit. Open Duration*. http://terikehaapoja.net/exhibitions/closed circuit/closedcircuit.htm.

Haapoja, Terike, *Media Age Landscapes*. Text published on the website www.katoava maisema.fi translated by Jenni Grey. 2008. http://www.terikehaapoja.net/pdf/TH%20Media%20age%20landscapes.pdf.

Haapoja, Terike, *On Environmental Crisis, Science, and Art*, 2010. http://www.terikehaapoja.net/pdf/TH%20On%20environmental....pdf.

HeHe

Brucker-Cohen, Johan, "GIZMODO Gallery: Social Commentary Meets Expressive Design with HeHe." Interview/article, September 4, 2007. http://gizmodo.com/gadgets/notag/gizmodo-gallery-social-commentary-meets-expressive-design-with-hehe-295417.php.

HeHe, An interview with Alessandro Ludovico for *Neural Magazine*, issue 33 (July 2009). http://hehe.org.free.fr/hehe/texte/neural/index.html.

Rodgers, Paul, and Michael Smyth, *Digital Blur: Creative Practice at the Boundaries of Architecture, Design and Art*. Oxfordshire, UK: Libri Publishing, 2010.

Natalie Jeremijenko

Natalie Jeremijenko: The Art of the Eco-Mindshift. TED Partner Series, filmed October 2009. http://www.ted.com/talks/natalie_jeremijenko_the_art_of_the_eco_mindshift.html.

"Natalie Jeremineko: The WorldChanging Interview by Emily Gertz," WorldChanging: Change Your Thinking, October 22, 2004. http://www.worldchanging.com/archives/001450.html.

Reeves, Audrey Elizabeth, *Natalie Jeremijenko: Engineering Art in the Age of Biopolitics* (manuscript). Annandale-on-Hudson, NY: Bard College, 2004.

Yun-Fei Ji

Fitzgerald, Shannon, Tan Lin, Gregory Volk, and Melissa Chiu, *Yun-Fei Ji: The Empty City*. Catalog. St. Louis, MO: Contemporary Art Museum of St. Louis, 2005.

Spears, Dorothy, "Part Traditionalist, Part Naturalist, Part Dissident," *New York Times*, February 20, 2010.

Yun-Fei Ji, *Mistaking Each Other for Ghosts*. New York: James Cohan Gallery, 2010.

Eduardo Kac

Hughes, Thomas P., *Human-Built World: How to Think about Technology and Culture*. Chicago: University of Chicago Press, 2005.

Kac, Eduardo, *Signs of Life: Bio Art and Beyond*. Leonardo Book Series. Cambridge, MA: MIT Press, 2009.

Kac, Eduardo, *Telepresence and Bio Art: Networking Humans, Rabbits and Robots*. Ann Arbor: University of Michigan Press, 2005.

Jae Rhim Lee

George, Alison, "Designing a Mushroom Death Suit." Interview of Jae Rhim Lee in CultureLab, *New Scientist*, July 20, 2011. http://www.newscientist.com/blogs/culturelab/2011/07/designing-a-mushroom-death-suit.html.

"The Infinity Burial Project: A Modest Proposal for the Postmortem Body," 2011. http://infinityburialproject.com/author/jrlee.

"N=1=NPK=KIMCHI=N," Vimeo. http://zonezerozerostudio.com/n1.

Maya Lin

Langmead, Donald, *Maya Lin: A Biography*. Westport, CT: Greenwood Publishers, forthcoming.

What Is Missing? Maya Lin's video on Metacafe. http://www.metacafe.com/watch/3588422/maya_lins_what_is_missing/.

What Is Missing? Maya Lin's video on YouTube. http://www.youtube.com/watch?v=1jCGiSDfIAM.

Michael Mandiberg

Holmes, Tiffany, "Eco-Visualization: Combining Art and Technology to Reduce Energy Consumption," *Reconstruction 6.3: Studies in Contemporary Culture*, Summer 2006.

Mandiberg, Michael, "A Case Study of the Real Costs," Eyebeam: Art + Technology Center. http://www.eyebeam.org/feeds/thoughts/a-case-study-of-the-real-costs.

Michael Mandiberg on Vimeo. http://vimeo.com/mandiberg.

Viet Ngo

Oakes, Baile, *Sculpting with the Environment*. Hoboken, NJ: John Wiley & Sons, 1995.

Steiner, Andy, "Viet Ngo, the Artist Engineer," *Civil Engineering*, Winter 2004. http://www.ce.umn.edu/news/stories/pdf/Civil_Engineer_Winter04.pdf.

Westfall, Katie, "Lemna's African Adventures: Lemna International Has Been Planting Infrastructure Projects throughout the World," *Twin Cities Business*, November 2008. http://www.tcbmag.com/industriestrends/economicdevelopment/106302p3.aspx.

Marjetica Potrč

Basualdo, Carlos, Liyat Esakov, Eyal Weissman, and Michael Rush, *Marjetica Potrč: Urgent Architecture*. Lake Worth, FL: Palm Beach Institute of Contemporary Art, 2004.

Potrč, Marjetica, "Five Ways to Urban Independence." http://www.favelapavilion.net/text/english/five%20ways%20to%20urban%20indepe.htm.

Potrč, Marjetica, *Marjetica Potrč: Fragment Worlds*. New York: Actar, 2006.

Red Earth

Lowenstein, Oliver, "Land, Sea and Sky: Red Earth's Seven Sisters Ritual." Courtesy Fourth Door Review, December 9, 2005. http://greenmuseum.org/generic_content.php?ct_id=251 Performance.

"Red Earth," The Ashden Directory: Bringing Together Environmentalism and Performing Arts. Database. http://www.ashdendirectory.org.uk/directoryView.asp?companyIdentifier=76.

Pedro Reyes

Cuevas, Tatiana, *Pedro Reyes*, interview on *BOMB* 94 (Winter 2006). http://bombsite.com/issues/94/articles/2779.

"Pedro Reyes Interview: 'Sanatorium' at Stillspotting NYC," *Designboom*, 2011. http://www.designboom.com/weblog/cat/10/view/15008/pedro-reyes-interview-sanatorium-at-stillspotting-nyc.html.

"San Francisco Planting," Palas por Pistolas, September 26, 2008. http://www.palasporpistolas.org/?p=37#more-37.

Tomás Saraceno

Manacorda, Francesco, *Radical Nature: Art and Architecture for a Changing Planet 1969–2009*. London: Koenig Books for Barbican Art Gallery, 2009, pp. 199–206.

Tomás Saraceno Microscale, Macroscale, and Beyond: Large-Scale Implications of Small-

Scale Experiments. Exhibition brochure, University of California, Berkeley Art Museum, 2008.
Tomás Saraceno's Visions of a Better World through Science, Art Tattler International. http://www.arttattler.com/archivetomassaraceno.html.

Simon Starling

Rosenberg, Angela, Julian Heynen, Dominic Eichler, and Simon Starling, *Simon Starling: Under Lime*. Dusseldorf: Walther Konig, 2009.
Starling, Simon, Fernando Rances, Martin Clark, and Montse Badia, *Simon Starling: Recent History*, Exhibition at Tate St. Ives, Cornwall, England. Malaga, Spain: Centro de Arte Contemporáneo Malaga, 2011.
Volz, Jochen, Kakteenhaus

Gerda Steiner/Jörg Lenzlinger

Steiner, Gerda, and Jörg Lenzlinger, *Brainforest*. Basel: Christoph Merian Verlag, 2005.
Steiner, Gerda, and Jörg Lenzlinger, *Good and Silly Miracles: Biennale Venice 2003*. Zurich: Lars Muller Publishers, 2003.
Steiner, Gerda, and Jörg Lenzlinger, *The Mystery of Fertility*. Basel: Christoph Merian Verlag, 2010.

Tavares Strachan

Heller, Maxwell, "Tavares Strachan: Hermetically Sealed," *Brooklyn Rail*, December 2006–January 2007.
Heller, Maxwell, Franklin Sirmans, and Tavares Strachan, *Tavares Strachan: Orthostatic Tolerance: Launching Into an Infinite Distance*. Kansas City: Grand Arts, 2010.
Hobbs, Robert, *The Distance Between What We Have and What We Want*. New York: Pierogi Gallery and Ronald Feldman Fine Arts, 2006.

SUPERFLEX

Berger, Doris, Charles Esche, Mika Hannula, and Andreas Spiegl, *SUPERFLEX/Tools*. Edited by Barbara Steiner. Cologne: Walther Konig, 2003.
Bradley, Will, *Biogas in Africa*. Published for the exhibition Emergencies at MUSAC, Museo de Arte Contemporaneo de Castilla y Leon, 2005. http://www.superflex.net/text/articles/willbradley.shtml.
Cameron, Dan, "Into Africa," *Afterall, A Journal of Art*, Spring/Summer 1999.

Reverend Billy Talen

Reverend Billy's Freakstorm, weekly podcast on Reverend Billy Talen's website. http://revbilly.com/work/freakstorm.
Talen, Bill, Savitri D., and Alisa Solomon, *The Reverend Billy Project: From Rehearsal Hall to Super Mall with the Church of Life After Shopping (Critical Performances)*. Ann Arbor: University of Michigan Press, 2011.
Talen, William, *What Should I Do If Reverend Billy Is in My Store?* New York: New Press, 2005.
What Would Jesus Buy? A movie directed by Rob VanAlkemade, closed-captioned, color, DVD. Art Alliance America, 2008.

Tissue Culture & Art Project

Catts, Oron, and Ionat Zurr, "The Ethics of Experiential Engagement with the Manipulation of Life," *Tactical Biopolitics Art, Activism, and Technoscience*. Edited by Beatriz da Costa and Kavita Philip. Cambridge, MA: MIT Press, 2008, pp. 143–157.

Catts, Oron, and Ionat Zurr, "The Semi Living Art," *Signs of Life: Bio Art and Beyond*. Edited by Eduardo Kac. Cambridge, MA: MIT Press, 2006, pp. 231–249.

Catts, Oron, and Ionat Zurr, "The Tissue Culture and Art Project: Semi-Livings as Agents of Irony," *Performance and Technology: Practices of Virtual Embodiment and Interactivity*. Edited by Sue Broadhurst and Josephine Machon. Hampshire, UK: Palgrave/Macmillan, 2006, pp. 153–168.

Lily Yeh

Healing Arts, Healing Hearts: Lily Yeh in China. http://aworldofpossibilities.org/program/healing-arts-healing-hearts-lily-yeh-in-china.

Moskin, Bill, and Jill Jackson, *Warrior Angel: The Work of Lily Yeh*, 2004. http://www.barefootartists.org/Lilys_Warrior_Angel_11_2.pdf.

Yeh, Lily, *Awakening Creativity: Dandelion School Blossoms*. Oakland, CA: New Village Press, 2011.

Marina Zurkow

Connor, Michael, *Marina Zurkow: Crossing the Waters*. Bennington, VT: Usdan Gallery, Bennington College, 2010. http://o-matic.com/press/crossing.pdf.

Zurkow, Marina, *The Poster Children*. Three-minute version, animated loop, color, silent, single channel, 2009. http://www.o-matic.com/play/poster/2.html.

Zamudio, Raul, "Marina Zurkow: The Poster Children and Other Heroes of the Revolution," *EyeBall*, Media Arts Webzine, September 29, 2009. http://eyeball2ng.tistory.com/entry/New-York-Marina-Zurkow-The-Poster-Children-and-Other-Heroes-of-the-Revolution.

Index

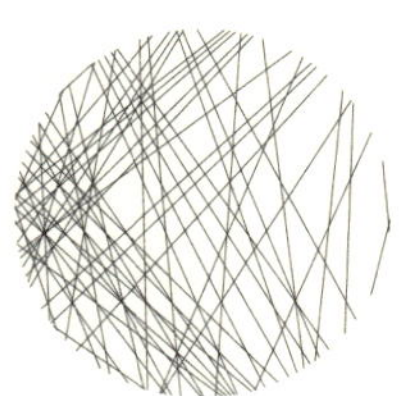

SPONSORING EDITORS	DEBORAH KIRSHMAN AND KARI DAHLGREN
BOOK DESIGNER	NICOLE HAYWARD
COPYEDITOR	LOUISE DOUCETTE
INDEXER	LEONARD ROSENBAUM
TEXT	KYRIAL 9/13.5
DISPLAY	KYRIAL
PACKAGER	BOOKMATTERS
PRINTER AND BINDER	THOMSON-SHORE